The Student's Greek Grammar

A GRAMMAR

OF THE

GREEK LANGUAGE

By DR. GEORGE CURTIUS
PROFESSOR IN THE UNIVERSITY OF LEIPZIG

TRANSLATED UNDER THE REVISION OF THE AUTHOR

EDITED BY

WILLIAM SMITH, LL.D.
CLASSICAL EXAMINER IN THE UNIVERSITY OF LONDON, AND EDITOR OF THE CLASSICAL
AND LATIN DICTIONARIES

With an Appendix
CONTAINING VERSIFICATION AND LIST OF VERBS
By J. B. SEWALL, A.M.
PROFESSOR OF ANCIENT LANGUAGES, BOWDOIN COLLEGE

Wipf & Stock
PUBLISHERS
Eugene, Oregon

Wipf and Stock Publishers
199 W 8th Ave, Suite 3
Eugene, OR 97401

A Grammar of the Greek Language
By Curtius, George
ISBN: 1-59752-669-X
Publication date 5/3/2006
Previously published by Harper & Brothers, 1880

EDITOR'S PREFACE.

THE Greek Grammar of Dr. Curtius is acknowledged by the most competent scholars, both in this country and in Germany, to be the best representative of the present advanced state of Greek scholarship. It is, indeed, almost the only Grammar which exhibits the inflexions of the language in a really scientific form; while its extensive use in the schools of Germany, and the high commendations it has received from practical teachers in that country, are sufficient proof of its excellence as a school-book. It is surprising to find that many of the public and private schools in this country continue to use Grammars which ignore all the improvements and discoveries of modern philology, and still cling to the division of the substantives into ten declensions, the designation of the Second Perfect as the Perfect Middle, and similar exploded errors. Dr. Curtius has stated so fully in his Preface the principles on which this Grammar is constructed, that it is unnecessary to say more by way of introduction. It only remains to add that the translation has been made from the fifth edition of the original work (1862), with the author's sanction, and that the proof-sheets have enjoyed the advantage of his final correction and revision.

An abridgment for the use of the lower forms is published simultaneously with the present work.

W. S.

LONDON, *March,* 1863.

FROM THE AUTHOR'S PREFACE.

THE fact that within a few years the present Grammar has found its way into a large number of schools in various countries of Europe seems to me a satisfactory answer to the question whether a thorough knowledge of Greek is attainable by the method I have adopted. Much, therefore, of what I thought it necessary to state on the first appearance of the book does not now require to be repeated; but I consider it incumbent upon me to make some observations upon the objects and the use of the Grammar, and I beg to recommend these to the careful consideration of teachers.

Few sciences have within the last half century been so completely reformed as the science of language. Not only has our insight into the nature and history of human speech been greatly advanced, but—and this is justly regarded as a matter of still greater importance — quite a different method in treating language in general has been discovered, after a new era had been opened up by the philosophical inquiries of William von Humboldt, and the historical investigations of Francis Bopp and Jacob Grimm. No one, unless he desires to exclude schools from the progress thus made, and to confine them to the mechanical repetition of imperfect and antiquated rules, will probably doubt that the new knowledge, the principles of which have stood the test of nearly half a century, ought to exercise its influence on the teaching of language.

If the teaching of a language in our schools is intended

to lead not only to a thorough understanding of the master-works of literature, but at the same time to cultivate and stir up the youthful mind by independent exertion, and by occupation with a subject so immensely rich, and so harmoniously quickening the most different mental powers as language, such teaching can not possibly continue to keep aloof from the progress of scientific inquiry, which is, unfortunately, still the case in many places. The teaching of Greek, however, seems to be specially called upon to make a commencement. The modern science of language has, indeed, exercised its influence on every part of grammar, but none has been more affected by it than the first, commonly called the accidence. In Latin, scientific inquiry into the structure of the forms has not yet reached the same completeness as in Greek. The structure of the Latin language is less transparent, and we miss so many aids which we possess for the Greek in the high antiquity of its literature and in its dialects. A scientific treatment of the structure of the Latin language in schools is, moreover, a matter of great practical difficulty, on account of the early age at which the elements must necessarily be learned. We ought not, however, on this account, to separate the teaching of Latin from all contact with scientific inquiry, the influence of which can show itself with advantage, at least, in a more suitable arrangement and distribution of the matter. Granting, therefore, that our boys, as heretofore, must commit to memory a large portion of Latin forms; granting that the most important object in learning Latin consists, perhaps, more in the acquisition of fixed laws of syntax, which obviously form the principal strength of the Latin language, the case of the Greek is different. The Greeks are justly called an artistic people, and the Greek language is the most ancient work of art which they have reared upon a very primitive basis. The student, who approaches the Greek after he has already gone through a considerable preparation by the study of Latin, ought to be impressed with the idea that the structure of this language is one of the most marvelous productions of the intellectual powers acting unconsciously. Every thing lies here clear before us: the sources of our knowledge are more varied, and the necessity of analyzing the given forms is rendered so absolute, even on account of the Homeric dialect, that this analysis has, in fact, never been entirely wanting, and after the first appearance of Buttmann, in 1782, made considerable progress. The attempt, therefore, to connect in a still higher degree the practice of the school with the spirit of science, can here point to numerous precedents; and it is, no doubt, mainly owing to this circumstance that it has met with so favorable a reception. My object has been to produce a consistent system, a careful selection, and a clear and precise exposition, rather than an entirely new system.

In selecting and expounding the results of scientific inquiry, I have always kept in view the idea that the book was intended for practical use in schools. The first requisite, therefore, was not to admit any thing which is beyond the sphere of the school, to explain only that which is necessary, and to admit only that which is absolutely certain; for a school-book must speak categorically, must exclude all matters of mere opinion, and has no space for discussion and inquiry. It is, however, perfectly indifferent whether a result has been obtained by special researches into the Greek language or by the more general inquiries of comparative philology.

I was farther obliged to admit only those things which find their explanation in the Greek language itself, or at most in a comparison with the Latin; but even within these limits I have confined myself to such innovations as really afford an important insight into the structure of the forms, whereas all that belongs to philological learning and many other things have been passed over because they seemed unnecessary. Among such superfluous innovations I include especially all changes of terminology, and the entire alteration of whole parts of grammar which are often still less necessary, but to which formerly too much importance used to be attached.

The new technical terms I have introduced have generally been approved of, and the principle stated in my Preface to the first edition, though not followed with pedantic consistency, " if possible, to put significant names in the place of dead numbers," as, for e. g., A Declension, O Declension, instead of First and Second Declension, will scarcely be found fault with, for a name with a meaning at once gives a piece of information, and therefore facilitates learning. Doubts have been raised only about the expressions *strong* and *weak*, which I have employed to distinguish the two Aorists and Perfects. I am as well aware now as I was at the first that, from the point of view of scientific inquiry, much may be said against the expressions, but I nevertheless feel that I can not give them up. For the old designation by numbers is unsatisfactory, unless we are prepared for its sake either to sacrifice a more consistent arrangement of the verb, or to mislead the pupil by calling the Aorist which is treated of first the second, and first the one with which he is made acquainted afterward. But a common name to distinguish the two forms of the Aorist Active Middle and Passive, and of the Perfect Active, is indispensable in a system of Greek Grammar. An innovation had here become necessary, for both negative and positive reasons. The expressions *strong* and *weak* have this advantage—that, after being introduced by Grimm into his German Grammar, they have also been adopted by English grammarians; and, though I use them not quite in the same sense, they are easily intelligible. It will surely not be difficult to make a pupil understand that those forms are called *strong* which spring from the root, as it were, by an internal agency, and *weak* those which are formed by syllables added externally, especially as he may easily compare the English *take, took*, and *love, loved*. I still know of no designation which, with so few disadvantages, offers so many advantages as this, and I shall retain it until a better one is suggested; and, after all, in necessary innovations, it is often more important *that* men agree than *on what* they agree.

The fact that the most essential changes I have made in the arrangements of the subjects—as, for example, the strict adherence to the system of Stems in all the inflexions, and especially the division of the verb according to temporal Stems—have met with the approval of practical teachers, has been to me a source of great gratification, it being a clear proof that the demands of scientific inquiry are by no means so much opposed to a right system of teaching as is still imagined by many. The arrangement of temporal Stems is made less upon scientific than upon didactic grounds, in such a manner that kindred forms are joined together, and due regard is paid to the progress from that which is easy to that which is more difficult.

The chapter on the formation of words, though somewhat enlarged, has, for the same reasons, still been kept very brief. But, in treating of the verbs, I have directed attention to the formation of verbal nouns: in treating of the verbs of the different classes, I have always directed attention, by a number of characteristic examples, to the application of the different Stems in the formation of words. By this means the learner has an opportunity, during the study of his grammar, of making himself acquainted with a number of words, and I have no doubt that teachers will give their sanction to this arrangement.

In regard to Syntax, the positive results of recent linguistic inquiries are as yet less numerous. In this part of the Grammar, therefore, I follow the principle of stating the essential idioms of the Greek language with the utmost possible precision and in the utmost logical order. Only in some chapters, especially in that on the use of the tenses, does my system present considerable differences from the usual one. All minute disquisitions, conjectures, and more or less probable theories—among them especially the ever-repeated theory about the original local meaning of the cases, with which I can not agree at all—have been rigorously excluded. In this part, also, I have never neglected to compare the phenomena of the Greek language with the corresponding ones of Latin, and occasionally also of English, where this could be done with brevity and advantage; for as the usage of a language must be mainly comprehended by a feeling of language, I imagine that every appeal to a Latin usage already embodied with our feeling of language, or to an English usage familiar to us from childhood, advances our knowledge much more than philosophical definitions or technical terms of vague or various meanings. For the same reason, I every where attach great importance to an accurate translation of a Greek idiom into English or Latin. I need hardly guard myself against the opinion that I considered such a translation to be a philosophical explanation of a linguistic phenomenon. A real explanation is beyond the problem of a Grammar.

PREFACE. xi

I scarcely need repeat here that the present book is not intended, like an Elementary Grammar, to be committed to memory paragraph by paragraph; but, in teaching, a suitable selection, according to the degree of the pupil's advancement, should be made by the teacher. By a difference in type I have myself, at least partially, indicated this.

It may be remarked in general that the first business every where is that of memory, and only when the actual forms, with the aid of the paradigms, have been committed to memory, analysis may be added. First *knowledge*, then *understanding:* this ought to be the leading principle; but, as I have said in another place, "Memory can neither accurately grasp the great variety of Greek forms nor retain them, unless it be supported by an analyzing and combining intelligence, which furnishes, as it were, the hooks and cement to strengthen that which has been learned, and permanently to impress it upon the mind." If details learned at different times and carefully committed to memory, during a subsequent repetition variously combine with one another and form various groups; if, then, many things, at first sight strange, appear to the pupil in the light of a law pervading the language, such insight is certainly not a mere support of memory, but animates the desire to learn, and incites to exercise the power of thought in a variety of ways. The present book offers to teachers abundant opportunities for such exercises, and acquires its highest efficacy under the guidance of thinking teachers who are truly familiar with it, and take a delight in its subjects. That the book has actually found such teachers has been proved to me in various ways, and caused me sincere gratification. G. C.

TABLE OF CONTENTS.

INTRODUCTION.
THE GREEK LANGUAGE AND ITS DIALECTS.

FIRST PART.—ETYMOLOGY.

I. Letters and Sounds.

CHAPTER I.
THE GREEK CHARACTERS.

A. Letters .... § 1–9
B. Other Characters 10–16
C. Accents 17–22
D. Punctuation 23

CHAPTER II.
THE SOUNDS.

A. The Vowels 24–29
B. The Consonants 30–34

CHAPTER III.
COMBINATIONS AND CHANGES OF SOUNDS.

A. Vowels in Combination 35–39
B. Other kinds of Vowel Changes 40–43
C. Consonants in Combination with one another 44–54
D. Other Changes in the Middle of a Word 55–62
E. Changes of Sound at the End of a Word 63–69

CHAPTER IV.
DIVISION OF SYLLABLES AND THEIR QUANTITY.

A. Division of Syllables 70–73
B. Quantity 74–78

CHAPTER V.

ACCENTS 79–99

xiv   CONTENTS.

II. Inflexion.
A. INFLEXION OF NOUNS AND PRONOUNS.

CHAPTER VI.
DECLENSION OF SUBSTANTIVES AND ADJECTIVES.

FIRST PRINCIPAL (OR VOWEL) DECLENSION.
A. The A Declension .... § 112–113
    (*commonly called the First Declension.*)
    1. Feminines 114–119
    2. Masculines 120–123
B. The O Declension 124–131
    (*commonly called the Second Declension.*)
Attic Declension 132–133
SECOND PRINCIPAL (OR CONSONANT) DECLENSION 135–143
    (*commonly called the Third Declension.*)
    1. Consonant Stems:
        a. Guttural and Labial Stems 144–145
        b. Dental Stems 146–149
        c. Liquid Stems 150–153
    2. Vowel Stems:
        a. Soft Vowel Stems 154–158
        b. Diphthong Stems 159–161
        c. O Stems 162–163
    3. Stems suffering Elision:
        a. Sigma Stems 164–167
        b. r-Stems 168–169
        c. ν-Stems 170–171
    Irregularities in Declension 174–177
    Case-like Terminations 178–179

CHAPTER VII.
OTHER INFLEXIONS OF THE ADJECTIVE.

A. Gender 180–191
B. Comparison 192–200
C. Adverbs of Adjectives 201–204

CHAPTER VIII.
INFLEXION OF PRONOUNS 205–219

CHAPTER IX.
THE NUMERALS 220–224

CONTENTS. XV

B. INFLEXION OF VERBS.
General Remarks .... § 225-230

LIST OF PARADIGMS.   Table.
Εἰμί, *I am* .... I.
Synopsis of λύω, *I loose* (exhibiting the meanings of the Tenses)   II.

VERBS IN Ω.
A. Vowel Stems:
 1. Uncontracted, λύω .... III.
 2. Contracted, τιμάω, ποιέω, δουλόω .... IV.
B. Consonant Stems:
 1. Guttural Stems, πλέκω, φεύγω, τάσσω .... V.
 2. Dental Stems, ψεύδομαι, πείθω, κομίζω .... VI.
 3. Labial Stems, πέμπω, λείπω, καλύπτω .... VII.
 4. Liquid Stems, δέρω, ἀγγέλλω, σπείρω .... VIII.

VERBS IN MI.
First Class, τίθημι, δίδωμι, ἵστημι .... IX.
Second Class, δείκνυμι .... X.

CHAPTER X.
FIRST PRINCIPAL CONJUGATION, OR VERBS IN Ω.

I. The Present-Stem:
 A. Inflexion of the Present-Stem .... § 231-233
 B. The Augment 234-242
 C. Contracted Verbs 243-244
 D. Distinction of the Present-Stem from the Verbal
   Stem 245-253
II. The Strong Aorist-Stem 254-257
III. The Future-Stem 258-266
IV. The Weak Aorist-Stem 267-271
V. The Perfect-Stem 272
 1. Perfect Active 276-282
 2. Pluperfect Active 283
 3. Perfect Middle and Passive 284-289
 4. Pluperfect Middle and Passive 290-291
VI. Forms of the Strong Passive Stem 292-295
VII. Forms of the Weak Passive Stem 296-299
Verbal Adjectives 300
Verbs which leave their Stem-Vowel short 301

CHAPTER XI.

SECOND PRINCIPAL CONJUGATION, OR VERBS IN MI.

Preliminary Remarks .... § 302–304
1. First Class 305–317
2. Second Class 318–319

CHAPTER XII.

IRREGULAR VERBS OF THE FIRST CONJUGATION . 320–327
Anomalies in Signification 328–330
Outlines of the Accentuation of Verbal Forms 331–333
Peculiar Verbal Forms of the Ionic Dialect .... 334 D.–338 D.

III. Derivation.

CHAPTER XIII.

A. *Simple Derivatives* 339–340
   1. The most important Suffixes for forming Substantives 341–349
   2. The most important Suffixes for forming Adjectives.. 350–352
   3. Derivative Verbs 353
B. *Compound Derivatives:*
   1. Form of the Combination 354–358
   2. Meaning of Combination 359–360

SECOND PART.—SYNTAX.

Preliminary Remarks 361

CHAPTER XIV.

NUMBER AND GENDER 362–367

CHAPTER XV.

THE ARTICLE 368–391

CHAPTER XVI.

USE OF CASES:

A. Nominative 392–393
B. Vocative 394
C. Accusative 395–406
D. Genitive 407–428
E. Dative 429–443

CONTENTS. xvii

CHAPTER XVII.

THE PREPOSITIONS .... § 444
General View of the Prepositions 448
1. Prepositions which take only One Case................ 449–457
2. Prepositions which take Two Cases 458–461
3. Prepositions which take Three Cases 462–468

CHAPTER XVIII.

THE PRONOUNS 469–475

CHAPTER XIX.

THE KINDS OF VERBS 476–483

CHAPTER XX.

USE OF THE TENSES 484
1. The forms for the Incomplete Action................... 486–491
2. The forms for the Indefinite (Aorist) Action............ 492–498
3. The Future.. 499–501
4. The forms for the Complete Action................... 502–506

CHAPTER XXI.

USE OF THE MOODS.

A. In Simple Sentences:
  1. Indicative 507
  2. Subjunctive 508–513
  3. Optative.. 514–517
  4. Imperative...................................... 518
B. In Compound Sentences:
  Connexion of Sentences with one another............ 519–524
  1. Dependent, Declarative, and Interrogative Sentences 525–529
  2. Sentences expressing a purpose.................... 530–533
  3. Conditional Sentences 534–550
  4. Relative Sentences 551–555
  5. Temporal Sentences.............................. 556–558

CHAPTER XXII.

THE INFINITIVE.

1. Use of the Infinitive in general 559–566
2. The Case of the Subject and Predicate with the Infinitive 567–572
3. The Infinitive with the Article 573–574
4. The Infinitive with ἄν 575–576
5. The Infinitive instead of the Imperative............... 577

CHAPTER XXIII.

ON PARTICIPLES.

1. Attributive Use .... § 578
2. Appositive Use 579–583
3. The Participle with an Absolute Case 584–586
4. Supplements to Participles 587–588
5. The Predicative Participle 589–594
6. The Participle with ἄν 595
7. Verbal Adjectives 596

CHAPTER XXIV.

SOME PECULIARITIES IN RELATIVE SENTENCES .. 597–605

CHAPTER XXV.

INTERROGATIVE SENTENCES 606–611

CHAPTER XXVI.

THE NEGATIVES.

1. Use of Simple Negatives 612–618
2. Several Negatives combined 619–621
3. Some Negative Phrases 622

CHAPTER XXVII.

THE PARTICLES.

A. Conjunctions 623
   1. Copulative Conjunctions 624–625
   2. Disjunctive   "   626–627
   3. Adversative   "   628–630
   4. Comparative   "   631–632
   5. Declarative   "   633
   6. Temporal   "   634–635
   7. Causal   "   636
   8. Inferential   "   637
   9. Final   "   638
   10. Hypothetical "   639
   11. Concessive   "   640
B. Emphatic Particles 641–643

                                                   Page

ENGLISH INDEX 353
GREEK INDEX 357

THE STUDENT'S GREEK GRAMMAR.

INTRODUCTION.

THE GREEK LANGUAGE AND ITS DIALECTS.

THE Greek language is the language of the Ancient Hellenes ("Ελληνες), the inhabitants of Greece, with all its islands and numerous colonies. It is related to the languages of the Indians, Persians, Romans, Slavonians, Lithuanians, Germans, and Celts. These are all sister-languages, and together form the Indo-European family.

The Greeks were early divided into races, each of which spoke a different dialect. The chief dialects of the Greek language are the Æolic, Doric, and Ionic. At first each race employed its own dialect both in poetry and in prose.

1. The IONIC dialect was spoken by the Ionic race, especially in Asia Minor and Attica, in numerous islands, and in the Ionic colonies. It was the first of the dialects developed by poetry, and produced three different but nearly related dialects, viz.:

a) The *Old-Ionic* or *Epic* dialect, which is preserved in the poems of Homer and Hesiod as well as of their followers.

b) The *New-Ionic* dialect, which we know chiefly from the history of Herodotus.

Obs.—The Old and New Ionic dialects are also designated by the common name *Ionic*, as distinguished from the Attic.

c) The *Attic* dialect, in which are written the numerous works in poetry and prose produced at Athens in the time of her glory. The principal writers of the Attic dialect are — the tragedians Æschylus, Sophocles, Euripides, the comic writer Aristophanes, the historians Thucydides and Xenophon, the philosopher Plato, the great orators Lysias, Demosthenes, and Æschines. Through the importance of Athens in Greece, and the excellence of the Attic literature, the Attic became the chief dialect of the Greek language.

Obs.—A less important distinction is made between the earlier and later Attic writers. The tragedians and Thucydides belong to the earlier Attic, and the remaining authors to the later. The language of Plato is intermediate between the two: that of the tragedians has also many other peculiarities.

2. The ÆOLIC dialect was spoken by the Æolians, particularly in Asia Minor, Bœotia, and Thessaly. Alcæus and Sappho wrote in this dialect.

3. The DORIC dialect was spoken by the Dorians, chiefly in Northern Greece, in the Peloponnesus, in Crete, and in the numerous Doric colonies, especially Sicily and Lower Italy. Doric is essentially the dialect of Pindar's lyric poems and Theocritus's bucolics (herdsman's poetry). The choruses in the tragedies also contain some Doric forms.

4. After Athens ceased to be the leading city in Greece, the Attic dialect still remained the language of educated Greeks. But it soon began to degenerate from its primitive purity and excellence, and thus, from the third century before Christ, the common Greek dialect (ἡ κοινὴ διάλεκτος) was distinguished from the Attic.

On the boundary-line between the older Attic and the common Greek dialect stands the great philosopher *Aristotle*. Among later authors, the most important are—the historians *Polybius, Plutarch, Arrian, Dion Cassius;* the geographer *Strabo;* the rhetoricians *Dionysius* of *Halicarnassus* and *Lucian*.

PART FIRST.
ETYMOLOGY.

I. LETTERS AND SOUNDS.

Chap. I.—The Greek Characters.

A. *Letters.*

§ 1. The Greek letters are the following:

Large Character.	Small Character.	Name.	Pronunciation.
A	α	Alpha	ă (short or long).
B	β	Beta	b.
Γ	γ	Gamma	g.
Δ	δ	Delta	d.
E	ε	Epsīlon	ĕ (only short).
Z	ζ	Zeta	z.
H	η	Eta	ē (only long).
Θ	θ	Theta	th.
I	ι	Iota	ĭ (short or long).
K	κ	Kappa	k.
Λ	λ	Lambda	l.
M	μ	Mu	m.
N	ν	Nu	n.
Ξ	ξ	Xi	x.
O	ο	Omīkron	ŏ (only short).
Π	π	Pi	p.
P	ρ	Rho	r.
Σ	σ, ς	Sigma	s.
T	τ	Tau	t.
Υ	υ	Upsīlon	ŭ (short or long).
Φ	φ	Phi	ph.
X	χ	Chi	ch.
Ψ	ψ	Psi	ps.
Ω	ω	Omĕga	ō (only long).

§ 2. For *s* there is a double sign in the small character: σ at the beginning and in the middle, and ς at the end of a word. Hence σύν, σείω, ἦσαν, but πόνος, κέρας. In compound words ς may also stand at the end of the first word in the compound: προς-ἔρχομαι, δύς-βατος.

§ 3. From the names of the first two letters arose the expression "Alphabet." The characters of the Greek alphabet do not essentially differ from those of the Latin and of modern languages. All come from the alphabet of the Phœnicians.

In regard to pronunciation, the following points are to be observed:

§ 4. All Greek letters are always pronounced alike. But γ is an exception, since, before γ, κ, χ, or ξ, it is pronounced *ng*. Hence in Latin it is represented by *n* : τέγγω is pronounced *tengo ;* συγκαλῶ, *syngkălo ;* λόγχη, *longchē ;* φόρμιγξ, *phorminx.*

§ 5. ζ is pronounced like the English *z*. It is of very different origin in different cases. Compare μείζων (for μέγιων) from μέγας; ζυγόν with Latin *jugum*, English *yoke*, etc.

§ 6. φ we pronounce as *f*, but probably the Greeks pronounced the *p* and *h* separately; hence *ph*, not *f*, is used in Latin for φ: φιλοσοφία, *philosophia ;* Φιλοκτήτης, *Philoctetes.*

§ 7. θ we pronounce like the English *th*.

§ 8. Of the diphthongs, αι and ει are both pronounced as *ei* in *height ;* οι, as *oy* in *boy ;* αυ, as *ou* in *sour ;* ου, as *ou* in *tour ;* υι, as *wi* in *wing ;* ευ and ηυ, as *ew* in *few*. The iota subscriptum (*underwritten*) is not pronounced in

---

§ 3. **Dialects.**—The Greek language had in the most ancient times another letter, ϝ, which was called *Digamma* (δίγαμμα= "double gamma") from its form, and *Vau* (ϝαῦ) from its pronunciation. It was pronounced like the Latin *v:* ϝοῖνος, *wine*=Lat. *vinum*. At a later time it was written only by the Æolians and Dorians.

§ 14. OTHER CHARACTERS. 5

ᾳ, ῃ, ῳ. It is not written under, but after capitals, as Αι, Ηι, Ωι, but still remains unpronounced.

§ 9. When two vowels, usually pronounced together, are to be pronounced separately, the latter has over it a diæresis (διαίρεσις = *separation*): thus πάϊς is pronounced *pa-is;* ἄϋπνος, *a-upnos*.

B. Other Characters.

§ 10. Besides the letters, the Greek language has also the sign ʽ, which is placed over the initial vowel to which it belongs, and represents the *h:* ἕξ is pronounced *hex;* ἅπαξ, *hapax*. This sign is called *spiritus asper*, "rough breathing."

§ 11. For more exact distinction, the Greeks also mark those initial vowels which have not this breathing with the sign ʼ, *i. e.*, the *spiritus lenis*, "gentle breathing." This sound indicates only the raising of the voice which is necessary for the pronunciation of a vowel when no consonant precedes: ἐκ is pronounced *ek;* ἄγω, *ago*.

§ 12. In diphthongs the breathing stands over the second vowel: οὗτος = *houtos;* εἶδον = *eidon*. But when the first vowel is in large character, the breathing stands before it: Ἅιδης = *Hades;* Ὠιδή = *Odē*.

§ 13. Every initial ρ has the spiritus asper over it: ῥαψῳδός, ῥεῦμα. In Latin the aspirate is written after the ρ: *rhapsodus, rheuma*. When two ρ's come together in a word, ʼ is usually placed over the first, and ʽ over the second: Πύῤῥος = *Pyrrhus;* Καλλιῤῥόη = *Callirrhoe*.

Obs.—Many write the double ρ without any breathing: Πύρρος; Καλλιρρόη.

§ 14. As in Latin, so in Greek, the sign ˉ over a vowel denotes that the vowel is long, ˘ that it is short, and ⁓ that it is sometimes one, sometimes the other. In Greek they are used only with the vowels α, ι, υ, since ε, η, ο, ω, are distinguished by their form.

§ 15. The sign ' at the junction of two words indicates the omission of a vowel or diphthong, and is then called an *apostrophe* : παρ' ἐκείνῳ for παρὰ ἐκείνῳ, *with that one;* μὴ 'γώ for μὴ ἐγώ (*ne ego*).

§ 16. The same sign has the name *coronis* (κορωνίς) when it stands over the junction of two words contracted into one: τοὔνομα for τὸ ὄνομα, *the name ;* κἀγαθός for καὶ ἀγαθός, *and good*. It indicates that a *crasis* (κρᾶσις, *mixture*) or contraction of two words has taken place, and, like the breathing, stands over the second vowel of a diphthong: ταὐτό for τὸ αὐτό, *the same*.

C. Accents.

§ 17. The Greeks also indicate the tone or ACCENT (προςῳδία) of words. The sign ' over a vowel is called the *acute accent* (ὀξεῖα προςῳδία), that is, the sharp or *raised* tone : λόγος, τούτων, παρά, ἕτερος. The syllable thus marked must be raised above the rest.

A word having the acute accent upon the last syllable is called *oxytone* (ὀξύτονον): παρά, εἰπέ, βασιλεύς.

A word having the acute accent upon the last but one is called *paroxytone* (παροξύτονον) : λέγω, φαίνω.

A word having the acute accent upon the last but two is called *proparoxytone* (προπαροξύτονον): λέγεται, εἴπετε.

§ 18. *Obs*.—A *proparoxytone*, having a long vowel or diphthong in the second syllable of the word, ought to be pronounced so as to give the accent on the third syllable, and yet preserve the length of the second syllable : βέβηκα should be pronounced *bébēka;* ἀπόβαινε, *apóbaine*.

§ 19. The sign ` over a vowel is called the *grave accent* (βαρεῖα προςῳδία). It indicates a *low* tone, that is, that a syllable is not raised in tone. Thus in ἀπόβαινὲ, the last two might have the grave accent. The marking of them, however, would be superfluous, the absence of the acute being a sufficient guide. All words without an accent on the final syllable are therefore called *barytone* (βαρύτονα): λέγω, ἕτερος.

§ 20. The sign ʽ, however, also denotes a subdued acute, and occupies the place of an acute in every oxytone not immediately followed by a pause: ἀπό, *from*, but ἀπὸ τούτου, *from this;* βασιλεύς, *a king,* but βασιλεὺς ἐγένετο, *he became king.* Oxytones, therefore, retain their accent unchanged only at the end of a sentence.

§ 21. The sign ˜ over a vowel is called the *circumflex accent* (περισπωμένη προςῳδία), from its shape. The circumflex is a combination of the acute and the grave, ˆ.

A word having a circumflex on the last syllable is called *perispomenon* (περισπώμενον): ἀγαθοῖς, σκιᾶς.

A word having a circumflex on the last syllable but one is called *properispomenon* (προπερισπώμενον): φεῦγε, βῆτε.

§ 22. In diphthongs, the accent, like the breathing (§ 12), is put over the second vowel: φεύγει, τοῦτο.

When the circumflex accent and the breathing meet upon the same vowel, the accent is placed over the breathing: οὗτος, ἦθος, Ὦτος. The acute, in a similar case, stands to the right of the breathing: ἄγε, ἔρχομαι, Ἴων.

Obs.—The acute is placed between the two points of a diæresis (9), ἀίδιος, but the circumflex over them, πραῦναι.

D. *Punctuation.*

§ 23. For the purpose of dividing sentences and periods, the Greeks employ the comma and the full-point. For the sign of interrogation they use the semicolon: τί εἶπας; *what did you say?* For the colon or semicolon they place a point at the upper part of the line: ἐρωτῶ ὑμᾶς· τί ἐποιήσατε; *I ask you: what did you do?* ἑσπέρα ἦν· τότε ἦλθεν ἄγγελος, *it was evening; then a messenger came.*

Chap. II.—The Sounds.

A. *The Vowels.*

§ 24. The Greek language, like the Latin, has five vowels, of which the first four are like the Latin, *a, e, o, i*. But instead of the Latin *u*, the Greeks have υ (pronounced nearly like the French *u* and the German *ü*).

§ 25. The vowels, apart from the distinction of long and short, are divided into two classes—the *hard* and the *soft* vowels: α, ε, η, ο, ω, are hard; υ, ι, soft.

§ 26. From the union of *hard* and *soft* vowels together arise *diphthongs* (δίφθογγοι, *i. e.*, double-sounds). They are:

αυ, from α and υ.   ου, from ο and υ.
αι,   "   α " ι.   οι,   "   ο " ι.
ευ,   "   ε " υ.   ηυ,   "   η " υ.
ει,   "   ε " ι.

§ 27. The union of *long hard* vowels with ι produces the

---

§ 24. **Dialects.**—The Dialects, in many words and forms, admit different vowels from those usual in the Attic dialect. Thus:

1. The *Ionic* (Epic and New-Ionic) dialect prefers η for Attic ā: Att. θώραξ, Ion. θώρηξ, *breastplate;* Att. ἀγορά, Ion. ἀγορή, *market;* Att. ναῦς, Ion. νηῦς, *ship;* but Ion. μεσαμβρίη for Att. μεσημβρία, *midday.*

2. The *Doric*, on the contrary, prefers ā: Att. δῆμος, Dor. δᾶμος, *people;* Att. μήτηρ, *mother*, Dor. μάτηρ (comp. Latin *māter*); Dor. Ἀθάνα for Ἀθηνᾶ, *goddess Athena*, even in Attic poets.

3. The Ionic dialect often changes ε to ει, and ο to ου: Att. ξένος, Ion. ξεῖνος, *foreign;* At. ἕνεκα, Ion. εἵνεκα, *on account of;* Att. μόνος, Ion. μοῦνος, *alone;* Att. ὄνομα, Ion. οὔνομα, *name*. Rarely ο to οι, or α to αι: Att. ἠγνόησε, Ion. ἠγνοίησε, *he knew not.*

§ 26. **Dialects.**—The New-Ionic dialect has moreover the diphthong ωυ, which, however, only comes in place of αυ in the other dialects. θωῦμα for θαῦμα, *wonder;* ἑωυτοῦ for ἑαυτοῦ, *of himself:* ωυ must be pronounced as *ou*.

spurious diphthongs ᾳ, ῃ, ῳ, in which the underwritten iota is not heard. (Compare § 8.)

§ 28. The Greek language also combines υ with ι, but only before vowels: μυῖα, *a fly*.

§ 29. We farther distinguish the obscure o-sound (o, ω), the medium a-sound (α), and the clear e-sound (ε, η), and the more obscure υ from the clearer ι.

B. *The Consonants.*

§ 30. The consonants are divided: I. According to the position in the mouth where they are produced, *i. e.*, according to their *organ* (ὄργανον, "instrument"), into:

1. GUTTURALS (throat-sounds), κ, γ, χ.
2. DENTALS (teeth-sounds), τ, δ, θ, ν, λ, ρ, σ.
3. LABIALS (lip-sounds), π, β, φ, μ.

§ 31. II. According to their *power*, that is, whether they can be pronounced with or without a vowel, into:

§ 32. 1. MUTES (mutæ):

(*a.*) *hard* (tenues), κ, τ, π.
(*b.*) *soft* (mediæ), γ, δ, β.
(*c.*) *aspirated* (aspiratæ), χ, θ, φ.

Obs.—The aspirated consonants contain each a *hard* consonant with the rough breathing, χ therefore = κ' (kh); θ = τ' (th); φ = π' (ph).

§ 33. 2. VOCALS (semivocales):

(*a.*) *Liquids* (liquidæ), λ, ρ.
(*b.*) *Nasals* (nasales), γ (γ before gutturals, § 4), ν, μ.
(*c.*) *Sibilant* (sibilans), σ (ς).

---

§ 32. **Dialects.**—In the Ionic dialect the aspirates often lose the breathing: δέκομαι for Attic δέχομαι, *accept;* αὖτις for Attic αὖθις, *again.* The New-Ionic sometimes transposes the breathing: κιθών for Attic χιτών, *tunic;* ἐνθεῦτεν for Attic ἐντεῦθεν.

§ 34. The *double consonants* belong to both kinds: ξ, ψ, ζ: for ξ = κσ, ψ = πσ, ζ = δ, with a soft sibilant (§ 5).

Obs.—κσ only occurs in compounds with ἐκ: ἐκσώζω, *I rescue*.

Chap. III.—Combinations and Changes of Sounds.

A. *Vowels in Combination.*

§ 35. In the inner part of a word not all vowels may

§ 34. **Dialects.**—A peculiarity of the Greek language is the want of the breathing *v*. The *v*, however, was not altogether wanting; for—

1. The digamma (§ 3, D.) occurred in the Homeric dialect in the beginning of the following words: ἄγνυμι, *break;* ἅλις, *numer-ous;* ἀλίσκομαι, *am caught;* ἄναξ, *ruler;* ἀνάσσω, *rule;* ἀνδάνω, *please;* ἀραιός, *tender;* ἄστυ, *city;* ἔαρ, *spring* [*ver*]; ἔθνος, *swarm, people;* εἴκοσι, *twenty* [Doric Ϝίκατι, Latin *viginti*]; εἴκω, *yield;* εἴλω, *press;* ἕκητι, *willingly;* ἑκυρός, *father-in-law;* ἑκών, *willing;* ἔλπομαι, *hope;* the pronominal Stem ἑ (ἕο, *sui*), ἔοικα, *appear;* ἔπος, *word;* εἶπον, *spoke;* ἔργον, *work;* ἔργω, *close in;* ἔῤῥω, *go on;* ἐρύω, *draw;* ἐρέω, *shall say;* ἰσθής, *clothing;* εἷμα, *dress* (Stem Ϝες, Latin *vestis*); ἔτης, *relative;* ἡδύς, *agreeable;* Ἴλιος, *city Ilios;* ἴσος, *equal;* οἶκος, *house;* οἶνος, *wine* (*vinum*). On the operation of the digamma, see § 63, D., 75, D.

2. The Ϝ in the middle occurred in ὄϊς, *sheep*, from ὄϜις (Latin *ovis*): νη-ός, *of the ship*, from νᾶϜος (Latin *navis*), Gen. of ναῦ-ς.

3. The Dorians and Æolians retained the digamma at the beginning of many words: Æol. Ϝέτος, *year*, Dor. Ϝίδιος, *own.*

4. In Homer, at the beginning of many words, ε stands for Ϝ. ἐέ, *him, self;* ἐείκοσι, *twenty;* ἐίση, *equal;* ἔεδνον, *marriage-gift* = ἕδνον.

§ 35. **Dialects.**—The Dialects vary much in regard to the combinations of vowels. The *Epic* and *New-Ionic* leave many syllables uncontracted: ἰύ = εὖ, *well;* οἴομαι = οἶμαι, *I think;* πάϊς = παῖς, *boy;* νόος = νοῦς, *sense;* φιλέητε = φιλῆτε (*ametis*); ἀέκων = ἄκων, *unwilling.* Some of the forms usually uncontracted are, on the

§ 37. VOWELS IN COMBINATION. 11

combine. The dissimilar vowels pair with one another best:

1. The *soft* generally remain *unchanged* before the *hard* vowels: σοφία, *wisdom ;* λύω, *I loosen ;* ἰαύω, *I slumber ;* ὕει, *it rains ;* εὔνοια, *benevolence.*

2. *Hard* vowels *before soft ones* become diphthongs: ἐΰ, εὖ, *good ;* πάϊς, παῖς, *boy ;* γένεϊ, γένει, *to the race.*

Obs.—Diphthongs sometimes lose their second part before vowels: βου-ός becomes βο-ός (*bov-is*); καί-ω, κά-ω, *burn.* Compare §§ 160, 248, *Obs.*

§ 36. *Similar* (§ 25) vowels can not well stand together, and hence, when they meet, are often *contracted* according to the following laws:

1. Two *similar* vowels melt into one long vowel: λᾶας becomes λᾶς, *stone ;* ζηλόω, ζηλῶ, *I am zealous ;* Χίιος, Χῖος, *a Chian ;* φιλέητε, φιλῆτε, *ametis,* in which cases ε and η, ο and ω, are similar.

Still it must be observed that ε ε usually become ει, and ο ο become ου: ποίεε, ποίει, *do ;* πλόος, πλοῦς, *passage by sea.* Vowels before a similar one beginning a diphthong disappear: πλόου, πλοῦ, *of a passage ;* οἰκέει, οἰκεῖ, *dwells ;* φιλέῃ, φιλῇ, *amet.*

§ 37. 2. *Dissimilar* vowels form a compound in which

---

contrary, contracted in these dialects: ἱρός = ἱερός, *holy ;* βώσας = βοήσας, *one who has called.*

2. The abbreviation in the diphthongs ending in υ is explained by this letter first becoming ϝ, and then being quite dropped (compare § 34, D., 2): βου-ός — βοϝ-ός [*bov-is*] — βο-ός.

§ 37. Dialects.—1. The Dialects supply many exceptions. Thus, in New-Ionic especially, εο and εου are contracted into ευ, not into ου: ποιέομεν, ποιεῦμεν, *we make ;* ποιέουσι, ποιεῦσι, *they make.*

2. In the Ionic dialect, ᾱο (ηο) often changes to εω: Ἀτρείδαο, Ἀτρείδεω, *of Atrides ;* ἵλαος, ἵλεως, *merciful.* α before ω is often changed into the thinner sound ε: Ποσειδέων = Ποσειδάων, Att. Ποσειδῶν, *the god Poseidon.*

3. In Doric, αο, αω, are contracted into ᾱ: Ἀτρείδαο = Ἀτρείδα, Ποσειδάων = Ποσειδᾶν, θεάων (*dearum*) = θεᾶν.

a) the **obscurer** vowel overpowers the **clearer** (§ 29).
Thus from

αο	comes ω	in	τιμάομεν,	τιμῶμεν,	*we honor.*
ηο	" ω	"	νη-όδυνος,	νώδυνος,	*painless.*
οα	" ω	"	αἰδόα,	αἰδῶ,	*pudorem.*
οη	" ω	"	ζηλόητε,	ζηλῶτε,	*ye may be jealous.*
εο	" ου	"	γένεος,	γένους,	*of the race.*
οε	" ου	"	ζήλοε,	ζήλου,	*be jealous.*
αοι	" ῳ	"	ἀοιδή,	ᾠδή,	*song.*
αου	" ω	"	τιμάου,	τιμῶ,	*be honored.*
ηου	" ω	"	μὴ οὖν,	μῶν,	*surely not.*
εου	" ου	"	χρυσέου,	χρυσοῦ,	*of the golden.*
εοι	" οι	"	χρύσεοι,	χρυσοῖ,	*the golden.*
οει	" οι	"	ζηλόεις,	ζηλοῖς,	*thou art jealous.*
"	" ου	"	οἰνόεις,	οἰνοῦς,	*abounding in wine.*

Obs.—οει become ου when the ει represents the lengthening of ε (§ 42).

§ 38. *b)* When the **medium** a-sound and **clearer** e-sound meet, the first in order gains the upper hand:

αε	become ᾱ	in	ἀέκων,	ἄκων,	*unwilling.*
αη	" ᾱ	"	τιμάητε,	τιμᾶτε,	*honoretis.*
αει	" ᾳ	"	ἀείδω,	ᾄδω,	*I sing.*
αῃ	" ᾳ	"	τιμάῃς,	τιμᾷς,	*honores.*
εα	" η	"	ἔαρ,	ἦρ,	*spring.*
εαι	" ῃ	"	λύεαι,	λύῃ,	*thou art loosened.*
ηαι	" ῃ	"	λύηαι,	λύῃ,	*solvaris.*

Obs.—In the contractions of αει and εαι, sometimes αι takes the place of ᾳ, ει that of ῃ. So from ἀεικής, *unfit,* comes αἰκής; from ἀείρω, *I lift up,* comes αἴρω; from λύεαι comes λύει (with λύῃ). Exceptions, §§ 130, 183, 243 (τιμᾶν), 244.

§ 39. Another mode of treating vowels which meet together is called *Synizesis* (συνίζησις, *i. e., sinking*). It consists in the first vowel being written but not pronounced as a vowel: θεός—as one syllable.

---

§ 39. **Dialects.**—*Synizesis* is frequent in Homer, especially after ε: Πηληϊάδεω, *of Pelides;* χρυσέοις, *aureis;* νέα, *navem;* also πόλιας, *cities;* ὄγδοος, *the eighth.*

§ 43. OTHER VOWEL CHANGES.

B. *Other kinds of Vowel changes.*

§ 40. Another change of the vowels consists in their being lengthened. Two kinds of lengthening are distinguished, viz.:

1. *Organic lengthening, i. e.,* that which is required by inflexion or derivation. By organic lengthening—

ᾰ generally becomes	η,	τιμάω, *I honor*,	Fut.	τιμήσω.
ο always	"	ω, ζηλόω, *I am jealous*,	"	ζηλώσω.
ε "	"	η, ποιέω, *I make*,	"	ποιήσω.
ῐ either	"	ῑ, τίω, *I honor*,	"	τίσω;
or	"	ει, St. λιπ,	Pres.	λείπω, *I leave:*
sometimes	"	οι, " λιπ,	Adj.	λοιπός, *remaining*.
ῠ either	"	ῡ, λύω, *I loose*,	Fut.	λύσω;
or	"	ευ, St. φυγ,	Pres.	φεύγω, *I flee*.

§ 41. *Obs.*—After ε, ι, and ρ, α is changed to ᾱ instead of η: ἐάω, *I leave, allow;* fut. ἐάσω; St. ἰα, *heal;* ἰᾱτρός, *physician;* St. ὀρα, *see;* ὄρᾱμα, *a view.* The Attic dialect is altogether averse to the combinations εη, ιη, ρη, and frequently puts εᾱ, ιᾱ, ρᾱ in their place.

§ 42. 2. *Compensatory lengthening, i. e.,* that which is used as a compensation for lost consonants. By it ᾰ, even when ε, ι, or ρ does not precede, is often changed to ᾱ: πᾶς, *every,* from πᾰ-ντ-ς — ε generally becomes ει: εἰμί, *I am,* from ἐσ-μι (§ 315) — ο generally becomes ου: διδούς for διδο-ντ-ς [Lat. *da-n-s*] — ῐ always becomes ῑ, and ῠ always ῡ: δεικνύ-ς for δεικνυ-ντ-ς, *showing.*

Obs.—Exceptions, in which ε becomes η, and ο becomes ω, are given in § 147, and in which α becomes η in § 270.

§ 43. The three short hard vowels often interchange in one and the same Stem, when, generally, ε is regarded as the Stem-vowel: τρέπω, *I turn;* ἔτραπον, *I turned;*

---

§ 40. Dialects.—The extension of υ to ου appears in εἰλήλουθα, *am come,* from Stem ἐλυθ (§ 327, 2).

§ 41. Dialects.—The Old and New-Ionic dialect does not avoid the combinations εη, ιη, and ρη: ἰτέη = Attic ἰτέᾱ, *willow;* ἰητρός = Attic ἰᾱτρός, *physician;* πειρήσομαι = Attic πειράσομαι, *I will try.*

The Doric dialect, on the contrary, regularly lengthens ᾰ into ᾱ: τιμᾱ́σω = τιμήσω, *I will honor* (§ 24, D., 2).

τρόπος, *turning;* Stem γενες, Nom. γένος, *race* [compare Lat. generis, Nom. gen*us*]; φλέγω, *I burn;* φλόξ, *flame.* η also is at times changed to ω: ἀρήγω, *I help;* ἀρωγός, *helper.*

C. *Consonants in combination with one another.*

§ 44. Consonants, in regard to their combination, are subject to still greater limitation and change than the vowels. Those which are *dissimilar* (comp. §§ 32, 33) *agree best* with one another, especially the mutes with the liquids.

That discordant consonants may continue together, they are either made more like one another (assimilated) or more unlike (dissimilated). The essential laws for the necessary changes of consonants are the following:

§ 45. 1. Before *mute dentals* (§§ 30, 31), only consonants of *other organs* which are of the *same order* (that is, both hard, both soft, or both aspirated, § 32) can stand; consequently, the only allowable combinations of sounds are—κτ, πτ, γδ, βδ, χθ, φθ.

When a different mute stands before the dental, through inflexion or derivation, it must be *assimilated* to the order of the latter. Consequently—

κδ and χδ become γδ.	πδ and φδ become βδ.
κθ " γθ " χθ.	πθ " βθ " φθ.
γτ " χτ " κτ.	βτ " φτ " πτ.

Therefore—

πλεκ-θηναι	becomes	πλεχθῆναι,	from	πλέκω, *I weave*.
λεγ-τος	"	λεκτός,	"	λέγω, *I say*
				[*lectus* instead of *leg-tus*].
λεγ-θηναι	"	λεχθῆναι,	"	λέγω, *I say.*
δεχ-τος	"	δεκτός,	"	δέχομαι, *I receive*
				[*tractus* instead of *trah-tus*, from *traho*].
τυπ-θηναι	"	τυφθῆναι,	from	τύπτω, *I strike.*
γραφ-τος	"	γραπτός,	"	γράφω, *I write.*
γραφ-δην	"	γράβδην,	"	" "

Obs.—The preposition ἐκ, *out of* (Lat. *ex*), remains unchanged in all combinations: ἔκθεσις, *casting out;* ἐκδρομή, *running out.*

§ 48. CONSONANTS IN COMBINATION. 15

§ 46. 2. Before *mute dentals,* mute *dentals* to be audible are changed into σ (*Dissimilation*). Therefore—

ττ, δτ, and θτ become στ.

τθ, δθ, " θθ " σθ: hence

ἀνυτ-τος becomes ἀνυστός, *accomplished*, from ἀνύτω, *I accomplish.*
ᾀδ-τεον " ᾀστέον, *canendum est*, " ᾄδω, *I sing.*
πειθ-θηναι " πεισθῆναι, *to be persuaded*, " πείθω, *I persuade.*

§ 47. 3. Before μ a *guttural* becomes γ, a *dental* σ, a *labial* μ. Therefore—

διωκ-μος becomes διωγμός, *persecution*, from διώκω, *I pursue.*
βε-βρεχ-μαι " βέβρεγμαι, *I have been wetted*, from βρέχω, *I wet.*
ἰδ-μεν " ἴσμεν, *we know*, from οἶδα, *I know.* [*plish.*
ἤνυτ-μαι " ἤνυσμαι, *I have been perfected*, from ἀνύτω, *I accom-*
πε-πειθ-μενος " πεπεισμένος, *persuaded*, from πείθω, *I persuade.*
κοπ-μος " κομμός, *a striking*, from κόπ-τω, *I strike* [*summus*, from *sup-mus*].
τε-τριβ-μαι " τέτριμμαι, *I have been rubbed*, from τρίβω, *I rub.*
γραφ-μα " γράμμα, *letter*, from γράφω, *I write.*

Obs.—Sometimes in derivation the gutturals and dentals remain unchanged: ἀκμή, *bloom;* ῥυθμός, *movement*, *rhythm;* ἀριθμός, *number.*

The preposition ἐκ leaves its κ unchanged: ἐκμάσσω, *I wipe out.*

§ 48. 4. Before σ, as a hard consonant, γ and χ become κ, and β becomes π (*Assimilation*): κσ is then written ξ, and πσ ψ. Therefore—

ἀγ-σω becomes ἀκ-σω, written ἄξ-ω, *I shall lead*, from ἄγω, *I lead* [*rexi* instead of *reg-si*, from *reg-o*].
δεχ-σομαι " δεκ-σομαι, written δέξομαι, *I shall receive*, from δέχομαι, *I receive* [*traxi* instead of *trah-si*, from *trah-o*].
τριβ-σω " τριπ-σω, written τρίψω, *I shall rub*, from τρίβω, *I rub* [*scripsi* instead of *scrib-si*, from *scrib-o*].
γραφ-σω " γραπ-σω, written γράψω, *I shall write*, from γράφ-ω, *I write.*

Obs.—It is clear from § 34 that every κ and π with σ must become

§ 47. Dialects.—The changes of dentals and gutturals before μ is frequently omitted in Ionic: ἴκ-μενος, *favorable*, from St. ἰκ (ἱκάνω, *I come*); ἀκαχμένος, *pointed*, from St. ἀκ (Lat. *acuo*); ἀϋτμή, *breath;* ὀδμή, *smell*, from St. ὀδ (ὄζω) [*od-or*], Att. ὀσ-μή; ἴδ-μεν, *we know* = Att. ἴσ-μεν; κεκορυθμένος, *equipped*, from St. κορυθ (κορύσσω) = Att. κεκορυσμένος.

16 CONSONANTS IN COMBINATION. § 49.

ξ and ψ: hence πλεκ-σω becomes πλέξω, from πλέκω, *I weave;* λειπ-σω becomes λείψω, from λείπω, *I leave.*

§ 49. 5. The dentals, when standing separately before σ, are dropped *without compensation;* in like manner ν disappears before ζ. Therefore—

ἀνυτ-σις becomes ἄνυσις, *accomplishment,* from ἀνύτω, *I accomplish.*
ἡδ-σομαι " ἥσομαι, *I shall rejoice,* from ἥδομαι, *I rejoice* [*laesi* for *laed-si,* from *laed-o*].
κορυθ-σι " κόρυσι, *to the helmets,* from κόρυς, Gen. κόρυ-θος, *helmet.*
δαιμον-σι " δαίμοσι, *to the dæmons,* from δαίμων, *dæmon.* [*yoke.*
συν-ζυγος " σύζυγος, *yoked together,* from σύν, *together,* and ζυγόν,

Hence σ before another σ is lost: τειχεσ-σι becomes τείχε-σι, *to walls* (from τεῖχος, *wall*); ἐσ-σομαι, ἔ-σομαι.

Obs. 1.—ν is not always dropped before σ or ζ in composition. In the preposition ἐν, the ν remains for the sake of clearness: ἐν-στάζω, *I trickle in;* ἐνζεύγνυμι, *I harness.* The ν in πᾶν, *all, every,* and πάλιν, *again,* either remains unchanged or is assimilated to the following σ: πάνσοφος, *all-wise;* π α λ ί σ σ υ τ ο ς, from παλίν-συτος, *starting back.* The ν in σύν, *with,* is dropped before ζ or σ with a consonant following: σύζυγος (see above); σύστημα, *system;* it is assimilated before a simple σ: συσσίτιον, from συν-σιτιον, *common meal.*

2. Sometimes ν remains unchanged before σ in the 2d Pers. Sing. of the Perf. Mid. : πέ-φαν-σαι, *thou hast appeared.*

3. In exceptional cases, compensatory lengthening (§ 42) takes place when a single ν is omitted : for instance—
a) In some Nominatives Sing. : μελᾱ-ς, *black,* for μελαν-ς.
b) In the 3d Pers. Plur. of the chief tenses, where σ has taken the place of τ: λύ-ον-σι, *they loosen,* instead of λυ-ον-σι (originally λυ-ον-τι) (§ 60).
c) Often in derivation : γερουσία, *senate,* instead of γεροντια, from St. γεροντ, Nom. γέρων, *old man.*

§ 50. 6. The *combinations* ντ, νθ, νδ, are likewise omitted before σ, but cause a *compensatory lengthening* (§ 42):

παντ-σι becomes πᾶσι, *to all,* from St. παντ-, Nom. πᾶ-ς.
τιθεντ-ς " τιθείς, *putting,* " " τιθεντ.
γεροντ-σι . " γέρουσι, *to old men,* " " γεροντ, Nom. γέρων.

§ 49. Dialects.—Homer often assimilates a mute to the following σ: ποσσί=Att. ποσί for ποδ-σι (*pedibus*). He often preserves one σ before another: ἔσ-σομαι, *I shall be.*

§ 51. CONSONANTS IN COMBINATION. 17

δεικνυντ-σι becomes δεικνῦσι, { to those / who show }, from St. δεικνυντ, Nom. δεικνῦ-ς.

σπενδ-σω " σπείσω, { I will pour / libations }, " " σπενδ, Pres. σπένδω.

πενθ-σομαι " πείσομαι, I shall suffer, " " πενθ, Pres. πάσχω.

Obs. 1.—ντ disappears, without compensation, in the Dat. Plur. of Stems of Adjectives in εντ, Nom. ει-ς: St. χαριεντ, Nom. χαρίεις, Dat. Plur. χαρίε-σι for χαριεντ-σι.

2.—Of νθ before σ, ν remains in ἕλμιν-ς, *tape-worm,* instead of ἑλμινθ-ς, Stem ἑλμινθ: Τίρυν-ς, *the city Tiryns,* instead of Τιρυνθ-ς, Stem Τιρυνθ.

§ 50*b.* In later Attic σ is readily assimilated to a preceding ρ: Old Att. χερσόνησος, New Att. χερρόνησος, *peninsula;* Old Att. θαρσῶ, New Att. θαρρῶ, *I am courageous.*

§ 51. 7. ν remains unchanged before mute dentals; it becomes the *nasal* γ before *gutturals* (§ 4), μ before *labials,* and is assimilated before liquid consonants:

συν-τίθημι, *I put together,* is unchanged.
συν-καλεω, *I call together,* becomes συγκαλέω.
συν-χρονος, *contemporaneous,* " σύγχρονος.
ἐν-πειρος, *experienced,* " ἔμπειρος, from ἐν and πεῖρα, *proof* [so in-peritus becomes im-peritus].
ἐν-ψυχος, *inspirited,* " ἔμψυχος, from ἐν and ψυχή, *soul;*
ἐν-μετρος, *metrical,* " ἔμμετρος, from ἐν and μέτρον, *measure* [so in-modicus becomes im-mod- icus].
συν-ρεω, *I flow together,* " συρρέω, from σύν and ῥέω, *I flow* [so con-ruo becomes cor-ruo].
συν-λεγω, *I collect,* " συλλέγω, from σύν and λέγω, *I gather* [so con-ligo becomes col-ligo].

Obs. 1.—ν in the preposition ἐν remains unchanged before ρ: ἔν-ρυθμος, *rhythmical.*

2.—ν is combined with ρ by means of δ in ἀν-δ-ρός, Gen. of ἀνήρ, *man.* So is μ with ρ by β in μεσημ-β-ρία, *midday,* instead of μεσημ(ε)ρια (μέσος and ἡμέρα, compare § 61, *c*).

---

§ 51. **Dialects.**—In the Epic dialect β is often inserted between μ and ρ, and between μ and λ: μέ-μ-β-λωκα, *I have gone,* from Stem μολ, by metathesis (§ 59). μ before λ or ρ becomes β at the beginning of a word: βλώ-σκω, *I go,* Present of the Stem μολ; βροτός, *mortal,* for μροτος, from the Stem μρο or μορ [*mor-ior, mortuus sum*].

§ 52. 8. *Hard mutes* (tenues) unite with a following *rough breathing* (spiritus asper) into *aspirates* (χ, θ, ϕ): hence,

ἐπ' (ἐπί) and ἡμέρα, *day*, become ἐφήμερος, *for a day*.
δεκ' (δέκα) " ἡμέρα, *day*, " δεχήμερος, *for ten days*.
ten
ἀντ' (ἀντί) " ὕπατος, *consul*, " ἀνθύπατος, *proconsul*.

§ 53. 9. At the end of a word, when the following word begins with a spiritus asper, the hard mute is changed into an aspirate:

οὐχ οὗτος, *not this*, for οὐκ οὗτος.
ἀφ' ἑστίας, *from the hearth*, " ἀπ' (ἀπὸ) ἑστίας.
καθ' ἡμέραν, *by day*, " κατ' (κατὰ) ἡμέραν.

Obs.—If another hard mute stands before the one to be aspirated, the first must also be aspirated (§ 45): ἑπτά and ἡμέρα form ἐφθήμερος, *for seven days;* νύκτα and ὅλην become νύχθ' ὅλην, *totam noctem*.

§ 53*b*. 10. Two syllables immediately following one another can not both begin with aspirates in the following cases:

a) In reduplication the corresponding hard mute takes the place of the aspirate:

κε-χώρηκα for χε-χώρηκα, *I have proceeded*, from χωρέω, *I proceed*.
τί-θημι " θι-θημι, *I put*.
πέ-φυκα " φε-φυκα, *I have become*.

b) The Aorists Passive of the verbal Stems θε (τίθημι, *I put*), θυ (θύω, *I sacrifice*), adopt the same modification: ἐ-τέ-θην, *I was put*, for ἐ-θε-θην; ἐ-τύ-θην, *I was sacrificed*, for ἐ-θυ-θην. (Compare § 298.)

c) In the Imperative of the First Aorist Passive (§ 297), on the contrary, *the second* aspirate is changed to a tenuis: σώ-θη-τι, *be saved*, for σω-θη-θι.

d) Isolated instances are: ἀμπέχω, *embrace*, for ἀμφεχω; ἐκεχειρία, for ἐχεχειρια, *armistice*, from ἔχειν, *to hold*, and χείρ, *hand*.

§ 52 and 53. Dialects.—The aspiration is omitted in New Ionic: ἐπήμερος, *for a day;* ἀπίημι, *I send away;* οὐκ οὕτως = οὐχ οὗτος, *not so;* ἀπ' οὗ, *from the time when*, Att. ἀφ' οὗ.

§ 55.   OTHER CHANGES OF SOUND.   19

Obs.—Sometimes the spiritus asper is changed to the lenis, because the following syllable begins with an aspirate: ὄ-φρα, *till*, for ὀ-φρα, from the relative Stem ὁ (§ 213, 217), ἔχω for ἕχω, from St. ἐχ (§ 327, 6).

§ 54. Some Stems beginning with τ change this letter to θ when an aspirate at the end can not be retained (§ 45). This happens:

a) In the Substantive Stem τριχ, whose Nominative is θρίξ, *hair*, Dat. Plur. θριξί. The other cases are regular, formed from the Stem τριχ (Gen. τριχός, Nom. Plur. τρίχες).

b) In ταχύς, *quick*, whose comparative is θάσσων for ταχιων (§ 57; compare § 198).

c) In the following Verbal Stems:

τاφ, Pres. θάπτω, *I bury*,   Fut. θάψω, Aor. Pass. ἐτάφην, Subs. ταφός, *grave*.
τρεφ,   "   τρέφω, *I nourish*,   "   θρέψω, Subs. θρέμμα, *cattle*.
τρεχ,   "   τρέχω, *I run*,   "   θρέξομαι ⎫
τρυφ,   "   θρύπτω, *I rub to pieces*, "   θρύψω   ⎬ (§ 260).
τυφ,   "   τύφω, *I smoke*,   "   θύψω   ⎭

Obs.—In the Passive First Aorist (§ 296), and in the Infinitive of the Perf. Mid., the aspirate of the Stem remains unchanged, yet the initial tenuis is aspirated, because the Stem-consonant is not felt to be necessarily an original aspirate, as it might have been modified by the influence of the θ after it (§ 45): ἐθρέφθην, τεθράφθαι.

D. *Other changes of Consonants and Vowels in the middle of a Word.*

§ 55. Important changes of sounds are produced by the modifications of the soft vowel ι in connection with consonants (compare §§ 186, 198, 199, 250–253). Frequently, for instance,

1. ι after ν or ρ is put a syllable farther back, where it forms a diphthong with the preceding vowel. Hence,

τείνω, from τεν-ιω, I stretch, St. τεν [tendo].
μαίνομαι, " μαν-ιομαι, I rage, " μαν.
ἀμείνων, " ἀμεν-ιων, better, " ἀμεν.
κείρω, " κερ-ιω, I shear, " κερ.
δότειρα, " δοτερ-ια, the giver, fem. " δοτερ (δοτήρ, giver).
χείρων, " χερ-ιων, worse, " χερ.

§ 56. 2. ι is assimilated to a preceding λ:
μᾶλλον, from μαλ-ιον, more, from μάλα, much.
ἅλλομαι, " ἀλ-ιομαι, I spring, St. ἀλ [salio].
ἄλλος, " ἀλ-ιος, another [alius].
στέλλω, " στελ-ιω, I send, St. στελ.

§ 57. 3. Gutturals (τ and θ less frequently) coalesce with a following ι to σσ (New Att. ττ):
ἥσσων, from ἡκ-ιων, less, St. ἡκ, superl. ἥκιστα.
Θρᾷσσα, " Θρακ-ια, Thracian, fem. (masc. Θρᾷξ), St. Θρᾳκ.
τάσσω, " ταγ-ιω, I arrange, St. ταγ.
ἐλάσσων, " ἐλαχ-ιων, smaller, " ἐλαχ, superl. ἐλάχιστος.
Κρῆσσα, " Κρητ-ια, Cretan, fem. (masc. Κρῆς), St. Κρητ.
κορύσσω, " κορυθ-ιω, I arm, St. κορυθ (κόρυς, helmet).

§ 58. 4. δ and sometimes γ coalesce with a following ι to ζ.
ἕζομαι, from ἑδ-ιομαι, I sit, St. ἑδ (τὸ ἕδος, the seat).
κράζω, " κραγ-ιω, I cry, " κραγ (Perf. κέ-κρᾱγ-α).

Other changes of Sounds are:

§ 59. 1. Transposition (μετάθεσις), which most frequently occurs with λ, ρ, also with μ and ν:
θράσος, together with θάρσος, boldness.
θρώσκω, from the St. θορ, I spring, Second Aorist ἔθορον.
βέ-βλη-κα, " βαλ, I have thrown, " " ἔβαλον.
τέ-θνη-κα, " θαν, I am dead, " " ἔθανον.
τμῆ-σις, " τεμ, a cut, Pres. τέμνω, I cut.

Obs.—In the last four examples the vowel is moreover lengthened.

§ 59. Dialects.—Transposition is more frequent in the Homeric dialect (compare § 295, D.): καρτερός and κρατερός, strong; κάρτιστος = Att. κράτιστος, the strongest, from κράτος, strength; τραπ-είομεν (compare § 295, D.) for ταρπ-είομεν, we desire to rejoice, St. τερπ (τέρπομαι). So also in ἔδρακον, I saw, St. δερκ (δέρκομαι); ἔπραθον, I destroyed, St. περθ (πέρθω). Homer: ἀταρπός = Att. ἀτραπός; path.

§ 62.   OTHER CHANGES OF SOUND.   21

§ 60. 2. The *weakening* of single consonants. The most important weakenings are:

a) The very frequent one, especially before ι, of τ to σ: ἀναισθησία, *want of feeling*, for ἀναισθητια, from ἀναίσθητος, *without feeling*. φᾶσί for φαντι, *they say*.

On the rejection of ν and the compensation for it, which frequently occur in this case, see § 49, *Obs.* 3, c; compare § 187.

b) The weakening of initial σ before vowels to the spiritus asper:

ὕς, *swine*, together with σῦς. Compare Lat. *su-s*.
ἵ-στη-μι for σι-στη-μι, *I place*. Compare Lat. *si-sto* (§§ 308, 327, 5, 6).

§ 61. 3. The entire *rejection* of sounds. The following cases are important:

a) σ is rejected where it would have to stand between two consonants in inflexion:

γεγράφ-θαι for γεγραφ-σθαι, *to be written*, St. γραφ, Pres. γράφω.
τέτυφ-θε   " τε-τυφ-σθε, *be ye struck*,   " τυπ,   " τύπτω.

b) σ between two vowels is very often rejected:

λέγε-αι, λέγῃ (§ 38), for λεγεσαι, *thou art said*, St. λ ε γ, Pres. λέγω.
ἐδύνα-ο, ἐδύνω, for ἐδύνασο, *thou couldst*, Pres. δύναμαι.
γένε-ος for γενεσος, *of the race*, St. γ ε ν ε σ (§ 166).

c) The rejection of a vowel between consonants in the middle of a word is called *syncope* (συγκοπή): ἐ-πτ-ό-μην for ἐ-πετ-ο-μην, *I flew*, St. π ε τ (§ 326, 34). Compare § 51, *Obs.* 2.

§ 62. 4. The *doubling* of a consonant. This is rare,

§ 60. **Dialects.**—The Dorians retain τ: φαντί=φᾶσί(ν), *they say*. The older Att. less frequently: τήμερον = σήμερον, *to-day*.
§ 61. **Dialects.**—Syncope is more frequent in Homer: τίπτε for τίποτε, *why ever? why?* ἐκέκλετο = ἐ-κε-κελέτο, *he called*, St. κελ.
§ 62. **Dialects.**—In Homer simple consonants are readily doubled; the mutes more rarely: ὅππως = Attic ὅπως, *how;* ὁπποῖος = Attic ὁποῖος, *qualis;* ὅττι = Attic ὅτι, *that;* the vocal consonants often:

when it has not arisen through the assimilations mentioned above (§§ 47, 50b, 51, 56). The liquid ρ is the most frequently doubled: ἔρριψα for ἔριψα, *I hurled;* ἄρρηκτος for ἄ-ρηκτος, *not breakable.* The aspirates can be doubled only by the corresponding tenuis: Βάκχος, Σαπφώ, Ἀτθίς.

E. *Changes of Sound at the end of a Word.*

§ 63. When a word *ending* in a vowel is followed by another *beginning* with a vowel, whether accompanied by a spiritus lenis or asper, there is a *hiatus*. The Greeks very often suffer the hiatus in prose; but frequently the hiatus is avoided, especially if the first word is a shorter one and of itself of little importance. This is done in three ways, that is, either by *elision* (rejection of the final vowel), or by *crasis* (contraction of the two vowels), or by *synizesis* (collapse of two syllables into one).

ἔλλαβε = Attic ἔλαβε, *he took;* φιλομμειδής = Attic φιλομειδής, *readily smiling;* ἐϋννητος = Attic εὔ-νητος, *well-woven;* ὅσσον = Attic ὅσον, *how great;* νέκυσσι = Attic νέκυσι, *to the corpses;* ὀπίσσω = Attic ὀπίσω, *back.* On the contrary, Homer sometimes has a single ρ where the Attic has double: ὠκύροος = ὠκύρροος, *swift-flowing.* Often also both forms are usual together: Ἀχιλεύς and Ἀχιλλεύς, Ὀδυσεύς and Ὀδυσσεύς.

§ 63. Dialects.—The Homeric dialect admits the hiatus in many cases: the most important are:

1. The hiatus is only apparent in words with the digamma: κατὰ οἶκον for κατὰ Ϝοῖκον, *at home.*
2. It is allowed after weak vowels in forms with which elision is not usual: παιδὶ ὄπασσεν, *he gave to the son.*
3. It is softened by a pause or a caesura after the first short syllable of the third foot: κάθησο, ἐμῷ δ' ἐπιπείθεο μύθῳ, *sit down, and obey my word;* τῶν οἱ ἓξ ἐγένοντο ἐνὶ μεγάροισι, *of which six were born to him in the chambers.*
4. A long vowel or diphthong before another in the thesis becomes short, and causes only an *improper* or *weak* hiatus: Ἀτρεῖδαί τε καὶ ἄλλοι ἐϋκνήμιδες Ἀχαιοί, *Ye Atridæ and ye other well-greaved Achæans.* Compare § 75, D., 2.

§ 65. ELISION.—CRASIS. 23

§ 64. 1. *Elision*, or the rejection of the final vowel, of which the apostrophe (§ 15) is the sign, occurs only with short final vowels, but never with υ; most frequently at the end of dissyllabic prepositions, conjunctions, and adverbs: ἐπ' αὐτῷ, *with him*, for ἐπὶ αὐτῷ; οὐδ' ἐδύνατο, *he could not even*, ἀλλ' ἦλθεν, *but he came;* less frequently at the end of nouns and verbs: οἱ πάντ' εἰςαγγέλλοντες, *i. e.*, οἱ πάντα εἰςαγγέλλοντες, *who reported the whole.*

Obs. 1.—The prepositions περί, *round*, ἄχρι and μέχρι, *till*, and the conjunction ὅτι, *that*, never suffer elision.

2. In compounds also the elision occurs, without, however, being indicated by the apostrophe: ἐπ-έρχομαι, from ἐπι-έρχομαι, *I come up;* but περιέρχομαι, *I go round*.

3. On the change of consonants occurring with elision (ἐφ' ἡμέρᾳ), see § 52.

§ 65. 2. *Crasis* (κρᾶσις, *mixing*) is governed, on the

§ 64. Dialects.—Elision is much more frequent with the poets than in prose; thus, not only ε and ι even in nominal and verbal forms are elided, but also the diphthongs αι and οι, in the verbal terminations μαι, σαι, ται, σθαι, and in the forms μοι and τοι. In Homer, ι in ὅτι, *that*, is also sometimes elided.

A change of the final vowel, occurring only in poets, is the *apocope* (ἀποκοπή). It is the rejection of a short final vowel before a word beginning with a *consonant*. The apocope is frequent in Homer with the prepositions ἀνά, κατά, παρά, and with the conjunction ἄρα, *now*, seldom with ἀπό and ὑπό: it takes place in compounds as well as at the meeting of two separate words. The ν of ἀν(ά) then suffers the changes described in § 51; the τ of κατ(ά), the π of ἀπ(ό) and ὑπ(ό), are made like the following consonant: ἀνδύεται = ἀναδύεται, *emerges;* κἀπ πεδίον = κατὰ πεδίον, *on the plain;* κάλλιπε = κατέλιπε, *left behind;* πάρθετο = παρέθετο, *put before;* ἀππέμψει = ἀποπέμψει, *will send away;* κατθανεῖν = καταθανεῖν, *die.*

§ 65. Dialects.—Crasis in Homer is very rare, but very frequent in the Attic poets: *e. g.*, οὐξ = ὁ ἐξ, κὠδύρεται = καὶ ὀδύρεται, *and laments;* ὦναξ = ὦ ἄναξ, *O king;* χὠπόσοι = καὶ ὁπόσοι, *and how many.*—Herod. ὧλλοι = οἱ ἄλλοι, *the rest.* The loss of a short initial vowel is sometimes indicated by the apostrophe (§ 15): μὴ 'γώ = μὴ ἐγώ, *ne ego;* ἤδη 'ξέρχεται = ἤδη ἐξέρχεται, *he is already coming out.*

whole, by the laws given for contraction (§ 36–39). It occurs chiefly after forms of the article, of the relative pronoun (especially ὅ, *quod*, and ἅ, *quæ*), after the preposition πρό, *for*, *before*, Latin *pro*, and the conjunction καί, *and*. The syllable produced by crasis is *necessarily long*. The sign of crasis is the coronis (§ 16): τἀγαθά, *bona*, from τὰ ἀγαθά; τἄλλα, from τὰ ἄλλα, *the other things;* τοὔνομα, *the name*, from τὸ ὄνομα; ταὐτό, *the same*, for τὸ αὐτό.

Obs. 1.—The rough breathing of the article or relative maintains its place in spite of crasis: ἀνήρ, *the man*, irregular for ὁ ἀνήρ, in which case the coronis disappears; in θοἰμάτιον, from τὸ ἱμάτιον, *the dress*, the spiritus asper has changed τ into θ (§ 52); so also θάτερον, irregular for τὸ ἕτερον, *the other*.
2. The new syllable, formed by crasis, has ι subscript only when ι is the last of the contracted vowels: καὶ ἐν, *and in*, becomes κἀν, but καὶ εἶτα, *and then*, becomes κᾆτα.
On the accent with crasis, § 89.

§ 66. 3. *Synizesis* (*sinking*, compare § 39) occurs at the meeting of two words only after a long vowel, especially after the conjunctions ἐπεί, *as*, ἤ, *or*, ἦ, *num*, μή, *not*, and after ἐγώ, *I:* ἐπεὶ οὐ, *as not;* μὴ ἄλλοι, *ne alii;* ἐγὼ οὐ, *I not*. It is perceptible only in the poets, who reckon the two syllables as one.

§ 67. *No Greek word ends in any consonant except the vocal ones*, ν, ρ, *and* ς (ξ, ψ). The only exceptions are: the negative οὐκ (before consonants οὐ) and the preposition ἐκ, *out of* (before vowels ἐξ), which attach themselves so closely to the following word that their κ can hardly be looked upon as final.

When any other consonant, except these three, appears at the end of a word, it is usually rejected:

μέλι, *honey* (*mel*), for μελιτ (Gen. μέλιτ-ος)	} compare § 147b.
σῶμα, *body*, " σωματ (Gen. σώματ-ος)	
ἦσαν, *they were*, " ἦσαντ (compare Lat. *erant*).	

§ 68. MOVABLE CONSONANTS. 25

But mute Dentals in this case are often changed into vocal ς:

πρός for προτ, from προτί, to (Hom.).
δός " δοθ, " δοθι, give.
τέρας " τεραт, Gen. τέρατ-ος, miracle.

§ 68. Certain words and forms have, after a short vowel at the end, a *movable* ν (ν ἐφελκυστικόν). This ν is used before words which begin with a vowel—by which the hiatus is avoided—and before longer pauses. Poets employ it also before consonants, especially at the end of the word, to make it more sonorous.

The words and forms which have a movable ν are the following:

1. The Dat. Plur. in σι(ν): πᾶσιν ἔδωκα, *I gave to all;* but πᾶσι δοκεῖ οὕτως εἶναι, *to all it seems to be so.*

2. The designations of place in σι(ν): Ἀθήνησιν ἦν, *he was at Athens;* but Ἀθήνησι τόδε ἐγένετο, *this happened at Athens.*

3. The single words εἴκοσι(ν), *twenty;* πέρυσι(ν), *last year;* and παντάπασι(ν), *entirely;* εἴκοσιν ἄνδρες, *twenty men;* but εἴκοσι γυναῖκες, *twenty women.*

4. The third person Sing. in ε(ν): ἔσωσεν αὐτούς, *he saved them;* but ἔσωσε τοὺς Ἀθηναίους, *he saved the Athenians.*

5. The third person Plur. as well as Sing. in σι(ν): λέγουσιν εὖ, *they speak well,* but λέγουσι τοῦτο, *they say this;* δείκνυσιν ἐκεῖσε, *he points there,* but δείκνυσι τὸν ἄνδρα, *he points out the man.*

---

§ 68. Dialects.—To the words which have a movable ν there are added in Homer the adverbs of place in θε(ν): ἄνευθε(ν), *from afar;* πάροιθε(ν), *from before, formerly*; the particles κέ(ν), *perhaps,* and νύ(ν), *now.*

The New-Ionic dialect, which admits the immediate succession of vowels, omits the movable ν. On the κ in οὐκ before a spiritus asper, § 52, D.

B

§ 69. *Obs*. 1.—In like manner, οὐ, *not*, takes κ only before vowels, which becomes χ before the spiritus asper (§ 52): οὔ φησι, *he says not;* οὐκ αὐτός, *not he himself;* οὐχ οὕτως, *not so*. The κ appears also in οὐκέτι and μηκέτι, *no more*.
2. ἐκ, *out of*, is ἐξ before vowels (Lat. *ex*): ἐκ τῆς πόλεως, *out of the city;* ἐξ ἀκροπόλεως, *out of the acropolis* or *castle;* ἐκλέγω, *I speak out;* ἐξέλεγον, *I spoke out.*
3. Without any definite reason, the words οὕτως, *thus* (adverb of οὗτος, *this*), ἄχρις, μέχρις, *till*, very frequently lose their final ς; but πολλάκις, *many times*, loses it only in the poets.

Chap. IV.—Division of Syllables and their Quantity.

A. *Division of Syllables*.

§ 70. The Syllables (συλλαβή; *collection*) in Greek words are divided according to the following rules. Every vowel which stands before another, but does not form a diphthong with it, or collapse with it by synizesis (§ 39), is reckoned a separate syllable: ἰ-ατρός; *physician*, trisyllabic.

§ 71. A consonant which stands between two vowels belongs to the second syllable: ἔ-χει, *has;* οὗ-τος, *this;* ἱ-κα-νός, *capable.*

Two or more consonants usually belong to the following vowel: ἁ-πλοῦς, *simple;* ἁ-ρι-στε-ρός, *on the left hand;* ἔ-σχον, *I had;* ἀ-μνός, *lamb;* ἐ-χθρός, *inimical;* likewise double consonants: ὄ-ψο-μαι, *I shall see;* ἔ-ζω, *I place.*

§ 72. Exceptions. 1. Liquids and nasals join the preceding vowel: ἅρ-μα, *carriage;* ἀδελ-φός, *brother;* καγ-χάζω, *I laugh;* ἔν-δον, *within;* ἄμ-φω, *both, ambo.* μν only join the following vowel: κά-μνω, *I suffer.* 2. When a consonant is doubled, the first belongs to the preceding, the second to the following syllable: ἵπ-πος, *horse;* βάλ-λω, *I throw;* Πύρ-ρος. The same takes place when aspirates follow the corresponding tenues: Ἀτ-θίς, Βάκ-χος, Σαπ-φώ.

§ 73. Compounds are divided into the elements out of which they are formed: συν-έχω, *I hold together;* ἐξ-άγω, *I drive out.*

B. *Quantity*

§ 74. With regard to the quantity (length or shortness) of syllables, the same rules, in general, hold good for the Greek as for the Latin. An important exception, however, consists in one vowel before the other not needing to be *short* in Greek: θωή, *penance;* λᾱός, *people;* βέλτῖον, *better.* Nor do the special Latin rules for final syllables hold good in Greek.

§ 75. A syllable is long *by nature* when it contains a long vowel or diphthong: ὑμεῖς, *you;* κρίνω, *I decide;* ᾄδω, *I sing.* The recognition of quantity in Greek is rendered much easier by the characters: δόμος, *room, house;* δῶμα, *house;* in other cases by the accent (§§ 83, 84); the rest can be learned only by practice and from the lexicon.

Obs.—Every contracted syllable must, of course, be long: ἄκων, *unwilling* = ἀέκων, ἱρός = ἱερός, *holy.*

§ 76. A syllable is long *by position* when a vowel is fol-

---

§ 74. **Dialects.**—Diphthongs and long vowels are very seldom shortened before vowels in the same word: Hom. οἷος (*qualis* ⁻ ⁻), and βέ-βληαι, with short η.

§ 75. **Dialects.**—1. The quantity of the common vowels is very uncertain generally, but especially in Hom. ἴωμεν, *let us go;* Ἄρες, Ἄρες, *O Ares, Ares.*

2. A final syllable ending in a long vowel or diphthong in Homer and the tragic choruses is shortened before a following vowel: οἴκοι ἔσαν, *they were at home* (⁻ ⁻ ⁻ ⁻); ἡμένη ἐν, *sitting in* (⁻ ⁻ ⁻). Compare § 63, D. 4. But those words which began with digamma (§ 34, D.) leave a preceding vowel long in Hom.: κάλλεϊ τε στίλβων καὶ εἵμασιν (⁻ ⁻ ⁻ ⁻ ⁻ ⁻ ⁻), *glittering with beauty and garments.*

lowed by two or more consonants, or a double consonant, whether—

a) both consonants or the double consonant stand in the same word: χάρμα, *joy* (˘ ˘); ἕξις, *mien* (˘ ˘); Κάστωρ (¯ ¯); or
b) the first concludes the first word, and the rest begin the second: θεὸς δέ, *but God* (˘ ¯ ˘); ἐν τούτῳ, *meanwhile* (¯ ¯ ¯); or
c) both or the double consonant stand at the beginning of the second word: τὰ κτήματα, *the goods* (¯ ¯ ˘ ˘); ὁ ζῶν, *the living one* (¯ ¯).

Obs.—When the vowel thus placed is already long by nature, this must be indicated in the pronunciation: the α in πράσσω, *I act*, sounds differently from that of τάσσω, *I arrange*, though both words make a spondee in verse; that in μᾶλλον different from that of κάλλος, *beauty*, though both form a trochee.

§ 77. When a vowel short by nature stands before a mute with λ, ρ, ν, μ following, the syllable may be long or short: τέκνον, *child* (˘ ˘); τυφλός, *blind* (˘ ˘); τί δρᾷς, *what art thou doing* (˘ ¯)?

The syllable, however, is necessarily long in the following cases:

§ 78. *a)* when the mute stands at the end of the first, the liquid or nasal at the beginning of the second word: ἐκ νηῶν, *out of the ships* (¯ ¯ ¯); and in compounds in which the mute belongs to the first element: ἐκλέγω, *I speak out* (¯ ˘ ¯);

b) when a soft mute (β, γ, δ) is followed by λ, μ, or ν: βίβλος, *book* (¯ ˘); τάγμα, *task* (¯ ˘); ἔχιδνα, *snake* (˘ ¯ ˘).

---

§ 77. **Dialects.**—In Homer, a mute with λ, ρ, ν, μ following, almost *regularly* makes position: τέκνον τί κλαίεις, *child, why weepest thou* (¯ ¯ ¯ ¯ ˘)? ὕπνος πανδαμάτωρ, *all-subduing sleep* (¯ ¯ ¯ ¯ ˘ ¯). Nay, even λ, ρ, ν, μ, at the beginning of words, have often the power of lengthening the short final vowel of the preceding word: καλήν τε μεγάλην τε, *a beautiful and great* (¯ ¯ ˘ ˘ ˘ ¯ ˘). δ in the Stem δει (δεῖσαι), *fear*, and in δήν, *long*, has the same effect.

Chap. V.—Accents.

§ 79. The general rules for the *accentuation* of words are the following:

1. Every word *must* have *one*, and can *never* have *more* than *one* principal accent, which is called simply the accent: πολυπραγμοσύνη, *busy occupation;* ἀπαρασκεύαστος, *unprepared.* On the designation of words according to the accent, see §§ 17, 19, 21.

§ 80. 2. There are two kinds of accents, the *sharp* accent or the *acute* (ὀξεῖα), and the lengthened or the *circumflex* (περισπωμένη). On the mode of using both, see §§ 17, 21.

§ 81. 3. The *acute* may be upon long or short syllables, the *circumflex* only upon such syllables as are long *by nature:* as, λέγω, *I say;* λήγω, *I cease;* καλός, *beautiful;* ἀληθής, *true;* ἄνθρωπος, *man;* κείμενος, *lying;* κεῖται, *he lies;* σῶμα, *body;* εὖ, *well.*

§ 82. 4. The *acute accent* can be only on *one of the last three* syllables, and on the last but two only when the *last* is *short :* ἄποικος, *colonist,* but not ἀποίκου (Gen.); ἔλεγον, *I said,* but not ἔλεγην, *I was said.*

§ 83. 5. The *circumflex* can be only on *one of the last two* syllables, and on the last but one only when the *last* is *short* by nature: σῦκον, *fig,* but not σύκου (Gen.); σῶμα, *body,* but not σώματος (Gen.); πρᾶξις, *act,* but not πράξεις (Nom. Plur.).

Obs. 1.—When the last syllable is long by position, it does not hinder the circumflex from being on the last syllable but one: αὖλαξ, *furrow,* Gen. αὔλακος, but it does when it is long by nature as well as by position: θώραξ, *breast-plate,* Gen. θώρακος. Compare § 145.

2. Exceptions to 4 and 5 will be adduced separately in the chapters on inflexions. It is specially to be observed that most of

the exceptions occur with the final syllables in αι and οι: ἄποικοι, although οι is long; γνῶμαι, opinions; τύπτεται, he is struck. Compare §§ 108, 122 D. 3, 133, 157, 229, 268.

§ 84. 6. A last syllable but one, when long by nature, can have no other accent but the circumflex if the last is short by nature: φεῦγε, flee, not φεύγε; ἦρχον, I reigned, not ἤρχον; ἦλῐξ, of the same age, not ἦλιξ (Gen. ἥλῐκος); Κρατῖνος, not Κρατίνος. It may, however, be without an accent: εἰπέ, speak; ἄνθρωπος, man.

Obs. 1.—Apparent exceptions, such as ὥστε, so that, ἥδε, this, are explained in § 94.

2. So fixed is the rule, apart from these cases, that the quantity of the final syllable, or of the last but one, may often be inferred from the accent: ἴθι (ἰ), go; πρῶτα [prima, Nom. Plur.] (ἄ); γυναῖκας (ᾰ), women, Acc. Plur.; γνώμας (ᾱ), opinions, Acc. Plur.

§ 85. 7. Compound words have the accent on the last part but one of the word, as far as is possible according to § 82, etc.: ἄπιθι, go away; ἄφιλος, friendless; φιλόγυνος, friendly to women; ἀπόδος, give back; παρένθες, put in besides. (Compare § 359, *Obs.* 2.)

§ 86. The accent of a word is variously altered by the changes which a word undergoes, as well as by the connexion of a word with others in a sentence. That is:

1. Every oxytone subdues its sharp tone when followed by another word, so that the grave takes the place of the acute. (Compare § 20.)

§ 87. 2. In a contraction in the middle of a word, the syllable produced by contraction acquires no accent if none of the syllables to be contracted had it: γένεος, γένους, of the race; τίμαε, τίμα, honor. The accent of a contracted last syllable but one is manifest of itself from the general rules on accent; hence τιμῶντες, honoring (Nom. Plur.), from τιμάοντες, τιμώντων (Gen. Plur.), from τιμαόντων (according to §§ 83 and 84). A contracted final syllable has *a)* the *circumflex*, when the *first* of the uncontracted syllables was accented: τιμάει, τιμᾷ, *he honors;* χρυσέου, χρυσοῦ, *of golden;*

b) the *acute*, when the *last* was accented: ἑσταώς, ἑστώς, *standing.*

§ 88. 3. With *elision* (§ 64), oxytone prepositions and conjunctions entirely lose their accent; all other kinds of words throw it upon the previous syllable as acutes: ἐπ' αὐτῷ, *on him* = ἐπὶ αὐτῷ; οὐδ' ἐδυνάμην, *I could not even* = οὐδὲ ἐδυνάμην; εἴμ' Ὀδυσεύς, *I am Odysseus* = εἰμὶ Ὀδυσεύς; ἔπτ' ἦσαν, *there were seven* = ἑπτὰ ἦσαν.

§ 89. 4. With *crasis* (§ 65) the accent of the first word is lost: τἀγαθά, *bona* = τὰ ἀγαθά; θοἰμάτιον, *the dress* = τὸ ἱμάτιον. Only when paroxytones change the first syllable by crasis into one long by nature, this receives a circumflex: τὰ ἄλλα, *alia*, gives τἆλλα; τὸ ἔργον, *the work*, τοὔργον.

On the changes of the accent in declension, see §§ 107–109; on the accent of verbs, see §§ 229, and 331–333.

§ 90. The dissyllabic *prepositions*, with the exception of ἀμφί, ἀντί, ἀνά, διά, when placed after the *noun* or *verb* to which they belong, throw their accent on to the first syllable: τούτων πέρι, *about those* (περὶ τούτων); in like manner, when used adverbially, they include the substantive verb, as πάρα = πάρεστι, *it is there, near;* ἔνι = ἔνεστι, *it is therein, is possible.* This drawing back of the accent is called *anastrophe*. Compare § 446.

§ 91. Some words of one and of two syllables unite so closely with the *preceding* word that they throw their accent on to it. Such words are called *enclitics* (ἐγκλιτικαὶ

---

§ 90. **Dialects.**—Prepositions, whose final syllable is lost by elision, have not the accent even when they occupy the position indicated in § 90. Homeric τῇσι παρ' εἰνάετες χάλκευον, *among them I forged nine years long*.

λέξεις, *i. e.*, *inclining words*), and the *throwing back of the accent is called inclination*.

§ 92. The following are *enclitics:*

1. The indefinite pronoun τὶς, τὶ, *some one, something,* through all forms (§ 214).

2. The three personal pronouns, in the forms μοῦ, μοί, μέ, *mei, mihi, me;* σοῦ, σοί, σέ, *tui, tibi, te;* οὗ, οἷ, ἕ, *sui, sibi, se;* σφωΐν, *to them two;* and σφίσι(ν), *to them*.

3. The Indicative Present of εἰμί, *I am*, and of φημί, *inquam*, with the exception of the second Pers. Sing. εἶ and φῄς.

4. The indefinite adverbs πού or ποθί, *somewhere;* πή, *somehow;* ποί, *somewhither;* ποθέν, *from somewhere;* ποτέ, *sometime;* πώς, *somehow;* πώ, *yet*.

5. The particles γέ, *quidem;* τέ, *and;* τοί, *truly;* νύν or νύ, *now;* Hom. κέν or κέ, *perhaps, I suppose;* ῥά (ἄρα), *then;* Hom. θήν, *truly;* πέρ, *very;* and δέ '(meaning *toward*, and as a demonstrative appendage). Compare § 212.

§ 93. These words throw their accent back on the preceding word, in the following manner:

a) A preceding *oxytone* leaves its sharp tone 'unsubdued (§ 20), and this then serves also for the enclitic: ἀγαθόν τι, *something good;* αὐτός φησιν, *he himself says*.

b) After a *perispome* the accent of the enclitic is entirely lost: ὁρῶ τινας, *I see some;* εὖ ἐστιν, *it is well;* τιμῶ σε, *I honor thee*.

c) After a *paroxytone*, enclitics of one syllable entirely lose their accent; but those of two syllables retain their accent on the last syllable: φίλος μου, *my friend;* λόγος τις, *a speech;* but λόγοι τινές, *some speeches*, λόγων τινῶν (Gen. Plur.).

---

§ 92. **Dialects.**—The Ionic additional form of εἱ = εἵς, is enclitic, so also σφέας (Acc. Plur.), *them* = Att. σφᾶς, and μίν, *him, her,* § 205, D.

§ 97. ENCLITICS. 33

d) *Proparoxytones* and *properispomes* retain their accent, but receive also from the following enclitic another accent as acute on the last syllable, which remains unsubdued: ἄνθρωπός τις, *a man;* βέβαιοί εἰσιν, *they are firm;* σῶμά γε, *the body at least;* παῖδές τινες, *some boys.*

e) Atona (§ 97) receive the accent of following enclitics as acutes: οὔ φησιν, *he says not:* ὥς τε, *and how.*

§ 94. *Obs.*—Several words of one syllable form *one* word with enclitics following: thus, ὥςτε, *so that;* εἴτε, *sive;* οὔτε, *neque;* μήτε, *neque;* οἰόςτε, *capable;* ὅςτις, *whoever;* ἤτοι, *truly;* καίτοι, *and yet;* to this also belongs the δέ mentioned in § 92, 5: ὅδε, *this one;* οἴκαδε, *homewards.* These words form partly apparent exceptions to §§ 79 and 84.

§ 95. *f*) When several enclitics follow one another, each throws its accent upon the preceding: εἴ τίς μοί φησί ποτε, *if any one ever says to me.*

§ 96. The enclitics in certain cases retain their accent (become *orthotoned*), viz.:

1. when an enclitic forms the first word in the sentence, and therefore has nothing on which to throw its accent: τινὲς λέγουσι, *some say.* This position, however, is rare.

2. when an enclitic is made emphatic: σὲ λέγω, *I mean you—no one else;* εἰ ἔστιν, *if it is really so.* When ἔστι denotes *exist, be allowed, possible,* it retains the accent, and that, too, on the last syllable but one: ἔστι θεός, *there is a God;* οὐκ ἔστιν, *it is not allowed, not possible.* Compare § 315, *Obs.* 2.

3. After elision: ταῦτ' ἔστι ψευδῆ, *this is false=*ταῦτά ἐστι ψευδῆ.

4. Enclitics of two syllables, in the case mentioned § 93, *c.*

§ 97. *Atona, i. e.,* words without accent, also called *proclitics,* or inclining forward, are several words of one syl-

B 2

lable, which have so little independence that, in regard to accent, they combine with the *following* word.

They are the following:
1. of the article, the forms ὁ, ἡ, οἱ, αἱ;
2. the prepositions, ἐν (*in*, with the Dat.), ἐς or εἰς (*into*, with the Acc.), ἐκ or ἐξ, *out of;*
3. the conjunctions, εἰ, *if,* and ὡς, *how, that;* the latter also in its use as preposition *to;*
4. the negative οὐ or οὐκ (οὐχ).

Obs.—οὐχί, a more emphatic οὐ, is always accented.

§ 98. Atona receive the accent only in two cases, viz.:

a) when they are at the end of a sentence, and therefore have no following word on which they can rest: φῂς ἢ οὔ; *do you say so or not?* so always ὥς when placed after the word with which a comparison is made: θεὸς ὥς, *like a god,* Hom.;

b) when followed by an enclitic, which throws back its accent: οὔ φησι, *he says not.* Compare § 93, *c.*

§ 99. The following particles are distinguished according to the accent: ἤ, *than,* or, and ἦ, *truly,* or interrogative, Lat. *num;* ἄρα, *then, consequently,* and ἆρα as an interrogative; νῦν, *now,* and enclitic. νυ(ν), *now,* particle of transition; ὡς, *how,* and ὥς, *so;* οὐκοῦν, *therefore,* and οὔκουν, *not therefore.*

II. INFLEXION.

A. INFLEXION OF NOUNS AND PRONOUNS.

Chap. VI.—Declension of Substantives and Adjectives.

§ 100. Inflexion is the change which nouns, pronouns, and verbs undergo to indicate their relation in a sentence. A distinction must be made in inflexion between *Stem* and *Termination*. Stem is the fixed part, Termination the changeable part which is appended to the Stem to indicate the different relations.

The inflexion of nouns and pronouns is called *Declension*. As the nominal and pronominal Stems are modified according to *Cases*, the terminations added to them are called *Case-endings*. The form which arises from a case-ending being added to a Stem is called the *Case-form*. Thus πράγματ-ος is a case-form of the Stem πραγματ, formed by means of the case-ending -ος.

Great care must be taken not to confound the Stem and the Nominative case. The Nominative is itself a case-form, often quite different from the Stem. Thus the Nominative of the Stem πραγματ is πρᾶγμα, *thing*. λόγος, *speech*, is the Nominative of the Stem λογο, which appears, for example, in the compound word λογογράφο-ς, *a writer of speeches*.*

The Greeks distinguish in the Declension:

1. *Three Numbers*: the *Singular* for one, the *Dual* for two, the *Plural* for several.
2. *Five Cases*: Nominative, Genitive, Dative, Accusative, Vocative. The Dual has only two case-forms, one for the Nom., Acc., and Voc., the other for the Gen. and Dat. In the Plur., the Voc. is always like the Nom.
3. *Three Genders*: Masculine, Feminine, Neuter.

---

* The Stem will always be left unaccented.

§ 101. The gender is known:

1. From certain *general* characteristics of sex, in which the Greek language almost entirely coincides with the Latin. Besides the rule founded in the nature of things, that the designations of male persons are masculine, those of females feminine, the following rules are to be observed:

§ 102. *a*) The names of *rivers* and *winds* (gods of rivers and winds), and *months* (ὁ μήν, *the month*), are *masculine:* ὁ Εὐρώτας, *the River Eurotas;* ὁ Ζέφυρος, *the west wind;* ὁ Ἑκατομβαιών, *the month Hecatombæon.*

§ 103. *b*) The names of *trees, lands* (ἡ γῆ, *the land*), *islands* (ἡ νῆσος, *the island*), and *most cities,* are *feminine:* ἡ δρῦς, *the oak;* ἡ Ἀρκαδία, *Arcadia;* ἡ Λέσβος, *the island of Lesbos;* ἡ Κολοφών, *the city of Colophon.* Most *abstract* substantives also, *i. e.*, those which denote a condition, relation, act, or property, are feminine: ἡ ἐλπίς, *hope;* ἡ νίκη, *victory;* ἡ δικαιοσύνη, *righteousness;* ἡ ταχυτής, *quickness.*

§ 104. *c*) Many names of *fruits* are *neuter:* τὸ σῦκον, *the fig;* most diminutives also, both of masculine and feminine words: τὸ γερόντιον, dimin. of ὁ γέρων, *the old man;* τὸ γύναιον,* dimin. of ἡ γυνή, *the woman.* Farther, every name and word which is adduced merely as a word: τὸ ἄνθρωπος, *the name "man;"* τὸ δικαιοσύνη, *the idea of "righteousness;"* and the names of the letters, τὸ ἄλφα, τὸ σῖγμα.

§ 105. 2. From the *ending* of the *Stem* the gender is known according to §§ 113, 125, 137–140.

3. In *Declension,* the Neuter may be distinguished from the Masculine and Feminine, for all Neuters have

a) no Accusative or Vocative distinct from the Nom.

b) no ς as case-sign of the Nom. Sing.

c) the ending ἄ in Nom. Acc. and Voc. Pl.

§ 106. The Greek language, like the English, employs the definite *Article.* The forms of the Article are the following:

	Masc.	Fem.	Neut.	
Singular.				
Nom.	ὁ	ἡ	τό	the.
Gen.	τοῦ	τῆς	τοῦ	of the.
Dat.	τῷ	τῇ	τῷ	to the.
Acc.	τόν	τήν	τό	the.
Dual.				
N. A.	τώ	τά or τώ	τώ	the.
G. D.	τοῖν	ταῖν or τοῖν	τοῖν	of or to the.
Plural.				
Nom.	οἱ	αἱ	τά	the.
Gen.	τῶν	τῶν	τῶν	of the.
Dat.	τοῖς	ταῖς	τοῖς	to the.
Acc.	τούς	τάς	τά	the.

The following general rules on *accentuation* apply to all the declensions of substantives.

§ 107. *a*) The accent remains unaltered on the syllable on which it stood in the Nominative as long as the general laws of accent allow: ἄνθρωπος, *man,* ἄνθρωπε (Voc.); σῦκον, *fig,* σῦκα (Nom. Plur.). Exceptions, §§ 121 and 142, 181, 2.

b) But when the original accentuation becomes impossible by the length of the final syllable or by increase at the end, the accent is shifted only as near to the end of the word, and is changed only as much, as is absolutely necessary: ἄνθρωπος, *man,* ἀνθρώπου (Gen. Sing.), ἀνθρώποις (Dat. Plur.); σῶμα, *body,* σώματος (Gen. Sing.), σωμάτων (Gen. Plur.); τεῖχος, *wall,* τείχους (Gen. Sing.).

§ 108. *c*) The terminations οι and αι are not considered long in regard to accent; hence ἄνθρωποι, γνῶμαι (γνώμη, *opinion*).

§ 109. *d*) The Genitives and Datives of all numbers, if the last syllable is long, can never have the acute upon this syllable, but only the circumflex: ποταμοῦ, Gen. Sing.

THE A DECLENSION.

of ποταμός, *river ;* τιμῇ, Dat. Sing. of τιμή, *honor ;* ποδῶν, Gen. Plur. of πούς, *foot ;* μηνοῖν, Gen. Dual of μήν, *month.*

§ 110. Originally there was only a single declension, for which reason much has still remained common, which we shall put together below, § 173. But we distinguish *Two Principal Declensions* according to the ending of the Stems:

1. the *First Principal Declension* (*vowel declension*), which comprehends the Stems ending in α and ο ; and
2. the *Second Principal Declension* (*consonant declension*), which comprehends the Stems ending in consonants, but also those in the soft vowels ι, υ, in diphthongs, and a small number of Stems in ο.

First Principal Declension.
(*Vowel-declension.*)

§ 111. The first principal declension is subdivided into two, viz.:

  A. *The* A *Declension.*
  B. *The* O *Declension.*

What is common to both is put together below, § 134.

A. The A Declension
(*commonly called the First Declension*).

§ 112. The A Declension comprehends those words whose Stems end in α. In certain cases, however, this α becomes η. Hence the A Declension of the Greeks corresponds both to the A, or first, and to the E, or fifth, Declension of the Latin language.

§ 113. The A Declension contains only *Masculines* and *Feminines.* The two genders are most easily distinguished in the Nom. Sing., in which the masculines take ς, the feminines no case-ending. Hence the terminations of

§ 115. THE A DECLENSION. 39.

The Nom. Sing. are in the feminine α, η, in the masculine ᾱς, ης.

§ 114. 1. *Feminines.*

	Examples. Stems.	χώρα, *land.* χ ω ρ α [terra]	γλῶσσα, *tongue.* γ λ ω σ σ α	τιμή, *honor.* τ ῑ μ α
Singular.	Nom.	χώρᾱ [terra]	γλῶσσᾰ	τιμή
	Gen.	χώρᾱς	γλώσσης	τιμῆς
	Dat.	χώρᾳ [terræ]	γλώσσῃ	τιμῇ [re-i]
	Acc.	χώρᾱ-ν [terra-m]	γλῶσσᾰ-ν	τιμή-ν [re-m]
	Voc.	χώρᾱ [terra]	γλῶσσᾰ	τιμή
Dual.	N. A. V.	χώρᾱ	γλώσσᾱ	τιμά
	G. D.	χώραιν	γλώσσαιν	τιμαῖν
Plural.	Nom.	χῶραι [terræ]	γλῶσσαι	τιμαί
	Gen.	χωρῶν	γλωσσῶν	τιμῶν
	Dat.	χώραις	γλώσσαις	τιμαῖς
	Acc.	χώρᾱς [terras]	γλώσσᾱς	τιμάς
	Voc.	χῶραι [terræ]	γλῶσσαι	τιμαί

Examples for Declension.

θεά, *goddess.*   δόξα, *opinion.*   γῆ, *earth.*
σκιά, *shadow.*   πύλη, *gate.*   γνώμη, *opinion.*
βία, *jorce.*

§ 115. In certain cases in the Singular, but never in the Dual and Plural, α becomes η. Hence the following rules:
1. In order to form the Nom. Sing. from the Stem, or from a given case-form of the Dual or Plural:

---

§§ 11ΰ-117. **Dialects.**—1. The Doric dialect *never changes a into η*: τιμά, τιμᾶς; γλῶσσα, γλώσσᾱς.
2. The Ionic dialect changes *every* long α in the Singular into η: σοφίη, πέτρη, βασιλείης, μοίρῃ. Short ἁ is generally unchanged, as βασίλειᾰ, μοῖρᾰν: but in abstract substantives in -ειᾰ, -οιᾰ, α is likewise changed into η: ἀληθείη, *truth*, Att. ἀλήθεια; εὐπλοίη, *good passage;* and also in κνίσση, *steam from fat*, Σκύλλη. The ᾱ remains in θεά and some proper names.
3. The Voc. of νύμφη, *young woman*, is in Homer νύμφᾰ.

a) α remains in the Nom. Sing. after ε, ι, or ρ (§ 41):
St. σοφια, Nom. Sing. σοφία, *wisdom ;* Dat. Plur. πέτραις,
Nom. Sing. πέτρᾱ, *rock.*

b) α remains in the Nom. Sing. after σ, and after the
double consonants ζ, ξ, ψ, σ σ (or τ τ), λλ, as well as in the
feminine designations in -αινα: St. ἅμαξα, Nom. Sing.
ἅμαξᾰ, *carriage;* Gen. Plur. λεαινῶν, Nom. Sing. λέαινᾰ,
lioness.

c) After other vowels and consonants α is generally
changed into η in the Nom. Sing.: St. βοα, Nom. Sing.
βοή, *cry;* Acc. Plur. γνώμᾱς, Nom. Sing. γνώμη (opinion).

More important exceptions are: to *a)* κόρη, *girl;* κόῤῥη, *temple;*
δείρη, *neck*—to *b)* ἕρση, *dew*—to *c)* στοά, *hall;* χρόα, *color;* τόλμα,
boldness; δίαιτα, *mode of life.*

§ 116. 2. In order to form the other cases in the Singular according to a given Nom. Sing.:

a) If the Nom. Sing. ends in η, this letter remains
throughout the Sing.: δίκη, *justice,* δίκης, δίκῃ, δίκην, δίκη.

b) If the Nom. Sing. ends in α, this letter remains *always*
in the Acc. and Voc.: ἅμαξα, ἅμαξαν.

c) If the Nom. Sing. ends in α, this letter remains *also* in
the Gen. and Dat. when preceded by a *vowel* or ρ (§ 41):
Nom. Sing. σοφία, *wisdom,* Gen. σοφίας ; Nom. Sing. στοά,
colonnade, Dat. στοᾷ: also in some proper names with long
α : Nom. Sing. Λήδᾱ, Gen. Λήδας ; and in μνᾶ (contracted
from μνάα), Gen. μνᾶς.

d) Otherwise α of Nom. Sing. becomes η in Gen. and
Dat. : Nom. Sing. μοῦσα, Gen. μούσης ; Nom. Sing. δίαιτα,
Dat. διαίτῃ.

§ 117. For the *quantity* of α in the Nom. and Acc. Sing.,
the general rule is : α *purum* (after vowels) and α after ρ is
long, every other α is short : θεά, *goddess;* ἅμιλλᾰ, *fight.*

The exceptions are generally shown by the accent (§ 84, *Obs.* 2).
The most important are the fem. designations in -τρια and -εια :
ψάλτριᾰ, *female player;* βασίλεια, *queen* (but βασιλεία, *dominion*);
and several words with diphthongs in the last syllable but one,
as σφαῖρᾰ, *ball;* εὔνοιᾰ, *good will;* μοῖρᾰ, *fate.*

§ 120. THE A DECLENSION. 41

§ 118. The Gen. Plur. has the ending ων, which combines with the Stem α to form άων, contr. ῶν. This is the reason that the *Gen. Plur. of all words in this declension has the circumflex:* χώρα, χωρῶν ; λέαινα, λεαινῶν (Exceptions, § 181. Compare § 123).

§ 119. The Dat. Plur. originally ended in σι, before which ι is added to the α of the Stem. The αισι thus formed is usually shortened into αις, but the original form is found even in Attic writers in poetry and prose. (Compare § 128, D.)

§ 120. 2. *Masculines*.

Examples. Stems.	νεανίας, *youth.* νεανια	πολίτης, *citizen.* πολιτα	Ἑρμῆς, *god Hermes.* Ἑρμη (from Ἑρμεα)
Singular.			
Nom.	νεανία-ς	πολίτη-ς	Ἑρμῆ-ς
Gen.	νεανίου	πολίτου	Ἑρμοῦ
Dat.	νεανίᾳ	πολίτῃ	Ἑρμῇ
Acc.	νεανία-ν	πολίτη-ν	Ἑρμῆ-ν
Voc.	νεανία	πολῖτα	Ἑρμῆ
Dual.			
N. A. V.	νεανία	πολίτα	Ἑρμᾶ, *statues of Hermes.*
G. D.	νεανίαιν	πολίταιν	Ἑρμαῖν
Plural.			
Nom.	νεανίαι	πολῖται	Ἑρμαῖ
Gen.	νεανιῶν	πολιτῶν	Ἑρμῶν
Dat.	νεανίαις	πολίταις	Ἑρμαῖς
Acc.	νεανίας	πολίτας	Ἑρμᾶς
Voc.	νεανίαι	πολῖται	Ἑρμαῖ

§ 118. **Dialects.**—4. The -αων of the Gen. Plur. is preserved in the Hom. dialect: κλισιάων (κλισία, *tent*), ἀγοράων (ἀγορά, *speech*); but -εων also occurs, in which case ε is generally lost by synizesis (§ 39): πασέων, *of all*, fem.
The Dorians contract -αων into ᾶν (§ 37, D. 3): θεᾶν, *dearum*.

§ 119. **Dialects.**—5. The Dat. Plur. in Ionic ends in -ῃσι(ν), -ῃς (but also in the Attic -αις): κλισίῃσι, πέτρῃς.

THE A DECLENSION. § 121.

Examples for Declension.

ταμίας, *treasurer.* στρατιώτης, *warrior.* ἀδολέσχης, *babbler.*
Νικίας, *Nicias.* παιδοτρίβης, *wrestling-* Ἀλκιβιάδης.
κριτής, *judge.*   *master.*

§ 121. In the Masculines, as well as in the Feminines, when a vowel or ρ precedes, the α of the Stem *remains* and is long; after every other letter it becomes η in the Nom. Dat. and Acc. Sing.

Those words which in the Nom. Sing. end in τη-ς, names of peoples, and compound words, have α short in the Voc. Sing.: πολῖτᾰ, Πέρσᾰ (Nom. Sing. Πέρση-ς, *Persian*); γεωμέτρᾰ (Nom. Sing. γεωμέτρη-ς, *land-measurer*). The Voc. δέσποτᾰ (Nom. Sing. δεσπότη-ς, *lord*) draws back the accent, contrary to § 107, *a*, to the first syllable. All others have η in the Vocative: Κρονίδη (Nom. Sing. Κρονίδη-ς).

§ 122. The Declension of the *Masculines* is distinguished from that of the Feminines:

1. in the Nom. Sing. by ς being added to the Stem;
2. by the Gen. Sing. ending in ο υ.

Obs.—The termination of the Gen. Sing. of the masculines is properly *-ο*, which, with the α of the Stem, forms *-αο* (see the Homeric *dialect*); by weakening α to ε (§ 118, D.) and contraction (§ 37) arises ου: πολίτᾱο (πολιτεο), πολίτου.

---

§§ 121 and 122. **Dialects.**—1. The Epic dialect in some words omits the ς of the Nom. Sing., in which cases the α remains short: ἱππότᾰ, *horseman;* νεφεληγερέτᾰ, *cloud-gatherer.* (Compare Lat. *poëta, scriba.*)

2. The Dorians also in the masculines put ᾱ for η, and contract ᾱ ο into ᾱ. (§§ 24, D.; 37, D. 3.)

3. Homer has three forms in the Gen. Sing.:

a) the original *-ᾱο* : Ἀτρείδᾱο;
b) *-εω* with the quantity transposed (where ε is lost by synizesis, §§ 37, D., 39, D.) : Ἀτρείδεω. The accent remains unchanged, in spite of the ω in the final syllable. The New-Ionic form is the same.
c) *-ω* by contraction: Ἑρμείω (Nom. Sing. Ἑρμείᾱ-ς = Attic Ἑρμῆς), βορέω (Nom. Sing. βορέᾱς). Compare § 37, *a*.

§ 125.   THE O DECLENSION.   43

βορρᾶς (contracted from βορέα-ς, *north wind*), contracts the original $\bar{a}$ o in the Gen. Sing., after Doric fashion, into $\bar{a}$: βορρᾶ. The same takes place with some Doric and Roman proper names, and a few other words: Σύλλας, *Sulla;* ὀρνιθοθήρας, *fowler*, Gen. Sing. ᾱ.

§ 123. In the Dual and Plural the Declension of the Masculines is the same as that of the Feminines.

Exceptions to the accentuation prescribed in § 118 are χρήστη-ς, *usurer;* ἐτησίαι, *trade-winds*, Gen. Plur. χρήστων (χρηστῶν in the O declension, from χρηστός, *good*) and ἐτησίων.

B. THE O DECLENSION
(*commonly called the Second Declension*).

§ 124. The O Declension comprehends those words whose Stems end in o, together with a few whose Stems end in ω (§ 132). It answers to the *o-* or Second Declension in Latin.

§ 125. The O Declension is the complement of the A Declension in regard to gender. It contains *Masculines* and *Neuters*, but only few *Feminines*.

The termination of the Masculines and Feminines in the Nom. Sing. is o-ς, that of Neuters o-ν [Lat. *u-s, u-m*].

The Masculines and Feminines are declined alike; the Neuters are distinguished from them (compare § 105) only by—

1. The Nom. and Voc. Sing. taking the Accusative ending ν: δῶρο-ν (*gift*) [*donu-m*].

2. The Nom. Acc. and Voc. Plur. ending in ᾰ: δῶρα [*dona*].

44   THE O DECLENSION.   § 126.

§ 126.

Examples. Stems.	ὁ ἄνθρωπο-ς, man ἀνθρωπο	ἡ ὁδό-ς, way. ὁδο	τὸ δῶρο-ν, gift. δωρο
Singular.			
Nom.	ἄνθρωπο-ς [dominu-s]	ὁδό-ς	δῶρο-ν [donu-m]
Gen.	ἀνθρώπου	ὁδοῦ	δώρου
Dat.	ἀνθρώπῳ [domino]	ὁδῷ	δώρῳ [dono]
Acc.	ἄνθρωπο-ν [dominu-m]	ὁδό-ν	δῶρο-ν [donu-m]
Voc.	ἄνθρωπε [domine]	ὁδέ	δῶρο-ν [donum-]
Dual.			
N. A. V.	ἀνθρώπω	ὁδώ	δώρω
G. D.	ἀνθρώποιν	ὁδοῖν	δώροιν
Plural.			
Nom.	ἄνθρωποι [domini]	ὁδοί	δῶρα [dona]
Gen.	ἀνθρώπων	ὁδῶν	δώρων
Dat.	ἀνθρώποις	ὁδοῖς	δώροις
Acc.	ἀνθρώπους [domino-s]	ὁδούς	δῶρα [dona]
Voc.	ἄνθρωποι [domini]	ὁδοί	δῶρα [dona]

Examples for Declension.

θεός, God.	ποταμός, river.	σῦκον, fig.
νόμος, law.	πόνος, trouble.	μέτρον, measure.
κίνδυνος, danger.	βίος, life.	ἱμάτιον, dress.
ταῦρος, bull.	θάνατος, death.	

§ 127. *Obs.*—The *Feminines* are partly known by the general rules already given (§§ 101, 103): ἡ φηγός, *esculent oak;* ἡ ἄμπελος, *vine;* ἡ νῆσος, *island;* ἡ ἤπειρος, *continent;* Κόρινθος.
The following also are feminine:

1. The names of different kinds of *earth* and *stones:* ψάμμος, *sand;* κόπρος, *dung;* γύψος, *chalk;* πλίνθος, *brick;* σποδός, *ashes;* ψῆφος, *pebble;* βάσανος, *touch-stone.*
2. Different words for *way:* ὁδός, κέλευθος, ἀτραπός, *path;* ἁμαξιτός, *carriage-road.* In the same manner, ἡ τάφρος, *dike,* but ὁ στενωπός, *narrow way.*
3. Words conveying the idea of a *cavity:* χηλός, *chest of drawers;* γνάθος, *jaw;* κιβωτός, *chest;* σορός, *coffin;* ληνός, *wine-vat;* κάρδοπος, *kneading-trough;* κάμῖνος, *oven.*
4. Several adjectives used as substantives: ἡ διάμετρος (supply γραμμή, *line*), *diameter;* σύγκλητος (supply βουλή, *council*), *meeting of the council.*

§ 130. THE O DECLENSION. 45

5. Single words: βίβλος, *book*; ῥάβδος, *staff*; διάλεκτος, *dialect*; νόσος, *disease*; δρόσος, *dew*; δοκός, *beam*. Many designations of personal beings are *common*, that is, with the same form they are masculine when they denote a male, feminine when they denote a female: ὁ θεός, *god*; ἡ θεός, *goddess*; ὁ ἄνθρωπος and ἡ ἄνθρωπος.

§ 128. The ending of the Gen. Sing. is -ο, which, with the ο of the Stem, is contracted into ου (compare § 122): ἀνθρωπο-ο = ἀνθρώπου.

§ 129. The Nominative form is sometimes used instead of the Vocative form: the Vocative of θεός is always the same as the Nom.: ὦ θεός [Lat. *deus*]: ἀδελφός, *brother*, has ἄδελφε in the Vocative with the accent thrown back.

Contracted Declension.

§ 130. Several words which have ε or ο before the last letter of the Stem may contract these vowels with the ο. The rules of §§ 36 and 37 are here applied: εα, however, contrary to § 38, is contracted into ā.

---

§ 128. **Dialects.**—The Epic dialect in the Gen. Sing. has the older form ιο for the ending; ιο with ο of the St. produces οιο: ἀνθρώποιο, πεδίοιο (πεδίο-ν), *field*. We also, however, find the Attic ου.

Other Epic peculiarities are: -οιιν = οιν in the Gen. and Dat. Dual: ὤμοιιν (ὦμος, *shoulder*):—οισι(ν) = οις in the Dat. Plur.: ἀνθρώποισι(ν), which is also New-Ionic, and is found even in Attic writers (compare § 119).

§ 130. **Dialects.**—The Ionic dialect leaves the forms uncontracted.

Examples. Stems.	ὁ νοῦ-ς, sense. νοο		τὸ ὀστοῦν, bone. ὀστεο	
Singular.				
Nom.	νόο-ς	νοῦς	ὀστέο-ν	ὀστοῦ-ν
Gen.	νόου	νοῦ	ὀστέου	ὀστοῦ
Dat.	νόῳ	νῷ	ὀστέῳ	ὀστῷ
Acc.	νόο-ν	νοῦ-ν	ὀστέο-ν	ὀστοῦ-ν
Voc.	νόε	νοῦ	ὀστέο-ν	ὀστοῦ-ν
Dual. N. A. V.	νόω	νώ	ὀστέω	ὀστώ
G. D.	νόοιν	νοῖν	ὀστέοιν	ὀστοῖν
Plural.				
Nom.	νόοι	νοῖ	ὀστέα	ὀστᾶ
Gen.	νόων	νῶν	ὀστέων	ὀστῶν
Dat.	νόοις	νοῖς	ὀστέοις	ὀστοῖς
Acc.	νόους	νοῦς	ὀστέα	ὀστᾶ
Voc.	νόοι	νοῖ	ὀστέα	ὀστᾶ

Examples for Declension.

πλοῦς, *voyage*. ῥοῦς, *stream*. ἀδελφιδοῦς, *brother's son*.

§ 131. Some irregularities of accentuation occur in the contraction, viz.:

1. the Nom. Dual is made oxytone, contrary to § 87.
2. compound words leave the accent on the last syllable but one, also contrary to § 87: περίπλῳ, Dat. of περίπλους, *circumnavigation*, for περιπλῴ, from -όῳ.
3. the word κάνεον, *basket*, is contracted into κανοῦν, contrary to § 87.

On contracted adjectives, see § 183.

Attic Declension.

§ 132. A small number of words, instead of the short O-sound (ο), have the long (ω). This ω at the end of the

---

§ 131. Dialects.—A Gen. ending -ο appears in Homer in Πετεῶ-ο, Gen. Sing. from the Nominative Πετεώ-ς.

§ 134.   ATTIC O DECLENSION.   47

Stem goes through all the cases, but at the same time takes the case-endings as far as possible. Most of these words have ε before ω, and for -εω there also occurs the additional form -āo : νεώ-ς, *temple*, together with νāό-ς ; λεώ-ς, *people*, together with λāό-ς (compare § 37, D.). This Declension is called the *Attic*.
On adjectives in ω-ς, see § 184; on some words which fluctuate between this and the second principal declension, see § 174.

Examples. Stems.	ὁ νεώ-ς, *temple*. ν ε ω	τὸ ἀνώγεω-ν, *upper room*. ἀ ν ω γ ε ω
Singular. Nom. Gen. Dat. Acc.	νεώ-ς νεώ νεῴ νεώ-ν	ἀνώγεω-ν ἀνώγεω ἀνώγεῳ ἀνώγεω-ν
Dual. N. A. V. G. D.	νεώ νεῴν	ἀνώγεω ἀνώγεῳν
Plural. Nom. Gen. Dat. Acc.	νεῴ νεών νεῴς νεώς	ἀνώγεω ἀνώγεων ἀνώγεῳς ἀνώγεω

Another example: κάλως, *rope*.

§ 133. The accentuation in these words has a twofold irregularity, viz. :

1. εω passes always for only *one syllable* in regard to accent: Μενέλεως, apparently contrary to § 82;

2. even upon the Genitives and Datives, when they are accented, the accent is put, not as a circumflex, but as an acute, contrary to § 109.

§ 134. The A and O Declensions, that is, the Vowel or First Principal Declension, have the following points in common:

1. the masculines have in the Nom. Sing. the ending -ς.
2. the masculines have in the Gen. Sing. (§§ 122, 128) the ending -ου.
3. all three genders have ι subscriptum with a long vowel in the Dat. Sing.
4. all three genders have -ν in the Acc. Sing.
5. all three genders have the Stem vowel lengthened in the Nom. Acc. and Voc. Dual.
6. all three genders affix -ιν to the Stem vowel in the Gen. and Dat. Dual.
7. all three genders have -ων in the Gen. Plur.
8. all three genders affix -σιν or ς with preceding ι to the Stem vowel in the Dat. Plur.
9. the masculines and feminines affix -ι to the Stem vowel in the Nom. Plur.
10. the masculines and feminines affix -ς (for νς) in the Acc. Plur., lengthening the Stem vowel to compensate for the ν dropped (§ 42).

The difference, therefore, is only in the formation of the Gen. Sing. of the feminines and in the accentuation of the Gen. Plur.

SECOND PRINCIPAL DECLENSION.

CONSONANT-DECLENSION

(*commonly called the Third Declension*).

§ 135. The Second Principal Declension comprehends all the Stems which end in *consonants*, the *soft vowels* ι and υ, or *diphthongs*, and a small number of Stems in ο (Nom. ω). The Stem is best recognized in the Gen. Sing., where what remains after rejecting the termination ο ς may generally be considered as the Stem: Gen. λέοντ-ος, St. λεοντ (Nom. λέων, *lion*); Gen. φύλακ-ος, St. φυλάκ (Nom. φύλαξ, *guard*).

§ 139. CONSONANT DECLENSION. 49

Hence, for the exact recognition of a word of this declension, not only the Nominative, but also the Stem or the Genitive is necessary: as, Nom. δαίς, St. δαιτ, or Gen. δαιτός, *meal* [Lat. *rex*, St. *reg*, or Gen. *regis*].

To the second principal declension correspond in Latin the third and fourth declensions. In it the case-endings usually appear pure, *i. e.*, not mixed up with the end of the Stem.

The Stems ending in the soft vowels follow the third declension, because the soft vowels (§ 35, 1) can be used together with the vowels of the terminations: Gen. πίτυ-ος (Stem πιτυ, Nom. πίτυ-ς, *pine-tree*). In the Stems ending in diphthongs, the υ is sometimes resolved into ϝ: for example, the Stem βου (Nom. βοῦ-ς, *ox*) was originally in some forms βοϝ (Latin *bov*), as Gen. βοϝ-ός (=*bov-is*). See § 35, *Obs*. The O Stems have probably lost a final consonant.

§ 136. The Second Principal Declension comprehends all three genders.

The *Neuters* may be recognized by the inflexion, according to § 105, from their having the Nom. and Acc. alike, and these cases in the Plur. always with the ending -α: σώματ-α (St. σωματ, Nom. Sing. σῶμα, *body*).

§ 137. For determining the *gender* from the Stem, the following are the most important rules:

a) *Masculine* are the Stems in ευ (Nom. εὔ-ς), τ η ρ (Nom. τηρ), τ ο ρ (Nom. τωρ), ν τ (with Nom. ς or ν preceded by a long vowel), as well as most Stems in ν (of various Nominatives) with a preceding long vowel: St. γ ρ α φ ε υ, Nom. γραφεύς, *writer;* St. and Nom. σωτήρ, *savior;* St. ῥ η τ ο ρ, Nom. ῥήτωρ, *orator;* St. λ ε ο ν τ, Nom. λέων, *lion, leo ;* St. and Nom. ἀγών, *contest*.

§ 138. *b*) *Feminine* are all Stems in δ (Nom. -ἴς, -ἄς), most in ι (Nom. -ι-ς), those in ο (Nom. -ω or -ω-ς), and the names of qualities in τητ (Nom. -τη-ς): St. ἐλπιδ, Nom. ἐλπίς, *hope ;* St. πολι, Nom. πόλις, *city ;* St. πειθο, Nom. πειθώ, *persuasion ;* St. ἰσοτητ, Nom. ἰσότης, *equality*.

§ 139. *c*) *Neuter* are the Stems in μ α τ (Nom. μα), the substantive Stems in ς with Nom. ος or ας, those in ι or υ which append no ς in the Nominative, and those in ρ pre-

C

ceded by a short vowel in the Nom.: St. σ ω μ α τ, Nom. σῶμα, *body;* St. γ ε ν ε ς, Nom. γένος, *genus;* St. and Nom. γῆρας, *age;* St. and Nom. σίνᾱπι, *mustard;* St. and Nom. ἄστυ, *city;* St. and Nom. ἦτορ, *heart.*

§ 140. The following words must be noticed separately: ἡ γαστήρ (St. γ α σ τ ε ρ), *belly;* ὁ πούς (St. π ο δ), *foot;* ἡ χείρ (St. χ ε ι ρ), *hand;* τὸ οὖς (St. ὠ τ), *ear;* ὁ πῆχυς (St. π η χ υ), *forearm;* ἡ φρήν (St. φ ρ ε ν), *diaphragm, mind;* ὁ πέλεκυς (St. π ε λ ε κ υ), *axe;* ὁ βότρυς (St. β ο τ ρ υ), *bunch of grapes;* ὁ στάχυς (St. σ τ α χ υ), *ear of corn;* ὁ σφήξ (St. σ φ η κ), *wasp;* ὁ μῦς (St. μ ῡ ς), *mouse* [*mus*]; ὁ ἰχθύς (St. ἰ χ θ υ), *fish;* ὁ ἀήρ (St. ἀ ε ρ), *air;* τὸ πῦρ (St. π ῡ ρ), *fire;* τὸ ὕδωρ (St. ὑδατ), *water.*

Of two genders (common) are several names of animals, as: ὁ and ἡ ἀλεκτρυών (St. ἀ λ ε κ τ ρ υ ο ν), *cock* and *hen;* ὁ and ἡ ὗς or σῦς (St. ὑ or σ υ), *swine* [*sus*]; ὁ and ἡ αἴξ (St. α ἰ γ), *goat;* ὁ and ἡ βοῦς (St. β ο υ), *ox;* and many names of persons: ὁ and ἡ παῖς (St. π α ι δ), *boy* and *girl;* ὁ and ἡ δαίμων (St. δ α ι μ ο ν), *god* and *goddess;* ὁ and ἡ μάντις, *prophet* and *prophetess.*

§ 141. The endings of the consonant declension are the following:

	Masculines and Feminines.	Neuters.
Singular.		
Nom.	ς, or compensation by lengthening	no ending.
Gen.	ος	
Dat.	ἰ	
Acc.	ἀ or ν	no ending.
Voc.	no ending, or as in the Nom.	"
Dual.		
N. A. V.	ε	
G. D.	οιν	
Plural.		
Nom.	ες	ἀ
Gen.	ων	
Dat.	σι(ν)	
Acc.	ἀς	ἀ
Voc.=Nom.	ες	ἀ

§ 141. **Dialects.**—The Hom. dialect has ο ι ι ν for ο ι ν in Gen. and Dat. Dual (compare § 129, D.), ποδ-οῖιν, and in Dat. Plur. *frequently* ε σ σ ι(ν) for σ ι(ν) : πόδ-εσσι(ν), seldom ε σ ι(ν) : αἴγ-εσι(ν).

§ 143. CONSONANT DECLENSION.

§ 142. The accent in the Second Principal Declension deviates from the rules laid down in § 107 in the following point:

Words of *one syllable* accentuate the *Gen.* and *Dat.* of all numbers on the case-ending (circumflex if the vowel be long, § 109): ποδ-ός, ποδ-ί (but πόδ-α), ποδοῖν, ποδῶν, ποσί.

EXCEPTIONS.—1. Participles, as: ὤν, *being*, ὄντος; βάς, *going*, βάντος —accentuate the Genitive and Dative of all numbers on the last syllable but one.

2. πᾶς, *omnis*, has παντός, παντί, but πάντων, πᾶσι(ν).

3. The words παῖς, *boy;* δμώς, *slave;* θώς, *jackal;* Τρώς, *Trojan;* τὸ φῶς, *light;* ἡ φῷς, *blister;* ἡ δᾷς, *torch;* τὸ οὖς, *ear;* ὁ σής, *moth,* are paroxytones in Gen. Plur. and Dual: παίδ-ων, δμώ-ων, θώ-ων, Τρώ-ων, φώτ-ων, φῴδ-ων, δᾴδ-ων, ὤτ-οιν, σέ-ων (compare farther § 177, 9).

4. The words which have become monosyllables by contraction: ἦρ = ἔαρ, *spring* (*ver*), ἦρος, ἦρι.

§ 142 *b.* In regard to the *quantity*, it must be observed that several monosyllables, in spite of the short Stem-vowel, are lengthened: St. π ο δ, Nom. Sing. πούς, *foot;* St. π α ν τ, Nom. Sing. Neut. πᾶν, *every thing;* St. πῠρ, Nom. Sing. πῦρ, *fire;* St. σ ῠ, Nom. Sing. σῦς, *boar.*

§ 143. The Stems of the Second Principal Declension are divided into three Classes with different subdivisions:

I. CONSONANT STEMS.
1. Guttural and Labial Stems.
2. Dental Stems.
3. Liquid Stems.

II. VOWEL STEMS.
1. Soft-vowel Stems.
2. Diphthong Stems.
3. ο Stems.

III. ELIDED STEMS.
1. ς Stems.
2. τ Stems.
3. ν Stems.

I. Consonant Stems.

§ 144. 1. *Guttural and Labial Stems,*
i. e., Stems in κ, χ, γ, π, φ, β.

Examples. Stems.	ὁ φύλαξ, *guard.* φυλακ	ἡ φλέψ, *vein.* φλεβ
Singular.		
Nom. V.	φύλαξ [dux]	φλέψ [pleb-s]
Gen.	φύλᾰκ-ος [duc-is]	φλεβ-ός [plĕb-is]
Dat.	φύλᾰκ-ῐ [duc-i]	φλεβ-ῐ [plĕb-i]
Acc.	φύλᾰκ-ᾰ [duc-e-m]	φλέβ-ᾰ [plĕb-e-m]
Dual.		
N. A. V.	φύλᾰκ-ε	φλέβ-ε
G. D.	φυλάκ-οιν	φλεβ-οῖν
Plural.		
Nom. V.	φύλᾰκ-ες [duc-es]	φλέβ-ες
Gen.	φυλάκ-ων [duc-um]	φλεβ-ῶν
Dat.	φύλαξι(ν)	φλεψί(ν)
Acc.	φύλᾰκ-ᾰς [duc-es]	φλέβ-ᾰς

Examples for Declension.

Ὁ μύρμηξ, *ant*, St. μυρμηκ. ἡ φόρμιγξ, *lyre*, St. φορμιγγ.
ἡ μάστιξ, *whip*, St. μαστιγ. ὁ Αἰθίοψ, *Æthiopian*, St. Αἰθιοπ.
ἡ βήξ, *cough*, St. βηχ.

§ 145. All these Stems are Masc. or Fem. The Nom. Sing. is formed by affixing ς to the Stem: the ς with the final consonant of the Stem forms ξ, ψ, as in the Dat. Plur. (§ 48). The Voc. is always the same as the Nom.

Obs.—The Stem ἀλωπεκ has the vowel irregularly lengthened in the Nom. Sing.: ἀλώπηξ, *fox;* while, on the contrary, the long vowel in the Stems κηρῡκ, φοινῑκ, is shortened in the Nom.: κῆρυξ, *herald;* φοῖνιξ, *palm-tree*, where the accent shows that the υ and ι are short by nature (compare § 83, *Obs.* 1). τριχ has Nom. Sing. θρίξ, *hair*, Dat. Plur. θριξί(ν) (compare § 54, *a*).

§ 147. CONSONANT DECLENSION. 53

§ 146. 2. *Dental Stems, i. e.*, Stems in τ, θ, δ, ν.

Examples. Stems.	ἡ λαμπάς λ α μ π ᾰ δ *lamp.*	τὸ σῶμα σ ω μ ᾰ τ *body.*	ὁ γέρων γ ε ρ ο ν τ *old man.*	ὁ ἡγεμών ἡ γ ε μ ο ν *leader.*
Singular.				
Nom.	λαμπᾰ́-ς	σῶμα	γέρων	ἡγεμών
Gen.	λαμπᾰ́δ-ος	σώμᾰτ-ος	γέροντ-ος	ἡγεμόν-ος
Dat.	λαμπᾰ́δ-ῐ	σώμᾰτ-ῐ	γέροντ-ῐ	ἡγεμόν-ῐ
Acc.	λαμπᾰ́δ-ᾰ	σῶμα	γέροντ-α	ἡγεμόν-ᾰ
Voc.	λαμπᾰ́-ς	σῶμα	γέρον	ἡγεμών
Dual.				
N. A. V.	λαμπᾰ́δ-ε	σώμᾰτ-ε	γέροντ-ε	ἡγεμόν-ε
G. D.	λαμπᾰ́δ-οιν	σωμᾰ́τ-οιν	γερόντ-οιν	ἡγεμόν-οιν
Plural.				
N. V.	λαμπᾰ́δ-ες	σώμᾰτ-ᾰ	γέροντ-ες	ἡγεμόν-ες
Gen.	λαμπᾰ́δ-ων	σωμάτ-ων	γερόντ-ων	ἡγεμόν-ων
Dat.	λαμπᾰ́-σι(ν)	σώμᾰ-σι(ν)	γέρου-σι(ν)	ἡγεμό-σι(ν)
Acc.	λαμπᾰ́δ-ᾰς	σώμᾰτ-ᾰ	γέροντ-ᾰς	ἡγεμόν-ᾰς

Examples for Declension.

ἡ πατρί-ς, *native country*, St. π α τ ρ ι δ.
τὸ ὄνομα, *name*, St. ὀ ν ο μ α τ.
ἡ νύξ, *night* [*nox* for *noets*], St. ν υ κ τ [*noct*].
ἡ κακότη-ς, *badness*, St. κ α κ ο τ η τ.
τὸ μέλι, *honey* [*mel*], St. μ ε λ ι τ.
ὁ ὀδούς, *tooth* [*den-s* for *dent-s*], St. ὀ δ ο ν τ [*dent*].
ὁ δελφίς, *dolphin*, St. δ ε λ φ ῑ ν.
ὁ ποιμήν, *shepherd*, St. π ο ι μ ε ν.
ὁ Ἕλλην, *Hellen*, St. Ἑ λ λ η ν.
ὁ ἀγών, *contest*, St. ἀ γ ω ν.

Adjectives:

πένη-ς, *poor*, St. π ε ν η τ.
ἄκων, neut. ἆκον, *unwilling*, St. ἀ κ ο ν τ.
ἀπράγμων, neut. ἆπραγμον, *inactive*, St. ἀ π ρ α γ μ ο ν.

§ 147. In the dental Stems, as in the Stems to be noticed below, the Nom. Sing. Masc. and Fem. may be formed in two ways, viz. :

1. *With Sigma* affixed to the Stem. Before this sigma

the consonants τ, δ, θ, when they stand alone, disappear altogether (§ 49): λαμπαδ-ς, λαμπἄ-ς ; κορυθ-ς, κόρῠ-ς, *helmet ;* but ν and ντ have the short vowels of the Stem lengthened by way of compensation (§ 42), so that ἄ, ἴ, ῠ become ᾱ, ῑ, ῡ; but ε becomes ει, and ο, ου : παντ-ς, πᾶ-ς, *every ;* ἑν-ς, εἷ-ς, *one ;* ὀδοντ-ς, ὀδού-ς, *tooth.*

EXCEPTIONS.—The monosyllabic Stem π ο δ [*ped*] (§ 142 *b*) has the vowel lengthened exceptionally : πού-ς [Lat. *pē-s, i. e., ped-s*]; δ α μ α ρ τ has Nom. Sing. ἡ δάμαρ, *spouse,* for δαμαρς, because of its harshness.

2. *Without Sigma* being affixed to the Stem; but in its stead the Stem-vowel, in case it is short, *is lengthened,* so that by *this* lengthening (§ 42, *Obs.*) ε becomes η, and ο becomes ω : St. π ο ι μ ε ν, Nom. ποιμήν, *shepherd ;* St. ἡ γ ε μ ο ν, Nom. ἡγεμών. If the Stem-vowel is long of itself, the Nom. Sing. is like the Stem : ὁ ἀγών, *contest.*

The τ of the Stems in ν τ in this formation is rejected, according to § 67 : γ ε ρ ο ν τ, Nom. γέρων (for γερωντ). The simple τ of the Participial Stems in ο τ is changed into ς : St. λ ε λ υ κ ο τ, Nom. Sing. λελυκώς (for λελυκωτ), *having loosened.*

Obs. 1. The vowel ω shows that ς is not a mere affix in λελυκώς, *one who has loosened.* Compare χάρῐ-ς, *favor,* St. χαριτ.

Obs. 2. The Stems in δ, θ, as well as those in α ν τ, ε ν τ, always form the Nom. Sing. *with* sigma; but Stems of substantives in ο ν τ and the Stems in ν generally *without* ς.

§ 147 *b*. The *Neuter* has the pure Stem in the Nom. Acc. and Voc. Sing. (§ 136), as far as the laws of sound in regard to final consonants (§ 67) admit it: λυθέν(τ), *loosened* (see § 187), λελυκός (for λ ε λ υ κ ο τ); γάλα, *milk,* from the Stem γ ἄ λ α κ τ (Gen. γάλακτ-ος = Lat. *lact-is*). On πᾶν (Stem παντ), see § 142 *b*.

Obs.—On the Acc. Sing. in ν, belonging to some Stems in ιτ, ιθ, ιδ, νθ, νδ, see § 156.

§ 149. CONSONANT DECLENSION. 55

§ 148. The *Vocative* of masculines and feminines sometimes has the pure Stem, as far as is possible: Ἄρτεμι (St. Ἀρτεμιδ), Αἶαν (St. Ἀιαντ), γέρον (St. γεροντ); sometimes it is like the Nom. (necessarily so when the accent is on the last syllable): ἡγεμών; and in *all* participles even when the accent is not on the last syllable: λέγων (St. λεγοντ), *speaking*.
The Voc. παῖ, *boy*, from the St. παιδ, is specially to be observed.

Obs.—The Stems Ἀπόλλων, Ποσειδῶν, which are like the Nom., shorten the vowel and draw back the accent in the Vocative: Ἄπολλον, Πόσειδον. The accent is also drawn back in many compound words: Ἀγάμεμνον, Ἀριστόγειτον (§ 85).

§ 149. The formation of the Dat. Plur. results from the laws of sound (§§ 49, 50). τ, δ, θ, and simple ν, are dropped before σι(ν) without leaving any trace; but ντ is dropped with the previous vowel lengthened by way of compensation.

EXCEPTION.—The *adjectives* (not participles) in εντ admit no lengthening of the vowel by way of compensation: St. χαριεντ (Nom. Sing. χαρίεις, *graceful*, Dat. Plur. χαρίεσι(ν). See Inflexion, § 187).

§ 148. Dialects.—The Vocative of the Stem ἀνακτ (Nom. Sing. ἄναξ, *ruler*) is in Homer ἄνα (shortened from ἀνακτ: compare the neuter γάλα, § 147 *b*); some Stems in ντ lose the ν in the Voc.: Ἄτλᾶ for Ἄτλαν(τ).

§ 149. Dialects.—Homer forms the Dat. Plur. ποσσί(ν) instead of ποδ-σι(ν), Att. ποσίν (πούς, *foot*); the δ being assimilated instead of being rejected.

§ 150. 3. Liquid Stems, i. e., Stems in λ and ρ.

Examples. Stems.	ὁ ἅλς 'ἅλ salt.	ὁ ῥήτωρ ῥητορ orator.	ἡ μήτηρ μητερ mother.	ὁ θήρ θηρ game.
Singular.				
Nom.	ἅλ-ς [sal]	ῥήτωρ	μήτηρ [mater]	θήρ
Gen.	ἁλ-ός [sal-is]	ῥήτορ-ος	μητρ-ός [matr-is]	θηρ-ός
Dat.	ἁλ-ί [sal-i]	ῥήτορ-ι	μητρ-ί [matr-i]	θηρ-ί
Acc.	ἅλ-α [sal-e-m]	ῥήτορ-α	μητέρ-α [matr-e-m]	θῆρ-α
Voc.	ἅλ-ς	ῥῆτορ	μῆτερ	θήρ
Dual.				
N. A. V.	ἅλ-ε	ῥήτορ-ε	μητέρ-ε	θῆρ-ε
G. D.	ἁλ-οῖν	ῥητόρ-οιν	μητέρ-οιν	θηρ-οῖν
Plural.				
N. V.	ἅλ-ες [sal-es]	ῥήτορ-ες	μητέρ-ες [matr-es]	θῆρ-ες
Gen.	ἁλ-ῶν [sal-um]	ῥητόρ-ων	μητέρ-ων [matr-um]	θηρ-ῶν
Dat.	ἁλ-σί(ν)	ῥήτορ-σι(ν)	μητρά-σι(ν)	θηρ-σί(ν)
Acc.	ἅλ-ας	ῥήτορ-ας	μητέρ-ας	θῆρ-ας

Examples for Declension.
τὸ νέκταρ, nectar. ὁ κρατήρ, mixing-jug, St. κ ρ α τ η ρ.
ὁ αἰθήρ, æther, St. α ι θ ε ρ. ὁ φώρ, thief (fur), St. φ ω ρ.

§ 151. The only Stem in λ which forms the Nom. Sing. with sigma is ἁλ; all Masc. and Fem. Stems in ρ form the Nom. Sing. without sigma (§ 147, 2); hence with long Stem-vowels the Nom. Sing. is like the Stem; short Stem-vowels, however, are lengthened, i. e., ε into η, ο into ω.
The neuter has the pure Stem in the Nom. Sing.: τὸ ἦτορ, heart.
Only the monosyllabic Stem π ῦ ρ lengthens the υ: τὸ πῦρ, fire (§ 142, b).

§ 152. The Voc. Sing. has the pure Stem: ῥῆτορ. The Stem σ ω τ η ρ (Nom. σωτήρ, savior) shortens η into ε, and draws back the accent (compare § 148): Voc. σῶτερ.

§ 153. The Stems π α τ ε ρ, μ η τ ε ρ, θ υ γ α τ ε ρ, γ α σ τ ε ρ,

§ 150. Dialects.—ἡ ἅλς, poet., the sea.
§ 153. Dialects.—The ε is often retained in the Gen. and Dat. by poets: μητέρος; while it is rejected in other cases: θύγατρα. Instead of α σ ι (ν) in the Dat. Plur., there may be the ε σ σ ι (ν) mentioned, § 141, D.: θυγατέρεσσι(ν).

Δ η μ η τ ε ρ (Noms. πατήρ, *father;* μήτηρ, *mother;* θυγάτηρ, *daughter;* γαστήρ, *belly;* Δημήτηρ), reject ε in the Gen. and Dat. Sing. (§ 61, c). The first four throw the accent on the case-ending; the last draws it back (πατρός, Δήμητρος). The ε is accented where it appears: μητέρα, in spite of μήτηρ, except in the Voc., where the accent is drawn back: πάτερ, in spite of πατήρ, but Acc. Sing. Δήμητρα. In the Dat. Plur. the syllable τ ε ρ becomes by metathesis (§ 59) τ ρ α : μητρά-σι(ν).

Obs.—The Stem ἀστερ (Nom. Sing. ἀστήρ, *star*) belongs to these words only in the formation of the Dat. Plur.: ἀστράσι(ν). For ἀνήρ (St. ἀ ν ε ρ), see, under the irregular words, § 177, 1.

II. Vowel Stems.

§ 154. 1. *Soft-vowel Stems, i. e.,* Stems in ι and υ.

Examples. Stems.	ἡ πόλις, *city.* π ο λ ι	ἡ σῦς, *sow.* σ υ	τὸ ἄστυ (ἀστύ), *city.*
Singular.			
Nom.	πόλι-ς	σῦ-ς	ἄστυ
Gen.	πόλε-ως	σῦ-ός	ἄστε-ος or ἄστε-ως
Dat.	(πόλε-ϊ) πόλει	σῦ-ΐ	(ἄστε-ϊ) ἄστει
Acc.	πόλι-ν	σῦ-ν	ἄστυ
Voc.	πόλι	σῦ-ς	ἄστυ
Dual.			
N. A. V.	πόλε-ε	σύ-ε	(ἄστε-ε) ἄστη
G. D.	πολέ-οιν	σύ-οῖν	ἀστέ-οιν
Plural.			
N. V.	(πόλε-ες) πόλεις	σύ-ες	(ἄστε-α) ἄστη
Gen.	πόλε-ων	σύ-ῶν	ἄστε-ων
Dat.	πόλε-σι(ν)	σύ-σί(ν)	ἄστε-σι(ν)
Acc.	(πόλε-ας) πόλεις	σύ-ας or σῦς	(ἄστε-α) ἄστη

Examples for Declension.

ὁ βότρυ-ς, *bunch of grapes,*
ἡ πίτυ-ς, *pine-tree,* } according to § 157.
ὁ πῆχυ-ς, *fore-arm,*

ἡ δύναμι-ς, *power,* } both according to § 157.
ἡ στάσι-ς, *party, faction,*

Adjectives, § 185.

§ 155. The Nom. Sing. Masc. and Fem. is always formed by Sigma. The Neuter Sing. as well as the Vocative Sing. of all genders has the pure Stem. Yet sometimes the Nom. form is used for the Vocative, and this is the case in all monosyllables. In the Acc. Sing. Masc. and Fem. ν is affixed to the Stem. On the lengthening of monosyllabic Stems, § 142 b. But this lengthening takes place also in the Nom. and Acc. Sing. of some polysyllabic words.

§ 156. *Barytones* in ιτ, ιδ, ιθ, υδ, υθ (Nom. ι ς, υ ς), form the Acc. Sing. generally by affixing ν after rejecting the Stem-consonant: St. ἐ ρ ι δ (Nom. ἔρι-ς, *strife*), Acc. ἔρι-ν; St. κ ο ρ υ θ (Nom. κόρυ-ς, *helmet*), Acc. κόρυ-ν; St. ὀ ρ ν ῑ θ (Nom. ὄρνῑ-ς, *bird*), Acc. ὄρνῑ-ν. The *Oxytones*, on the contrary, always have α: ἐλπί-ς, *hope*, Acc. ἐλπίδα; κλείς, *key*, stands alone; St. κ λ ε ι δ, Acc. κλεῖν (seldom κλεῖδ-α), Acc. Plur. κλεῖς or κλεῖδας.

Examples. ἡ ἔρι-ς, *strife*.   ἡ ἐλπί-ς, *hope*.
Stems.   ἐ ρ ι δ.   ἐ λ π ι δ.
Singular. ἔρι-ς.   ἐλπί-ς.
           ἔριδ-ος.   ἐλπίδ-ος.
           ἔριδ-ι.   ἐλπίδ-ι.
           ἔρι-ν.   ἐλπίδ-α.

§ 157. Most Stems in ι, as well as adjective and some substantive Stems in υ, *change* their final vowel to ε in Gen. and Dat. Sing., and in all the cases of the Dual and

---

§ 156. **Dialects.**—The Acc. Sing. in α of dental Stems is more frequent in Homer: γλαυκώπιδ-α (γλαυκῶπις, *bright-eyed*), ἔριδ-α; κλείς is κληῒς, Acc. κληῒδ-α.

§ 157. **Dialects.**—The Ionic dialect leaves ι unchanged: Gen. πόλι-ος, Dat. πόλῑ (from πόλι-ι), Nom. Plur. πόλι-ες, Gen. πολί-ων, Dat. in Herod. πόλι-σι(ν), Homer πολί-εσσι(ν), Acc. πόλι-ας (Herod. also πόλις). Other additional forms of the Homeric dialect are: Gen. Sing. πόλη-ος, Dat. Sing. πόλε-ϊ and πόλη-ϊ, Nom. Plur. πόλη-ες, Acc. Plur. πόλη-ας.

The Stems in υ have always ο ς in the Gen. Sing. The Dat. Sing. only is contracted: πήχει. εὐρύ-ς, *broad*, has the additional form εὐρέα in the Acc. Sing.

§ 158. CONSONANT DECLENSION. 59

Plur. Before the ending of the Gen. Sing. this ε remains unchanged; in the Stems, however, in ι, and in some substantive Stems in υ, ε is followed by ω ς (instead of ος), called the *Attic* termination, which does not prevent the accent from being on the antepenult: πόλε-ως, πελέκε-ως (πέλεκυ-ς, *axe*).

In the Dat. Sing. ε ϊ is contracted into ε ι, in the Nom. Plur. ε ε ς and Acc. ε α ς into ε ι ς, and ε α of neuter *substantives* into η. Adjectives maintain the uncontracted form εα: ἄστη, but γλυκέα.

§ 158. The contraction of ε ε to η in the Nom. Acc. and Voc. Dual is rare. The Gen. Plur. of Stems in ι follows the accent of the Gen. Sing.: πόλε-ων like πόλε-ως.

Most substantive Stems in υ leave this vowel unchanged; but others, like ἄστυ, follow the analogy of Stems in ι, and change υ into ε. υ ε are sometimes contracted into ῡ in the Nom. Acc. and Voc. Dual; in the Acc. Plur. also we find ἰχθῦς, with ἰχθύ-ας (ἰχθύ-ς, *fish*), and ὀφρῦς, Acc. Plur. of ὀφρύ-ς, *eyebrow*.

ἔγχελυ-ς, *eel*, retains υ in the Sing.: Gen. ἐγχέλυ-ος; but changes it in the Dual and Plur. into ε: Nom. Plur. ἐγχέλεις.

The adjective ἴδρι-ς, *acquainted with*, St. ἴ δ ρ ι, keeps its ι unchanged through all the cases.

§ 158. Dialects.—The Dat. ἰχθύϊ is in Homer contracted into ἰχθυῖ. In the Dat. Plur. σ is sometimes doubled: νέκυ-σσι(ν) with νεκύ-εσσι(ν) (νέκυ-ς, *corpse*).

§ 159. 2. *Diphthong Stems, i. e.*, Stems in ε υ, α υ, ο υ.

Examples. Stems.	ὁ βασιλεύς βασιλευ *king.*	ἡ γραῦς γραυ *old woman.*	ὁ and ἡ βοῦς βου *ox* or *cow.*
Singular.			
Nom.	βασιλεύ-ς	γραῦ-ς	βοῦ-ς [bo-s]
Gen.	βασιλέ-ως	γρᾱ-ός	βο-ός [bov-is]
Dat.	(βασιλέ-ϊ) βασιλεῖ	γρᾱ-ΐ	βο-ΐ [bov-i]
Acc.	βασιλέ-ᾱ	γραῦ-ν	βοῦ-ν [bov-e-m]
Voc.	βασιλεῦ	γραῦ	βοῦ
Dual.			
N. A. V.	βασιλέ-ε	γρᾶ-ε	βό-ε
G. D.	βασιλέ-οιν	γρᾱ-οῖν	βο-οῖν
Plural.			
N. V.	(βασιλέ-ες) βασιλῆς or βασιλεῖς	γρᾶ-ες	βό-ες [bov-es]
Gen.	βασιλέ-ων	γρα-ῶν	βο-ῶν [bo-um]
Dat.	βασιλεῦ-σι(ν)	γραυ-σί(ν)	βου-σί(ν)
Acc.	βασιλέ-ας	γραῦ-ς	βοῦ-ς

Examples for Declension.

ὁ γονεύ-ς, *parent.*   ὁ ἱερεύ-ς, *priest.*   'Οδυσσεύ-ς, 'Αχιλλεύ-ς.

§ 160. *All* diphthong Stems affix ς in the Nom. Sing. and σι(ν) in the Dat. Plur.; those in αυ and ου affix ν in the Acc. Sing. to the full Stem. In the Voc. Sing. the Stem appears pure.

Before vowel case-endings, *i. e.*, in all other forms, the υ of the Stem was changed into ϝ (§ 34, D.): βοϝ-ός [*bov-is*], and then was entirely lost: βο-ός [βο-ῶν=*bo-um*] (§ 35, D. 2).

Obs.—An isolated diphthong Stem is ο ἰ, Nom. οἶ-ς, *sheep* [*ovi-s*]: οἰός, οἰΐ, οἶν; Plur. οἶες, οἰῶν, οἰσί(ν), οἶς. Compare § 34, D.

§ 159. **Dialects.**—Homer has γρηῦς for γραῦ-ς, Dat. γρηΐ, Voc. γρηῦ or γρηῢ; from βοῦ-ς, Acc. Plur. βό-ᾰς, Dat. βό-εσσι(ν). The forms βῶς, Nom., βῶν, Acc. Sing., are Doric.

§ 160. **Dialects.**—Ionic ὄϊς (*ovis*) for οἶς, Gen. ὄϊος, Dat. Plur. ὀΐ-εσσι or ὄεσσι, Acc. ὄϊς.

§ 162. CONSONANT DECLENSION. 61

Some compounds of πού-ς, *foot*, form the Acc. Sing. like Stems in ου: τρίπους, *three-footed*, Acc. τρίπουν. For ναῦ-ς, see among the irregular words, § 177, 11.

§ 161. The Stems in ε υ, moreover, have in the
a) Gen. Sing., ως for ος. Compare § 157.
b) Dat. Sing., ε ι always contracted for ει.
c) Acc. Sing. and Plur., α is long and not contracted.
d) Nom. and Voc. Plur., ε ε ς contracted by older Attic writers into η ς, by the later into ε ι ς.
e) Words which have a vowel before ε υ may be contracted also in the Gen. and Acc. Sing., and in the Acc. Plur.: St. Π ε ι ρ α ι ε υ, Nom. Πειραιεύ-ς, *port of Athens*, Gen. Πειραιῶς, Acc. Πειραιᾶ ; χοεύ-ς, *measure*, Acc. Plur. χοᾶς.

Obs.—The Gen. in -ε ω ς has arisen by transmutation of quantity (§ 37, D. 2) out of the Hom. η ο ς. Hence the length of the final syllable. In the same manner, the Acc. Sing. εᾱ has arisen out of ηᾰ: still εᾰ is also found, like εᾰς in the Acc. Plural; εας is contracted by later writers into εις.

§ 162. 3. O *Stems, i. e.*, Stems in o and ω.

Examples. Stems.	ἡ πειθώ, *persuasion*. π ε ι θ ο		ὁ ἥρως, *hero*. ἡ ρ ω	
Singular.				
Nom.	πειθώ		ἥρω-ς	Plur. ἥρω-ες
Gen.	(πειθό-ος) πειθοῦς		ἥρω-ος	ἡρώ-ων
Dat.	(πειθό-ϊ) πειθοῖ		ἥρω-ι	ἥρω-σι(ν)
Acc.	(πειθό-α) πειθώ		ἥρω-α ἥρω	ἥρω-ας or
Voc.	πειθοῖ		ἥρω-ς	ἥρως
Dual and Plural of πειθώ are formed as in the o declension.			Dual ἥρω-ε ἡρώ-οιν	

§ 161. **Dialects.**—The Epic dialect lengthens the ε of Stems in ε υ into η before vowels: βασιλῆ-ος, βασιλῆ-ι, βασιλῆ-α, βασιλῆ-ες, βασιλή-ων,

Examples for Declension.

ἡ ἠχώ (St. ἠ χ o), echo.
Καλυψώ, Λητώ, δμώ-ς (St. δ μ ω), slave.
μήτρω-ς (St. μ η τ ρ ω), avunculus.

§ 163. The Stems in o, all feminine, form the Nom. Sing. without sigma, except the Stem α ἰ δ o, Nom. Sing. αἰδώ-ς, shame, Acc. αἰδῶ. The Acc., which is like the Nom., is oxytone (contrary to § 87): πειθώ, not πειθῶ. The Vocative ends in o ι ; all other cases are contracted. The Acc. of Stems in ω usually remains uncontracted. The Stem ἑ ω, Nom. ἡ ἕω-ς, dawn, has Gen. Sing. ἕω, Dat. ἕῳ (according to § 132), Acc. ἕω (from ἕωα).

Obs.—Several Stems in o ν follow the above declension in some of their forms : ἀηδών, nightingale, Gen. ἀηδοῦς, with ἀηδόνος ; εἰκών, image, Gen. εἰκοῦς (compare § 171).

ἀριστή-εσσι(ν) (ἀριστεύ-ς, prince) ; still there are Genitives also in ε ο ς and ε ῦ ς ('Οδυσεῦς), Datives in ε ϊ, ε ι, and Accusatives in ε α, η : Τυδῆ. The New-Ionic dialect leaves ε frequently uncontracted : βασιλέ-ες.

§ 163. **Dialects.**—Homer contracts ἥρωϊ into ἥρῳ, Μίνωα into Μίνω. The old and poetic form for ἕω-ς is ἠώ-ς (St. ἠ o), declined like αἰδώ-ς. Some proper names in ω in the Nom. Sing. have in the New-Ionic dialect an Acc. in οῦν : Λητοῦν, Ἰοῦν.

§ 165. CONSONANT DECLENSION. 63

III. ELIDED STEMS, *i. e.*, Stems which reject the final consonant in certain forms.

§ 164. 1. Σ *Stems, i. e.*, Stems which elide sigma.

Examples. Stems.	τὸ γένος, *race.* γενες	M. εὐγενής, N. εὐγενές, *of good family.* εὐγενες
Singular.		
Nom.	γένος [genus]	M. εὐγενής N. εὐγενές
Gen.	(γένε-ος) γένους	(εὐγενέ-ος) εὐγενοῦς
Dat.	(γένε-ϊ) γένει	(εὐγενέ-ϊ) εὐγενεῖ
Acc.	γένος	(εὐγενέ-α) εὐγενῆ N. εὐγενές
Voc.	γένος	εὐγενές · N. εὐγενές
Dual.		
N. A. V.	(γένε-ε) γένη	(εὐγενέ-ε) εὐγενῆ
G. D.	(γενέ-οιν) γενοῖν	(εὐγενέ-οιν) εὐγενοῖν
Plural.		
N. V.	(γένε-α) γένη	(εὐγενέ-ες) εὐγενεῖς N. (εὐγενέα) εὐγενῆ
Gen.	(γενέ-ων) γενῶν	(εὐγενέ-ων) εὐγενῶν
Dat.	γένε-σι(ν)	εὐγενέ-σι(ν)
Acc.	(γένε-α) γένη	(εὐγενέ-ᾱς) εὐγενεῖς N. (εὐγενέα) εὐγενῆ

Examples for Declension.

τὸ εἶδος, *form.* κάλλος, *beauty.* μέλος, *song.* ἄχθος, *burden.*
Adjectives:
σαφής, Neut. σαφές, *clear.* ἀκριβής, Neut. ἀκριβές, *exact.*
εὐήθης, Neut. εὔηθες, *simple.*

§ 165. The sigma Stems retain their final consonant only when it stands at the end, *i. e.*, in the Nom. Acc. and Voc. Sing. Neuter, and in the Nom. and Voc. Sing. Masc. and Fem.

The Neuter substantives change the Stem-vowel ε into ο in the Nom. Acc. and Voc. Sing.: St. γενες, γένος.

§ 165. **Dialects.**—The Epic dialect *frequently*, the New-Ionic *always*, leaves the vowels of the sigma Stems uncontracted: γένεος, γένεϊ. Hom. sometimes has the Gen. Sing. ευς (from εος, § 37, D. 1): θάρσευς (θάρσος, *courage*).

In the Dative Plur. Homer has three endings: ε-εσσι(ν), εσ-σι(ν), and the usual ε-σι(ν): βελέ-εσσι(ν), βέλεσ-σι(ν), βέλε-σι(ν), (βέλος, *dart*).

Neuter adjectives leave ε unchanged: εὐγενές. Masculines and Feminines form the Nom. Sing. by lengthening ες into ης (§ 147, 2), as ς can not be affixed: εὐγενής from εὐγενες, like ποιμήν from ποιμεν.

Masculines and Feminines have the pure Stem in the Voc. Sing., and in compound words which are not oxytone in Nom. Sing. the accent is on the last syllable but two (compare §§ 148, 85): Nom. Σωκράτης, Voc. Σώκρατες; Nom. Δημοσθένης, Voc. Δημόσθενες.

Obs.—The Neuter ἀληθές (Masc. ἀληθής, *true*) draws back the accent in interrogations: ἄληθες; *really?*

§ 166. In all other forms ς is rejected (§§ 61 and 49): γένε-ϊ for γένεσ-ι [*gener-i*]. Wherever two vowels meet they are contracted: εε in the Nom. Acc. and Voc. Dual become η; εα generally η; but when another vowel stands before ε they sometimes become ᾱ, according to § 41: St. ἐνδεες, Nom. ἐνδεής, *defective*, Acc. ἐνδεᾶ; St. ὑγιες, Nom. ὑγιής, *healthy*, Acc. ὑγιᾶ, but also ὑγιῆ; St. χρεες, Nom. τὸ χρέος, *debt*, Neut. Plur. χρέα. The adjectives in -φυής (St. φυες) have φυῆ and φυᾶ: εὐφυής, *well-disposed*, εὐφυῆ and εὐφυᾶ.

Obs.—Barytone adjectives have the accent in the Gen. Plur. on the last syllable but one, contrary to § 87: αὐτάρκων (Nom. αὐτάρκης, *self-sufficient*). So also τριήρης, *trireme*, used as a substantive, Gen. Plur. τριήρων.

§ 167. Proper names in -κλεης, compounded with κλέος, *glory* (St. κλεες), have a double contraction in the Dat. Sing., and a single one in all the other cases: Nom. (Περικλεης) Περικλῆς, Gen. (Περικλεεος) Περικλέους, Dat. (Περικλεεϊ, Περικλέει) Περικλεῖ, Acc. (Περικλεεα) Περικλέᾱ, Voc. (Περικλεες) Περίκλεις.

§ 166. **Dialects.**—A vowel before ε is often contracted with it in Homer: σπέος or σπεῖος, *cave*, Gen. σπείους, Dat. σπῆ-ι (from σπέεϊ), Dat. Plur. σπήεσσι(ν) and σπέσσι(ν); εὐκλεής, *glorious*, Acc. εὐκλεῖας (from εὐκλέεας), but ἀκλεεῖς (from ἀκλεής, *inglorious*). Herodotus ἐνδεέες (ἐνδεής, *defective*), ἀνθρωποφυέας (ἀνθρωποφυής, *human*).

§ 167. **Dialects.**—The Epic dialect forms Ἡρακλῆς, Ἡρακλῆ-ος, Ἡρακλῆ-ι, Ἡρακλῆ-α; the New-Ionic, Ἡρακλέης, Ἡρακλέ-ος, Ἡρακλέ-ϊ, Ἡρακλέ-α.

§ 168. 2. T *Stems, i. c.*, Stems which elide τ.

Examples. Stems.	τὸ κέρας, *horn.* κεράτ			τὸ κρέας, *meat.* κρεατ	
Singular.					
N. A. V.	κέρᾰς			κρέας	
Gen.	κέρᾱτ-ος	(κέραος)	κέρως	(κρέαος)	κρέως
Dat.	κέρᾱτ-ι	(κέραϊ)	κέρᾳ	(κρέαϊ)	κρέᾳ
Dual.					
N. A. V.	κέρᾱτ-ε	(κέραε)	κέρᾱ		
G. D.	κεράτ-οιν	(κεράοιν)	κερῷν		
Plural.					
N. A. V.	κέρᾱτ-α	(κέραα)	κέρᾱ	(κρέαα)	κρέᾰ
Gen.	κεράτ-ων	(κεράων)	κερῶν	(κρεάων)	κρεῶν
Dat.	κέρᾰ-σι(ν)			κρέᾰ-σι(ν)	

§ 169. τ becomes ς in Nom. Acc. and Voc. Sing., according to § 67. In the other cases some words always reject it: *e. g.*, κρέας, σέλας, *splendor ;* γῆρας, *age ;* κνέφας, *gloom.* Others, like κέρας, retain both forms together, with and without τ. The vowels which meet are regularly contracted. The quantity of α is very fluctuating. The Dat. Sing. is written also αι : σέλαι.

In prose, only a few Neuters (Nom. α ς) have a movable τ.

§ 169. **Dialects.**—Homer has δέπα-εσσι(ν) or δέπασ-σι(ν), Dat. Plur. of δέπας, *goblet.* In Ionic α often becomes ε : Homer οὔδας, *ground,* Gen. οὔδε-ος, κῶας, *fleece,* Nom. Plur. κώε-α ; κέρας, New-Ionic Gen. κέρεος.

A movable τ appears also in the Stems ἱ δ ρ ω τ, γ ε λ ω τ, χ ρ ω τ (Nom. ἱδρώς, *sweat ;* γέλως, *laughter ;* χρώς, *skin*), Dat. ἱδρῷ, Acc. ἱδρῶ, together with Gen. ἱδρῶτος ; γέλω ; and regularly in Homer χρο-ός, χρο-ΐ (poet. χρῷ), χρό-α. Compare αἰδώς, ἠώς, § 163.

§ 170. 3. N *Stems, i. e.*, Stems which elide ν.

Examples. Stems.	M. F. μείζων, greater. μειζον		N. μεῖζον
Singular. *N. V.* *Gen.* *Dat.* *Acc.*	μείζων μείζον-ος μείζον-ι μείζον-α [μειζοα] μείζω		N. μεῖζον N. μεῖζον
Dual. *N. A. V.* *G. D.*	μείζον-ε μειζόν-οιν		
Plural. *N. V.* *Gen.* *Dat.* *Acc.*	μείζον-ες [μειζοες] μείζους μειζόν-ων μείζο-σι(ν) μείζον-ας [μειζοας] μείζους		N. μείζονα [μειζοα] μείζω N. μείζονα [μεεζοα] μείζω

Examples for Declension.

βελτίων, *better.*   αἰσχίων, *more hateful.*   ἀλγίων, *more painful.*

§ 171. The full and the contracted forms are equally in use. But the open ones (μειζοα) never occur. Comparatives of more than two syllables throw back the accent in the Nom. Acc. and Voc. Sing. Neuter upon the last syllable but two: βέλτιον, αἴσχιον.

Besides the *comparatives* (Nom. ω ν, ο ν), there are only the two proper names, Ἀπόλλων (Stem. and Nom.) and Ποσειδῶν (Stem and Nom.), Acc. Ἀπόλλω (also Ἀπόλλων-α), Ποσειδῶ (also Ποσειδῶν-α). On the Vocative, see § 148, *Obs.* We may compare several Stems which fluctuate between ο ν and ο (§ 163).

§ 171. **Dialects.**—Homer forms the Acc. κυκεῶ or κυκειῶ from κυκεών, *mixture.*

§ 172. CONSONANT DECLENSION. 67

§ 172. Synopsis of terminations in the Second Principal Declension.

Nom.	Stem.		Gen.
in -α	-ατ	τὸ σῶμα, *body.*	σώματος
-αις	-αιδ -αιτ	ὁ παῖς, *boy.* ἡ δαίς, *meal.*	παιδός δαιτός
-ᾶν M. -αν N.	-αν -αντ	Πάν, *Pan.* Adj. τὸ πᾶν, *the whole.*	Πανός παντός
-αρ	-αρ -αρτ -α(ρ)τ	τὸ ἔαρ, *spring.* ἡ δάμαρ, *wife.* τὸ φρέαρ, *fountain.*	ἔαρος δάμαρτος φρέατος
-ᾰς F. -ᾰς N.	-αδ -α(τ)	ἡ λαμπάς, *lamp.* τὸ κρέας, *meat.*	λαμπάδος κρέως
-ᾶς M.	-αντ -αν	ὁ γίγας, *giant.* Adj. μέλας, *black.*	γίγαντος μέλανος
-αυς F.	-α(υ)	ἡ γραῦς, *old woman.*	γραός
-ειρ	-ειρ	ἡ χείρ, *hand.*	χειρός
-εις M. F.	-εντ -εν -ειδ	Part. λυθείς, *loosed.* Adj. εἷς, *one.* ἡ κλείς, *key.*	λυθέντος ἑνός κλειδός
-εν N.	-εντ -εν	Part. λυθέν, *loosed.* Adj. ἄρρεν, *male.*	λυθέντος ἄρρενος
-ες N.	-ε(ς)	Adj. σαφές, *clear.*	σαφοῦς
-ευς M.	-ε(υ)	ὁ φονεύς, *murderer.*	φονέως
-ην M.	-εν -ην	ὁ λιμήν, *harbor.* ὁ Ἕλλην, *Greek.*	λιμένος Ἕλληνος
-ηρ	-ερ -ηρ	ὁ αἰθήρ, *æther.* ὁ θήρ, *game.*	αἰθέρος θηρός

CONSONANT DECLENSION. § 172.

Nom.	Stem.		Gen.
-ης	-ητ -ε(ς)	ἡ βαρύτης, *weight.* ὁ, ἡ τριήρης, *trireme.*	βαρύτητος τριήρους
-ι N.	-ι -ιτ	Adj. ἴδρι, *acquainted with.* τὸ μέλι, *honey.*	ἴδριος μέλιτος
-ιν	-ιν	ὁ δελφίν, *dolphin.*	δελφῖνος
-ις	-ι -ιδ -ιτ -ῑθ -ιν	ἡ πόλις, *city.* ἡ ἐλπίς, *hope.* ἡ χάρις, *favor.* ὁ, ἡ ὄρνις, *bird.* ἡ Σαλαμίς, *Salamis.*	πόλεως ἐλπίδος χάριτος ὄρνῑθος Σαλαμῖνος
-ον N.	-ον -οντ	Adj. εὔδαιμον, *fortunate.* Part. λῦον, *loosing.*	εὐδαίμονος λύοντος
-ος N.	-ε(ς) -οτ	τὸ γένος, *race.* Part. πεφῡκός, *having become.*	γένους πεφῡκότος
-ους	-οντ -οδ -ο(υ)	ὁ ὀδούς, *tooth.* ὁ πούς, *foot.* ὁ, ἡ βοῦς, *ox, cow.*	ὀδόντος πόδος βοός
-υ N.	-υ	τὸ ἄστυ, *city.*	ἄστεος
-υν M. N.	-υν -υντ	ὁ μόσῡν, *wooden tower.* Part. δεικνύν, *showing.*	μόσῡνος δεικνύντος
-υς M. F.	-υντ -υ -υδ	Part. δεικνύς, *showing.* ὁ ἰχθύς, *fish.* ὁ πῆχυς, *ell.* ἡ χλαμύς, *cloak.*	δεικνύντος ἰχθύος πήχεως χλαμύδος
-ω F.	-ο	ἡ πειθώ, *persuasion.*	πειθοῦς
-ων M.	-ον -ων -οντ	ἡ ἀηδών, *nightingale.* ὁ ἀγών, *contest.* ὁ λέων, *lion.*	ἀηδόνος ἀγῶνος λέοντος
-ωρ	-ορ	ὁ ῥήτωρ, *orator.*	ῥήτορος

§ 173. CONSONANT DECLENSION. 69

Nom.	Stem.		Gen.
-ως M.	-ω -ο -οτ -ωτ	ὁ ἥρως, *hero.* ἡ αἰδώς, *shame.* Part. πεφῡκώς, *having become.* ὁ ἔρως, *love.*	ἥρωος αἰδοῦς πεφῡκότος ἔρωτος
-ψ	-π -β -φ	ὁ γύψ, *vulture.* ὁ χάλυψ, *steel.* ἡ κατῆλιψ, *upper story.*	γῡπός χάλυβος κατήλῑφος
-ξ	-κ -γ -χ -κτ	ὁ φύλαξ, *guard.* ἡ φλόξ, *flame.* ὁ ὄνυξ, *nail.* ἡ νύξ, *night.*	φύλακος φλογός ὄνῠχος νυκτός

§ 173. The Second Principal Declension agrees with the First in the following particulars:

1. Masculines have ς for the Nom. Sing. (or compensation for it); feminines are less consistent in this.
2. The Dat. Sing. affixes ι (subscribed in the First Principal Declension)..
3. Vowel, and in part diphthongal, Stems take ν in the Acc. Sing.

Obs.—The original ending of the Acc. Sing. was also in the Second Principal Declension every where ν. This consonant was, however, connected with consonant-Stems by the connecting vowel α: ὀδοντ-α-ν=Lat. *dent-e-m.* Subsequently ν was dropped, and α left, generally as the only sign: ὀδόντ-α.

4. The Gen. and Dat. Dual have ιν (αιν, οιν).
5. The Gen. Plur. ων.
6. The Dat. Plur. σι(ν) originally every where.
7. The Acc. Plur. ς every where.

Obs.—The original ending of all Acc. Plur. was νς, but ν was dropped after vowels of the First Principal Declension, and was compensated for by the lengthened ᾱς, ους. After consonants there was the same process as in the Acc. Sing.: ὀδόντ-α(ν)-ς, Lat. *dent-ē-s* for *dent-em-s.*

8. Neuters all have ᾰ in Nom. Acc. and Voc. Plur.

The principal differences in the endings are:
1. In the Gen. Sing., where the Second Principal Declension always has ο ς (ως).
2. In the Nom. Plur., where Masc. and Fem. of the Second Principal Declension always have ε ς.

Irregularities in Declension.

§ 174. The mixing of two Stems which may have *one* Nom. is called *Heteroclizing* (ἑτεροκλισία, *different inflexion*): Nom. σκότος, *darkness*, Gen. σκότου (O-Declension), and σκότους (Second Principal Declension); λαγώς, *hare*, according to the Attic declension, but Acc. λαγῶ. An important irregularity of this kind occurs with proper names in η ς: Σωκράτης (Στ. Σωκρατες), but Acc. Σωκράτην (as if from Stem Σωκρατα of the A-Declension) with Σωκράτη. But those in -κλῆς (§ 167) follow the Second Principal Declension exclusively.

§ 175. The formation of some cases from a Stem which can not be that of the Nom. is called *Metaplasm* (μεταπλασμός, *change of formation*): Nom. Sing. τό δένδρον, *tree*, Dat. Plur. δένδρεσι(ν), as if from Stem δ ε ν δ ρ ε ς ; Nom. Sing. τὸ δάκρυον, *tear*, Dat. Plur. δάκρυσι(ν), from St. δακρυ (poet. Nom. δάκρυ); τὸ πῦρ, *fire*, Plur. τὰ πῦρά, Dat. τοῖς πυροῖς (O-Declension); Nom. Sing. ὄνειρο-ς, *dream*, Gen. ὀνείρατος, Nom. Plur. ὀνείρατα.

§ 176. A peculiar irregularity appears in several Neuter

---

§ 174. **Dialects.**—Several Masc. Stems in α, Nom. η ς in Herodotus, have ε α for η ν in the Acc. Sing.: δεσπότη-ς, *master*, δεσπότεα. ὁ ὄχο-ς, *carriage*, in Homer has Plur. τὰ ὄχεα, ὀχεσφι(ν), from the St. ὀ χ ε ς. Οἰδίπους has poet. forms from a St. Ο ἰ δ ι π ο δ α, Gen. Sing. Οἰδιπόδαο, trag. Οἰδιπόδᾱ. Homeric Σαρπηδών, Stems Σ α ρ π η δ ο ν and Σ α ρ π η δ ο ν τ. Μίνως, Acc. Sing. Μίνωα (§ 163) and Μίνων.

§ 175. **Dialects.**—Hom. metaplasms are: Dat. Plur. ἀνδραπόδεσσι(ν), Nom. Sing. ἀνδράποδον, *slave*; Nom. Acc. Plur. προσώπατα, Nom. Sing. πρόσωπον, *countenance*; δέσματα, *bonds*, Sing. ὁ δεσμός ; ἐρίηρο-ς, *trusty*, Nom. Plur. ἐρίηρες ; ἀλκή, *strength*, Dat. Sing. ἀλκ-ί ; ὑσμίνη, *battle*, ὑσμῖνι; ἰχώρ, *divine blood*, Acc. Sing. ἰχῶ.

§ 177. IRREGULARITIES IN DECLENSION. 71

Stems in αρτ, as φρεαρτ. They reject τ in the Nom. Acc. and Voc. Sing. and ρ in the other cases: τὸ φρέαρ, *well*, Gen. φρέατος (also φρητός); τὸ ἦπαρ, *liver*, Gen. ἤπᾰτος; τὸ ἄλειφαρ and ἄλειφᾰ, *salve*, Gen. ἀλείφᾰτος. To these correspond the Stems σκα(ρ)τ and ὑδα(ρ)τ: Nom. σκώρ, *dirt*, Gen. σκᾰτός; ὕδωρ, Gen. ὕδᾰτος.

§ 177. Special irregularities in alphabetical order:

1. ἀνήρ, *man* (compare § 153), rejects ε of the Stem ἀνερ, and inserts δ in its place (§ 51, *Obs.* 2): ἀν-δ-ρ-ός, ἀνδρί, ἄνδρα; Voc. ἄνερ; Dual, ἄνδρε, ἀνδροῖν; Plur. ἄνδρες, ἀνδρῶν, ἀνδράσι(ν), ἄνδρᾰς.

2. Ἄρης (*the god Ares*): St. Ἄρες, Gen. Ἄρεως and Ἄρεος, Acc. Ἄρην, together with Ἄρη; Voc. regul. Ἄρες.

3. ἀρν, without Nom.: Gen. τοῦ and τῆς ἀρν-ός, *of the lamb*, ἀρνί, ἄρνα; Dat. Plur. ἀρνᾰσι(ν).

4. τὸ γόνυ, *knee* (*genu*), Nom. Acc. Voc. All the rest from St. γονατ, Gen. γόνατος.

5. ἡ γυνή, *woman*. All the rest from St. γυναικ-, Gen. γυναικός, Dat. γυναικί, Acc. γυναῖκα, Voc. γύναι; Dual γυναῖκε, γυναικοῖν; Plur. γυναῖκ-ες, -ῶν, -ξί(ν), -ας.

6. τὸ δόρυ, *wood, spear*: St. δορατ (comp. 4.). Gen. δόρατος, poet. δορός, Dat. δορί and δόρει.

7. Ζεύς (*the god Zeus*), Gen. Διός, Dat. Διί, Acc. Δία, Voc. Ζεῦ.

8. ὁ and ἡ κύων, *dog*, with Voc. κύον, from St. κυον. All the rest from κυν: Gen. κυνός, Dat. κυνί, Acc. κύνα; Plur. κύνες, κυνῶν, κυσί(ν), κύνας.

9. ὁ λᾶ-ς, *stone*, from Hom. λᾶα-ς, Gen. λᾶ-ος, Dat. λᾶ-ϊ,

---

§ 177. Dialects.—The following forms are peculiar to dialects:

1. ἀνήρ, poet. 'ἀνέρ-ος, 'ἄνέρ-ι, 'ἀνέρ-α; Dat. Plur. ἄνδρεσσι(ν).
2. Ἄρης, Homer Ἄρηος, Ἀρηϊ, Ἄρηα.
4. γόνυ, Ion. and poet. γούνᾰτ-ος, γούνατ-ᾰ, γούνᾰσι(ν); Ep. Gen. Sing. γουνός, Plur. γοῦνᾰ, γούνων, γούν-εσσι(ν).
6. δόρυ, δούρατος, Ep. δουρός, δουρί, δοῦρε, δοῦρα, δούρων, δούρεσσι(ν).
7. Ζεύς, poet. St. Ζην: Ζην-ός, Ζην-ί, Ζῆν-α (also Ζῆν, from Ζη).

Acc. λᾶα-ν, λᾶν; Plur. λᾶ-ες, λά-ων, λά-εσσι(ν) or λά-εσι(ν), λᾶ-ας.

10. ὁ μ ά ρ τ ῠ - ς; *witness*, with Dat. Plur. μάρτυσι(ν), from St. μαρτυ. The rest from the St. μαρτυρ : μάρτυρος, μάρτυρι, etc.

11. ἡ ν α ῦ - ς, *ship*, νε-ώς, νη-ί, ναῦ-ν ; Plur. νῆ-ες, νε-ῶν, ναυ-σί(ν), ναῦς. Compare § 159.

Obs.—The Nom. Acc. Sing. and Dat. Acc. Plur. rest on the St. ναυ. Before vowels ναυ becomes (according to § 35, D. 2) νηF, νη; νε-ώς is for νη-ός (§ 37, D. 2).

12. ὁ and ἡ ὄρνῑ-ς, *bird*, St. ὀρνιθ and ὀρνι : ὄρνῑθ-ος, ὄρνῑθι, ὄρνῑθα, and ὄρνιν ; Plur. ὄρνῑθες and ὄρνεις, ὄρνεων.

13. τὸ ο ὖ ς, *ear.* All the rest from St. ὠτ : ὠτός, ὠτί ; Plur. ὦτα, ὤτων, ὠ-σί(ν). (On the accent, § 142, 3.)

14. ἡ Π ν ύ ξ (*the Pnyx*), St. πυκν, Πυκν-ός; Πυκν-ί, Πύκν-α.

15. ὁ πρέσβυ-ς, *the aged*, has in the Gen. and Dat. Sing., and throughout the Plur., its forms from πρεσβυτα (Nom. Sing. πρεσβύτης) : πρέσβεις, πρέσβεων, πρέσβεσι(ν), signifies *embassadors*, to which the Sing. is πρεσβευτής.

16. τ ά ν. Only Voc. ὦ τάν or ὦ τᾶν, *friend* or *friends*, a defective Stem.

17. ὁ υἱός, *son*, St. υἱο, υἱ, υἱευ, Gen. υἱέος, Dat. υἱεῖ, Acc. υἱέα (rare), Plur. υἱεῖς, υἱέων, υἱέσι(ν), υἱεῖς. But also regularly υἱοῦ, etc.

18. ἡ χεῖρ, *hand*, St. χειρ, Dual χεροῖν, Dat. Pl. χερσί(ν).

Dialects.—11. ναῦ-ς, from St. ν η υ, Ion. νηῦ-ς, Hom. Acc. Sing. νῆ-α, Dat. Plur. νήεσσι(ν), νηυσί(ν), Acc. νῆας.
from St. ν ε υ, Ion. νε-ός, νε-ί, νέ-α, νέ-ες, νε-ῶν, νέ-εσσι, νέ-ας.
from St. ν α υ, Dor. νᾶ-ός, να-ί (*navi*), νά-εσσι(ν).
13. οὖς, Ion. οὖας, οὖατ-ος ; Plur. οὔατ-α, Dor. ὦς, ὠτ-ός.
17. υἱό-ς, Ep. Gen. υἷ-ος, υἷ-ι, υἷ-α, υἷ-ες, υἱ-άσι(ν), υἷ-ας.
18. χείρ, poet. and New-Ion. χερ-ός, χερ-ί, Ep. Dat. Plur. χείρ-εσι or χείρ-εσσι(ν).

To these add the words which are anomalous only in dialects:
19. Homer Ἀίδη-ς (Att. Ἅιδης), St. Ἀϊδ, Gen. Ἀϊδ-ος, Ἀϊδ-ι, also Ἀϊδωνεύ-ς, with regular inflexion, according to § 159.

Case-like Terminations.

§ 178. Besides the case-endings, there occur certain suffixes or appendages, which in meaning very nearly resemble case-endings. To these belong:

1. -θι, answering to the question *where*: ἄλλο-θι, *elsewhere*;
2. -θεν, answering to the question *whence*: οἴκο-θεν, *from home*;
3. -δε, answering to the question *whither*: οἴκα-δε, *homewards*.

Dialects—20. ὁ ἔρως, *love*, Stems ἐ ρ ω τ and ἐ ρ ο, poet. Acc. ἔρο-ν.
21. θέμις, *justice*, St. θ ε μ ι and θεμιστ, Plur. θέμιστ-ες, θέμιστ-ας.
22. τὸ κάρα, *head*, Hom. St. κ α ρ η τ, κ α ρ η α τ, κ ρ ᾶ α τ, κ ρ ᾶ τ, κ α ρ. Hom. Nom. Sing. κάρη.
    Gen.   "   κάρητ-ος, καρήατ-ος, κράατ-ος, κρᾱτ-ός.
    Dat.   "   κάρητ-ι, καρήατ-ι, κράατ-ι, κρᾱτ-ί (trag. κάρᾳ).
    Acc.   "   κάρη, τὸν κρᾱτ-α, τὸ κάρ.
    Nom. Plur. κάρᾱ, καρήατ-α, κράατ-α, secondary form κάρηνα.
    Gen.   "   κράτων, καρήνων.
    Dat.   "   κρᾱσί(ν).
    Acc.   "   = Nom. (also τοὺς κρᾱτ-ας).
23. ἡ μάστιξ, *whip*, Hom. Dat. μάστῑ, Acc. μάστι-ν.
24. ὁ μείς, *month*, Ion. = Att. μήν.
25. ὄσσε, *eyes*. Nom. Acc. Dual, Neut. in Homer. The trag. have Gen. Plur. ὄσσων, Dat. ὄσσοις or ὄσσοισι(ν).

§ 178. **Dialects.**—The three local suffixes are very frequent in Hom. : οἴκοθι, *at home*; Ἰλιόθι πρό, *in front of Ilios*; οὐρανόθεν, *from heaven*; ἀγορῆθεν, *from the assembly*. θ ε ν also supplies the place of the Gen.-ending : κατὰ κρῆθεν, *down from the head, entirely*; ἐξ ἁλόθεν, *out of the sea*. -δε is generally affixed to the Acc. : οἰκόνδε, *homewards*; κλισίηνδε, *into the tent*; πόλινδε, *into the city*; φόβονδε, *into flight*. φύγαδε, *into flight*, and ἔραζε, *to the earth*, are peculiar.

A suffix peculiar to the Hom. language is φ ι (ν); it is added to the Stem of nouns, and supplies the place of the Gen. or Dat. termination in both Sing. and Plur., as :

1. A- decl.: βίη-φι, *with force*; κλισίη-φι, *in the tent*; ἀπὸ νευρῆ-φιν, *from the bow-string*.
2. O- decl.: θεό-φιν, *from the gods*; Ἰλιό-φιν, *from Ilios*.
3. Cons.-decl.: κοτυληδον-ό-φιν, *with the suckers* (on the feelers of the polypus); ἀπ' ὄχεσ-φι(ν), *from the carriage*; παρὰ ναῦ-φι(ν), *alongside the ships*; ἀπὸ κράτεσ-φιν, *from the head*. (§ 177, D. 22.)

D

These suffixes are joined to the Stem of the noun: Ἀθήνηθεν, *from Athens* (with Ion. η); κυκλόθεν, *from the circle* (κυκλό-ς). Sometimes ο comes in place of the A-sound: ῥιζόθεν (*radicitus*), from ῥίζα (*radix*); it also serves as a connecting vowel with consonant-stems: πάντ-ο-θεν, *from all sides*. The ο is sometimes accented, contrary to § 107, *a*: κυκλ-ό-θεν, Μαραθων-ό-θεν, *from Marathon*. The enclitic suffix δε (§ 92, 5) is often also combined with the Acc. form: Μέγαρά-δε, *to Megara;* Ἐλευσῖν-ά-δε, *to Eleusis*. οἴκ-α-δε, *home*, from Stem οἶκο, is irregular.

For δε we find σε, ζε, with the same meaning: ἄλλοσε, *elsewhither;* Ἀθήναζε, *to Athens;* Θήβαζε, *to Thebes;* θύραζε (*foras*).

§ 179. Moreover, a few words have an old *Locative* in ι for the Sing., and σι(ν) (without a preceding ι) for the Plur., answering the question *where:* οἴκοι, *at home;* Πυθοῖ, *at Pytho;* Ἰσθμοῖ, *on the Isthmus;* Ἀθήνησι(ν), *in Athens;* Πλαταιᾶσι(ν), *in Platœa;* θύρᾶσι(ν), *at the door* (*foris*); ὥρᾶσι(ν), *at the right time*.

Chap. VII.—Other Inflexions of the Adjective.

A. *Inflexion according to Genders*.

Adjectives of the Vowel Declension.

§ 180. The most numerous class of adjectives is that which in the Masc. and Neut. follows the O-Declension, and in the Fem. the A-Declension; which, consequently, has in the Nom. Sing. ος, η (or ᾱ), ον [Lat. *us, a, um*].

§ 180. **Dialects.**—The Ionians have frequently here also η for Att. ᾱ: αἰσχρή.

§ 182. INFLEXIONS OF ADJECTIVES. 75

Singular.	Masc.	Fem.	Neut.	Masc.	Fem.	Neut.
Nom.	ἀγαθός	ἀγαθή	ἀγαθόν	φίλιος	φιλία	φίλιον
Gen.	ἀγαθοῦ	ἀγαθῆς	ἀγαθοῦ	φιλίου	φιλίας	φιλίου
Dat.	ἀγαθῷ	ἀγαθῇ	ἀγαθῷ	φιλίῳ	φιλίᾳ	φιλίῳ
Acc.	ἀγαθόν	ἀγαθήν	ἀγαθόν	φίλιον	φιλίαν	φίλιον
Voc.	ἀγαθέ	ἀγαθή	ἀγαθόν	φίλιε	φιλία	φίλιον
Dual.						
N. A. V.	ἀγαθώ	ἀγαθά	ἀγαθώ	φιλίω	φιλία	φιλίω
G. D.	ἀγαθοῖν	ἀγαθαῖν	ἀγαθοῖν	φιλίοιν	φιλίαιν	φιλίοιν
Plural.						
Nom.	ἀγαθοί	ἀγαθαί	ἀγαθά	φίλιοι	φίλιαι	φίλια
Gen.	ἀγαθῶν	ἀγαθῶν	ἀγαθῶν	φιλίων	φιλίων	φιλίων
Dat.	ἀγαθοῖς	ἀγαθαῖς	ἀγαθοῖς	φιλίοις	φιλίαις	φιλίοις
Acc.	ἀγαθούς	ἀγαθάς	ἀγαθά	φιλίους	φιλίας	φίλια

In the Nom. Sing. Fem. α stands after a *vowel* or ρ, elsewhere η: δίκαιος, δικαία, δίκαιον, *just;* αἰσχρός, αἰσχρά, αἰσχρόν, *hateful;* σοφύς, σοφή, σοφόν, *wise.*

Exception:—η stands after ο, except when ρ precedes ο:
ἁπλόος, ἁπλόη, ἁπλόον, *simple.*
ἀθρόος, ἀθρόα, ἀθρόον, *assembled.*

§ 181. Though the declension of these adjectives conforms to §§ 114, 126, the following points must be observed:

1. α in the Nom. Sing. is always long.
2. In the accent of the Nom. and Gen. Plur. the Fem. follows the Masc.: βέβαιος, *firm,* Nom. Plur. Masc. βέβαιοι, Fem. βέβαιαι (§ 108 would require βεβαῖαι, from Nom. Sing. βεβαία); Gen. of all genders, βεβαίων (not even in the Fem. βεβαιῶν, as would be required by § 118).

§ 182. Many adjectives of this class have only *two* end-

---

§ 181. **Dialects.**—δῖα, Fem. of δῖος, *heavenly,* has in Hom. ἄ: δῖα θεάων, *the heavenly one among the goddesses.*

§ 182. **Dialects.**—The poets form a peculiar Fem. from many compound adjectives: ἀβρότη (Masc. ἄμβροτος, *immortal*), ἀντιθέη (Masc. ἀντίθεος, *godlike*).

ings, the Masc. being used for the Fem.: Masc. and Fem. ἥσυχος, Neut. ἥσυχον, *quiet. Compound adjectives especially are all of only two endings:* ἄτεκνος, *childless;* καρποφόρος, *fruitful.*

§ 183. Adjectives ending in ε ο ς and ο ο ς in the Nom. Masc. are generally contracted (§ 130): χρύσεος, *golden,* and ἁπλόος, *simple,* are thus contracted:

Singular.	Masc.	Fem.	Neut.	Masc.	Fem.	Neut.
Nom.	χρυσοῦς	χρυσῆ	χρυσοῦν	ἁπλοῦς	ἁπλῆ	ἁπλοῦν
Gen.	χρυσοῦ	χρυσῆς	χρυσοῦ	ἁπλοῦ	ἁπλῆς	ἁπλοῦ
Dat.	χρυσῷ	χρυσῇ	χρυσῷ	ἁπλῷ	ἁπλῇ	ἁπλῷ
Acc.	χρυσοῦν	χρυσῆν	χρυσοῦν	ἁπλοῦν	ἁπλῆν	ἁπλοῦν
Voc.	χρυσοῦς	χρυσῆ	χρυσοῦν	ἁπλοῦς	ἁπλῆ	ἁπλοῦν
Dual.						
N. A. V.	χρυσώ	χρυσᾶ	χρυσώ	ἁπλώ	ἁπλᾶ	ἁπλώ
G. D.	χρυσοῖν	χρυσαῖν	χρυσοῖν	ἁπλοῖν	ἁπλαῖν	ἁπλοῖν
Plural.						
Nom.	χρυσοῖ	χρυσαῖ	χρυσᾶ	ἁπλοῖ	ἁπλαῖ	ἁπλᾶ
Gen.	χρυσῶν	χρυσῶν	χρυσῶν	ἁπλῶν	ἁπλῶν	ἁπλῶν
Dat.	χρυσοῖς	χρυσαῖς	χρυσοῖς	ἁπλοῖς	ἁπλαῖς	ἁπλοῖς
Acc.	χρυσοῦς	χρυσᾶς	χρυσᾶ	ἁπλοῦς	ἁπλᾶς	ἁπλᾶ

The Fem. ε α is contracted to η, except when preceded by a *vowel* or ρ; it is then contracted to ᾱ: ἀργυρέα, ἀργυρᾶ (*argentea*). The Nom. Plur. ο α, ο α ι, produce ᾱ: αι : ἁπλᾶ, ἁπλαῖ.

The contracted final syllable also receives the circumflex, contrary to § 87: χρύσεος, χρυσοῦς. But compound adjectives retain the accent on the last syllable but one: εὔνους, *well-disposed,* Gen. εὔνου, Dat. εὔνῳ, Nom. Plur. εὔνοι.

§ 184. A few adjectives in ω ς in the Nom. follow the

---

§ 183. **Dialects.**—The adjectives in ε ο ς, ο ο ς, often remain uncontracted: Hom. χρυσέῳ (where ε disappears by synizesis), καλλίρροος, *beautifully-flowing.*

§ 184. **Dialects.**—Hom. ἰλᾱος, πλεῖος, πλείη, πλεῖον; New-Ion. ε ο ς = Att. ε ω ς; for Att. σῶς (*salvus*), Hom. σόος, η, ον, comparative σαώτερος.

§ 185. INFLEXIONS OF ADJECTIVES. 77

Attic O-Declension (§ 132): ἵλεως, Neut. ἵλεων, *gracious;* ἀξιόχρεως, Neut. *-ων, considerable;* πλέως, πλέα, πλέων, *full.* σῶς (from σάος, *salvus*) has in the Nom. Sing. Fem. and Neut. Plur. σᾶ; but also the forms σῶος, σώα, Plur. σῶοι, σῶαι.

ADJECTIVES OF THE CONSONANT DECLENSION.

§ 185. Other adjectives in the Masc. and Neut. follow the Consonant Declension, and form from the Stem a peculiar Fem. with the ending ια, which, however, undergoes various changes in combination with the Stem. Such adjective-stems of three denominations are:

1. *Stems in* υ (Masc. and Neut., § 154). The Fem. is formed from the Stem as it appears in the *Gen.* (ἡ δ ε); ε and ια are contracted, and the accent remains on the last syllable of the Stem: hence—

	Masc.	Fem.	Neut.
Nom.	ύ-ς	ειᾰ	ύ
Singular.			
Nom.	ἡδύ-ς, *sweet.*	ἡδεῖα	ἡδύ
Gen.	ἡδέος	ἡδείας	ἡδέος
Dat.	ἡδεῖ	ἡδείᾳ	ἡδεῖ
Acc.	ἡδύν	ἡδεῖαν	ἡδύ
Dual.			
Nom. Acc.	ἡδέε	ἡδείᾱ	ἡδέε
Gen. Dat.	ἡδέοιν	ἡδείαιν	ἡδέοιν
Plural.			
Nom.	ἡδεῖς	ἡδεῖαι	ἡδέα
Gen.	ἡδέων	ἡδειῶν	ἡδέων
Dat.	ἡδέσι(ν)	ἡδείαις	ἡδέσι(ν)
Acc.	ἡδεῖς	ἡδείας	ἡδέα

§ 185. Dialects.—Hom. sometimes has εη for Att. εια: βαθέη (βαθεῖα, *deep*); the Ion. εα for εια: Hom. ὠκέα Ἴρις, *swift Iris.* Besides θῆλυς, *feminine,* we find also ἡδύς, πουλύς (πολύς, *much*), as Fem. Sometimes εα is used for υν in the Acc. Sing. Masc.: εὐρέα πόντον, *the wide sea.*

Examples for Declension.

γλυκύς, *sweet*.   βραχύς, *short*.   εὐρύς, *broad*.
βραδύς, *slow*.   ταχύς, *swift*.

Obs.—θῆλυς, *female*, differing also in accent, occurs as a Feminine.

§ 186. 2. *Stems in* ν. The ι in ι α is transferred to the preceding syllable (§ 55): St. μ ε λ α ν, Nom. Masc. μέλᾱς, Fem. μέλαινα (from μελαν-ια), Neut. μέλᾰν, *black*.

	Masc.	Fem.	Neut.
Singular.			
Nom.	μέλᾱς	μέλαινα	μέλᾰν
Gen.	μέλᾰνος	μελαίνης	μέλᾰνος
Dat.	μέλανι	μελαίνῃ	μέλανι
Acc.	μέλανα	μέλαιναν	μέλαν
Voc.	μέλαν	μέλαινα	μέλαν
Dual.			
N. A. V.	μέλανε	μελαίνα	μέλανε
G. D.	μελάνοιν	μελαίναιν	μελάνοιν
Plural.			
Nom.	μέλανες	μέλαιναι	μέλανα
Gen.	μελάνων	μελαινῶν	μελάνων
Dat.	μέλασι	μελαίναις	μέλασι
Acc.	μέλανας	μελαίνας	μέλανα

Examples for Declension.

St. τ α λ α ν, τάλᾱς, τάλαινα, τάλᾰν, *unfortunate*.
St. τ ε ρ ε ν, τέρην, τέρεινα, τέρεν, *tender*.

§ 187. 3. *Stems in* ν τ. To these belong especially the numerous participial forms. In the Fem. the ν τ combines with the ending ι α to form σ α, the previous vowel being lengthened by compensation (§ 50): λεγοντ-ια becoming λέγουσα.

The *adjectives* in ε ν τ have ε σ σ α in the Fem.: χαρίεις, χαρίεσσα, χαρίεν, *pleasing*, St. χ α ρ ι ε ν τ. For the Dat. Plur., see § 149.

---

§ 187. **Dialects.**—Adjectives in ε ν τ (Nom. Masc. εις) are sometimes contracted: Hom. τιμῇς=τιμήεις, *honorable;* λωτεῦντα=λωτόεντα, *abounding in lotuses;* poet. πτεροῦσσα=πτερόεσσα, *winged*.

§ 187. INFLEXIONS OF ADJECTIVES. 79

	Masc.	Fem.	Neut.	Masc.	Fem.	Neut.
Sing.	*loosing.*			*loosing.*		
Nom.	λύσᾱς	λύσᾱσα	λῦσάν	λύων	λύουσα	λῦον
Gen.	λύσαντος	λυσάσης	λύσαντος	λύοντος	λυούσης	λύοντος
Dat.	λύσαντι	λυσάσῃ	λύσαντι	λύοντι	λυούσῃ	λύοντι
Acc.	λύσαντα	λύσασαν	λῦσαν	λύοντα	λύουσαν	λῦον
Voc.	λύσας	λύσασα	λῦσαν	λύων	λύουσα	λῦον
Dual.						
N. A. V.	λύσαντε	λυσάσα	λύσαντε	λύοντε	λυούσα	λύοντε
G. D.	λυσάντοιν	λυσάσαιν	λυσάντοιν	λυόντοιν	λυούσαιν	λυόντοιν
Plural.						
Nom.	λύσαντες	λύσασαι	λύσαντα	λύοντες	λύουσαι	λύοντα
Gen.	λυσάντων	λυσασῶν	λυσάντων	λυόντων	λυουσῶν	λυόντων
Dat.	λύσᾱσι	λυσάσαις	λύσᾱσι	λύουσι	λυούσαις	λύουσι
Acc.	λύσαντας	λυσάσας	λύσαντα	λύοντας	λυούσας	λύοντα
Sing.	*loosed.*			*giving.*		
Nom.	λυθείς	λυθεῖσα	λυθέν	διδούς	διδοῦσα	διδόν
Gen.	λυθέντος	λυθείσης	λυθέντος	διδόντος	διδούσης	διδόντος
Dat.	λυθέντι	λυθείσῃ	λυθέντι	διδόντι	διδούσῃ	διδόντι
Acc.	λυθέντα	λυθεῖσαν	λυθέν	διδόντα	διδοῦσαν	διδόν
Voc.	λυθείς	λυθεῖσα	λυθέν	διδούς	διδοῦσα	διδόν
Dual.						
N. A. V.	λυθέντε	λυθείσα	λυθέντε	διδόντε	διδούσα	διδόντε
G. D.	λυθέντοιν	λυθείσαιν	λυθέντοιν	διδόντοιν	διδούσαιν	διδόντοιν
Plural.						
Nom.	λυθέντες	λυθεῖσαι	λυθέντα	διδόντες	διδοῦσαι	διδόντα
Gen.	λυθέντων	λυθεισῶν	λυθέντων	διδόντων	διδουσῶν	διδόντων
Dat.	λυθεῖσι	λυθείσαις	λυθεῖσι	διδοῦσι	διδούσαις	διδοῦσι
Acc.	λυθέντας	λυθείσας	λυθέντα	διδόντας	διδούσας	διδόντα
Sing.	*pleasing.*			*showing.*		
Nom.	χαρίεις	χαρίεσσα	χαρίεν	δεικνύς	δεικνῦσα	δεικνύν
Gen.	χαρίεντος	χαριέσσης	χαρίεντος	δεικνύντος	δεικνύσης	δεικνύντος
Dat.	χαρίεντι	χαριέσσῃ	χαρίεντι	δεικνύντι	δεικνύσῃ	δεικνύντι
Acc.	χαρίεντα	χαρίεσσαν	χαρίεν	δεικνύντα	δεικνῦσαν	δεικνύν
Voc.	χαρίεν	χαρίεσσα	χαρίεν	δεικνύς	δεικνῦσα	δεικνύν
Dual.						
N. A. V.	χαρίεντε	χαριέσσα	χαρίεντε	δεικνύντε	δεικνύσα	δεικνύντε
G. D.	χαριέντοιν	χαριέσσαιν	χαριέντοιν	δεικνύντοιν	δεικνύσαιν	δεικνύντοιν
Plural.						
Nom.	χαρίεντες	χαρίεσσαι	χαρίεντα	δεικνύντες	δεικνῦσαι	δεικνύντα
Gen.	χαριέντων	χαριεσσῶν	χαριέντων	δεικνύντων	δεικνυσῶν	δεικνύντων
Dat.	χαρίεσι	χαριέσσαις	χαρίεσι	δεικνῦσι	δεικνύσαις	δεικνῦσι
Acc.	χαρίεντας	χαριέσσας	χαρίεντα	δεικνύντας	δεικνύσας	δεικνύντα

Obs.—The form of the Fem. is explained from τ before ι becoming σ, according to § 60, ι being dropped after σ, and ν before σ being thrown out and compensated for by a lengthening of the vowel: παντια, πανσια, πανσα, πᾶσα; λυοντια, λυονσια, λυοῦσα, λύουσα.

§ 188. 4. *Stems in* ο τ. The participles of the Perfect Active in ο τ (Nom. Sing. Masc. ω ς, Neut. ο ς) have υ ι α in the Fem.: λελυκώς, λελυκυῖα, λελυκός, *one who has freed.* See §§ 146, 147.

Singular.	Masc.	Fem.	Neut.
Nom.	λελυκώς	λελυκυῖα	λελυκός
Gen.	λελυκότος	λελυκυίας	λελυκότος
Dat.	λελυκότι	λελυκυίᾳ	λελυκότι
Acc.	λελυκότα	λελυκυῖαν	λελυκός
Voc.	λελυκώς	λελυκυῖα	λελυκός
Dual.			
N. A. V.	λελυκότε	λελυκυία	λελυκότε
G. D.	λελυκότοιν	λελυκυίαιν	λελυκότοιν
Plural.			
Nom.	λελυκότες	λελυκυῖαι	λελυκότα
Gen.	λελυκότων	λελυκυιῶν	λελυκότων
Dat.	λελυκόσι	λελυκυίαις	λελυκόσι
Acc.	λελυκότας	λελυκυίας	λελυκότα

Obs.—The strange difference of the Fem. from the Stem of the Masc. and Neut. is explained by the ϝ which was originally before the ο. From ϝοτ-ια came first ϝοσ-ια (§ 60), then by a peculiar contraction (ϝο becoming υ) υσ-ια, finally (σ being dropped, § 61, *b*) υ-ῖα and υ ι α.

§ 189. The most important adjectives of *two endings* with Stems according to the Second Principal Declension are:

1. *Stems in* ς (Inflexion given under §§ 164, 165), as:

    σαφής   σαφές, *clear.*   Gen. σαφοῦς.
    ἀληθής   ἀληθές, *true.*   " ἀληθοῦς.

Other Examples for Declension.

πλήρης, *full.*   ψευδής, *false.*   ἀσφαλής, *safe.*   δυσμενής, *hostile.*

2. *Stems in* ν (Inflexion given under §§ 146, 147), as:

    πέπων   πέπον, *ripe.*   Gen. πέπον-ος.
    εὐδαίμων   εὔδαιμον, *happy.*   " εὐδαίμον-ος.
    σώφρων   σῶφρον, *reasonable.*   " σώφρον-ος.

§ 189. **Dialects.**—Herod. ἔρσην for ἄρσην.

§ 191. INFLEXIONS OF ADJECTIVES. 81

Other Examples for Declension.

μνήμων, *mindful of.* ἐπιλήσμων, *forgetful of.*
πολυπράγμων, *much occupied.*

3. Isolated forms, as:
ἴδρις   ἴδρι, *acquainted with.*   Gen. ἴδρι-ος.
(Inflexion according to § 157, D.)
ἄῤῥην (ἄρσην), ἄῤῥεν, *male.*   Gen. ἄῤῥεν-ος.
Compounds of substantives, such as ἀπάτωρ, Neut. ἄπατορ, St. π α τ ε ρ
(Nom. πατήρ), *fatherless;* δυσμήτωρ, μήτηρ, *unmotherly;* φιλόπολις, -ι,
Gen. -ιδ-ος, *loving the city;* εὔελπις (Gen. εὐέλπιδ-ος), *hopeful.*

§ 190. 4. Besides these, there is a large number of adjectives which have only *one* ending, because either their meaning or form excludes a Neuter: ἅρπαξ, *rapacious,* St. ἁ ρ π α γ ; φυγάς, *fugitive,* St. φ υ γ α δ ; ἀγνώς, *unacquainted,* St. ἀ γ ν ω τ ; ἄπαις, *childless,* St. ἀ π α ι δ ; μακρόχειρ, *long-handed ;* πένης, *poor,* St. π ε ν η τ ; γυμνής, *light-armed,* St. γ υ μ ν η τ. Some adjectives of one ending follow the A-Declension, and are almost substantives, as: ἐθελοντής, Gen. ἐθελοντοῦ, *voluntary;* they occur only in the Masc.

§ 191. The following adjectives are irregular: μέγας, *great ;* πολύς, *much ;* and πρᾷος, *gentle,* the forms of each being derived from different Stems, viz., in μέγας, from

§ 190. Dialects.—Hom. has also many adjectives in the Fem. only: καλλιγύναικα, Acc. Sing. *e. g.,* Σπάρτην, *abounding in beautiful women ;* βωτιάνειρα, *e. g.* Φθίη, *men nourishing.*

§ 191. Dialects.—In Hom. both Stems, π ο λ υ and π ο λ λ ο, in Masc. and Neut., are almost completely declined; the Fem. is regularly πολλή.

Sing. *N.* πολύς   πουλύς or πολλός   *N.* πολύ   πουλύ   πολλόν
  G. πολλοῦ or πολέος
  D.   πολλῷ
  A. πολύν   πουλύν   πολλόν   *N.* πολύ   πουλύ   πολλόν
Plur. *N.* πολέες   (πολεῖς)   πολλοί   πολλά
  G. πολλῶν or πολέων
  D. πολέεσσι(ν) πολέσσι(ν)   πολέσι(ν) or πολλοῖς
  A. πολέας   πολλούς   *N.* πολλά

Herod. has scarcely any forms except from the Stem π ο λ λ ο : πολ-λόν, πολλοί.

D 2

the Stems μ ε γ a and μ ε γ α λ ο; in πολύς, from π ο λ υ and π ο λ λ ο; in πρᾷος, from π ρ ᾳ ο and πραΰ.

Sing.	Masc.	Fem.	Neut.	Masc.	Fem.	Neut.
Nom.	μέγας	μεγάλη	μέγα	πολύς	πολλή	πολύ
Gen.	μεγάλου	μεγάλης	μεγάλου	πολλοῦ	πολλῆς	πολλοῦ
Dat.	μεγάλῳ	μεγάλῃ	μεγάλῳ	πολλῷ	πολλῇ	πολλῷ
Acc.	μέγαν	μεγάλην	μέγα	πολύν	πολλήν	πολύ
Voc.	μέγα	μεγάλη	μέγα	πολύ	πολλή	πολύ
Dual.						
N. A. V.	μεγάλω	μεγάλα	μεγάλω			
G. D.	μεγάλοιν	μεγάλαιν	μεγάλοιν			
Plural.						
Nom.	μεγάλοι	μεγάλαι	μεγάλα	πολλοί	πολλαί	πολλά
Gen.	μεγάλων	μεγάλων	μεγάλων	πολλῶν	πολλῶν	πολλῶν
Dat.	μεγάλοις	μεγάλαις	μεγάλοις	πολλοῖς	πολλαῖς	πολλοῖς
Acc.	μεγάλους	μεγάλας	μεγάλα	πολλούς	πολλάς	πολλά
Sing.				Plural.		
Nom.	πρᾷος	πραεῖα	πραΰ	πρᾷοι, or πραεῖς	πραεῖαι	πραέα
Gen.	πρᾴου	πραείας	πρᾴου	πραέων	πραειῶν	πραέων
Dat.	πρᾴῳ	πραείᾳ	πρᾴῳ	πρᾴοις, or πραέσι(ν)	πραείαις	πρᾴοις, or πραέσι(ν)
Acc.	πρᾷον	πραεῖαν	πρᾷον	πρᾴους	πραείας	πραέα

B. *Comparison.*

§ 192. *The first and most frequent* ending of the Comparative is τ ε ρ ο (Nom. τερος, τερα, τερον); of the Superlative τ α τ ο (Nom. τατος, τατη, τατον), with the usual inflexion of adjectives (§ 180). These endings are affixed to the pure Stem of the Masc., as:

Positive.	Stem.	Comparative.	Superlative.
κοῦφος, *light*.	κ ο υ φ ο	κουφότερος, α, ον	κουφότατος, η ον
γλυκύς, *sweet*.	γ λ υ κ υ	γλυκύτερος	γλυκύτατος
μέλας, *black*.	μ ε λ α ν	μελάντερος	μελάντατος
χαρίεις, *graceful*.	χ α ρ ι ε ν τ	χαριέστερος	χαριέστατος

(from χαριεντ-τερος, according to §§ 46 and 49).

σαφής, *clear*.	σ α φ ε ς	σαφέστερος	σαφέστατος
μάκαρ, *happy*.	μ α κ α ρ	μακάρτερος	μακάρτατος
πένης, *poor*.	π ε ν η τ	πενέστερος	πενέστατος

(for πενητ-τερος, τατος, according to § 46, η being shortened).

§ 197. COMPARISON OF ADJECTIVES. 83

§ 193. The following points are to be observed:

1 The Stems in ο leave ο unchanged only when the preceding syllable is long (§ 74, etc.), but lengthen it to ω when that is short: πονηρό-τερος, *worse;* πικρό-τατον, *most bitter;* σοφώ-τερος, *wiser;* ἀξιω-τάτη, *most worthy.* Every syllable with a vowel followed by two consonants or a double consonant is here considered long (§§ 76, 77).

§ 194. 2. The ο is always rejected after α ι in the adjective γεραιός, *senex,* sometimes in παλαιός, *antiquus,* and σχολαῖος, *at leisure:* γεραίτερος, παλαίτατος.

§ 195. 3. The ο or ω is changed to α ι in μέσος, *medius;* ἴσος, *like;* εὔδιος, *clear;* πρώϊος, *early;* ὕψιος, *late:* μεσαίτατος, πρωϊαίτερον. ἥσυχος, *peaceful,* has ἡσυχαίτερος, and ἡσυχώτερος; φίλος, *dear,* besides φιλώτερος, -τατος, also φίλτερος, -τατος, and φιλαίτερος, -τατος; πλησιαίτερος, πλησιαίτατος, belong to πλησίον, *near,* and παραπλησιαίτερος, *more like,* to the same; προὐργιαίτερος to προὔργου, from πρὸ ἔργου, *advantageously.*

§ 196. 4. The endings ε σ τ ε ρ ο -ς, ε σ τ α τ ο -ς, are inorganically applied:

a) to Stems in ον: σωφρονέστερος (St. σ ω φ ρ ο ν, Nom. σώφρων, *reasonable*), εὐδαιμονέστερος (St. ε ὐ δ α ι μ ο ν, Nom. εὐδαίμων, *fortunate*). πιότερος, -τατος, from πίων, *fat,* and πεπαίτερος, -τατος, from πέπων, *ripe,* are exceptional.

b) to the Stems of ἄκρᾱτος, *unmixed;* ἐῤῥωμένος, *strong;* ἄσμενος, *willing:* ἀκρατέστερος, ἐῤῥωμενέστερος. More seldom to others.

c) to some Stems in ο ο contracted: εὐνούστερος for εὐνοέστερος, from εὔνους, *well-disposed.*

§ 197. 5. ι σ τ ε ρ ο ς, ι σ τ α τ ο ς, occur with λάλος, *talkative;* πτωχός, *beggarly;* ὀψοφάγος, *epicure;* μονοφάγος, *eating alone;* and some adjectives of one ending, as κλέπτη-ς, *thievish:* λαλίστερος, πτωχίστατος, κλεπτίστερος.

Others of one gender in η-ς follow the rule of those in ο: ὑβριστότερος, from ὑβριστής, *haughty.*

§ 193. Dialects.—The quantity of the O-sound in poets is rather doubtful: Hom. ὀϊζυρώτατος, *the most wretched.*

Hom. has ἰθύντατα, from ἰθύς, *straight;* φαάντατος, from φαεινός, *glittering;* ἀχαρίστερος (for ἀχαριτ-τερος, according to § 46), from ἄχαρις, *graceless.*

The compounds of χάρις, *grace, favor*, form their Comparative and Superlative as if they ended in χαριτο-ς: ἐπιχαριτώτερος, *more obliging*.

§ 198. The *second and rarer* termination of the Comparative is ι ο ν (Nom., Masc., and Fem. ι ω ν, Neut. ι ο ν); of the Superlative, ι σ τ ο (Nom. ιστος, ιστη, ιστον). The Stem-vowel is rejected before ι. The accent is placed as far as possible from the end in the Comp. and Superl. Inflexion of the Comp., § 170. So is formed from:

Positive.	Stem.	Comparative.	Superlative.
ἡδύς, *agreeable*.	ἡ δ υ	ἡδίων, -ον	ἥδιστος, -η, -ον
ταχύς, *swift*.	τ α χ υ	θάσσων, -ον	τάχιστος, -η, -ον
		(from ταχιων, according to §§ 54, 57).	
μέγας, *large*.	μ ε γ α	μείζων, -ον	μέγιστος.
		(from μεγιων, according to § 58).	

Obs.—The length of α in θᾶσσον (compare μᾶλλον, § 202), and the diphthong of μείζων, is explained from the ι passing into the preceding syllable, as in ἀμείνων (compare § 55).

Farther with suppression of ρ:

ἐχθρό, -ς, *hostile*. ἐχθίων, -ον Superl. ἔχθιστος.
αἰσχρό, -ς, *shameful*. αἰσχίων, -ον " αἴσχιστος.
οἰκτρό, -ς, *pitiable*. " οἴκτιστος.

ἐχθρ-ός and οἰκτρ-ός also have the forms in τερο-ς and τατο-ς.

§ 199. This comparison occurs also in connection with

---

§ 198. **Dialects.**—The endings ι ω ν, ι σ τ ο ς, are more frequent in the poets: Hom. φιλίων (φίλος, *dear*); γλυκίων (γλυκύς, *sweet*); ὤκιστος (ὠκύς, *swift*); βάθιστος (βαθύς, *deep*); βράσσων = βραχίων (βραχύς, *short*), Sup. poet. βράχιστος, Hom. Superl. βάρδιστος (βραδύς, *slow*, § 59, D.); πάσσων = παχίων (παχύς, *thick*); μάσσων = μᾱκίων (μᾱκρός, *long*), Sup. μήκιστος (Dor. μᾱκιστος); κυδίων (κυδρός, *famous*); μέζων, New-Ion. for μείζων.

§ 199. **Dialects.**—1. Hom. Comp. ἀρείων, Positive κρατύ-ς, Superl. κάρτιστος; Comp. λωΐτερος; New-Ion. κρέσσων = κρείσσων; poet. βέλτερος, βέλτατος, φέρτερος, φέρτατος, or φέριστος, *more excellent, most excellent*.

2. Hom. κακώτερος; χέρης, χερείων, χερειότερος, χειρότερος; New.-Ion. ἕσσων = ἥσσων. (Compare κρέσσων, μέζων, § 198, *Obs.*)

4. Hom. ὑπ-ολίζων.

§ 199. COMPARISON OF ADJECTIVES. 85

other peculiarities in the following adjectives, where the changes of sound of §§ 55-58 are often applied:

1. For the idea of *good:*

Positive	Comparative.	Superlative.
ἀγαθός		
[St. ἀ μ ε ν]	ἀμείνων, ἄμεινον	
[St. ἀ ρ ε ς]	[ἀρείων, Hom.]	ἄριστος, η, ον
[St. β ε λ τ ο]	βελτίων, βέλτιον	βέλτιστος, η, ον
[St. κ ρ α τ υ]	κρείσσων (κρείττων)	κράτιστος, η, ον
	N. κρεῖσσον (κρεῖττον)	
[St. λ ω υ]	λωίων or λώων	λῷστος, η, ον
	N. λώϊον or λῷον	

Obs.—ἀμείνων and ἄριστος rather express *excellence, capacity;* κρείσσων, κράτιστος, *strength, preponderance* (Lat. *superior*); ἥσσων is opposed to κρείσσων.

2. For the idea of *bad:*

Positive.	Comparative.		Superlative.
κακός	κακίων	*N.* κάκιον	κάκιστος
[St. χ ε ρ]	χείρων (*deterior*),	*N.* χεῖρον	χείριστος
[St. ἥ κ υ]	ἥσσων (*inferior*),	*N.* ἧσσον *N. Pl.* ἥκιστα, *least of all.*

3. μικρὸς, *small*, besides μικρότερος μικρότατος
   μείων, *smaller*, *N.* μεῖον

4. ὀλίγος, *little*, ὀλίγιστος
   [St. ἐ λ α χ υ], ἐλάσσων *N.* ἔλασσον ἐλάχιστος

5. πολύς, *much*, πλείων (πλέων) πλεῖστος
   N. πλέον (also πλεῖν)

6. κᾰλός, *beautiful*, as if from
   κάλλος, *beauty* καλλίων *N.* κάλλιον κάλλιστος

7. ῥᾴδιος, *easy*,
   [St. ῥ α], ῥᾴων *N.* ῥᾷον ῥᾷστος

8. ἀλγεινός, *painful*, as if from
   ἄλγος, *pain*, ἀλγίων *N.* ἄλγιον ἄλγιστος

Dialects.—5. Homer contracts πλέον to πλεῦν, πλέονες to πλεῦνες; Plur. also πλέες, πλέας, πλέα.
7. Ion. ῥηΐδιος; Hom. ῥηίτερος, ῥήϊστος, ῥήϊτατος. Hom. forms single degrees from substantives: κύντερος, *more doggish* (κύων, *dog*); ῥίγιον, *worse;* ῥῖγος, *cold, shudder.*

Defectives: ἔνερτεροι, also tragic νέρτεροι (*inferi*, for which Positive ἔνεροι); Hom. πύματος and λοῖσθος, λοίσθιος, *last;* ὑστάτιος = ὕστατος, δεύτατος, in a like sense, πρώτιστος = πρῶτος, *the first.*

§ 200. Finally observe farther the Defectives:

ὕστερος, later, ὕστατος, ultimus.
ἔσχατος, extremus.
(νέος, new), νέατος, novissimus.
(ὑπέρ, over), ὕπατος, summus.
(πρό, before), πρότερος, prior, πρῶτος, primus.
(πέραν, on the other side), περαίτερος.

C. Adverbs of Adjectives.

§ 201. Adverbs are derived from the Adjective Stem by affixing to it the syllable ω ς. The o of the Stem is entirely dropped: φίλος, adv. φίλως. The Stems of the Second Principal Declension have the same form as in the Genitive: ταχύς, *swift*, ταχέως; σαφής, *clear*, σαφέως, contr. σαφῶς; σώφρων, *reasonable*, σωφρόνως. Contraction occurs only where the Genitive also has it. The accent of the adverb is always the same as that of the Genitive Plural of the corresponding adjective: ψυχρός, *cold*, ψυχρῶς; δίκαιος, *just*, δικαίως; πᾶς (St. π α ν τ), πάντως, *every way*.

The Neuter Accusative, both of the Singular and the Plural, is moreover very often used as an adverb.

§ 202. An older adverbial form is that in ἄ, as: τάχἄ, from ταχύς, *quick* (meaning, in Att. prose, *perhaps*); ἅμα, *at the same time;* μάλα, *very.* The Comp. of μάλα is μᾶλλον (*potius*)=μάλιον (§ 56); Superl. μάλιστα (*potissimum*). εὖ, *well*, as an adverb to ἀγαθός, *good*, stands alone.

§ 203. Adverbs in ω ς are also formed from Comparatives and Superlatives: βεβαιοτέρως, *more firmly;* καλλιόνως, *more beautifully.* But, as a rule, the *comparative* has the

§ 202. **Dialects.**—The adverbs in α are more numerous in Homer: ὦκα (*quickly*, ὠκύς); λίγα, *aloud*, λιγύς; κάρτα, *strongly, very*, to κρατύς, compare § 59, D.; σάφα (*clearly*, σαφής).
Homer has for εὖ or ἰύ the adjective ἰύς or ἠύς, *good*.

§§ 203, 204. **Dialects.**—Homeric ἑκαστέρω, ἑκαστάτω (from ἑκάς, *far*); ἆσσον (=ἄγχιον), ἀσσοτέρω (ἄγχι, *near*), ἄγχιστα; New-Ion. ἀγχοτάτω, ἀγχότατα. In addition to this, there is the Hom. ἐπασσύτεροι, *crowded*, with υ instead of ο.

§ 205. PERSONAL PRONOUNS. 87

Neut. Acc. Sing., the superlative the *Neut. Acc. Plur.*, as an adverb: βεβαιότερον, κάλλιον; βεβαιότατα, κάλλιστα.

§ 204. Adverbs in ω, like ἄνω, *above;* κάτω, *below;* ἔσω, *inside;* ἔξω, *outside*, have no ς in Compar. and Superl.: ἀνωτέρω, κατωτέρω, likewise ἀπωτέρω, *farther* (from ἀπό); ἐγγυτέρω (or ἐγγύτερον), ἐγγυτάτω (or ἐγγύτατα), from ἐγγύς, *near*, and some others.

Chap. VIII.—Inflexion of Pronouns.

§ 205. The *Personal Pronouns* are:

Singular.			
Nom.	ἐγώ, *I* [ego]	σύ, *thou* [tu]	
Gen.	ἐμοῦ, μοῦ	σοῦ	οὗ, *of him.*
Dat.	ἐμοί, μοί	σοί	οἱ
Acc.	ἐμέ, μέ [me]	σέ [te]	ἕ [se]
Dual.			
N. A.	(νῶι) νώ, *we.*	(σφῶι) σφώ, *ye.*	(σφωέ), *they.*
G. D.	(νῶιν) νῷν	(σφῶιν) σφῷν	(σφωίν)
Plural.			
Nom.	ἡμεῖς, *we.*	ὑμεῖς, *you.*	σφεῖς, *they.* *N.* σφέα
Gen.	ἡμῶν	ὑμῶν	σφῶν
Dat.	ἡμῖν	ὑμῖν	σφί-σι(ν)
Acc.	ἡμᾶς	ὑμᾶς	σφᾶς *N.* σφέα

§ 205. **Dialects.**—The following are special additional forms of the Ion. Dialect. (Those in brackets are merely New-Ion.)

Sing. *Nom.* ἐγών   τύνη [tu]
Gen. {ἐμέο, ἐμεῦ, μεῦ   {σέο, σεῦ {ἕο, εὖ
       {ἐμεῖο, ἐμέ-θεν (§ 178, D.) {σεῖο, σέ-θεν {εἷο, ἕ-θεν
Dat.   τοί, τείν   ἐοί} compare § 34,
Acc.   ἑέ }   D. 4.
Plur. *Nom.* (ἡμέες) ἄμμες   (ὑμέες) ὕμμες
Gen. ἡμέων, ἡμείων   ὑμέων, ὑμείων   σφέων, σφείων
Dat.   ἄμμι(ν)   ὕμμι(ν)   σφί(ν)
Acc. ἡμέας, ἄμμε   ὑμέας, ὕμμε   σφάς,   σφέας,
                                                     σφεῖας, σφέ

An isolated Ionic form for the Accusative Sing. of the third person is μίν, trag. νίν, both enclitic; in a like sense σφέ occurs in the poets. νίν seldom stands for the Plural.

§ 206. The Stems of the Sing. are: ἐ μ ε, for the first person; σ ε, for the second; ἑ, for the third. The Nominative, however, is formed differently from them: ἐγώ, σύ, and that of the third person is entirely wanting.

Obs.—The σ of the Stem σε has arisen from τ (§ 60, *a*) [*te*], which remains in many dialect-forms. The Stem ἑ goes back to Ϝε, and this to a still older form, σϜε [Lat. *se* for *sve*]. (§ 60, *b*.) In the form σφε, the Ϝ is hardened into φ.

The Stems of the Dual are: ν ω [*no-s*], σφω, σφω. The Dual of the third person does not occur in prose.

The Stems of the Plural are: ἡ μ ε, ὑ μ ε, σ φ ε (ε is generally contracted with the ending, hence the circumflex: see Dialects).

§ 207. When there is no emphasis on the Personal Pronouns, it becomes enclitic in the forms mentioned in § 92, 2; in that case the first person has the forms beginning with μ. But when emphatic, as well as generally after prepositions, it retains its accent, and the first person has the fuller forms: δοκεῖ μοι, *it seems to me;* ἐμοὶ οὐ σοὶ τοῦτο ἀρέσκει, *this pleases me, not you.*

The Gen., Dat., and Acc. Plur. of the first and second persons, when not emphatic, sometimes have the accent on the first syllable : ἥμων, ὕμιν, and in this case the final syllable of the Dat. and Acc. is usually shortened : ἥμιν, ἥμας (Hom.). When emphatic, with the final syllable shortened, they are written ἡμίν, ὑμίν.

§ 208. The *Possessive Pronouns* are formed from the Stems of the Personal Pronouns :

St. ἐ μ ε, ἐμός, *my*.
" σ ε, σός, *thy*.
" ἑ, ὅς, *his, her*.

St. ἡ μ ε, ἡμέτερος, *our*.
" ὑ μ ε, ὑμέτερος, *your*.
" σ φ ε, σφέτερος, *their*.

Obs.—The ending τ ε ρ ο ς is that of the comparative (§ 192).

§ 208. **Dialects.**—Hom. additional forms of the Possessives: τεός [*tuus*], ἑός [*suus*], ἀμός (properly Dor.), ὑμός, σφός. From the Dual Stems νω, σφω: νωΐτερος, *nos-ter;* σφωΐτερος, *belonging to you two;* ἁμός (also ἀμός) often means *my*, ὅς sometimes means *own*, without any reference to a particular person.

§ 211. REFLEXIVE AND OTHER PRONOUNS. 89

§ 209. αὐτό-ς, αὐτή, αὐτό, *self*, is declined like a common adjective, except that the Neuter in the Nom. Acc. Voc. Sing. has no ν (compare the article τό).
ὁ αὐτός (αὑτός), ἡ αὐτή (αὑτή), τὸ αὐτό (ταὐτό or ταὐτόν), *the same*, Lat. *idem*.

§ 210. The Stems of the Personal Pronouns, combined with αὐτός, produce the *Reflexive Pronouns*.

Singular.	Gen. M. N. F.	Dat. M. N. F.	Acc. M. F. N.	
1st person,	ἐμαυτοῦ -ῆς	ἐμαυτῷ -ῇ	ἐμαυτόν -ήν,	*myself*.
2d person,	σεαυτοῦ -ῆς	σεαυτῷ -ῇ	σεαυτόν -ήν,	*thyself*.
or	σαυτοῦ -ῆς	σαυτῷ -ῇ	σαυτόν -ήν	
3d person,	ἑαυτοῦ -ῆς	ἑαυτῷ -ῇ	ἑαυτόν -ήν -ό,	*himself, her-*
or	αὑτοῦ -ῆς	αὑτῷ -ῇ	αὑτόν -ήν -ό,	*self, itself*.

In the plural, both Stems are declined together:

Plural.	Gen. M. F. N.	Dat. M. N. F.	Acc. M. F.	
1st person,	ἡμῶν αὐτῶν	ἡμῖν αὐτοῖς -αῖς	ἡμᾶς αὐτούς -άς,	*ourselves*.
2d person,	ὑμῶν αὐτῶν	ὑμῖν αὐτοῖς -αῖς	ὑμᾶς αὐτούς -άς,	*yourselves*.
3d person,	σφῶν αὐτῶν	σφίσιν αὐτοῖς -αῖς	σφᾶς αὐτούς -άς,	*themselves*.

Neut. σφέα αὐτά

Yet the 3d person plural has also the compound form:

ἑαυτῶν	ἑαυτοῖς -αῖς	ἑαυτούς -άς -ά
or αὑτῶν	αὑτοῖς -αῖς	αὑτούς -άς -ά

§ 211. ἄλλο-ς, ἄλλη, ἄλλο, *another* (*alius*), is declined like αὐτός.

The Stem ἄλλο combined with itself produces the *Reciprocal Pronoun* ἀλλ-ηλο (for ἀλλ-αλλο), occurring only in the Dual and Plural.

---

§ 209. **Dialects.**—New-Ionic ωὑτός, ωὑτή, τωὑτό; Homeric ωὑτός = ὁ αὐτός.

§ 210. **Dialects.**—The Epic dialect declines both Stems together even in the sing.: ἐμὲ αὐτόν = ἐμαυτόν, οἷ αὐτῷ = ἑαυτῷ, etc.
New-Ionic ἐμεωυτοῦ, σεωυτοῦ, ἑωυτοῦ, stand for the forms with αυ.

90   DEMONSTRATIVE PRONOUNS.   § 212.

	Masc.	Fem.	Neut.
Dual. G. D.	ἀλλήλοιν	ἀλλήλαιν	ἀλλήλοιν
Acc.	ἀλλήλω	ἀλλήλα	ἀλλήλω
Plural. Gen.	ἀλλήλων	ἀλλήλων	ἀλλήλων
Dat.	ἀλλήλοις	ἀλλήλαις	ἀλλήλοις
Acc.	ἀλλήλους	ἀλλήλας	ἄλληλα

§ 212. The two most important *Demonstrative Pronouns* are:

ὅδε, ἥδε, τόδε, *that*.   οὗτος, αὕτη, τοῦτο, *this*.

ὅδε consists of the article ὁ and the demonstrative enclitic δέ, and is therefore declined entirely like the article with δε affixed. οὗτος corresponds to the article with regard to the rough breathing and the τ at the beginning; it also has the diphthong αυ in the last syllable but one where the article has α or η (A-sound), and ου where the article has ο, ω, or ου (O-sound).

	Singular.			Plural.	
Nom.	ὁ ἡ τό		οἱ	αἱ	τά
	ὅδε ἥδε τόδε		οἵδε	αἵδε	τάδε
	οὗτος αὕτη τοῦτο		οὗτοι	αὗται	ταῦτα
Gen.	τοῦ τῆς τοῦ		τῶν		
	τοῦδε τῆςδε τοῦδε		τῶνδε		
	τούτου ταύτης τούτου		τούτων		
Dat.	τῷ τῇ τῷ		τοῖς	ταῖς	τοῖς
	τῷδε τῇδε τῷδε		τοῖςδε	ταῖςδε	τοῖςδε
	τούτῳ ταύτῃ τούτῳ		τούτοις	ταύταις	τούτοις
Acc.	τόν τήν τό		τούς	τάς	τά
	τόνδε τήνδε τόδε		τούςδε	τάςδε	τάδε
	τοῦτον ταύτην τοῦτο		τούτους	ταύτας	ταῦτα

§ 212. **Dialects.**—In Homer, the article itself is a demonstrative pronoun, with these special forms: Nom. ὅ; Gen. τοῖο; Gen. Dat. Dual τοῖιν; Nom. Plur. τοί, ταί; Gen. Plur. Fem. τάων; Dat. Plur. τοῖσι(ν), τῇσι(ν), or τῇς.

From ὅδε we have Dat. Plur. τοῖσδεσι or τοῖσδεσσι(ν), and κεῖνος, poet. for ἐκεῖνος.

§ 214. RELATIVE AND INTERROG. PRONOUNS. 91

Dual.

N. A. V. { τώ   τά   τώ   *G. D.* { τοῖν   ταῖν   τοῖν
         { τώδε   τάδε   τώδε   { τοῖνδε   ταῖνδε   τοῖνδε
         { τούτω ταύτā τούτω   { τούτοιν ταύταιν τούτοιν

The adverb of ὅδε is ὧδε; that of οὗτος, οὕτως or οὕτω, *in this way.*

Like οὗτος are declined:

τοσοῦτος   τοσαύτη   τοσοῦτο   or τοσοῦτον, *so great (tantus)*;
τοιοῦτος   τοιαύτη   τοιοῦτο   or τοιοῦτον, *such (talis)*;
τηλικοῦτος   τηλικαύτη   τηλικοῦτο or τηλικοῦτον, *so old;*

in which, however, the τ of the forms beginning with τ is dropped; ταῦτα, but τοσ-αῦτα; by affixing the enclitic δέ, we have the forms τοσόςδε, *so large;* τοιόςδε, *of such quality;* τηλικός-δε, *of such an age,* with a regular adjective declension before the syllable δε.

ἐκεῖνο-ς, ἐκείνη, ἐκεῖνο, *that,* is declined like αὐτός.

A long accented ι is often affixed to the Demonstrative Pronouns to strengthen the meaning without affecting the declension, but the ε of δε is lost: οὑτοςί, ὁδί, ἐκεινωνί, αὑτηί, τοιςδί. Compare the Lat. *ce* in *his-ce, has-ce.*

§ 213. The *Relative Pronoun* has the rough breathing in all cases, as:

	Singular.			Plural.			Dual.		
	Masc.	Fem.	Neut.	Masc.	Fem.	Neut.	Masc.	Fem.	Neut.
Nom.	ὅς, *who.*	ἥ	ὅ	οἵ	αἵ	ἅ	*N. A.* ὥ	ἅ	ὥ
Gen.	οὗ	ἧς	οὗ		ὧν		*G. D.* οἷν	αἷν	οἷν
Dat.	ᾧ	ᾗ	ᾧ	οἷς	αἷς	οἷς			
Acc.	ὅν	ἥν	ὅ	οὕς	ἅς	ἅ			

Obs.—In the phrases καὶ ὃς ἔφη, *and he said,* and ἣ δ' ὅς, *but he said,* ὅς is used as a Demonstrative (compare the Dialects).

§ 214. The *Interrogative Pronoun* has the same Stem as the *Indefinite Pronoun,* from which it is distinguished

§ 213. **Dialects.**—Hom. ὅ = ὅς, ὅου = οὗ, ἕης = ἧς, and signifies *he.* Ion. οἷο = οὗ, and the forms of the *Article* which begin with τ, are used instead of those of the *Relative:* τοῦ = οὗ, *cujus;* τῷ = ᾧ, *cui;* τοῖς = οἷς, *quibus.*

§ 214. **Dialects.**—Hom., partly also New-Ion. forms are: Gen. τέο, τεῦ; Dat. τέῳ, τῷ; Gen. Plur. τέων; Dat. Plur. τέοισι(ν); Neut. Plur. ἅσσα. The

only by the accent. The Interrogative Pronoun has the accent always on the Stem syllable; the Indefinite is enclitic: hence τίς, *who* ? τὶς, enclitic, *some one*.

	Interrogative.		Indefinite.	
	Singular.		Singular.	
Nom.	τίς	τί	τὶς	τὶ
Gen.	τίνος		τινός	
Dat.	τίνι		τινί	
Acc.	τίνα	τί	τινά	τὶ
	Dual.		Dual.	
Nom. Acc.	τίνε		τινέ	
Gen. Dat.	τίνοιν		τινοῖν	
	Plural.		Plural.	
Nom.	τίνες	τίνα	τινές	τινά (ἄττα)
Gen.	τίνων		τινῶν	
Dat.	τίσι(ν)		τισί(ν)	
Acc.	τίνας	τίνα	τινάς	τινά (ἄττα)

Obs.—1. τοῦ, τῷ, which as indefinites are enclitic, are often used for τίνος, τίνι, and for τινός, τινί.

Obs.—2. The Relative and Indefinite combine to form ὅστις, ἥτις, ὅ τι, *who*. Both Stems are declined together: οὗτινος, ἧςτινος, ᾧτινι, οἵντινοιν (§ 93, *b*). A space is left between *o* and *τι* in ὅ τι, *which*, to distinguish it from the conjunction ὅτι, *that*.

The shorter forms of τὶς are also used with ὅς; but the Stem ὁ is not declined: Gen. ὅτου; Dat. ὅτῳ; more rarely Gen. Plur. ὅτων, Dat. ὅτοισι(ν). ἄττα is an additional form for ἅτινα, not to be confounded with ἄττα for τινά.

§ 215. Another Indefinite Pronoun is δεῖνα, of three genders, *quidam*, sometimes undeclined, sometimes declined as follows:

Sing. ὁ, ἡ, τὸ δεῖνα,   δεῖνος, δεῖνι, δεῖνα.
Plur. οἱ, αἱ,   δεῖνες,   δείνων,   δεῖνας.

The following are special forms of the compound Relative in Hom. and also in New-Ion.:

Sing. ὅτις, N. ὅττι;   ὅτευ, ὅττεο, ὅττευ; ὅτεῳ;   ὅτινα, N. ὅττι
Plur.   N. ἅσσα; ὅτεων   ὁτέοισι; ὅτινας, N. ἅσσα
(for ἅτια, according to § 57).

The Stem of the Relative thus often remains unchanged.

§ 216. The following are called *Correlative Pronouns:*

Interrogative.	Indefinite.	Demonstrative.	Relative.
τίς, *who?*	τὶς, *some one.*	ὅδε, οὗτος, *this.*	ὅς, ὅςτις, *who.*
πότερος, *uter?* *which of two?*	πότερος, *one of two* (alteruter).	ἕτερος, *the one of two* (alter).	ὑπότερος, *which of two.*
πόσος, *how great?* *how much?* (*quantus, quot*).	ποσός, *of some size or number.*	τόσος, τόσοςδε, τοσοῦτος, *so great, so much* (*tantus, tot*).	ὅσος, ὁπόσος, *how great, how much* (*quantus, quot*).
ποῖος, *of what quality?* (*qualis*).	ποιός, *of some quality.*	τοῖος, τοιόςδε, τοιοῦτος, *of such a quality* (*talis*).	οἷος, ὁποῖος, *of what quality* (*qualis*).
πηλίκος, *how old?*	πηλίκος, *of some age.*	τηλίκος, τηλίκοςδε, τηλικοῦτος, *of such age.*	ἡλίκος, ὁπηλίκος, *of what age.*

Obs.—On the ending τ ε ρ ο ς, see §§ 192, 208, *Obs.*

In Attic prose of the Demonstratives generally only those in -δε and -ουτο-ς are used.

§ 217. *Correlative Adverbs* are formed from the same Pronominal Stems.

§ 216. **Dialects.**—ὅσσος (add. form ὁσσάτιος), τόσσος, are Epic for ὅσος, τόσος. For every Interrogative π the New-Ion. dialect has κ: κόσος, κοῖος, κότε, κοῦ.

§ 217. **Dialects.**—πόθι is Epic = ποῦ; ποθί = πού; dem. τόθι, *there,* rel. ὅθι, *where.* In poetry, τόθεν is dem. to πόθεν, New-Ion. ἐνθαῦτα for ἐνταῦθα, ἐνθεῦτεν for ἐντεῦθεν.

ὥς in the Poets, like οὕτως, means *so,* to be distinguished from ὡς (without accent), *how;* it is written also ὧς, with the meaning *yet:* καὶ ὧς, *and yet.* With the meaning *so*, τώς also occurs. ἧχι is an additional form of ᾖ. The π is doubled: ὅππως, ὅπποτε (§ 62, D.).

94 CORRELATIVE ADVERBS. § 218.

Interrogative.	Indefinite.	Demonstrative.		Relative.	
ποῦ, where? (ubi?)	πού (ali- cubi) { some- where.	ἔνθα ἐνθάδε ἐνταῦθα } there (ibi).		οὗ ὅπου } where (ubi).	
πόθεν, whence? (unde?)	ποθέν (ali- cunde) { from some- where.	ἔνθεν ἐνθένδε ἐντεῦθεν } from there (inde).		ὅθεν ὁπόθεν } whence (unde).	
ποῖ, whither? (quo?)	ποί (ali- quo) { some- whither.	ἔνθα ἐνθάδε ἐνταῦθα } thither (eo).		οἷ ὅποι } whither (quo).	
πότε, when?	ποτέ, sometime.	τότε, then.		ὅτε, ὁπότε, when.	
πηνίκα { at what time?		τηνίκα τηνικάδε τηνικαῦτα } at that time.		ἡνίκα ὁπηνίκα } at what time.	
πῶς, how?	πώς, somehow.	ὥς ὧδε οὕτως } thus.		ὡς, ὅπως, as.	
πῇ { whither? in what way?	πῄ { some whither, in some way.	τῇδε ταύτῃ } thither, in this way.		ᾗ, ὅπῃ { whither, in what way.	

Obs.—ἔνθα and ἔνθεν, in their original demonstrative sense, occur only in a few combinations in Attic prose (ἔνθα δή, *just then*; ἔνθα καὶ ἔνθα, *here and there*); but they are regularly used in a relative sense: *where, whence.*

To the Correlative Adverbs there belong also ἕως, *quamdiu* (Relative, *as long*); τέως, *tamdiu* (Demonstrative, *so long*), as well as the poetic ὄφρα (for ὄφρα, § 53, c, *Obs.*) used in the same meaning as ἕως, and τόφρα as τέως.

To the simple ἐκεῖνος (*that*, § 212) correspond among the Adverbs of place ἐκεῖ, *there*; ἐκεῖθεν, *from there*; ἐκεῖσε, *thither*. The Demonstrative ὥς occurs in Attic prose only in καὶ ὥς, *even thus*, and οὐδ' ὥς, *not even thus*. It is also written ὧς in these combinations.

§ 218. The conjunctions δή, δήποτε, and οὖν (meaning *ever*, Latin *cunque*), and the enclitic περ, may be joined to any relative pronoun or adverb to give prominence: ὅστις δή ποτε, *whosoever;* ὅπως οὖν (*utcunque*), ὥσπερ, *just as.*

Sometimes ἤ is affixed to the interrog. τί in the sense of *why?* and to the corresponding indirect interrogative ὅ τι: τίη, ὅτίη, *why?*

§ 219. There are also negative pronouns and adverbs to be noticed: οὔτις, μήτις, *no one;* οὐδέτερος, μηδέτερος, *neither, neuter;* οὐδαμοῦ, μηδαμοῦ, *nowhere;* οὐδαμῶς, μηδαμῶς, *in no way.*

CHAP. IX.—THE NUMERALS.

§ 220. The *Cardinal, Ordinal,* and *Adverbial* Numerals, with their value and signs, are:

			ὁ πρῶτος, *the first.*	ἅπαξ, *once.*
1	α΄	εἷς, μία, ἕν, *one.*		
2	β΄	δύο	δεύτερος	δίς
3	γ΄	τρεῖς, τρία	τρίτος	τρίς
4	δ΄	τέσσαρες, τέσ- σαρα, or τέττά- ρες, τέττάρα	τέταρτος	τετράκις
5	ε΄	πέντε	πέμπτος	πεντάκις
6	ϛ΄	ἕξ	ἕκτος	ἑξάκις
7	ζ΄	ἑπτά	ἕβδομος	ἑπτάκις
8	η΄	ὀκτώ	ὄγδοος	ὀκτάκις
9	θ΄	ἐννέα	ἔνατος (ἔννατος)	ἐνάκις (ἐννάκις)
10	ι΄	δέκα	δέκατος	δεκάκις
11	ια΄	ἕνδεκα	ἑνδέκατος	ἑνδεκάκις
12	ιβ΄	δώδεκα	δωδέκατος	δωδεκάκις
13	ιγ΄	τριςκαίδεκα	τριςκαιδέκατος	
14	ιδ΄	τεσσαρεςκαίδεκα τεσσαρακαίδεκα	τεσσαρακαιδέκατος	
15	ιε΄	πεντεκαίδεκα	πεντεκαιδέκατος	
16	ιϛ΄	ἑκκαίδεκα	ἑκκαιδέκατος	
17	ιζ΄	ἑπτακαίδεκα	ἑπτακαιδέκατος	
18	ιη΄	ὀκτωκαίδεκα	ὀκτωκαιδέκατος	
19	ιθ΄	ἐννεακαίδεκα	ἐννεακαιδέκατος	
20	κ΄	εἴκοσι(ν)	εἰκοστός	εἰκοσάκις
30	λ΄	τριάκοντα	τριᾱκοστός	τριᾱκοντάκις
40	μ΄	τεσσαράκοντα	τεσσαρᾱκοστός	τεσσαρᾱκοντάκις
50	ν΄	πεντήκοντα	πεντηκοστός	πεντηκοντάκις
60	ξ΄	ἑξήκοντα	ἑξηκοστός	ἑξηκοντάκις
70	ο΄	ἑβδομήκοντα	ἑβδομηκοστός	ἑβδομηκοντάκις
80	π΄	ὀγδοήκοντα	ὀγδοηκοστός	ὀγδοηκοντάκις
90	ϟ΄	ἐνενήκοντα	ἐνενηκοστός	ἐνενηκοντάκις
100	ρ΄	ἑκατόν	ἑκατοστός	ἑκατοντάκις
200	σ΄	διᾱκόσιοι, αι, α	διακοσιοστός	διακοσιάκις
300	τ΄	τριᾱκόσιοι, αι, α	τριακοσιοστός	
400	υ΄	τετρᾱκόσιοι, αι, α	τετρακοσιοστός	
500	φ΄	πεντᾱκόσιοι, αι, α	πεντακοσιοστός	
600	χ΄	ἑξᾱκόσιοι, αι, α	ἑξακοσιοστός	
700	ψ΄	ἑπτᾱκόσιοι, αι, α	ἑπτακοσιοστός	
800	ω΄	ὀκτᾱκόσιοι, αι, α	ὀκτακοσιοστός	
900	ϡ΄	ἐνᾱκόσιοι, αι, α ἐννᾱκόσιοι, αι, α	ἐνακοσιοστός or ἐννακοσιοστός	
1000	,α	χίλιοι, αι, α	χιλιοστός	χιλιάκις
2000	,β	διςχίλιοι, αι, α	διςχιλιοστός	
3000	,γ	τριςχίλιοι, αι, α	τριςχιλιοστός	
10000	,ι	μύριοι, αι, α	μυριοστός	μυριάκις

Obs.—The letters of the alphabet are used in numbers also in uninterrupted succession. In the most frequent designation, given above, stigma (ς') is inserted after ε for the number 6 : ά to θ' are therefore units ; ί is 10, κ' 20 ; after π' (= 80), Ϥ' (koppa = 90) is inserted ; and after ώ (= 800) ϡ (sampi = 900). The alphabet begins again at 1000, but here each letter has the accent under it; hence ͵βτμδ' = 2344, ͵αωξβ' = 1862.

§ 221. The Cardinal Numbers 1 to 4 are declined:

1. *Nom.*	εἷς	μία	ἕν	2. *N. A.* δύο
Gen.	ἑνός	μιᾶς	ἑνός	*G. D.* δυοῖν
Dat.	ἑνί	μιᾷ	ἑνί	
Acc.	ἕνα	μίαν	ἕν	

3. *Nom.*	τρεῖς	*N.* τρία	4. τέσσαρες	*N.* τέσσαρα
Gen.	τριῶν		τεσσάρων	
Dat.	τρισί(ν)		τέσσαρσι(ν)	
Acc.	τρεῖς	*N.* τρία	τέσσαρας	*N.* τέσσαρα

οὐδείς, οὐδεμία, οὐδέν, and μηδείς, *no one*, are declined like εἷς. δύο is also used without inflexion. δυεῖν is another form for δυοῖν. ττ occurs for σσ in all forms and derivations of τέσσαρες. ἄμφω (*ambo, both*), Gen. Dat. ἀμφοῖν, is sometimes represented by the Plur. ἀμφότεροι, αι, α, of which the Singular ἀμφότερον, *both*, is also in use.

---

§§ 220-223. Dialects.—1, Homer has the fem. ἴα, ἰῆς, ἰῇ : also Neut. Dat. ἰῳ.
2, δύω for all cases : δοιώ, δοιοί, δοιαί, δοιά ; Dat. δοιοῖς ; Acc. δοιούς, άς, ά.
3, τρίτατος = τρίτος.
4, Hom. Æol. πίσυρες, New-Ion. τέσσερες, Hom. τέτρατος (§ 59, D.).
7, ἑβδόματος. 8, ὀγδόατος. 9, εἴνατος.
12, Hom. δυώδεκα, and δύο καὶ δέκα, δυοδέκατος.
20, Hom. ἐείκοσι, ἐεικοστός. 30, Hom. τριήκοντα. 80, ὀγδώκοντα. 90, ἐννήκοντα. 200, etc., also διηκόσιοι; Herod. πεντηκόσιοι, εἰνακόσιοι.
9000, Hom. ἐνεάχιλοι. 10,000, δεκάχιλοι.
δίχα, Hom. διχθά ; likewise τριχθά, τετραχθά, *threefold, fourfold ;* also τριπλῇ, τετραπλῇ.

§ 224. NUMERALS. 97

§ 222. The numerals 5 to 199 are indeclinable.

We also find τρεῖς, τρία καὶ δέκα, τέσσαρες, τέσσαρα καὶ δέκα, for 13 and 14. The units and tens are united by καί, in any order: εἴκοσι καὶ πέντε and πέντε καὶ εἴκοσι; or without καί when the tens are first: εἴκοσι πέντε, 25; so also ἑκατὸν δέκα. For twenty-first we have εἷς καὶ εἰκοστός, or πρῶτος καὶ εἰκοστός, and εἰκοστὸς πρῶτος, etc.

The Cardinal numerals from 200 are, like the Ordinal, regular adjectives of three terminations: διακόσιοι, αι, α. The Ordinal numerals have the endings of the superlative, except δεύτερος, which has that of the comparative (compare § 192).

§ 223. By combination with σύν, the numeral Stems form Distributives: σύνδυο, *two and two;* σύντρεις, *three and three;* Multiplicatives, by the syllable πλοῦς (from πλόος, Lat. *plex*): ἁπλοῦς, *simple;* διπλοῦς, τριπλοῦς, πενταπλοῦς, etc. Observe also δισσός, *twofold;* τρισσός, *threefold;* διπλάσιος, *twice as much;* τριπλάσιος, etc., πολλαπλάσιος, *many times as much.* Adverbs: μοναχῇ, *simply* (μόνος, *alone*); διχῇ or δίχα, *doubly.* Substantives: μονάς (St. μοναδ), *unity;* δυάς, τριάς, τετράς, πεμπάς, ἑξάς, ἑβδομάς, ὀγδοάς, ἰννεάς, δεκάς, εἰκάς, ἑκατοντάς, χιλιάς, μυριάς; hence τρεῖς μυριάδες = 30,000.

§ 224. The most important *general* Adjectives of quantity are: ἕκαστος, *each;* ἑκάτερος, *either;* πᾶς, πᾶσα, πᾶν (St. παντ), *all;* ποστός, ὁπόστος [quotus]; and the adverbs: πολλάκις, *many times, often;* ἑκαστάκις, *every time;* ὁσάκις, *as often as;* τοσαυτάκις, *so often;* πλειστάκις, *very often;* ὀλιγάκις, *seldom.*

E

B. INFLEXION OF VERBS.

General Remarks.

§ 225. The Greeks distinguish in the Verb—
1. *Three Numbers:* Singular, Dual, and Plural.
2. *Three Voices:*
    Active : ἔλυσα, *I loosed ;*
    Middle : ἐλυσάμην, *I loosed for myself ;*
    Passive : ἐλύθην, *I was loosed.*

Verbs which occur only in the Middle or Passive are called *Deponents :* δέχομαι, *I receive.*

Obs.—Only the Aorist and the Future have special forms for the Passive; and only the Aorist special forms for the Middle: in all other tenses the Middle forms have *also* a Passive meaning.

3. *Two* classes of *Tenses :*
    A. *Principal,* viz. :
        1. *Present :* λύω, *I loose ;*
        2. *Perfect :* λέλυκα, *I have loosed ;*
        3. *Future :* λύσω, *I shall loose.*
    B. *Historical,* viz. :
        1. *Imperfect :* ἔλυον, *I was loosing ;*
        2. *Pluperfect :* ἐλελύκειν, *I had loosed ;*
        3. *Aorist :* ἔλυσα, *I loosed.*

4. *Four Moods,* viz. :
Finite Verb.
{ 1. *Indicative :* λύω, *I loose ;*
  2. *Subjunctive :* λύω, *I may loose ;*
  3. *Optative :* λύοιμι, *I would loose ;*
  4. *Imperative :* λῦε, *loose.*

5. *Three Verbal Nouns,* viz. :
    1. *Infinitive :* λύειν, *loose ;*
    2. *Participle :* λύων, *loosing ;*
    3. *Verbal Adjective :* λυτέος, *to be loosed,* sol‑vendus.

§ 227. THE PERSONAL ENDINGS.—TENSE-STEMS. 99

§ 226. The *Personal Endings* had originally the following forms :

	Active.			Middle.	
	Principal Tenses.	Hist. Tenses.		Principal Tenses.	Hist. Tenses.
Sing. 1.	-μι	-ν		-μαι	-μην
2.	-σι	-ς		-σαι	-σο
3.	-τι	—		-ται	-το
Dual 1.	-μεν			-μεθον	
2.	-τον			-σθον	
3.	-τον	-την		-σθον	-σθην
Plur. 1.	-μεν			-μεθα	
2.	-τε			-σθε	
3.	-ντι	-εν		-νται	-ντο

The Active personal endings of the principal tenses are most easily observed in the verb :

εἰ-μί, *I am.*   ἐσ-μέν   ἐσ-μέν.
ἐσ-σί (contr. εἶ)   ἐσ-τόν   ἐσ-τέ.
ἐσ-τί(ν)   ἐσ-τόν   εἰ-σί(ν) (σι = ντι, § 60).

The endings of the three persons in the Sing. are really the personal pronouns affixed, *I, thou, he*, and to be compared with the Stems of the Personal Pronouns : μι (St. μ ε), σι (σ ε), τι (the Stem of the article, τ ο). The 1 Dual in the Active is always identical with the 1 Plur. The ending of the 1 Sing. of the Historical Tenses was originally μ (Lat. *era-m*), which at the end of the word was changed into ν, according to § 67, *Obs.* The ending of the 3 Sing. was originally τ, which, however, could not continue at the end according to § 67 (compare § 233, 2) ; and that of the 3 Plur. ντ (Lat. *era-nt*) ; but the τ was dropped (§ 67).

§ 227. The tenses, moods, and verbal nouns are classified according to the *Stems* (*Tense-Stems*) from which they are formed. The Tense-Stems are the following :

1. The *Present Stem*, from which the Present and Imperfect are formed.

§ 226. Dialects.—Instead of νται, ντο, the Ion. (especially New-Ion.) often has αται, ατο, in 3 Plur. Mid. The vowel α is here properly a connecting vowel, as in the Acc. Sing. of the Second Principal Declens. (§ 173, 3, *Obs.*) ; and ν is dropped in both alike ; hence α-ται, α-το, for α-νται, α-ντο (compare §§ 287, 302, 3).

2. The *Strong Aorist Stem*, from which the Second or Strong Aorist Act. and Mid. are formed.
3. The *Future Stem*, from which the Future Act. and Mid. are formed.
4. The *Weak Aorist Stem*, from which the First or Weak Aorist Act. and Mid. are formed.
5. The *Perfect Stem*, from which the Perfect, Pluperfect, and Future-Perfect are formed.

These five Stems belong to the Active and Middle. There are added to them, for the special forms of the Passive:

6. The *Strong Passive Stem*, from which the Second or Strong Aorist Passive and Second Future Passive are formed.
7. The *Weak Passive Stem*, from which the First or Weak Aorist Passive and First Future Passive are formed.

The form from which all the Tense-Stems of a verb may be derived is called the *Verbal Stem*.

§ 228. The *Subjunctive* is indicated between the Stem and the ending. Long vowels are peculiar to it: λύ-ω-μεν, *solv-ā-mus*; λύ-η-τε, *solv-ā-tis*.

The vowel ι is characteristic of the *Optative*, which generally becomes a diphthong with other vowels: λύ-οι-μεν, *we would loose*. The *Subjunctive* has the endings of the *principal tenses;* the *Optative* (except 1 Sing. Act.) those of the *historical tenses*.

The *Imperative* has the following peculiar endings:

	Active.	Middle.
Sing. 2.	-θι	-σο
3.	-τω	-σθω
Dual 2.	-τον	-σθον
3.	-των	-σθων
Plur. 2.	-τε	-σθε
3.	-ντων or -τωσαν	-σθων or -σθωσαν

§ 229. The general law for the *accentuation* of the verb is *that the accent is placed as far back as possible from*

§ 228. **Dialects.**—The Hom. dialect often shortens the long vowel of the Subjunctive in the Dual and Plural.

§ 230. CONJUGATIONS. 101

the end, final α ι not being considered long except in the optative: λύω, λύετε, λύομαι.

Obs.—An exception is formed by the *Participles*, which in declension (chap. vii.), if possible (§§ 79-87), always keep the accent on the *same* syllable as in the Nom. Sing. Masc.: Part. Pres. Act. βασιλεύων, *regnans*, Neut. βασιλεῦον (not βασίλευον, according to § 84), Part. Fut. Act. βασιλεύσων, *regnaturus*, Neut. βασιλεῦσον. (The special exceptions, see §§ 331-333.)

§ 230. We distinguish *Two Principal Conjugations*:

1. The *First*—the far more frequent—connects the personal endings with the first two Tense-Stems by a connecting vowel: λύ-ο-μεν. The verbs belonging to it are called verbs in ω because the first Person Sing. Pres. Act. ends in ω: λύω.

2. The *Second*—the less frequent, but older—affixes the personal endings to the first two Tense-Stems *without a connecting vowel:* ἐσ-μέν. They are called verbs in μι because the 1 Sing. Pres. Act. preserves the original ending μι: εἰ-μί.

The forms of the other five Tense-Stems are common to both Conjugations.

The Paradigms of the verbs are given first: the formation of each Tense-Stem is then explained in order.

LIST OF THE PARADIGMS.

Εἰμί, *I am* .... Table I.
Synopsis of λύω, *I loose* (exhibiting the meanings of the Tenses) .... " II.

VERBS IN Ω.
A. *Vowel Stems.*
 1. Uncontracted, λύω .... " III.
 2. Contracted, τιμάω, ποιέω, δουλόω .... " IV.
B. *Consonant Stems.*
 1. Guttural Stems, πλέκω, φεύγω, τάσσω .... " V.
 2. Dental Stems, ψεύδομαι, πείθω, κομίζω .... " VI.
 3. Labial Stems, πέμπω, λείπω, καλύπτω .... " VII.
 4. Liquid Stems, δέρω, ἀγγέλλω, σπείρω .... " VIII.
VERBS IN MI.
 First Class, τίθημι, δίδωμι, ἵστημι .... " IX.
 Second Class, δείκνυμι .... " X.

PARADIGMS OF VERBS.

Εἰμί, *I am.* Stem ἐς.

Moods.	Numbers.	Persons.	Present.	Imperfect.	Future.
Indicative.	S.	1	εἰμί	ἦν or ἦ	ἔσομαι
		2	εἶ	ἦσθα	ἔσῃ or ἔσει
		3	ἐστί(ν)	ἦν	ἔσται
	D.	1			ἐσόμεθον
		2	ἐστόν	ἦστον or ἦτον	ἔσεσθον
		3	ἐστόν	ἤστην or ἤτην	ἔσεσθον
	P.	1	ἐσμέν	ἦμεν	ἐσόμεθα
		2	ἐστέ	ἦστε or ἦτε	ἔσεσθε
		3	εἰσί	ἦσαν	ἔσονται
Subjunctive.	S.	1	ὦ		
		2	ᾖς		
		3	ᾖ		
	D.	2	ἦτον		
		3	ἦτον		
	P.	1	ὦμεν		
		2	ἦτε		
		3	ὦσι		
Optative.	S.	1	εἴην		ἐσοίμην
		2	εἴης		ἔσοιο
		3	εἴη		ἔσοιτο
	D.	1			ἐσοίμεθον
		2	εἴητον or εἶτον		ἔσοισθον
		3	εἰήτην or εἴτην		ἐσοίσθη
	P.	1	εἴημεν or εἶμεν		ἐσοίμεθα
		2	εἴητε or εἶτε		ἔσοισθε
		3	εἴησαν or εἶεν		ἔσοιντο
Imperative.	S.	2	ἴσθι		
		3	ἔστω		
	D.	2	ἔστον		
		3	ἔστων		
	P.	2	ἔστε		
		3	ἔστωσαν or ἔστων		
Infinitive.			εἶναι		ἔσεσθαι
Participle.			ὤν		ἐσόμενος
			οὖσα		ἐσομένη
			ὄν (Stem ο ν τ)		ἐσόμενον

NOTE.—The formation of the tenses of this verb is explained in § 315, but they are inserted in this place because some of them are required in conjugating the Middle and Passive Voices of ordinary verbs.

Table II.   PARADIGMS OF VERBS.   103

Synopsis of the Verb λύ-ω, to loose (exhibiting the meanings of the Tenses).

Tense.	Mood.	Act. Voice.		Middle Voice.		Passive Voice.	
Pres.	Ind.	λύω	*I am loosing (or I loose).*	λύομαι	*I am loosing for myself.*	λύομαι	*I am loosed* (continued).
	Subj.	λύω	*I may or can be loosing.*	λύωμαι			*I may, etc., be loosed.* "
	Opt.	λύοιμι	*I might, could, would, or should be loosing.*	λυοίμην			*I might, etc., be loosed.* "
	Imp.	λῦε	[*be loosing.*]	λύου			*be thou loosed* "
	Inf.	λύειν	*to be loosing.*	λύεσθαι			*to be loosed* "
	Part.	λύων	*loosing.*	λυόμενος			*being loosed*
Imperf.	Ind.	ἔλυον	*I was loosing.*	ἐλυόμην		like the middle	*I was loosed* (continued).
Fut.	Ind.	λύσω	*I shall loose.*	λύσομαι		λυθήσομαι	*I shall be loosed.* [after].
	Opt.	λύσοιμι	*I might, etc., loose* (hereafter).	λυσοίμην		λυθησοίμην	*I might, etc., be loosed* (hereafter).
	Inf.	λύσειν	*to loose* (hereafter).	λύσεσθαι		λυθήσεσθαι	*to be loosed* (hereafter).
	Part.	λύσων	*about to loose.*	λυσόμενος		λυθησόμενος	*about to be loosed.*
1 Aor. (Weak)	Ind.	ἔλυσα	*I loosed.*	ἐλυσάμην		ἐλύθην	*I was loosed.*
	Subj.	λύσω	*I may or can loose.*	λύσωμαι		λυθῶ	*I may, etc., be loosed.*
	Opt.	λύσαιμι	*I might, could, would, or should* [*loose.*]	λυσαίμην		λυθείην	*I might, etc., be loosed.*
	Imp.	λῦσον	*loose thou.*	λῦσαι		λύθητι	*be thou loosed.*
	Inf.	λῦσαι	*to loose.*	λύσασθαι		λυθῆναι	*to be loosed.*
	Part.	λύσας	*loosing or having loosed.*	λυσάμενος		λυθείς	*loosed or having been loosed.*
1 Perf. (Weak)	Ind.	λέλυκα	*I have loosed.*	λέλυμαι			*I have been loosed.*
	Subj.	λελύκω	*I may, etc., have loosed.*	λελυμένος ὦ			*I may, etc., have been loosed.*
	Opt.	λελύκοιμι	*I might, etc., have loosed.*	λελυμένος εἴην			*I might, etc., have been loosed.*
	Imp.	λέλυκε	*do thou have loosed.*	λέλυσο			*do thou have been loosed.*
	Inf.	λελυκέναι	*to have loosed.*	λελύσθαι			*to have been loosed.*
	Part.	λελυκώς	*having loosed.*	λελυμένος			*having been loosed.*
Plup.	Ind.	ἐλελύκειν	*I had loosed.*	ἐλελύμην		like the middle	*I had been loosed.*

Fut. Perf. Ind. λελύσομαι, Mid. *I shall have loosed for myself*, Pass. *I shall have been loosed.*
 Opt. λελυσοίμην, Inf. λελύσεσθαι, Part. λελυσόμενος.
Verbal Adject. λυτός, *loosed or loosable* ; λυτέος, (requiring) *to be loosed.*

104 PARADIGMS OF VERBS.—VERBS IN Ω. Table III.

A. VOWEL STEMS.

ACTIVE

Tenses.	Numbers.	Persons.	Indicative.		Subjunctive.
			Present.	Imperfect.	
Present.	S.	1	λύω	ἔλυον	λύω
		2	λύεις	ἔλυες	λύῃς
		3	λύει	ἔλυε(ν)	λύῃ
	D.	2	λύετον	ἐλύετον	λύητον
		3	λύετον	ἐλυέτην	λύητον
	P.	1	λύομεν	ἐλύομεν	λύωμεν
		2	λύετε	ἐλύετε	λύητε
		3	λύουσι(ν)	ἔλυον	λύωσι(ν)
Future.	S.	1	λύσω		
		2	λύσεις		
		3	λύσει		
	D.	2	λύσετον		
		3	λύσετον		
	P.	1	λύσομεν		
		2	λύσετε		
		3	λύσουσι(ν)		
1 Aorist	S.	1	ἔλυσα		λύσω
(Weak).		2	ἔλυσας		λύσῃς
		3	ἔλυσε(ν)		λύσῃ
	D.	2	ἐλύσατον		λύσητον
		3	ἐλυσάτην		λύσητον
	P.	1	ἐλύσαμεν		λύσωμεν
		2	ἐλύσατε		λύσητε
		3	ἔλυσαν		λύσωσι(ν)
			Perfect.	Pluperfect.	
1 Perfect	S.	1	λέλυκα	ἐλελύκειν	λελύκω
(Weak).		2	λέλυκας	ἐλελύκεις	λελύκῃς
		3	λέλυκε(ν)	ἐλελύκει	λελύκῃ
	D.	2	λελύκατον	ἐλελύκειτον	λελύκητον
		3	λελύκατον	ἐλελυκείτην	λελύκητον
	P.	1	λελύκαμεν	ἐλελύκειμεν	λελύκωμεν
		2	λελύκατε	ἐλελύκειτε	λελύκητε
		3	λελύκᾱσι(ν)	ἐλελύκεσαν or ἐλελύκεισαν	λελύκωσι(ν)
2 Aorist (Strong).			Wanting.		
2 Perfect and Pluperf.(Strong).			Wanting.		

Examples for
θύω, *I sacrifice;* θεραπεύω, *I serve;* βουλεύω, *I advise;* χορεύω, *I dance;*
ἐπαύσθην ;

Table III. PARADIGMS OF VERBS.—VERBS IN Ω. 105

1. UNCONTRACTED.
VOICE.

Optative.	Imperative.	Infinitive.	Participle.
λύοιμι		λύειν	λύων
λύοις	λῦε		λύουσα
λύοι	λυέτω		λῦον
λύοιτον	λύετον		
λυοίτην	λυέτων		Gen. λύοντος
λύοιμεν			λυούσης
λύοιτε	λύετε		λύοντος
λύοιεν	λυόντων or λυέτωσαν		St. λυοντ
λύσοιμι		λύσειν	λύσων
λύσοις			
λύσοι			λύσουσα
λύσοιτον			λῦσον
λυσοίτην			Gen. λύσοντος
λύσοιμεν			λυσούσης
λύσοιτε			λύσοντος
λύσοιεν			St. λυσοντ
λύσαιμι		λῦσαι	λύσας
λύσαις or λύσειας	λῦσον		λύσασα
			λῦσαν
λύσαι or λύσειε(ν)	λυσάτω		Gen. λύσαντος
λύσαιτον	λυσάτον		λυσάσης
λυσαίτην	λυσάτων		λύσαντος
λύσαιμεν			St. λυσαντ
λύσαιτε	λύσατε [σαν		
λύσαιεν or λύσειαν	λυσάντων or λυσάτω-		
λελύκοιμι		λελυκέναι	λελυκώς
λελύκοις	λέλυκε		λελυκυῖα
			λελυκός
λελύκοι	λελυκέτω		Gen. λελυκότος
λελύκοιτον			λελυκυίας
λελυκοίτην	λελύκετον		λελυκότος
λελύκοιμεν	λελυκέτων		St. λελυκοτ
λελύκοιτε	λελύκετε		
λελύκοιεν	λελυκόντων or λελυκέτωσαν		

Conjugation.
δακρύω, I weep; παύω, I make to cease (Mid., I cease). [1 Aor. Pass.
Verbal, παυστέος.]

106 PARADIGMS OF VERBS.—VERBS IN Ω. Table III.—

A. VOWEL STEMS.
MIDDLE AND
Tenses common to

Tenses.	Nos.	Persons.	Indicative.	Subjunctive.
Present.	S.	1	λύομαι	λύωμαι
		2	λύῃ or λύει	λύῃ
		3	λύεται	λύηται
	D.	1	λυόμεθον	λυώμεθον
		2	λύεσθον	λύησθον
		3	λύεσθον	λύησθον
	P.	1	λυόμεθα	λυώμεθα
		2	λύεσθε	λύησθε
		3	λύονται	λύωνται
Imperfect.	S.	1	ἐλυόμην	
		2	ἐλύου	
		3	ἐλύετο	
	D.	1	ἐλυόμεθον	
		2	ἐλύεσθον	
		3	ἐλυέσθην	
	P.	1	ἐλυόμεθα	
		2	ἐλύεσθε	
		3	ἐλύοντο	
Future.	S.	1	λύσομαι [ομαι etc., as in the Pres. λύ-	
Perfect.	S.	1	λέλυμαι	λελυμένος ὦ
		2	λέλυσαι	
		3	λέλυται	
	D.	1	λελύμεθον	
		2	λέλυσθον	
		3	λέλυσθον	
	P.	1	λελύμεθα	
		2	λέλυσθε	
		3	λέλυνται	
Pluperfect.	S.	1	ἐλελύμην	
		2	ἐλέλυσο	
		3	ἐλέλυτο	
	D.	1	ἐλελύμεθον	
		2	ἐλέλυσθον	
		3	ἐλελύσθην	
	P.	1	ἐλελύμεθα	
		2	ἐλέλυσθε	
		3	ἐλέλυντο	
Future Perfect.	S.	1	λελύσομαι [ομαι etc., as in the Pres. λύ-	

Continued. PARADIGMS OF VERBS.—VERBS IN Ω. 107

I. UNCONTRACTED.
PASSIVE VOICES. (§ 225, *Obs.* 2.)
both Voices.

Optative.	Imperative.	Infinitive.	Participle.
λυοίμην	λύου	λύεσθαι	λυόμενος
λύοιο			λυομένη
λύοιτο	λυέσθω		λυόμενον
λυοίμεθον			
λύοισθον	λύεσθον		
λυοίσθην	λυέσθων		
λυοίμεθα			
λύοισθε	λύεσθε		
λύοιντο	λυέσθων or		
	λυέσθωσαν		
λυσοίμην [οίμην		λύσεσθαι	λυσόμενος
etc., as in the Pres. λυ-			λυσομένη
			λυσόμενον
λελυμένος εἴην	λέλυσο	λελύσθαι	λελυμένος
			λελυμένη
	λελύσθω		λελυμένον
	λέλυσθον		
	λελύσθων		
	λέλυσθε		
	λελύσθων or		
	λελύσθωσαν		
λελυσοίμην [οίμην		λελύσεσθαι	λελυσόμενος
etc., as in the Pres. λυ-			λελυσομένη
			λελυσόμενον

108 PARADIGMS OF VERBS.—VERBS IN Ω. Table III.—

A. VOWEL STEMS.
MIDDLE AND
Tenses peculiar to

Tenses.	Numbers.	Persons.	Indicative.	Subjunctive.
1 Aorist (Weak).	S.	1	ἐλυσάμην	λύσωμαι
		2	ἐλύσω	λύσῃ
	D.	3	ἐλύσατο	λύσηται
		1	ἐλυσάμεθον	λυσώμεθον
		2	ἐλύσασθον	λύσησθον
		3	ἐλυσάσθην	λύσησθον
	P.	1	ἐλυσάμεθα	λυσώμεθα
		2	ἐλύσασθε	λύσησθε
		3	ἐλύσαντο	λύσωνται
2 Aorist (Strong).			Wanting.	

Tenses peculiar to

1 Aorist (Weak).	S.	1	ἐλύθην	λυθῶ
		2	ἐλύθης	λυθῇς
	D.	3	ἐλύθη	λυθῇ
		2	ἐλύθητον	λυθῆτον
		3	ἐλυθήτην	λυθῆτον
	P.	1	ἐλύθημεν	λυθῶμεν
		2	ἐλύθητε	λυθῆτε
		3	ἐλύθησαν	λυθῶσι(ν)
1 Future (Weak).	S.	1	λυθήσομαι	
		2	λυθήσῃ or λυθήσει	
		3	λυθήσεται	
	D.	1	λυθησόμεθον	
		2	λυθήσεσθον	
		3	λυθήσεσθον	
	P.	1	λυθησόμεθα	
		2	λυθήσεσθε	
		3	λυθήσονται	
2 Aorist (Strong).			Wanting.	
2 Future (Strong).			Wanting.	

Verbal Adjectives: λυτός, ή, όν. 2. λυτέος, α, ον.

Continued. PARADIGMS OF VERBS.—VERBS IN Ω. 109

I. UNCONTRACTED.
PASSIVE VOICE.
the Middle Voice.

Optative.	Imperative.	Infinitive.	Participle.
λυσαίμην		λύσασθαι	λυσάμενος
λύσαιο	λῦσαι		λυσαμένη
λύσαιτο	λυσάσθω		λυσάμενον
λυσαίμεθον			
λύσαισθον	λύσασθον		
λυσαίσθην	λυσάσθων		
λυσαίμεθα			
λύσαισθε	λύσασθε		
λύσαιντο	λυσάσθων or		
	λυσάσθωσαν		

the Passive Voice.

λυθείην		λυθῆναι	λυθείς
λυθείης	λύθητι		λυθεῖσα
			λυθέν
λυθείη	λυθήτω		Gen. λυθέντος
λυθείητον or λυθεῖτον			λυθείσης
λυθειήτην or λυθείτην	λύθητον		λυθέντος
λυθείημεν or λυθεῖμεν	λυθήτων		St. λ υ θ ε ν τ
λυθείητε or λυθεῖτε	λύθητε		
λυθείησαν or λυθεῖεν	λυθήτωσαν or		
	λυθέντων		
λυθησοίμην		λυθήσεσθαι	λυθησόμενος
λυθήσοιο			
λυθήσοιτο			λυθησομένη
λυθησοίμεθον			λυθησόμενον
λυθήσοισθον			
λυθησοίσθην			
λυθησοίμεθα			
λυθήσοισθε			
λυθήσοιντο			

110 PARADIGMS OF VERBS.—VERBS IN Ω. Table IV.

A. VOWEL STEMS.
Present and

		τῑμάω, I honor [compare Lat. am(a)o].		ποιέω, I make [comp. Lat. moneo].		δουλόω, I subjugate.	
		Stems: τιμα		ποιε		δουλο	
		Active.					
Pres. Indicative.	S. 1	τιμάω	τιμῶ	ποιέω	ποιῶ	δουλόω	δουλῶ
	2	τιμάεις	τιμᾷς	ποιέεις	ποιεῖς	δουλόεις	δουλοῖς
	3	τιμάει	τιμᾷ	ποιέει	ποιεῖ	δουλόει	δουλοῖ
	D. 1						
	2	τιμάετον	τιμᾶτον	ποιέετον	ποιεῖτον	δουλόετον	δουλοῦτον
	3	τιμάετον	τιμᾶτον	ποιέετον	ποιεῖτον	δουλόετον	δουλοῦτον
	P. 1	τιμάομεν	τιμῶμεν	ποιέομεν	ποιοῦμεν	δουλόομεν	δουλοῦμεν
	2	τιμάετε	τιμᾶτε	ποιέετε	ποιεῖτε	δουλόετε	δουλοῦτε
	3	τιμά-ουσι(ν)	τιμῶ-σι(ν)	ποιέου-σι(ν)	ποιοῦ-σι(ν)	δουλόου-σι(ν)	δουλοῦ-σι(ν)
Subjunctive.	S. 1	τιμάω	τιμῶ	ποιέω	ποιῶ	δουλόω	δουλῶ
	2	τιμάῃς	τιμᾷς	ποιέῃς	ποιῇς	δουλόῃς	δουλοῖς
	3	τιμάῃ	τιμᾷ	ποιέῃ	ποιῇ	δουλόῃ	δουλοῖ
	D. 1						
	2	τιμάητον	τιμᾶτον	ποιέητον	ποιῆτον	δουλόητον	δουλῶτον
	3	τιμάητον	τιμᾶτον	ποιέητον	ποιῆτον	δουλόητον	δουλῶτον
	P. 1	τιμάωμεν	τιμῶμεν	ποιέωμεν	ποιῶμεν	δουλόωμεν	δουλῶμεν
	2	τιμάητε	τιμᾶτε	ποιέητε	ποιῆτε	δουλόητε	δουλῶτε
	3	τιμάω-σι(ν)	τιμῶ-σι(ν)	ποιέω-σι(ν)	ποιῶ-σι(ν)	δουλόω-σι(ν)	δουλῶ-σι(ν)
Optative.	S. 1	τιμάοιμι (-αοίην)	τιμῷμι (-ῴην)*	ποιέοιμι (εοίην)	ποιοῖμι (-οίην)	δουλόοιμι (-οοίην)	δουλοῖμι (-οίην)
	2	τιμάοις (-αοίης)	τιμῷς (-ῴης)	ποιέοις (-εοίης)	ποιοῖς (-οίης)	δουλόοις (-οοίης)	δουλοῖς (-οίης)
	3	τιμάοι (-αοίη)	τιμῷ (-ῴη)	ποιέοι (-εοίη)	ποιοῖ (-οίη)	δουλόοι (-οοίη)	δουλοῖ (-οίη)
	D. 1						
	2	τιμάοιτον (-αοίητον)	τιμῷτον (-ῴητον)	ποιέοιτον (-εοίητον)	ποιοῖτον (-οίητον)	δουλόοιτον (-οοίητον)	δουλοῖτον (-οίητον)
	3	τιμαοίτην (-αοιήτην)	τιμῴτην (-ῴήτην)	ποιεοίτην (-εοιήτην)	ποιοίτην (-οιήτην)	δουλοοίτην (-οοιήτην)	δουλοίτην (-οιήτην)
	P. 1	τιμάοιμεν (-αοίημεν)	τιμῷμεν (-ῴημεν)	ποιέοιμεν (-εοίημεν)	ποιοῖμεν (-οίημεν)	δουλόοιμεν (-οοίημεν)	δουλοῖμεν (-οίημεν)
	2	τιμάοιτε (-αοίητε)	τιμῷτε (-ῴητε)	ποιέοιτε (-εοίητε)	ποιοῖτε (-οίητε)	δουλόοιτε (-οοίητε)	δουλοῖτε (-οίητε)
	3	τιμάοιεν	τιμῷεν	ποιέοιεν (-εοίησαν)	ποιοῖεν (-οίησαν)	δουλόοιεν	δουλοῖεν

* *Obs.*—The more usual forms are those printed in spaced type.

Table IV. PARADIGMS OF VERBS.—VERBS IN Ω. 111

II. CONTRACTED.
Imperfect Tenses.

Middle and Passive.

τιμάομαι	τιμῶμαι	ποιέομαι	ποιοῦμαι	δουλόομαι	δουλοῦμαι
τιμάῃ, ει	τιμᾷ	ποιέῃ, ει	ποιῇ, εῖ	δουλόῃ, ει	δουλοῖ
τιμάεται	τιμᾶται	ποιέεται	ποιεῖται	δουλόεται	δουλοῦται
τιμαόμεθον τιμώμε-		ποιεόμεθον ποιούμε-		δουλοόμε-	δουλούμε-
θον		θον		θον	θον
τιμάεσθον τιμᾶσθον		ποιέεσθον ποιεῖσθον		δουλόεσθον	δουλοῦσθον
τιμάεσθον τιμᾶσθον		ποιέεσθον ποιεῖσθον		δουλόεσθον	δουλοῦσθον
τιμαόμεθα τιμώμεθα		ποιεόμεθα ποιούμεθα		δουλοόμεθα	δουλούμεθα
τιμάεσθε τιμᾶσθε		ποιέεσθε ποιεῖσθε		δουλόεσθε	δουλοῦσθε
τιμάονται τιμῶνται		ποιέονται ποιοῦνται		δουλόονται	δουλοῦνται
τιμάωμαι τιμῶμαι		ποιέωμαι ποιῶμαι		δουλόωμαι	δουλῶμαι
τιμάῃ τιμᾷ		ποιέῃ ποιῇ		δουλόῃ	δουλοῖ
τιμάηται τιμᾶται		ποιέηται ποιῆται		δουλόηται	δουλῶται
τιμαώμε- τιμώμε-		ποιεώμεθον ποιώμε-		δουλοώμε-	δουλώμε-
θον θον		θον		θον	θον
τιμάησθον τιμᾶσθον		ποιέησθον ποιῆσθον		δουλόησθον	δουλῶσθον
τιμάησθον τιμᾶσθον		ποιέησθον ποιῆσθον		δουλόησθον	δουλῶσθον
τιμαώμεθα τιμώμεθα		ποιεώμεθα ποιώμεθα		δουλοώμεθα	δουλώμεθα
τιμάησθε τιμᾶσθε		ποιέησθε ποιῆσθε		δουλόησθε	δουλῶσθε
τιμάωνται τιμῶνται		ποιέωνται ποιῶνται		δουλόωνται	δουλῶνται
τιμαοίμην τιμῴμην		ποιεοίμην ποιοίμην		δουλοοίμην	δουλοίμην
τιμάοιο τιμῷο		ποιέοιο ποιοῖο		δουλόοιο	δουλοῖο
τιμάοιτο τιμῷτο		ποιέοιτο ποιοῖτο		δουλόοιτο	δουλοῖτο
τιμαοίμε- τιμῴμε-		ποιεοίμεθον ποιοίμε-		δουλοοίμε-	δουλοίμε-
θον θον		θον		θον	θον
τιμάοισθον τιμῷσθον		ποιέοισθον ποιοῖσθον		δουλόοι-	δουλοῖσθον
				σθον	
τιμαοίσθον τιμῴσθον		ποιεοίσθην ποιοίσθην		δουλοοί-	δουλοίσθην
				σθην	
τιμαοίμεθα τιμῴμεθα		ποιεοίμεθα ποιοίμεθα		δουλοοίμε-	δουλοίμεθα
				θα	
τιμάοισθε τιμῷσθε		ποιέοισθε ποιοῖσθε		δουλόοισθε	δουλοῖσθε
τιμάοιντο τιμῷντο		ποιέοιντο ποιοῖντο		δουλόοιντο	δουλοῖντο

112 PARADIGMS OF VERBS.—VERBS IN Ω. Table IV.—

A. VOWEL STEMS.

Present and Imperfect Tenses,

τιμάω, I honor [compare Lat. am(a)o]. Stems: τιμα	ποιέω, I make [comp. Lat. moneo]. ποιε	δουλόω, I subjugate. δουλο

Active.

			τίμαε τίμα	ποίεε ποίει	δούλοε δούλου
Imperative.	S.	2	τίμαε τίμα	ποίεε ποίει	δούλοε δούλου
		3	τιμαέτω τιμάτω	ποιεέτω ποιείτω	δουλοέτω δουλούτω
	D.	2	τιμάετον τιμᾶτον	ποιέετον ποιεῖτον	δουλόετον δουλοῦτον
		3	τιμαέτων τιμάτων	ποιεέτων ποιείτων	δουλοέτων δουλούτων
	P.	2	τιμάετε τιμᾶτε	ποιέετε ποιεῖτε	δουλόετε δουλοῦτε
			τιμαόν- τιμών-	ποιεόν- ποιούν-	δουλοόν- δουλούν-
		3	των των	των των	των των
			τιμαέτω- τιμάτω-	ποιεέτω- ποιείτω-	δουλοέτω- δουλούτω-
			σαν σαν	σαν σαν	σαν σαν

Infin.	τιμάειν τιμᾶν	ποιέειν ποιεῖν	δουλόειν δουλοῦν

Participle.	τιμάων τιμῶν	ποιέων ποιῶν	δουλόων δουλῶν
	τιμάουσα τιμῶσα	ποιέουσα ποιοῦσα	δουλόουσα δουλοῦσα
	τιμάον τιμῶν	ποιέον ποιοῦν	δουλόον δουλοῦν

Imperfect.	S.	1	ἐτίμαον ἐτίμων	ἐποίεον ἐποίουν	ἐδούλοον ἐδούλουν
		2	ἐτίμαες ἐτίμας	ἐποίεες ἐποίεις	ἐδούλοες ἐδούλους
		3	ἐτίμαε(ν) ἐτίμα	ἐποίεε(ν) ἐποίει	ἐδούλοε(ν) ἐδούλου
	D.	1			
		2	ἐτιμάε- ἐτιμᾶ-	ἐποιέετον ἐποιεῖ-	ἐδουλοέ- ἐδουλοῦ-
			τον τον	τον	τον τον
		3	ἐτιμαέ- ἐτιμά-	ἐποιεέ- ἐποιεί-	ἐδουλοέ- ἐδουλού-
			την την	την την	την την
	P.	1	ἐτιμάο- ἐτιμῶ-	ἐποιέομεν ἐποιοῦ-	ἐδουλόο- ἐδουλοῦ-
			μεν μεν	μεν	μεν μεν
		2	ἐτιμάετε ἐτιμᾶτε	ἐποιέετε ἐποιεῖτε	ἐδουλόετε ἐδουλοῦτε
		3	ἐτίμαον ἐτίμων	ἐποίεον ἐποίουν	ἐδούλοον ἐδούλουν

The other Tenses are conjugated like the same Tenses in λύω.

Examples for

τολμάω, I dare.   ἐάω, I let (§ 236).
σιγάω, I am silent.   ἀσκέω, I practise.
βοάω, I call out.   κοσμέω, I adorn.

Continued. PARADIGMS OF VERBS.—VERBS IN Ω. 113

II. CONTRACTED.
Indicative Mood.

Middle and Passive.

τιμάου	τιμῶ	ποιέου	ποιοῦ	δουλόου	δουλοῦ
τιμαέσθω	τιμάσθω	ποιεέσθω	ποιείσθω	δουλοέσθω	δουλούσθω
τιμάεσθον	τιμᾶσθον	ποιέεσθον	ποιεῖσθον	δουλόεσθον	δουλοῦσθον
τιμαέσθων	τιμάσθων	ποιεέσθων	ποιείσθων	δουλοέσθων	δουλούσθων
τιμάεσθε	τιμᾶσθε	ποιέεσθε	ποιεῖσθε	δουλόεσθε	δουλοῦσθε
τιμαέσθων	τιμάσθων	ποιεέσθων	ποιείσθων	δουλοέσθων	δουλούσθων
τιμαέσθω- σαν	τιμάσθω- σαν	ποιεέσθω- σαν	ποιείσθω- σαν	δουλοέσθω- σαν	δουλούσθω- σαν
τιμάεσθαι	τιμᾶσθαι	ποιέεσθαι	ποιεῖσθαι	δουλόεσθαι	δουλοῦσθαι
τιμαόμε- νος	τιμώμε- νος	ποιεόμε- νος	ποιούμε- νος	δουλοόμε- νος	δουλούμε- νος
τιμαομένη	τιμωμένη	ποιεομένη	ποιουμένη	δουλοομένη	δουλουμένη
τιμαόμε- νον	τιμώμε- νον	ποιεόμε- νον	ποιούμε- νον	δουλοόμε- νον	δουλούμε- νον
ἐτιμαόμην	ἐτιμώμην	ἐποιεόμην	ἐποιούμην	ἐδουλοόμην	ἐδουλούμην
ἐτιμάου	ἐτιμῶ	ἐποιέου	ἐποιοῦ	ἐδουλόου	ἐδουλοῦ
ἐτιμάετο	ἐτιμᾶτο	ἐποιέετο	ἐποιεῖτο	ἐδουλόετο	ἐδουλοῦτο
ἐτιμαόμε- θον	ἐτιμώμε- θον	ἐποιεόμε- θον	ἐποιούμε- θον	ἐδουλοόμε- θον	ἐδουλούμε- θον
ἐτιμάε- σθον	ἐτιμᾶ- σθον	ἐποιέεσθον	ἐποιεῖ- σθον	ἐδουλόε- σθον	ἐδουλοῦ- σθον
ἐτιμαέ- σθην	ἐτιμά- σθην	ἐποιεέσθην	ἐποιεί- σθην	ἐδουλοέ- σθην	ἐδουλού- σθην
ἐτιμαόμε- θα	ἐτιμώμε- θα	ἐποιεόμε- θα	ἐποιούμε- θα	ἐδουλοόμε- θα	ἐδουλούμε- θα
ἐτιμάεσθε	ἐτιμᾶσθε	ἐποιέεσθε	ἐποιεῖσθε	ἐδουλόεσθε	ἐδουλοῦσθε
ἐτιμάοντο	ἐτιμῶντο	ἐποιέοντο	ἐποιοῦντο	ἐδουλόοντο	ἐδουλοῦντο

A Synopsis of these Tenses is given in the following Table:

Conjugation.

ἀριθμέω, *I count*.
δηλόω, *I make clear*.
στεφανόω, *I crown*.
ζημιόω, *I punish*.
χρυσόω, *I gild*.

114 PARADIGMS OF VERBS.—VERBS IN Ω. Table IV.—

A. VOWEL STEMS.
(Uncontracted

Tenses.	Indicative.	Subjunctive.	Optative.
	Active Voice.		
Future.	τιμήσω ποιήσω δουλώσω		τιμήσοιμι ποιήσοιμι δουλώσοιμι
1 Aorist (Weak).	ἐτίμησα ἐποίησα ἐδούλωσα	τιμήσω ποιήσω δουλώσω	τιμήσαιμι ποιήσαιμι δουλώσαιμι
1 Perfect (Weak).	τετίμηκα πεποίηκα δεδούλωκα	τετιμήκω πεποιήκω δεδουλώκω	τετιμήκοιμι πεποιήκοιμι δεδουλώκοιμι
1 Pluperfect (Weak).	ἐτετιμήκειν ἐπεποιήκειν ἐδεδουλώκειν		
	Middle and Passive Voices.		
Future.	τιμήσομαι ποιήσομαι δουλώσομαι		τιμησοίμην ποιησοίμην δουλωσοίμην
Perfect.	τετίμημαι πεποίημαι δεδούλωμαι	τετιμημένος ὦ πεποιημένος ὦ δεδουλωμένος ὦ	τετιμημένος εἴην πεποιημένος εἴην δεδουλωμένος εἴην
Pluperfect.	ἐτετιμήμην ἐπεποιήμην ἐδεδουλώμην		
Future Perfect.	τετιμήσομαι πεποιήσομαι δεδουλώσομαι		τετιμησοίμην πεποιησοίμην δεδουλωσοίμην
1 Aorist Passive (Weak).	ἐτιμήθην ἐποιήθην ἐδουλώθην	τιμηθῶ ποιηθῶ δουλωθῶ	τιμηθείην ποιηθείην δουλωθείην
2 Future Passive Weak).	τιμηθήσομαι ποιηθήσομαι δουλωθήσομαι		τιμηθησοίμην ποιηθησοίμην δουλωθησοίμην

Verbal Adjectives : 1. τιμητός 2. τιμητέος
ποιητός ποιητέος
δουλωτός δουλωτέος

Continued. PARADIGMS OF VERBS.—VERBS IN Ω. 115

1. UNCONTRACTED.
Tenses.)

Imperative.	Infinitive.	Participle.
	Active Voice.	
	τιμήσειν ποιήσειν δουλώσειν	τιμήσων ποιήσων δουλώσων
τίμησον ποίησον δούλωσον	τιμῆσαι ποιῆσαι δουλῶσαι	τιμήσας ποιήσας δουλώσας
τετίμηκε πεποίηκε δεδούλωκε	τετιμηκέναι πεποιηκέναι δεδουλωκέναι	τετιμηκώς πεποιηκώς δεδουλωκώς

	Middle and Passive Voices.	
	τιμήσεσθαι ποιήσεσθαι δουλώσεσθαι	τιμησόμενος ποιησόμενος δουλωσόμενος
τετίμησο πεποίησο δεδούλωσο	τετιμῆσθαι πεποιῆσθαι δεδουλῶσθαι	τετιμημένος πεποιημένος δεδουλωμένος

	τετιμήσεσθαι πεποιήσεσθαι δεδουλώσεσθαι	τετιμησόμενος πεποιησόμενος δεδουλωσόμενος
τιμήθητι ποιήθητι δουλώθητι	τιμηθῆναι ποιηθῆναι δουλωθῆναι	τιμηθείς ποιηθείς δουλωθείς
	τιμηθήσεσθαι ποιηθήσεσθαι δουλωθήσεσθαι	τιμηθησόμενος ποιηθησόμενος δουλωθησόμενος

116 PARADIGMS OF VERBS.—VERBS IN Ω. Table V.

B. CONSONANT STEMS.

πλέκω, *I plait* (Class 1); φεύγω, *I flee* (Class 2);

Tenses.	Indicative.		Subjunctive.

Active.

	Present.	Imperfect.	
Present.	πλέκω φεύγω τάσσω	ἔπλεκον ἔφευγον ἔτασσον	πλέκω φεύγω τάσσω
Future.	πλέξω φεύξομαι τάξω		
1 Aorist (Weak). 2 Aorist (Strong). 1 Aorist (Weak).	ἔπλεξα ἔφυγον ἔταξα		πλέξω φύγω τάξω
	Perfect.	Pluperfect.	
1 Perfect (Weak). 2 Perfect (Strong). 1 Perfect (Weak).	πέπλεχα πέφευγα τέταχα	ἐπεπλέχειν ἐπεφεύγειν ἐτετάχειν	πεπλέχω πεφεύγω τετάχω

Middle and Passive.

	Present.	Imperfect.	
Present.	πλέκομαι τάσσομαι	ἐπλεκόμην ἐτασσόμην	πλέκωμαι τάσσωμαι
Future.	πλέξομαι τάξομαι		
1 Aorist Middle (Weak).	ἐπλεξάμην ἐταξάμην		πλέξωμαι τάξωμαι
	Perfect.	Pluperfect.	
Perfect.	πέπλεγμαι τέταγμαι	ἐπεπλέγμην ἐτετάγμην	πεπλεγμένος ὦ τεταγμένος ὦ
Future Perfect.	πεπλέξομαι τετάξομαι		
2 Aorist Pass. (Strong). 1 Aorist Pass. (Weak).	ἐπλάκην ἐτάχθην		πλακῶ ταχθῶ
2 Future Pass. (Strong). 1 Future Pass. (Weak).	πλακήσομαι ταχθήσομαι		

Verbal Adjectives : 1. πλεκτός, φευκτός, τακτός.

Examples for
ἄγω, *I drive* (Aor. ἤγαγον, Perf. Act. ἦχα); ἄρχω, *I rule*, both of Class (Pres. -σσω, rarely -ξω), see § 250. Nouns are formed from the Pure ἡ ἀρχ-ή, *the government.*

Table V. PARADIGMS OF VERBS.—VERBS IN Ω. 117

I. GUTTURAL STEMS.

τάσσω, *I arrange* (Class 4). Verbal Stems: πλεκ, φυγ, ταγ.

Optative.	Imperative.	Infinitive.	Participle.
Active.			
πλέκοιμι	πλέκε	πλέκειν	πλέκων
φεύγοιμι	φεῦγε	φεύγειν	φεύγων
τάσσοιμι	τάσσε	τάσσειν	τάσσων
πλέξοιμι		πλέξειν	πλέξων
φευξοίμην		φεύξεσθαι	φευξόμενος
τάξοιμι		τάξειν	τάξων
πλέξαιμι	πλέξον	πλέξαι	πλέξας
φύγοιμι	φύγε	φυγεῖν	φυγών
τάξαιμι	τάξον	τάξαι	τάξας
πεπλέχοιμι	πέπλεχε	πεπλεχέναι	πεπλεχώς
πεφεύγοιμι	πέφευγε	πεφευγέναι	πεφευγώς
τετάχοιμι	τέταχε	τεταχέναι	τεταχώς
Middle and Passive.			
πλεκοίμην	πλέκου	πλέκεσθαι	πλεκόμενος
τασσοίμην	τάσσου	τάσσεσθαι	τασσόμενος
πλεξοίμην		πλέξεσθαι	πλεξόμενος
ταξοίμην		τάξεσθαι	ταξόμενος
πλεξαίμην	πλέξαι	πλέξασθαι	πλεξάμενος
ταξαίμην	τάξαι	τάξασθαι	ταξάμενος
πεπλεγμένος εἴην	πέπλεξο	πεπλέχθαι	πεπλεγμένος
τεταγμένος εἴην	τέταξο	τετάχθαι	τεταγμένος
πεπλεξοίμην		πεπλέξεσθαι	πεπλεξόμενος
τεταξοίμην		τετάξεσθαι	τεταξόμενος
πλακείην	πλάκηθι	πλακῆναι	πλακείς
ταχθείην	τάχθητι	ταχθῆναι	ταχθείς
πλακησοίμην		πλακήσεσθαι	πλακησόμενος
ταχθησοίμην		ταχθήσεσθαι	ταχθησόμενος

2. πλεκτέος, φευκτέος, τακτέος.

Conjugation.

1.; ὀρύσσω, *I dig*, Stem ὀρυχ, Class 4, *a;* for other guttural Stems Verbal Stems, as τὸ πλέγ-μα, *the wreath* (§ 47); ἡ τάξι-ς, *arrangement;*

PARADIGMS OF VERBS.—VERBS IN Ω. Table VI.

B. CONSONANT STEMS.

ψεύδομαι, *I lie* (Class 1); πείθω, *I persuade* (Class 2);

Tenses.	Indicative.		Subjunctive.
	Active.		
	Present.	Imperfect.	
Present.	πείθω	ἔπειθον	πείθω
	κομίζω	ἐκόμιζον	κομίζω
Future.	πείσω		
	κομιῶ		
1 Aorist (Weak).	ἔπεισα		πείσω
	ἐκόμισα		κομίσω
	Perfect.	Pluperfect.	
2 Perfect (Strong).	πέποιθα	ἐπεποίθειν	πεποίθω
1 Perfect (Weak).	κεκόμικα	ἐκεκομίκειν	κεκομίκω
	Middle and Passive.		
	Present.	Imperfect.	
Present.	ψεύδομαι	ἐψευδόμην	ψεύδωμαι
	πείθομαι	ἐπειθόμην	πείθωμαι
	κομίζομαι	ἐκομιζόμην	κομίζωμαι
Future.	ψεύσομαι		
	πείσομαι		
	κομιοῦμαι		
1 Aorist Middle) (Weak).	ἐψευσάμην		ψεύσωμαι
	ἐπεισάμην		πείσωμαι
	ἐκομισάμην		κομίσωμαι
	Perfect.	Pluperfect.	
Perfect.	ἔψευσμαι	ἐψεύσμην	ἐψευσμένος ὦ
	πέπεισμαι	ἐπεπείσμην	πεπεισμένος ὦ
	κεκόμισμαι	ἐκεκομίσμην	κεκομισμένος ὦ
1 Aorist Passive (Weak).	ἐψεύσθην		ψευσθῶ
	ἐπείσθην		πεισθῶ
	ἐκομίσθην		κομισθῶ
1 Future Passive (Weak).	ψευσθήσομαι		
	πεισθήσομαι		
	κομισθήσομαι		
	Verbal Adjectives: 1. ψευστός, πειστός, κομιστός.		

Examples for

σπένδω, *libo*, Fut. σπείσω, Perf. ἔσπεικα, Perf. Mid. ἔσπεισμαι, Aor. Pass. For verbs of a Dental Stem, with the Present ending in -σσω, see § 250, the *lie;* ἡ πίσ-τι-ς, *the faith;* ἡ σπονδ-ή, *the libation;* ὁ κλύδ-ων, Gen.

Table VI. PARADIGMS OF VERBS:—VERBS IN Ω.

II. DENTAL STEMS.

κομίζω *I carry* (Class 1, *b*). Verbal Stems: ψευδ, πιθ, κομιδ.

Optative.	Imperative.	Infinitive.	Participle.
		Active.	
πείθοιμι	πεῖθε	πείθειν	πείθων
κομίζοιμι	κόμιζε	κομίζειν	κομίζων
πείσοιμι		πείσειν	πείσων
κομιοῖμι		κομιεῖν	κομιῶν
πείσαιμι	πεῖσον	πεῖσαι	πείσας
κομίσαιμι	κόμισον	κομίσαι	κομίσας
πεποίθοιμι	πέποιθε	πεποιθέναι	πεποιθώς
κεκομίκοιμι	κεκόμικε	κεκομικέναι	κεκομικώς

Middle and Passive.

ψευδοίμην	ψεύδου	ψεύδεσθαι	ψευδόμενος
πειθοίμην	πείθου	πείθεσθαι	πειθόμενος
κομιζοίμην	κομίζου	κομίζεσθαι	κομιζόμενος
ψευσοίμην		ψεύσεσθαι	ψευσόμενος
πεισοίμην		πείσεσθαι	πεισόμενος
κομιοίμην		κομιεῖσθαι	κομιούμενος
ψευσαίμην	ψεῦσαι	ψεύσασθαι	ψευσάμενος
πεισαίμην	πεῖσαι	πείσασθαι	πεισάμενος
κομισαίμην	κόμισαι	κομίσασθαι	κομισάμενος
ἐψευσμένος εἴην	ἔψευσο	ἐψεῦσθαι	ἐψευσμένος
πεπεισμένος εἴην	πέπεισο	πεπεῖσθαι	πεπεισμένος
κεκομισμένος εἴην	κεκόμισο	κεκομίσθαι	κεκομισμένος
ψευσθείην	ψεύσθητι	ψευσθῆναι	ψευσθείς
πεισθείην	πείσθητι	πεισθῆναι	πεισθείς
κομισθείην	κομίσθητι	κομισθῆναι	κομισθείς
ψευσθησοίμην		ψευσθήσεσθαι	ψευσθησόμενος
πεισθησοίμην		πεισθήσεσθαι	πεισθησόμενος
κομισθησοίμην		κομισθήσεσθαι	κομισθησόμενος

2. ψευστέος, πειστέος, κομιστέος.

Conjugation.
ἐσπείσθην; κλύζω, *I wash against;* ἁρπάζω, *I snatch;* ἐλπίζω, *I hope.* *Obs.* Nouns are formed from the Pure Verbal Stem, as: τὸ ψεῦδ-ος, κλύδων-ος, *the wave;* ἡ ἁρπαγ-ή, *plunder.*

PARADIGMS OF VERBS. — Table VII.

B. CONSONANT STEMS.

πέμπω, *I send* (Class 1); λείπω, *I leave* (Class 2);

Tenses.	Indicative.		Subjunctive.
	Active.		
	Present.	Imperfect.	
Present.	πέμπω λείπω καλύπτω	ἔπεμπον ἔλειπον ἐκάλυπτον	πέμπω λείπω καλύπτω
Future.	πέμψω λείψω καλύψω		
Aorist 1 (Weak). 2 (Strong). 1 (Weak).	ἔπεμψα ἔλιπον ἐκάλυψα		πέμψω λίπω καλύψω
	Perfect.	Pluperfect.	
2 Perfect (Strong). 2 Perfect (Strong).	πέπομφα λέλοιπα	ἐπεπόμφειν ἐλελοίπειν	πεπόμφω λελοίπω
	Middle and Passive.		
	Present.	Imperfect.	
Present.	πέμπομαι λείπομαι καλύπτομαι	ἐπεμπόμην ἐλειπόμην ἐκαλυπτόμην	πέμπωμαι λείπωμαι καλύπτωμαι
Future.	πέμψομαι λείψομαι καλύψομαι		
Aorist { 1 (Weak). Middle { 2 (Str'ng). { 1 (Weak).	ἐπεμψάμην ἐλιπόμην ἐκαλυψάμην		πέμψωμαι λίπωμαι καλύψωμαι
	Perfect.	Pluperfect.	
Perfect.	πέπεμμαι λέλειμμαι κεκάλυμμαι	ἐπεπέμμην ἐλελείμμην ἐκεκαλύμμην	πεπεμμένος ὦ λελειμμένος ὦ κεκαλυμμένος ὦ
Future Perfect.	λελείψομαι κεκαλύψομαι		
1 Aorist Passive (Weak).	ἐπέμφθην ἐλείφθην ἐκαλύφθην		πεμφθῶ λειφθῶ καλυφθῶ
1 Future Passive (Weak).	πεμφθήσομαι λειφθήσομαι καλυφθήσομαι		
	Verbal Adjectives: 1. πεμπτός, λειπτός, καλυπτός.		

Examples for τρέπω, *I turn* (Class 1); ἀλείφω, *I anoint* (Class 2); τρίβω, *I rub* (§ 249). Nouns are formed from the Pure Verbal Stems, as ὁ πομπ-ό-ς, *ing, manner;* τὸ ἄλειφ-αρ, *the ointment;* ὁ τάφ-ο-ς, *the tomb.*

Table VII. PARADIGMS OF VERBS. 121

III. LABIAL STEMS.

καλύπτω, *I cover* (Class 3). Verbal Stems: πεμπ, λιπ, καλυβ.

Optative.	Imperative.	Infinitive.	Participle.
Active.			
πέμποιμι	πέμπε	πέμπειν	πέμπων
λείποιμι	λεῖπε	λείπειν	λείπων
καλύπτοιμι	κάλυπτε	καλύπτειν	καλύπτων
πέμψοιμι		πέμψειν	πέμψων
λείψοιμι		λείψειν	λείψων
καλύψοιμι		καλύψειν	καλύψων
πέμψαιμι	πέμψον	πέμψαι	πέμψας
λίποιμι	λίπε	λιπεῖν	λιπών
καλύψαιμι	κάλυψον	καλύψαι	καλύψας
πεπόμφοιμι	πέπομφε	πεπομφέναι	πεπομφώς
λελοίποιμι	λέλοιπε	λελοιπέναι	λελοιπώς
Middle and Passive.			
πεμποίμην	πέμπου	πέμπεσθαι	πεμπόμενος
λειποίμην	λείπου	λείπεσθαι	λειπόμενος
καλυπτοίμην	καλύπτου	καλύπτεσθαι	καλυπτόμενος
πεμψοίμην		πέμψεσθαι	πεμψόμενος
λειψοίμην		λείψεσθαι	λειψόμενος
καλυψοίμην		καλύψεσθαι	καλυψόμενος
πεμψαίμην	πέμψαι	πέμψασθαι	πεμψάμενος
λιποίμην	λιποῦ	λιπέσθαι	λιπόμενος
καλυψαίμην	κάλυψαι	καλύψασθαι	καλυψάμενος
πεπεμμένος εἴην	πέπεμψο	πεπέμφθαι	πεπεμμένος
λελειμμένος εἴην	λέλειψο	λελεῖφθαι	λελειμμένος
κεκαλυμμένος εἴην	κεκάλυψο	κεκαλύφθαι	κεκαλυμμένος
λελειψοίμην		λελείψεσθαι	λελειψόμενος
κεκαλυψοίμην		κεκαλύψεσθαι	κεκαλυψόμενος
πεμφθείην	πέμφθητι	πεμφθῆναι	πεμφθείς
λειφθείην	λείφθητι	λειφθῆναι	λειφθείς
καλυφθείην	καλύφθητι	καλυφθῆναι	καλυφθείς
πεμφθησοίμην		πεμφθήσεσθαι	πεμφθησόμενος
λειφθησοίμην		λειφθήσεσθαι	λειφθησόμενος
καλυφθησοίμην		καλυφθήσεσθαι	καλυφθησόμενος

2. πεμπτέος, λειπτέος, καλυπτέος.

Conjugation.

(Class 2), as to its Perf., see § 279; θάπτω, *I bury* (Class 3), Stem ταφ, *the escort;* λοιπ-ό-ς, *remaining;* ἡ καλύβ-η, *the hut;* ὁ τρόπ-ο-ς, *the turn-*

122 PARADIGMS OF VERBS. Table VIII.

B. CONSONANT STEMS.

δέρω, *I skin* (Class 1); ἀγγέλλω, *I announce* (Class 4, c); σπείρω, *I sow* (Class

Tenses.	Indicative.		Subjunctive.
	Present.	Imperfect.	
Active. Present.	δέρω ἀγγέλλω σπείρω μιαίνω	ἔδερον ἤγγελλον ἔσπειρον ἐμίαινον	δέρω ἀγγέλλω σπείρω μιαίνω
Future.	δερῶ ἀγγελῶ σπερῶ μιανῶ		
1 Aorist (Weak).	ἔδειρα ἤγγειλα ἔσπειρα ἐμίᾱνα	-	δείρω ἀγγείλω σπείρω μιάνω
	Perfect.	Pluperfect.	
1 Perfect (Weak).	ἤγγελκα ἔσπαρκα μεμίαγκα	ἠγγέλκειν ἐσπάρκειν ἐμεμιάγκειν	ἠγγέλκω ἐσπάρκω μεμιάγκω
	Present.	Imperfect.	
Mid. and Passive. Present.	δέρομαι ἀγγέλλομαι σπείρομαι μιαίνομαι	ἐδερόμην ἠγγελλόμην ἐσπειρόμην ἐμιαινόμην	δέρωμαι ἀγγέλλωμαι σπείρωμαι μιαίνωμαι
Future.	δεροῦμαι ἀγγελοῦμαι σπεροῦμαι μιανοῦμαι		
1 Aorist Middle (Weak).	ἐδειράμην ἠγγειλάμην ἐσπειράμην ἐμιανάμην		δείρωμαι ἀγγείλωμαι σπείρωμαι μιάνωμαι
	Perfect.	Pluperfect.	
Perfect.	δέδαρμαι ἤγγελμαι ἔσπαρμαι μεμίασμαι	ἐδεδάρμην ἠγγέλμην ἐσπάρμην ἐμεμιάσμην	δεδαρμένος ὦ ἠγγελμένος ὦ ἐσπαρμένος ὦ μεμιασμένος ὦ
Aorist Passive {2 Strong. 1 Weak. 2 Strong. 1 Weak.	ἐδάρην ἠγγέλθην ἐσπάρην ἐμιάνθην		δαρῶ ἀγγελθῶ σπαρῶ μιανθῶ
Future Passive {2 Strong. 1 Weak. 2 Strong. 1 Weak.	δαρήσομαι ἀγγελθήσομαι σπαρήσομαι μιανθήσομαι		

Verbal Adjectives: 1. δαρτός, ἀγγελτός, σπαρτός, μιαντός.

Table VIII. PARADIGMS OF VERBS. 123

IV. LIQUID STEMS (λ, μ, ν, ρ).

4, d); μιαίνω, I soil (Class 4, d). Verbal Stems: δερ, αγ.γελ, σπερ, μιαν.

Optative.	Imperative.	Infinitive.	Participle.
δέροιμι	δέρε	δέρειν	δέρων
ἀγγέλλοιμι	ἄγγελλε	ἀγγέλλειν	ἀγγέλλων
σπείροιμι	σπεῖρε	σπείρειν	σπείρων
μιαίνοιμι	μίαινε	μιαίνειν	μιαίνων
δεροῖμι		δερεῖν	δερῶν
ἀγγελοῖμι		ἀγγελεῖν	ἀγγελῶν
σπεροῖμι		σπερεῖν	σπερῶν
μιανοῖμι		μιανεῖν	μιανῶν
δείραιμι	δεῖρον	δεῖραι	δείρας
ἀγγείλαιμι	ἄγγειλον	ἀγγεῖλαι	ἀγγείλας
σπείραιμι	σπεῖρον	σπεῖραι	σπείρας
μιάναιμι	μίανον	μιᾶναι	μιάνας
ἠγγέλκοιμι	ἤγγελκε	ἠγγελκέναι	ἠγγελκώς
ἐσπάρκοιμι	ἔσπαρκε	ἐσπαρκέναι	ἐσπαρκώς
μεμιάγκοιμι	μεμίαγκε	μεμιαγκέναι	μεμιαγκώς
δεροίμην	δέρου	δέρεσθαι	δερόμενος
ἀγγελλοίμην	ἀγγέλλου	ἀγγέλλεσθαι	ἀγγελλόμενος
σπειροίμην	σπείρου	σπείρεσθαι	σπειρόμενος
μιαινοίμην	μιαίνου	μιαίνεσθαι	μιαινόμενος
δεροίμην		δερεῖσθαι	δερούμενος
ἀγγελοίμην		ἀγγελεῖσθαι	ἀγγελούμενος
σπεροίμην		σπερεῖσθαι	σπερούμενος
μιανοίμην		μιανεῖσθαι	μιανούμενος
δειραίμην	δεῖραι	δείρασθαι	δειράμενος
ἀγγειλαίμην	ἄγγειλαι	ἀγγείλασθαι	ἀγγειλάμενος
σπειραίμην	σπεῖραι	σπείρασθαι	σπειράμενος
μιαναίμην	μίαναι	μιάνασθαι	μιανάμενος
δεδαρμένος εἴην	δέδαρσο	δεδάρθαι	δεδαρμένος
ἠγγελμένος εἴην	ἤγγελσο	ἠγγέλθαι	ἠγγελμένος
ἐσπαρμένος εἴην	ἔσπαρσο	ἐσπάρθαι	ἐσπαρμένος
μεμιασμένος εἴην	μεμίασο	μεμιάνθαι	μεμιασμένος
δαρείην	δάρηθι	δαρῆναι	δαρείς
ἀγγελθείην	ἀγγέλθητι	ἀγγελθῆναι	ἀγγελθείς
σπαρείην	σπάρηθι	σπαρῆναι	σπαρείς
μιανθείην	μιάνθητι	μιανθῆναι	μιανθείς
δαρησοίμην		δαρήσεσθαι	δαρησόμενος
ἀγγελθησοίμην		ἀγγελθήσεσθαι	ἀγγελθησόμενος
σπαρησοίμην		σπαρήσεσθαι	σπαρησόμενος
μιανθησοίμην		μιανθήσεσθαι	μιανθησόμενος

2. δαρτέος, ἀγγελτέος, σπαρτέος, μιαντέος.

124   PARADIGMS OF VERBS.—VERBS IN μι.   Table IX.

VERBS IN μι.

			τί-θη-μι, *I put.*	δί-δω-μι, *I give.*	ἵ-στη-μι, *I place.*
			Pure Stems θ ε	δ ο	σ τ α
			Present Stems τι - θ ε	δ ι - δ ο	ἱ - σ τ α
			Present. Active.		
Indicative.	S.	1	τί-θη-μι	δί-δω-μι	ἵ-στη-μι
		2	τί-θη-ς	δί-δω-ς	ἵ-στη-ς
		3	τί-θη-σι(ν)	δί-δω-σι(ν)	ἵ-στη-σι(ν)
	D.	1			
		2	τί-θε-τον	δί-δο-τον	ἵ-στᾰ-τον
		3	τί-θε-τον	δί-δο-τον	ἵ-στᾰ-τόν
	P.	1	τί-θε-μεν	δί-δο-μεν	ἵ-στᾰ-μεν
		2	τί-θε-τε	δί-δο-τε	ἵ-στᾰ-τε
		3	τι-θέ-ᾱ-σι(ν)	δι-δό-ᾱ-σι(ν)	ἱ-στᾰ-σι(ν)
Subjunctive.	S.	1	τι-θῶ	δι-δῶ	ἱ-στῶ
		2	τι-θῇ-ς	δι-δῷ-ς	ἱ-στῇ-ς
		3	τι-θῇ	δι-δῷ	ἱ-στῇ
	D.	1			
		2	τι-θῆ-τον	δι-δῶ-τον	ἱ-στῆ-τον
		3	τι-θῆ-τον	δι-δῶ-τον	ἱ-στῆ-τον
	P.	1	τι-θῶ-μεν	δι-δῶ-μεν	ἱ-στῶ-μεν
		2	τι-θῆ-τε	δι-δῶ-τε	ἱ-στῆ-τε
		3	τι-Ͽῶ-σι(ν)	δι-δῶ-σι(ν)	ἱ-στῶ-σι(ν)
Optative.	S.	1	τι-θείη-ν	δι-δοίη-ν	ἱ-σταίη-ν
		2	τι-θείη-ς	δι-δοίη-ς	ἱ-σταίη-ς
		3	τι-θείη	δι-δοίη	ἱ-σταίη
	D.	1			
		2	τι-θείη-τον or τιθεῖτον	δι-δοίη-τον or διδοῖτον	ἱ-σταίη-τον or ἱσταῖτον
		3	τι-θειή-την or τιθείτην	δι-δοιή-την or διδοίτην	ἱ-σταιή-την or ἱσταίτην
	P.	1	τι-θείη-μεν or τιθεῖμεν	δι-δοίη-μεν or διδοῖμεν	ἱ-σταίη-μεν or ἱσταῖμεν
		2	τι-θείη-τε or τιθεῖτε	δι-δοίη-τε or διδοῖτε	ἱ-σταίη-τε or ἱσταῖτε
		3	τι-θείη-σαν or τιθεῖεν	δι-δοίη-σαν or διδοῖεν	ἱ-σταίη-σαν or ἱσταῖεν
Imperative.	S.	2	τί-θει	δί-δου	ἵ-στη
		3	τι-θέ-τω	δι-δό-τω	ἱ-στᾰ-τω
	D.	2	τί-θε-τον	δί-δο-τον	ἵ-στᾰ-τόν
		3	τι-θέ-των	δι-δό-των	ἱ-στά-των
	P.	2	τί-θε-τε	δί-δο-τε	ἵ-στα-τε
		3	τι-θέ-ντων or τι-θέ-τωσαν	δι-δό-ντων or δι-δό-τωσαν	ἱ-στά-ντων or ἱ-στά-τωσαν
Infin.			τι-θέ-ναι	δι-δό-ναι	ἱ-στά-ναι
Part.			τι-θεί-ς, τι-θεῖ-σα, τιθέν G. τιθέντ-ος	δι-δού-ς, δι-δοῦ-σα, διδόν G. δι-δόντ-ος	ἱ-στά-ς, ἱ-στᾱ-σα, ἱστάν G. ἱ-στάντ-ος

Table IX. PARADIGMS OF VERBS.—VERBS IN μι. 125

FIRST CLASS.

This First Class consists of Verbs which affix their terminations directly to the Stem.

Present.	Middle and Passive.	
τί-θε-μαι	δί-δο-μαι	ἵ-στᾰ-μαι
τί-θε-σαι	δί-δο-σαι	ἵ-στᾰ-σαι
τί-θε-ται	δί-δο-ται	ἵ-στᾰ-ται
τι-θέ-μεθον	δι-δό-μεθον	ἱ-στά-μεθον
τί-θε-σθον	δί-δο-σθον	ἵ-στα-σθον
τί-θε-σθον	δί-δο-σθον	ἵ-στα-σθον
τι-θέ-μεθα	δι-δό-μεθα	ἱ-στά-μεθα
τί-θε-σθε	δί-δο-σθε	ἵ-στα-σθε
τί-θε-νται	δί-δο-νται	ἵ-στα-νται
τι-θῶ-μαι	δι-δῶ-μαι	ἱ-στῶ-μαι
τι-θῇ	δι-δῷ	ἱ-στῇ
τι-θῆ-ται	δι-δῶ-ται	ἱ-στῆ-ται
τι-θώ-μεθον	δι-δώ-μεθον	ἱ-στώ-μεθον
τι-θῆ-σθον	δι-δῶ-σθον	ἱ-στῆ-σθον
τι-θῆ-σθον	δι-δῶ-σθον	ἱ-στῆ-σθον,
τι-θώ-μεθα	δι-δώ-μεθα	ἱ-στώ-μεθα
τι-θῆ-σθε	δι-δῶ-σθε	ἱ-στῆ-σθε
τι-θῶ-νται	δι-δῶ-νται	ἱ-στῶ-νται
τι-θεί-μην	δι-δοί-μην	ἱ-σταί-μην
τι-θεῖ-ο	δι-δοῖ-ο	ἱ-σταῖ-ο
τι-θεῖ-το	δι-δοῖ-το	ἱ-σταῖ-το
τι-θεί-μεθον	δι-δοί-μεθον	ἱ-σταί-μεθον
τι-θεῖ-σθον	δι-δοῖ-σθον	ἱ-σταῖ-σθον
τι-θεί-σθην	δι-δοί-σθην	ἱ-σταί-σθην
τι-θεί-μεθα	δι-δοί-μεθα	ἱ-σταί-μεθα
τι-θεῖ-σθε	δι-δοῖ-σθε	ἱ-σταῖ-σθε
τι-θεῖ-ντο	δι-δοῖ-ντο	ἱ-σταῖ-ντο
τί-θε-σο	δί-δο-σο	ἵ-στᾰ-σο
τι-θέ-σθω	δι-δό-σθω	ἱ-στά-σθω
τί-θε-σθον	δί-δο-σθον	ἵ-στα-σθον
τι-θέ-σθων	δι-δό-σθων	ἱ-στά-σθων
τί-θε-σθε	δί-δο-σθε	ἵ-στα-σθε
τι-θέ-σθων or	δι-δό-σθων or	ἱ-στά-σθων or
τι-θέ-σθωσαν	δι-δό-σθωσαν	ἱ-στά-σθωσαν
τί-θε-σθαι	δί-δο-σθαι	ἵ-στα-σθαι
τι-θέ-μενο-ς, η, ο-ν	δι-δό-μενο-ς, η, ο-ν	ἱ-στᾰ-μενο-ς, η, ο-ν

126 PARADIGMS OF VERBS.—VERBS IN μι. Table IX.—

VERBS IN μι.

		τί-θη-μι, *I put.*	δί-δω-μι, *I give.*	ἵ-στη-μι, *I place.*
		Pure Stems θ ε Present Stems τι-θε	δο δι-δο	στα ι-στη
Imperfect.	S. 1	ἐ-τί-θη-ν	ἐ-δί-δω-ν	ἵ-στη-ν
	2	ἐ-τί-θη-ς	ἐ-δί-δω-ς	ἵ-στη-ς
	3	ἐ-τί-θη	ἐ-δί-δω	ἵ-στη
	D. 1			
	2	ἐ-τί-θε-τον	ἐ-δί-δο-τον	ἵ-στᾰ-τον
	3	ἐ-τι-θέ-την	ἐ-δι-δό-την	ἱ-στά-την
	P. 1	ἐ-τί-θε-μεν	ἐ-δί-δο-μεν	ἵ-στᾰ-μεν
	2	ἐ-τί-θε-τε	ἐ-δί-δο-τε	ἵ-στᾰ-τε
	3	ἐ-τί-θε-σαν	ἐ-δί-δο-σαν	ἵ-στᾰ-σαν
		Second or Strong Aorist. Active.		
Indicative.	S. 1	[ἔ-θη-ν]	[ἔ-δω-ν]	ἔ-στη-ν
	2	[ἔ-θη-ς]	[ἔ-δω-ς]	ἔ-στη-ς
	3	[ἔ-θη]	[ἔ-δω]	ἔ-στη
	D. 1			
	2	ἔ-θε-τον	ἔ-δο-τον	ἔ-στη-τον
	3	ἐ-θέ-την	ἐ-δό-την	ἐ-στή-την
	P. 1	ἔ-θε-μεν	ἔ-δο-μεν	ἔ-στη-μεν
	2	ἔ-θε-τε	ἔ-δο-τε	ἔ-στη-τε
	3	ἔ-θε-σαν	ἔ-δο-σαν	ἔ-στη-σαν
Subj.		θῶ θῇ-ς	δῶ δῷ-ς	στῶ στῇ-ς etc., as in the
Opt.		θείη-ν	δοίη-ν	σταίη-ν etc., as in the
Imperative.	S. 2	θέ-ς	δό-ς	στῆ-θι
	3	θέ-τω	δό-τω	στή-τω
	D. 2	θέ-τον	δό-τον	στῆ-τον
	3	θέ-των	δό-των	στή-των
	P. 2	θέ-τε	δό-τε	στῆ-τε
	3	θέ-ντων or θέ-τωσαν	δό-ντων or δό-τωσαν	στά-ντων or στή-τωσαν
Infin.		θεῖ-ναι	δοῦ-ναι	στῆ-ναι
Part.		θεί-ς, θεῖ-σα, θέ-ν G. θέντ-ος	δού-ς, δοῦ-σα, δό-ν G. δόντ-ος	στά-ς, στᾰ-σα, στάν G. στάντ-ος

The following Tenses are formed

Active.

Future.	θήσω	δώσω	στήσω
First or Weak Aorist.	ἔθηκα	ἔδωκα	ἔστησα
Perfect.	τέθεικα	δέδωκα	ἔστηκα
Pluperfect.	ἐτεθείκειν	ἐδεδώκειν	ἐστήκειν or εἱστήκειν
Verbals.			

Continued. PARADIGMS OF VERBS.—VERBS IN μι.

FIRST CLASS.

This First Class consists of Verbs which affix their terminations directly to the Stem.

ἐ-τι-θέ-μην	ἐ-δι-δό-μην	ἰ-στά-μην
ἐ-τί-θε-σο	ἐ-δί-δο-σο	ἵ-στα-σο
ἐ-τί-θε-το	ἐ-δί-δο-το	ἵ-στα-το
ἐ-τι-θέ-μεθον	ἐ-δι-δό-μεθον	ἰ-στά-μεθον
ἐ-τί-θε-σθον	ἐ-δί-δο-σθον	ἵ-στα-σθον
ἐ-τι-θέ-σθην	ἐ-δι-δό-σθην	ἰ-στά-σθην
ἐ-τι-θέ-μεθα	ἐ-δι-δό-μεθα	ἰ-στά-μεθα
ἐ-τί-θε-σθε	ἐ-δί-δο-σθε	ἵ-στα-σθε
ἐ-τί-θε-ντο	ἐ-δί-δο-ντο	ἵ-στα-ντο

Second or Strong Aorist. Middle and Passive.

ἐ-θέ-μην	ἐ-δό-μην	Wanting.
ἔ-θου	ἔ-δου	
ἔ-θε-το	ἔ-δο-το	
ἐ-θέ-μεθον	ἐ-δό-μεθον	
ἔ-θε-σθον	ἔ-δο-σθον	
ἐ-θέ-σθην	ἐ-δό-σθην	
ἐ-θέ-μεθα	ἐ-δό-μεθα	
ἔ-θε-σθε	ἔ-δο-σθε	
ἔ-θε-ντο	ἔ-δο-ντο	

θῶ-μαι	δῶ-μαι	Wanting.
θῇ	δῷ	
Pres. Subjunctive.		
θεί-μην	δοί-μην	Wanting.
Pres. Optative.		
θοῦ	δοῦ	Wanting.
θέ-σθω	δό-σθω	
θέ-σθον	δό-σθον	
θέ-σθων	δό-σθων	
θέ-σθε	δό-σθε	
θέ-σθων or θέ-σθωσαν	δό-σθων or δό-σθωσαν	

θέ-σθαι	δό-σθαι	Wanting.
θέ-μενο-ς, η, ο-ν	δό-μενο-ς, η, ο-ν	Wanting.

on the analogy of Verbs in Ω.

Middle and Passive.

θήσομαι	δώσομαι	στήσομαι
PASSIVE. τεθήσομαι	δοθήσομαι	σταθήσομαι
MIDDLE. Wanting	Wanting	ἐστησάμην
PASSIVE. ἐτέθην	ἐδόθην	ἐστάθην
τέθειμαι	δέδομαι	ἔσταμαι
ἐτεθείμην	ἐδεδόμην	ἐστάμην
θετός	δοτός	στατός
θετέος	δοτέος	στατέος

128 PARADIGMS OF VERBS.—VERBS IN μι. Table X.

VERBS IN μι. SECOND CLASS.

This Second Class consists of Verbs which form the Present-Stem by adding νυ to the Pure Stem.

δείκνυμι, *I show.* Pure Stem δεικ. Present Stem δεικ-νυ.

		Present Active.	Middle and Passive.
Indicative.	S. 1	δείκ-νῡ-μι	δείκ-νῠ-μαι
	2	δείκ-νῡ-ς	δείκ-νῠ-σαι
	3	δείκ-νῡ-σι(ν)	δείκ-νῠ-ται
	D. 1		δείκ-νῠ-μεθον
	2	δείκ-νῠ-τον	δείκ-νυ-σθον
	3	δείκ-νῠ-τον	δείκ-νυ-σθον
	Pl. 1	δείκ-νῠ-μεν	δείκ-νῠ-μεθα
	2	δείκ-νῠ-τε	δείκ-νυ-σθε
	3	δεικ-νύ-ᾱσι(ν)	δείκ-νυ-νται
Subjunctive.		δεικνύω, ῃς, ῃ, etc.	δεικνύωμαι, ῃ, ῃται, etc.
Optative.		δεικνύοιμι, οις, οι, etc.	δεικνυοίμην, οιο, οιτο, etc.
Imperative.	S. 2	δείκ-νῡ	δείκ-νῠ-σο
	3	δεικ-νῠ-τω	δεικ-νύ-σθω
	D. 2	δείκ-νῠ-τον	δείκ-νυ-σθον
	3	δείκ-νῠ-των	δεικ-νύ-σθων
	Pl. 2	δείκ-νῠ-τε	δείκ-νυ-σθε
	3	δεικ-νύ-ντων or	δεικ-νύ-σθων or
		δεικ-νῠ-τωσαν	δεικ-νύ-σθωσαν
Infinitive.		δεικ-νῠ-ναι	δείκ-νυ-σθαι
Participle.		δεικ-νύς, δεικ-νῦσα, δεικ-νύν Stem δεικ-νυ-ντ	δεικ-νῠ-μενος, η, ον
Imperfect Indicative.	S. 1	ἐ-δείκ-νῡ-ν	ἐ-δεικ-νύ-μην
	2	ἐ-δείκ-νῡ-ς	ἐ-δείκ-νῠ-σο
	3	ἐ-δείκ-νῡ	ἐ-δείκ-νῠ-το
	D. 1		ἐ-δεικ-νῠ-μεθον
	2	ἐ-δείκ-νυ-τον	ἐ-δείκ-νυ-σθον
	3	ἐ-δεικ-νῠ-την	ἐ-δεικ-νύ-σθην
	Pl. 1	ἐ-δείκ-νῠ-μεν	ἐ-δεικ-νῠ-μεθα
	2	ἐ-δείκ-νυ-τε	ἐ-δείκ-νυ-σθε
	3	ἐ-δείκ-νυ-σαν	ἐ-δείκ-νυ-ντο
Future.		δείξω	δείξομαι PASSIVE. δειχθήσομαι
First or Weak Aorist.		ἔδειξα	MIDDLE. ἐδειξάμην PASSIVE. ἐδείχθην
Perfect.		δέδειχα	δέδειγμαι
Pluperfect.		ἐδεδείχειν	ἐδεδείγμην

Chap. X.—First Principal Conjugation,
or Verbs in ω.

I. The Present-Stem.

A. *Inflexion of the Present-Stem.*

§ 231. The Present-Stem is the form which remains after rejecting ω in the 1 Sing. Pres. Act.
On the distinction of the Present-Stem from the Verbal-Stem, see § 245, etc.

The following Table exhibits the way in which the Personal Endings are affixed to the Present-Stem by means of the connecting vowels.

§ 232.		Active.		Middle and Passive.
Present Indicative.	1 Sing.	λύ-ω	[solv-o]	λύ-ο-μαι
	2 "	λύ-ει-ς	[solv-i-s]	λύ-ῃ or λύ-ει
	3 "	λύ-ει	[solv-i-t]	λύ-ε-ται
	1 Dual			λυ-ό-μεθον
	2 "	λύ-ε-τον		λύ-ε-σθον
	3 "	λύ-ε-τον		λύ-ε-σθον
	1 Plur.	λύ-ο-μεν	[solv-i-mus]	λυ-ό-μεθα
	2 "	λύ-ε-τε	[solv-i-tis]	λύ-ε-σθε
	3 "	λύ-ου-σι(ν)	[solv-u-nt]	λύ-ο-νται
Present Subjunctive.	1 Sing.	λύ-ω	[solv-a-m]	λύ-ω-μαι
	2 "	λύ-ῃ-ς	[solv-a-s]	λύ-ῃ
	3 "	λύ-ῃ	[solv-a-t]	λύ-η-ται
	1 Dual			λυ-ώ-μεθον
	2 "	λύ-η-τον		λύ-η-σθον
	3 "	λύ-η-τον		λύ-η-σθον
	1 Plur.	λύ-ω-μεν	[solv-a-mus]	λυ-ώ-μεθα
	2 "	λύ-η-τε	[solv-a-tis]	λύ-η-σθε
	3 "	λύ-ω-σι(ν)	[solv-a-nt]	λύ-ω-νται

130   I. THE PRESENT-STEM.   § 232.

		Active.	Middle and Passive.
Present Optative.	1 Sing.	λύ-οι-μι	λυ-οί-μην
	2 "	λύ-οι-ς	λύ-οι-ο
	3 "	λύ-οι	λύ-οι-το
	1 Dual		λυ-οί-μεθον
	2 "	λύ-οι-τον	λύ-οι-σθον
	3 "	λυ-οί-την	λυ-οί-σθην
	1 Plur.	λύ-οι-μεν	λυ-οί-μεθα
	2 "	λύ-οι-τε	λύ-οι-σθε
	3 "	λύ-οι-εν	λύ-οι-ντο
Present Imperative.	2 Sing.	λῦ-ε [solv-e]	λύ-ου
	3 "	λυ-έ-τω [solv-i-to]	λυ-έ-σθω
	2 Dual	λύ-ε-τον	λύ-ε-σθον
	3 "	λυ-έ-των	λυ-έ-σθων
	2 Plur.	λύ-ε-τε [solv-i-te]	λύ-ε-σθε
	3 "	λυ-ό-ντων [solv-u-nto] or λυ-έ-τωσαν	λυ-έ-σθων or λυ-έ-σθωσαν
Present Infinitive.		λύ-ειν	λύ-ε-σθαι
Present Participle.		Stem λυ-ο-ντ [solv-e-nt] λύ-ων λύ-ουσα λῦ-ον Gen. λύ-ο-ντ-ος [solv-e-nt-is]	λυ-ό-μενο-ς λυ-ο-μένη λυ-ό-μενο-ν
Imperfect.	1 Sing.	ἔ-λυ-ο-ν	ἐ-λυ-ό-μην
	2 "	ἔ-λυ-ε-ς	ἐ-λύ-ου
	3 "	ἔ-λυ-ε(ν)	ἐ-λύ-ε-το
	1 Dual		ἐ-λυ-ό-μεθον
	2 "	ἐ-λύ-ε-τον	ἐ-λύ-ε-σθον
	3 "	ἐ-λυ-έ-την	ἐ-λυ-έ-σθην
	1 Plur.	ἐ-λύ-ο-μεν	ἐ-λυ-ό-μεθα
	2 "	ἐ-λύ-ε-τε	ἐ-λύ-ε-σθε
	3 "	ἔ-λυ-ο-ν	ἐ-λύ-ο-ντο

§ 233. PERSONAL ENDINGS. 131

§ 233. *Obs.*—1. The E-sound (ε, η, ε ι) is used as a connecting vowel except before nasals, where the O-sound (ο, ω, ο υ) is used.

2. In 1 Sing. Ind. Act. ω is the connecting vowel lengthened, the ending μι being dropped. In the 2 Sing. ε ι ς is for ε σ ι. In the 3 Sing. ε ι for ε τ ι: λύ-ει-ς for λυ-ε-σι, λύ-ει for λυ-ε-τι [compare *solv-i-t*]. The ου of the 3 Plur. has arisen out of ο by compensative lengthening (§ 42): λύ-ου-σι, from λυ-ο-νσι, for the original and Doric λύ-ο-ντι [compare *solv-u-nt*]. In the 3 Sing. Imperf. ε (ν) stands for original ε-τ—compare *solveba-t*—as τ at the end could not maintain its ground (§ 67).

3. In the 2 Sing. Indic. Pres. Mid. ῃ or ε ι arose from ε (σ) α ι (§§ 61, 38): λύῃ, from λυε(σ)αι; the ending ει is the Old Attic one exclusively used in οἴει, *thou thinkest;* βούλει, *thou wishest;* ῃ is the one later in general use. Compare the Fut. ὄψει (§ 259).

4. The Subjunctive has always ω, η, ῃ, for ο (ου), ε, ε ι; the ῃ of the 2 Sing. Mid. is contracted from η (σ) α ι (compare § 228).

5. In the 2 Sing. Imperat. Act. the termination after the connecting vowel is quite lost. ο υ in the 2 Sing. Imperat. and Imperf. Mid. has arisen from ε (σ) ο, ε ο : λύου = λυε(σ)ο, ἐλύου = ἐλυε(σ)ο (§§ 61, 37); ο ι ο in the 2 Sing. Opt. Mid. arose from ο ι (σ) ο.

---

§ 233. **Dialects.**—1. The Epic dialect sometimes has the original ending μ ι of the 1 Sing. in the *subjunctive:* ἐθέλω-μι, *velim;* the 2 Sing. Subj. and Opt. often has the fuller ending σ θ α (for ς): ἐθέλῃ-σθα = ἐθέλῃς, κλαίοι-σθα = κλαίοις (κλαίω, *I weep*); the 3 Sing. Subj. has the old ending σ ι (ν), from τ ι : ἐθέλη-σι(ν) = ἐθέλῃ.

2. The long vowels of the subjunctive are often shortened in Homer: ἰθύνετε for ἰθύνητε (ἰθύνω, *I put straight*) (compare § 228, D.).

3. The Epic dialect often has μ ε ν α ι or μ ε ν in the Inf. Act. connected with the Stem by an accented ε : ἀμῦν-έ-μεναι or ἀμῦν-έ-μεν = ἀμύνειν, *to defend.*

4. The 2 Sing. Mid. often remains uncontracted in the Ion. dialect: λιλαίεαι, *thou wishest;* Subj. ἔχηαι (*habearis*), also shortened, μίσγεαι (*miscearis*); Imperat. ἕπεο, *follow;* Imperf. ἰδεύεο, *thou wast in want of.* ε ο is also contracted to ε υ (§ 37, D.) : ἕπευ.

5. The 1 Dual and 1 Plur. Mid. in poetry often has σ θ for θ : βουλόμεσθον, -μεσθα, *we wish.*

6. α τ ο (§ 226, D.) occurs in the Ion. dialect regularly for ντο in 3 Plur. Opt. : μαχοίατο (= μάχοιντο), *they may fight*. In New-Ion. αται, αται, are also sometimes found in other forms where ε is the connecting vowel instead of ο : κηδ-έ-αται = κήδ-ο-νται, *they care :* ἐβουλ-έ-ατο = ἐβούλοντο.

B. *The Augment.*

§ 234. The Augment (*Augmentum, increase*) is the sign of the *past* in the Indicative of all the historical tenses (§ 225, 3. B.). It has two forms; that is, it appears either—

a) As a *Syllabic* Augment, in the syllable ε prefixed, or

b) As a *Temporal* Augment, in the lengthening of the initial vowel.

All verbs beginning with a *consonant* have the *Syllabic* Augment: ἔ-λυ-ο-ν, ἐ-τυπτ-ό-μην, *I was struck*. ρ is doubled after ε: ἔρριπτον, from ῥίπτω, *I hurl*.

Obs.—The Syllabic Augment appears in the stronger form of η instead of ε in ἤ-μελλ-ο-ν, *I was about to*, from μέλλω; ἠ-βουλ-ό-μην, *I wished*, from βούλομαι; ἠ-δυνά-μην, *I could*, from δύναμαι.

§ 235. The *Temporal* Augment is used in all verbs which begin with a *vowel*, whether aspirated or not. The Temporal Augment changes

α	to η:	ἄγω, *I lead*.	Imperfect	ἦγ-ο-ν
ε	" η:	ἐλαύνω, *I drive*.	"	ἤλαυν-ο-ν
ο	" ω:	ὀνειδίζω, *I reproach*.	"	ὠνείδιζ-ο-ν
ῐ	" ῑ:	ἱκετεύω, *I beseech*.	"	ἱκέτευ-ο-ν

---

7. Homer, quite peculiarly, has in the 3 Dual Imperf. τον, σθον, for την, σθην: ἐτεύχετον, *the two made;* and Attic writers have την for the 2 Dual of an historic sense: εἰχέτην, *ye two had;* εὑρέτην, *ye two found*.

§ 234. Dialects.—In Homer, and also in other poets, the *Augment* may be entirely *omitted*: τεῦχε, *he made;* ἔχεν, *he had*. λ, μ, ν, σ are also sometimes doubled after the Syllabic Augment: ἐλλίσσετο (from λίσσομαι, *I beseech*); δ only in the Stem δι: ἔδδεισα (*I feared*, § 317, 5). On the contrary, ρ is sometimes left single: ἐράπτομεν (ῥάπτω, *I sew, spin*).

§ 235. Dialects.—By the Temporal Augment ᾰ becomes ᾱ in Doric: ᾶγον. The Temporal Augment is very often wanting in Herodotus, especially in the case of diphthongs.

§ 233. THE AUGMENT. 133

ŭ to ū :	'ὑβρίζω, I insult.	Imperfect	'ὑβρίζ-ο-ν
αι "	ῃ : αἰσθάνομαι, I perceive.	"	ᾐσθαν-ό-μην
αυ "	ηυ : αὐξάνω, I increase.	"	ηὔξαν-ο-ν
οι "	ῳ : οἰκτείρω, I pity.	"	ᾤκτειρ-ο-ν

Before vowels, ă becomes ā, not η : 'ἀίω, I hear, 'ἀιον.
The long vowels η, ω, ῑ, ῡ, and usually the diphthongs
ε ι, ε υ, ο υ, remain *without Augment*.

εἰκάζω, I conjecture, εἴκαζ-ο-ν (also ᾔκαζον);
εὑρίσκω, I find,   εὕρισκ-ο-ν (seldom Aorist ηὗρον);

also α υ and ο ι immediately before a vowel : αὑαίνω, I dry,
αὕαινον ; οἰακίζω, I steer, οἰάκιζον ; and other diphthongs
in isolated instances.

Obs. — The rough breathing precedes the augmented
form when the verb in its unaugmented form had it.

§ 236. ε becomes ε ι (instead of η) in some verbs, viz., in
ἐάω, I leave ; ἐθίζω, I accustom ; ἑλίσσω, I roll ; ἕλκω or
ἑλκύω, I draw ; ἕπομαι, I follow ; ἐργάζομαι, I work ; ἕρπω
or ἑρπύζω, I creep ; ἑστιάω, I entertain hospitably ; ἔχω, I
have. Compare below the Aorists : εἵμην (§ 313), εἷλον (αἱρέω, I take, § 327, 1), εἷσα, I placed (§ 269, D., and § 275).

Obs.—These verbs originally began with a consonant, and therefore
had the Syllabic Augment : Ϝεργαζ-ο-μαι (§ 34, D.), ἐ-Ϝεργαζ-ο-μην ;
σεχ-ω (§ 327, 6), ἐ-σεχ-ο-ν. Then the consonant was dropped :
ἐ-εργαζ-ο-μην, ἐ-εχ-ο-ν ; finally εε was regularly contracted to ει
(§ 36) : εἰργαζ-ό-μην, εἰχ-ο-ν.

§ 237. ἑορτάζω, I celebrate, has the Augment in the second vowel :
ἑώρταζον for ἡόρταζον (compare § 37, D. 2). Verbs which originally began with a digamma (§ 34, D.), consequently with a consonant, have the Syllabic Augment in spite of their initial vowel :
ἀνδάνω, I please, ἐ-άνδανον ; οὐρέω, I make water ; ὠθέω, I push ;
ὠνέομαι, I buy (§ 275). Both Augments, Syllabic and Temporal,
are combined in ὁράω, I see, ἑώραον (ἑώρων) ; ἀν-οίγ-ω, I open,
ἀν-έῳγ-ο-ν.

§ 238. *Verbs compounded with a preposition have the*

§ 237. **Dialects.**—Homer forms ἐῳνοχόει from οἰνοχοέω, I pour out
wine ; ἐήνδανον (Herod. ἑάνδανον) and ἥνδανον from ἁνδάνω, I please.
Compare § 34, D., 1 and 4.

Augment immediately *after* the preposition: εἰς-φέρ-ω, *I carry in*, εἰς-έ-φερ-ο-ν; προς-άγ-ω, *I lead to*, προς-ῆγ-ο-ν; ἐκ, *out of*, becomes ἐξ before the Augment: ἐξ-ῆγ-ο-ν, *I led out*. The true forms of ἐν, *in*, and σύν, *with*, altered by assimilation (§ 51) in the Present, appear again before ε: συλ-λέγ-ω, *I collect*, συν-έ-λεγ-ο-ν; ἐμ-βάλλ-ω, *I invade*, ἐν-έ-βαλλ-ο-ν.

The final vowel of a preposition is elided: ἀπ-έ-φερ-ο-ν, *I carried away*, from ἀπο-φέρ-ω; only περί and πρό never lose their final vowel; but πρό is often contracted with ε: πρού-βαινον, from προ-έ-βαιν-ο-ν, *I marched on.*

§ 239. EXCEPTIONS.—Some verbs, which are not merely compounded with prepositions, but derived from already compound nouns (Decomposita), have the Augment at the *beginning*: ἐναντιόομαι (from ἐναντίος, *against*), ἠναντιούμην (from οομην), *I was against;* poet. ἤναρον, from ἐναίρω, *I slay;* παρρησιάζομαι (from παρρησία, *freedom of speech*), ἐπαρρησιαζόμην, *I spoke freely;* but the majority nevertheless have it in the *middle*: ἐκκλησιάζω, *I assemble*, from ἐκκλησία, *assembly*, ἐξεκλησίαζον; ὑποπτεύω, *I suspect*, from ὕποπτος, *suspicious*, ὑπώπτευον; κατηγορέω, *I accuse*, κατηγόρουν (from εον). παρανομέω, *I act contrary to law* (from παρά-νομος, *contrary to law*), has irregularly παρηνόμουν (εον).

§ 240. Many prepositions have in some compounds so far lost their distinctive meanings that the verbs are treated as simple: καθεύδω, *I sleep*, ἐκάθευδον, yet καθηῦδον also; καθίζω, *I sit*, ἐκάθιζον. Compare the verbs ἵημι (ἀφίημι, § 313), ἔννυμι (ἀμφιέννυμι, § 319, 5), ἧμαι (κάθημαι, § 315, 2). Some verbs also have a double Augment: ἀνέχομαι, *I endure*, ἠνειχόμην; ἀνορθόω, *I raise up*, ἠνώρθουν (οον); ἐνοχλέω, *I encumber*, ἠνώχλουν (εον); παροινέω, *I act as a drunkard*, ἐπαρῴνουν. So also διαιτάω, *I live* (from δίαιτα, *mode of life*), ἐδιῄτων (αον); διακονέω, *I serve*, ἐδιηκόνουν (εον).

§ 241. δύς, *bad, ill*, in composition is *preceded* by the Augment when the second word begins with a consonant or long vowel: δυςτυχέω, *I am unfortunate*, ἐδυςτύχουν (εον); δυςωπέω, *I make a sour face*, ἐδυςώπουν (εον); but short vowels receive the Temporal Augment *after* δύς: δυςἀρεστέω, *I displease*, δυςηρέστουν (εον).

Compounds with εὖ generally have no Augment: εὐτύχουν (εον), *I was fortunate;* but short vowels occasionally receive the Temporal Augment after εὖ: εὐηργέτουν (εον), together with εὐεργέτουν, from εὐεργετέω, *I do good.*

§ 242. All other compounds have the Augment at the beginning: ἠθύμουν, from ἀθυμέω, *I am without courage*.

C. *Contracted Verbs*

§ 243. Verbs whose Present-Stem ends in α, ε, or ο, regularly contract these vowels in all forms of the Present-Stem with the connecting vowel, and hence are called *Contracted Verbs*. The laws of contraction given in §§ 36-38

§ 243. **Dialects.**—The Ion. dialect *very often* does not contract; but the three kinds of contracted verbs are treated differently.

A. Homer inflects the α-Stems in three ways:

1. The syllables regularly contracted by the Attic writers remain *open* and unchanged: ἀοιδιά-ει, *he sings;* ναιετά-ουσι, *they dwell;* and the Fem. Part. ναιετάωσα for ναιετάουσα, with a remarkable change of ου to ω.

2. *Contraction* takes place: ἀρετᾷ = ἀρετά-ει, *he thrives*, from ἀρετάω; προς-ηύδα = προς-ηύδα-ε, from προς-αυδάω, *I address*. Sometimes α ε becomes η (not ᾱ): προς-αυδήτην (3 Dual Imperf.), ὄρηαι—also with regular accent—(from ὁρά-εαι) = Att. ὁρᾷ (2 Sing. Pres. Ind. Mid.).

3. *Extension* instead of contraction takes place when a vowel of the same kind is inserted before the long one which results from contraction: ὁράω, *I see*, contracted ὁρῶ, extended ὁρόω.

a) This inserted vowel is usually *short*. Hence ὁράω is thus inflected:

			Act. Pr. Ind.	ὁρά-ω	Att.	ὁρῶ	Hom.	ὁρόω
				ὁρά-εις	"	ὁρᾷς	"	ὁράᾳς
				ὁρά-ει	"	ὁρᾷ	"	ὁράᾳ
				ὁρά-ουσι	"	ὁρῶσι	"	ὁρόωσι
			Subj.	ὁρά-ω	"	ὁρῶ	"	ὁρόω
				ὁρά-ῃς	"	ὁρᾷς	"	ὁράᾳς, etc.
			Opt.	ὁρά-οιμι	"	ὁρῷμι	"	ὁρόῳμι
			Inf.	ὁρά-ειν	"	ὁρᾶν	"	ὁράαν
			Part.	ὁρά-ων	"	ὁρῶν	"	ὁρόων
				ὁρά-ουσα	"	ὁρῶσα	"	ὁρόωσα
			Gen.	ὁρά-οντος	"	ὁρῶντος	"	ὁρόωντος
Mid.	2.	Sing. Ind.		ὁρά-ῃ	"	ὁρᾷ	"	ὁράᾳ
	3.	Plur.		ὁρά-ονται	"	ὁρῶνται	"	ὁρόωνται
Opt.	3.	Plur.		ὁρά-οιντο	"	ὁρῷντο	"	ὁρόῳντο
Inf.				ὁρά-εσθαι	"	ὁρᾶσθαι	"	ὁράασθαι
	3.	Plur. Impf.		ἑωρά-οντο	"	ἑωρῶντο	"	ὁρόωντο

are observed. Paradigms of the three verbs τιμάω, ποιέω, δουλόω, are given on p. 110–113.

Obs.—As the ε ι in the Infinitive ε ι ν is not original, α ε ι ν, ο ε ι ν do not become ᾷ ν, ο ι ν, but ᾶ ν, ο υ ν (§ 37, *Obs.*).

Dialects.
b) sometimes *long, e. g.*,
ἡβά-ουσα   Att. ἡβῶσα   Hom. ἡ β ώ ω σ α
from ἡβάω, *I am youthful;* so also from δράω, *I do;*
δρά-ουσι   Att. δρῶσι   Hom. δ ρ ώ ω σ ι
and from μνάομαι, *I remember;*
μνά-εσθαι   Att. μνᾶσθαι   Hom. μ ν ά α σ θ α ι.

After *long vowels*, the one following is sometimes shortened:

μνα-όμενος   Att. μνώμενος   Hom. μ ν ω ό μ ε ν ο ς
ἡβά-οντες   "   ἡβῶντες   "   ἡ β ώ ο ν τ ε ς

The metre chiefly determines which of the vowels should be long or short. Such forms, for instance, as ἀρετάᾳ (͝ ͝ ͝ ͝), ἡβώωντες (͝ ͝ ͝ ͝), are inadmissible.

In Herod., the Stems in α often pass over into the conjugation of the Stems in ε : ὁρέω (but ὁρᾷς, ὁρᾷ), ὁρέομεν, ὁρέουσι, ὁρέοντες. Instead of εο we also find 'εω : ὁρέωντες. Homer also has ἤντεον = Att. ἤντων (from ἀντά-ω, *I meet*) ; χρεώμενος = Att. χρώμενος, *making use of*.

B. *Stems in* ε fluctuate between the open and contracted forms. ε ο is *often* monosyllabic by synizesis (§ 39) : ἐθρήνεον, *I complained;* often also in Ionic contracted to ε υ : Hom. νεῦμαι = Att. νέομαι, *I return home.* ε ο υ rarely becomes ε υ : νεικεῦσι = νεικοῦσι, *they quarrel*. ε ε becomes η irregularly in Hom. : ὁμαρτήτην (ὁμαρτέω, *I meet with*), ἀπειλήτην (ἀπειλέω, *I threaten*), δορπήτην (δορπέω, *I sup*), Inf. φορήμεναι = Att. φορεῖν, *to carry*. An utterly anomalous Infinitive is φορῆναι. The second ε in the 2 Sing. Mid. is sometimes dropped : μυθέαι for μυθέεαι (Att. μυθῇ, μυθεῖ, *thou sayest*) ; πωλέο = Att. ἐπωλοῦ, *thou hadst intercourse;* sometimes ε ε are contracted to ε ι : μυθεῖαι. The first way is usual in Herod. Homer also prolongs ε to ει without contraction : νεικείω = Att. νεικῶ ; ἐτελείετο = Att. ἐτελεῖτο (τελῶ, *I complete*).

C. *Stems in* ο are mostly contracted : γουνοῦμαι, *I supplicate.* Some have an extension like those in α : ἀρόωσι(ν) = Att. ἀροῦσι(ν), *they plow;* δηϊόψεν = Att. δηϊοῖεν, *they would destroy;* ὑπνώοντας = Att. ὑπνοῦντας, *the sleepers.*
In Herod. ο sometimes changes to ε, and with ο is contracted to ε υ : ἐδικαιεῦν = Att. ἐδικαίουν, *deemed right.*

§ 244. *Obs.*—1. Monosyllabic Stems in ε admit only the contraction ε ι. All syllables which, contracted, would produce another sound, remain uncontracted.

Stem π λ ε (Pres. πλέω, *I sail*, Inf. πλεῖν)
πλέεις   πλεῖς,   but   πλέω
πλέει   πλεῖ,   "   πλέουσι
ἔπλεες· ἔπλεις, "   ἔπλεον

δέω, *I bind*, forms an exception, having τὸ δοῦν (δέον), δοῦμαι, etc., to distinguish them from forms of δέω, *I am in want of;* δεῖ, *it is necessary;* τὸ δέον, *duty*.

2. Some Stems in α have a preference for η, which they admit in the place of ᾱ: ζά-ω, *I live*, ζῇς, ζῇ, ζῆτε, ζῆν; πεινά-ω, *I am hungry*, πεινῆν; διψά-ω, *I thirst*, διψῆν; so also κνά-ω, *I scratch;* σμά-ω, *I stroke;* ψά-ω, *I scrape;* and χρά-ομαι, *I make use of*.

3. ῥιγό-ω, *I freeze*, has ω and ῳ for ο υ and ο ι: Inf. ῥιγῶν, Opt. ῥιγῴην.

4. λούω, *I wash, lav-o*, has a peculiar contraction; that is, the connecting vowel after ο υ disappears: ἔ-λου for ἔ-λου-ε; λοῦ-μαι for λού-ο-μαι, etc. In like manner, οἴ-ο-μαι is often contracted to οἶ-μαι, *I think*, and the Imperf. ᾠ-ό-μην to ᾤ-μην.

D. *Distinction of the Present-Stem from the Verbal-Stem.*

§ 245. We call that part of a verb the Verbal Stem from the combination of which with the terminations of persons, tenses, moods, infinitives, and participles, consistently with the laws of euphony, all the forms of the verb may be explained: λ υ, Pres. λύω, Perf. λέλυκα, Fut. λύσω; τ ι μ α, Pres. τιμάω, Perf. τετίμηκα, Fut. τιμήσω.

Obs.—From the Verbal-Stem also *nouns* are formed by means of the nominal suffixes: λύ-σι-ς, *loosing;* λυ-τήρ, *looser;* λύ-τρο-ν, *redemption fee;* τί-μη-σι-ς, *valuation;* τιμη-τή-ς, *censor*.

When the Verbal-Stem can not be traced farther back, it is called a *Root:* λ υ, and a verb formed from it, a *Root-Verb:* λύω. But when the Verbal-Stem is itself a Nom-

---

§ 244. **Dialects**:—2. For χρῆται Herod. has χρᾶται.
4. Hom. 3 Sing. Imperf. λόε (for λοϝε, § 35, *Obs.*) = λοῦε, ἔλουε.

inal-Stem formed by means of a nominal suffix, it is said to be *derived :* τ ι μ a is at once the Nominal-Stem of τιμή, *honor*, formed by the nominal suffix μ ā from the root τ ι, and the verb formed from it is a *derivative* one: τιμάω.

> *Obs.*—*Roots* are almost all of one syllable; derived Stems are of two or more syllables.

§ 246. The *Verbal-Stem* is not always like the *Present-Stem*, but the Present-Stem is frequently an *extension* of the Verbal-Stem: Pres. λείπ-ω, *I leave*, Present-Stem λ ε ι π, Verbal-Stem λ ι π (Aorist ἔλιπον).

Such additions are called *enlargements of the Present;* the Verbal-Stem divested of them is the *pure* Verbal-Stem.

> *Obs.*—Where the Verbal-Stem differs from the Present-Stem, nouns are usually formed from the former, not from the latter : Verbal-Stem φ υ γ, Present-Stem φ ε υ γ, substantive φυγ-ή (*fug-a*), adj. φυγ-ά(δ)-ς, *fugitive.*

§ 247. The relation of the Present-Stem to the Verbal-Stem produces four classes of verbs with some subdivisions.

1. FIRST CLASS (unenlarged).
The Present-Stem is like the Verbal-Stem.
This comprises, first of all, the *pure verbs, i. e.*, verbs whose stem ends in a vowel (with the exception of a small number in ε ω, § 248, and many others besides: τιμά-ω, δουλό-ω, παιδεύ-ω, *I educate;* λύ-ω, *I loose;* τί-ω, *I honor;* ἄρχ-ω, *I rule;* ἄγ-ω, *I lead;* λέγ-ω, *I say.*

§ 248. 2. SECOND CLASS (lengthened class).
The Stem vowel is lengthened in the Present-Stem.
This comprises several verbs whose Stem ends in a *mute*, and which in the Present have a diphthong or a long vowel, as:

---

§ 248. **Dialects.**—To these belongs the Hom. σεύω, *I hurry*, from the Stem συ.

§ 249. PRESENT AND VERBAL-STEMS. 139

φεύγ-ω, *I flee*,   Pure Stem φ υ γ (φὔγ-ή, *flight*, Lat. *fuga*).
λείπ-ω, *I leave*,   "   "   λ ι π
πείθ-ω, *I persuade*, "   "   πιθ (πιθ-ανό-ς, *persuasive*).
τήκ-ω, *I melt*,   "   "   τ ἄ κ
τρίβ-ω, *I rub*,   "   "   τρῐβ

But, besides these, there are also six verbs in ε ω, viz. :

πλέω, *I sail*,   Pure Stem π λ ὐ
πνέω, *I blow*,   "   "   π ν υ
νέω, *I sail*,   "   "   ν υ
ῥέω, *I flow*,   "   "   ῥ υ
θέω, *I run*,   "   "   θ υ
χέω, *I pour*,   "   "   χ υ

Obs.—The υ of these Stems was lengthened to ε υ, but resolved to εϝ before vowels (compare § 35, D. 2) ; finally the ϝ was dropped : πλυ-πλευω-πλεϝω-πλέω. The diphthong appears in the substantives unresolved : πνεῦ-μα, *breath ;* ῥεῦ-μα, *stream*. Compare § 260, 2.

§ 249. 3. THIRD CLASS (T-class).

The Present-Stem affixes τ *to the Verbal-Stem.*

This comprises only verbs whose Pure Stems end in *Labials*, as :

τύπτ-ω, *I strike*,   Pure Stem τ υ π (τύπος, *stroke*).
βλάπτ-ω, *I injure*,   "   "   β λ α β (βλᾰβή, *injury*).
βάπτ-ω, *I dip*,   "   "   β α φ (βᾰφή, *a dip*).

and, besides—

τίκτ-ω, *I bring forth*, "   "   τ ε κ (τέκος, *child*).

The final consonant of the Pure Stem is called here, as in the verbs of the following class, the *character*. On the changes of sound, see § 45.

Other Examples.

κόπτω, *I cut*,   Stem κ ο π
κλέπτω, *I steal*,   "   κ λ ε π
κρύπτω, *I hide*,   "   κ ρ υ φ or κ ρ υ β
θάπτω, *I bury*,   "   τ α φ (§ 54, *c*).

§ 249. Dialects.—The Stem βλαβ in Hom. has a Pres. βλάβεται, like class 1.

§ 250. 4. Fourth Class (I-class).

The Present-Stem adds ι to the Verbal-Stem [Latin *fug-i-o*, Pure Stem *fug*]. The ι is here subject to the various changes and transpositions discussed in §§ 55–58, viz.:

a) The *Gutturals* κ, γ, χ form, with ι, the group σσ (New-Att. ττ) (§ 57):

φυλάσσω, *I guard*, instead of φυλακιω, Pure Stem φυλακ (φυλακή, a *guard*).
τάσσω, *I arrange,*   "   ταγιω,   "   "   ταγ (ταγός, *arranger*).
ταράσσω, *I confuse,*   "   ταραχιώ,   "   "   ταραχ (ταραχή, *confusion*).

Other Examples.

ἑλίσσω(κ), *I roll.*   πράσσω(γ), *I do.*   ὀρύσσω(χ), *I dig.*
κηρύσσω(κ), *I proclaim.*   σφάττω(γ), *I slay.*

Obs.—The character of the Presents ἁρμόττω, *I fit;* πάσσω, *I scatter;* πλάσσω, *I shape;* βράσσω, *I seethe;* ἐρέσσω, *I row;* πτίσσω, *I stamp;* βλίττω, *I abstract honey*, is a dental; πέσσω, *I boil*, has Stem πεπ irregularly.

§ 251. b) δ, and more rarely γ, with ι, form ζ (§ 58): ἕζομαι, *I sit*, instead of ἑδίομαι, Pure Stem ἑδ (ἕδ-ος, *seat*, Latin *sedes*); κράζω, *I cry*, instead of κραγιω, Pure Stem κραγ.

Other Examples.

φράζω(δ), *I say.*   ὄζω(δ), *I smell.*   σχίζω(δ), *I split.*

Obs.—Present-Stems in ζ which express a sound have the Verbal-Stem in γ: στενάζω, *I sigh;* οἰμώζω, *I wail;* οἰμωγ-ή, a *wailing;* moreover, στάζω, *I trickle;* στίζω, *I prick*, Lat. *in-stig-o;* μαστίζω;

§ 250. Dialects.—The Stems of the Presents ἱμάσσω, *I whip;* λίσσομαι, *I beseech;* κορύσσω, *I arm;* Herod. ἀφάσσω, *I touch*, end in Dentals (λιτ, κορυθ); Hom. ἐνίσσω, *I blame*, has irregularly the Stem ἐνιπ.

§ 251. Dialects.—In all dialects, Presents in -ζω much more frequently have a Guttural for their character, in Hom. especially in ἀλαπάζω, *I conquer;* δαΐζω, *I divide;* μερμηρίζω, *I ponder;* πολεμίζω, *I war;* στυφελίζω, *I strike*, etc.

§ 253. PRESENT AND VERBAL STEMS. 141

I whip, and some others. κλάζω, *I call*, Stem κλαγγ, κλαγγ-ή, *a call;* πλάζω, *I mislead;* σαλπίζω, *I blow a trumpet*, have a Pure Stem in γγ; νίζω, *I wash*, has irregularly the Stem ν ι β.

§ 252. *c*) λ with ι forms λ λ (§ 56):

βάλλω, *I throw*, for βαλιω, Pure Stem β α λ (βέλ-ος, *a shot*).
ἄλλομαι, *I leap*, " ἁλιομαι, "   " ἁ λ [*sal-i-o*].
τίλλω, *I pluck*, " τιλιω, "   " τ ι λ

Other Examples.

θάλλω, *I bloom*.   σφάλλω, *I cause to stagger*.   στέλλω, *I send*.
πάλλω, *I wield*.   ἀγγέλλω, *I announce*.   ψάλλω, *I play on the lyre*.

§ 253. *d*) ν and ρ throw the ι into the preceding syllable of the Stem (§ 55):

τείνω, *I stretch*, for τενιω, Pure Stem τ ε ν (τόν-ο-ς, *a stretching*, Latin *tendo*).
φθείρω, *I corrupt*, " φθεριω, "   " φ θ ε ρ (φθορ-ά, *corruption*).
φαίνω, *I show*, " φανιω, "   " φ α ν (ἀ-φᾰν-ής, *invisible*).

Other Examples.

μαίνομαι, *I rage*.   σπείρω, *I sow*.   ἐγείρω, *I awaken*.
αἴρω, *I raise*.   ἀγείρω, *I collect*.   ὑφαίνω, *I weave*.

Obs.—If the Stem syllable has ι or υ for its vowel, this is lengthened by the retreating ι: κρίνω, *I sever, judge*, from κρῐν-ιω; σύρω, *I drag*, from σῠρ-ιω.

A single Stem in λ also follows this formation, viz.: ὀ φ ε λ, Pres. ὀφείλω, *I owe*, for ὀφελιω, to distinguish it from ὀφέλλω, *I increase*, with the same Stem.

The ι unites immediately with the final vowels of the Stems καυ and κλαυ, which then sacrifice their υ (ϝ): κα-ίω, *I burn;* κλα-ίω, *I weep*. Additional forms in Attic are κάω, κλάω (§ 35, *Obs.*).

N.B.—The other less usual classes of verbs are given below.

§ 253. Dialects.—Homer joins ι immediately with Vowel Stems: δα-ίω, *I burn*, Stem δ α : μα-ίομαι, *I seek*, Stem μ α; να-ίω, *I dwell*, Stem ν α; and he uses ὀφέλλῳ in the sense of the Att. ὀφείλω; but, on the other hand, he has εἴλω, *I press*, from the Stem ἐ λ for which one might expect ἔλλω (Class 4, *c*).

II. THE STRONG OR SECOND AORIST-STEM.

§ 254. The Strong or Second Aorist Active and Middle is formed from the Strong Aorist-Stem, which is like the Pure Verbal-Stem, except the few cases named in § 257.

Pres. Stem	λείπ-ω, *I leave.* λῐπ	τύπτ-ω, *I strike.* τῠπ	βάλλ-ω, *I throw.* βᾰλ
		Active.	
Aorist Ind.	ἔ-λῐπ-ο-ν, *I left.* ἔ-λιπ-ε-ς	ἔ-τῠπ-ο-ν, *I struck.* ἔ-τυπ-ε-ς	ἔ-βᾰλ-ο-ν, *I threw.* ἔ-βαλ-ε-ς
	etc., like the Imperfects ἔλειπον, ἔτυπτον, ἔβαλλον		
Subj.	λίπ-ω λίπ-ῃ-ς	τύπ-ω τύπ-ῃ-ς	βάλ-ω βάλ-ῃ-ς
	etc., like the Pres. Subjunctive λείπω, τύπτω, βάλλω		
Opt.	λίπ-οι-μι λίπ-οι-ς	τύπ-οι-μι τύπ-οι-ς	βάλ-οι-μι βάλ-οι-ς
	etc., like the Pres. Optative λείποιμι, τύπτοιμι, βάλλοιμι		
Imper.	λίπ-ε λιπ-έ-τω	τύπ-ε τυπ-έ-τω	βάλ-ε βαλ-έ-τω
	etc., like the Pres. Imper. λεῖπε, τύπτε, βάλλε		
Infin.	λιπ-εῖν	τυπ-εῖν	βαλ-εῖν
Part.	λιπ-ών, λιπ-οῦσα, λιπ-όν, *Gen.* λιπ-όντος	τυπ-ών, τυπ-οῦσα, τυπ-όν, *Gen.* τυπ-όντος	βαλ-ών, βαλ-οῦσα, βαλ-όν, *Gen.* βαλ-όντος
		Middle.	
Indic.	ἐ-λιπ-ό-μην ἐ-λίπ-ου	ἐ-τυπ-ό-μην ἐ-τύπ-ου	ἐβαλ-ό-μην ἐ-βάλ-ου
	etc., like the Imperf. ἐλειπόμην, ἐτυπτόμην, ἐβαλλόμην		
Subj.	λίπ-ω-μαι λίπ-ῃ	τύπ-ω-μαι τύπ-ῃ	βάλ-ω-μαι βάλ-ῃ
	etc., like the Pres. Subj. λείπωμαι, τύπτωμαι, βάλλωμαι		
Opt.	λιπ-οί-μην λίπ-οι-ο	τυπ-οί-μην τύπ-οι-ο	βαλ-οί-μην βάλ-οι-ο
	etc., like the Pres. Opt. λειποίμην, τυπτοίμην, βαλλοίμην		
Imper.	λιπ-οῦ λιπ-έ-σθω	τυπ-οῦ τυπ-έ-σθω	βαλ-οῦ βαλ-έ-σθω
	etc., like the Pres. Imper. λείπου, τύπτου, βάλλου		
Infin.	λιπ-έ-σθαι	τυπ-έ-σθαι	βαλ-έ-σθαι
Part.	λιπ-ό-μενο-ς, η, ο-ν	τυπ-ό-μενο-ς, η, ο-ν	βαλ-ό-μενο-ς, η, ο-ν

§ 257. II. THE STRONG OR SECOND AORIST-STEM. 143

§ 255. 1. The *Inflexion* of the Strong Aorist-Stem differs from that of the Present-Stem (Imperfect and Present tenses) only in the accent of the following forms: the Infin. Act. is perispome (λιπεῖν), the Infin. Mid. paroxytone (λιπέσθαι), the Part. Act. accents the O-sound (λιπών, λιποῦσα), the 2 Sing. Imper. Mid. is perispome (λιποῦ).

2. The Aorist Middle has not, like the Present Middle, the meaning also of the Passive: thus ἐβαλόμην means only *I threw for myself*, but not *I was thrown*.

On the Augment of the Indicative, §§ 234-242.

§ 256. The Strong Aorist can be formed only from such verbs as have a Present-Stem *different* from the Pure Verbal-Stem, therefore *not* from the verbs of the *First* (unenlarged) *Class* (§ 247). Also it is not usually formed from many verbs of other classes, and scarcely occurs at all from any but *Root-Verbs* (§ 245).

Obs.—On the Aorists of the verbs δύ-ω and φύ-ω (class 1), see §§ 316, 16, 17.

§ 257. In a few verbs the Strong Aorist Stem is distinguished from the Pure Verbal Stem; viz., instead of ε of the latter, the Strong Aor. sometimes has ἄ, by which τρέπ-ω, *I turn*, though belonging to the first class, has a Strong Aor.: ἔ-τρᾰπ-ο-ν (Impf. ἔ-τρεπ-ο-ν), ἐ-τραπ-ό-μην. An isolated formation is Pres. τρώγ-ω, *I gnaw*, Aor. ἔ-τρᾰγ-ο-ν. ἄγ-ω, *I drive*, likewise belonging to the first class, by doubling the Verbal-Stem forms the Aorist-Stem ἀγ-αγ, whence Ind.: ἤγ-ᾰγ-ο-ν, Subj. ἀγ-άγ-ω, Inf. ἀγ-αγ-εῖν.

§ 255. Dialects.—1. All the peculiarities enumerated § 233, D., extend likewise to the Strong Aorist: 2 Sing. Subj. βάλησθα, 3 Sing. βάλησι, etc. The Inf. Aor. Act. ends in Hom. also in ἐειν instead of εῖν (βαλέειν).

2. The Middle Aorist forms of the Stems κ τ α (§ 316, 4), β λ η (§ 316, 19), ο ὐ τ α (§ 316, 20), exceptionally have a *Passive* meaning.

III. THE FUTURE-STEM.

§ 258. From the Future-Stem are formed the Fut. Active and Middle.

	First Future (*The σ Future*).	Second Future (*Contracted Future*).
Pres.	λύω, Stem λ ῠ	Pres. φαίνω, *I show*, Stem φ ᾰ ν
Fut.	Stem λ ῡ σ	Fut. Stem φ ᾰ ν ε

Active.

Indic.	λύσ-ω, *I shall loose.* λύσ-εις, etc. like the Pres. λύω	φᾰνέω, ῶ, *I shall show.* φᾰνέ-εις, εῖς, etc. like the Present ποιῶ
Opt. Infin. Part.	λύσ-οι-μι λύσ-ειν Masc. λύσ-ων Fem. λύσ-ουσα Neut. λῦσ-ον Gen. λύσ-οντος	φανε-οίην, οίην φανέ-ειν, εῖν φανέ-ων, ῶν φανέ-ουσα, οῦσα φανέ-ον, οῦν φανέ-οντος, οῦντος

Middle.

Indic.	λύσ-ο-μαι, *I shall loose for myself.* like the Present λύομαι	φανέ-ο-μαι, οῦμαι, *I shall appear.* like the Present ποιοῦμαι
Opt. Infin. Part.	λυσ-οί-μην λύσ-ε-σθαι λυσ-ό-μενος, η, ον	φανε-οί-μην, οίμην φανέ-ε-σθαι, εῖσθαι φανε-ό-μενος, ούμενος, η, ον

§ 257. Dialects.—Hom., in the case of several Stems with ρ, forms the Strong Aorist by metathesis (§ 59), and by changing ε into α: δέρκ-ο-μαι, *I see*, ἔ-δρακ-ον; πέρθ-ω, *I destroy*, ἔ-πρᾰθ-ο-ν; in others by the syncope of ε (§ 61, c): ἐ-πτ-ό-μην (πέτ-ομαι, *I fly*), ἔ-γρ-ε-το (Stem ἐ γ ε ρ, Pres. class 4, d, ἐγείρω, *I awake*); Part. ἀγρ-ό-μενοι, *assembled;* Inf. ἀγερ-έσθαι (Pres. class 4, d, ἀγείρω).

Reduplication occurs in Homer in a great many Aorists: ἐ-πέ-φρᾰδ-ε-ν (Stem φ ρ α δ, Pres. class 4, b, φράζω, *I indicate*); πέ-πῐθ-ο-ν (Stem π ῐ θ, Pres. class 2, πείθω, *I persuade*); πε-πᾰλ-ών (Pres. class 4, c, πάλλω, *I brandish*); Aor. Mid. 3 Sing.: τε-τάρπ-ε-το (τέρπ-ο-μαι, *I rejoice*);

§ 259. 1. The Inflexion of the Future-Stem is the same as that of the Present-Stem, *i. e.*, that of the σ Future is the ordinary Inflexion, that of the contracted future is the Inflexion of the contracted Present of ε Stems (§§ 231, 232, and 243).

§ 260. The σ Future forms the Future-Stem by adding σ to the Verbal-Stem: λ υ, λῦσ. All Stems ending in a vowel or a mute have the σ Future. The σ, according to § 48, with gutturals makes ξ, with labials ψ, and admits of no dentals before it (§ 49): ἄγ-ω, *I drive*, Fut. ἄξ-ω; γράφ-ω, *I write*, Fut. γράψ-ω; ᾄδ-ω, *I sing*, Fut. ᾄσ-ω; σπένδ-ω, *libo*, Fut. σπείσ-ω for σπενδ-σω (§ 50). About θρέψω, Stem τ ρ ε φ, θύψω, Stem τ υ φ, and others, see § 54.

2. Verbs of the second or extended class (§ 248) retain the extended Stem also in the Future: λείπ-ω, λείψ-ω; the six verbs in εω mentioned in § 248 show their strengthened form in the Fut., though it is not seen in the Present: πλέω, πλεύσομαι; in like manner, κλαίω brings out its Pure Stem κ λ α υ in κλαύσω, and καίω in καύσω (§ 253). About χέω, see § 265.

3. Of verbs of the third or T class, and of those of the fourth or I class (§ 249, etc.), the Pure Stem must be found in order to form the Future: τύπτω (class 4), Pure Stem τ υ π, Fut. τύψω; φυλάσσω, Pure Stem φ υ λ α κ, Fut.

Stem φ ι δ (class 2), φείδομαι, Inf. Aor. πε-φιδ-έ-σθαι, also Fut. πε-φιδ-ή-σομαι. Isolated Aorists are: ἐ-κέ-κ(ε)λ-ε-το, *he called*, from κέλομαι; πέ-φν-ο-ν, *I killed* (Stem φ ε ν); τέ-τμ-ο-ν (*I hit*, Stem τ ε μ); τε-ταγ-ών (*seizing*, Stem τ α γ, Lat. *tango*). ἠν-ίπ-απ-ο-ν (*I scolded*, Pres. ἐνίπτω), along with ἐν-ενῑπ-ο-ν, and ἠρύκ-ακ-ο-ν (*I kept back*, Pres. ἐρύκω), have the reduplication in the middle of the word. The reduplication in this case every where belongs to the Tense-Stem, and, as in the Perfect-Stem (§ 273), is preserved in all the moods, in the Infin., and the Participle. The Indic. may add the Augment or omit it before the reduplication. (§ 234, D.)

§ 259. Dialects.—About the contraction, see § 243, D.

G

φυλάξω ; φράζω, Pure Stem φ ρ α δ, Fut. φράσω. Accordingly, verbs ending in the Present in -σσω or -ττω generally make the Fut. in -ξω, and those having the Present in ζω generally have their Future in -σω.

According to this rule, let the Future be formed of ελίσσω, *I roll;* κηρύσσω, *I proclaim;* πράσσω, *I do;* σχίζω, *I split;* δικάζω, *I judge;* οπλίζω, *I arm;* and let the Presents be found to the Futures ορύξω, σφάξω, βιάσομαι, λογίσομαι.

Verbs with a dental character ending in the Present in -σσω or -ττω, naturally (§ 250, *Obs.*) make the Future in -σω : πλάσω (Pres. πλάσσω, *I shape*), αρμόσω (Pres. αρμόττω, *I fit*); and, on the other hand, those with the character γ, which have the Present in -ζω (§ 251, *Obs.*), make their Future in -ξω : στενάξω (Pres. στενάζω, *I sigh*); στίξω (Pres. στίζω, *I prick*).

§ 261. Vowel-Stems have their vowels *long* before σ ; α becomes ā if preceded by ε, ι, or ρ (§ 41), in all other cases it becomes η. Every other short vowel is changed into the corresponding long one : εά-ω, *I leave*, εάσ-ω ; ιά-ομαι, *I heal*, ιάσ-ομαι ; δρά-ω, *I do*, δράσ-ω ; but τιμά-ω, τιμήσ-ω ; βοά-ω, *I cry out*, βοήσ-ομαι ; εγγυά-ω, *I hand over*, εγγυήσ-ω ; ποιέ-ω, ποιήσ-ω, δουλόω, δουλώσ-ω.

The Stem χ ρ α (χράω, *I give an oracle;* χράομαι, *I use*) exceptionally has η in the Future : χρήσω, χρήσομαι ; whereas ακροάομαι, *I listen*, has ακροάσομαι.

Respecting the Future with a short vowel, see § 301.

§ 262. The contracted Future forms the Future-Stem

§ 261. **Dialects.**—The Ion. dialect has η even after ε, ι, ρ : πειρήσομαι, *I shall endeavor.* The Ep. dialect sometimes doubles the σ when the vowel is short : αιδέσσομαι (αιδέομαι, *I feel shame*). The Hom. Futures αλαπάξω, πολεμίξω, στυφελίξω, and others, with their Presents in -ζω, are explained in § 251, D.

§ 262. **Dialects.**—Stem θ ε ρ has in Hom. the Fut. θέρσομαι, Pres. θέρομαι, *I grow warm;* Stem κ ε ρ (Pres. class 4, *d*, κείρω, *I shave*), Fut. κέρσω ; Stem φ υ ρ, Pres. φύρω, *I mix*, Fut. φύρσω.

§ 264. III. THE FUTURE-STEM. 147

by adding ε to the Verbal-Stem: φάν, φάνε. This form of the Future occurs in Stems ending in λ, μ, ν, ρ; and the Stem vowel is short : νέμω, I distribute, Fut. νεμῶ; ἀμύνω, I defend, ἀμυνῶ. Verbs of the seventh class here show their Pure Stem (§§ 252, 253): βάλλω, I throw, βαλῶ; φαίνω, φανῶ; κτείνω, I kill, κτενῶ; φθείρω, φθερῶ; ἀγγέλλω, ἀγγελῶ. According to this rule, let the Future be formed of σφάλλω, I cause to fall; στέλλω, I send; μαίνομαι, I rave; αἴρω, I lift; and the Present (class 4) of σπερῶ, ποικιλῶ, σημανῶ, ἡδυνῶ.

Exceptions.—The Stems κ ε λ (κέλλω, class 4, c, I knock against) and κ υ ρ (κυρέω, I meet) have the σ form of the Future : κέλσω, κύρσω.

Obs.—The contracted Future is properly a peculiar form of the σ Future, for φανέ-ω has arisen from φαν-έ-σ-ω (§ 61, b), in which ε is the connecting vowel.

§ 263. Several Stems in ε (Pres. εω), αδ (Pres. αζω), and ιδ (Pres. ιζω), throw out the σ in the Future. Those in ε and αδ then contract the vowels ε and α with the connecting vowel: τελέ-ω, I complete, τελέσ-ω, τελέω, τελῶ; 1 Plur. τελέομεν, τ ε λ ο ῦ μ ε ν (as in the Present); βιβάζω, I bring, βιβάσ-ω, βιβάω, βιβῶ; 1 Plur. βιβάομεν, βιβῶμεν. To these also belongs ἐλάω, ἐλῶ, 2 Sing. ἐλᾷς, 3 Sing. ἐλᾷ, from the irregular Present ἐλαύνω, I drive; compare § 321, 2.

Stems in ιδ after dropping the σ insert ε, which is contracted with the connecting vowel : κομίζω, I carry, Fut. Act. κομίσ-ω, κομι-έ-ω, κ ο μ ι ῶ, 1 Plur. κομιέομεν, κομιοῦμεν; Fut. Mid. κ ο μ ι ο ῦ μ α ι.
This form of the Future is called the *Attic*.

§ 264. Some verbs take an ε after the σ of the Future, which is contracted with the connecting vowel: πνέω, I breathe, Stem π ν υ, πνευσοῦμαι; πλέω, I sail, Stem π λ υ,

---

§ 263. **Dialects.**—The Futures in αω in the Hom. dialect are treated exactly like the Presents (§ 243, D. A.), hence ἐλόω, ἐλάᾳς, ἐλάᾳ.

πλευσοῦμαι along with πλεύσομαι; φεύγω, *I flee*, Stem φ υ γ, φευξοῦμαι and φεύξομαι. This kind of Future, which occurs only in the Middle voice with an Active meaning, is called the *Doric*.

§ 265. Few verbs form their Future without any tense sign: χέω, *I pour*, Fut. Act. χέω, Mid. χέομαι, and so also among the irregular verbs ἔδομαι, *I shall eat* (§ 327, 4), and πίομαι, *I shall drink* (§ 321, 4).

§ 266. The Future Middle generally has a Middle sense, but in many verbs it has a Passive, and in not a few an Active meaning; the last is the case especially in verbs denoting a bodily activity: ᾄδω, *I sing;* ἀκούω, *I hear;* ἀπαντάω, *I meet;* ἀπολαύω, *I enjoy;* βαδίζω, *I walk* (βαδιοῦμαι); βοάω, *I call out;* γελάω, *I laugh;* οἰμώζω, *I bewail;* σιγάω and σιωπάω, *I am silent;* σπουδάζω, *I am zealous*. Irregular verbs (§ 320, etc.) very frequently have a Middle Future with Active meaning.

---

§ 265. **Dialects** —The Hom. βείομαι or βέομαι, *I shall live*, akin to βιόω, *I live*, is likewise formed without a tense sign.

§ 267. IV. THE WEAK OR FIRST AORIST-STEM. 149

IV. THE WEAK OR FIRST AORIST-STEM.

§ 267. From the Stem of the Weak or First Aorist are formed the *Weak* (or *First*) Aorist Active and Middle.

Pres. Stem	λύ-ω λ υ		φαίν-ω Pure Stem φăν	
	1. σ Form.		2. Supplementary Form.	
	Stem of Weak Aorist λ ῦ σ ă		φ η ν ă	
	Active.	Middle.	Active.	Middle.
Indic.	ἔ-λῡσα, *I loosed.*	ἐ-λυσά-μην, *I loosed for myself.*	ἔ-φηνα, *I showed.*	ἐ-φηνά-μην
	ἔ-λυσα-ς	ἐ-λύσω	ἔ-φηνα-ς	ἐ-φήνω
	ἔ-λυσε(ν)	ἐ-λύσα-το	ἔ-φηνε(ν)	ἐ-φήνα-το
		ἐ-λυσά-με-θον		ἐ-φηνά-με-θον
	ἐ-λύσα-τον	ἐ-λύσα-σθον	ἐ-φήνα-τον	ἐ-φήνα-σθον
	ἐ-λυσά-την	ἐ-λυσά-σθην	ἐ-φηνά-την	ἐ-φηνά-σθην
	ἐ-λύσα-μεν	ἐ-λυσά-μεθα	ἐ-φήνα-μεν	ἐ-φηνά-με-θα
	ἐ-λύσα-τε	ἐ-λύσα-σθε	ἐ-φήνα-τε	ἐφήνα-σθε
	ἔ-λυσα-ν	ἐ-λύσα-ντο	ἔ-φηνα-ν	ἐ-φήνα-ντο
Subjunct.	λύσω	λύσω-μαι	φήνω	φήνω-μαι
	λύσῃς	λύσῃ	φήνῃς	φήνῃ
	etc., like the Pres. Act. and Mid.			
Optative.	λύσαι-μι	λυσαί-μην	φήναι-μι	φηναί-μην
	λύσαι-ς or λύσειας	λύσαι-ο	φήναι-ς or φήνειας	φήναι-ο
	λύσαι or λύσειε(ν)	λύσαι-το	φήναι or φήνειε(ν)	φήναι-το
		λυσαί-μεθον		φηναί-μεθον
	λύσαι-τον	λύσαι-σθον	φήναι-τον	φήναι-σθον
	λυσαί-την	λυσαί-σθην	φηναί-την	φηναί-σθην
	λύσαι-μεν	λυσαί-μεθα	φήναι-μεν	φηναί-μεθα
	λύσαι-τε	λύσαι-σθε	φήναι-τε	φήναι-σθε
	λύσαι-εν or λύσει-αν	λύσαι-ντο	φήναι-εν or φήνει-αν	φήναι-ντο
Imperat.	λῦσο-ν	λῦσαι	φῆνο-ν	φῆναι
	λυσά-τω	λυσά-σθω	φηνά-τω	φηνά-σθω
	λύσα-τον	λύσα-σθον	φήνα-τον	φήνα-σθον
	λυσά-των	λυσά-σθων	φηνά-των	φηνά-σθων
	λύσα-τε	λύσα-σθε	φήνα-τε	φήνα-σθε
	λυσά-ντων or λυσά-τωσαν	λυσά-σθων or λυσά-σθωσαν	φηνά-ντων or φηνά-τωσαν	φηνά-σθων or φηνά-σθωσαν
Infinitive.	λῦσαι	λύσα-σθαι	φῆναι	φήνα-σθαι
Particip.	λύσᾱ-ς, ᾱσα, αν Gen. λύσαντ-ος	λυσά-μενο-ς, η, ο-ν	φήνᾱ-ς, ᾱσα, αν φήναντ-ος	φηνά-μενο-ς, η, ο-ν

§ 268. The characteristic vowel in the inflexion of the Weak Aorist is ă, which in the 3 Sing. Ind. Act. becomes ε, but every where else remains unchanged before the personal and modal signs. In the Subj. α is lengthened to ω and η, whereby the endings become the same as those of the Present. In the Optat. Act., the forms with ει in the 2 and 3 Sing. and 3 Plur. are more common than those with αι : λύσειας, λύσειε(ν), λύσειαν. In the 2 Sing. Imperat. Act. ν is added, by which the ᾰ is rendered so obscure as to become ο : λῦσο-ν ; and in 2 Imp. Mid. ι is added, which, with the α, makes αι. In the 2 Sing. Ind. Mid. σ is thrown out, as in the Pres. and Fut., so that ἰ-λύσα(σ)ο becomes ἐλύσω, according to § 37.

Obs. 1.—Three forms of the Weak Aorist are the same, the 3 Sing. Opt. Act., the Infin. Active, and the 2 Imperat. Mid.; but in accent they differ; for, as the αι of the Optat. is regarded as long (§ 229), the first of these three forms is always paroxytone : λῦσαι, γράψαι (γράφω, *I write*), παιδεῦσαι (παιδεύω, *I educate*) ; the Infin. always has the accent on the penultima : λῦσαι, παιδεῦσαι, γράψαι ; the 2 Sing. Imperat. Mid., where possible, has the accent on the antepenultima : παίδευσαι, λῦσαι, γράψαι.

Obs. 2.—The 2 Sing. Imperat. of the Weak Aor. Act. is the same in form as the Neut. Partic. Fut. λῦσον, but in Verbal-Stems of more than one syllable it differs from it by the accent : παίδευσον, but the Neut. Part. Fut. is παιδεῦσον (§ 229).

§ 269. The σ form of the Aorist differs from the Stem

---

§ 268. **Dialects.**—In the Ion. dialect, the 2 Sing. Indic. Mid. frequently leaves the vowels uncontracted : ἐλύσαο.
Some Aorists in Hom. take the vowels ο and ε instead of α : ἷξον, *I came*, ἷξες ; ἐβήσετο (βαίνω, *I walk*) ; δύσετο (*he set* or *went down*, δύω) ; so also the Imperatives ὄρσεο, *arise* ; ἄξετε, *bring* ; οἶσε, *bring* ; λέξεο, *lie down* ; πελάσσετον = πελάσατον, from πελάζω, *I approach*.

§ 269. **Dialects.**—ἀφύσσω, *I draw water*, has in Hom. the Fut. ἀφύξω, but the Aor. ἄφυσσα. Irregular Hom. forms without σ are : ἔχευα for ἔχευσα, from Pres. χέω, *I pour* ; ἕκηα, 1 Plur. Subj. κήομεν or κείομεν, Imperat. κῆον or κεῖον, Infin. κῆαι or κεῖαι, from Pres. καίω, *I burn* ; Stem καυ (Att. ἔκαυσα) ; ἔσσευα, Pres. σεύω, *I drive away* ; the Infinitives ἀλεύασθαι or ἀλέασθαι, *to avoid* ; δατέασθαι, from δατέομαι, *I distribute*.

§ 270. IV. THE WEAK OR FIRST AORIST-STEM. 151

of the Future only by the addition of the α : λῦσ, λῦσα; γράψ, γράψα ; φύλαξ, φύλαξα. Respecting the change of vowels and consonants before σ, compare §§ 260, 261. The irregular χέω (§ 265) has the Aorist ἔχεα for ἔχευσα. Compare the irregularity in εἶπα, *I spoke;* ἤνεγκα, *I bore*, § 327, 12 and 13.

§ 270. The Stems in λ, μ, ν, ρ, forming their Future without σ, reject this consonant also in the Weak Aorist, which gives rise to the supplementary form, for the vowel of the Stem is lengthened by compensation for the loss of the σ.

ἄ after ι and ρ becomes ᾱ: Pres. περαίνω (class 4, d), *I penetrate*, Stem περαν, Fut. περανῶ, Aor. ἐ-πέρᾱνα (§ 41);
otherwise η : Pres. φαίνω (class 4, d), Stem φαν, Fut. φανῶ, Aor. ἔ-φηνα.
ε becomes ει : Pres. ἀγγέλλω (class 4, c), *I announce*, Stem ἀγγελ, Fut. ἀγγελῶ, Aor. ἤγγειλα.
. " " Pres. νέμω (class 1), *I distribute*, Fut. νεμῶ, Aor. ἔ-νειμα.
ῐ " ῑ: Pres. κρίνω (class 4, d), *I judge*, Stem κριν, Fut. κρῑνῶ, Aor. ἔ-κρινα.
ῠ " ῡ: Pres. ἀμύνω (class 4, d), *I defend*, Stem ἀμυν, Fut. ἀμῡνῶ, Aor. ἤμυνα.

Obs.—The Stems ἀρ (αἴρω, *I lift*) and ἀλ (ἄλλομαι, *I leap*) have in the Indic. η because of the Augment : ἦρα, ἡλάμην, but in the other forms α : ἄρας, ἀλάμενος. ᾱ instead of η occurs in some

εἶσα, *I placed*, is a defective poet. Aorist; the Hom. Infin. is ἕσσαι, Part. εἵσας and ἕσσας (ἀνέσας), 3 Sing. Mid. ἑέσσατο. On the doubling of the σ, see § 261, D. : λόεσσα (λοϝ-ε-σσα) = ἔλουσα (λούω, *I wash*), with ε inserted. (Compare § 35, *Obs.*)

§ 270. **Dialects.**—1. Homer makes the Aorist of several Stems in λ, μ, ν, ρ with σ: ἔλσα, from εἴλω, *I press ;* the defective ἀπόερσα, *I tore away*.
2. In the Æol. dialect, σ is assimilated to preceding λ, μ, ν, ρ ; an example of it in Hom. is ὤφελλα for ὤφελ-σα = Att. ὤφειλα, Pres. ὀφέλλω, *I increase*.
3. The Augment of the Hom. Aor. ἤειρα, Pres. εἴρω, *I join*, is quite irregular. Compare § 275, D. 2.

few verbs: κερδαίνω, *I gain;* ὀργαίνω, *I cause anger;* σημαίνω, *I indicate*—ἐσήμᾶνα along with ἐσήμηνα. On the other hand, η instead of ᾱ, in spite of the ρ, occurs in τετραίνω, *I bore,* ἐτέτρηνα.

§ 271. The Weak Aorist is the usual form in all verbs which, according to § 256, can not form the Strong Aorist, that is, in all derivative verbs and in verbs of the first class; but radical verbs of other classes, especially those with Stems in λ, μ, ν, ρ, also have the Weak Aorist.

The Weak Aorist Middle, like the Strong one, has only a Middle sense, and is never Passive (§ 477, etc.).

V. The Perfect-Stem.

§ 272. From the Perfect-Stem are formed the Perfect, and Pluperfect Active and Middle, and the third Future (*Futurum exactum*), which occurs only in the Middle.

§ 273. The essential characteristic of the Perfect-Stem is the *reduplication* (compare πέ-πηγ-α with Lat. *pe-pig-i*), which generally takes the first place; but in verbs compounded with prepositions is put, like the Augment, after the preposition (§ 238): λέ-λυ-κα, but ἐκ-λέ-λυ-κα.

The reduplication belongs to the Perfect-Stem, and is therefore, unlike the Augment, preserved in all the moods, infinitives, and participles (compare 258, D.).

In verbs beginning with a consonant, it consists in the initial consonant with ε being placed before the Stem: Stem λυ, Perfect-Stem λελυ, 1 Sing. Perf. Ind. Act. λέ-λυ-κα.

---

§ 273. **Dialects.**—The reduplication can not, like the Augment, be omitted in the Epic dialect; δέγ-μαι forms an exception (3 Plur. δέχ-αται), though we also find δέ-δεγ-μαι, *I expect* or *receive*, Part. δε-δεγ-μένος, from Pres. δέχ-ο-μαι (compare § 316, 34). Some verbs beginning with a vowel do not lengthen it in the Perfect in the New-Ionic dialect.

§ 273. V. THE PERFECT-STEM. 153

I. Active.

	Present λύ-ω Stem λυ Perfect Stem λελυ Perfect: 1. Weak form	φαίν-ω Pure Stem φᾰν π ε φ η ν 2. Strong form
Indic.	λέ-λῠ-κ-α, *I have loosed.* λέ-λυ-κ-α-ς λέ-λυ-κ-ε-(ν) λε-λύ-κ-α-τον λε-λύ-κ-α-τον λε-λύ-κ-α-μεν λε-λύ-κ-α-τε λε-λύ-κ-ᾱ-σι(ν)	πέ-φην-α, *I have appeared.* πέ-φην-α-ς πέ-φην-ε(ν) πε-φήν-α-τον πε-φήν-α-τον πε-φήν-α-μεν πε-φήν-α-τε πε-φήν-ᾱ-σι(ν)
Subj.	λε-λύ-κ-ω λε-λύ-κ-ῃ-ς etc., like the Subj. Present, § 232.	πε-φήν-ω πε-φήν-ῃ-ς
Optat.	λε-λύ-κ-οι-μι or λελυκοίην etc., like the Optat. Present, § 232.	πε-φήν-οι-μι or πεφηνοίην
Imperat.	λέ-λυ-κ-ε etc., like the Imperat. Present, § 232.	πέ-φην-ε
Infin.	λε-λυ-κ-έναι	πε-φην-έναι
Partic.	M. λε-λυ-κ-ώς F. λε-λυ-κ-υῖα N. λε-λυ-κ-ός Gen. λε-λυ-κ-ότ-ος (Inflexion, § 147, 2.)	πε-φην-ώς πε-φην-υῖα πε-φην-ός πε-φην-ότ-ος

Pluperfect.

Indic.	ἐ-λε-λύ-κ-ει-ν, *I had loosed.* ἐ-λε-λύ-κ-ει-ς ἐ-λε-λύ-κ-ει ἐ-λε-λύ-κ-ει-τον ἐ-λε-λυ-κ-εί-την ἐ-λε-λύ-κ-ει-μεν ἐ-λε-λύ-κ-ει-τε ἐ-λε-λύ-κ-ε-σαν or ἐλελύκεισαν	ἐ-πε-φήν-ει-ν, *I had appeared.* ἐ-πε-φήν-ει-ς ἐ-πε-φήν-ει ἐ-πε-φήν-ει-τον ἐ-πε-φην-εί-την ἐ-πε-φήν-ει-μεν ἐ-πε-φήν-ει-τε ἐ-πε-φήν-ε-σαν or ἐπεφήνεισαν

II. Middle and Passive.

Perfect.

Indic.	λέ-λῠ-μαι, *I have loosed for myself*, or *have been loosed*.	λε-λύ-μεθον	λε-λύ-μεθα
	λέ-λυ-σαι		λέ-λυ-σθε
	λέ-λυ-ται	λέ-λυ-σθον	λέ-λυ-νται
		λέ-λυ-σθον	
Subj.	λε-λυ-μένος, ὦ, ᾖς, ᾖ, etc., § 315.		
Optat.	λε-λυ-μένος, εἴην, εἴης, εἴη, etc., § 315.		
Imperf.	λέ-λυ-σο	λέ-λυ-σθον	λέ-λυ-σθε
	λε-λύ-σθω	λε-λύ-σθων	λε-λύ-σθων or
			λε-λύ-σθωσαν
Infin.	λε-λύ-σθαι		
Partic.	λε-λυ-μένο-ς, η, ο-ν		

Pluperfect.

Indic.	ἐ-λε-λύ-μην, *I had loosed for myself*, or *had been loosed*.	ἐ-λε-λύ-μεθον	ἐ-λε-λύ-μεθα
	ἐ-λέ-λυ-σο		ἐ-λέ-λυ-σθε
	ἐ-λέ-λυ-το	ἐ-λέ-λυ-σθον	ἐ-λέ-λυ-ντο
		ἐ-λε-λύ-σθην	

Future Perfect.

Indic. λε-λύ-σ-ο-μαι, *I shall have been loosed*.
λε-λύ-σ-ῃ, etc., like the usual Fut. Mid. (§ 258).

| Opt. λε-λυ-σ-οί-μην | Inf. λε-λύ-σ-ε-σθαι | Part. λε-λυ-σ-ό-μενο-ς |

§ 274. The following points, however, are to be observed:

1. An aspirate, according to § 53, *a*, is represented by the

---

§ 274. **Dialects.**—The full reduplication, in spite of the initial ρ, occurs in the Hom. ῥε-ρυπω-μένο-ς, *soiled*; on the other hand, the Perfects ἔμ-μορ-α (Pres. μείρομαι, class 4, *d, I obtain*) and ἔσ-σῠ-μαι (Pres. σεύω, class 2, *I hasten*), instead of μέμορα, σέσυμαι, are treated like Stems with ρ.

§ 275. V. THE PERFECT-STEM. 155

corresponding tenuis: Stem χ ω ρ ε, χωρῶ, *I retreat*, κε-χώρη-κα; Stem θ υ, θύω, *I sacrifice*, τέ-θυ-κα; Stem φ α ν, πέ-φην-α.

2. When a verb begins with two consonants, only the first appears in the reduplication, and even this only when it is a *mute* followed by λ, μ, ν, or ρ: Stem γ ρ α φ, γράφω, *I write*, γέ-γραφ-α; Stem π λ ᾰ γ, πλήσσω, *I strike*, πέ-πληγ-α; Stem π ν υ, πνέω, *I breathe*, πέ-πνευ-κα.

3. In every other case a Stem beginning with two consonants takes only ε for its reduplication: Stem κ τ ε ν, κτείνω, *I kill*, ἔ-κτον-α; Stem ζ η τ ε, ζητῶ, *I seek*, ἐ-ζήτη-κα.

4. Stems beginning with ρ likewise have only ε, after which the ρ is doubled: Stem ρ ι φ, ῥίπτω, *I throw*, ἔρ-ριφ-α (compare §§ 62, 234).

EXCEPTIONS.—Verbs beginning with γν, γλ, and sometimes those beginning with βλ, have a simple ε for their reduplication. Stem γ ν ω, ἔ-γνω-κα, *I have come to know;* Stem β λ α σ τ ε (βλαστῶ, *I germinate*), ἐ-βλάστη-κα. The Stems κ τ α (κτῶμαι, *I acquire*), and μ ν α, on the other hand, have κέ-κτη-μαι and μέ-μνη-μαι, *I remember, me-min-i.* Compare πέ-πτω-κα, *I have fallen*, and πέ-πτα-μαι, *I am spread out*, §§ 319, 3, 327, 15.

Instead of the reduplication ει appears in εἴ-ληφ-α, *I have taken* (§ 322, 25); εἴ-ληχ-α, *I have obtained* (§ 322, 27); εἴ-λοχα (from λέγω, *I gather*); δι-εί-λεγ-μαι (from διαλέγομαι, *I converse*); εἴ-ρη-κα, *I have said* (§ 327, 13); and in the aspirated εἴ-μαρ-ται, *it is fated*, Stem μ ε ρ.

§ 275. Initial vowels are lengthened as in the case of the

---

§ 275. Dialects.—1. The Attic reduplication is more frequent in Homer, as: ἀρ-ήρο-ται, from ἀρόω, *I plough;* ἀλ-άλη-μαι, from ἀλά-ο-μαι, *I wander;* ἄρ-ηρ-α, *I am joined*, Stem ἀ ρ; ὄδ-ωδ-α, *I smell*, ὄζω, compare *od-or;* ὄπ-ωπ-α, *I have seen*, from the Stem ὀ π; and with a ν inserted: ἐμν-ήμυν-κα, from the Pres. ἡμύ-ω, *I droop the head.* Herod. has ἀρ-αίρη-κα, from αἱρέω, *I take.*

2. Instead of εἴ-ωθα, Hom. also has ἔ-ωθα, which is the only form used by Herod. From the Stem ἐ λ π (originally Ϝ ε λ π) ἔ-ολπ-α, *I hope;* from Stem ἐ ρ γ (Ϝ ε ρ γ), ἔ-οργ-α, *I have done.* From the Stem ἐ ρ (Lat. *sero*), Pres. εἴρω, 3 Sing. Pluperf. Mid. ἔερτο, Part. Perf. Mid.

Temporal Augment (§ 235): Stem ὀρθο, ὀρθῶ, *I raise up*, ὤρθω-κα. The verbs mentioned in § 236 have ει here also: εἴλιγμαι, Pres. ἑλίσσω, *I roll*.

1. Some Stems beginning with α, ε, or ο exceptionally take what is called the *Attic reduplication* instead of the mere lengthening of the vowel. This reduplication consists in the initial vowel with its following consonant being repeated, and the vowel of the second syllable being lengthened: Stem ἀλιφ (ἀλείφω, class 2, *I anoint*), ἀλ-ήλιφ-α; Stem ἀκο, ἀκούω, *I hear*, ἀκ-ήκο-α (for ἀκήκοϝα, § 35, *Obs.*), but Mid. ἤκουσμαι; Stem ὀρυχ (ὀρύσσω, class 4, *I dig*) ὀρ-ώρυχ-α; Stem ἀγερ (ἀγείρω, class 4, *d, I collect*), ἀγ-ήγερ-κα; Stem ἐλα (Pres. ἐλαύνω, *I drive*, § 321, 2), ἐλ-ήλἄ-κα, Mid. ἐλ-ήλα-μαι; Stem ἐλεγχ, Pres. ἐλέγχω, *I refute* (class 1), Perf. Mid. ἐλ-ήλεγ-μαι (compare § 286, *Obs.*); ἐγρ-ήγορ-α, *I am awake*, from the Stem ἐγερ, Pres. ἐγείρω, *I awaken* (class 4, *d*), is irregular.

2. The Stems ἀλω (ἀλίσκομαι, § 324, 17, *I am made prisoner*), ἀγ (ἄγνυμι, § 319, 13, *I break*), εἰκ (not used in the Pres., § 317, 7), and ὠνε (ὠνέομαι, *I buy*) are likewise irregular; but originally they had an initial consonant (§ 34, D.): ἐ-άλω-κα, ἔ-αγ-α, ἔ-οικ-α, ἐ-ώνη-μαι; the Stem ἀνοιγ (ἀνοίγω, *I open*) has ἀν-έῳγ-α. To these may be added εἴ-ωθ-α, *I am accustomed*, from the Stem ἰθ, originally ϝεθ (compare §§ 236, 237).

1. *The Perfect Active.*

§ 276. The terminations of the principal tenses are appended to the Perfect-Stem in the Indicative by means of the connecting vowel α. The first person has no personal ending at all; in the third, α is changed into ε. The Subjunctive, Optative, and the Imperative (which rarely occurs) have the vowels of the Present; the Infinitive ends in -έναι (always paroxytone), and the Participle in -ώς, -υῖα, -ός, Gen. -ότος (Stem οτ, § 188).

ἱερμένος (compare § 270, D., 3). The following two are defective Perfects in Hom.: ἀν-ήνοθ-ε(ν), *it gushes forth;* ἐν-ήνοθ-ε(ν), *it is upon.* Both also occur as Pluperfects.

§ 276. **Dialects.**—In the Hom. dialect, the Part. Perf. Act. sometimes has ω instead of ο: τεθνηῶτος = Att. τεθνηκότος (from θνήσκω, *I die*); κεκλήγωτες for κεκληγότες, *calling,* from Pres. κλάζω.

§ 278. THE PERFECT ACTIVE. 157

Obs.—The Subjunctive and Optative are not unfrequently formed periphrastically by the Participle with the corresponding forms of εἰμί, *I am.*

§ 277. The Perfect Active is formed in two different ways:

1. THE STRONG PERFECT (SECOND PERFECT) is formed, like the Strong Aorist, directly from the Stem: Stem π ρ ᾱ γ, Pres. (Class 4, *a*) πράσσω, *I do*, Perf. πέ-πρᾱγ-α. The Strong Perfect, like the Strong Aorist, occurs almost exclusively in the case of radical verbs (§ 245), and is generally the older and rarer form.

§ 278. The following changes of vowels are to be observed in its formation:

ᾰ after ρ becomes ᾱ : Stem κ ρ ᾰ γ, Pres. κράζω, *I scream*, Perf. κέ-κρᾱγ-α.
ᾰ otherwise becomes η : Stem π λ ᾰ γ, Pres. πλήσσω, *I strike*, Perf. πέ-πληγ-α.
Stem φ ᾰ ν, Pres. φαίνω, *I show*, Perf. πέ-φην-α.
ε becomes ο : Stem σ τ ρ ε φ, Pres. στρέφω, *I turn*, Perf. ἔ-στροφ-α.
ι " οι : Stem λ ῐ π, Pres. λείπω, *I leave*, Perf. λέ-λοιπ-α.
υ " ευ : Stem φ υ γ, Pres. φεύγω, *I flee*, Perf. πέ-φευγ-α.

Compare § 40 to § 43.

The change of ᾰ into ω is quite isolated: Stem ρ ᾰ γ, Perf. ἔρ-ρωγα, *I am torn*, Pres. ῥήγνῡ-μι (§ 319, 24), and

---

§ 277–280. Dialects.—The Hom. dialect is partial to the Strong Perfect; the aspiration does not occur in it: Stem κ ο π (κόπτω), κεκοπώς. The Part. πε-φυζ-ότ-ες, from Stem φ υ γ (φεύγω), is quite an isolated Hom. form. Hom. forms the Weak Perfect only from Vowel-Stems, and even here he has sometimes strong secondary forms: Stem φ υ, 3 Plur. Perf. Act. πεφύασι = Att. πεφύκασι, from φύω, *I beget;* Stem κ ο τ ε (κοτέω, *I am angry*), Part. Perf. κεκοτηώς, § 317, D. In the Fem: Part. Perf. shortenings of vowels often occur: Stem ἀ ρ, Masc. Part. Perf. ἀρ-ηρ-ώς, *joined,* Fem. ἀρ-ᾰρ-υῖα; Stem θ α λ (θάλλω, *I bloom*), Masc. Part. Perf. τε-θηλ-ώς, Fem. τε-θᾰλ-υῖα. The Perf. τέ-τρηχ-α, *I am restless,* Pres. ταράσσω, *I disturb,* Stem τ [α] ρ α χ, is irregular.

so also that of ε into ω: Stem ἐ θ, Perf. εἴ-ωθ-α, *I am accustomed* (§ 275). With the Attic reduplication, and in some other cases also, there is no lengthening of the vowel: Stem ὀρῠχ, ὀρ-ώρῠχ-α, Pres. ὀρύσσω, *I dig;* γέ-γρᾰφ-α, from γράφω, *I write*.

§ 279. Some Stems ending in the consonants κ, γ, π, β, change these into the corresponding aspirates, generally without any lengthening of the vowels:

Stem κ η ρ υ κ, Pres. κηρύσσω, *I proclaim*, Perf. κε-κήρυχ-α.
" ἀ γ, " ἄγω, *I lead*, " ἦχα (ἀγήοχ-α).
" κ ο π, " κόπτω, *I hew*, " κέ-κοφ-α.
" β λ ἀ β, " βλάπτω, *I hurt*, " βέ-βλᾰφ-α.

In spite of the aspiration, the vowels are changed in κέ-κλοφ-α, Stem κ λ ε π, Pres. κλέπτω, *I steal;* πέ-πομφ-α, Stem π ε μ π, Pres. πέμπω, *I send;* τέ-τροφ-α, Stem τ ρ ε π, τρέπω, *I turn*, which is in form the same as the Perf. of the Stem τ ρ ε φ (Pres. τρέφω, *I nourish*); εἴ-λοχ-α (compare § 274), Stem λ ε γ, Pres. λέγω, *I gather*.

Obs. 1.—Few verbs have both forms with and without the aspirate: the Stem π ρ α γ (Pres. πράσσω, *I do*) has both πέ-πρᾱγ-α (intransitive, *I have fared*) and πέ-πρᾱχ-α (transitive, *I have done*); Stem ἀ ν ο ι γ, Pres. ἀνοίγω, *I open*, Perf. ἀν-έῳγ-α (intrans., *I stand open*) and ἀν-έῳχ-α (transit., *I have opened*).

2. The aspirated form of the Perfect, contrary to § 277, occurs also in a number of derivative verbs: Stem ἀ λ λ α γ, ἀλλάσσω, *I change*, from ἄλλος, Perf. ἤλλαχ-α.

§ 280. 2. The Weak Perfect (First Perfect) is formed from the Stem by the insertion of κ: Stem λ υ, λέ-λυ-κ-α. The Weak Perfect is the more recent form, and with all Vowel-Stems it is the only one in use, while it is the more common with Stems ending in τ, δ, θ, and those in λ, μ, ν, ρ.

Obs.—The only complete Strong Perfect of a Vowel-Stem in Attic prose is ἀκήκοα (§ 275, 1); but compare § 317.

§ 281. In regard to the vowel, the Weak Perfect follows the σ Future (§§ 260, 261): Stem δ ρ α, δράσω, δέ-δρᾱ-κα;

§ 283. THE PLUPERFECT ACTIVE. 159

Stem τ ι μ α, τιμήσω, τετίμηκα; Stem π λ υ, πλεύσω, πέπλευκα; Stem π ι θ (πείθω, I persuade), πείσω, πέπεικα. χέω, I pour, Perf. κέχυκα, is an exception (§ 265). For other exceptions, see § 301.

Stems in τ, δ, θ throw out these consonants before. α, without any other change : Stem κ ο μ ι δ, κομίζω, I carry, κεκόμικα.

§ 282. The monosyllabic Stems in λ, ν, ρ, having ε in the Stem syllable, change this ε in the Weak Perf. into α : Stem σ τ ε λ, στέλλω, I send, Perf. ἔ-σταλ-κα; Stem φ θ ε ρ, φθείρω, I destroy, Perf. ἔ-φθαρ-κα. Several in ν throw out the ν: Stem κ ρ ῖ ν, κρίνω, I judge, Perf. κέ-κρῐ-κα; Stem κ λ ῖ ν, κλίνω, I incline, Perf. κέ-κλῐ-κα; Stem π λ ῠ ν, πλύνω, I wash, Perf. πέ-πλῠ-κα; Stem τ ε ν, τείνω, I stretch, Perf. τέ-τᾰ-κα. Wherever ν is not thrown out before κ, it becomes, according to § 51, a nasal γ : Stem φ α ν, φαίνω, I show, Perf. πέ-φαγ-κα.

Other Stems of this kind, and some in μ, admit of metathesis (§ 59) : Stem β α λ, βάλλω, I throw, Perf. βέ-βλη-κ-α; Stem κ α μ, κάμνω, I grow tired, Perf. κέ-κμη-κ-α (§ 321, 9).

2. *The Pluperfect Active.*

§ 283. The Pluperfect takes the Augment before the Perfect-Stem ; its terminations are those of the historical tenses. Between the Stem and the termination the diphthong ει steps in, which in the 3 Plur. is reduced to. ε.

Obs.—The 3 Plur. in εισαν is rare and more modern.

The Temporal Augment of verbs beginning with a vowel is not recognizable, because their Perfect-Stem has already

---

§ 282. Dialects.—The Hom. μέ-μβλω-κα for μέ-μλω-κα, from the Stem μ ο λ (Aor. ἔμολον, I went), is explained by metathesis. Compare §§ 51, D., 324, 12.

§ 283. Dialects.—The Ionic dialect has the antiquated endings of the Pluperf.: 1 Sing. εα, 2 Sing. εας, 3 Sing. εε(ν), contracted ει, ειν, or η; the 2 Plur. New-Ion. εα-τε. Hom. ἐτε-θήπ-εα, I was astonished ; 3 Sing. δεδειπνήκ-ειν, from δειπνέω, I dine.

ἐ-μέμηκ-ον (Perf. μέμηκα, I bleat) and ἤνωγον, along with ἠνώγεα (Perf. ἄνωγα; I compel), are formed quite irregularly, according to the manner of Imperfects.

a long vowel: Verbal-Stem ἀγ, ἄγω, *I drive*, Perfect-Stem ἦχ, ἦχ-ει-ν. The Syllabic Augment is often omitted. The 1 and 3 Sing. in the older Attic dialect have η instead of ει and ειν, as ἐ-λελύκ-η.

The formation of the Pluperfect is exactly the same as that of the Perfect, and, like it, it is either strong or weak, and has the vowel long or short, or unchanged.

§ 284. 3. *The Perfect Middle and Passive* can be formed only in one way, that is, by appending the personal endings of the principal tenses of the Middle, without any connecting vowel, to the Perfect-Stem, *i. e.*, to the reduplicated Verbal-Stem: Stem λυ, Perf. Mid. λέ-λυ-μαι.

The Infinitive and the Participle always have the accent on the penultima: λελύσθαι, λελυμένος; Stem παιδευ, πεπαιδεῦσθαι, from παιδεύω, *I educate*.

§ 285. The vowels are treated in the same way as in the Weak Perfect: Stem τιμα, τετίμηκα, τετίμημαι; Stem πιθ, πέπεικα, πέπεισμαι; Stem φθερ, ἔφθαρκα, ἔφθαρμαι; Stem βαλ, βέβληκα, βέβλημαι. The verbs τρέφω, *I nourish*, τρέπω, *I turn*, and στρέφω, *I turn*, also take α instead of ε: τέ-θραμ-μαι, τέ-τραμ-μαι, ἔ-στραμ-μαι.

§ 286. The final Consonants of Consonantal-Stems change according to the general laws of sound (§§ 45–49):

§ 284. Dialects.—In the Hom. dialect, the σ of the 2 Sing. Perf. and Pluperf. Mid. is sometimes thrown out between two vowels: μέμνηαι = μέμνησαι (*meministi*), contracted μέμνῃ; so also in the New-Ionic the Imperat. μέμνεο for μέμνησο.

§ 285. Dialects.—The Hom. πέ-πρω-ται, Stem πορ (Strong Aorist ἔπορον, *I gave*), is explained by metathesis. The following have a short vowel: τέτυγμαι, from τεύχω, *I prepare*, 3 Plur. τετεύχαται; πεφυγμένος, from φεύγω, *I flee;* ἔσσυμαι, from σεύω, *I hasten;* ῡ instead of ευ: πέ-πνῡ-μαι, from πνέω, § 248.

§ 286. Dialects.—The θ of the Stem κορυθ (κορύσσω, *I arm*) remains unchanged in Homer: κε-κορυθ-μένος. αἰσχύνω, *I put to shame*, has ᾔσχυμμαι.

§ 287. THE PERFECT MIDDLE. 161

1. Before all terminations beginning with μ
every guttural becomes γ : Stem π λ ε κ, πλέκω, *I twist*, πέ-πλεγ-μαι ;
" dental   "   σ : Stem π ι θ, πείθω, *I persuade*, πε-πείσ-μεθα ;
" labial   "   μ : Stem γ ρ α φ, γράφω, *I write*, γε-γραμ-μένος.

Obs.—When a guttural or labial is preceded by a nasal, the latter is thrown out before μ : Stem κ α μ π, κάμπτω, *I bend*, κέκαμμαι ; Stem ἐ λ ε γ χ,.ἐλέγχω, *I refute*, ἐλέλεγμαι (§ 275, 1). Some Stems in ν, by way of exception, do not change the ν before μ into σ, but into μ : ὤξυμμαι, from ὀξύνω, *I sharpen;* those which throw out the ν in the Perf. Active do the same here (§ 282) : κέκριμαι (compare πέ-φασ-μαι, from the Stem φ ά ν) : σπένδω, *I offer a libation*, Fut. σπείσω, has ἔσπεισμαι.

. Before σ
every guttural becomes κ, and this with σ becomes ξ : πέ-πλεξαι ;
" labial   "   π,   "   "   "   ψ : γέ-γραψαι ;
" dental is thrown out: πέ-πεισαι.

3. Before τ
every guttural becomes κ : πέ-πλεκται ; Stem λ ε γ, λέ-λεκ-ται ;
" labial   "   π : γέ-γραπται ;
" dental (exc. ν) "   σ : πέ-πεισ-ται (Stem φ α ν, πέ-φαν-ται).

4. The σ of σθ after consonants (§ 61) is dropped, and then

every guttural becomes χ : πέ-πλεχ-θον for πε-πλεκ-σθον ;
" labial   "   φ : γέ-γραφ-θε for γε-γραφ-σθε ;
" dental (exc. ν) "   σ : πε-πεῖσ-θαι for πε-πειθ-σθαι.

ν, λ, and ρ remain unchanged before the θ which has arisen from σθ : Stem φ α ν, πεφάνθαι ; Stem ἀ γ γ ε λ, ἠγγέλθαι.

§ 287. The ending νται of the 3 Plur. is irreconcilable with Consonantal-Stems. Sometimes the Ionic αται takes

---

§ 287. **Dialects.**—In the Ion. dialect, the forms αται and ατο·for the 3 Plur. are common : Hom. has βε-βλή-αται (βάλλω, *I throw*), πεποτήατο (ποτάομαι, *I flutter*), δεδαίαται (δαίω, *I divide*), ἔρχαται, ἵερχατο (εἴργω, *I shut in*, § 319, 15) ; in New-Ionic, παρεσκευάδατο (παρασκευάζω, *I prepare*), κεκοσμέαται (κοσμέω, *I adorn*). Three Homeric forms insert δ : ἐρρά-δ-αται (ῥαίνω, *I besprinkle*), ἀκηχέ-δ-ατο (ἄχνυμαι, *I am grieved*), ἐληλά-δ-ατο (Stem ἐ λ α, ἐλαύνω, *I drive*) ; ἐρηρέδαται, from ἐρείδω, *I support*, is irregular.

its place (§ 226, D.), before which γ, κ, β, and π are aspirated: γε-γράφ-αται, τε-τάχ-αται (Stem τ α γ, τάσσω, *I arrange*), τε-τρίφ-αται (Stem τ ρ ι β, τρίβω, *I rub*). But the common practice is to use the periphrasis by means of the Participle with εἰ-σί(ν): γεγραμμένοι εἰσίν. Compare Lat. *scripti sunt* and § 276, *Obs.*
The following paradigms supply examples of the above-mentioned changes.

	Perfect Middle and Passive.	
Guttural Stems.	Dental Stems.	Labial Stems.
πέ-πλεγ-μαι	πέ-πεισ-μαι	γέ-γραμ-μαι
πέ-πλεξαι	πέ-πεισαι	γέ-γραψαι
πέ-πλεκ-ται	πέ-πεισ-ται	γέ-γραπ-ται
πε-πλέγ-μεθα	πε-πείσ-μεθα	γε-γράμ-μεθα
πέ-πλεχ-θε	πέ-πεισ-θε	γέ-γραφ-θε
πε-πλεγ-μένοι εἰσί	πε-πεισ-μένοι εἰσί	γε-γραμ-μένοι εἰσί

§ 288. After Vowel-Stems, σ is frequently inserted before the terminations beginning with μ and τ, but more especially when the Stems have the vowel short: Stem τ ε λ ε, τελῶ, *I complete*, Perf. τε-τέλε-σ-μαι; Stem σ π ᾰ, σπάω, *I draw*, 3 Sing. ἔ-σπα-σ-ται; but it also occurs in not a few Stems with long vowels and diphthongs: ἀκούω, *I hear*, ἤκουσμαι; κελεύω, *I order*; κυλίω, *I roll*; λεύω, *I stone to death*; ξύω, *I polish*; παίω, *I strike*; πλέω (πέπλευσται), *I sail*; πρίω, *I saw*; σείω, *I shake*; χρίω, *I anoint*; ψαύω, *I touch*. Others fluctuate: κλείω or κλῄω, *I close*; κρούω, *I push*.

§ 289. The Subjunctive and Optative are generally formed by periphrasis with the Participle and the corresponding forms of εἰμί. (Compare Lat. *solutus sim, essem.*) These moods are but rarely evolved out of Vowel-Stems themselves: κτάομαι, *I acquire*, κέ-κτη-μαι, Subj. κε-κτῶ-μαι, κε-κτῇ, κέ-κτη-ται, Opt. κε-κτῴ-μην (from κε-κταοί-μην), κε-κτῷ-το; besides these, we also have κεκτῄμην, ᾖο, ᾖτο.

---

§ 289. Dialects.—The Hom. Subj. from Stem μ ν α (μέμνημαι, *memini*), 1 Plur. μεμνώμεθα (New-Ion. μεμνεώμεθα), Opt. μεμνῄμην; 3 Sing. λελῦτο, 3 Plur. λελῦντο, instead of λελυ-ι-το, λελυ-ι-ντο, § 28.

§ 290. 4. *The Pluperfect Middle and Passive* differs in every verb from the corresponding Perfect only by the addition of the Augment and the personal endings, which are those of the historical tenses. Respecting the 3 Plur. in νто and ατο, and their places being supplied by periphrasis, see § 287, which is here applicable also.

§ 291. 5. *The Future Perfect or Futurum Exactum* adds σ to the Perfect-Stem with the Inflexion of the Future-Middle; the σ produces the same changes in the preceding consonants as in the ordinary Future Middle: πεπράξεται (Stem π ρ a γ, πράσσω, *I do*), *it will have been done;* γεγράψεται (Stem γ ρ a φ, γράφω, *I write*), *it will have been written.*

There are two isolated Future Perfects with Active endings: ἑστήξω (§ 311), *I shall stand,* and τεθνήξω (§ 324, 4), *I shall be dead,* from the Perf. ἕστηκα, τέθνηκα.

Otherwise its place in the Active is supplied by the Part. of the Perf. with the Fut. of εἰμί, *I am* (ἔσομαι): λελυκὼς ἔσομαι, *I shall have loosed* (*solvero*).

VI. The Strong Passive Stem.

§ 292. From the Strong Passive Stem are formed the *Strong* or *Second Aorist*, and the *Strong* or *Second Future Passive*.

Present: φαίνω, Pure Stem φ ἄ ν, Strong Passive Stem φ ἄ ν ε.

1. Strong or Second Aorist Passive.

	Indicative.	Subjunctive.	Optative.
	ἐ-φάνη-ν, *I appeared*.	φᾰνῶ	φανείη-ν
	ἐ-φάνη-ς	φανῇ-ς	φανείη-ς
	ἐ-φάνη	φανῇ	φανείη
	ἐ-φάνη-τον	φανῆ-τον	φανείη-τον or φανεῖτον
	ἐ-φανή-την	φανῆ-τον	φανείη-την or φανείτην
	ἐ-φάνη-μεν	φανῶ-μεν	φανείη-μεν or φανεῖμεν
	ἐ-φάνη-τε	φανῆ-τε	φανείη-τε or φανεῖτε
	ἐ-φάνη-σαν	φανῶ-σι(ν)	φανείη-σαν or φανεῖεν

Imperative.		Inf.	φανῆ-ναι	Part.	φανείς, φανεῖσα, φανέν
φάνη-θι					Gen. φανέ-ντ-ος
φανή-τω					
φάνη-τον					
φανή-των					
φάνη-τε					
φανή-τωσαν or φανέ-ντων					

2. Strong or Second Future Passive.

Ind.	φανή-σομαι	
Opt.	φανη-σοίμην	etc., the same as the Future Middle.
Inf.	φανή-σεσθαι	
Part.	φανη-σόμενος, η, ον	

§ 293. The personal endings of the Aorist Passive are of an *Active* nature, those of the Future Passive of the nature of the *Middle*. They are appended, as in the Sec-

§ 293. **Dialects.**—The Hom. dialect has the shorter ending εν in the 3 Plur. Ind. Aor. Pass.: ἐ-φάνε-ν or φάνε-ν; τράφε-ν = ἐτράφησαν, from τρέφω. The Ion. dialect leaves the ε in the Subj. uncontracted: μῐγέ-ω (μίσγω, *I mix*). Homer often lengthens the ε in the Subj., sometimes to ει: δᾰμείω = δαμῶ, Stem δ ᾰ μ, Pres. δάμνημι, *I tame;* and some-

§ 295. VI. THE STRONG PASSIVE STEM. 165

ond Principal Conjugation (§ 302), to the Stem without a connecting vowel, and the ε of the Stem is lengthened in the Indicative and Imperative to η. In the Subjunctive, the ε is contracted with the vowels of the Subjunctive: φᾰνέ-ω, φᾰνῶ; in the Optative, the ε, combined with the modal sign ιη, becomes ειη: φανε-ίη-ν. The Infinitive always has the circumflex on the penultima, and the Participle in the Nom. Sing. Masc. the acute on the last.

§ 294. The Strong Passive Stem, just like the Strong Aorist Active and Middle (§ 256), is formed very rarely from derivative Stems; but it occurs in verbs of all classes, even the first (§ 247), ε being added to the pure Verbal-Stem: Pres. ῥάπτ-ω (class 3, *I sew*), Pure Stem ῥ ᾰ φ, Strong Passive Stem ῥ ᾰ φ ε, Aor. Pass. ἐρράφη-ν; σφάττω (class 4, *I slaughter*), Pure Stem σ φ α γ, Strong Passive Stem σ φ α γ ε, Aor. Pass. ἐσφάγη-ν, Fut. Pass. σφάγη-σομαι; Pres. γράφ-ω (class 1), Strong Pass. Stem γ ρ.ᾰ φ ε, Aor. Pass. ἐγράφη-ν. The Strong Passive Aor. occurs only in such verbs as have *no* Strong Active Aorist. The only exception is τρέπω, *I turn*, Aor. Act. ἔ-τρᾰπ-ο-ν, Pass. ἐ-τράπη-ν.

Obs.—By way of exception, ἠλλάγην is formed from the derivative Stem ἀ λ λ α γ, Pres. ἀλλάσσω, *I change.*

§ 295. As in the Strong Aorist Active (§ 257), the ε is sometimes changed into ᾰ: κλέπ-τ-ω, *I steal*, ἐ-κλάπη-ν; στέλλω, *I send*, ἐ-στάλη-ν; τρέφ-ω, *I nourish*, ἐ-τράφη-ν; πλέκ-ω, *I twist*, ἐ-πλέκη-ν and ἐ-πλᾰκη-ν; πλήσσω, *I strike*,

times to η: φᾰνή-ῃ = φᾰνῇ. In the Dual and Plur., the modal vowel is shortened where this lengthening of the ε occurs: δαμεί-ετε (for δαμέητε, Att. δαμῆτε). In the Infinitive we find the Hom. μεναι or μεν: μιγήμεναι, δαμῆμεν.

§ 295. **Dialects.**—Homer here also employs metathesis (§ 59), as in the Strong Aor. Act. and Mid. (§ 357, D.): Pres. τέρπ-ω, *I delight*, Aor. Pass. ἐ-τάρπη-ν, Subj. τρᾰπέ-ω, 1 Plur. τρᾰπείομεν (*gaudeamus*), Inf. τρᾰπή-μεναι.

has ἐ-πλήγη-ν, πληγή-σομαι, but in composition ἐξ-ε-πλάγη-ν, ἐκ-πλἄγή-σομαι ; the Pure Stem of verbs of the second class here reappears : σήπ-ω (Stem σᾰπ, *I corrupt*), ἐ-σάπη-ν ; τήκ-ω (Stem τᾰκ, *I melt*), ἐ-τάκη-ν ; ῥέω (Stem ῥῠ, *I flow*), ἐ-ῤῥύη-ν, ῥυή-σομαι.

VII. THE WEAK PASSIVE STEM.

§ 296. From the Weak Passive Stem are formed the *Weak* or *First Aorist* and the *Weak* or *First Future Passive*.

Pres. λύω, Stem λυ, Weak Passive Stem λυθε.

1. *Weak* or *First Aorist Passive.*

Ind. ἐ-λύθη-ν, *I was loosed.* ἐ-λύθη-ς	Subj. λυθῶ λυθῇ-ς	Opt. λυθείη-ν λυθείη-ς
etc., like the Strong or Second Aorist Passive.		
Imp. λύθη-τι λυθή-τω	Inf. λυθῆ-ναι	Part. λυθεί-ς, λυθεῖσα, λυθέν Gen. λυθέντ-ος
etc., like the Strong or Second Aorist Passive.		

2. *Weak* or *First Future Passive.*

Ind. λυθή-σομαι	Opt. λυθη-σοίμην	Inf. λυθή-σεσθαι Part. λυθη-σόμενο-ς, η, ο-ν

§ 297. The inflexion of the Weak Passive Stem is entirely like that of the Strong. Respecting the τ of λύθη-τι, instead of λυθη-θι, see § 53, *c*.

---

§ 296. **Dialects.**—The Weak Fut. Pass. is wanting in the Homeric dialect.

§ 297. **Dialects.**—Respecting the inflexion, see § 293, D.

§ 298. **Dialects.**—The Hom. dialect after some Vowel-Stems inserts ν before θ : ἀμπνύ-ν-θη (Stem πνυ, πνέω, *I breathe*), ἱδρύ-ν-θη (ἱδρύω, *I set firm*), and changes the ε of the Stem φαεν (φαείνω, φαίνω, *I make appear*) into α, φαάνθην.

§ 298. The Weak Passive Stem is formed from the Verbal-Stem by appending the syllable θε. Before this syllable the vowels of Vowel-Stems are lengthened as in the Future, the Weak Aorist Active, and the Perfect: τ ι μ α, ἐτιμήθην; π ε ι ρ α, ἐπειράθην, *I tried*. As to the exceptions, see § 301. As in the Perfect Middle, σ is inserted before θ, especially after short vowels, but often also after long ones: ἐ-τελέ-σ-θην, from τελέω, *I complete;* ἐ-κελεύ-σ-θην, from κελεύω, *I order;* and this is the case in the verbs mentioned in § 288, and especially in γελάω, *I laugh*, ἐγελάσθην; δράω, *I do*, ἐδράσθην; παύω, *I cause to cease*, ἐπαύσθην, but also ἐπαύθην. The Aor. Passive of σώζω, *I save*, on the other hand, is formed from the shorter Stem σω without the σ: ἐσώθην.

As in the Weak Perfect Active and the Perfect Middle, the ε before λ, ν, ρ is sometimes changed into α: Stem τ ε ν (τείνω, *I stretch*), ἐ-τάθη-ν (compare § 282).

The changes of the consonants before θ are explained by the laws of sound (§ 45): Stem π ρ ᾱ γ, πράσσω, *I do*, ἐ-πράχ-θη-ν; Stem ψ ε υ δ, ψεύδω, *I deceive*, ἐ-ψεύσ-θη-ν; Stem π ε μ π, πέμπω, *I send*, ἐ-πέμφ-θη-ν. Respecting ἐθρέφθην (Pres. τρέφω), ἐθάφθην (Pres. θάπτω), see § 54, Obs., and respecting ἐτέθην, ἐτύθην (Stems θ ε, θ υ), see § 53, b.

§ 299. The Weak Aorist Passive and the Weak Future Passive are, on the whole, more common than the Strong, and in the case of derivative verbs, as of nearly all Vowel-Stems, they are the only customary forms of the Aorist and Future Passive.

There are some primitive verbs of which both Passive Stems are in use: Stem βλαβ, Pres. βλάπτω, *I hurt*, Aor. Pass. ἐβλάβην and ἐβλάφθην.

Verbal Adjectives.

§ 300. The Verbal Adjectives are a kind of Passive Participles.

Pres. λύω, Stem λ υ, 1. λῠ-τός, ή, όν, *loosed, capable of being loosed*.

2. λῠ-τέο-ς, α, ον, *to be loosened, solvendu-s, a, um.*

The First Verbal Adjective is formed by means of the syllable το (Nom. το-ς, τη, το-ν) from the Verbal-Stem, and has the meaning either of a Participle Perfect Passive, λυ-τό-ς = *solu-tu-s*, or of possibility, *capable of being loosened*.

The Second Verbal Adjective is formed by means of the syllable τέο (Nom. τέο-ς, τέα, τέο-ν), which is never contracted, from the Verbal-Stem, and has the meaning of necessity, like the Latin gerundive: λυ-τέο-ς, *one who is to be loosened;* λυτέον ἐστί, *loosening must take place, solvendum est.*

The vowels preceding the τ are in general treated exactly in the same manner as in the Weak Passive Aorist; σ is inserted in the same cases as in the Aor. Pass.: τελε-σ-τός, κελευ-σ-τέον. The consonants before τ are treated in accordance with the laws of sound: πρακ-τό-ς (Stem π ρ ᾱ γ, Pres. πράσσω); γραπ-τό-ς(γράφω); κομισ-τέο-ν(Stem κ ο μ ι δ, κομίζω, *I carry*).

Verbs which leave their Stem Vowel short in the formation of their Tenses.

§ 301. The Vowel remains short throughout in:

---

§ 300. Dialects.—δοα-τό-ς is derived by metathesis (§ 59) from the Stem δ ε ρ (δέρω, *I flay*).

§ 301. Dialects.—The Hom. dialect ἐράω, *I love*, Aor. Mid. ἠρᾰσάμην; ἀρκέω, *I ward off*, ἤρκεσα; κορέω, *I satisfy*, ἐκόρεσα; κοτέω, *I grudge*, κοτέσσατο; ἐρύω, *I draw*, εἴρῠσα. On the usual doubling of the σ after short vowels (ἐράσσατο, ἐρύσσατο), see § 261, D.

§ 301. VERBS WITH A SHORT VOWEL. 169

γελάω,	I laugh,	Fut. γελάσομαι,	Aor. Act. ἐγέλᾰσα,
			Aor. Pass. ἐγελάσθην,
			Fut. Pass. γελασθήσομαι.
θλάω,	I squeeze,	Fut. θλάσω,	Aor. Act. ἔθλᾰσα,
			Verb. Adj. θλαστός.
κλάω,	I break,	Fut. κλάσω,	Aor. Pass. ἐκλάσθην,
			Perf. Mid. κέκλασμαι.
σπάω,	I draw,	Fut. σπάσω,	Aor. Act. ἔσπᾰσα,
			Aor. Pass. ἐσπάσθην, Perf. Act. ἔσπᾰκα,
			Perf. Mid. ἔσπασμαι, Verb. Adj. σπαστός.
χαλάω,	I slacken,	Fut. χαλάσω,	Aor. Pass. ἐχαλάσθην.
αἰδέομαι,	I dread,	Fut. αἰδέσομαι,	Aor. Pass. ᾐδέσθην (328),
			Perf. ᾔδεσμαι.
ἀκέομαι,	I heal,	Fut. ἀκέσομαι,	Aor. ἠκεσάμην.
ἀλέω,	I grind,	Fut. ἀλέσω (ῶ),	Perf. Act. ἀλήλεκα,
			Perf. Mid. ἀλήλεσμαι.
ἀρκέω,	I satisfy,	Fut. ἀρκέσω,	Aor. Act. ἤρκεσα.
ἐμέω,	I vomit,		Aor. Act. ἤμεσα.
ζέω,	I seethe,	Fut. ζέσω,	Aor. Act. ἔζεσα,
			Verb. Adj. ζεστός.
ξέω,	I scrape,	Fut. ξέσω,	Verb. Adj. ξεστός.
τελέω,	I finish,	Fut. τελέσω (ῶ),	Aor. Act. ἐτέλεσα,
			Aor. Pass. ἐτελέσθην,
			Verb. Adj. τελεστός,
			Perf. Act. τετέλεκα,
			Perf. Mid τετέλεσμαι.
ἀρόω,	I plow,	Fut. ἀρόσω,	Aor. Act. ἤροσα,
			Aor. Pass. ἠρόθην.
ἀρύω,	I draw,	Fut. ἀρύσω,	Aor. Act. ἤρῠσα.
addit. form ἀρύτω.			
ἑλκύω,	I draw,		Aor. Act. εἵλκῠσα.
		Fut. Pass. ἑλκυσθήσομαι,	Perf. Act. εἵλκυκα,
			Perf. Mid. εἵλκυσμαι.
πτύω,	I spit,		Aor. Act. ἔπτῠσα.
			Verb. Adj. πτυστός.

2. *The vowel is long* in the Weak Aor. Act., and short in the Perf., the Aor. Pass., and the Verbal Adjective in

δέω,	I bind,	Fut. δήσω,	Aor. Act. ἔδησα,
			Perf. Act. δέδεκα,
			Aor. Pass. ἐδέθην,
			Verb. Adj. δετός,
			Perf. Mid. δέδεμαι,
			3 Fut. δεδήσομαι.

H

θύω, *I sacrifice*, Fut. θύσω, Aor. Act. ἔθῦσα,
Perf. Act. τέθῠκα, Aor. Pass. ἐτυθην,
Perf. Mid. τέθῠμαι.
λύω, *I loose*, Fut. λύσω, Aor. Act. ἔλῡσα,
Perf. Act. λέλῠκα, Aor. Pass. ἐλῠθην,
Verb. Adj. λῠτός, Perf. Mid. λέλῠμαι.

3. *The Vowel is short* in the Future and Weak Aorist Active and Middle, but *long* in the Perfect, Aorist Passive, and Verbal Adjective of καλέω, *I call*, καλέσω, κέκληκα, ἐκλήθην, κλητός; αἰνέω, *I praise*, has αἰνέσω, ᾔνεκα, ᾐνέθην, αἰνετός, but Perf. Mid. ᾔνημαι.

4. ποθέω, *I long for;* πονέω, *I toil;* and δύω, *I sink*, fluctuate between the short and long vowels: ποθέσομαι and ποθήσω; πονέσω, ἐπονησάμην; δύσω, Aor. Pass. ἐδύθην.

CHAP. XI.—SECOND PRINCIPAL CONJUGATION, or Verbs in μι.

PRELIMINARY OBSERVATIONS.

§ 302. The Second Principal Conjugation differs from the First only in the inflexion of the *Present* and *Strong Aorist-Stems*, and in the case of a few verbs also in the Perfect and Pluperfect Active.

The special terminations of this conjugation are:

1. The 1 Sing. Pres. Ind. Act. retains the ancient μι: φη-μί, *I say* (§ 226).
2. The 3 Sing. Pres. Ind. Act. retains the ancient σι(ν) (for τι): φησί(ν) (§ 226).
3. The 3 Plur. Pres. Ind. Act. inserts the vowel α before the termi-

---

§ 302. **Dialects.**—The Hom. dialect often has the ending σθα in the 2 Sing. Ind. Act.: τίθη-σθα, *thou puttest;* ἔ-φη-σθα; and μεναι or μεν instead of ναι in the Inf.: φά-μεναι, φά-μεν; and a short ν instead of the σαν of the 3 Plur. of the Preterite: ἔ-φᾰ-ν.

The Hom. dialect sometimes lengthens the Stem-vowel in the Subj. and shortens the Modal-vowel as in the Aor. Pass. (§ 298): 'ἴομεν = 'ἴωμεν (*eamus*).

§ 304. SECOND PRINCIPAL CONJUGATION. 171

nation σι (for ντι) (§ 226, compare Dialects), and this a is lengthened by compensation (ῖ-ᾱσι(ν), *they go*, from the Stem ἰ), and unites with the α of the Stem : φᾶσι(ν).

4. In the Optative, ιη (ιε, ι), the Modal-sign attaches itself directly to the Stem : φα-ίη-ν; compare § 293.
5. The 2 Sing. Imperat. has the ending θι: φά-θι. } Compare § 292.
6. The Infinit. has the ending ναι: φά-ναι.   }
7. The 3 Plur. of the Preterite has σαν: ἔ-φἄ-σαν (3 Plur. Imperf.).

All terminations of these two tenses are appended to the Stem *without a connecting vowel*: φἄ-μέν (compare τιμά-ο-μεν), φά-τω (compare τιμα-έ-τω) ; in the Participle, also, ντ attaches itself directly to the Stem : φ α-ν τ, of which the Nom. is formed by the addition of σ: φάς; Stem δο, δούς (compare § 147, 1). In the Subjunctive alone the final vowels of the Stems are contracted with the long connecting vowels, as in the ordinary contracted verbs (§ 243): φά-ω, φῶ ; τι-θέ-ω, τι-θῶ ; δό-ω-μαι, δῶμαι.

§ 303. In the vowel-Stems of this conjugation a change of quantity takes place in such a manner that vowels in themselves short are lengthened in the Singular Indicative Active, α and ε becoming η, ο ω, and ὔ ῡ : φη-μί, *I say*, Plur. φἄ-μέν, ἔ-φη-ν, Dual ἔ-φἄ-τον ; [ἔ-θη-ν, *I placed*], Plur. ἔ-θε-μεν ; δείκνῡ-μι, *I show*, Plur. δείκνῠ-μεν.

Obs.—Those forms which always have the vowel long are specially noticed below.

§ 304. All verbs in μι are divided into 2 classes :

1. Those which in the Present join their terminations directly to the Stem : φη-μί ;
2. Those which form the Present-Stem by adding νυ to the Pure Stem: δείκ-νῡ-μι, *I show*, Pure Stem δ ε ι κ, Present-Stem δ ε ι κ ν υ.

I. First Class of Verbs in μι.

§§ 305 and 306. The Paradigms of this Class of Verbs are inserted on p. 124, fol. *sqq.*

§ 307. Some few forms of the Verbs in μι are formed

§§ 305, 306. Dialects.—The following are Ionic secondary forms, those inclosed in brackets being the New-Ionic.

Active.

2 Sing. Pres. Ind. τί-θη-σθα	δι-δοῖ-σθα, also δι-δοῖ-ς	
3 " " " τι-θεῖ	δι-δοῖ	[ἱ-στᾷ]
3 Plur. " " τι-θεῖσι(ν)	δι-δοῦσι(ν)	[ἱ-στέ-ᾶσι(ν)]
also (προ)θέουσι(ν)		
2 Sing. Pres. Imperat.	δί-δω-θι	(καθ)-ί-στα
Inf. Pres. τι-θή-μεναι	δι-δό-μεν	
	δι-δοῦ-ναι	
Imperf. 1 Sing. [ἐ-τί-θε-α]	[ἐ-δί-δου-ν]	
3 " [ἐ-τί-θε-ε]		[ἵ-στα]

Middle.

3 Plur. Pres. Ind. [τι-θέ-αται	δι-δό-αται	ἱ-στέ-αται]
3 " Imperf. "		[ἱ-στέ-ατο]
Pres. Part. τι-θή-μενος .		

Active.

2 Aor. Ind. 3 Plur. ἔστᾰν
 ἔστᾰσαν

" Subj. 1 Sing. θείω [θέω]
" " 2 " θείῃς or θήῃς   δῷς   στήῃς
" " 3 " θείῃ   δῶσι(ν) or
 δώῃσι(ν) :
" " 2 D.   στήετον (§ 302, D.)
" " 1 Plur. θέωμεν or   δώομεν   στέωμεν or
 • θείομεν   στείομεν
" " 3 "   δώωσι(ν)   [στέωσι] ·
" Inf.   θέμεναι, θέμεν   δόμεναι, δόμεν   στήμεναι·

Middle.

" Ind.   ἔθεο, ἔθευ (§ 37, D., 1)
 [Herod. προςθήκαντο]
" Subj.   [θέωμαι] θείομαι
" Imper.   θέο, θεῦ.

after the First Principal Conjugation, as, e. g., the 2 Sing. Imperf. ἐτίθεις, the 3 Sing. ἐτίθει, as if from the Stem τ ι θ ε. In the Imperf., the forms ἐδίδουν, ἐδίδους, ἐδίδου are the only ones in use from the Stem δ ι δ ο; they are formed in the same manner as those of contracted verbs (§ 243). Other similar forms will be noticed in treating of the separate verbs.

In the 3 Plur. Pres. Ind. contraction is sometimes employed: τιθεῖσι, διδοῦσι.

In the 2 Sing. Imperat. Pres. Act. the real ending θι is dropped, and the Stem-vowel is lengthened to compensate for it: δίδου for δίδοθι.

In the same person of the Aorist after a short vowel ι only is dropped, and the remaining θ, according to § 67, is changed to ς: δο-θι, δός, but στῆ-θι, which only in compounds sometimes appears as στᾶ, e. g., κατάστα.

In the 2 Sing. Mid. of the Present and Imperfect the σ between the two vowels is preserved: τίθε-σαι, τίθε-σο, ἐτίθε-σο; only the 2 Sing. of the Subj. is treated entirely like the contracted verbs of the First Principal Conjugation. In the 2 Sing. Mid. of the Strong Aorist, on the other hand, the σ is thrown out, which gives rise to a contraction: ἔ-θε-σο, ἔ-θε-ο, ἔ-θου; Imper. θέ-σο, θέ-ο, θοῦ.

Obs.—The forms of the 2 Sing. Imperat. Mid. compounded with monosyllabic prepositions, after contraction, throw the accent as a circumflex upon the last syllable: προ-θοῦ; but Homer has σύν-θεο and περί-θου.

§ 308. The three verbs conjugated above (p. 124) distinguish the *Present-Stem* from the *Pure Stem* by *reduplication*, that is, the initial consonant with ι is prefixed before the Stem: δο, διδο; θε, τιθε (§ 53 b); ἱ-στα for σι-στα, according to § 60, b (compare Latin *si-sto*). In like manner, the Stem χρα in the Pres. becomes κι-χρα (κί-χρη-μι, *I lend*); πλα and πρα, with the insertion of a nasal, become πι-μ-πλα, πι-μ-πρα (πίμπλημι, *I fill*; πίμπρημι, *I burn*); but συμ-πί-πλη-μι, ἐμ-πί-πλη-μι; the

Stem ἑ becomes ἵ-η-μι, *I send;* and, with the reduplication within the Stem itself, ὀ ν α becomes ὀ-νί-νη-μι, *I benefit.*

§ 309. The Deponents δύναμαι, *I can;* ἐπίσταμαι, *I understand;* κρέμαμαι, *I hang;* together with the Aorists ἐπριάμην, *I bought;* ὠνήμην, *I benefited,* withdraw the accent, even in the Subjunctive and Optative, as far as possible from the end: δύνωμαι, ἐπίσταιντο (compare ἱστῶμαι, ἱσταῖντο).

Other peculiarities of verbs of this class are:

§ 310. The three Stems θ ε (τίθημι), δ ο (δίδωμι), and ἑ (ἵημι) form an irregular Weak Aorist in κα : ἔθηκα, ἔδωκα, ἧκα, but in the Middle we find only ἡκάμην. In the Sing. of the Indicative the Active forms are customary instead of those of the Strong Aorist, but in the Dual and Plural of the Indicative they are rare. The other moods and the Participles have the strong forms exclusively.

The really customary forms of the Aorist, therefore, are these:

Ind.	Subj. θῶ	Mid. ἐθέμην
ἔθηκα	Opt. θείην	Subj. θῶμαι
ἔθηκας	Imp. θές	etc.
ἔθηκε(ν)	Inf. θεῖναι	
ἔθετον	Part. θείς	
ἐθέτην		
ἔθεμεν (seldom ἐθήκαμεν)		
ἔθετε (" ἐθήκατε)		
ἔθεσαν (" ἐθήκαν).		

§ 311. 2. The *rough breathing* instead of the σ of the Stem στα is also used in the Perf. (§ 60, b): ἕ-στη-κα for σε-στη-κα. On the shorter forms, ἕσταμεν, etc., see § 317, 4. ἑστήξω, *I shall stand,* is a Third Future Active. The Perfects of θ ε and ἑ are τέθεικα, εἷκα; the same vowel also remains in the Perf. Mid. τέθειμαι, εἷμαι. The Stems δ ο and στ α leave their vowel *short* in the Perf. Mid. and Aor.

---

§ 310. **Dialects.**—From the Stem δ ο Hom. has sometimes Fut. διδώ-σω instead of δώσω.

Pass., and θ ε in the Aor. Pass.: δέ-δο-μαι, ἐδόθην, ἐστάθην, ἐτέθην, τεθήσομαι. On the meaning of the different forms of ἵστημι, see § 329, 1.

§ 312. To the *First* Class of the Verbs in μι there also belong:
A) Verbs whose Stem ends in α (compare ἵστημι):
1. ἤ-μί (compare Lat. *ā-io*), *I say*, only in the Imperf. ἦν, 3 Sing. ἦ (compare § 213, *Obs.*).
2. ὀ-νί-νη-μι (Stem ὀ ν α, § 308), *I benefit*, Mid. ὀνίναμαι (§ 309), *I have advantage*, Strong Aor. Mid. ὠνήμην, ὤνησο, ὤνητο; Opt. ὀναίμην, Imperat. ὄνησο, Inf. ὄνασθαι, Fut. ὀνήσω, ὀνήσομαι; Aor. Pass. ὠνήθην.
3. πί-μ-πλη-μι (Stem π λ α, § 308). Additional form, πλήθω, *I fill* [Lat. *ple-o*], Fut. πλήσω, Perf. Mid. πέπλησμαι, Aor. Pass. ἐπλήσθην.
4. πί-μ-πρη-μι (Stem π ρ α). Additional form, πρήθω (quite like 3).
5. φη-μί (Stem φ α), *I say*, 2 Sing. Imperf. ἔφησθα (enclitic in Pres. Ind. except 2 Sing., compare § 92, 3). Imperat. φάθί or φάθι; compare φάσκω, 324, 8.
6. χρή (Stem χ ρ α, χ ρ ε), *one must*, Subj. χ ρ ῇ, Opt. χ ρ ε ί η, Inf. χ ρ ῆ ν α ι, Part. χρεών (only Neut. from χ ρ ᾶ ο ν according to § 37, D.). Imperf. ἐχρῆν or χρῆν, Fut. χρήσει; ἀ π ό χ ρ η, *it suffices*, also 3 Plur. ἀ π ο χ ρ ῶ σ ι(ν), etc., as above ἀποχράω.
7. κί-χρη-μι (Stem χ ρ α, § 308); *I lend*, Inf. κ ι χ ρ ά ν α ι, Fut. χ ρ ή σ ω, Aor. ἔ χ ρ η σ α. Farther the *deponents*:
8. ἄγα-μαι (Stem ἄ γ ἄ), *I admire*, Fut. ἀγάσομαι, Aor. Pass. ἠγάσθην, Verb. Adj. ἀγαστός.
9. δύνἄ-μαι (Stem δ υ ν ἄ), *I can*, 2 Sing. Ind. δύνῃ is rare (§ 309), Imperf. ἐδυνάμην, 2 Sing. ἐδύνω, Fut. δυνήσομαι,

---

§ 312. **Dialects.**—3. Hom. has the Aor. πλῆτο, *it was filled*, 3 Plur. πλῆντο, Opt. πλήμην or πλείμην, Imper. [ἐμ]πλησο.
6. Herod. ἀπέχρα.
8. Hom. ἀγάομαι, ἀγαίομαι.

Aor. ἐδυνήθην, seldom ἐδυνάσθην. The Augment is frequently η (§ 234, Obs.), Perf. δεδύνημαι, Verb. Adj. δυνατός, capable, possible.

10. ἐπίστα-μαι (Stem ἐ π ι σ τ ă), I understand, 2 Sing. ἐπίστασαι, Imperf. ἠπιστάμην, ἠπίστω, Fut. ἐπιστήσομαι, Aor. ἠπιστήθην, Verb. Adj. ἐπιστητός.

11. ἔρα-μαι (Stem ἐ ρ ă), poetic, I love (commonly ἐράω), Aor. Pass. ἠράσθην.

12. κρέμα-μαι (Stem κ ρ ε μ ă), I hang (§ 309). Fut. κρεμήσομαι, Aor. ἐκρεμάσθην. Additional forms, § 319, 2.

Obs.—The following may serve as examples of the formation of words: τὸ θέ-μα, the position; ὁ δο-τήρ, the giver; ἡ στά-σι-ς, the rise; ἡ ὄνη-σι-ς, the benefit, from the Pure Verbal-Stem, differing from the Present-Stem; ἡ φή-μη, fā-ma, talk; ἡ δύναμι-ς, power; ἡ ἐπιστή-μη, knowledge, from the Verbal-Stem, which is the same as that of the Present.

Dialects.—13. Hom. ἄμεναι, satiate, Stem ἀ, Subj. ἕωμεν.
14. Stem β α, Part. βιβάς, stepping.
14. b. Stem δ ε α, 3 Sing. Imperf. δέατο, seemed, Aor. δοά-σσατο.
15. Stem ἰ λ α, ἱλάσκομαι, ἱλάομαι, I am gracious, Hom. Imperat. ἵληθι.
16. Stem κ ε ρ α (compare κεράννυμι, I mix), Hom. 3 Plur. Subj. Mid. κέρωνται. To these belong also, in regard to the inflexion of the Present-Stem, those Hom. verbs which either are used only in the Present-Stem, or form the Present-Stem from the Verbal Stem by affixing the syllable -να:

a) δ ά μ-ν η-μ ι (also δαμ-νά-ω), I tame, Mid. δάμ-νă-μαι, Fut. δαμόω, δαμάςς, Weak Aor. Inf. δαμάσαι, δαμάσασθαι, Perf. δέδμημαι, Aor. Pass. ἐδμήθην, δαμάσθην, and Strong Aor. Pass. ἐδάμην (Subj. δαμείω).

b) κ ί ρ ν η μ ι (also κεράννυμι, § 319, 1), I mix, Part. κιρνάς, 3 Sing. Imperf. ἐκίρνā. Compare § 319, 1.

c) κ ρ ή μ ν ă μ α ι, poetic additional form of κρέμα-μαι (12). Compare also § 319, 2.

d) μ ά ρ ν ă μ α ι, I contend, 2 Sing. Imperf. ἐμάρνăο.

e) π έ ρ ν η μ ι, I sell, Part. περνάς, περνάμενος.

f) π ί λ ν α μ α ι, I approach, Stem π ε λ, Aor. 3 Sing. ἔ-πλη-το.

g) π ί τ ν η μ ι, I spread, Part. πιτνάς, Imperf. πίτναντο. Compare 319, 3.

h) σ κ ί δ ν η μ ι, I scatter, σκίδνăται. Compare § 319, 4.

§ 313. FIRST CLASS OF VERBS IN μι. 177

§ 313. B) Verbs whose Stem ends in ε (compare τίθημι):
1. ἵ-η-μι (Stem ἑ, Present-Stem ἱ-ε, i. e., ἱ-ἑ, according to § 308), *I send*.
Act. Pres. 3 Plur. Ind. ἱᾶσι(ν), Opt. ἱείην (secondary forms ἵοιμι, 3 Plur. ἵοιεν).
Imperf. ἵη-ν (secondary forms [ἵουν], ἵεις, ἵει), Plur. ἵεμεν, 3 Plur. ἵε-σαν, ἀφίει and ἠφίει (ἀφίημι, *I send away*). Compare § 240.
Aor. ἧ-κ-α, ἧκας, ἧκε(ν), εἷτον, εἵτην, εἷμεν, εἷτε, εἷ-σαν.
Subj. ὧ, Opt. εἵην, Imperat. ἕς, Inf. εἷναι, Part. εἵς (Stem ἑ ν τ). On this Aor., compare § 310.
Fut. ἥσω, Perf. εἷ-κ-α.
Mid. Pres. ἵ-ε-μαι, *I hasten, strive*, Subj. ἱῶμαι, ἱῇ, etc.
Opt. ἱείμην (additional form ἱοίμην), Imperat. ἵεσο or ἵου, Imperf. ἱ-έμην.
Aor. εἵμην, εἷσο, εἷτο, Subj. ὧμαι, Opt. εἵμην (additional form οἵμην).

Obs.—The ει of the Ind. εἵ-μην is caused by the Augment (§ 236), that of the Opt. by the Mood-sign (§ 302, 4).

Fut. ἥ-σομαι, Perf. εἷ-μαι, Plup. εἵ-μην.

---

§ 313. Dialects.—1. Hom. 2 and 3 Sing. Pres. ἵεις, ἵει; 3 Plur. ἱεῖσι(ν); 1 Sing. Imperf. ἵειν, ἵεις, ἵει; 3 Plur. ἵεν, 3 Sing. Subj. ἵησι(ν); Inf. ἱέμεναι; Aor. Act. ἕηκα; 3 Plur. ἕσαν; Subj. εἵω; Aor. Mid. 3 Plur. ἕντο.
2. Fut. ἥσω and (ἀν)έσω [Herod. μεμετιμένος, as a Part. Perf. of με-τίημι = μεθίημι, § 52, D., as if from μετίω, with irregular reduplication].
Moreover:
3. Stem ἀ(F)ε, Pres. ἄημι, *I blow*, 2 Dual ἄητον, 3 Sing. Imperf. ἄη and ἄει, Inf. ἀῆναι and ἀήμεναι, Part. Aor. Nom. Plur. ἀέντες, Mid. ἀήμενος.
4. Stem διε, (ἐν) δίεσαν, *they frightened;* δίενται, *they flee;* Opt. δίοιτο.
5. Stem διζε, δίζημαι, additional form, δίζω, *I seek;* 2 Sing. δίζηαι, Inf. δίζησθαι, Fut. διζήσομαι.
6. Pres. κίχημι (compare § 322, 18), *I obtain;* Subj. κιχείω, Opt. κιχείην, Inf. κιχῆναι, Part. κιχείς, Mid. κιχήμενος.
Imperf. 2 Sing. ἐκίχεις, 3 Dual κιχήτην.

H 2

178 FIRST CLASS OF VERBS IN μι. § 314.

Aor. Pass. εἴθην, Subj. ἐθῶ. Fut. ἐθήσομαι.
Verb. Adj. ἑτός, ἑτέος.

2. δί-δη-μι (Stem δ ε), *I bind*, a rare additional form of δέ-ω (§ 244, 1).

§ 314. C) Verbs whose Stem ends in ι:

1. εἶ-μι (Stem· ι, Lat. *i-re*), *I go*.

Pres. Ind. εἶ-μι   ἴ-μεν   Subj. ἴ-ω   ἴ-ῃς, etc.
       εἶ   ἴ-τον   ἴ-τε   Opt. ἰ-οίην ἴ-οις, etc.
       εἶ-σι(ν) ἴ-τον   ἴ-ᾱσι(ν)   Imperat. ἴ-θι   ἴ-τω, etc.
                             3 Plur. ἰ-όντων or ἴ-τωσαν
Inf. ἰ-έ-ναι   Part. ἰ-ών, ἰ-οῦσα, ἰ-όν (Gen. ἰ-όντ-ος, compare Lat. *e-unt-is*)

Imperf. ᾔειν or ᾖα   ᾔειμεν or ᾖμεν
       ᾔεις " ᾔεισθα, ᾔειτον, ᾖτον, ᾔειτε " ᾖτε
       ᾔει " ᾔειν, ᾔείτην, ᾔτην, ᾔεσαν

Verbal Adj. ἰτός, ἰτέος (additional form ἰτητέον, *it is necessary to go*.

Obs.—The Present, especially in the Indicative, has a *Future* meaning; the Imperfect has the endings of a Pluperfect; ᾐ is produced by the Augment preceding ε ι.

2. κεῖ-μαι (Stem κ ε ι), *I lie*, has the Inflexion of a Perfect. 2 Sing. κεῖ-σαι, 3 Plur. κεῖνται, Subj. 3 Sing. κέηται, Opt. κέοιτο, Imperat. κεῖσο, Inf. κεῖσθαι, Part. κείμενος; the compound παράκειμαι, Inf. παρακεῖσθαι. (Compare ἧμαι, § 315, 2).

---

§ 314. **Dialects.**—1. Stem ἰ, 2 Sing. Pres. Ind. εἶσθα, Subj. ἴησθα, ἴῃσιν, 1 Plur. ἴομεν, ἴομεν, and ἴωμεν, Opt. ἴοι, ἰείη or εἴη, Inf. ἴμεναι, ἴμεν.
Imperf. ᾔϊα and ᾔϊον, 3 Sing. ᾔϊε(ν) or ἴε(ν), 1 Plur. ᾔομεν, 3 Plur. ᾔϊον, ᾔϊσαν, with ἴτην, ἴμεν, ἴσαν.
Fut. εἴσομαι, Aor. εἰσάμην and ἰεισάμην.

2. Stem κ ε ι, 3 Plur. κείαται, κέαται, κέονται, Imperf. κείατο, κέατο [κέεται = κεῖται], Part. Fut. κέων, *cubiturus*, Inf. κειέμεν.

ὀ ν ο is an Hom. Stem in ο, Pres. ὄνομαι, *I vituperate*, ὄνοσαι, 3 Sing. Opt. ὄνοιτο (§ 309), Fut. ὀνόσσομαι, Aor. ὠνοσάμην, and, from the Stem ὀ ν, ὠνάμην.

ρ ῠ or ἐ ρ ῠ is an Hom. Stem in υ, 3 Plur. εἰρύαται, *they rescue, protect*, Inf. ῥῦσθαι, ἔρυσθαι, εἰρύμενος, Imperf. 2 Sing. ἔρυσο, 3 Plur. ῥύατο, ἔρυατο, εἴρυντο; moreover, Inf. Act. εἰρύμεναι, *to draw*; Aor. Mid. ῥύσατο, *he rescued;* ἐρύσσατο, *he drew*.

§ 315. FIRST CLASS OF VERBS IN μι. 179

Obs.—When compounded with prepositions, κεῖμαι is almost identical in meaning with the Perf. Pass. of the corresponding compounds of τίθημι : ὑποτίθημι, *I lay as a foundation ;* ὑπόκειται, *it is laid as a foundation.*

§ 315. D) Verbs whose Stem ends in a consonant (σ):
1. εἰμί (Stem ἐ ς, Lat. *es-se*), *I am.*

Pres. Ind. εἰ-μί (for ἐσμι)   ἐσ-μέν
    εἶ (for ἐσ-σι)   ἐσ-τόν   ἐσ-τέ (*es-tis*)
    ἐσ-τί(ν) (Lat. *es-t*)   ἐσ-τόν   εἰ-σί(ν)
Subj. ὦ   ὦμεν   Opt. εἴην   εἴημεν or εἶμεν
    ᾖς ἦτον ἦτε   εἴης εἴητον or εἶτον εἴητε or εἶτε
    ᾖ ἦτον ὦσι(ν)   εἴη εἰήτην or εἴτην εἴησαν or εἶεν
Imperat. ἴσθι ἔστον ἔστε   Inf. εἶναι
    ἔστω ἔστων ἔστωσαν   Part. ὤν οὖσα ὄν (Stem ο ν τ)
    (Lat. *esto*) ἔστων, ὄντων
Imperf. ἦν or ἦ   ἦμεν
    ἦσθα   ἦστον or ἦτον   ἦτε or ἦστε
    ἦν   ἤστην or ἤτην   ἦσαν
Imperf. Mid. ἤμην (rare)
Fut. ἔσομαι, 3 Sing. ἔσται
Verb. Adj. ἰστέον.

Obs.—1. The loss of the σ of the Stem is compensated for by the vowel being lengthened in the 1 Sing. (§ 42) : εἰμί for ἐσμί, in the 2 Sing. εἶ for ἐσι, which has arisen from the ἐσσί preserved in Homer (compare §§ 49, 61, *b*). In the 3 Sing. the original ending τ ι is retained : ἐστί(ν), the 3 Plur. has εἰσί(ν), from ἐσ-ντι. The Subj. ὦ stands for ἔω (Hom.), from ἔσω ; the Opt. εἴην for

§ 315. Dialects.—*Ionic additional forms :* 2 Sing. ἐσ-σί or εἶς, 1 Plur. ἐ᾿μέν, 3 Plur. ἔασι(ν) ; ἐσσί is also enclitic, but not ἔασι(ν).
Subj. 1 Sing. ἔω, εἴω, 2 Sing. ἔῃς, 3 Sing. ἔησι(ν), ἤσι(ν), ἔῃ, 3 Plur. ἔωσι(ν).
Opt. also ἔοις, ἔοι, 2 Sing. Imperat. Mid. ἴσσο, 3 Act. ἔστω, 3 Plur. ἔστων.
Inf. ἔμμεναι (for ἐσ-μεναι), ἔμμεν, ἔμεναι, ἔμεν.
Part. ἐών, ἐοῦσα, ἐόν (Stem ἐ ο ν τ).
Imperf. 1 Sing. ἦα, ἔα, ἔον ; 2 Sing. ἔησθα [ἔας], 3 Sing. ἦεν, ἔην, ἤην
· [2 Plur. ἔατε], 3 Plur. ἔσαν ; 3 Plur. Mid. εἴατο (ἧντο).
Fut. ἔσσομαι, 3 Sing. ἔσεται, ἔσσεται, ἐσσεῖται (§ 264).
2. From ἧμαι, 3 Plur. ἔαται, εἴαται, Imperf. ἔατο, εἴατο.
3. Inf. ἔδμεναι, *to eat*, Pres. ἔσθω, ἐσθίω, ἔδω [Lat. *es-tis = editis*]. Compare § 327, 4.
4. 2 Plur. Imperf. φέρτε = φέρετε, *bring* [Lat. *ferte*].

180   FIRST CLASS OF VERBS IN μι.   § 316.

ἰσ-ιην, as the Inf. εἶναι for ἰσ-ναι; ὧν for ἰων (Hom.), from ἰσ-ών. In the Imperf. the Dual has most fully preserved the σ.

Obs. 2.—εἰμί is enclitic in the Pres. Ind. except the 2 Sing. εἶ (compare § 92, 3); ἔστι is paroxytone when it denotes existence, or means the same, as, ἔξεστι, "*it is possible*," as well as at the beginning of a sentence and after the particles οὐ, μή, εἰ, ὡς, καί: ἔστι θεός, *there is a God;* οὐκ ἔστι, *it is not possible.* When merely external causes prevent it from being enclitic (§ 93, c), ἐστί(ν) is oxytone: φίλος. ἐστὶν ἐμοῦ, *he is my friend.*

Obs. 3.—In the compounds of εἰμί the accent remains on the Stem-syllable; *e. g.*, in the Imperf. παρῆν, in the Subj. and Opt. ἀπῶ, ἀπεῖεν, in the Inf. and Part. ἀπεῖναι, παρών, in the 3 Sing. Fut. παρέσται.

2. ἦμαι (Stem ἡ ς), *I sit*, has, like κεῖμαι, the Inflexion of a Perfect.

Pres. ἦμαι ἥμεθον ἥμεθα.   Imperat. ἦσο.
      ἦσαι   ἦσθον   ἦσθε   ἦσθω, etc.
      ἦσται ἦσθον   ἦνται   Inf.   ἦσθαι.
                              Part.   ἥμενος.

Impf. ἥμην ἦσο, etc.

In Attic prose we find almost exclusively the compound κάθημαι, of which 3 Sing. κάθηται, Subj. καθῶμαι; Opt. καθοίμην, 3 Plur. καθοῖντο, Imperat. κάθησο or κάθου (from καθεσο), Inf. καθῆσθαι, Part. καθήμενος, Imperf. ἐκαθήμην (§ 240) or καθήμην, 3 Sing. ἐκάθητο or καθῆστο, 3 Plur. ἐκάθηντο or καθῆντο.

§ 316. The following *Strong Aorists*, formed *without a connecting vowel* from verbs whose Present-Stem mostly follows the First Principal Conjugation, likewise belong to the First Class of Verbs in μι:

Stems in a.

1. ἔ-βη-ν (Stem β a), Pres. βαίνω, *I go*, Imperat. βῆθι; in compounds also βᾱ (κατάβᾱ), Inf. βῆναι, Part. βάς.

---

§ 316. Dialects.—1. 3 Plur. ἔβᾱν, Subj. β:ίω, βήῃ or βείῃ, βείομεν [Her. βέωμεν], Inf. βήμεναι.

§ 316. FIRST CLASS OF VERBS IN μι. 181

2. γηρᾶ-ναι (Stem γ η ρ a), Inf. to the Pres. γηρά-σκω, *I grow old*, § 324, 1.
3. ἔ-δρᾶ-ν (Stem δ ρ ᾱ), Pres. δι-δρά-σκω, § 324, 2, *I run*, Inf. δρᾶ-ναι, Part. δράς.
4. ἔ-κτᾰ-ν (Stem κ τ ᾰ), Pres. κτείνω, *I kill*, Part. κτά-ς, Part. Mid. κτά-μενος (*killed*).
5. ἔ-πτη-ν (Stem π τ a, π τ ε), Pres. πέτομαι, *I fly*, Part. πτάς, Mid. πτάμενος, Inf. πτέσθαι.
6. ἔ-τλη-ν (Stem τ λ ᾱ), *I endured*, Subj. τλῶ, Opt. τλαίην, Imperat. τλῆθι, Inf. τλῆναι, Fut. τλήσομαι, Perf. τέτληκα (§ 317, D., 10).
7. ἔ-φθη-ν (Stem φ θ a), Pres. φθάνω, *I anticipate*, Inf. φθῆναι.
8. ἐ-πριά-μην (Stem π ρ ι a), *I bought*, Imperat. πρίω.

Stems in ε.

9. ἔ-σβη-ν (Stem σ β ε), Pres. σβέννῡμι, *I quench*, § 319, 7, Inf. σβῆναι.
10. ἔ-σκλη-ν (Stem σ κ λ ε), Pres. σκέλλω, *I dry*, Inf. σκλῆναι.
11. Imperat. σχέ-ς, from σχέ-θι (Stem σ χ ε), Pres. ἔχω, § 327, 6, 1 Sing. Ind. ἔ-σχ-ο-ν.

Stems in ω.

12. ἑ-άλω-ν (Stem ἁ λ ω), *I was caught*, Pres. ἁλίσκομαι (§ 324, 17), Opt. ἁλοίην, Inf. ἁλῶναι, Part. ἁλούς.
13. ἐ-βίω-ν (Stem β ι ω), Pres. βιόω, *I live*, Opt. βιῴην, Inf. βιῶναι, Part. βιούς.

Dialects.—2. Part. γηράς.
3. [Her. ἔδρην.]
4. 3 Sing. ἔκτᾰ, 3 Plur. ἔκτᾰν, Subj. κτέωμεν, Inf. κτάμεναι, Mid. ἔκτᾰτο (*he was killed*, § 225, D., 2), Pass. Aor., 3 Plur. ἔκτᾰθεν.
5. Mid. ἔπτᾰτο, Subj. πτῆται, Dor. 1 Sing. Act. ἐπτᾶν.
6. 3 Plur. ἔτλᾰν.
7. Subj. 3 Sing. φθῇ or φθῆσι(ν), (παρα)φθαίησι(ν), 1 Plur. φθέωμεν.
12. ἥλων, Subj. ἁλώω, Opt. 3 Sing. ἁλοίη, Inf. ἁλώμεναι.

14. ἔ-γνω-ν (Stem γ ν ω), Pres. γι-γνώ-σκω, *I come to know* (§ 324, 14), Opt. γνοίην, Imperat. γνῶθι, Inf. γνῶναι, Part. γνούς.

Stems in ι.

15. Imperat. πῖ-θι (Stem π ι), Pres. πίνω, *I drink*, 1 Sing. Aor. Ind. ἔπιον (§ 321, 4).

Stems in υ.

16. ἔ-δῡ-ν (Stem δ υ), Pres. δύω, *I dive*, Imperat. δῦθι, Inf. δῦναι, Part. δύς. As to its meaning, see § 329, 4.
17. ἔ-φῡ-ν (Stem φ υ), *I became*, Pres. φύω, *I produce*, Inf. φῦναι.

Dialects.—14. Subj. γνώω, Inf. γνώμεναι.
15. Imperat. πίε.
16. 3 Plur. ἔδῡ-ν, Subj. δύω, δύῃς, 3 Sing. Opt. δύῃ (from δυ-ίη), Inf. δῦμεν.
17. 3 Plur. ἔφῦν.

Besides these, the following are peculiar to the Ep. Dialect:
18. Part. ἀπούρας, Pres. ἀπαυράω, *I take away*.
19. Stem β λ η, Pres. βάλλω, *I throw*, 3 Dual ξυμβλήτην (*met together*), Fut. ξυμβλήσομαι, Mid. ἔβλητο (*was hit*, § 255, D. 2), Subj. βλή-ε-ται, 2 Sing. Opt. βλεῖο, Inf. βλῆσθαι, Part. βλήμενος (*hit*).
20. Stem ο ὐ τ α, Pres. οὐτάω, *I wound*, 3 Sing. οὐτᾰ, Inf. οὐτάμεναι, Part. Mid. οὐτάμενος (*wounded*), Verb. Adj. οὐτᾶτος.
21. Stem π τ α, Pres. πτήσσω, *I stoop*, 2 Dual ἐ-πτή-την, Part. Perf. πεπτηώς.
22. Stem π λ α, Pres. πελάζω, *I approach*, Aor. Mid. πλῆτο.
23. Stem β ρ ω, Pres. βι-βρώ-σκω, *I eat* (§ 324, 13), Aor. ἔβρων.
24. Stem π λ ω, Pres. πλώω, *I sail*, 2 Sing. Aor. ἔπλως, Part. πλώ-ς.
25. Stem κ τ ι, Pres. κτίζω, *I found*, Part. Aor. Mid. ἐϋ-κτί-μενος (*well-founded*).
26. Stem φ θ ι, Pres. φθίνω, *I waste away*, Subj. Aor. Mid. φθίεται, Opt. φθίμην, φθῖτο, Inf. φθίσθαι, Part. φθίμενος.
27. Stem κ λ υ, Pres. κλύω, *I hear*, Imperat. Aor. κλῦθι or κέκλυθι, κλῦτε or κέκλυτε.
28. Stem λ υ, Pres. λύω, *I loose*, Aor. Mid. λύμην, λύτο or λῦτο.
29. Stem π ν υ, Pres. πνέω, *I breathe*, Aor. Mid. ἄμπνῦτο (*he recovered breath*).
30. Stem σ υ, Pres. σεύω, *I scare*, Aor. Mid. σύτο, Part. σύμενος.
31. Stem χ υ, Pres. χέω, *I pour* (§ 248), Aor. Mid. ἔχυτο, χύτο, Part. χύμενος.

§ 317. FIRST CLASS OF VERBS IN μι. 183

§ 317. Several *Perfects* also have some forms without a connecting vowel:
A) *Vowel Stems.*
A number of Vowel-Stems form the Sing. Perf. Ind. Act. regularly, but in the Dual and Plural of the Perfect and Pluperf. Ind., in the other moods, and in the Infinitive and Participle, may connect the endings immediately with the Perfect-Stem.

1. Stem β α, Pres. βαίνω, *I go* (§ 321, 1).
Perf. Ind. βέβηκ-α   βέβᾰ-μεν
         βέβηκ-ας   βέβᾰ-τον   βέβᾰ-τε
         βέβηκ-ε.   βέβᾰ-τον   βεβᾱ-σι(ν)
3 Plur. Subj. βεβῶσι(ν), Part. βεβώς, βεβῶσα, Gen. βεβῶτος.

2. Stem γα (for γεν), Pres. γίγνομαι, *I become*, Perf. γέ-γον-α, Plur. also γέ-γᾰ-μεν (§ 327, 14), Part. γεγώς, Gen. γεγῶτος.

Dialects.—32. Stem ἀλ (ἄλλομαι, *I spring*), Aor. Mid. ἆλσο, ἆλτο, Subj. ἄλεται, Part. ἄλμενος.
33. Stem γεν, only in γέντο, *he took.*
34. Stem δεχ (Pres. δέχομαι, *I accept*), Aor. ἐδέγμην, 3 Sing. δέκτο, Imperat. δέξο, Inf. δέχθαι (compare § 273, D.).
35. Stem λεγ (λέγω, *I collect*), Aor. Mid. λέκτο, *he counted.*
36. Stem λεχ (no Pres.), Aor. Mid. λέκτο (*he laid himself*), Imperat. λέξο, Inf. λέχθαι, Part. (κατα)λέγμενος, Aor. Act. ἔλεξα, Mid. ἐλέξατο, Fut. λέξομαι.
37. Stem μιγ, Pres. μίσγω, *I mix*, Aor. Mid. ἔμικτο, μίκτο.
38. Stem ὀρ, ὄρνυμι, *I excite*, Aor. Mid. ὦρτο, Imperat. ὄρσο or ὄρσεο (ὄρσευ), Inf. ὄρθαι, Part. ὄρμενος.
39. Stem παγ (πήγνυμι, *I fix*), Aor. Mid. ἔπηκτο, *it was fixed.*
40. Stem παλ (πάλλω, *I wield*), Aor. Mid. πάλτο.
41. Stem περθ (πέρθω, *I destroy*), Inf. Aor. Mid. πέρθαι (*to be destroyed*).

To these are to be added the Participles which have become Adjectives, ἄσμενός, *glad* (Stem ἀδ, ἀνδάνω, *I please*); ἴκμενος, *favorable* (Stem ἰκ, ἰκνέομαι, *I come*).

§ 317. Dialects.—1. Hom. 3 Plur. βεβάασι(ν), Part. βεβαώς, Dual βεβαῶτε.
2. Hom. 3 Plur. γεγάασι(ν), Part. γεγαώς, γεγαυῖα, Gen. γεγαῶτος, 3 Dual Plup. (ἐκ)γεγάτην.

184　FIRST CLASS OF VERBS IN μι.　§ 317.

3. Stem θνα, Pres. θνή-σκω, I die, Perf. τέ-θνη-κα, Plur. τέ-θνά-μεν, etc., Inf. τεθνάναι, Part. τεθνεώς, τεθνεῶσα, τεθνεός, Pluperf. 3 Plur. ἐτέθνασαν (§ 324, 4).

4. Stem στα, Pres. ἵ-στη-μι, Perf. ἕ-στη-κα, I stand, Plur. ἕ-στά-μεν, Subj. ἑστῶμεν, ἑστῶσι(ν), Opt. ἑσταίην, Imperat. ἕστᾰθι, ἑστάτω, ἕστᾰτον, ἕστᾰτε, Inf. ἑστάναι, Part. ἑστώς, ἑστῶσα, ἑστός, Gen. ἑστῶτος, 3 Plur. Pluperf. ἕστᾰσαν (§ 306, etc.).

5. Stem δι, Perf. δέ-δϊ-α or δέ-δοι-κα, I fear, Plur. δέδιμεν, δεδίασι(ν), Subj. δεδίω, Opt. δεδιείην, Imperat. δέδιθι, Inf. δεδιέναι, Part. δεδιώς, Pluperf. ἐδεδίειν, 3 Dual ἐδεδίτην, 3 Plur. ἐδέδισαν, also Aor. ἔδεισα, Fut. δείσομαι.

Obs.—The regular and irregular forms are mostly both in use.

B) *Consonant Stems.*

In these the peculiar changes of the vowels (§ 303) and consonants (§§ 45–49) must be observed.

6. Stem ἰδ (Aor. εἶδον, I saw, § 327, 8).
Perf. Ind. οἶδ-α, I know,　　ἴσ-μεν, Subj. εἰδῶ　　　　εἰδῶμεν
　　οἶ-σθα　ἴσ-τον　ἴσ-τε　　εἰδῇς　　εἰδῆτον εἰδῆτε
　　οἶδ-ε(ν) ἴσ-τον ἴσ-ᾱσι(ν)　εἰδῇ　　εἰδῆτον εἰδῶσι(ν)
Opt. εἰδείην, Imp. ἴσ-θι　ἴσ-τον ἴσ-τε　　Inf. εἰδέναι
　　　　　　ἴσ-τω　ἴσ-των ἴσ-τωσαν　Part. εἰδώς, εἰδυῖα,
　　　　　　　　　　　　　　　　　εἰδός, Gen. εἰδότ-ος
Plup. ᾔδειν　or ᾔδη (I knew)　　　　　ᾔδειμεν or ᾖσμεν
　　ᾔδεισθα " ᾔδησθα　ᾔδειτον or ᾖστον　ᾔδειτε " ᾖστε
　　ᾔδει(ν) " ᾔδη　ᾔδείτην " ᾔστην　ᾔδεσαν " ᾖσαν
Fut. εἴσομαι, Verb. Adj. ἰστέον.

Dialects.—3. Imperat. τέθναθι, Inf. τεθνάμεν(αι), Gen. Part. τεθνεῶτος, τεθνηῶτος, τεθνειῶτος, τεθνηότος, τεθνειότος, Fem. τεθνηυῖα.
4. 2 Plur. Ind. also ἕστητε, Part. ἑσταώς, Gen. ἑσταότος [Her. ἑστεώς, ἑστεῶσα].
5. δείδια, δείδιμεν, Imperat. δείδιθι, 1 Sing. Perf. also δείδοικα, Aor. ἔδδεισα (compare § 77, D.).
6. 1 Plur. ἴδ-μεν [Herod. and sometimes also in Att. writers οἴδαμεν, 3 Plur. οἴδασι], Subj. εἰδέω or ἰδέω, Plur. εἴδομεν, εἴδετε, Inf. ἴδμεν(αι), Fem. Part. ἰδυῖα, Plup. [ᾔδεα] ᾔείδης, ᾔδεε(ν) or ἠείδη [2 Plur. ᾔδεατε], 3 Plur. ἴσαν, Fut. εἰδήσω.

§ 318. SECOND CLASS OF VERBS IN μι. 185

Obs.—Besides οἶσθα, we rarely have οἶδας, more frequently ᾔδεις, ᾔδης, together with ᾔδεισθα, and ᾔδεμεν, ᾔδετε, instead of ᾔδειμεν, ᾔδειτε.

7. Stem ἰκ, only in the Perf. ἔοικα, *I resemble, appear*, 1 Plur. poet. ἔοιγμεν, 3 Plur. quite irregularly εἴξᾱσι(ν) (compare ἴσασι), Inf. εἰκέναι (poet. with ἐοικέναι), Part. εἰκώς (with ἐοικώς), εἰκυῖα, εἰκός, Plur. ἐῴκειν.

8. Stem κραγ, Pres. κράζω, *I cry*, Perf. κέκρᾱγα, Imperat. κέ-κραχ-θι.

II. SECOND CLASS OF VERBS IN μι.

§ 318. 1. The Second Class of the Verbs in μι belongs to this conjugation only in regard to the inflexion of the

---

Dialects.—7. Imperf. εἶκε, Perf. [Her. οἶκα, οἰκώς]; Dual εἴκτον, 3 Dual Plup. εἴκτην, 3 Sing. Plup. Mid. ᾔικτο or εἴκτο.
Besides:
9. Stem μα, 2 Dual Perf. μέμᾰτον, *strive*, μέμᾰμεν, μέμᾰτε, μεμάᾱσι, Imperat. μεμάτω, Part. μεμαώς, υῖα, ός, Gen. ὦτος, 3 Plur. Plup. μέμᾱσαν.
10. Stem τλα, Perf. τέτληκα, *I am patient*, 1 Plur. τέτλᾰμεν, Opt. τετλαίην, Imperat. τέτλᾰθι, Inf. τετλαμεν(αι), Part. τετληώς, ηυῖα, Gen. τετληότος.
11. Stem ἀνωγ, Perf. ἄνωγα, *I command*, 1 Plur. ἄνωγμεν, Imperat. ἄνωχθι, 3 Sing. ἀνώχθω, 2 Plur. ἄνωχθε, Plup. ἠνώγεα.
12. Stem ἐγερ, Perf. ἐγρ-ήγορ-α, *I am awake*, 2 Plur. Imperat. ἐγρήγορθε, 3 Plur. Ind. ἐγρηγόρθᾱσι(ν).
13. Stem ἐλυθ, Perf. εἰλήλουθα, *I have come*, 1 Plur. εἰλήλουθμεν.
14. Stem πενθ, Perf. πέπονθα (Pres. πάσχω, *I suffer*, § 327, 9), 2 Plur. πέποσθε (for πεπονθ-τε), Fem. Part. πεπᾱθυῖα.
15. Stem πιθ, Perf. πέποιθα (Pres. πείθω, *I persuade*), 1 Plur. Plup. ἐπέπιθμεν, Imperat. πέπεισθι.
Farther the Participles:
16. Stem βρω (βιβρώσκω, *I eat*, § 324, 13), Part. Perf. βεβρώς, Gen. βεβρῶτος.
17. Stem πτε, πτω (πίπτω, *I fall*, § 327, 15), Perf. πέπτωκα, Part. Gen. πεπτεῶτος, Nom. πεπτώς.

§ 318. Dialects.—Ion. 3 Plur. Pres. Ind. Act. -ῦσι(ν), together with -ύᾱσι(ν). Hom. 2 Sing. Imperat. -ῦ and -ῦθι (δαίνῦ, ὄμνῦθι), Inf. Hom. -ύμεναι, ύμεν (ζευγνυμεν). Hom. forms from δαίνυμαι, *I feast*, the Opt. δαινῦτο, for δαινυ-ι-το. Similar cases see below, § 319, 32. In

Present-Stem. The Present-Stem of this Second Class is formed by adding the syllable ν υ to the Pure Stem.

2. The quantity of the υ is determined by the rules in § 303, hence δείκνῡμι, but ἐδείκνῠμεν.

3. Vowel-Stems double ν in the Present-Stem: Stem κ ε ρ α, κερά-ννῡμι, *I mix.*

4. Here also numerous additional forms are in use according to the First Principal Conjugation (δεικνύω), especially in the 3 Plur. Pres. Ind.: δεικνύουσι(ν); and these forms are exclusively used in the Pres. Subj. and Opt.

5. Most of the Verbs of this class have the *Weak Aorist;* only σβέννυμι, *I quench* (Stem σ β ε), forms the 2 Aorist ἔσβην, Inf. σβῆναι. Compare §§ 316, 9; 319, 7.

The Paradigms of this Class of Verbs are inserted on p. 128.

§ 319. The following verbs belong to the Second Class of Verbs in μ ι :

Stems in a.

1. κ ε ρ ά ν ν υ μ ι (Stem κ ε ρ ᾰ, κ ρ ᾱ), *I mix.*
   Aor. ἐκέρᾰσα   Perf. Act. κέκρᾱκα   Aor. Pass. { ἐκράθην
                  " Mid. κέκρᾱμαι   { ἐκεράσθην
2. κ ρ ε μ ά ν ν υ μ ι (Stem κ ρ ε μ α), *I hang,* trans. Mid. κρέμαμαι, *I hang,*
                       intrans. (§ 312, 12)
   Fut. κρεμῶ (§ 263)   ἐκρεμάσθην
   Aor. ἐκρέμᾰσα
3. π ε τ ά ν ν υ μ ι (Stem π ε τ α), *I spread.*
   πετῶ (§ 263)   ἐπετάσθην
   ἐπέτᾰσα   πέπ(ε)τᾰμαι [*pate-o*]
4. σ κ ε δ ά ν ν υ μ ι (Stem σ κ ε δ α), *I scatter;* additional form σκίδνημι
                       (§ 312, D. 16, *h*)
   σκεδῶ (§ 263)   ἐσκεδάσθην
   ἐσκέδᾰσα   ἐσκέδαςμαι.

---

the New-Ion. Dialect the ι of the Stem δ ε ι κ is lost in δέξω, ἔδεξα, δέδεγμαι, ἰδέχθην; Hom. Pf. (δείδεγμαι, *I salute*) 3 Plur. δειδέχαται.

§ 319. **Dialects.**—1. Compare § 312, D. 16, and § 312, D. 16, *b*. Other forms : κεράω, κεραίω, Aor. ἔκρησα.

2. Fut. κρεμόω, κρεμάᾳς (§ 243, D.).

§ 319. SECOND CLASS OF VERBS IN μι. 187

Stems in ε.

Obs.—Several of these Stems originally ended in ς.

5. ἕννυμι (Stem originally Ϝες, compare Lat. *ves-tis*), *I clothe* (only
           ἀμφι-έννυμι is in use).
  ἀμφι-ῶ (§ 263)
Fut. Mid. ἀμφι-έσομαι ἠμφίεσμαι
  Aor. ἠμφί-εσα (§ 240)
Inf. Aor. Mid. ἐπιέσασθαι
6. κορέννυμι (Stem κορε), *I satisfy.*
 ἐκόρεσα   ἐκορέσθην
      κεκόρεσμαι
7. σβέννυμι (Stem σβε), *I quench.*
 σβέσω } transitive ἔσβεσμαι   ἐσβέσθην
 ἔσβεσα }
 ἔσβην   ἔσβηκα }
 (§ 316, 9)   } intransitive (§ 329, 5)
Fut. σβήσομαι   }
8. στορέννυμι (Stem στορε) (compare 11 and 25), *I spread*
        (compare Lat. *ster-n-o*)
 στορῶ (§ 263). ἐστόρεσμαι
 ἐστόρεσα.
     Stems in ω.
9. ζώννυμι (Stem ζω), *I gird.*
 ζώσω   ἔζωσμαι
 ἔζωσα (Mid.)   ἐζωσάμην
10. ῥώννυμι (Stem ῥω), *I strengthen.*
 ῥώσω   ἔρρωμαι (*I am strong*) . ἐρρώσθην
11. στρώννυμι (Stem στρω). Compare No. 8.
 στρώσω   ἔστρωμαι   ἐστρώθην
 ἔστρωσα
12. χρώννυμι (Stem χρω), *I color.*
 ἔχρωσα   κέχρωσμαι   ἐχρώσθην.

Consonant-Stems.

13. ἄγνυμι (Stem ἀγ, originally Ϝαγ, § 34, D.), *I break.*
 ἄξω·   ἔᾱγα (*I am broken*) ἐάγην
 ἔαξα (§ 237)   (§ 275, 2)

Dialects.—5. Imperf. εἵννυον for ἑσ-νυον [Inf. Pres. εἵνυσθαι], Fut. ἀμφιέσω, ἕσσω, Aor. ἕσσα, Mid. ἑέσσατο, Perf. Mid. εἷμαι, ἕσσαι, Part. εἱμένος, 2 Sing. Plup. ἕσσο, 3 Sing. ἕστο, ἕεστο, 3 Plur. εἵατο.
6. Aor. Mid. κορέσσατο, Part. Perf. Act. κεκορηώς, *satiated*, Mid. κεκόρημαι.
13. ἦξα with ἔαξα [Her. Perf. ἔηγα].

14. δείκνυμι, see § 318.
15. εἵργνυμι (Stem εἰργ), *I shut in* (addit. form εἵργω)
εἵρξω εἵρχθην
εἶρξα Part. ἔρξας, εἴργμαι
16. ζεύγνυμι (Stem ζυγ), *I bind*.
ζεύξω ἐζύγην
ἔζευξα ἔζευγμαι [ἐζεύχθην]
17. κτίννυμι (Stem κτεν), *I kill*, with κτείνω (§ 253)
18. μίγνυμι (Stem μιγ), *I mix*, with μίσγω (§ 327, 7)
μίξω μέμιχα { ἐμίχθην
ἔμιξα μέμιγμαι { ἐμίγην
19. οἴγνυμι (Stem οἰγ), *I open* (with οἴγω)
οἴξω ἔῳχα and ἔῳγα (§ 279) ἐῴχθην
ἔῳξα (§ 237) ἔῳγμαι
20. ὄλλυμι (Stem ὀλ and ὀλε), for ὀλνυμι, *I destroy*.
ὀλῶ (§ 262) ὀλώλεκα (§ 275, 1)
ὤλεσα
Fut. Mid. ὀλοῦμαι ὄλωλα } intrans., *I perish*.
ὠλόμην
21. ὄμνυμι (Stem ὀμ, ὀμο), *I swear*.
ὀμοῦμαι (Act.) ὀμώμοκα (§ 275, 1) ὠμόσθην
ὤμοσα 3 Sing. Perf. Mid. { ὀμώμοται Verb. Adj. (ἀν)ώμοτος
{ ὀμώμοσται
22. ὀμόργνυμι (Stem ὀμοργ), *I wipe. out*.
ὤμορξα (Mid.) ὠμόρχθην
23. πήγνυμι (Stem πᾰγ), *I fix* [compare Lat. *pango*]
ἔπηξα πέπηγα (*I am fixed*) { ἐπήχθην
{ ἐπάγην
24. ῥήγνυμι (Stem ῥαγ), *I tear*.
ἔρρηξα (Mid.) ἔρρωγα (*I am torn*) ἐρράγην
(§ 278) ῥαγήσομαι
25. στόρνυμι (Stem στορ), with στορέννυμι (8) and στρώννυμι (11)
26. φράγνυμι (Stem φραγ), also φάργνυμι, and, according to
Class 4, a, φράσσω, *I shut in, lock in*.

Dialects.—15. Imperf. ἱέργνῦ, with ἱέργω [ἔργω], 3 Plur. Perf. Mid.
ἔρχαται, Plup. ἔρχατο (§ 287), Part. Perf. ἱεργμένος, Aor. Pass. ἑρχθείς,
with Imperf. ἔργαθον.
18. Aor. Mid., § 316, 37.
19. ὦϊξα, ᾦξα [ἄνοιξα], Imperf. ὠΐγνυντο.
20. ὀλέσσω [ὀλέω], Part. Aor. οὐλόμενος (*destructive*), with ὀλέκω.
21. ὤμοσσα or ὄμοσσα.
To these also belong:
27. αἴνυμαι, ἀποαίνυμαι, *I take away*, used only in the Pres.

§ 320. IRREGULAR VERBS. 189

Obs.—Nouns are formed from the Pure Verbal-Stems, as : ἡ δεῖξι-ς, *the announcement ;* ὁ κρᾱ-τήρ, *the mixing bowl ;* τὸ εἶ-μα, *the clothing*—for Ϝεσ-μα ; ἡ ζώ-νη, *the girdle ;* ἡ ῥώ-μη, *the strength ;* τὸ στρῶ-μα, *the carpet ;* τὸ ζυγ-ό-ν, *the yoke ;* ὁ ὄλε-θρο-ς, *the ruin ;* ὁ συν-ωμό-τη-ς, *the conspirator ;* ὁ πάγ-ο-ς, *the frost, hoar-frost.*

Chap. XII.—Irregular Verbs of the First Principal Conjugation.

§ 320. The irregularities of the Greek Verb chiefly consist in the Present-Stem differing from the Verbal-Stem in a way different from that which has been pointed out above, § 245, etc. To *the four classes there enumerated the following four classes* are to be added.

Obs.—In these as well as in the following lists, the principal forms only are given, from which the rest are easily formed. (Mid.), added to a tense, denotes that, in addition to the Active, the

Dialects:—28. ἄνυμι (and ἀνύω), *I complete,* only Imperf. Mid. ἤνῠτο.
29. ἄρνυμαι, *I acquire,* Aor. ἠρόμην, Inf. ἀρέσθαι, 1 Aor. 2 Sing. ἤραο, 3 Sing. ἤρατο.
30. ἄχνυμαι, *I grieve,* Aor. ἀκάχοντο (§ 257, D.), Perf. ἀκάχημαι (§ 275, 1), 3 Plur. ἀκηχέδαται (§ 287, D.), 3 Plur. Plup. ἀκαχείατο, Part. ἀκαχήμενος and ἀκηχέμενος. Moreover, the Active ἀκαχίζω (*I grieve*), Aor. ἤκαχον and ἀκάχησα (compare § 326).
31. γάνυμαι, *I rejoice,* Fut. γανύσσεται.
32. δαίνυμι, *I entertain,* Opt. Pres. Mid. 3 Sing. δαινῦτο (§ 318, D.), 3 Plur. δαινύατ', Fut. δαίσω (Mid.), Aor. ἔδαισα (Mid.).
33. καίνυμαι (Stem κ α δ), *I surpass,* Perf. κέκασμαι (*I am distinguished*).
34. κίνυμαι, *I move,* additional form of κινέω, Preterite ἐ-κι-ο-ν, *I went,* Subj. κί-ω, Opt. κί-οι-μι, Part. κι-ών.
35. τίνῡμι, τίνῠμαι, additional form of τίνω, § 321, D. 5.
36. ὀρέγνυμι, additional form of ὀρέγω, *I stretch out,* 3 Plur. Perf. Mid. ὀρωρέχαται (§ 287).
37. ὄρνυμι (Stem ὀρ), *I excite,* Fut. ὄρσω, Aor. ὤρορον (§ 257, D.), Perf. ὄρωρα (§ 275, 1), *I have arisen* [Lat. *or-ior*], Aor. Mid. 3 Sing. ὦρτο, *arose* (§ 316, 38), Perf. Mid. 3 Sing. Ind. ὀρώρ-ε-ται, Subj. ὀρώρηται, with Imperf. Mid. ὀρέοντο.
38. τάνυμαι, with τανύω, τείνω, *I extend, stretch.*

corresponding Middle form is also in use; *e. g.*, in addition to ἔτισα (No. 5) ἐτισάμην also is used.

Fifth, or Nasal Class.

§ 321. The Verbal-Stem is strengthened by the addition of ν, or of a syllable containing ν, to form the Present-Stem.

a) ν alone, often united with lengthening of the vowel, is added to the following Stems:

1. Stem β α, Pres. βαίνω, *I go*.

Aor. Act.   Fut.   Perf.   Pass.
ἔ-βη-ν (§ 316, 1)   βήσομαι   βέβηκα (§ 317, 1)
ἔβη-σα   βήσω (§ 329, 2)   Verb. Adj. βατός

2. Stem ἐ λ α,   Pres. ἐ λ α ύ ν ω, *I drive*.

ἤλἄ-σα   ἐλῶ (§ 263)   ἐλήλακα (§ 275, 1)   ἠλάθην
                                                           ἐλήλαμαι   Verb. Adj. ἐλατέος

3. Stem φ θ α, Pres. φ θ ά ν ω, *I anticipate*.

{ ἔ-φθη-ν (§ 316, 7)   φθήσομαι   ἔφθακα
{ ἔ-φθἄ-σα-

4. Stem π ι,   Pres. π ί ν ω, *I drink* (additional Stem π ο). Compare § 327, 10.

ἔ-πι-ο-ν (§ 316, 15)   πίομαι (§ 265)
5. Stem τ ι,   Pres. τ ί ν ω, *I pay penalty*.
ἔ-τί-σα (Mid.)   τίσω   τέτικα   ἐτίσθην
                                    τέτισμαι

6. Stem φ θ ι, Pres. φ θ ί ν ω, *I perish, waste away*.
ἔ-φθι-σα   φθίσομαι   ἔφθιμαι   ἐφθίθην

7. Stem δ υ, Pres. δ ύ ν ω (with δύω, Class 1), *I immerge*.
ἔ-δῦ-ν (§ 316, 16)   δύσω   δέδυκα   ἐδύθην
ἔδυσα, *I dipped*.

8. Stem δ ἄ κ, Pres. δ ά κ ν ω, *I bite*.
ἔ-δἄκ-ο-ν   δήξομαι   δέδηχα   ἐδήχθην

§ 321. Dialects.—1. Aor. Mid. ἐβήσετο, § 268, D.
2. Pres. ἐλάω, Fut. ἐλόω, ἐλάᾳς, § 243, D., Aor. ἔλασσα, Mid. ἠλἄσάμην.
3 Plup. Mid. ἐληλάδατο (§ 287, D.) [ἠλάσθην].
3. Ep. φθάνω, Part. Aor. Mid. φθάμενος.
5. Ep. τίνω, with τί-ω and τίνυμι, § 319, D. 35.
6. Ep. φθίνω, φθίω, Aor. ἐφθίμην, ἔφθιτο, § 316, D. 26; with Pres. φθινύθω.
7. Aor. Mid. ἐδύσετο, § 268, D. [Pres. ἐνδυνέω, *I put on*. Compare § 323].

§ 322. FIFTH, OR NASAL CLASS. 191

9. Stem κ ά μ, Pres. κ ά μ ν ω, *I weary.*
ἔ-καμ-ο-ν   καμοῦμαι   κέκμηκα (§ 282).
10. Stem τ ε μ, Pres. τ έ μ ν ω, *I cut.*
ἔ-τεμ-ο-ν (ἔταμον)   τεμῶ   τέτμηκα (§ 282)   ἐτμήθην

§ 322. *b*) The syllable ἄ ν is added to the following Stems:

11. Stem αἰσθ, Pres. αἰ σ θ - ά ν - ο - μ α ι, *I perceive.*
ᾐσθ-ό-μην   αἰσθ-ή-σομαι   ᾔσθ-η-μαι
12. Stem ἁμαρτ, Pres. ἁ μ α ρ τ - ά ν - ω, *I err, sin.*
ἥμαρτ-ο-ν   ἁμαρτ-ή-σομαι   ἡμάρτ-η-κα   ἡμαρτή-θην
13. Stem αὐξ, Pres. αὐ ξ - ά ν - ω and αὔξω, *I increase* [*aug-eo*]
ηὔξ-η-σα   αὐξήσω   ηὔξηκα   ηὐξήθην
                    αὐξήσομαι (Passive)
14. Stem βλαστ, Pres. β λ α σ τ ά ν ω, *I bud.*
ἐ-βλαστ-ο-ν.   βλαστ-ή-σω   ἐβλάστηκα (§ 274 exc.)
15. Stem δαρθ, Pres. δ α ρ θ ά ν ω, *I sleep.*
ἐ-δαρθ-ο-ν.   δαρθ-ή-σομαι   δεδάρθηκα
16. Stem ἐχθ, Pres. (ἀπ)ε χ θ ά ν ο μ α ι, *I am hated.*
(ἀπ)ηχθ-ό-μην   (ἀπ)εχθ-ή-σομαι   (ἀπ)ήχθημαι
17. Stem ἱζ, Pres. ἱ ζ ά ν ω and ἵζω, *I seat myself.*
18. Stem κιχ, Pres. κῑ χ ἄ ν ω, *I meet* (compare § 313, D. 6).
ἔ-κιχ-ο-ν   κῑχ-ή-σομαι
19. Stem οἰδ, Pres. ο ἰ δ ά ν ω and ο ἰ δ έ ω, *I swell.*
                    οἰδή-σω   ᾤδηκα
20. Stem ὀλισθ, Pres. ὀ λ ι σ θ ά ν ω, *I slip.*
ὤλισθο-ν   ὀλισθ-ή-σω
21. Stem ὀσφρ, Pres. ὀ σ φ ρ α ί ν ο μ α ι, *I smell.*
ὠσφρ-ό-μην   ὀσφρ-ή-σομαι
22. Stem ὀφλ, Pres. ὀ φ λ - ι σ κ - ά ν - ω (compare § 324) and
                  ὀφείλω, *I owe.*
ὤφλ-ο-ν   ὀφλ-ή-σω   ὤφληκα

Dialects.—9. Part. Perf. κεκμηώς, Gen. κεκμηῶτος.
10. With τμήγω, Aor. Pass. 3 Plur. ἔτμαγεν, with Pres. τέμει.
Peculiar to the Hom. dialect are: Aor. φά-ε(ν), *illuxit*, Fut. πε-φή-σομαι, from Stem φα, Pres. φαίνω (φαείνω), *I shine, show*, Aor. Pass. φαάνθην.
§ 322. **Dialects.**—12. Aor. ἤμβροτον for ἡμάρτον (§ 257, D. Compare § 51, D.).
13. ἀ(ϝ)έξω.
15. Aor. ἔδραθον (§ 257, D.).
18. Ep. κῑχάνω.
21. [Herod. ὀσφράμην, 1 Aor.]

23. Stem ἁδ, Pres. ἁνδάνω, *I please.*
24. Stem θῐγ, Pres. θιγγάνω, *I touch.*
ἔ-θῐγ-ο-ν θίξομαι
25. Stem λᾰβ, Pres. λαμβάνω, *I take.*
ἔ-λᾰβ-ο-ν λήψομαι εἴληφα (§ 274) ἐλήφθην
  εἴλημμαι (seldom λέλημμαι)
26. Stem λᾰθ, Pres. λανθάνω, *I am hidden,* with λήθω (Class 3),
  Mid., *I forget.*
ἔ-λᾰθ-ο-ν λήσω λέληθα
Mid. ἐλαθόμην λήσομαι λέλησμαι
27. Stem λᾰχ, Pres. λαγχάνω, *I attain.*
ἔ-λᾰχ-ο-ν λήξομαι εἴληχα (§ 274)
  εἴληγμαι
28. Stem μᾰθ, Pres. μανθάνω, *I learn.*
ἔ-μᾰθ-ο-ν μαθ-ή-σομαι μεμάθηκα
29. Stem πῠθ, Pres. πυνθάνομαι, *I learn,* with πεύθομαι, Class 2.
ἐ-πῠθ-ό-μην , πεύσομαι πέπυσμαι
30. Stem τῠχ, Pres. τυγχάνω, *I meet,* with τεύχω, *I prepare,* Cl. 2.
ἔ-τυχ-ο-ν τεύξομαι τε-τύχ-η-κα
  seldom τέτευχα
31. Stem φυγ, Pres. φυγγάνω, *I flee,* with φεύγω (Class 2).

Obs. 1.—The verbs in 23–31, whose Stem forms a short syllable, insert another nasal in addition to the affix αν. In βαίνω (1) and ὀσφραίνομαι (21) ι has crept in (§ 253), as well as in κερδαίνω, *I gain,* which forms only the Perf. κεκέρδηκα, from the Stem κερδα; all the other forms are regular, according to Class 4. A large part of the verbs (No. 11–16, 18–22, 28, and 30) form either some or all the tenses, except those of the Present-Stem, from a Stem in ε (compare below, § 326).

Obs. 2.—The following may serve as examples of the formation of nouns: τὸ βῆ-μα, *the step;* ἡ φθί-σι-ς, *the consumption;* ὁ κάμ-ατο-ς,

Dialects.—23. Imperf., § 237, D., Aor. [ἔαδον] εὔαδον (§ 237), [ἀδήσω] ἔαδα.
25. [Her. Fut. λάμψομαι, Perf. λελάβηκα, Aor. Pass. ἐλάμφθην.
  λέλαμμαι, Verb. Adj. λαμπτός.]
Hom. Inf. Aor. Mid. λελαβέσθαι (§ 257, D.).
26. Pres., with ἐκληθάνω, *cause to forget,* Aor. ἔλησα and λέλᾰθον (§ 257, D.), λελαθόμην (*I forgot*), Perf. Mid. λέλασμαι.
27. Aor. λέλαχον, *I shared with* [Fut. λάξομαι], Perf. λέλογχα.
29. Aor. Opt. πεπύθοιτο (§ 257, D.).
30. Also τεύχω, Aor. τετυκεῖν, Mid. τετύκοντο, Perf. τέτυγμαι, 3 Plur. τετεύχαται, Aor. ἐτύχθην, with the Pres. τιτύσκομαι (§ 324, D. 37), *I aim at,* Aor. ἐτύχησα, *I met* (§ 326).

§ 324. SIXTH CLASS, OR INCHOATIVE VERBS. 193

the exhaustion; τὸ λῆμ-μα, *the assumption;* ἡ λήθ-η, *the forgetting;* ἡ τύχ-η, *the chance, accident;* and from Stems which are lengthened by ε: ἡ αἴσθ-η-σι-ς, *the sensation;* τὸ ἁμάρτ-η-μα, *the error;* ὁ μαθ-η-τή-ς, *the scholar.*

§ 323. *c)* The syllable νε is added to the following Stems:

32. Stem βυ, Pres. βύνω, *I stop up.*
ἔ-βῡ-σα   βύσω   Mid. βέβυσμαι
33. Stem ἱκ, Pres. ἱκνοῦμαι, *I come,* with ἱκάνω, according to § 322
ἱκ-ό-μην   ἵξομαι   ἷγμαι
34. Stem κῠ, Pres. κυνέω, *I kiss.*
ἔ-κυ-σα
35. Stem πετ, Pres. πιτνέω, *I fall* (compare πίπτω, § 327, 15)
ἔ-πεσ-ο-ν (for ἔ-πετ-ο-ν), together with ἔ-πιτν-ο-ν
36. Stem ὑπεχ, Pres. ὑπισχνοῦμαι, *I promise* (compare. ἔχω, § 327, 6)
ὑπεσχόμην   ὑποσχήσομαι   ὑπέσχημαι
so likewise ἀμπισχνοῦμαι, *I wear* (also ἀμπέχομαι), Aor. ἤμπισχον, Inf. ἀμπισχεῖν.

§ 324. *Sixth Class,* or *Inchoative Verbs.*

The Verbal-Stem is enlarged by affixing σκ to form the Present-Stem. This σκ is added to Vowel-Stems (exc. 21) at once, but to Consonant-Stems after the insertion of the connecting vowel ι. Several of the verbs belonging to this class (Nos. 2, 6, 7, 13, 14, 16, 20) farther strengthen the Present-Stem by means of a reduplication with the vowel ι: γι-γνώ-σκ-ω [Lat. *(g)-no-sc-o*].

---

§ 323. Dialects.—32. [Herod. βύνω.]
33. ἵκω, Aor. ἷξον (§ 268, D.), Part. ἵκμενος, *favorable* (§ 316, D.).
34. κύσσα.
Moreover (to a—c), the Verbs:
37. Stem ἀλιτ, Pres. ἀλιταίνω, *I sin,* Aor. ἤλιτον, Mid. ἀλίτοντο, Part. Perf. ἀλιτήμενος, *sinful.*
38. Stem ἀλφ, Pres. ἀλφάνω, *I acquire,* Aor. ἤλφον.
39. ἀγινέω, only in Pres., *I lead,* with ἄγω.
40. ἐρυγγάνω, *I roar,* Aor. ἤρυγον, Pres. also ἐρεύγομαι.
41. Stem χᾰδ, Pres. χανδάνω, *I embrace,* Aor. ἔχαδον, Fut. χείσομαι, Perf. κέχανδα.

I

194   SIXTH CLASS, OR INCHOATIVE VERBS.   § 324.

As many of these verbs denote a beginning or coming into being, all of them are usually called Inchoatives.

Stems in α.

1. Stem γηρα, Pres. γηρά-σκ-ω, *I grow old* (seldom γηρά-ω). Compare *sene-sc-o*
ἐ-γήρᾱ-σα   γηρά-σομαι   γε-γήρα-κα
Inf. γηρᾱ-ναι (§ 316, 2)
2. Stem δρα, Pres. δι-δρά-σκ-ω, *I run* (used only in compounds)
ἔ-δρᾱ-ν   δρά-σομαι   δέ-δρᾱ-κα (§ 316, 3)
3. Stem ἡβα, Pres. ἡβά-σκ-ω, *I become marriageable* (compare *pube-sc-o*)
ἥβη-σα
4. Stem θνα (from θάν), Pres. θνή-σκ-ω, *I die* (usually ἀποθνήσκω)
ἔ-θαν-ον   θάν-οῦμαι   τέ-θνη-κα (§ 317, 3).
                        Fut. 3, τεθνήξω, § 291   θνη-τό-ς
                                                    (*mortal*)
5. Stem ἱλα, Pres. ἱλά-σκ-ομαι, *I conciliate.*
Mid. ἱλᾰ-σά-μην   ἱλά-σ-ο-μαι   ἱλά-σθη-ν
6. Stem μνα, Pres. μι-μνή-σκ-ω, *I remember.*
ἔ-μνη-σα   μνή-σω   ἐ-μνή-σθη-ν
                μέ-μνη-μαι   μνη-σθήσομαι
                [*memini*]
7. Stem πρα, Pres. πι-πρά-σκ-ω, *I sell.*
(for the Aor. and Fut. ἀπεδόμην   πέ-πρᾱ-κα   ἐ-πρά-θην
            ἀποδώσομαι)   πέ-πρᾱ-μαι   πρα-θήσομαι
                                πε-πρά-σομαι
8. Stem φα, Pres. φά-σκ-ω, *I say.* Compare φη-μί, § 312, 5.
9. Stem χα and χᾰν, Pres. χά-σκ-ω, *I open the mouth.*
ἔ-χᾰν-ον   χάν-οῦμαι   κέ-χην-α.

Stem in ε.

10. Stem ἀρε, Pres. ἀρέ-σκ-ω, *I please.*
ἤρε-σα   ἀρέ-σω   ἠρέ-σθην.

Stems in ω.

11. Stem βιω, Pres. (ἀνα)βιώ-σκ-ομαι, *I revive.*
(ἀν)ε-βίω-ν (§ 316, 13)
(ἀν)εβιωσάμην, *I revived.* Compare § 329.

§ 324. SIXTH CLASS, OR INCHOATIVE VERBS. 195

12. Stem βλω (from μολ, § 51, D.), Pres. βλώ-σκ-ω, *I go.*
ἔ-μολ-ον   μολ-οῦμαι
13. Stem βρω, Pres. βι-βρώ-σκ-ω, *I consume.*
βέ-βρω-κα (Part. βεβρώς, § 317,
D. 16)
βέ-βρω-μαι
14. Stem γνω, Pres. γι-γνώ-σκ-ω, *I recognize* [Lat. *(g)no-sc-o*]
ἔ-γνω-ν (§ 316, 14)   γνώ-σομαι   ἔ-γνω-κα   ἐ-γνώ-σθην
ἔ-γνω-σ-μαι
15. Stem θρω (from θορ), Pres. θρώ-σκ-ω, *I leap.*
ἔ-θορ-ον
16. Stem τρω, Pres. τι-τρώ-σκ-ω, *I wound.*
ἔ-τρω-σα   τρώ-σω   τέ-τρω-μαι   ἐ-τρώ-θην
17. Stem ἀλ and ἀλω, Pres. ἀλ-ί-σκ-ο μ α ι, *I am taken.*
{ ἑ-άλω-ν   ἀλώ-σομαι   ἑ-άλω-κα or ἥλω-κα
{ ἥλων (§ 316, 12)   (compare § 237)
18. Stem ἀμβλ and ἀμβλω, Pres. ἀμβλ-ί-σκ-ω, *I miscarry.*
ἤμβλω-σα   ἤμβλω-κα
19. Stem ἀναλ and ἀναλω, Pres. ἀνᾱλ-ί-σκ-ω, *I expend.*
ἀνάλω-σα or ἀνήλωσα ἀνᾱλώ-σω   { ἀνάλω-κα   { ἀνᾱλώ-θην
also ἠνάλω-σα   { ἀνήλω-κα   { ἀνηλώ-θην.

Stem in ι.

20. Stem πι, Pres. πι-πί-σκ-ω, *I give to drink.* Compare πί-ν-ω,
§ 321, 4.
ἔ-πῑ-σα   πί-σω

Stems in υ.

21. Stem κυ, Pres. κυ-ί-σκ-ω, *I fructify.*
22. Stem μεθυ, Pres. μεθύ-σκ-ω, *I make drunk,* Mid., *I become drunk.*
ἐ-μέθῠ-σα   ἐ-μεθύ-σθην.

Consonant-Stems.

23. Stem ἀμπλᾰκ, Pres. ἀμπλᾰκ-ί-σκ-ω, *I fail.*
ἤμπλᾰκ-ον   ἀμπλᾰκ-ή-σω
24. Stem (ἐπ)αὐρ, Pres. (ἐπ)αὐρ-ί-σκ-ο μ α ι, *I enjoy.*
ἐπηυρ-όμην
Inf. ἐπαυρ-έσθαι

§ 324. Dialects. — 12. Perf. μέ-μ-β-λω-κα (compare § 51, D., and § 282, D.).
13. Aor. ἔ-βρω-ν (§ 316, D. 23), with the Pres. βεβρώθω.
15. 3 Plur. Fut. θορέονται [with θόρ-νυ-μαι, according to § 319].
16. With τρώ-ω.
24. Aor. ἐπηῦρον, Inf. ἐπαυρεῖν.

196   SIXTH CLASS, OR INCHOATIVE VERBS.   § 324.

25. Stem εὑρ,   Pres. εὑρ-ί-σκ-ω, *I find*.
εὗρ-ον (Mid.)   εὑρ-ή-σω   εὕρ-η-κ-α   εὑρ-έ-θην
                                                          εὕρ-η-μαι   εὑρ-ε-θή-σομαι
26. Stem στερ,   Pres. στερ-ί-σκ-ω, *I deprive* (with στερῶ, Mid.
                  στέρομαι, *I am deprived*)
ἐ-στέρ-η-σα   στερ-ή-σω   ἐ-στέρ-η-κα   ἐ-στερ-ή-θην
                                        ἐ-στέρ-η-μαι
27. Stem ἁλυκ,   Pres. ἀλύ-σκ-ω, *I shun*.
ἤλυξα   ἀλύξω
28. Stem διδαχ,   Pres. διδά-σκ-ω, *I teach*.
ἐ-δίδαξα   διδάξω   δε-δίδαχ-α   ἐ-δι-δάχθην
                                        δε-δίδαγμαι
29. Stem λακ,   Pres. λά-σκ-ω, *I utter, speak*.
ἔ-λἄκ-ον   λακ-ή-σομαι   { λέ-ληκ-α
ἐ-λάκ-η-σα   { λέ-λᾱκ-α.

Obs. 1.—The last three Stems suppress a Guttural before σκ. Several of the Stems quoted form a part of the tenses by affixing ε to the Stem (compare § 322, *Obs.*, and § 326), especially Nos. 23, 25, 26, 29.

Obs. 2.—The following may serve as examples of the formation of nouns: ὁ θάν-α-το-ς, *death;* τὸ μνη-μεῖο-ν, *the memorial;* ὁ αὐτό-μολ-ο-ς, *the deserter;* ἡ γνώ-μη, *the opinion;* ἡ ἅλω-σι-ς, *the capture;* ὁ διδάσκ-αλο-ς (from the Present-Stem), *the teacher;* ἡ διδαχ-ή (from the Verbal-Stem), *the instruction;* and from Stems which are enlarged by ε : τὸ εὕρ-η-μα, *the discovery;* ἡ στέρ-η-σι-ς, *the deprivation*.

Dialects.—26. Aor. στερέσαι, Part. Pass. Aor. στερείς.
28. [διδασκῆσαι] a secondary Stem is δα, Aor. δίδαον, *I taught* (§ 320, D. 40).
29. Ion. form ληκέω (§ 325), Fem. Part. Perf. λελᾰκυῖα.

And the Special Verbs:
30. Stem ἁλδα, Pres. ἀλδήσκω, *I become great*, Aor. ἤλδανον, *I made great*.
31. Stem κλε, Pres. κικλήσκω, with καλέω, *I call*.
32. Stem φαν, Pres. [φαύ-σκ-ω] πι-φαύ-σκ-ω, *I call*.
33. Stem ἀπαφ (from ἀφ), Pres. ἀπ-αφ-ί-σκ-ω, *I deceive*, Aor. ἤπαφον, Subj. ἀπάφω.
34. Stem ἀρ, Pres. ἀρ-αρ-ί-σκ-ω, *I fit*, Aor. ἤραρον, *I fitted*, Perf. ἄρηρα, *I suit*, Fem. Part. ἀραρυῖα, Part. Mid. ἄρμενος, *suitable*, Weak Aor. ἦρσα, *I fitted*, Aor. Pass. ἄρθην.
35. Stem ἰκ, Pres. ἐ-ΐ-σκ-ω, *I make equal* (compare § 317, B. 7).
36. Imperf. ἴσκε(ν), *he spoke*.
37. Stem τυχ (compare § 322, 30), Pres. τιτύσκομαι, *I aim at*.

§ 325. Seventh, or E-class.

A short Stem alternates with one enlarged by ε.

A) The enlarged Stem in ε is the Present-Stem; the shorter serves to form the other tenses.

1. Stem γ α μ, Pres. γαμέ-ω, *I marry* (Act. *uxorem duco*, Mid. *nubo*)
ἔ-γημ-α   γάμ-ῶ (Mid.)   γε-γάμ-η-κα
                                       γε-γάμ-η-μαι
2. Stem γ η θ, Pres. γ η θ έ - ω, *I rejoice*.
                                γέ-γηθ-α, *I am rejoiced*.
3. Stem δ ο κ, Pres. δ ο κ έ - ω, *I seem*.
ἔ-δοξα   δόξω   Mid. δέδογ-μαι
4. Stem κ υ ρ, Pres. κ υ ρ έ - ω and κύρω, *I meet*.
ἔ-κυρ-σα   κύρσω
5. Stem μ α ρ τ υ ρ, Pres. μ α ρ τ ῠ ρ έ - ω, *I am witness*.
                        Mid. μαρτύρομαι, *I call to witness*.
6. Stem ξ υ ρ, Pres. ξ υ ρ έ ω, *I shave*.   Mid. ξ ῠ́ ρ ο μ α ι
ἐ-ξῦρ-άμην   ἐξύρ-η-μαι
7. Stem π ἄ τ, Pres. π α τ έ - ο μ α ι, *I eat*.
ἐ-πᾰσάμην   πέπασμαι
8. Stem ῥ ι φ, Pres. ῥ ι π τ - έ - ω and ῥίπτ-ω (according to § 249), *I throw*.
ἔρριψα   ῥίψω   ἔρριφα   { ἐρρίφην
                                     ἔρριμμαι   { ἐρρίφθην
9. Stem ὠ θ, Pres. ὠ θ έ - ω, *I push*.
ἔ-ωσα (§ 237)   ὤσω (ὠθήσω Mid.)   ἔ-ωσ-μαι   ἐ-ώσθην

---

§ 325. **Dialects.**—1 Fut. γαμ-έω, 3 Sing. Fut. Mid. γαμέσσεται, *she will marry*.
3. [δοκήσω, ἐδόκησα.]
8. 3 Sing. Plup. Mid. ἐρέριπτο.
Besides:
a) Stem γ ε γ ω ν, Pres. γεγωνέ-ω, *I call*, Perf. γέγωνα, Fut. γεγωνήσω.
b) Stem δ ἄ τ, Pres. δατέ-ομαι, *I distribute*, Fut. δάσομαι, Aor. δάσσατο, Perf. δέδασται.
c) Stem δ ο υ π, Pres. δουπέ-ω, *I make a sound*, Aor. ἐ(γ)δούπη-σα, Perf. δέ-δουπ-α.
d) Stem ε ἰ λ, ἐ λ, Pres. εἰ-λέ-ω, *I press*, Imperf. ἐείλεον (§ 237), Aor. 3 Plur. ἔλσαν, Perf. Mid. ἔελμαι, Aor. Pass. ἰάλην (§ 295), 3 Plur. ἄλεν, Inf. ἀλήμεναι.
e) Stem κ ε λ α δ, Pres. κελαδέ-ω, *I resound*, Part. κελάδ-ων.
f) Stem κ ε ν τ, Pres. κεντέ-ω, *I sting*, Aor. Inf. κέν-σαι.

Obs.—In some verbs the Stem with ε extends even farther than the Present-Stem. Examples of the formation of nouns : ὁ γάμ-ο-ς, *the wedding;* ἡ δόξα, *the appearance;* τὸ μαρτύρ-ιο-ν, *the testimony;* ἡ ὤ-σι-ς or ὤθη-σις, *pushing.*

§ 326. B) The shorter Stem is the Present-Stem; the enlarged one in ε serves to form the other tenses.

10. Stem αἰδ(ε), Pres. αἰδ-ο-μαι and αἰδέ-ομαι, *I am ashamed.*
11. Stem ἀλεξ(ε), Pres. ἀλέξ-ω, *I ward off.*
ἠλεξ-άμην   ἀλεξ-ή-σομαι
12. Stem ἀχθ(ε), Pres. ἄχθ-ο-μαι, *I am vexed.*
    ἀχθέ-σομαι   ἠχθέ-σθην
        ἀχθε-σθήσομαι
13. Stem βοσκ(ε), Pres. βόσκ-ω, *I pasture.*
    βοσκή-σω; from the Stem βο the Verb. Adj. βο-τός
14. Stem βουλ(ε), Pres. βούλ-ο-μαι, *I will.*
(Augment, § 234)   βουλή-σομαι   βε-βούλη-μαι   ἐ-βουλή-θην
15. Stem δε(ε), Pres. δέ-ω, *I need* (δεῖ, *it is necessary*), Mid. δέομαι, *I require.*
ἐ-δέη-σα   δεή-σω   δε-δέη-κα   ἐ-δεή-θην (§ 328, 2)
16. Stem ἐρ(ε), Pres. not usual (§ 327, 13)
ἠρ-όμην, *I asked.*   ἐρή-σομαι, Inf. ἐρέσθαι
17. Stem ἐρρ(ε), Pres. ἔρρ-ω, *I go away.*
ἤρρη-σα   ἐρρή-σω   ἤρρη-κα

Dialects.—*g*) Stem κτυπ, Pres. κτυπέ-ω, *I ring,* Aor. ἔκτυπ-ον.
h) Pres. πιέζω and πιεζέ-ω, *I press,* Aor. ἐπίεσα.
i) Stem ῥιγ, Pres. ῥιγέ-ω, *I shudder,* Perf. ἔρρῑγα.
k) Stem στυγ, Pres. στυγέ-ω, *I hate, shun,* Aor. ἔστυγον and στυγῆσαι, ἔστυξα, *I made dreadful.*
l) Stem φιλ, Pres. φιλέω, *I love,* Aor. ἐ-φῖλ-ά-μην.
m) Pres. χραισμέω, *I help,* Aor. ἔχραισμον.

Three Verbs in αω with a movable α are here to be noticed:
n) Stem γο, Pres. γοά-ω, *I wail,* Imperf. ἔ-γο-ον.
o) Stem μᾰκ, Pres. μηκά-ο-μαι, *I low,* Perf. μέ-μηκ-α, Aor. ἔ-μᾰκ-ον.
p) Stem μῠκ, Pres. μῡκά-ο-μαι, *I roar,* Perf. μέμῡκ-α, Aor. ἔμῠκ-ον.

§ 326. **Dialects.**—10. ᾐδέσατο, Imperat. αἰδέσσαι, Fut. αἰδέ-σομαι, Aor. Pass. 3 Plur. αἴδεσθεν.
11. ἄλαλκον (§ 257).
14. Pres. βόλεται, Imperf. ἐβόλοντο, Perf. βέβουλα.
15. Aor. ἐδεύησα, once δῆσα, *I was in want of,* also Pres. δεύομαι.
16. Pres. εἴρομαι, Fut. εἰρήσομαι.

§ 326. SEVENTH, OR E-CLASS. 199.

18. Stem εὐδ(ε), Pres. εὕδω, *I sleep* (generally καθεύδω) Augment, § 240 (καθ)ευδή-σω
19. Stem ἐψ(ε), Pres. ἕψ-ω, *I cook*.

ἥψη-σα   ἑψή-σομαι   ἥψη-μαι   ἡψή-θην
                                                  Verb. Adj. ἑφθός

20. Stem θελ(ε) or ἐθελ(ε), Pres. θέλ-ω or ἐθέλ-ω, *I will.*

ἠθέλη-σα   (ἐ)θελή-σω   ἠθέλη-κα

21. Stem ἰζ(ε), Pure Stem ἑδ, Pres. ἵζομαι, *I seat myself;* also ἱζάνω, Class 5. Compare ἕζομαι.

ἐκαθισάμην (§ 240)   καθιζήσομαι and καθεδοῦμαι (§ 263)
22. Stem κλαυ and κλαιε, Pres. κλαίω (κλάω), *I weep.* Compare § 253.

ἔκλαυ-σα   κλαιήσω   with κλαύσομαι
23. Stem μαχ(ε), Pres. μάχομαι, *I fight.*

ἐ-μαχε-σάμην   μαχοῦμαι (§ 263)   με-μάχη-μαι
24. Stem μελ(ε), Pres. μέλει μοι, *it is a care to me;* Mid. μέλομαι, *I care for, take care of.*

ἐ-μέλη-σε   μελή-σει   με-μέλη-κε   ἐ-μελή-θην
               (ἐπι)μελήσομαι

25. Stem μελλ(ε), Pres. μέλλ-ω, *I am on the point, hesitate.*

ἠ-μέλλη-σα   μελλή-σω
(§ 234, Obs.)

26. Stem μεν(ε), Pres. μέν-ω, *I remain* [*mane-o, man-si*], Verbal Adj. μεν-ε-τός

ἔ-μεινα   μεν-ῶ   με-μένη-κα
27. Stem μυζ(ε), Pres. μύζω, *I suck.*

ἐ-μύζη-σα   μυζή-σω
28. Stem νεμ(ε), Pres. νέμ-ω, *I assign.*

ἔ-νειμα   νεμ-ῶ   νε-νέμη-κα (Mid.) ἐ-νεμή-θην
29. Stem ὀζ(ε), Pure Stem ὀδ, Pres. ὄζ-ω, *I smell.*

ὤζη-σα   ὀζή-σω   ὄδ-ωδ-α (§ 275, D.) [Lat. *od-*or]
30. Stem οἰ(ε), Pres. οἴ-ομαι, *I think* (compare § 244)

    οἰή-σομαι   ᾠή-θην
31. Stem οἰχ(ε), Pres. οἴχ-ομαι, *I am off.*

    οἰχή-σομαι   οἴχ-ωκ-α

Dialects.—19. [Imperf. ἕψεε.]
23. μαχέ-ομαι, Part. μαχειόμενος or μαχεούμενος, Fut. μαχήσομαι. and μαχέσομαι.
24. Perf. μέμηλε, Plup. μεμήλει, Perf. Mid. μέ-μ-β-λε-ται (Plup. *-ro*), § 51, D.
26. Perf. μέμονα, *I am disposed, strive.*
30. Pres. ὀί-ομαι, ὀί-ω, Aor. Mid. ὀίσατο, Aor. Pass. ὠίσθην.
31. Perf. οἴχηκα (οἴχημαι), with the Pres. οἰχ-νέ-ω, according to § 323.

200   SEVENTH, OR E-CLASS.   § 326.

(οἴχ-ωκ-α, with irreg. Reduplication [§ 275] for οἰχ-ωχ-α. Compare § 35, a)

32. Stem ὀφειλ(ε), Pure Stem ὀφελ, Pres. ὀφείλω, *I owe* (§ 253, *Obs.*)
ὤφελ-ον [*utinam*]   ὀφειλή-σω   ὠφείλη-κα
ὠφείλη-σα.

33. Stem περδ(ε), Pres. πέρδω
ἔ-παρδ-ον   παρδή-σομαι   πέ-πορδ-α

34. Stem π(ε)τ(ε), Pres. πέτ-ομαι, *I fly*.
ἐ-π(ε)τ-ό-μην   π(ε)τή-σομαι
(§ 61, c)

35. Stem ῥυ(ε), Pres. ῥέω, *I flow* (§ 248).
ἐρρεύ-σα (rare, § 260, 2) · ῥυή-σομαι   ἐρρύη-κα   ἐρρύην
(with ῥεύσομαι)

36. Stem στιβ(ε), Pres. στείβ-ω, *I tread*.
                              ἐ-στίβη-μαι

37. Stem τυπτε, Pure Stem τυπ (§ 249), Pres. τύπτω, *I strike*.
ἔ-τυπ-ον   :τυπτή-σω   Mid. τέ-τυμ-μαι   ἐ-τύπ-ην

38. Stem χαιρε, Pure Stem χαρ, Pres. χαίρω, *I rejoice* (§ 253)
              χαιρή-σω   κε-χάρη-κα   ἐ-χάρ-ην
                         κε-χάρη-μαι

Obs.—The ε sometimes appears in all the tenses except the Present, sometimes only in some of them; sometimes it is added to the pure, sometimes to the strengthened Stem : μεν-ε, στιβ-ε, ιζε, ὀζε, τυπτε. The formation of nouns shows the same varieties: αἰδή-μων, *shame-faced ;* ἡ βούλη-σι-ς, *voluntas ;* ἐθελή-μων, *voluntary ;*

Dialects.—38. Part. Perf. κεχαρηώς, Fut. κεχαρήσω, Aor. ἐχήρατο, and 3 Plur. κεχάροντο, § 257, D.

Besides :

39. Stem ἀλθ(ε), Pres. ἄλθ-ομαι, *I become well*, Fut. ἀλθή-σομαι.
40. Stem δα, Aor. δέδαον (§ 257, D.), *I taught*, Aor. Mid. Inf. δεδάασθαι (*to get to know*), Aor. Pass. ἐδάην (*I learned*), besides Fut. δαήσομαι, Perf. δεδάηκα, Part. Perf. δεδαώς.
41. Stem κηδ(ε), Pres. κήδ-ω, *I grieve*, Fut. κηδή-σω, Perf. κέκηδ-α (*I am concerned*), Fut. κεκᾰδήσομαι.
42. Stem μεδ(ε), Pres. μέδ-ω, *I rule*, Mid., *I reflect*, Fut. μεδή-σομαι.
43. Stem πιθ, Pres. πείθω, *I persuade*, Fut. also πιθήσω, Part. Aor. πιθήσας.
44. Stem τορ(ε), Aor. ἔ-τορ-ον and ἐ-τόρη-σα, *I bored through*, Fut. τετορή-σω.
45. Stem φιδ, Pres. φείδομαι, *I spare*, Aor. Mid. πεφιδέσθαι (§ 257, D.), Fut. πεφιδή-σομαι.

§ 327. EIGHTH, OR MIXED CLASS. 201

ὁ μαχη-τή-ς, *the warrior;* ἡ μέλλη-σι-ς, *the delay;* μόν-ιμο-ς. *remaining;* ὁ νόμ-ο-ς, *the law;* ἡ ὀδ-μή, *the smell;* ἡ χαρ-ά, *the joy.*

§ 327. *Eighth, or Mixed Class.*

Several essentially different Stems unite to form one verb:

1. Present α ἱ ρ έ - ω, *I take;* Mid., *I choose;* Stems α ἱ ρ ε and ἑ λ.
εἶλ-ον (§ 236)   αἱρή-σω   ᾕρη-κα   ᾑρέ-θην
Inf. ἑλεῖν
εἱλόμην   αἱρή-σομαι   ᾕρη-μαι

2. Pres. ἔ ρ χ - ο μ α ι, *I go, come;* Stems ἐ ρ χ and ἐ λ (υ) θ
ἦλ[υ]θ-ον   ἐλεύ-σομαι   ἐλ-ήλῠθ-α (§ 275)
Imperat. ἐλθέ (§ 333, 12)
Inf. ἐλθεῖν. The place of the Fut. is generally supplied by εἶμι.

3. Pres. ἔ ρ δ - ω and ῥ έ ζ - ω, *I do;* Stems ἐ ρ δ, ἐ ρ γ, ῥ ε γ
ἔ-ρεξα   ἔρξω   ἐρέχθην

Obs.—The original Verbal-Stem is ϝ ε ρ γ, hence τὸ ϝέργ-ο-ν (§ 34, D.), Att. ἔργ-ο-ν, *work;* from (ϝ)ἔργ, by the addition of the enlargement of the Present ι (Class 4), arose (ϝ)ἔργ-ι-ω, and from this ἔρδ-ω. But by metathesis ϝ ε ρ γ became ϝ ρ ε γ, and, with loss of the ϝ, ῥ ε γ, whence the regular Present, according to Class 4, is ῥέζ-ω, *i. e.*, ῥεγ-ι-ω (§ 251).

4. Pres. ἐ σ θ ί - ω, *I eat;* Stem ἐ σ θ ι, ἐ δ (ε) [*ed-o*], and φ ᾰ γ
ἔ-φᾰγ-ον   Fut. ἔδ-ομαι   ἐδ-ήδοκα (§ 275)   ἠδέ-σθην
             (§ 265)   ἐδ-ήδεσμαι

5. Pres. ἕ π - ο μ α ι, *I follow* (Imperf. εἱπόμην, § 236); Stems ἑ π and
                σ (ε) π
ἑ-σπ-όμην   ἕψομαι   Subj. σπῶ-μαι   Inf. σπέσθαι

Obs.—The original Stem is σ ε π, from which ἑ π has arisen by weakening σ to the rough breathing (§ 60, *b*). In the Aor. Ind. the rough breathing is not organic, ε being properly only the Augment. Besides this there is a syncope (§ 61, *c*).

---

§ 327. Dialects.—1. [ἀραίρηκα, ἀραίρημαι, § 275.]
2. Aor. ἤλῠθον, Perf. εἰλήλουθα (§ 317, D. 13), Part. ἐληλουθώς.
3. [Pres. ἔρδ-ω] Perf. ἔοργα (§ 275, D. 2), Plup. ἰώργειν, Aor. ἔρξα and ἔρεξα.
4. Pres. ἔσθω and ἔδω, Inf. ἔδ-μεναι, Perf. ἔδ-ηδ-α, Mid. ἰδήδοται.
5. Pres. Act. ἕπω, *I am occupied*, Aor. ἔ-σπ-ον, Inf. σπεῖν, Part. σπών, Fut. ἕψω, Subj. Aor. Mid. ἕσπωμαι, ἐσποίμην, ἰσπέσθαι, ἰσπόμενος.

T 2

6. Pres. ἔχ-ω, *I have, hold* (Imperf. εἶχον, § 236); Stems ἐχ and σχ(ε)
ἔ-σχ-ον, *I seized*.   1. ἕξω (Mid.)
Subj. σχῶ, Opt. σχοίην
Inf. σχεῖν, Part. σχών   2. σχή-σω   ἔ-σχη-κα   ἐ-σχέ-θην
Imperat. σχέ-ς (§ 316, 11)   ἔ-σχη-μαι   ἐκτός   σχετός
Mid. ἐ-σχ-όμην, σχῶμαι, etc.
Ind. σχ-έσθαι

Obs.—The original Stem is σ ε χ, from which ἐχ has arisen by weakening σ to the rough breathing (§ 60, b). From σ ε χ by syncope came ἔ-σχ-ο-ν, by metathesis σ χ ε, from which σχέ-ς, ἔ-σχη-κα. From ἐ χ came the Future ἕξω and the Verbal Adj. ἐκ-τό-ς, while in the Present-Stem the rough breathing was changed into the soft breathing, because of the aspirate in the following syllable (§ 53, b, *Obs.*): ἔχ-ω for ἔχ-ω. Compare also ὑπισχνέομαι and ἀμπισχνέομαι, § 323, 36. All the Stem forms also appear in the formation of nouns: τὸ σχῆ-μα, *the form ;* ἡ ἕξι-ς, *the bearing ;* ἰσχυρό-ς, *firm, tenable.*

7. Pres. μίσγ-ω, *I mix, mise-eo*; Stems μ ι σ γ and μ ι γ, additional form μίγνυμι (§ 319, 18).

8. Pres. ὁ ρ ά - ω, *I see;* Stems ὁ ρ α, ἰ δ, ὀ π
εἶδ-ον   (Mid.) ὄψομαι   ἐ-ώρᾱ-κα   ὤφθην
        ὄπ-ωπ-α (§ 275)
Imperat. ἰδέ.   Mid. ἰδοῦ (333, 12).
Inf. ἰδ-εῖν   ἑώρᾱ-μαι   ὁρᾱτός
        ὦμ-μαι   ὀπτός

Obs.—On the irregular Augment of the Stem ὁ ρ α (Imperf. ἑώρων), § 237. The Stem ἰ δ was originally Ϝ ι δ (§ 34, D.). Compare *vid*-e-o ; the Aor. Ind. therefore, ἐ-Ϝιδ-ον, with Syllabic Augment, contracted to εἶδ-ο-ν, but Subj. ἴδ-ω, Opt. ἴδ-οι-μι. The Perf. of this Stem is οἶδα, *I know* (§ 317, 6). All three Stems appear also in the formation of nouns: τὸ ὁρᾱ-μα, *the spectacle ;* τὸ εἶδ-ος, *the form, appearance ;* ἡ ὄψι-ς, *the sight ;* τὸ ὄμ-μα, *the eye, look.*

9. Pres. π ά σ χ - ω, *I suffer;* Stem π α σ χ, π α θ (ε), π ε ν θ
ἔ-πᾱθ-ον   πεί-σομαι   πέ-πονθ-α   παθη-τός
(for πενθ-σόμαι, § 50)

Dialects.—6. Perf. ὄχ-ωκ-α (§ 326, 31), Perf.-Mid. ὤγμαι, 3 Plur. Plup. ὤχατο.

8. Aor. ἴδον, Weak Aor. Mid. ἐείσατο and εἴσατο, Part. ἐεισάμενος to the Pres. εἴδομαι, *I appear, resemble* (compare § 34, D. 4). As a shorter additional form of the Stem ὁ ρ ά, we find in Homer the Stem ὁ ρ (Ϝορ), thence 3 Plur. Pres. ἐπὶ ὁρ-ο-νται, *they overlook.*

9. 2 Plur. πέποσθε (§ 317, D. 14), Part. πεπαθυῖα.

§ 327. EIGHTH, OR MIXED CLASS. 203

Obs.—From the shorter Stems we have the nouns: τὸ πάθ-ος, *the suffering;* τὸ πένθ-ος, *the mourning.*

10. πίν-ω, *I drink;* Stems π ι ν, π ι, π ο [Latin *po*-tus]. Compare § 321, 4.

ἔ-πι-ον   Fut. πί-ομαι (§ 265)   πέ-πω-κα   ἐ-πό-θην
Imperat. πῖ-θι (§ 316, 15)   πέ-πο-μαι   πο-τός

Obs.—From the Stem π ο we have the nouns: ὁ πό-τη-ς, *po-tor;* ἡ πό-σι-ς, *po-tio;* τὸ πο-τήριο-ν, *po-culu-m.*

11. Pres. τ ρ έ χ - ω, *I run;* Stems τ ρ ε χ and δ ρ ε μ

ἔ-δράμ-ον   δράμοῦμ-αι   δε-δράμη-κα   θρεκτέον
          θρέξομαι (§ 54, c)

Obs.—Nouns from both Stems: ὁ τροχ-ό-ς, *the wheel;* ὁ δρομ-εύ-ς, *the runner.*

12. Pres. φ έ ρ - ω, *I carry* [*fero*] ; Stems φ ε ρ, ἐ ν ε (γ) κ, ο ἰ

ἤνεγκ-ον   οἴ-σω   ἐν-ήνοχ-α (§ 275)   οἰ-σ-θήσομαι
                        οἰ-σ-τός
ἤνεγκ-α (§ 269)   ἠνέχ-θην
ἠνεγκ-ά-μην   οἴσομαι   ἐν-ήνεγ-μαι   ἐνεχ-θήσομαι

Obs.—From the Stem φ ε ρ we have the nouns: τὸ φέρ-ε-τρο-ν, *the bier;* ὁ φόρ-ο-ς, *the contribution, tax;* ὁ φόρ-το-ς, *the burden.*

13. Aorist ε ἶ π ο ν, *I spoke;* Stems ε ἰ π, ἐ ρ, and ῥ ε.

εἶπ-ον
εἶπ-α (§ 269)   ἐρ-ῶ   εἴ-ρη-κα (§ 274, *Obs.*)   ἐρρήθην
Imperat. εἰπ-έ   Inf. εἰπ-εῖν   εἴ-ρη-μαι   ῥη-θήσομαι
      (§ 333, 12)
               εἰ-ρή-σ-ομαι   ῥη-τό-ς

Obs.—The Stem ε ἰ π has arisen by contraction from ἐ-επ, and ἐ-επ from Ϝε-Ϝεπ, the *reduplicated* Aorist-Stem of the Verbal-Stem Ϝεπ (ἔπος, *word*, § 34, D. 1). This is the reason why the diphthong ει belongs not to the Indicative alone (§ 257, D.). The Stem ἐ ρ (Fut. ἐρῶ), to which the Mid. ἐρέσθαι, *to ask* (§ 326, 16) belongs, has likewise lost Ϝ, it being originally Ϝερ (compare Lat. *ver*-bu-m). From Ϝερ, by metathesis (§ 59), arose Ϝρε, after the loss of the Ϝ, ῥε,

Dialects.—11. ἔθρεξα [δραμέομαι], δέδρομα.

12. 2 Plur. Imperat. Pres. φέρ-τε [Lat. *ferte*], Aor. ἤνεικα, 3 Sing. Opt. ἐνείκαι (ἐνείκοι) [Perf. ἐνήνειγμαι], Imperat. Aor. οἶσε, Inf. οἰσέμεναι (§ 268, D.).

13. Pres. εἴρω (Class 4, *d*), Aor. ἔσπ-ον (Stem σ ε π, compare 5), *I spoke*, Imperat. ἔσπ-ετε, Pres. ἐν-έπ-ω, Imperat. ἔννεπε (§ 62, D.), Aor. ἔνισπον, Subj. ἐνίσπω, Opt. 2 Sing. ἐνίσποις, Imperat. ἔνισπε and ἔνισπες, Fut. ἐνίψω and ἐνισπήσω.

hence εἴ-ρη-κα for Fε-Fρη-κα, ἰρρή-θη-ν for ε-Fρή-θη-ν, ῥη-τό-ς for Fρη-το-ς. As Present forms, φημί, λέγω, and, especially in compounds, ἀγορεύω may be used, e. g., ἀπαγορεύω, *I forbid;* Aor. ἀπεῖπον, Fut. ἀπερῶ, Perf. ἀπείρηκα. Nouns from the Stems ἰπ and ῥε : ἡ ὄψ, *the voice;* τὸ ῥῆ-μα, *the word;* ὁ ῥή-τωρ, *the orator.*

In addition to these, there are three verbs which reduplicate the Stem in the Present:

14. Present γ ί - γ ν - ο μ α ι (also γίν-ομαι), *I become.*
Stem γι-γ(ε)ν and γεν(ε) (Lat. *gi-g(e)n-o,* Perf. *gen*-ui)
ἐ-γεν-ό-μην   γενή-σομαι   γέ-γον-α
                                γε-γένη-μαι .

Obs.—From the Stem γ ε ν we have τὸ γέν-ος, *the race, genus;* οἱ γον-εῖς, *the parents,* from γ ε ν ε, ἡ γένε-σι-ς, *the origin.*

15. Pres. π ί - π τ - ω (from π ι - π ε τ - ω), *I fall;* Stem πῑπτ, πετ, πτω ἔ-πεσ-ον, from ἔ-πετ-ον (§ 60, *a*), πεσ-οῦμαι (§ 264), πέ-πτω-κα (compare § 323, 35).

Obs.—From the Stem π τ ω : ἡ πτῶ-σι-ς, τὸ πτῶ-μα, *the fall.*

16. Pres. τ ι - τ ρ ά - ω, *I bore;* Stems τ ι τ ρ α and τ ρ α
ἔ-τρη-σα   τρή-σω
(§ 270, *Obs.*).

IRREGULARITIES OF MEANING.

§ 328. The most important irregularities of meaning consist in the fluctuation between the Active, Middle, and Passive, as well as, on the other hand, between the transitive and intransitive meaning.

A) Active, Middle, and Passive Meaning.

1. Very many *Active* verbs have a *Middle* Future with *Active* meaning (§ 266). This is the case with most verbs of Classes 5 to 8.

2. The *Deponent* verbs are to be regarded as *Middle,*

Dialects.—14. Perf. 1 Plur. γέ-γἄ-μεν, § 317, D. 2. Compare § 329, 8.
15. Perf. Part. πε-πτε-ώς, § 317, D. 17.
Besides :
17. ἰ-αύω, Stem αὐ, ἀF, *I sleep* (ἰ as Reduplication, compare § 308), Aor. ἄεσα.

§ 329. IRREGULARITIES OF MEANING. 205

and also make most of their tenses in the *Middle* form. Those are called *Passive Deponents* whose Aorist has a Passive form : e. g., βούλομαι, *I wish*, ἐβουλήθην, *I wished*. The most important Passive Deponents are the following, of which those marked * have a Passive Future, which is used along with the Middle :

ἄγαμαι, *I admire* (§ 312, 8).   εὐλαβέομαι, *I am on my guard*.
*αἰδέομαι, *I dread* (§ 301, 1).   *ἥδομαι, *I rejoice*.
ἀλάομαι, *I ramble*.   *ἐν } θυμέομαι { *I take to heart*.
ἁμιλλάομαι, *I rival*.   προ }   { *I am inclined*.
*ἀρνέομαι, *I deny*.   *ἐπι }   { *I am anxious*.
*ἄχθομαι, *I am indignant* (§ 326, 12).   μετα } μέλομαι { *I repent*.
βούλομαι, *I wish* (§ 326, 14).   ἀπὸ }   { *I despair*.
δέομαι, *I need* (§ 326, 15).   *δια } νοέομαι { *I reflect*.
δέρκομαι, *I look*.   ἐν }   { *I ponder*.
*διαλέγομαι, *I converse*.   προ }   { *I anticipate*.
δύναμαι, *I can* (§ 312, 9).   οἴομαι, *I am of opinion* (§ 326, 30).
ἐναντιόομαι, *I am opposed*.   σέβομαι, *I reverence*.
ἐπίσταμαι, *I know* (§ 312, 10).   φιλοτιμέομαι, *I am ambitious*.

Obs.—Several of these verbs have the Middle Aorist as well as the Passive.

3. The *Passive Aorists* of several *Active* verbs have a *Middle* meaning : εὐφραίνω, *I rejoice*, εὐφράνθην, *I rejoiced;* στρέφω, *I cause to turn*, ἐστράφην, *I turned—myself;* φαίνω, *I show*, ἐφάνην, *I appeared*, etc.

4. The Passive forms of several *Deponents* have also a *Passive* meaning : ἰάομαι, *I heal*, ἰάθην, *I was healed;* δέχομαι, *I receive*, ἐδέχθην, *I was received;* in some even the *Middle* forms have both Active and Passive meaning : μιμέομαι, *I imitate*, μεμίμημαι, *I have imitated* or *have been imitated*.

§ 329. B) *Transitive and Intransitive Meaning*.

When the meaning of a verb fluctuates between Trans-

§ 329. **Dialects.**—The Strong Aor. ἔτραφον (τρέφω, *I nourish*) in Hom. has an intransitive meaning, *I grew up*. In Herod., ἀνέγνων (ἀναγιγνώσκω) means *I read*, ἀνέγνωσα, *I persuaded;* Hom. ἤριπον, *I fell*, Aor. to ἐρείπω (Class 2), *I throw down;* ἔνασσα, *I caused to dwell*, Aor. to ναίω, *I dwell*.

sitive and Intransitive, the *Strong Aorist* has the *intransitive*, and the *Weak Aorist* and *Future Active* the *transitive* meaning; when there are two Perfects, the *Strong* likewise has the *intransitive* and the *Weak* the *transitive* meaning; if there is only one Perfect, it is *intransitive*. The most important cases of this kind are:

1. Stem σ τ α, Pres. ἵστημι, *I place*, Weak Aor. ἔστησα, *I placed*, Fut. στήσω, *I shall place*, Pres. Mid. ἵσταμαι, *I place myself*, Strong Aor. ἔστην, *I placed myself—stood*, Perf. ἕστηκα, *I have placed myself, or stand* (§ 503), Plup. ἑστήκειν, *I stood*, Fut. ἑστήξω (§ 291), *I shall stand*.

Obs.—This same important distinction appears in the numerous compounds: ἀφίστημι, *I cause to revolt, to separate*, ἀπέστην, *I revolted—separated*, ἀφέστηκα, *I have revolted;* ἐφίστημι, *I put over*, ἐπέστην, *I put myself over*, ἐφέστηκα, *I am put over;* καθίστημι, *I put down*, κατέστην, *I put myself forward*, καθέστηκα, *I stand there* or *forward*. The Aor. Mid. has a specially Middle meaning, *e. g.*, κατεστήσατο, *he determined* for himself (compare § 479).

2. Stem β α, Pres. βαίνω, *I go*, is commonly intransitive with the Fut. βήσομαι; but in the poets, *I cause to go*, also in the Weak Aor. ἔβησα, Fut. βήσω; but intransitive in the Strong Aor. ἔβην, *I went*, βέβηκα, *I have advanced, stand firm* (βέβα-ιο-ς, *firm*).

3. Stem φ υ, Pres. φύω, *I beget*, Weak Aor. ἔφυσα, φύσω; but the Strong Aor. ἔφυν, *I was begotten*, πέφυκα, *I am by nature*, to which the Pres. is φύομαι.

4. Stem δ υ, Pres. δύω, *I sink, hide*, often transitive; καταδύω, *I cause to sink*, also ἔδυσα, δύσω; but ἔδυν, *I sunk myself, I dived;* ἐνέδυν, *I put on;* ἐξέδυν, *I put off*.

5. Stem σ β ε (ς), Pres. σβέννῡμι, *I quench*, Weak Aor. ἔ-σβε-σα, *I quenched*, Strong Aor. ἔσβην, *I was quenched*, ἔσβηκα, *I am quenched*. The Pres. to it is σβέννυμαι.

6. Stem σ κ ε λ, Pres. σκέλλω, *I dry*, but Aor. ἔσκλην, *I grew dry*, with the Pres. σκέλλομαι.

7. Stem πι, Aor. ἔπιον, I drank, ἔπισα (πιπίσκω), I caused to drink.
8. Stem γεν, Pres. γείνομαι (compare § 327, 14), I am born, Aor. ἐγεινάμην, I begat.
9. Stem ὀλ, Pres. ὄλλῡμι, I ruin, strong Perf. ὄλωλα, I am ruined, perii, Weak Perf. ὀλώλεκα, I have ruined, perdidi.

§ 330. In a number of verbs the *Strong Perfect* alone has only an intransitive meaning, as:
1. ἄγνυμι, I break, Perf. ἔᾱγα, I am broken (§ 275, 2).
2. ἐγείρω, I awake, " ἐγρήγορα, I am awake (§ 275, 1).
3. πείθω, I persuade, " πέποιθα, I trust (πείθομαι, I follow, obey).
4. πήγνυμι, I fasten, " πέπηγα, I stick fast.
5. ῥήγνυμι, I tear, " ἔρρωγα, I am torn (§ 278).
6. σήπω, I cause to rot, " σέσηπα, I am rotten.
7. τήκω, I melt, " τέτηκα, I am melted.
8. φαίνω, I show (rarely shine), Perf. πέφηνα, I have appeared (φαίνομαι, I appear).

On the distinction between ἀνέῳγα and ἀνέῳχα, and between πέπρᾱγα and πέπρᾱχα, see § 279.

§ 331. GENERAL VIEW OF THE ACCENTUATION OF VERBAL FORMS.

The general rule given in § 229, that in the verb the accent is removed *as far back as possible from the end*, is subject to the following exceptions:
For all contracted syllables the accentuation is seen from § 87. Hence δοκῶ, ἐλῶμεν (§ 263), πεσοῦμαι (πίπτω, § 327, 15), τιθῶμαι (§ 302), λυθῶ, λυθῇς (§ 296). Compare, however, § 307, *Obs*.

§ 330. Dialects.—9. Hom. δαίω, I set fire to, Perf. δέδηα, I have caught fire.
10. Hom. ἔλπω, I give hope, Perf. ἔολπα, I hope.
11. Hom. φθείρω, I destroy, Perf. (δι)έφθορα, I am destroyed.

§ 332. Compound Verbal forms follow the general rule laid down in § 85, with the following limitations:

1. The accent never goes back beyond the syllable on which the first word had it before the composition: ἀπό-δος, *give back* (ἀπό), not ἄποδος; ἐπίσχες, *hold in* (ἐπί), not ἔπισχες.

2. In double compounds the accent never goes back beyond the first: συνέκδος, *give out with;* παρένθες, *put in besides.*

3. The accent *never* passes *beyond the Augment or Reduplication:* ἀπῆλθε, *he went away;* ἀφῖκται, *he has arrived.* This is the case even when the Augment or Reduplication is not expressed: ὑπεῖκον, *I gave way;* ἀνεῦρε, *he found again;* σύνοιδα, *I know along with,* from οἶδα, *I know,* forms an exception.

§ 333. The other exceptions are:

1. All Infinitives in ν α ι have the accent on the penultima: τιθέναι, θεῖναι, λελυκέναι, λυθῆναι.
2. the Infinitive of the Strong Aorist Active of verbs in ω is perispome: λαβεῖν.
3. the same form in the Middle is paroxytone: λαβέσθαι.
4. the Infinitive of the Weak Aorist Active has the accent on the penultima: παιδεῦσαι, ἐπαινέσαι (§ 268, *Obs.* 1).
5. so likewise the Infinitive of the Perfect Middle: πεπαιδεῦσθαι, κεκομίσθαι.
6. the Participle of the Strong Aorist Active of verbs in ω is oxytone: λαβών.
7. the Participle of the Present and of the Strong Aorist Active of verbs in μ ι is oxytone: τιθείς, ἀποδούς.
8. so likewise the Participle of the Perfect Active: λελυκώς (υῖα, ός, Gen. ότος); and,
9. that of both Aorists Passive: λυθείς, γραφείς.

§ 337. FORMS OF VERBS IN THE IONIC DIALECT.

10. the Participle of the Perfect Middle is paroxytone: λελυμένος.

11. the contracted 2 Sing. Imperat. of the Strong Aorist Middle is perispome: λαβοῦ. Only the compounds of monosyllabic forms with dissyllabic prepositions form an exception: περίθου (περιτίθημι). Compare § 307, *Obs.*

12. The 2 Sing. Imperat. of the Strong Aorist Active in the following verbs is oxytone: εἰπέ, *speak ;* ἐλθέ, *come ;* εὑρέ, *find ;* ἰδέ, *see ;* λαβέ, *take.* But ἄπειπε, etc., according to § 85.

On the accentuation of the three equal forms of the Weak Aorist, see § 268, *Obs.* 1.

PECULIAR FORMS OF VERBS IN THE IONIC DIALECT.

§ 334. **Dialects.**—The *Iterative* form, denoting the repetition of an act, is frequent in Homer and Herodotus, though foreign to Attic prose. Its characteristic sign is the letters σκ affixed to the historical person-endings, in the Active as well as in the Middle, by means of the connecting vowels ο and ε; hence 1 Sing. Act. σκον, Mid. σκομην. The Augment is generally wanting, in Herod. always. The inflexion is quite the same as that of the Imperfect.

§ 335. **Dialects.**—The Iterative σκ may be affixed to the Present as well as to both the Strong and Weak Aorist-Stems; hence we distinguish *Iterative Imperfects*, as: ἔχ-ε-σκο-ν, *I used to have*, and *Iterative Aorists*, as: ἴδ-ε-σκ-ο-ν, *I used to see ;* ἐλάσα-σκ-ε-ν, *he used to drive ;* the former denote the repetition of continuance, the latter the repetition of the occurrence of an action (§ 492).

§ 336. **Dialects.**—In verbs of the First Principal Conjugation, ε is the constant connecting vowel for the Iterative Imperfects and the Iteratives of the Strong Aorist: μέν-ε-σκον (μένω, *I remain*), βοσκ-έ-σκοντο (βόσκω, *I pasture*), φύγ-ε-σκε (φεύγω, *I flee*); α occurs rarely in its stead: ῥίπτ-α-σκον (ῥίπτω, *I hurl*), κρύπτ-α-σκον (κρύπτω, *I hide*). Contracted verbs in the Iteratives either leave the two vowels uncontracted: καλέεσκον (καλέω, *I call*), or reject one of them: ὤθεσκον (ὠθέω, *I push*), εἴασκον (ἐάω, *I leave*); the Stems in α sometimes change αε to αα: ναιετάασκον (ναιετάω, *I inhabit*). Compare ναιετάᾳ, § 243, D.

§ 337. **Dialects.**—In verbs of the Second Principal Conjugation σκ is affixed immediately to the Stem: ἔ-φα-σκον (Stem φα, φημί, *I say*),

στά-σκον (ἔστην, I placed myself), ἴσκον instead of ἰσ-σκον (Stem ἰ ς, εἰμί, I am), κέ-σκετο (Stem κ ε ι, κεῖμαι, I lie), τί-θε-σκον (τίθημι, I put), ῥήγνυ-σκον (ῥήγνυμι, I tear). For the Stem ὀ λ, as in other formations (ὤλεσα, ὀλέσω), ε is the connecting vowel : ὀλ-έ-σκετο.
σκ is farther appended directly to the Weak Aorist-Stem : ἰρητύσα-σκε (ἰρητύω, I pacify), μνησά-σκετο (μνάομαι, I remember).

§ 338. **Dialects.**—Many Stems of the *Present* and *Strong Aorist* in poetry (seldom in Attic prose) have θ added without any particular modification of meaning. The Preterite is the most frequent of the Stems thus strengthened. The θ is connected with the Stems sometimes by α, sometimes by ε. The most important forms of this kind are :

διώκω, additional form διωκάθω, I pursue.
εἴκω,   "   "   εἰκάθω, I yield.
ἀμύνω,   "   "   ἠμύναθον, I warded off.
εἴργω,   "   "   ἐργάθον (ἐέργαθον), I separated, shut off.
κίω,   "   "   ἐκίαθον, I went.
ἀείρομαι,   "   "   ἠερέθονται, they hover.
ἀγείρω,   "   "   ἠγερέθοντο, they were assembled.
φθίνω,   "   "   φθινύθω.
ἔχω,   "   "   σχεθέειν, Aor. Inf., to hold.

III. DERIVATION.

Chap. XIII.

§ 339. A word is either *simple*, *i. e.*, sprung from a single Stem: λόγ-ος, *speech* (Stem λ ε γ), γράφ-ω, *I write* (Stem γ ρ α φ), or *compound*, *i. e.*, formed from two or more Stems: λογο-γράφο-ς, *speech-writer*.

A) Simple Derivation.

Simple words are either *primitive (Verbalia)*, *i. e.*, are formed directly from a *Verbal-Stem* (§ 245): ἀρχ-ή, *beginning*, from the Verbal-Stem ἀ ρ χ (ἄρχω, *I begin*), or *derived (Denominativa)*, *i. e.*, formed from a *Nominal-Stem* (§ 100): ἀρχα-ῖο-ς, *incipient, ancient*, from the Nominal-Stem ἀ ρ χ α, Nom. ἀρχή, *beginning*.

§ 340. *Nouns* are usually formed—whether from a Verbal or from a Nominal-Stem—by means of a termination. This termination, added to the Stem, is called a derivative-ending or *suffix*. Thus λόγο-ς is formed by means of the suffix ο from the Verbal-Stem λ ε γ, ἀρχα-ῖο-ς by means of the suffix ι ο from the Nominal-Stem ἀ ρ χ α. The suffixes serve more clearly to define the idea of the noun, or to mark the different relations in which the general idea of the Stem is to be conceived: Verbal-Stem π ο ι ε (ποιῶ, *I produce, compose*), ποιη-τή-ς, compos-*er ;* ποίη-σι-ς, composi-*tion ;* ποίη-μα(τ), composi*tion, poem ;* Verbal-Stem γ ρ α φ (γράφω, *I write*), γραφ-εύ-ς, writ*er ;* γραφ-ί-ς, writ*ing instrument ;* γράμ-μα, writ*ing ;* γραμ-μή, *a line ;* Nom.-Stem δ ι κ α (δίκη, *right*), δίκα-ιο-ς, *right, just ;* δικαιο-σύνη, righteous*ness ;* Nom.-Stem β α σ ι λ ε υ (βασιλεύ-ς, *king*), βασίλε-ιᾰ, *queen ;* βασιλε-ίᾱ, king*dom ;* βασιλικό-ς, king*ly*.

Obs. 1.—Only few primitive nouns are formed without a suffix: φύλαξ, *guard*, Nominal and Verbal-Stem φ υ λ α κ (φυλάσσω, Class 4, a, *I guard*); ὄψ, *voice*, Stem ὀ π, Verb.-Stem ἐ π (εἰπεῖν).

212   SUFFIXES FOR FORMING SUBSTANTIVES.   § 341.

Obs. 2.—The Consonant-Stems undergo the necessary changes before suffixes beginning with a consonant (§ 44, etc.) : γραφ, γράμ-μα, λεγ, λέξις, *word;* δικαδ (δικάζω), δικασ-τής, *judge.* Vowel-Stems readily lengthen the vowel and sometimes insert σ before several suffixes, as in the Perf. Mid. (§ 288), and in the Weak Passive-Stem (§ 298): ποίη-μα (compare πε-ποίη-μαι), σει-σ-μό-ς, *shaking* (compare σέ-σει-σ-μαι).

Obs. 3.—In many primitive words the Stem undergoes a change in its vowel, which generally is like that of the Strong Perfect (§ 278) : Stem λᾰθ, λήθ-η, *forgetfulness*, compare λέ-ληθ-α ; Stem πεμπ, πομπ-ή, *escort*, compare πέ-πομφ-α ; Stem λιπ, λοιπό-ς, *remaining*, compare λέ-λοιπ-α. The most frequent vowel-change is that of ε to ο : Stem πεμπ (πέμπω, *I escort*), πομπ-ή, *escort ;* Stem φλεγ (φλέγω, *I burn*), φλόξ, *flame ;* Stem τρεπ (τρέπω, *I turn*), τρόπ-ος, *turning, manner.*

Obs. 4.—A general rule for the accent of nouns is that the Neuters are almost all barytone (§ 19) : τὸ γέν-ος, *the race ;* δῶ-ρο-ν, *gift ;* λείψανο-ν, *remains ;* πνεῦ-μα, *breath.*

§ 341. I. *The most important Suffixes for forming Substantives.*

A) Substantives denoting an *agent* are called *nomina agentis.* The person *acting* or occupied in and belonging to something is indicated by the following suffixes :

1. ε υ, Nom. ευ-ς (always oxytone), Masc. (§ 137).

Examples of Primitive words are :

γραφ-εύ-ς, *writ*-ER, Verb.-Stem γραφ, Pres. γράφω (Class 1).
γον-εύ-ς, *begett*-ER,   "   γεν,   "   γίγνομαι (Class 8).
κουρ-εύ-ς, *barb*-ER,   "   κερ,   "   κείρω (Class 4, d).

An example of the not very numerous Denominatives is :

πορθμ-εύ-ς, *ferry*-MAN, Nom.-Stem πορθμο, Nom. πορθμός, *passage.*

Obs.—Several Masculines in ευ-ς have Feminines in εια (proparoxytones) : βασιλεύς, *king ;* βασίλεια, *queen.*

2. τηρ, Nom. τηρ   τειρα, Nom. τειρα
   τορ,   "   τωρ } Masc.   τρια,   "   τρια   } Fem.
   τα,   "   τη-ς   τριδ,   "   τρί-ς
                             τιδ,   "   τι-ς

§ 343. SUFFIXES FOR FORMING SUBSTANTIVES. 213

Examples of Primitive nouns are:

Stem and Nomin. σω-τήρ, deliver-ER, Masc. ⎫ Verb.-Stem σω (σώζω)
"   "   "   σώ-τειρα,   "   Fem. ⎭   (§ 298).
" ῥη-τορ, "   ῥή-τωρ, ora-TOR, Verb.-Stem ῥε, Fut. ἐρῶ (§ 327, 13).
" κρι-τα, "   κρι-τή-ς, judge,   "   κρι, Pres. κρίνω (§ 253,
                                               Obs.).
" ποιη-τα, "   ποιη-τή-ς, poet ⎫ "   ποιε, Pres. ποιέω (Cl. 1).
Stem and Nomin. ποιή-τρια, poetess ⎭
" αὐλη-τα, "   αὐλητή-ς, flute-play-ER, Masc. ⎫ Verbal-Stem αὐλε,
" αὐλη-τριδ, " αὐλητρί-ς,   "   Fem. ⎭ Pres. αὐλέω (Cl: 1).

Examples of Derived words are:

Stem πολῑ-τα, Nom. πολίτη-ς, citizen, Nom.-Stem πολι, Nom. πόλι-ς.
" οἰκε-τα,   "   οἰκέτη-ς, domestic, Masc. ⎫ Stem οἰκο, Nom.
" οἰκε-τιδ   "   οἰκέτι-ς,   "   Fem. ⎭ οἶκο-ς.

§ 342. B) Substantives expressing an *action* are called *nomina actionis;* the following suffixes are the most common for them:

1. τι, Nom. τι-ς
    σι,   "   σι-ς, from τι-ς, according to § 60, a [com- ⎫ Feminine,
                               pare Lat. *tio*]   ⎬ Barytones.
    σια,   "   σια   ⎭

All nouns of this kind are Primitives, as:

πίσ-τι-ς, *faith*,   Verb.-Stem πιθ, Pres. Mid. πείθομαι (Class 2).
μίμη-σι-ς, *imitation*,   "   μιμε, Pres. (Dep.) μιμέομαι (Class 1).
σκέψι-ς, *contemplation*,   "   σκεπ, "   "   σκέπτομαι (Class 3).
πρᾶξι-ς, *action*,   "   πρᾱγ, Pres. Act. πράσσω (Class 4, a).
γένε-σι-ς, *origin*,   "   γεν(ε), Pres. Mid. γίγνομαι (§ 327, 14).
δοκιμα-σί-α, *examination*, "   δοκιμαδ, Pres. δοκιμάζω (Class 4, b).

2. μο, Nom. μό-ς (always oxytone), Masc.
σπα-σ-μό-ς, *cramp*, Verb.-Stem σπα, Pres. σπάω (Class 1), *I draw*.
δε-σ-μό-ς, *bond*,   "   δε,   "   δέω,   "   *I bind*.
ὀδυρ-μό-ς, *wailing*,   "   ὀδυρ, "   ὀδύρομαι (Class 4, d, *Obs.*).

Obs.—From verbs in ευω substantives in εια are derived, which denote the action, and are all paroxytone : παιδεύω, *I educate*, παιδεία, *education;* βασιλεύω, *I am king*, βασιλεία, *king's rule*. Compare § 341, 1, *Obs.*

§ 343. C) The *result* of an action is indicated by:

214 SUFFIXES FOR FORMING SUBSTANTIVES. § 344.

1. ματ, Nom. μα, Neuter (accent, § 340, *Obs.* 4).
πρᾶγ-μα[τ], *the thing done*, Verb.-Stem πρᾶγ, Pres. πράσσω (Class 4, a)
 (almost the same as τὸ πεπραγμένον, Lat. *factum*).
ῥῆ-μα[τ], *word*, Verb.-Stem ῥε, Fut. ἐρῶ (§ 327, 13) (compare τὸ εἰρημένον, Lat. *dictum*).
τμῆ-μα[τ], *cut*, Verb.-Stem τεμ, Pres. τέμνω (§ 321, 10) (compare τὸ τετμημένον, *the piece cut off*).

2. ες, Nom. ος, Neuter (accent, § 340, *Obs.* 4). [27].
Stem λαχ-ες, Nom. λάχος, *lot*, Verb.-Stem λαχ, Pres. λαγχάνω (§ 322,
" ἐθ-ες, " ἔθος, *custom*, " ἐθ, Perf. εἴωθα (§ 275).
" τεκ-ες, " τέκος, *child*, " τεκ, Pres. τίκτω (Class 3).

Obs.—The same suffix in derived words denotes a quality:

βάρος, *weight*, Adjective-Stem βαρυ, Nom. βαρύ-ς.
βάθος, *depth*, " βαθυ, " βαθύ-ς.
μῆκος, *length*, " μακρο, " μακρό-ς.

§ 344. D) The *instrument* or means for an action is expressed by:

τρο, Nom. τρο-ν [Lat. *tru-m*] (accent, § 340, *Obs.* 4).
ἄρο-τρο-ν, *plow*, Verb.-Stem ἀρο, Pres. ἀρόω (Cl. 1) [*ara-tru-m*].
λύ-τρο-ν, *redemption money*, " λυ, " λύω (Class 1).
διδακ-τρο-ν, *a teacher's fee*, " διδαχ, " διδάσκω (§ 324, 28).

Obs.—The meaning of the kindred feminine suffix τρα is less fixed:
ξύ-ο-τρα (ξύω, *I scrape*), *scraper, instrument for rubbing;* ὀρχή-σ-τρα (ὀρχέομαι, *I dance*), *dancing place;* παλαί-σ-τρα (παλαίω, *I wrestle*), *wrestling school*.

§ 345. E) *Place* is indicated by:

1. τηριο, Nom. τηριο-ν, Neuter proparoxytone.
ἀκροα-τήριο-ν, *audi-toriu-m*, Verb.-Stem ἀκροα, Pres. ἀκροάομαι (Cl. 1).
δικασ-τήριο-ν, *judgment hall*, " δικαδ, " δικάζω (Cl. 4, b).

2. ειο, Nom. ειο-ν, Neuter properispome.
λογ-εῖο-ν, *speaking place*, from the Nom.-Stem λογο, Nom. λόγο-ς.
κουρ-εῖο-ν, *barber's shop*, " " κουρευ, " κουρεύ-ς.
Μουσ-εῖο-ν, *seat of the Muses*, " " Μουσα, " Μοῦσα.

3. ων, Nom. ων, Masc. oxytone,
denotes a place where any thing is in *abundance:* ἀμπελών, *vineyard;* ἀνδρών, *men's room;* οἰνών, *wine vault*.

§ 348. SUFFIXES FOR FORMING SUBSTANTIVES. 215

§ 346. F) Substantives of *quality* are derived from Adjective-Stems by means of the following suffixes:

1. τητ, Nom. τη-ς, Fem. [Lat. *tat, tut*, Nom. *tás, tús*].
Stem παχυ-τητ, Nom. παχύτης, *thickness*, Adj.-Stem παχυ, Nom. παχύ-ς.
" νεο-τητ,   " νεότης, *youth*,   " νεο, Nom. νέο-ς.
" ισο-τητ,   " ισότης, *equality*,   " ισο,   " ἴσο-ς.

2. συνα, Nom. σύνη, Fem. paroxytone.
δικαιο-σύνη, *justice*, Adj.-Stem δικαιο, Nom. δίκαιο-ς.
σωφρο-σύνη, *soberness*,   " σωφρον, " σώφρων.

3. ια, Nom. ια, Fem. paroxytone.
σοφ-ία, *wisdom*, Adj.-Stem σοφο, Nom. σοφό-ς.
εὐδαιμον-ία, *bliss*,   " εὐδαιμον, " εὐδαίμων.

The suffix ι α, with the vowel ε of the Adjective-Stems in -ες, Nom. -ης, becomes ειᾰ; and when the final o of an Adjective-Stem is preceded by another o, it becomes οια, οιᾰ (proparoxytone).

ἀληθε-ιᾰ, *truth*, Adj.-Stem ἀληθε[ς], Nom. ἀληθής (§ 165).
εὔνο-ια, *benevolence*,   " εὐνοο,   " εὔνου-ς.

4. ες, Nom. ος, Neuter, § 343, 2.

§ 347. G) *Diminutives* are formed from Nominal-Stems by the suffixes:

1. ιο, Nom. ιο-ν, Neuter.
παιδ-ίο-ν, *little boy*, Nom.-Stem παιδ, Nom. παῖ-ς.
κηπ-ίο-ν, *little garden*,   " κηπο,   " κῆπο-ς.

Obs.—Other forms of ιο are ιδιο (Nom. ιδιο-ν), αριο (Nom. αριο-ν), ὑδριο (Nom. ὑδριο-ν), υλλιο (Nom. υλλιο-ν): οἰκίδιο-ν, *a little house* (οἶκο-ς); παιδάριο-ν, *a little boy* (παῖ-ς); μελύδριο-ν, *a little song* (μέλος); εἰδύλλιο-ν, *a little picture* (εἶδος).

2. Masc. ισκο, Fem. ισκα, Nom. ισκο-ς, ισκη, paroxytone.
νεαν-ίσκο-ς, adolescen*tulus*, Nom.-Stem νεανια, Nom. νεανία-ς.
παιδ-ίσκη, *girl*,   " παιδ,   " παῖ-ς.
στεφαν-ίσκο-ς, *a little garland*, " στεφανο, " στέφανο-ς.

§ 348. H) *Patronymics* or substantives which denote *descent* from a father (or ancestor)—more rarely the descent from a mother—are most frequently formed by the suffix δα (Nom. δη-ς) for the Masculine, and only δ (Nom.

-ς) for the Feminine. The Masculines are paroxytone, the Feminines oxytone. This suffix is added to Stems in a without any connecting vowel:

Masc. Βορεά-δη-ς, Fem. Βορεα-ς, Nom.-Stem Β ο ρ ε α, Nom. Βορέα-ς.
" Αἰνειά-δη-ς, " Αἰνεια, " Αἰνεῖα-ς.

The same is affixed to *Consonant*-Stems by means of the *vowel* ι:

Masc. Κεκροπ-ί-δη-ς, Fem. Κεκροπ-ί-ς, Nom.-Stem Κ ε κ ρ ο π, Nom. Κέκροψ.

Stems in ευ and ο of the Second Principal Declension also adopt the connecting vowel ι, before which the υ of ευ is dropped:

Πηλε-ί-δη-ς, from the Nom.-Stem Π η λ ε υ, Nom. Πηλεύ-ς. Homeric additional form Πηληϊάδη-ς (compare § 161, D.).
Λητο-ί-δη-ς, from the Nom.-Stem Λ η τ ο, Nom. Λητώ, *son of Leto*.

The Stems of the O-Declension substitute ι for ο:

Masc. Τανταλ-ί-δ η-ς, Fem. Τανταλ-ί-ς, Nom.-Stem Τ α ν τ α λ ο, Nom. Τάνταλο-ς.
" Κρον-ί-δ η-ς, " Κ ρ ο ν ο, Nom. Κρόνο-ς.

Only those in ιο (Nom. ιο-ς) change these letters to ια:

Masc. Θεστιά-δ η-ς, Fem. Θεστιά-ς, Nom.-Stem Θ ε σ τ ι ο, Nom. Θέστιο-ς.
" Μενοιτιά-δ η-ς, " Μ ε ν ο ι τ ι ο, Nom. Μενοίτιο-ς.

Obs.—A more rare suffix for Patronymics is ἴ ο ν or ἴων, Nom. ιων: Κρονίων, *son of* Κρόνο-ς. The Poets take many liberties with regard to the metre.

§ 349. I) *Gentile* names, or substantives describing persons as natives of certain towns or countries, have the suffixes:

1. ευ, Nom. ευς (compare § 341), oxytone.
Μεγαρ-εύ-ς, Nom.-Stem Μ ε γ α ρ ο, Nom. τὰ Μέγαρα.
Ἐρετρι-εύ-ς, " Ἐ ρ ε τ ρ ι ο, " Ἐρέτρια.

2. τα, Nom. τη-ς, paroxytone.
Τεγεά-τη-ς (Τεγέα), Αἰγινή-τη-ς (Αἰγίνη), Ἠπειρώ-τη-ς (Ἤπειρο-ς), Σικελιώ-τη-ς (Σικελία).

§ 351. SUFFIXES FOR FORMING ADJECTIVES. 217

Obs.—The feminine *gentile names* end in δ (Nom. -ς) : Μεγαριδ, Nom. Μεγαρίς; Τεγεατιδ, Nom. Τεγεᾶτις; Σικελιωτιδ, Nom. Σικελιῶτις.

§ 350. II. *The most important Suffixes for forming Adjectives.*

1. ι ο, Nom. ιο-ς (proparoxytone), expresses the most general relation to the idea of the *substantive* from which the adjective is formed : οὐράν-ι ο-ς, heaven-*ly* (οὐρανός); ἑσπέρ-ι ο-ς, belonging to evening (ἑσπέρα). The ι sometimes combines with the final vowels of Vowel-Stems to diphthongs, which then frequently receive the circumflex : ἀγορα-ῖ ο-ς, for*ensis* (ἀγορά); αἰδο-ῖ ο-ς, *modest*, from the Stem α ἰ δ ο (Nom. αἰδώς); but δίκα-ιο-ς, *just*, from the Stem δ ι κ α (Nom. δίκη, *justice*); so also, after rejecting the ς, we have from the Stem θ ε ρ.ε ς (τὸ θέρος, *summer*), θέρε-ι ο-ς, *summer-like*. By the suffix ι ο, adjectives are also formed from *Adjective*-Stems : ἐλευθέρ-ιο-ς, liber-*alis* (ἐλεύθερο-ς, *liber*), and gentile adjectives (§ 349) from names of places, which, however, are also used substantively : Μιλήσ-ι ο-ς (for Μιλητ-ι ο-ς, from Μίλητο-ς, according to § 60), 'Αθηνα-ῖ ο-ς ('Αθῆναι).

§ 351. 2. κ ο, Nom. κό-ς (always oxytone), is mostly affixed to the Stem by the connecting vowel ι, and, in words derived from Verbal-Stems, denotes *fitness :* ἀρχ-ι-κό-ς, *suited* for governing ; γραφικός, *suited* for writing or painting (picturesque). Many Verbal-Stems insert the syllable τι before the suffix κο (§ 342) : αἰσθη-τι-κό-ς, *capable of perceiving ;* πρα-κτι-κό-ς, *suited for acting.* From Nominal-Stems the suffix κο, Nom. κο-ς, forms adjectives denoting what is *peculiar*, belonging or referable to the thing expressed by the noun : βασιλικός, *kingly ;* φυσικός, *natural ;* πολεμικός, *warlike.*

Obs.—By means of this suffix are formed the names of many arts and sciences, the Feminine being used substantively, originally with the addition of τέχνη, *art, science ;* ἡ μουσ-ι-κή, *music ;* ἡ

K

γραμματ-ι-κή, from τὰ γράμματα, litterœ, grammar, the art of writing; ἡ τακτ-ι-κή, tactics. The corresponding Masculine denotes one who is experienced in such art or science: ὁ μουσικό-ς, musician; ὁ γραμματικό-ς, grammarian; ὁ τακτικό-ς, tactician.

§ 352. 3. ι ν ο, Nom. ινο-ς, proparoxytone, and
4. ε ο, Nom. εο-ς [Lat. *eu-s*], proparoxytone (ους perispome, § 183), denote the *material* of which any thing consists: λίθ-ι ν ο-ς, *of stone* (λίθο-ς); ξύλ-ι ν ο-ς, *wood-en* (ξύλο-ν); χρύσ-ε ο-ς, χρυσοῦς, *gold-en* [*aur-eu-s*] (χρυσό-ς).

Obs.—ι ν ο, Nom. ινό-ς, oxytone, forms adjectives of time: χθεσ-ιν ό-ς, *yesterday's,* from χθές, *yesterday;* ἑαρ-ι ν ό-ς,̓ *vernus;* with enlarged suffix: νυκτ-ερ-ι ν ό-ς, *noct-ur-nu-s.*

5. ε ν τ, Nom. Masc. ει-ς, Fem. εσσα, Neut. εν,
denotes *abundance :* χαρί-ει-ς, grace-*ful* (χάρι-ς); ὑλή-ε ι-ς, wood-*y* (ὕλη); ἡμαθό-ε ι-ς, sand-*y* (ἄμαθο-ς). Compare Lat. *osu-s :* grati*osus*, silv*osus*, aren*osus*.

6. μ ο ν, Nom. Masc. μων, Neut. μον,
denotes the *bent* or *inclination* to something: μνή-μ ω ν, *mindful ;* τλή-μ ω ν, *patient ;* ἐπιλήσ-μ ω ν, *forgetful.*

Obs.—Adjective suffixes of less defined meanings are:

ν ο, Nom. νο-ς, oxytone, mostly passive: δει-ν ό-ς, *terrible;* σεμ-ν ό-ς (σέβ-ο-μαι), *venerable.*

λ ο, " λο-ς, mostly oxytone and active: ζει-λ ό-ς, *fearful;* ἀπατη-λ ό-ς, *deceitful.*

μ ο, " μο-ς, proparoxytone, partly active: μάχ-ι-μο-ς, *warlike;* and partly passive: ἀοίδ-ι-μ ο-ς, *capable of being sung;* akin to it is

σιμο, " σιμο-ς, proparoxytone : χρήσιμο-ς, *useful ;* φύξιμο-ς, *capable of being fled from, avoidable.*

ες, " ης, Neut. ες : ψευδ-ής, *false*, almost exclusively in compound words (§ 355).

§ 353. III. *Derived Verbs*

are formed in various ways from *Nominal*-Stems. The most important endings of derived verbs, differing little from one another in meaning, are the following, arranged according to their forms of the Present:

§ 353, b.   DERIVED VERBS.—ADVERBS.   219

1. ο-ω :   μισθό-ω, *I hire*   (μισθό-ς, *hire*).
           χρυσό-ω, *I gild*   (χρυσό-ς, *gold*).
           ζημιό-ω, *I punish*   (ζημία, *punishment*).
2. α-ω :   τιμά-ω, *I honor*   (τιμή, *honor*).
           αἰτιά-ομαι, *I blame*   (αἰτία, *blame*).
           γοά-ω, *I wail*   (γόο-ς, *wailing*).
3. ε-ω :   ἀριθμέ-ω, *I number*   (ἀριθμό-ς, *number*).
           εὐτυχέ-ω, *I am fortunate*   (εὐτυχής, *fortunate*).
           ἱστορέ-ω, *I search*   (ἵστωρ, *searcher*).
4. ευ-ω : βασιλεύ-ω, *I am king*   (βασιλεύ-ς, *king*).
           βουλεύ-ω, *I advise*   (βουλή, *advice*).
5. ιζ-ω : ἐλπίζ-ω, *I hope*   (ἐλπί-ς, *hope*).
           ἑλληνίζ-ω, *I speak Greek*   ("Ελλην).
           φιλιππίζ-ω, *I am inclined to Philip*   } (Φίλιππο-ς).
6. αζ-ω : δικάζ-ω, *I judge*   (δίκη, *justice*).
           ἐργάζ-ομαι, *I work*   (ἔργο-ν, *work*).
           βιάζ-ομαι, *I use violence*   (βία, *violence*).
7. αιν-ω : σημαίν-ω, *I sign*   (σῆμα, *sign*).
           λευκαίν-ω, *I whiten*   (λευκό-ς, *white*).
           χαλεπαίν-ω, *I am indignant*   (χαλεπό-ς, *severe, indignant*).
8. υν-ω : ἡδύν-ω, *I sweeten*   (ἡδύ-ς, *sweet*).
           λαμπρύν-ω, *I brighten*   (λαμπρό-ς, *bright*).

Obs. 1.—From a few Nominal-Stems verbs are derived with different endings and with different meanings; thus from δουλο, Nom. δοῦλο-ς, *slave*: δουλό-ω, *I enslave,* δουλεύ-ω, *I am a slave ;* from πολεμο, Nom. πόλεμο-ς, *war*, πολεμέ-ω and πολεμίζ-ω, *I make war*, πολεμό-ω, *I make hostile.*

Obs. 2.—A *desiderative* meaning belongs to verbs in σειω, as well as to several in αω and ιαω : γελασείω, *I am inclined to laugh ;* δρασείω, *I desire to do ;* φονάω, *I want to murder ;* κλαυσιάω, *I want to weep.* The verbs of the last two terminations frequently indicate a bodily weakness or illness: ὠχριάω, *I am pale ;* ὀφθαλμιάω, *I suffer in the eyes.*

IV. *Adverbs.*

§ 353, b. On the Adverbs formed from *Adjectives*, compare §§ 201-204.

From *Verbal* and *Substantive*-Stems adverbs are formed by the suffixes:

δόν, oxytone: ἀνα-φαν-δόν, *openly;* ἀγελη-δόν, *gregatim.*
δην (αδην), paroxytone: κρύβ-δην, *clam;* συλλήβ-δην, *collectively;*
briefly (Stem λαβ); σπορ-άδην, *scatteredly* (Stem σπερ), σπείρω,
I sow.
τί, oxytone: ὀνομασ-τί, *by name* (ὀνομάζω); ἑλληνισ-τί, *græce* (ἑλληνίζω).

B) COMPOSITION.

§ 354. I. *Form of Composition.*

A *noun*, standing *first* in a compound, appears in the form of its Stem: ἀστυ-γείτων, *neighbor to the city;* χορο-διδάσκαλο-ς, *teacher of the chorus;* σακές-παλος, *shaker of the shield* (τὸ σάκος).

Consonant-Stems are usually united to the second part by the *connecting-vowel* o: ἀνδριαντ-ο-ποιό-ς (ὁ ἀνδριά-ς), *maker of statues, statuary;* πατρ-ο-κτόνο-ς, *murderer of a father.* This o, farther, is frequently inserted after *weak* vowels: φυσι-ο-λόγο-ς, *acquainted with nature;* ἰχθυ-ο-φάγο-ς, *fish-eating;* and regularly stands in place of α in the Stem: ἡμερο-δρόμο-ς, *a runner by day;* χωρο-γράφο-ς, *describer of a country.* The o is dropped before vowels: χορ-ηγό-ς, *leader of the chorus;* πατρ-άδελφο-ς, *a father's brother;* it remains, however, where the word originally began with digamma (§ 34, D.): Hom. δημιοεργό-ς, Att. δημιουργός, *artisan.*

Obs.—Exceptions to these rules are frequent. Thus Stems in σ often appear in an abbreviated form in compounds: ξιφο-κτόνος, *killing with the sword* (Stem ξιφες); τειχο-μαχία, *a contest at the wall* (Stem τειχες); the final vowel of A-Stems is sometimes preserved as ᾱ or η: ἀρετᾱ-λόγος, *a speaker about virtue;* χοη-φόρος, *bearer of funeral offerings.* A case-form seldom occurs instead of the Stem-form: νεώς-οικος, *shed for ships;* ὀρεσσι-βάτης, *wandering on the hills.*

§ 355. The *ending* of a word is often somewhat altered in composition, especially when the compound word is an adjective: τιμή, φιλό-τιμο-ς, *ambitious;* πρᾶγμα, πολυ-πράγμων, *much occupied.* The ending η ς Masculine and

Feminine, ε ς Neuter, deserves special notice; this ending occurs:

a) in many adjectives formed directly from Verbal-Stems: ἀ-βλαβ-ής, *uninjured* (βλαβ, Pres. βλάπτω); αὐτάρκ-ης, *self-sufficient* (αὐτό-ς and ἀρκέω).

b) in adjectives, whose second part comes from a substantive in ε ς (Nom. ος): δεκα-ετής, *ten years old* (ἔτος); κακο-ήθης, *of a bad nature* (ἦθος).

Obs.—Observe also the compound adverbs in ει or ι, oxytone: αὐτο-χειρ-ί, *with one's own hand;* ἀ-μισθ-ί, *without pay;* παν-δημ-εί, *with the whole people.*

§ 356. A verb—without changing its nature—can only be compounded with a preposition. The looseness of the connection in such compounds is the reason for the position of the Augment mentioned in § 238: ἀποβάλλω, *I throw away;* ἀπέβαλον, *I threw away.* For the same reason, prepositions are frequently separated from their verbs in the poets and in Herodotus, and in some cases even in Attic prose (compare § 446). This separation is called *tmesis.*

When any other word is to be compounded with a Verbal-Stem, a noun is first formed of the two; *e. g.*, from λίθο-ς and Stem β α λ, λιθο-βόλο-ς, *throwing stones,* and thence λιθοβολέ-ω, *I throw stones;* so likewise from ναῦ-ς and μάχομαι comes first ναυ-μάχο-ς, *fighting at sea,* and thence ναυμαχέω; from εὖ and Stem ἐ ρ γ, εὐεργέτης, *benefactor,* εὐεργετέω, *I do good.*

§ 357. A substantive of an abstract meaning can only be compounded with a preposition without changing its termination: πρό and βουλή make προβουλή, *previous consultation.* In every other compound the abstract substantive must take a derivative ending: λίθος and βολή make λιθοβολία, *throwing stones;* ναῦς and μάχη, ναυμαχία, *sea-fight;* εὖ and πρᾶξις, εὐπραξία, *well-being.*

§ 358. Compounds having the first part formed directly

from a Verbal-Stem are rarely met with except in the poets. They are formed in two ways, viz.:

1. the Verbal or the Present-Stem is joined directly to Stems beginning with a vowel, and to those beginning with a consonant by means of the connecting-vowels ε, ι, or ο : δακ-έ-θυμο-ς (Pres. δάκν-ω, Class 5), *heart-gnawing;* πείθ-αρχο-ς, *obedient to order* (πείθομαι and ἀρχή); ἀρχ-ι-τέκτων, *master-builder;* μισ-ό-γυνο-ς, *hater of women* (μισέω).

2. A form strengthened by σ, and resembling the Weak Aorist-Stem, is joined in the same way to the second part of the word : λῡσ-ί-πονο-ς, *freeing from trouble;* πλήξ-ιππο-ς (πλήσσω, Class 4, a), *whipping horses;* στρεψί-δικο-ς (στρέφω, Class 1), *perverter of right.*

§ 359. II. *Meaning of Compounds.*

In regard to their meaning, compound Adjectives and Substantives are divided into *three* principal classes :

1. *Determinative* compounds. In them the second word is the principal, which, without in any way altering its meaning, is merely defined by the first. These compounds may be paraphrased by changing the first part either into an Adjective or an Adverb: ἀκρό-πολι-ς, *high town, castle,* i. e., ἄκρα πόλις (Hom. πόλις ἄκρη); μεσ-ημβρία, *midday,* i. e., μέση ἡμέρα ; ψευδο-κῆρυξ, i. e., ψευδὴς κῆρυξ, *false herald ;* ὁμό-δουλο-ς, *fellow-slave,* i. e., ὁμοῦ δουλεύων ; μεγαλοπρεπής, *grand,* properly, *appearing as great;* ὀψί-γονος, *late born,* i. e., ὀψὲ γενόμενος. This class is the least numerous.

2. *Attributive* compounds. In them the second word is indeed also defined by the first, yet so that the latter alters its meaning, and, together with the first, forms a new idea, which is attributed as a quality to another word. These compounds can generally be paraphrased by employing the Participle of ἔχω, or a verb akin to it in meaning, and adding to this the second word as an object, the first be-

§ 359. MEANING OF COMPOUNDS. 223

coming an attribute to the object: μακρό-χειρ, *longi-manus*, *long-handed*, *i. e.*, μακρὰς χεῖρας ἔχων (not the long hand itself); ἀργυρό-τοξο-ς, *provided with a silver bow*, *i. e.*, ἀργυροῦν τόξον φέρων; ὁμό-τροπο-ς, *of the same kind*, *i. e.*, ὅμοιον τρόπον ἔχων; γλαυκ-ῶπι-ς, *bright-eyed*, *i. e.*, γλαυκοὺς ὀφθαλμοὺς ἔχουσα; πικρό-γαμο-ς, *having a bitter wedding*; κουφό-νου-ς, *frivolous, trifling*; σώ-φρων, *of sound sense, sober*; δεκα-ετής, *ten years old*, *i. e.*, *having or lasting ten years*; αὐτό-χειρ, *making use of one's own hands*.

Obs.—To these belong the numerous adjectives in -ωδης and όειδης: γυναικώδης = γυναικο-ειδης (εἶδος), woman*like*, woman*ish*.

3. *Objective* compounds, or those of dependency. In them, either the first word is grammatically governed by the second or the second by the first, so that in the paraphrase one of the two must be put in an oblique case: ἡνί-οχο-ς=τὰ ἡνία ἔχων, *guiding the reins, driver*; λογο-γράφο-ς, *speech-writer*, *i. e.*, λόγους γράφων; ἀξιό-λογο-ς, *worth speaking*, *i. e.*, λόγου ἄξιος; φιλό-μουσο-ς, *loving the Muses*, *i. e.*, φιλῶν τὰς Μούσας; δεισι-δαίμων, *fearing the gods*, *i. e.*, δεδιὼς τοὺς δαίμονας; χειροποίητος, *made by hand*, *i. e.*, χερσὶ ποιητός; θεοβλαβής, *injured by God*, *i. e.*, ὑπὸ θεοῦ βεβλαμμένος; οἰκογενής, *born in the house*, *i. e.*, ἐν οἴκῳ γενόμενος.

Obs. 1.—Prepositions may be joined with substantives in any of the three principal classes—(1) *Determinative*: ἀμφι-θέατρον, *a round theatre*, *i. e.*, a theatre extending itself round in a circle; ἀπ-ελεύθερος, one who has been freed by another, not by himself, *i. e.*, *a freedman* (ὁ ἀπό τινος ἐλεύθερος ὤν); (2) *Attributive*: ἔν-θεος, *i. e.*, ἐν ἑαυτῷ θεὸν ἔχων, *carrying a god in himself, god-inspired*; ἀμφικίων, viz., *i. e.*, κίονας ἀμφ' ἑαυτὸν ἔχων, *a temple encompassed around with pillars*; (3) *Objective*: ἐγχώριος, *i. e.*, ἐν τῇ χώρᾳ ὤν, *at home*; ἐφίππιος, *i. e.*, ἐφ' ἵππῳ ὤν, *being on a horse, belonging to a horse*.

Obs. 2.—Against the general rule (§ 85), according to which compound words draw back the accent as far as possible from the end, those compounds in -ο-ς in the Nominative, whose second part comes directly from a Verbal-Stem (§ 356), usually *accent* this Stem if it has an *active* meaning. They are paroxytone when the last syllable but one is short, oxytone when it is long: λογο-γράφο-ς, *speech-writer;* μητρ-ο-κτόνος, *mother-murderer;* παιδαγωγό-ς, *boy-leader;* μελο-ποιός, *composer of songs.* When the meaning is *passive*, the second word remains *unaccented:* αὐτό-γραφο-ς, *written by one's self;* μητρ-ό-κτονο-ς, *murdered by the mother;* δυσ-άγωγος, *hard to guide.*

§ 360. The prefix ἀ ν [compare ἄνευ, *without*, Lat. *in-*, Engl. *un-*], before consonants ἀ [compare Lat. *i-* in *i-gna-ru-s*], called *alpha privative* on account of its meaning, is found in a very large number of compounds, which belong to the *determinative* class if the second part has arisen from a verb or an adjective, but chiefly to the *attributive* if from a substantive: ἄ-γραφος, *unwritten, i. e.*, οὐ γεγραμμένος; ἀν-ελεύθερος, *unfree, i. e.*, οὐκ ἐλεύθερος; ἀν-αιδής, *shameless, i. e.*, αἰδῶ οὐκ ἔχων; ἄπαι-ς, *childless, i. e.*, παῖδας οὐκ ἔχων. Determinatives with ἀ ν (ἀ) from substantives are rare and poetic: μήτηρ ἀμήτωρ, *an unmotherly mother, i. e.*, μήτηρ οὐ μήτηρ οὖσα.

Obs.—Words originally beginning with digamma (§ 34, D.) have ἀ, not ἀν: ἀ-έκων, contracted ἄκων, *unwilling;* ἀ-εικ-ής, contracted αἰκ-ής, *reproachful* (Stem ε ι κ, ἔοικα); ἀ-εργό-ς, contracted ἀργό-ς, *inactive* (ἔργο-ν, *work*).

The prefix δ υ ς corresponds to the English *mis*, and, as the opposite to εὖ, denotes something unfortunate, awkward, difficult: δυςάρεστος (§ 324, **10**), *displeased;* δύςβουλος, *ill advised, i. e.*, κακὰς βουλὰς ἔχων (attributive); δυςάλωτος, *hard to capture* (§ 324, **17**). Here, too, determinative compounds from substantives are rare: Hom. Δύςπαρις, *unfortunate Paris.*

PART SECOND.
SYNTAX.

Preliminary Remarks.

§ 361. 1. Syntax (σύνταξις, *arrangement*) teaches the use of the forms discussed in the first part of the grammar, and the way in which words are arranged into sentences, and sentences are combined together.

2. A sentence is either simple or compound. Every sentence is simple in which the necessary parts of a sentence occur only once.

3. The necessary parts of a sentence are:
a) the *Subject*, i. e., the person or thing about which something is stated;
b) the *Predicate*, i. e., that which is stated.

Obs. 1.—Every form of the finite verb (§ 225, 4) contains a complete sentence in itself, in which the personal ending contains the Subject and the Verbal-Stem the Predicate: φημί, *I say;* ἔφαμεν, *we said.*

Obs. 2.—In many cases the Subject remains *undefined:* φασί, *they say, people say;* or it is not defined, because readily understood by the Greeks: ὕει, *he̜* rains, i. e., Zeus, for he alone can cause rain; ἐσάλπιγξε, *he blew the trumpet*, i. e., the trumpeter, for it is his business. The Subject of the impersonal verbs δεῖ, χρή, *it is necessary*, is also undefined.

4. The *Predicate* is either *Verbal* or *Nominal;* it is Verbal when expressed in the form of a *finite verb:* Κῦρος ἐβασίλευσε, *Cyrus ruled;* it is *Nominal* when expressed in the form of a *noun* (substantive or adjective): Κῦρος βασιλεὺς ἦν, *Cyrus was king.*

5. The Predicate must agree with the Subject, viz., the Verbal Predicate in number, the Nominal in number and case, and, when it is an adjective, in gender also: οἱ πολί-

K 2

μιοι ενίκησαν, *the enemies conquered ;* ή μάχη μεγάλη ην, *the battle was great.*

Exceptions, §§ 362-366.

6. In many cases this agreement alone is sufficient to express the *relation* of a Nominal Predicate to the Subject: ὁ μέγας ὄλβος οὐ μόνιμος, *great prosperity is not lasting;* Λέριοι κακοί, *the Lerians* (inhabitants of the island of Leros) *are bad.* But mostly the Nominal Predicate is more clearly connected with its Subject by the verb *to be* (substantive verb): ὁ μέγας ὄλβος οὐ μόνιμός ἐστιν, Λέριοι κακοί εἰσιν. This verb, thus used, is called the *Copula.*

7. The intransitive and passive verbs, which denote *to become, be made, appear, be named, designated, chosen,* and the like, in order to produce a complete sentence, often require a Nominal Predicate along with the Verbal one. In this case also the Nominal Predicate must agree with the Subject: Κῦρος ἐγένετο βασιλεύς, *Cyrus became king, Cyrus rex factus est.* Compare § 392.

8. The Greek language expresses many definitions of time, order, and kind, less frequently of place, by *adjectives,* which are expressed in English by adverbs or prepositions with substantives. These adjectives, which must agree with the Subject, are to be considered as *supplementary Predicates :* τριταῖοι ἀπῆλθον, *they went away on the third day;* Λακεδαιμόνιοι ὕστεροι ἀφίκοντο, *the Lacedæmonians arrived later, posteriores advenerunt ;* ὅρκιός σοι λέγω, *I tell you on oath.*

On the similar use of the participle as a supplementary Predicate, see § 589, etc.

9. A simple sentence is enlarged by an *Object* being added to the verb. The Object is that to which the action of the verb extends: οἱ Ἀθηναῖοι ἀπέκτειναν τὸν Σωκράτην, *the Athenians killed Socrates.*

On the different kinds of Objects and the manner in which they are indicated, see §§ 395-402.

§ 361. PRELIMINARY REMARKS. 227

10. The Active verbs, which correspond in meaning to the Intransitive and Passive ones mentioned in 7, *i. e.*, the verbs which denote *to make, name, designate, choose*, and the like, frequently also require a *Nominal Predicate*. But, as this belongs to the Object, it must agree with it: οἱ Πέρσαι τὸν Κῦρον εἵλοντο βασιλέα, *the Persians chose Cyrus king* [*Persæ Cyrum regem elegerunt*]. Compare § 404. This kind of Predicate is called a *Dependent Predicate*. As the Dependent Predicate here appears in the Accusative, so it may in other cases appear in the Genitive or Dative. Compare § 438; *Obs.* § 589, etc.

11. Another enlargement of the sentence is the *Attribute, i. e.*, any nominal definition added to a substantive as essentially belonging to it and forming with it one idea: καλὸς ἵππος, *a fine horse;* ὁ παρὼν καιρός, *the present time* (the present).

Obs.—The Greek language in many cases adds an Attribute to the designation of a person; expressive of a generic idea : Ηοm. ἥρωες Δαναοί, *ye heroes Danai* (ye warring Danai); ἄνδρες δικασταί, *ye judges, judices*.

12. Different from the Attribute is the *Apposition*. Apposition is such a subordinate definition added to a substantive as does not exactly form *one* idea with it, but is superadded rather for describing or illustrating it, and hence might generally be expressed in the form of a descriptive clause : Παρύσατις, ἡ τοῦ Κύρου μήτηρ, τοῦτον μᾶλλον ἐφίλει ἢ τὸν Ἀρταξέρξην, *Parysatis, the mother of Cyrus*—who was Cyrus's mother—*loved him more than Artaxerxes;* ἐντεῦθεν Κῦρος ἐξελαύνει διὰ Φρυγίας εἰς Κολοσσούς, πόλιν οἰκουμένην, εὐδαίμονα καὶ μεγάλην, *from there Cyrus marches through Phrygia to Colossi, a populous, prosperous, and large city* (which was a ... city).

The Attribute and Apposition must agree with the substantive to which they belong, in the same way as the Predicate (5, 7).

Chap. XIV.—Number and Gender.

§ 362. The singular sometimes has a *collective* sense, denoting a plurality : ἐ σ θ ή ς, *clothing, clothes ;* π λ ί ν θ ο ς, *bricks ;* ἡ ἵ π π ο ς, *cavalry ;* ἡ ἀ σ π ί ς, *the heavy-armed.* Sometimes a Predicate or Apposition in the *Plural* refers to collective substantives in the Singular : 'Αθηναίων τὸ πλῆθος οἴονται "Ιππαρχον τύραννον ὄντα ἀποθανεῖν, *the mass of the Athenians believe Hipparchus died as ruler ;* τὸ στράτευμα ἐπορίζετο σῖτον κόπτοντες τοὺς βοῦς καὶ ὄνους, *the army obtained food by killing the oxen and asses.*

A Plural is formed in Greek from many words, especially abstracts, which have no plural in English, especially when the repetition of an idea is to be expressed : αἱ ἐπιφάνειαι καὶ λαμπρότητες ἐκ τῶν ἀγώνων γίγνεσθαι φιλοῦσιν, *celebrity and glory usually arise from the contests ;* ἐμοὶ αἱ σαὶ μεγάλαι εὐτυχίαι οὐκ ἀρέσκουσιν, *your* (repeated) *great success does not please me ;* Hom. πάντες θάνατοι στυγεροί, *all kinds of death are hateful.*

Obs. 1.—Poets frequently use the Plural in a generic sense where we employ the Singular with the indefinite article : οὐκ ἂν γυναικῶν ἥσσονες καλοίμεθ' ἄν, *I should not like to be called inferior to a woman ;* φίλοι, *a friend.* ὅ

Obs. 2.—The speaker often uses the first person Plural of himself [compare Lat. *nos*]. In this case the Masculine is used even when a woman is the speaker. Thus Electra says : πεσούμεθ', εἰ χρή, πατρὶ τιμωρούμενοι, *I will fall, if it must be, as my father's avenger.*

Obs. 3.—In Homer there are many Plurals of abstract ideas, which we express in the Singular ; the Plural, however, properly denotes the various manifestations of such ideas : ἱπποσύνῃς ἐκέκαστο, *by horsemanship he was distinguished ;* ἀφραδίῃσι νόοιο, *in the foolishness* (the foolish thoughts) *of his mind.*

§ 363. The Neuter Plural comes very near in its meaning to the Singular. This explains the peculiar Greek custom, *that the Neuter Plural has the verb in the Sin-*

§ 366. NUMBER AND GENDER. 229

gular : πῶς ταῦτα παύσεται; *how is this to end?* τὰ πράγματα ταῦτα δεινά ἐστιν, *these things are terrible.*

Obs. 1.—Some Plural Neuters, which denote a plurality of persons, sometimes have the verb in the Plural, as: τὰ τέλη, in the sense of *the authorities;* τὰ ἔθνη, *the peoples.*

Obs. 2.—The Homeric and the Common Greek Dialects (Introduction, 4) generally allow the Plural Verb with the Neuter Plural: Hom. σπάρτα λέλυνται, *the ropes are loosed.*

§ 364. With an indefinite Neuter Subject (in English, *it*) the Adjective Predicate is frequently in the Plural: ἀδύνατά ἐστιν ἀποφυγεῖν, *it is impossible to escape;* this is the case especially with the Verbal Adjective in τεο-ς : ἐπιχειρητέα ἦν, *it was to be attempted.*

§ 365. When *two* persons or things are spoken of, the Plural is always admissible as well as the Dual, and both numbers may be used in referring to the same thing: ἐγελασάτην ἄμφω, βλέψαντες εἰς ἀλλήλους, *they both laughed after looking at one another;* δότε παράδειγμα, ὦ Λάχης τε καὶ Νικία, *give an example, Laches and Nicias;* ὦ Λάχης τε καὶ Νικία, εἴπατον, *O Laches and Nicias say.*

§ 366. The Neuter of an adjective in the Singular as well as in the Plural easily becomes a substantive: ἐν μέσῳ, *in medio, in the midst;* ἐν τῷ παρόντι, *at the present moment, for the present;* ἐκ πολλοῦ, *for a long time;* δεινά, *terrible things.*

Hence a *Neuter Adjective* often stands as Predicate to one or more Masculine or Feminine substantives to express a class or genus in general: Hom. οὐκ ἀγαθὸν πολυκοιρανίη, *the government of many is not a good thing;* ὀρθὸν ἀληθεῖ ἀεί, *truth is always the right thing;* δεινὸν οἱ πολλοί, κακούργους ὅταν ἔχωσι προστάτας, *a bad thing is the many when they have base leaders;* ταραχαὶ καὶ στάσεις ὀλέθρια ταῖς πόλεσιν, *disturbance and discord are ruinous to states.*

§ 367. The demonstrative pronoun, instead of being in the Neuter as in German, frequently agrees in gender and number with the *Predicate* to which it refers, just as in Latin: οὗτοί εἰσιν ἄνδρες, *those are men;* οὗτος ὅρος ἐστὶ δικαιοσύνης ἀληθῆ τε λέγειν καὶ ἃ ἂν λάβῃ τις ἀποδιδόναι, *this is the idea of justice, to speak the truth, and to give back what we have received* [*hæc notio justitiæ est*].

The relative pronoun also often agrees in Gender and Number, not with the preceding substantive to which it refers, but with the substantive following, which is added as a *Predicate:* φίλου, ὃ μέγιστον ἀγαθόν ἐστιν, οὐ φροντίζουσιν, *they do not care for a friend, which is the greatest good.*

Chap. XV.—The Article.

§ 368. The Article ὁ, ἡ, τό is originally a *demonstrative pronoun*, and still employed as such in Homer, both in a substantive and adjective sense, and frequently also in the language of the other poets: Hom. τὴν ἐγὼ οὐ λύσω, her *I will not give up;* poet. τὸν, ὦ Ζεῦ πάτερ, φθίσον, him, *father Zeus, destroy;* Hom. φθίσει σε τὸ σὸν μένος, *this thy courage will be thy ruin.*

§ 369. The Article in this *demonstrative* sense is also employed in the following cases in Attic prose:
1. In connection with μέν and δέ: ὁ μέν, *the one;* ὁ δέ, *the other.*

Obs.—Used adverbially, τὸ (τὰ) μέν — τὸ (τὰ) δέ, mean *partly — partly.*

2. Sometimes also with καί and δέ: καὶ τὸν κελεῦσαι, *and that he ordered;* τὸν καὶ τόν, *the one and the other.*
3. In πρὸ τοῦ, *before that, formerly.*

§ 370. The real Article generally corresponds to the English *definite* article. It serves to set forth an object,

§ 374.   THE ARTICLE.   231

either as a single one (the individualizing article) or as a class (the generic article).

Obs.—ὁ, ἡ, τό in Homer almost always has a demonstrative power. Yet in many cases—compare especially § 379—the use of these forms approaches very near to that of the Attic Article. The Article, however, in Homer is *scarcely ever necessary*, and is frequently omitted also in the Tragic writers.

§ 371. 1. The *Individualizing* Article sets forth a single object above others of the same kind, and that:

a) as known or having been pointed out before : Herod. Χαλκιδέες τ ὰ ς ἐπ' Ἀρτεμισίῳ εἴκοσι νῆας παρείχοντο, *the Chalcideans furnished the* (before mentioned) *twenty ships at Artemision;* Ξέρξης ἀγείρας τὴν ἀναρίθμητον στρατιὰν ἦλθεν ἐπὶ τὴν Ἑλλάδα, *after having collected the* (well-known) *innumerable army, Xerxes marched against Greece.*

Obs.—In this sense proper names also, which in general do not need it, may take the Article: ὁ Σωκράτης, *Socrates,* whom you know, or who was mentioned before.

§ 372. *b*) A thing as distinguished from others by the addition of *distinguishing circumstances :* ὁ τῶν Ἀθηναίων δῆμος, *the Athenian people* (no other) ; ἡ πόλις ἣν πολιορκοῦμεν, *the city which we are besieging* (just this).

§ 373. The distinguishing circumstance expressed by the Article is often indicated in English by the *possessive* pronoun : ἕκαστος τῶν δημιουργῶν τ ὴ ν τέχνην καλῶς ἐξειργάζετο, *each of the artisans practised his art well.*

§ 374. In connexion with numerals, the Article sometimes denotes that the number to which it is added stands in a defined relation to another number : τὰ δύο μέρη, *two thirds ;* τῶν τριήρων τριακοσίων οὐσῶν τῶν πασῶν τ ὰ ς διακοσίας ἡ πόλις παρέσχετο, *of the triremes, of which there were three hundred in all, the city furnished two hundred.* The Article has a similar effect with quantitative adjectives of a more general kind : πολλοί, *many*—οἱ πολλοί, most; πλέονες, more—οἱ πλέονες, the greater part; ἄλλοι, alii—οἱ ἄλλοι, cæteri; ὀλίγοι, a few—οἱ ὀλίγοι, the oligarchs.

§ 375. 2. The *Generic* Article indicates a whole class of homogeneous objects: οἱ πολῖται, *all the citizens*; ὁ ῥήτωρ, *the orator* (by profession); δεῖ τὸν στρατιώτην τὸν ἄρχοντα μᾶλλον ἢ τοὺς πολεμίους φοβεῖσθαι, *the soldier must fear his superior rather than the enemy*.

> *Obs.*—Hence the Article may also be used with proper names in the plural when a whole class is to be described: οἱ Δημοσθένεις, *orators like Demosthenes* (a Demosthenes, compare § 362, *Obs.* 1).

§ 376. The Article is not used when a substantive only expresses an idea in general: ἀνθρώπου ψυχὴ τοῦ θείου μετέχει, *man's soul partakes of the divine*; so θεός denotes *the deity*; ὁ θεός, *a particular god*; so likewise, in many other current expressions, the more ancient method of not using the Article has been preserved: νυκτός, *by night*; ἡμέρας, *by day*; ἐπὶ θαλάσσῃ, *at sea*; πρὸς ἄστυ, *to town*; κατ' ἀγρόν, *in the country*; κατὰ γῆς, *under the earth*; ἐν δεξιᾷ, *on the right*; ἐξαιρῶ λόγου, *I exempt*.

§ 377. The Article is omitted with a number of substantives, which by custom have almost acquired the force of proper names: βασιλεύς, *the king* (of the Persians); πρυτάνεις, *the presidents* (as officials); ἐν ἀκροπόλει, *in the Acropolis* (Athens).

§ 378. The *Predicate* (§ 361, 3, 10) generally has *no* Article: Κῦρος ἐγένετο β α σ ι λ ε ὺ ς τῶν Περσῶν, *Cyrus became king of the Persians*; πόνος εὐκλείας π α τ ή ρ, *labor is father of fame*; οἱ Ἀθηναῖοι Περικλέα εἵλοντο σ τ ρ α τ η γ ό ν, *the Athenians chose Pericles general* (compare §§ 387, 392, 403, and 438, *Obs.*

§ 379. By means of the Article, any adjective, participle, or adverb, as well as the infinitive, may be made *a substantive*: Hom. ὁ γέρων, *the old man*; οἱ πλούσιοι, *the rich*; ὁ λέγων, *the speaker*; ὁ πέλας, *the neighbor*; οἱ

§ 385. THE ARTICLE. 233

παρόντες, *those present ;* τὰ κάτω, *the under* (part) ; οἱ πάλαι, *the ancients ;* τὸ μισεῖν, *hating* or *hatred.*

Obs.—With the Neuter Article, any word, or even a whole sentence, may be represented as one object.: τὸ ἀνήρ, the word ἀνήρ or the idea "man;" τὸ Γνῶθι σεαυτόν, the saying or rule "Know thyself."

§ 380. The Generic Article (§ 375) generalizes the idea of a *participle*, which then is to be translated by a relative phrase : ποιείτω τοῦτο ὁ βουλόμενος, *do that, who will ;* μὴ ζητεῖτε τὸν ταῦτα λέξοντα, *seek not* (one) *who will say this* (compare § 500).

§ 381. By the Article, many *adverbs*, placed between it and a substantive, become *attributive adjectives* : οἱ τότε ἄνθρωποι, *the people of that time ;* ἡ παραυτίκα ἡδονή, *the momentary pleasure ;* αἱ ἐνθάδε γυναῖκες, *the women of this place ;* ἡ ἄγαν ἐλευθερία, *the excessive freedom.*

§ 382. In the same way, a genitive, or a preposition with a substantive, placed between the Article and another substantive, becomes an *attributive clause* : τὰ τῶν Ἀθηναίων πράγματα, *the affairs of the Athenians ;* οἱ ἐν τῇ πόλει ἄνθρωποι, *the people in the city ;* ἡ καθ' ἡμέραν τροφή, *the daily nourishment ;* αἱ ἄνευ λυπῶν ἡδοναί, *the painless pleasures.*

§ 383. The Article often stands alone, sometimes with the Genitive of a substantive (compare §§ 409, 410), sometimes with a preposition followed by a substantive ; in such a construction the Article has the force of *a substantive* (§ 379): τὰ τῶν Ἀθηναίων, *the affairs* (possessions, interests) *of the Athenians ;* οἱ ἐν τῇ πόλει, *the* (people) *in the city ;* τὰ μετὰ ταῦτα, *what follows, the later* (events).

§ 384. When a substantive with an *attributive* (§ 361, 11) adjective has the Article, *the adjective stands between the substantive and the article :* ὁ ἀγαθὸς ἀνήρ, *the good man.*

§ 385. If the substantive alone is to be prominent, and the adjective to be added as *apposition* (§ 361, 12), the substantive stands first, and the *adjective with the article follows*, thus:

a) The *substantive without Article*, when the case is such that the substantive, if put alone, would have no article: τί διαφέρει ἄνθρωπος ἀκρατὴς θηρίου τοῦ ἀκρατεστάτου; *in what does an ungovernable man differ from the most ungovernable beast?* for if θηρίον stood alone it would be without Article, θηρίου, *from a beast.*

b) The *substantive has the Article* when by itself, even without an adjective, it must have the Article: οἱ Χῖοι τὸ τεῖχος περιεῖλον τὸ καινόν, *the Chians pulled down* (their) *wall—the new one* (which they themselves had built); for, even without the adjective, it would have to be τὸ τεῖχος περιεῖλον (§ 373).

§ 386. The same rule holds good with regard to the position of the attributive additions mentioned in §§ 381 and 382: ὁ Ἀθηναίων δῆμος, *the Athenian people;* ὁ δῆμος, ὁ τῶν Ἀθηναίων, *the people, that is, the Athenian;* ὁ μετὰ ταῦτα χρόνος, *the after time;* ὁ χρόνος ὁ μετὰ ταῦτα, *the time which followed this.*

§ 387. An adjective which, *without* the Article, either precedes or follows a substantive having the Article, is *predicative, i. e.*, the character is assigned to the substantive only by this word (§ 361, **4, 8,** and **10**): ἀγαθὸς ὁ ἀνὴρ or ὁ ἀνὴρ ἀγαθός (viz., ἐστίν), *the man is good;* ἅπαντες ἔχομεν τὸ σῶμα θνητόν, *we all have a body* (which is) *mortal.* The translation may often be effected by a relative clause: οἱ Ἀθηναῖοι ἡγοῦντο αὐτονόμων τὸ πρῶτον συμμάχων, *the Athenians had the lead of allies* (who) *at first* (were) *independent;* φαίνομαι μεγάλας τὰς ὑποσχέσεις ποιούμενος, *I seem to make promises which are great.* Compare § 378.

Obs.—With proper names, the use of the Article is very uncertain when the class is added to which they belong: ὁ Εὐφράτης ποταμός or ὁ ποταμὸς ὁ Εὐφράτης, *the river Euphrates;* ἡ Αἴτνη τὸ ὄρος, *Mount Etna;* Σικελία ἡ νῆσος, *the island of Sicily;* ἡ πόλις οἱ Ταρσοί, *the city of Tarsi.*

§ 388. The *possessive pronoun* is preceded by the Article when a single definite object is referred to: ὁ ἐμὸς

§ 391. THE ARTICLE. 235

ἑταῖρος, my (particular) *friend ;* ἐμὸς ἑταῖρος, *a friend of mine.*

§ 389. αὐτός, as a *predicate,* put before or after a substantive with the Article, means *self :* αὐτὸς ὁ πατήρ or ὁ πατὴρ αὐτός, *the father himself, ipse pater ;* but as an *attribute* it is put between the Article and the substantive, and means *same :* ὁ αὐτὸς ἀνήρ, *the same man, idem vir.*

With the *demonstrative pronouns* οὗτος, ὅδε, ἐκεῖνος, a substantive, not being a predicate, has regularly the Article: οὗτος ὁ ἀνήρ or ὁ ἀνὴρ οὗτος, *this man ;* ἐκεῖνο τὸ δῶρον, *that gift.* But when the substantive is a predicate the Article is wanting : ἐν Πέρσαις νόμος ἐστὶν οὗτος, *among the Persians this is law.* Compare § 367.

§ 390. πᾶς without the Article before a substantive without the Article means in the Singular *every :* πᾶσα πόλις, *every city.* The Article before πᾶς gives it the meaning of *whole :* ἡ πᾶσα πόλις, *the whole city ;* τοὺς πάντας ὁπλίτας, *the whole of the heavy-armed.* Most generally πᾶς as well as ὅλος without the Article precedes or follows a substantive provided with the Article : πᾶσαν ὑμῖν τὴν ἀλήθειαν ἐρῶ, *I will tell you the whole truth ;* τὸν ἀριθμὸν πάντα δίχα διελάβομεν, *we divided the whole number into two parts ;* τῆς ἡμέρας ὅλης διῆλθον οὐ πλέον πέντε καὶ εἴκοσι σταδίων, *during the whole day they proceeded no more than twenty-five stadia.*

Obs.—πᾶς, with the Article added to a numeral, may often be translated by " altogether" or " in all :" Δαρεῖος ἐβασίλευσε τὰ πάντα ἓξ καὶ τριάκοντα ἔτη, *Darius ruled altogether thirty-six years.*

§ 391. Expressions for measures are to be understood differently, according to the position of the Article : ἔσχατον τὸ ὄρος, *the extreme end of the mountain ;* τὸ ἔσχατον ὄρος, *the farthest mountain* (in contrast to other mountains); ἡ ἀγορὰ μέση, *the middle* (of the) *market-place ;* ἡ μέση ἀγορά, *the middle market,* that placed in the middle of several others. In Latin, *forum medium* means both.

Chap. XVI.—Use of the Cases.

A) *The Nominative.*

§ 392. The *Nominative* is the case of the *subject* and of the predicate belonging to the subject (§ 361, 3, 4).

Hence, as in Latin with *fio, dicor, videor, creor*, etc., so in Greek with verbs of the same meaning, the predicative noun referring to the subject is in the Nominative: καθίσταται βασιλεύς, *he is appointed king;* Ἀλέξανδρος θεὸς ὠνομάζετο, *Alexander deus appellabatur.* Compare § 361, 7; §§ 378, 403.

> *Obs.*—ἀκούω, *I hear*, in the sense of *I am called* [Lat. *audio*], also belongs to these verbs: οἱ ἐν Ἀθήναις φιλιππίζοντες κόλακες καὶ θεοῖς ἐχθροὶ ἤκουον, *the Philippizers in Athens were called flatterers and objects of the gods' hatred.*

§ 393. The Nominative is frequently used instead of the Vocative in addressing a person, especially in connection with οὗτος : ὁ Ἀπολλόδωρος οὗτος, οὐ περιμενεῖς; *You! Apollodorus, won't you stop?* and also in exclamations : νήπιος, *the fool!*

B) *The Vocative.*

§ 394. The person or thing addressed is in the Vocative. In Attic prose ὦ is generally put before it, except sometimes in animated discourse : μὴ θορυβεῖτε, ὦ ἄνδρες Ἀθηναῖοι, *don't make a disturbance, Athenians;* ἀκούεις Αἰσχίνη; *do you hear, Æschines?*

> *Obs.*—The Vocative, like interjections, does not belong to the structure of a sentence, whence a word in the Vocative is inclosed by commas.

C) *The Accusative.*

§ 395. The Accusative, Genitive, and Dative mark an object as dependent, whence they are called cases of dependence (*casus obliqui, oblique cases*).

The Accusative is the case of the *Object*, and therefore denotes generally the person or thing to which an action is directed.

§ 398. THE EXTERNAL OBJECT. 237

The Object is either external to the action by which it is affected : τύπτω τὸν δοῦλον, *I strike the slave*, or internal, *i. e.*, already contained in the action itself : τύπτω πεντήκοντα πληγάς, *I strike fifty blows*.

Obs.—The Accusative, therefore, in the great majority of cases, is dependent on a *verb*. Only in a very few cases does it happen that a *substantive* after the manner of a verb is followed by an Accusative : οἱ σύμμαχοι τεθνᾶσι τῷ δέει τοὺς τοιούτους ἀποστόλους, *the allies are dead* (beside themselves) *from fear of such embassadors*.

§ 396. 1. The *External Object* is expressed by the Accusative with *transitive* verbs as in other languages. Several verbs, however, are treated in Greek as transitive which in other languages are intransitive. Such verbs are :

a) Those which signify to *benefit* or *injure*, whether it be by act or speech : εὖ or ἀγαθὸν ποιέω, εὐεργετέω, *I benefit* (τοὺς εὐεργετήσαντας, *my benefactors*); ὀνίνημι, ὠφελέω, *I am useful ;* κακῶς or κακὸν ποιέω, κακόω, *I do ill ;* ἀδικέω, *I do wrong ;* ὑβρίζω, *I insult ;* βλάπτω, *I hurt,* etc. ; also κολακεύω, *I flatter*, and τιμωρέομαι, *I avenge myself* (τὸν ἐχθρόν, *on my enemy*); ὁ Σωκράτης οὐδένα τῶν πολιτῶν ἠδίκησεν, *Socrates acted unjustly to none of his fellow-citizens*.

§ 397. Not unfrequently the verb of a principal clause takes as its object what should properly be the subject of a subordinate clause : καί μοι τὸν υἱὸν εἰπέ, εἰ μεμάθηκε τὴν τέχνην, more animated than καί μοι εἰπέ, εἰ ὁ υἱὸς μεμάθηκε τὴν τέχνην, *and tell me about my son, whether he has learned his trade*. Compare § 519, 5, *Obs.* 2.

§ 398. *b*) The Accusative of the external Object is used with the verbs : φεύγω (compare *fugio*), ἀποδιδράσκω, *I run away from ;* φθάνω, *I get before ;* θηράω, θηρεύω, *I hunt after ;* μιμέομαι (compare *imitor*), ζηλόω, *I rival ;* ἀμείβομαι, *I repay, I respond to ;* λανθάνω (compare *lateo*), ἐκλείπω (compare *deficio*); ἐκλείπει με ἡ ἐλπίς, *spes me deficit*.

§ 399. *c*) This Accusative is farther used with verbs of *emotion:* αἰδέομαι, αἰσχύνομαι, *I am ashamed* (τὸν πατέρα, *before my father*); φυλάττομαι, εὐλαβέομαι, *I am on my guard against;* θαρρέω, *I have confidence* (τὴν ἰσχύν, *in my strength*); ἐκπλήττομαι, καταπλήττομαι, *I am amazed at;* similarly with ὄμνυμι, *I swear by* (τοὺς θεούς, *the gods*).

Obs.—As with ὄμνυμι, so in exclamations, the Accusative is used even without a governing verb: ναὶ μὰ τὸν Δία, *Yes, by Zeus!* (§ 643, 16).

§ 399*b*. The *Space and Time* over which an action extends are often expressed by the Accusative: κοινὴν ὁδὸν ἤλθομεν, *we came by a common road;* Hom. κλίμακα ὑψηλὴν κατεβήσετο, *she came down the high ladder;* πλεῖν θάλασσαν, *to navigate the sea;* ἐνταῦθα Κῦρος ἔμεινε ἡμέρας πέντε, *there Cyrus remained five days.* Compare § 405.

On the Accusative of the *aim,* see § 406.

§ 400. 2. The *Internal Object* is expressed by the Accusative not only with transitive, but also with intransitive and passive verbs.

The internal Object is:

a) a word of cognate *origin* with the verb: Hom. ἄλλοι δ' ἀμφ' ἄλλῃσι μ ά χ η ν ἐμάχοντο πύλῃσιν, *alii circa alias portas pugnam pugnabant;* τ ε ῖ χ ο ς τειχίζονται, *they wall* (build) *a wall;* πομπὴν πέμπειν, *to send an escort, make a solemn procession;* κακίστην δουλείαν ἐδούλευσεν, *he served the worst service* (endured the worst slavery); Hom. τῷ πείσεαι ὅς κεν ἀρίστην βουλὴν βουλεύσῃ, *you will obey him who advises* (gives) *the best advice;* τὴν ἐναντίαν νόσον νοσοῦμεν, *we suffer* (sicken) *from the opposite sickness;* μεγάλην τινὰ κρίσιν κρίνεται, *he is judged* (tried) *in a great trial;*

b) or a word *akin* to the verb in *meaning;* πληγὴν τύπτεται βαρυτάτην, *he is struck a very severe blow;* πάσας νόσους κάμνει, *he suffers from all diseases;* poet. ὀδύρματα γοᾶσθαι, *to moan lamentations;* πόλεμον ἐστράτευσαν τὸν ἱερὸν καλούμενον, *they marched out to the so-called holy war;* γραφὴν διώκειν, *to pursue with a writ* (compare γραφὴν γράφεσθαι);

c) or a substantive *defining* the verb: Ὀλύμπια νικᾶν, *to conquer in the Olympic games;* γάμους ἑστιᾶν, *to give a marriage-feast;* Hom. νόστον ὀδυρόμενοι, *weeping for the return;* μένεα πνείοντες Ἀχαιοί, *the courage-breathing Achæans;* ἀγγελίην ἐλθεῖν, *to go a message;* πῦρ ὀφθαλμοῖσι δεδορκώς, *looking fire with the eyes* (flashing fiery looks);

d) or the *result* of the action expressed by the verb: ἕλκος οὐτάσαι, *to strike a wound* (produce by blows); ὅρκια τάμνειν, *fœdus ferire, i. e., fœdus hostiam feriendo efficere;* poet. ἥδε (ἡ ἀναρχία) τροπὰς καταρρήγνυσι, *it* (anarchy) *breaks flight, i. e.,* produces flight by breaking through the ranks.

§ 401. Often, especially in the poets, a neuter adjective or pronoun in the Accusative is added to a verb as a special qualification, almost like an adverb (§ 400, *c*): ὀ λ ί γ ο ν ἀπεῖναι, *to be a little way off;* μ έ γ α ψεύδεται, *he tells a great lie* (compare μέγα ψ ε ῦ δ ο ς ψεύδεται); τ ο ῦ τ ο χαίρω, *at this I rejoice;* τί χρήσομαι τ ο ύ τ ῳ; *what use shall I make of this?* π ά ν τ α πείσομαι, *I will obey in all things.*

§ 402. 3. *Double Object.*

Many verbs have a double object, consequently a *double Accusative;* the following, which most frequently occur with this construction, may serve as examples: διδάσκω (ἐδίδαξαν τὸν παῖδα τὴν μουσικήν, *docuerunt puerum musicam*); κρύπτω, *I hide;* ἐρωτάω, *I ask;* αἰτέω, *I demand;* πράττομαι, *I acquire* (ἀργύριον τοὺς παρόντας, *money from those who are present*); κακὸν λέγω τοὺς ἐχθρούς, *I speak ill of my enemies;* ἀφαιρέομαι, ἀποστερέω, *I deprive of;* ἀναμιμνήσκω, *I remind of;* ἐνδύω, ἀμφιέννυμι, *I put on* (τινὰ χιτῶνα, *a coat on some one*); περιβάλλομαι, *I encircle* (τείχη τὴν πόλιν, *the city with walls*). Hom.: ἡ δὲ μέγαν ἱστὸν ὕφαινεν δίπλακα, *she wove a double garment at the loom* (§ 399, *b*).

Obs. 1.—In the passive construction the *thing* remains in the Accusative: διδάσκομαι τὴν μουσικήν; ἀφῄρημαι τὸν ἵππον, *I am robbed of the horse*.

Obs. 2.—Many other verbs besides these have a double Accusative, by an external object being added to the internal one: Hom. ὃν Ζεὺς φίλει παντοίην φιλότητα, *whom Zeus loved with multiform love, i. e.*, to whom Zeus manifested love in various ways (§ 400, *a*); Αἰσχίνης Κτησιφῶντα γραφὴν παρανόμων ἐδίωκεν, *Æschines prosecuted Ktesiphon with a charge of violating the law* (§ 400, *b*); poet. πολλά σε ὀδύρματα κατεῖδον τὴν Ἡράκλειον ἔξοδον γοωμένην, *many wailings I saw you give vent to about the departure of Heracles* (§ 400, *c*); Hom. ἕλκος ὅ με βροτὸς οὔτασεν ἀνήρ, *the wound which a mortal man struck me* (§ 400, *d*).

§ 404. 4. *The Accusative as a Predicate.*

A *dependent Predicate relating to an Object* is in the Accusative. Hence the verbs mentioned in §§ 361, 10, and 392, which signify *naming, deeming, making, appointing, choosing, representing,* and the like, have a *double* Accusative in the Active—one of the external Object, and one of the *Predicate:* οἱ κόλακες Ἀλέξανδρον θεὸν ὠνόμαζον, *the flatterers used to call Alexander a god;* αἱρεῖσθαί τινα στρατηγόν, *eligere aliquem ducem;* οὐ τοὺς πλεῖστα ἔχοντας εὐδαιμονεστάτους νομίζω, *I do not deem those possessing most the happiest;* παρέχω ἐμαυτὸν εὐπειθῆ, *I show myself obedient;* ἔλαβε τοῦτο δῶρον, *he received this* (as) *a gift.*

Obs.—The want of the Article often of itself distinguishes the predicative accusative from the objective (§ 378). In the passive construction both Accusatives must become Nominatives, according to § 392.

§ 404. 5. In a *freer way* the Accusative is joined to

§ 405. DOUBLE OBJECT. 241

verbs and adjectives, to point out to what the idea of these words refers, *in reference to what* they are to be understood: κάμνω τ ὴ ν κ ε φ α λ ή ν, *I suffer in the head* (compare § 400, *b*); ἄδικος π ᾶ σ α ν ἀ δ ι κ ί α ν, *unjust in every* (kind of) *injustice* (in every way, compare § 400, *a*); Ἕλληνές εἰσι τ ὸ γ έ ν ο ς, *they are Greeks in race;* εὖ ἔχομεν τ ὰ σ ώ μ α τ α, *we are well in body;* Hom. ὄμματα καὶ κ ε φ α λ ὴ ν ἴκελος Διὶ τερπικεραύνῳ, *in eyes and head like thunder-loving Zeus;* παρθένος καλὴ τ ὸ ε ἶ δ ο ς, *a maiden beautiful in form,* or *of* beautiful form (*facie pulchra*); οὐδεὶς ἄνθρωπος αὐτὸς π ά ν τ α σοφός, *no man is himself wise in every thing;* ὁ Μαρσύας ποταμὸς εἴκοσι καὶ πέντε πόδας εἶχε τ ὸ ε ὖ ρ ο ς, *the River Marsyas was twenty-five feet in breadth.* This Accusative is called the *Accusative of reference.*

Obs.—Hence a great number of independent, almost *adverbial*, Accusatives : τὸ ὄνομα, *in name, by name;* τὸ πλῆθος, *in number;* τὸν τρόπον, *in character;* τοῦτον τὸν τρόπον, *in this way;* τὴν φύσιν, *by nature;* πρόφασιν, *on the pretext, ostensibly;* δίκην, *like;* χάριν, *for the sake of* (*gratia*); τὸ πᾶν, *altogether, on the whole;* πολύ, *by far;* τί, *quid, what? why?* τί κλαίεις ; *why weepest thou?* αὐτὰ ταῦτα ἥκω, *for this very reason I have come.*

§ 405. In regard to the ideas of space and time, the Accusative expresses *extension* (compare § 399, *b*): Hom. π ᾶ ν ἦ μ α ρ φερόμην, *a whole day I was borne along, totum diem ferebar;* βασιλεὺς καὶ Ἕλληνες ἀπεῖχον ἀλλήλων τ ρ ι ά κ ο ν τ α σ τ ά δ ι α, *the king and the Hellenes were thirty stadia distant from each other;* Hom. λείπετο δουρὸς ἐ ρ ω ή ν, *he remained a spear's throw behind;* τὸν μὲν εὖ παθόντα δεῖ μεμνῆσθαι τ ὸ ν π ά ν τ α χ ρ ό ν ο ν, τὸν δὲ ποιήσαντα εὐθὺς ἐπιλελῆσθαι, *he who has received kindnesses ought to remember them throughout all time, but he who has done them immediately to forget them.*

Obs. 1.—An Accusative used with ordinal numerals, in regard to time, is to be translated by *since before* or *ago:* ἑβδόμην ἡμέραν ἡ θυγάτηρ αὐτῷ ἐτετελευτήκει, *his daughter had died seven days before.*

L

Obs. 2.—Freer Accusatives, referable chiefly to time, are: τοῦτον τὸν χρόνον, *at this time;* τὸ λοιπόν, *for the future, henceforth;* τέλος, *at last;* πρότερον, *formerly;* ἀρχήν, *up to the beginning,* hence *entirely;* τὴν ταχίστην, supply ὁδόν, *the quickest* (way); μακράν, *far, distant.*

§ 406. In the poets, the Accusative joined to verbs of motion also denotes the *place toward* which an action is directed: Hom. τοῦ δὲ κλέος οὐρανὸν ἵκει, *his fame reaches up to heaven;* πῶς ἦλθες Ἄργος; *quomodo Argos venisti?* On the absolute Accusative of participles, see § 586.

D) *The Genitive.*

§ 407. The Genitive generally denotes a thing *belonging* to another.

Obs.—Hence the Genitive is most commonly dependent on a *noun*, and, even where it is governed by a verb, its use resembles that with a noun.

§ 408. 1. *The Genitive with Substantives.*

One Substantive may be joined to another in various ways; the most common are:

1. Σωκράτης ὁ **Σωφρονίσκου** υἱός, *Socrates son of Sophroniscus: Origin.*
2. ἡ οἰκία **τοῦ πατρός**, *the father's house: Possession.*
3. νόμισμα **ἀργυρίου**, *a silver coin: Material.*
   Hom. δέπας **οἴνου**, *a cup of wine: Contents.*
4. οἱ πλεῖστοι **τῶν Ἑλλήνων**, *most of the Hellenes: Partitive Genitive.*
5. ὁ φόβος τῶν πολεμίων, *metus hostium, i. e.,* either
   a) *the fear of the enemy, i. e.,* the fear which the enemy feels (*Subjective* Genitive), or,
   b) *the fear about the enemy, i. e.,* the fear of which the enemy is the object (*Objective* Genitive).
6. δοῦλος πέντε μνῶν, *a slave worth five minæ: Value.*
7. γραφὴ κλοπῆς, *an accusation of theft: Cause.*
8. πολίτου ἀρετή, *a citizen's virtue: Quality.*

§ 412. THE GENITIVE. 243

9. Hom. Τροίης πτολίεθρον, *the city of* (called) *Troy: Designation.*

Which of the two substantives in any particular case has to be expressed by the Genitive is generally quite as clear from their meaning as in English.

But the following special peculiarities in the use of the different kinds of Genitives deserve to be noticed:

§ 409. *a*) The Genitive denotes descent from a father, even without the addition of a Substantive: Σωκράτης ὁ Σωφρονίσκου, *Socrates, the son of Sophroniscus;* Μιλτιάδης Κίμωνος, *Miltiades, son of Kimon;* poet., Διὸς Ἄρτεμις, *Artemis, daughter of Zeus.*

§ 410. *b*) The Neuter of the Article with a Genitive has very different meanings (compare § 383): τὰ τῶν Ἑλλήνων, *the affairs, interests, possessions of the Hellenes* (compare τὰ Ἑλληνικά); τὸ τῆς ὀλιγαρχίας, *the nature of the oligarchy;* on the other hand, τὸ τοῦ Δημοσθένους, *the word of Demosthenes;* τὰ τῶν φίλων κοινά, *the property of friends is common.*

§ 411. *c*) The idea of abode is to be supplied in the expressions: εἰς διδασκάλου φοιτᾶν, *to go to the master's* (house), *i. e.*, to go to school; ἐν or εἰς Ἅιδου (Homer, εἰν Ἀΐδαο δόμοις, *in Hades' dwelling, dominion*), *in or into the lower world.*

§ 412. *d*) The *Partitive* Genitive (4), denoting a whole to be divided, is most common with numerals and superlatives: πολλοὶ τῶν Ἀθηναίων, *multi Atheniensium;* πότερος τῶν ἀδελφῶν; *which of the two brothers?* πάντων ἄριστος, *omnium optimus;* but also with various adjectives: οἱ σπουδαῖοι τῶν πολιτῶν, *the assiduous among the citizens.* So, more freely in the Homeric poems: δῖα θεάων, *the divine one among goddesses;* δήμου ἀνήρ, *a man of the people;* and similarly, ἀνὴρ τῶν ῥητόρων, *a man from the number of the orators.*

The Partitive Genitive with names of places denotes the whole territory: Θῆβαι τῆς Βοιωτίας, *Thebes in Bœotia;* with Neuter pronouns it sometimes denotes a whole which is attained by degrees: εἰς τοῦτο ἀνοίας ἦλθον, *eo usque insaniæ progressi sunt.*

Obs.—Adjectives which have a Partitive Genitive sometimes follow the gender of the Genitive dependent upon them: ὁ ἥμισυς τοῦ χρόνου, the half of the time (instead of τὸ ἥμισυ τοῦ χρόνου); ἡ πλείστη τῆς χώρας, *most of the land.*

§ 413. *e*) The *Objective* Genitive (5, *e*) may be translated by various prepositions: εὔνοια τῶν φίλων, *benevolence toward friends;* ἀπορία σίτου, *want of food;* Hom., ἔρος ἐδητύος ἠδὲ ποτῆτος, *eagerness for food and drink;* ἡσυχία ἐχθρῶν, *peace from enemies;* ἀγῶνες λόγων, *contests in speeches;* ἀφορμὴ ἔργων, *stimulus to deeds;* ἀπόστασις τῶν Ἀθηναίων, *defection from the Athenians;* λύσις θανάτου, *deliverance from death;* βίᾳ πολιτῶν, *with violence against the citizens, in spite of the citizens.*

2. *Genitive with Adjectives and Adverbs.*

§ 414. The Genitive is joined to many *relative* adjectives and their adverbs, *i. e.*, to such adjectives and adverbs as are conceivable *only in reference to something*, and points out the person or thing they refer to. The most important adjectives of this kind are:

1. κοινός, *common;* ἴδιος, οἰκεῖος, *own, peculiar,* and others which imply *property* or *belonging to*, as: ναὸς ἱερὸς τοῦ Ἀπόλλωνος, *a temple sacred to Apollo* (possession, compare § 408, 2).

2. Adjectives denoting *plenty* and *want* (contents, § 408, 3), as: μεστός, ἔμπλεως, πλήρης, *full;* πλούσιος, *rich;* ἐνδεής, πένης, *necessitous;* farther, the adverb ἅλις, *enough:* πάντα εὐφροσύνης πλέα ἦν, *all was full of joy.*

3. Those signifying *acquainted* or *unacquainted with:* ἔμπειρος, *peritus;* ἄπειρος, *imperitus;* ἐπιστήμων, *skilled*

§ 416. THE GENITIVE. 245

(τέχνης, *in an art*); μνήμων, ἀμνήμων, *mindful* and *unmindful*.

4. ἄξιος, *worthy;* ἀνάξιος, *unworthy;* πλείστου ἄξιον, *worth most, the worthiest thing* (§ 408, 6).

5. Adjectives implying *participation* (§ 408, 4), whether it be positive or negative: μέτοχος τοῦ πόνου, *particeps laboris;* ἄμοιρος, *without a share;* αἴτιος, *author, guilty, reus.*

Obs.—To these belong many adjectives compounded with ἀν (ἀ, § 360) privative, which, especially in poets, are joined with the genitive: poet. αἰὼν κακῶν ἄγευστος, *a life which has not tasted of misfortunes;* φίλων ἄκλαυτος, *unwept by friends.*

6. Adjectives in -ικός (§ 351) denoting *capability* or *fitness for* (compare 3) something: διδασκαλικὸς γραμματικῆς, *capable of teaching grammar;* παρασκευαστικὸς τῶν εἰς τὸν πόλεμον, *skilled in obtaining the necessaries for war.*

§ 415. Many *Adverbs of Place* are joined with a Genitive, which is mostly of a Partitive nature (compare § 412): ποῦ γῆς; *where on earth?* so with ἐντός, *within;* εἴσω, *inside;* ἐκτός, *without;* ἔξω, *outside;* ἄγχι, ἐγγύς, *near;* πρόσω or πόρρω, *forward;* πέρα, *beyond;* εὐθύ, *straight towards;* πρόσθεν, ἔμπροσθεν, *in front;* ὄπισθεν, *behind;* ἀμφοτέρωθεν, *on both sides;* ἄνω, *upward* (ποταμῶν, *up-stream*); and corresponding with these also some adverbs of *time* and *manner:* πηνίκα τῆς ἡμέρας; *at what time of the day?* πῶς ἔχεις τῆς γνώμης; *what do you think?* λάθρα τῶν γονέων, *secretly from the parents.*

§ 416. The *Comparative* may have the object with which any thing is compared in the Genitive (as in the Ablative in Latin): μείζων τοῦ ἀδελφοῦ, *major fratre, i. e.,* ἢ ὁ ἀδελφός, *than the brother;* οὐ προςήκει τὸν ἄρχοντα τῶν ἀρχομένων πονηρότερον εἶναι, *i. e.,* ἢ τοὺς ἀρχομένους, *it is not becoming that the governor should be worse than the governed.*

Obs. 1.—This Genitive is used most frequently where it represents ἤ with the Nominative or Accusative; yet it may also more freely represent ἤ with the Dative: poet. πλείων χρόνος, ὃν δεῖ μ' ἀρέσκειν τοῖς κάτω τῶν ἐνθάδε (ἤ τοῖς ἐνθάδε), *longer is the time that I must please those below than that I must please those here.*

Obs. 2.—Like the Comparative, the Superlative is sometimes joined with the Genitive of the things with which any thing is compared: poet. φάος κάλλιστον τῶν προτέρων, *a light most beautiful in comparison with the former ones*, where we might have expected φάος κάλλιον τῶν προτέρων, *lux prioribus pulchrior*, or φάος κάλλιστον πάντων, *omnium pulcherrima.*

Obs. 3.—All adjectives expressive of a comparison follow the rule of Comparatives: διπλάσιος, *doubly* (as great as); δεύτερος (οὐδενός), *second (to none)*; ὕστερος, *later than;* ἕτερος, *another than.*

3. *The Genitive with Verbs.*

Very many verbs are joined with the Genitive on the general principles mentioned in § 408.

§ 417. 1. The Genitive represents a *Predicate* (§ 361, 7 and 10) with verbs which denote *being, becoming, making, deeming,* in order to predicate something of a substantive, as originating from, possessing, consisting of, or in any other way qualifying it, § 408: Σωκράτης Σωφρονίσκου ἦν, *Socrates was Sophroniscus's son* (§ 408, 1); ἡ οἰκία τοῦ πατρὸς ἐγένετο, *the house became the father's property* (§ 408, 2); τὸ τεῖχος λίθου πεποίηται, *the wall has been made of stone* (§ 408, 3); οἱ Θεσσαλοὶ τῶν Ἑλλήνων ἦσαν, *the Thessalians belonged to the Hellenes* (§ 408, 4); πολίτου ἀγαθοῦ νομίζεται θαρρεῖν, *to be courageous is deemed a good citizen's quality* (§ 408, 8).

Obs.—The Genitive often occurs with verbs of perception and observation in such a way that it is properly dependent on a noun or pronoun: τοῦτο ὑμῶν μάλιστα θαυμάζομεν, *this we most admire in you* (properly: this of you we most admire).

§ 418. 2. The Genitive of *Material* (§ 408, 3) is also used with verbs of *plenty* and *want* (compare § 414, 2): πίμπλημι, πληρόω, *I fill;* πλήθω, γέμω, *I am full;* δέομαι (δεῖ μοι), *I need;* τὰ ὦτα ἐνέπλησαν δαιμονίας σοφίας, *they filled the ears with wondrous wisdom;* ὁ παρὼν καιρὸς

§ 419. THE GENITIVE. 247.

πολλῆς φροντίδος καὶ βουλῆς δεῖται, *the present time is in need of much reflection and advice.*

§ 419. 3. The *Partitive Genitive* (§ 408, 4) is used with many verbs which *only partially* affect the object of the action:

a) With all verbs which contain the idea of *sharing* : μετέχω (μέτεστί μοι), *I have a share in;* μεταλαμβάνω, *I take a share in;* μεταδίδωμι, *I give a share* (τῆς λείας, *of the booty*); κοινωνέω, *I share* (compare § 414, 5); Hom. σῖτον δ' αἰδοίη ταμίη παρέθηκε χαριζομένη παρεόντων, *the modest stewardess brought bread supplying from the store.*

Obs.—ὄζω, *I smell*, also belongs to these : μύρων ὄζει, *he smells of myrrh.*

b) With verbs which denote *touching, laying hold of, seizing:* ἅπτομαι, ψαύω, *I touch;* ἔχομαι, *I hold by, border* (τινός) *on something;* ἀντέχομαι, ἐπιλαμβάνομαι, *I lay hold of;* λαμβάνω τινὰ τῆς χειρός, *I seize one by the hand;* ἄρχομαι, *I begin* (τῆς παιδείας, *with the education*); poet. θανόντων οὐδὲν ἄλγος ἅπτεται, *no pain touches the dead.*

c) With verbs which denote *striving, aiming at:* στοχάζομαι τοῦ σκοποῦ, *I aim at the goal;* ὀρέγομαι; *I strive;* διψάω, *I thirst;* τυγχάνω, *I hit, attain* (ἔτυχε τῶν ἄθλων, *he won the prizes*); ἐφικνοῦμαι, *I reach, attain;* ἥκω, *I have attained* (Herod. δυνάμιος, *power*).

d) With verbs which denote *enjoying:* ἐσθίω, *I eat;* πίνω, *I drink;* γεύω, *I give a taste;* ἑστιάω, *I entertain;* ἀπολαύω, *I enjoy* (μεγίστων ἀγαθῶν, *the greatest blessings*); ἑνὸς ἀνδρὸς εὖ φρονήσαντος πολλοὶ ἂν ἀπολαύσειαν, *many would enjoy a man who has thought sensibly.*

e) With verbs denoting the opposites of the ideas enumerated under *a—d*, that is, the *exclusion* from a share in something : ἀπέχομαι, *I refrain* (σίτου, *abstineo cibo*); χωρίζω, *I separate;* εἴργω, *I keep off;* στερίσκω, *I deprive;* παύομαι, *I cease;* εἴκω, παραχωρέω, *I yield;* λύω, *I loose;*

ἐλευθερόω, *I free;* φείδομαι, *I spare;* ἁμαρτάνω, *ἀποτυγ*-
χάνω, *I miss;* ψεύδομαι, σφάλλομαι, *I am deceived* (τῆς
ἐλπίδος, *in my hope*).

Obs.—Many of these verbs are also joined with an Accusative
when an object is to be expressed as *wholly* encompassed by the
action: πλεῖστον μέρος τινὸς μετέχειν, *to have the greatest part in
any thing;* πίνω οἶνον, *I drink wine;* οἴνου, *some wine;* λαγχάνω
τι, *I attain something;* τινός, *a share in something.*

§ 420. 4. The Genitive is joined with many verbs denoting a *sensuous* or *moral perception* or *emotion* (compare § 414, 3), as: ἀκούω, ἀκροάομαι, *I hear;* αἰσθάνομαι,
I perceive; μιμνήσκομαι, *I remember* (τοῦ φίλου, *memini
amici*); ἐπιλανθάνομαι, *I forget;* μέλει μοί τινος, ἐπιμελέομαι, *I am concerned about something, I care;* ἐντρέπομαι,
Hom. ἀλέγω, ἀλεγίζω, *I concern myself;* ἀμελέω, *I neglect;* ὀλιγωρέω, *I care little about;* ἐράω, *I love* (§ 419, c);
ἐπιθυμέω, *I desire;* πυνθάνομαί τί τινος, *I learn something
about one.*

Obs.—The Accusative also is admissible with several of these
verbs : with ἀκούω, if the object is directly audible : φθόγγον, *a
sound*, but τοῦ διδασκάλου, *the teacher.*

§ 421. 5. With verbs of *estimating, buying, selling,* etc.,
the Genitive denotes the *value* or *price* (compare § 408, 6,
and § 417): ὁ δοῦλος πέντε μνῶν τιμᾶται, *the slave is valued
at five minœ;* πολλοῦ ὠνεῖσθαι, *magni emere;* ταλάντου
ἀποδόσθαι, *to sell for a talent.*

§ 422. 6. With verbs of *judicial proceedings* the Genitive denotes the *cause* (§ 408, 7, § 414, 5): κλοπῆς γράφεσθαι αἰσχρόν, *furti accusari turpe est;* φόνου διώκειν, *to
prosecute for murder;* φεύγει παρανόμων, *he is charged
with violating the law;* ἀπέφυγε κακηγορίας, *he was acquitted of libel;* ἑάλωσαν προδοσίας, *proditionis condemnati sunt.*

Obs.—With verbs of emotion the Genitive likewise expresses the
cause, as : θαυμάζω σε τῆς σωφροσύνης, *I admire thee for thy moderation;* Hom. χωόμενος γυναικός, *angry about the woman.*

§ 423. 7. The Genitive is also joined with verbs which imply the meaning of a Comparative (§ 416), as: κρατέω (κρείττων εἰμί), ἄρχω (Κροῖσος Λυδῶν ἦρχεν, *Croesus ruled over the Lydians*); βασιλεύω, *I rule ;* περίειμι, περιγίγνομαι, *I am superior ;* ἡττάομαι (ἥττων εἰμί), *I am inferior ;* λείπομαι, ὑστερέω, *I am behind ;* διαφέρω τινός, *differo ab aliquo ;* βαρβάρων Ἕλληνας ἄρχειν εἰκός, *it is reasonable that Hellenes should rule over barbarians.*

§ 424. 8. The Genitive is joined with verbs compounded with prepositions, which either always, or in the sense which they have in the compound verb, require the Genitive (compare Chapter XVII.): ἐκβάλλω τινὰ τιμῆς, *I eject some one from office ;* προστατεύει τῆς πόλεως, *he presides over the state ;* ἰσχὺν τοῦ δικαίου προτίθησιν, *he prefers might before right ;* καταφρονεῖν τινος, *to despise any one ;* κατηγορεῖν τί τινος, *to accuse one of a thing ;* πάτριον ἦν τῇ Ἀθηναίων πόλει προεστάναι τῶν Ἑλλήνων, *it was a hereditary custom for the city of the Athenians to be at the head of the Hellenes.*

4. *Freer use of the Genitive.*

§ 425. The Genitive, without immediate connection with a noun or verb, expresses:

1. *Place* (local Genitive), almost exclusively in the language of poetry, and that either the place *from* which something is removed : ἵστασθε βάθρων, *get up from the steps ;* ὑπάγειν τῆς ὁδοῦ, *to go out of the way* (compare § 419, e) ;—or the space *within which* something takes place (compare §§ 412, 415): τῆς Ἰωνίας τοῦτο αἰσχρὸν νενόμισται, *within Ionia that is considered disgraceful ;* Hom. νέφος οὐ φαίνετο πάσης γαίης, *no cloud appeared within the compass of the whole earth ;* ἔρχονται πεδίοιο, *they go through or within the plain* (compare the German *ich gehe des Weges*).
On another local Genitive, see § 412.

§ 426. **2.** *Time* (temporal Genitive), in which case it is a Partitive Genitive expressing the *whole of a space of time* (§ 412) within which something takes place: τρὶς τοῦ ἐνιαυτοῦ, *thrice in the year;* ἡμέρας, *by day;* νυκτός, *by night;* τοῦ αὐτοῦ χειμῶνος, *in the same winter;* τοῦ λοιποῦ, *for the future;* χρόνου συχνοῦ, *for some time;* ἑκάστου ἔτους, *each year.*

§ 427. **3.** *Cause* (causal Genitive, compare § 408, 7, § 422), in exclamations: οἴμοι τῆς τύχης, *alas! for my fortune* (compare the German *O des Leides*); and in Infinitives with the Genitive of the Article (in order to). § 574, 3; *Obs.*

§ 428. **4.** Occasion, time, circumstances, etc., as an *absolute Genitive,* in connection with *participles,* just like the absolute Ablative in Latin: Κύρου βασιλεύοντος, *Cyro regnante,* § 584 (compare the German: *stehenden Fusses*).

Obs.—The absolute Genitive very rarely occurs, like the absolute Ablative of the Latins, without a participle; when the verb *to be* occurs in the clause the participle ὤν is to be used: *te puero,* σοῦ παιδὸς ὄντος.

E) *The Dative.*

§ 429. The Dative denotes, in general, the person or thing more *remotely connected* with an action.

Obs.—The Dative, therefore, depends just as often on verbs as on adjectives (adverbs), but very rarely on a substantive.

§ 430. **1.** Dative of the *person concerned.*

As in Latin and English, so in Greek, the person more remotely affected by something is in the Dative, and:

a) with transitive verbs it is the so-called *indirect object:* Hom. ἑπτὰ δέ οἱ δώσω εὐναιόμενα πτολίεθρα, *and I will give him seven flourishing cities.*

b) with intransitive verbs it expresses the person or a thing conceived as a person to which the action refers:

πρέπει μοί τι, *a thing becomes me;* δεῖ μοί τινος, *I need something;* ἐμοὶ οὕτω δοκεῖ ἔχειν, *it seems to me to be so;* βοηθῶ τοῖς συμμάχοις, succurro sociis; πείθου τοῖς νόμοις, *obey the laws;* εὔχεσθε τοῖς θεοῖς, *pray to the gods;* μέμφομαι τοῖς μαθηταῖς, *I reproach the scholars.*

Obs.—Substantives derived from such verbs are sometimes followed by the Dative: ἡ ἐν τῷ πολέμῳ τοῖς συμμάχοις βοήθεια, *the help to the allies in the war.*

c) with Adjectives: ὁ ἀγαθὸς τῷ ἀγαθῷ μόνος φίλος, *the good alone is dear to the good.*

431. 2. Dative of *interest.*

The Dative denotes the person *for* whom—for whose interest—something is or takes place; hence

a) the person *benefited or injured* (dat. commodi, incommodi): πᾶς ἀνὴρ αὑτῷ πονεῖ, *every man toils for himself;* φθόνος μέγιστον κακὸν τοῖς ἔχουσιν αὐτόν, *envy is the greatest evil to them that have it.*

432. b) the *possessor* with εἰμί, γίγνομαι, and similar verbs: πολλοί μοι φίλοι εἰσίν, *I have many friends.*

Obs.—The possessive Dative is sometimes, like the Genitive, joined with a Substantive: Herod., οἵ σφι βόες, *their oxen.*

§ 433. c) the *sympathizing* person (*ethical Dative*): poet. ὦ τέκνον, ἦ βέβηκεν ἥμιν ὁ ξένος; *O child, has the stranger left us?* τί γὰρ πατήρ μοι πρέσβυς ἐν δόμοισι δρᾷ; *for what is my aged father doing in the house?*

§ 434. d) the *acting* person with passive verbs (commonly ὑπό with the Genitive), which is then to be viewed as one interested in the action: Hom. πολέες δάμεν Ἕκτορι δίῳ, *many were overcome by godlike Hector;* τί πέπρακται τοῖς ἄλλοις; *what has been done by the rest?* This Dative is regularly joined with the Verbal Adj. in -τέος: ἐμοὶ πολεμητέον ἐστίν, *mihi pugnandum est.*

§ 435. e) the person remotely connected with an action: τέθνηχ' ὑμῖν πάλαι, *he died to you long ago;* Hom. πᾶσίν κεν Τρώεσσι κῦδος ἄροιο, *thou mightest get thee fame with all Trojans;* Hom. τοῖσιν ἀνέστη, *among them arose;* ὑπολαμβάνειν δεῖ τῷ τοιούτῳ ὅτι εὐήθης ἐστίν, *in regard to such a one we must suppose him simple.*

Obs.—In this manner *participles* are most frequently used, partly with, partly without, an accompanying noun : Hom. ἡμῖν εἰνατός ἐστι περιτροπέων ἐνιαυτὸς ἐνθάδε μιμνόντεσσιν, *it is the ninth year for us lingering here;* ἡ διαβάντι τὸν ποταμὸν πρὸς ἑσπέραν ὁδός, *the road westward when you have crossed the river;* γίγνεταί τι ἐμοὶ βουλομένῳ, *something happens to me as I wish;* συνελόντι or ὡς συνελόντι εἰπεῖν, *to speak briefly.*

§ 436. 3. Dative of *community.*

With verbs, adjectives, and adverbs, which denote community, agreement, friendly or hostile meeting, the person or thing *with* which such a community, agreement, or such a meeting takes place, is in the Dative.

a) *Verbs* of this kind are : κοινωνέω, *I share* (τινί τινος, *something with one*); συμφωνέω, ὁμολογέω, συνᾴδω, ὁμονοέω, *I agree;* ὁμοιόομαι, *I resemble.;* ὁμιλέω, *I associate with;* διαλέγομαι, *I converse;* διαφέρομαι, *I differ;* μάχομαι, *I fight;* ἐρίζω, *I dispute;* τὰ ἔργα οὐ συμφωνεῖ τοῖς λόγοις, *the deeds do not harmonize with the words;* poet. κακοῖσιν μὴ προςομίλει ἀνδράσιν, ἀλλ' αἰεὶ τῶν ἀγαθῶν ἔχεο, *with bad men do not associate, but always hold to the good.*

b) *Adjectives:* ἴσος, *like;* ὅμοιος, παραπλήσιος, *similar;* ὁ αὐτός, *the same;* οἰκεῖος, ἴδιος, *peculiar;* κοινός, *common* (compare 414, 1); ὁμώνυμος, *of like name;* συνώνυμος, *of like meaning;* διάφορος, *different;* ἐναντίος, *opposite:* ὡπλισμένοι ἦσαν τοῖς αὐτοῖς Κύρῳ ὅπλοις, *they were armed with the same weapons as Cyrus.*

c) *Adverbs:* besides those derived from the adjectives just mentioned, especially ἅμα, *at the same time;* ὁμοῦ, *together:* ἅμα τῷ ἑταίρῳ, *at the same time with his friend.*

§ 437. The Dative is used with many verbs which, com-

§ 440. THE DATIVE. 253

pounded with prepositions, denote a contact or union, especially with such as are compounded with ἐν, σύν, ἐπί, yet also with those compounded with πρός, παρά, περί, ὑπό, as: ἐπιστήμην ἐμποιεῖν τῇ ψυχῇ, *to bring knowledge into the soul;* ἐπικεῖσθαί τινι, *to press upon, to urge, one;* ἐπιτιμᾶν τινί τι, *to reproach one with something;* προςιέναι τῷ δήμῳ, *to come before the people;* παρίστασθαι, παρεῖναί τινι, *to support one;* περιπίπτειν τινί, *to meet one.*

§ 438. 4. The *Instrumental* Dative, answering to the Latin Ablative, denotes that *by* or *by means of* which an action is brought about: hence

a) the *means* or *instrument* (compare διά, § 458): Hom. τὸν μὲν κατὰ στῆθος βάλε δουρί, *the one he struck on the breast with the spear;* ὁρῶμεν τοῖς ὀφθαλμοῖς, *we see with the eyes;* οὐδεὶς ἔπαινον ἡδοναῖς ἐκτήσατο, *no one gained praise by pleasures;* ζημιοῦν τινα θανάτῳ, *to punish one with death;* Hom. τίσειαν Δαναοὶ ἐμὰ δάκρυα σοῖσι βέλεσσιν, *may the Danai pay for my tears by thy darts.*

Obs.—Hence the Dative is used with χρῆσθαι, *to make use of;* as the Ablative with *uti* in Latin. A second predicative Dative is often added (§ 361, 10): τούτων τισὶ φύλαξιν ἐχρῆτο, *some of them he used as guards.*

§ 439. *b)* the *operating power* or *cause* from which an action proceeds: ἄνθρωπος φύσει πολιτικόν, *man (is) by nature fitted for the state;* πολλάκις ἀγνοίᾳ ἁμαρτάνομεν, *we often err from ignorance;* φόβῳ, *from fear.*

Obs.—With verbs of emotion, the Dative expresses the ground or occasion of the emotion: ἥδομαι, χαίρω τῇ μουσικῇ, *I delight in music;* λυποῦμαι, *I am grieved;* χαλεπαίνω, *I am angry;* στέργω, ἀγαπῶ, *I am satisfied* (*with* something); αἰσχύνομαι, *I am ashamed* (*about* something).

§ 440. *c)* the *measure, by which* a thing is measured, *by which* one thing surpasses another, *by which* it is distinguished: τὰ μέλλοντα κρίνομεν τοῖς γεγενημένοις, *the fu-*

ture we judge of by the past; δέκα έτεσι πρὸ τῆς ἐν Σαλαμῖνι μάχης· οἱ Ἀθηναῖοι ἐν Μαραθῶνι ἐνίκησαν, ten years before the battle of Salamis the Athenians conquered at Marathon; πολλῷ μείζων, multo major (also πολύ, § 404, Obs.); διαφέρειν τινὸς φρονήσει, to differ from any one in insight.

§ 441. 5. The *freer use* of the Dative expresses:

a) the way and manner, or an accompanying circumstance: τούτῳ τῷ τρόπῳ, in this way; βίᾳ, by force; σπουδῇ, with zeal; σιγῇ, in silence; ἔργῳ, in fact; τῷ ὄντι, in truth; ἰδίᾳ, privatim; δημοσίᾳ, publice; Hom. νηπιέῃσι, in his folly (§ 362, Obs.).

Obs.—The Dative with αὐτός should be particularly noticed: ὁ Φίλιππος πεντακοσίους ἱππέας ἔλαβεν αὐτοῖς τοῖς ὅπλοις, Philip took five hundred horse together with their armor. (Compare the Dative of community, § 436.)

§ 442. *b*) The *place where* something happens is expressed by the Dative more rarely in prose than in poetry: Μαραθῶνι, at Marathon; Hom. Ἑλλάδι οἰκία ναίων, inhabiting his house in Hellas; Hom. τόξ᾽ ὤμοισιν ἔχων, having the bow on his shoulders; poet. ὁδοῖς, on the way.

§ 443. *c*) *Time* is expressed by the Dative as definitely limited in answer to the question *when*: τῇδε τῇ νυκτί, hac nocte; τῇ ὑστεραίᾳ, on the following day; τετάρτῳ ἔτει, in the fourth year; Ὀλυμπίοις, at the Olympic games; poet. χειμερίῳ νότῳ, in a stormy south wind.

Obs.—Notice the difference between the Accusative (§ 405) and the Genitive (§ 426), in their application to relations of time.

Chap. XVII.—The Prepositions.

§ 444. Prepositions have a double use. Either they are combined with a verb, to define the direction which the action of the verb takes, or they are used independently, and serve, in connection with different cases, to point out the relation of single words in a sentence to one another more distinctly than could be done by the cases alone.

§ 445. *Obs.* 1.—As the name *præpositio* (πρόθεσις) points to the first of these uses, those prepositions which are not combined with verbs, such as: ἄνευ, *without* (poet. δίχα, χωρίς); ἄχρι, μέχρι, *till;* μεταξύ, *between;* ἕνεκα, *on account of;* πλήν, *besides*, are called *spurious*. They are all used with the Genitive (compare § 415), except ὡς, *to*, which has the Accusative.

§ 446. *Obs.* 2.—All Prepositions were originally *adverbs;* many of them are still used as such in poetry, and a few even in prose: περί, *beyond, very;* μετά, *later;* πρός, *in addition*. On account of this origin, their position in Homer is very free; they may be separated from their verb as well as from their substantive : Hom. ἐν δ' αὐτὸς ἐδύσετο νώροπα χαλκόν, *and he himself put on the glittering brass;* ἀμφὶ δὲ χαῖται ὤμοις ἀΐσσονται, *and the manes wave around the shoulders*. On the *anastrophe* in placing the Prepositions behind, see § 90. In prose only περί is sometimes thus used.

§ 447. With regard to the cases joined with Prepositions, the following general rules are to be noticed:

1. The *Accusative* with Prepositions expresses the object *upon* which, *over* which, *toward* which an action extends (§§ 395, 405), and with many Prepositions the *goal* of an action itself (§ 406).

2. The *Genitive* frequently denotes the *place from* which an action proceeds (§ 425), often also a moral relation (§ 408, etc.), while it depends on other Prepositions in the same way as on the adverbs mentioned in § 415.

3. The *Dative* denotes a more external connection (§§ 435, 442).

General View of the Prepositions.

§ 448. I. Prepositions which can have only *one case:*
A) the *Accusative:* εἰς, ὡς.
B) the *Genitive:* ἀντί, ἀπό, ἐκ (ἐξ), πρό—ἄνευ, ἄχρι, μέχρι, μεταξύ, ἕνεκα, πλήν.
C) the *Dative:* ἐν, σύν (ξύν).

II. Prepositions which can have two cases:
A) the *Genitive* and *Accusative:* διά, κατά, ὑπέρ.
B) the *Dative* and *Accusative:* ἀνά.

III. Prepositions which can have all the *three* oblique cases: ἀμφί, ἐπί, μετά, παρά, περί, πρός, ὑπό.

I. Prepositions which can have only one Case.

§ 449. A) *Prepositions with the Accusative.*

1. εἰς or ἐς (Lat. *in,* c. Accus., and *inter*), *to, into;* points out the *goal toward* which the action is directed. The opposite is ἐξ, *out.* εἰς is used:

a) *of place:* οἱ Λακεδαιμόνιοι εἰσέβαλον εἰς τὴν Ἀττικήν, *the Lacedæmonians invaded Attica;* εἰς δικαστήριον εἰσιέναι, *to come into court;* λέγειν εἰς τὸ πλῆθος, *to speak to the multitude;* εἰς ἄνδρας ἐγγράφειν, *to enroll among men.* Compare ἐν, § 456, *a.*

b) *of time:* εἰς τὴν ὑστεραίαν, *in diem proximum, for the next day;* εἰς ἑσπέραν, *toward evening;* poet. ἔτος εἰς ἔτος, *year by year;* εἰς καιρόν, *for the right time.*

c) *of measure* and *number:* εἰς διακοσίους, *up to two hundred;* εἰς δύναμιν, *up to one's power, as much as is in one's power.*

d) *of purpose:* χρήσιμον εἰς τὸν πόλεμον, *useful for the war;* εἰς τόδε ἥκομεν, *for that we have come.*

In compounds it is to be translated by *into, in, to.*

§ 450. 2. ὡς (compare § 631), *to,* only of persons: Hom.

§ 453. PREPOSITIONS WITH THE GENITIVE. 257

αἰεὶ τὸν ὁμοῖον ἄγει θεὸς ὡς τὸν ὁμοῖον, *God always brings like to like.*

§ 451. B) *Prepositions with the Genitive.*

1. ἀντί (compare Hom. ἄντα, ἄντην, ἀντικρύ), originally *opposite to* (compare ἐν-αντί-ος), then *instead of, for :* Hom. ἀντὶ κασιγνήτου ξεῖνός θ' ἱκέτης τε τέτυκται, *a stranger and a suppliant is instead of a brother* (like a brother); ἀντὶ θνητοῦ σώματος ἀθάνατον δόξαν ἀλλάξασθαι, *to exchange a mortal body for immortal glory.*
In compounds it signifies *against.*

§ 452. 2. ἀπό (Lat. *ab, a*, Engl. *off*), *from*, in the sense of *separation, severance,* and *origin :*

a) of place : Hom. ἀφ' ἵππων ἆλτο χαμᾶζε, *he sprang off the chariot to the ground.*

b) of time : from, since : ἀπ' ἐκείνης τῆς ἡμέρας, *from that day.*

c) of cause : by, from, through : αὐτόνομος ἀπὸ τῆς εἰρήνης, *independent through the peace.*

Phrases : ἀπὸ σκοποῦ, *far from the goal;* ἀπὸ γνώμης, *contrary to expectation;* ἀπὸ στόματος λέγειν, *to speak from memory;* οἱ ἀπὸ σκηνῆς, *those of the stage, the actors.*
In compounds it signifies *from, off, away.*

§ 453. 3. ἐκ, before vowels ἐξ (Lat. *ex, e*), *out of* (opposed to εἰς), denotes removal from within or from among :

a) of place : ἐκ Σπάρτης φεύγει, *he is banished out of Sparta.*

b) of time : ἐκ παίδων, *from boyhood (a pueris).*

c) of origin : ἐκ πατρὸς χρηστοῦ ἐγένετο, *he sprang from a brave father;* seldom with a Passive verb : τιμᾶσθαι ἔκ τινος, *to be honored by any one.*

d) close connection and *conformity with : after, secundum :* λόγον ἐκ λόγου λέγειν, *to deliver speech after speech;*

ἐκ τῶν ὁμολογουμένων, *according to the agreement* (Lat. *secundum*).

Phrases: ἐκ δεξιᾶς, *on the right;* ἐξ ἴσου, *equally;* δῆσαι, κρεμάσαι τι ἔκ τινος, *to fasten, to hang one thing to another* (Lat. *pendēre ex, ab aliqua re*).

In compounds: *out, away*.

§ 454. 4. πρό (Lat. *pro*), *for, before, instead.*

a) *of place, before :* πρὸ θυρῶν, *before the door.*
b) *of time :* πρὸ τῆς μάχης, *before the battle.*
c) *of preference :* πρὸ τούτων τεθνάναι μᾶλλον ἂν ἕλοιτο, *he would choose death before this,* i. e., rather than this.
d) *for*, a rare use : πρὸ παίδων μάχεσθαι, *to fight for the children.*

Phrase : πρὸ πολλοῦ ποιεῖσθαι (*c*), *to prefer greatly.*
In compounds : *before, forth, beforehand, forward.*

§ 455. The spurious Prepositions :
5. ἄνευ, *without* (poet. χωρίς, δίχα, ἄτερ).
6. ἄχρι, μέχρι, *until.*
7. μεταξύ, *between.*
8. ἕνεκα, also ἕνεκεν, εἵνεκα (poet. οὕνεκα), *for the sake of* an *object* to be attained (Lat. *causā*): τῆς ὑγιείας ἕνεκα χρώμεθα τῷ ἰατρῷ, *we employ a physician for the sake of health.* (Compare διά with Acc., § 458, B.)
9. πλήν, *besides* (*præter*).

Obs.—πλήν is often used quite adverbially without governing a case : poet. οὐκ ἄρ' Ἀχαιοῖς ἄνδρες εἰσὶ πλὴν ὅδε; *have then the Achæans no men but this?* It might be πλὴν τοῦδε, *besides this?*

§ 456. C) *Prepositions with the Dative.*

1. ἐν (Hom. ἐνί, ἐν, Lat. *in*, c. Ablat., and *inter*), *in*, answers to the question *where?*

a) *of place :* ἐν Ἀθήναις, *in Athens;* also *among* (*inter*): ἐν τούτοις, *among them;* ἐν δήμῳ λέγειν, *to speak before the people* (compare § 449, *a*).

§ 458. PREPOSITIONS WITH THE GEN. AND ACC.

b) *of time :* ἐν τούτῳ τῷ ἔτει, *in that year.*
c) *a moral relation : with :* ἐν τῷ θεῷ τὸ τῆς μάχης τέλος, *the result of the battle rests with God.*

Phrases: ἡ ἐν Μαραθῶνι μάχη, *the battle at Marathon ;* ἐν τοῖς πρῶτος, *first by far ;* ἐν καιρῷ, *at the right time ;* ἐν προςθήκης μέρει, *in addition ;* ἐν χερσὶ τιθέναι, *to put into the hands* (compare Lat. *in mensa ponere*).
In compounds: *in, into, on.* The accented ἔνι = ἔνεστι signifies *it is in, it exists, it is possible.*

§ 457. 2. σύν or ξύν (Lat. *cum*), *with,* denotes companionship (opposed to ἄνευ, compare μετά with Gen., § 464, B) ; σὺν Ἀθήνῃ ἐνίκησεν, *he conquered (with the help of) Athene ;* σὺν νόμῳ, *in accordance with the law* (opposed to παρά with Acc., § 465, C, *b*).
In compounds : *with, together.*

II. PREPOSITIONS WHICH CAN HAVE TWO CASES.

The Genitive and Accusative.

Obs.—Here, as every where in what follows, that use of a Preposition is placed first in which its original meaning is most manifest.

§ 458. 1. διά (akin to δύο, as *between* is to *two* [*twain*]), originally *between,* then *through.*

A) with the *Genitive :*

a) *of space :* most frequently *through* (Lat. *per*): Hom. διὰ μὲν ἀσπίδος ἦλθε φαεινῆς ὄβριμον ἔγχος, *through the glittering shield pierced the mighty lance.*
b) *instrumental : by* or *with :* διὰ τῶν ὀφθαλμῶν ὁρῶμεν, *by (by means of) the eyes we see* (compare § 438).
c) *of space* and *time : among* (*inter*), *during, in :* διὰ χειρῶν ἔχειν, *to have in hand ;* διὰ νυκτός, *during night ;* διὰ φιλίας ἰέναι, *to be on friendly terms.*
Phrases: διὰ στόματος ἔχειν, *to have in the mouth,* to

be talking about; δι' οὐδενὸς ποιεῖσθαι, *to deem as nothing;* διὰ μακροῦ, *after a long interval, interruption.*

B) with the *Accusative:*

a) of space and *time,* almost exclusively in the poets: *through, during:* Hom. διὰ δώματα, *through the rooms;* διὰ νύκτα, *during night.*

b) usually *causal: on account of* (the operating cause) (compare ἕνεκα, § 455, 8): διὰ τὴν νόσον χρώμεθα τῷ ἰατρῷ, *we employ the physician on account of the illness.*

Phrases: αὐτὸς δι' ἑαυτόν, *by himself;* διὰ τί; *why?*

In compounds, διά is *through,* or denotes *separation,* like Lat. *dis-* : διαφέρω=*differre,* διαιρέω, *I sever.*

§ 459. 2. κατά (compare Adv. κάτω, *down*), originally *downward, down* (the opposite to ἀνά).

A) with the *Genitive:*

a) of space: down from: Hom. βῆ δὲ κατ' Οὐλύμποιο καρήνων, *he came down from the heights of Olympus;* below (*sub*): τὰ κατὰ γῆς, *things below the earth.*

b) tropically: *about, against:* λέγειν κατά τινος, *to speak about, against one.*

Phrases: πόλιν κατ' ἄκρας ἑλεῖν, *to capture a city completely;* κατὰ νώτου, *behind.*

B) with the *Accusative* it denotes in its most general sense extension *over,* relation *to,* direction *toward* something:

a) of place: κατὰ ῥόον, *down a stream;* κατὰ γῆν καὶ θάλασσαν, *by land and sea;* Hom. Ζεὺς ἔβη κατὰ δαῖτα, *Zeus went to the feast.*

b) of time: κατ' ἐκεῖνον τὸν χρόνον, *at that time;* οἱ καθ' ἡμᾶς, *our contemporaries.*

c) of other relations: κατὰ τοῦτον τὸν τρόπον, *in this way;* κατὰ πάντα, *in every respect;* κατὰ δύναμιν, *according to ability, as much as possible;* κατὰ τοὺς νόμους, *in accordance with the laws;* κατ' ἐμέ, *as regards me;* κατὰ Πίνδαρον ἄριστον ὕδωρ, *according to Pindar, water is best.*

§ 461. PREPOSITIONS WITH THE DAT. AND ACC. 261

d) *distributive* in divisions: Hom. κατὰ φῦλα, *by tribes;* κατὰ τρεῖς, *by threes;* καθ' ἡμέραν, *daily.*

In compounds: *down, downward, against, toward*, very often untranslatable.

§ 460. **3.** ὑπέρ, Hom. also ὑπείρ (Lat. *super*), radical meaning *over.*

A) with the *Genitive:*

a) *of space:* ὁ ἥλιος ὑπὲρ ἡμῶν πορεύεται, *the sun passes over us.*

b) tropically, *for:* μάχεσθαι ὑπέρ τινος, *to fight for any one* (originally *over*, e. g., over a corpse): ὁ ὑπὲρ τῆς πατρίδος κίνδυνος, *the danger for one's country; instead of:* ἐγὼ ὑπὲρ σοῦ ἀποκρινοῦμαι, *I will answer instead of you.*

B) with the *Accusative:*

over, beyond—of space and *measure:* Hom. ὑπὲρ οὐδὸν ἐβήσετο, *he went over or beyond the threshold;* ὑπὲρ δύναμιν, *beyond (his) power.*

In compounds: *over, away over, excessively, for.*

With the Dative and Accusative.

§ 461. **4.** ἀνά (compare adv. ἄνω, *above*), originally *upon, up* (opposed to κατά).

A) with the *Dative* only poet., *on the top of, upon:* Hom. χρυσέῳ ἀνὰ σκήπτρῳ, *on the top of a golden staff.*

B) with the *Accusative* ἀνά denotes the direction *upward, up toward* something, then spreading out *over* something (compare κατά).

a) *of space:* ἀνὰ ῥόον, *up the stream;* ἀνὰ πᾶσαν τὴν γῆν, *over the whole earth, over the whole country.*

b) *of time:* ἀνὰ πᾶσαν τὴν ἡμέραν, *per totum diem.*

c) *tropically:* ἀνὰ λόγον, *in accordance with.*

d) *distributive:* ἀνὰ τέτταρας, *by fours* (four men *deep*, compare κατά, § 459, *d*).

Phrase: ἀνὰ στόμα ἔχειν, *to have in the mouth, to be talking about* (compare διά).

In compounds: *up, upward, again, back.*

III. Prepositions which can have three Cases.

Obs.—The original meaning is usually most manifest in connection with the Dative.

§ 462. 1. ἀμφί (Lat. *amb-*, German *um*, akin to ἄμφω, *both*), radical meaning *around* (*i. e.*, on both sides, compare περί).

A) with the *Dative:*
only poet.: Hom. ἱδρώσει τελαμὼν ἀμφὶ στήθεσσι, *the belt around the breast will sweat;* ἀμφὶ φόβῳ, *from fear.*

B) with the *Genitive:*
Hom. ἀμφὶ φιλότητος ἀείδειν, *to sing about love.*

C) with the *Accusative:*
of place, time, measure, occupation: ἀμφὶ τὰ ὅρια, *about the boundaries;* ἀμφὶ τοῦτον τὸν χρόνον, *about this time;* ἀμφὶ τὰ ἑξήκοντα, *circiter sexaginta;* ἀμφὶ δεῖπνον πονεῖν, *to be occupied about a meal.*

Phrase: οἱ ἀμφί τινα, *any one with his attendants;* hence even: οἱ ἀμφὶ Πλάτωνα, *Plato and his followers.*

In compounds: *about, around, on two sides, doubly.*

§ 463. 2. ἐπί, radical meaning *upon, on, on the surface, by.*

A) with the *Dative:*
a) of space: Hom. ἐπὶ χθονὶ σῖτον ἔδοντες, *eating bread on earth;* ἐπὶ τῇ θαλάσσῃ οἰκεῖν, *to dwell by the sea.*

b) of time: ἐπὶ τούτοις, *thereupon.*

c) of an ethical relation: ἐπὶ τοῖς πράγμασιν εἶναι, *to preside over the business;* ἐπὶ τοῖς πολεμίοις εἶναι, *to be in the power of the enemy;* ἐπί τινι χαίρειν, *to rejoice at a thing;* especially also of *purpose:* ἐπὶ παιδείᾳ τοῦτο ἔμαθες, *you learned this for education;* and of *condition:* ἐπὶ τόκοις δανείζειν, *to lend on interest;* ἐπὶ τούτῳ, *on this condition.*

B) with the *Genitive:*
a) of space, in answer to the question *where:* Κῦρος

§ 465. PREPOSIT. WHICH CAN HAVE THREE CASES. 263

προὐφαίνετο ἐφ' ἅρματος, *Cyrus appeared on a chariot;* and to the question *whither:* ἐπὶ Σάμου πλεῖν, *to sail to Samos.* (Compare § 419, c.)

b) of time: ἐπὶ Κροίσου ἄρχοντος, *in the reign of Crœsus;* also in many connections: *near, by.*

C) with the *Accusative:*
on, on-to: ἀναβαίνειν ἐφ' ἵππον, *to mount (on-to) a horse;* ἐπὶ δεξιά, *on the right.*

Phrases: ὡς ἐπὶ τὸ πολύ, *for the most part;* τὸ ἐπ' ἐμέ, *for my part.*

In compounds: *on, at, by, in addition, be-*, very often untranslatable.

§ 464. 3. μετά (German *mit*), radical meaning *in the midst.*

A) with the *Dative:*
in poet. only: *amid, among (inter):* Hom. Ἕκτορα, ὃς θεὸς ἔσκε μετ' ἀνδράσι, *Hector, who was a god among men.*

B) with the *Genitive:*
with, in the sense of participation *with* (compare σύν, § 457): μετὰ τῶν ξυμμάχων κινδυνεύειν, *to fight with* (in alliance with) *the allies;* μετὰ δακρύων, *with tears.*

C) with the *Accusative:*
a) into the midst, among: poet.: Hom. ἰὼν μετὰ ἔθνος ἑταίρων, *going among the crowd of companions.*

b) usually *after:* Hom. οἴχονται μετὰ δεῖπνον, *they go after (for) a meal;* μετὰ τὸν Πελοποννησιακὸν πόλεμον, *after the Peloponnesian War.*

c) seldom *in* (as with the Dative): μετὰ χεῖρας ἔχειν, *to have in hand* (compare διά): μεθ' ἡμέραν, *interdiu.*

In compounds: *with, after, trans-* (μετατιθέναι, *transpose*).

§ 465. 4. παρά (Hom. πάρ, παραί), radical meaning *beside, near.*

A) with the *Dative:*
at or *near:* Hom. παρὰ νηυσὶ κορωνίσι μιμνάζειν, *to linger*

near the curved ships; καὶ παρ' ἐμοί τις ἐμπειρία ἐστίν, I also have some experience (with me also is, etc.).

B) with the *Genitive*:

a) *from*, with verbs of motion, and such as denote receiving either bodily or mentally: Hom. ἀπονοστεῖν παρὰ νηῶν, *to return from the ships;* λαμβάνειν, μανθάνειν παρά τινος, *to receive, learn from some one.*

b) *by*, very rare, and only poet.: ναιετῶν παρ' Ἰσμήνου ῥείθρων, *dwelling by the waters of the Ismenus.*

C) with the *Accusative*:

a) *to*: Hom. τὼ δ' αὖτις ἴτην παρὰ νῆας, *they went again to the ships.*

b) *along, near by*:

of place: Hom. παρὰ θῖνα θαλάσσης, *along the sea beach.*

of time: *during*: παρ' ὅλον τὸν βίον, *per totam vitam, during the whole of life;*

compared with: δεῖ τὰς πράξεις παρ' ἀλλήλας τιθέναι, *you must put the acts by the side of* (or compare with) *one another;* with the comparative: μεῖζόν τι παρὰ τοῦτο, *something greater than this;*

on account of (compare *propter, near,* and *on account of*): παρὰ τὴν ἡμετέραν ἀμέλειαν Φίλιππος αὔξεται, *on account of our neglect Philip becomes great.*

Taken negatively; *besides:* ἔχομέν τι παρὰ ταῦτα ἄλλο λέγειν, *we have something else to say besides this;*

contrary to (opposed to κατά with the Acc.: παρὰ τὸν νόμον, *contrary to the law,* properly past the law, by evading the law.

Phrases: παρὰ μικρόν, *nearly;* παρ' οὐδὲν ποιεῖσθαι, *to deem as nothing.*

In compounds: *near, at, past, beyond, over* (παραβαίνειν, *overstep*).

§ 466. 5. περί (Hom. adv. περί, *very*=Lat. *per* in *permagnus*), radical meaning *around* (from above), compare ἀμφί.

§ 467. PREPOSIT. WHICH CAN HAVE THREE CASES. 265

A) with the *Dative:*
round, around, near, for: Hom. περὶ Σκαιῇσι πύλῃσι, *round the Skœan gate;* περὶ τοῖς φιλτάτοις κυβεύειν, *to gamble for what is dearest.* Hom. περὶ κῆρι, *at heart;* περὶ φόβῳ, *from fear.*

B) with the *Genitive:*
a) mostly in a figurative sense, *about,* Lat. *de: τίνα* δόξαν ἔχεις περὶ τούτων; *what opinion have you about this?* βουλεύονται περὶ τοῦ πολέμου, *they consult about the war.*

b) in Hom. *over, above:* περὶ πάντων ἔμμεναι ἄλλων, *to be above all others;* hence the prose phrases: περὶ πολλοῦ ποιεῖσθαι, *to place above much, i. e., estimate highly;* περὶ οὐδενὸς ποιεῖσθα, *place above nothing, i. e., estimate at nothing at all.*

C) with the *Accusative:*
almost the same as ἀμφί (§ 462): περὶ Αἴγυπτον (*around, i. e.,* every where in *Egypt*), *about the country of Egypt;* figuratively: *in regard to, about, concerning:* περὶ φιλοσοφίαν σπουδάζειν, *to be zealous about philosophy.*

In compounds (with adjectives = Latin *per-*): *round, round about, besides, over.*

§ 467. 6. πρός (Hom. προτί, ποτί), akin to πρό, radical meaning *at, to* (toward the front), compare παρά.

A) with the *Dative:*
a) at, near: ὁ Κῦρος ἦν πρὸς Βαβυλῶνι, *Cyrus was near Babylon.*

b) on, to: Hom. ποτὶ δὲ σκῆπτρον βάλε γαίῃ, *he threw the staff on the ground;* τὸν νοῦν προςέχετε πρὸς τούτῳ, *give your mind to this.*

c) besides, in addition to: πρὸς τούτοις, *besides this;* πρὸς τοῖς ἄλλοις, *besides the rest.*

B) with the *Genitive:*
a) with, in the sense of community: Hom. πρὸς γὰρ Διός εἰσιν ἅπαντες ξεῖνοί τε πτωχοί τε, *with* (protected by)

M

Zeus are all strangers and the poor; πρός τινος είναι, to be with (on the side of) any one; πρὸς ιατροῦ ἐστιν, it is with (belongs to) a physician, medici est; πρός τινος λέγειν, to speak for (in behalf of) any one; πρὸς θεῶν, with (in presence of, by) the gods, per deos, form of an oath.

b) toward (versus): πρὸς μεσημβρίας, toward the south, compare πρός with Acc.

c) from, by (compare παρά with Gen.): ὄλβος πρὸς θεῶν, blessing from the gods; sometimes with Passive verbs: πρός τινος φιλεῖσθαι, to be loved by some one.

C) with the *Accusative*:

a) to: ἔρχονται πρὸς ἡμᾶς πρέσβεις, embassadors come to us; πρὸς τὸν δῆμον ἀγορεύειν, to speak to the people.

b) toward, against (versus, adversus, erga): πρὸς βορρᾶν, toward the north (compare πρός with Gen.); δικάζεσθαι πρός τινα, to enter an action against any one; πιστῶς διακεῖσθαι πρός τινα, to be faithfully disposed toward some one; πρὸς βασιλέα σπονδὰς ποιεῖσθαι, to make a treaty toward (with) the king.

c) in regard to, according to: διαφέρειν πρὸς ἀρετήν, to differ in regard to virtue; πρὸς τὰ κάλλιστα τῶν ὑπαρχόντων δεῖ τὰ λοιπὰ πράττειν, we ought to arrange the future according to the best of the present means; πρὸς ταῦτα, according to this.

Phrases: πρὸς ἡδονήν, according to pleasure; πρὸς χάριν, in favor of; πρὸς βίαν, by force; οὐδὲν πρὸς ἐμέ, nothing to me.

In compounds: to, in addition, near, together with.

§ 468. 7. ὑπό (Hom. also ὑπαί, Lat. *sub*), radical meaning *under, below*.

A) with the *Dative*:

under: Hom. τῶν ὑπὸ ποσσὶ μέγα στεναχίζετο γαῖα, under their feet the earth loudly groaned; ὑπ' Ἀθηναίοις εἶναι, to be under (subject to) the Athenians; poet. χερσὶν ὑφ' ἡμετέρῃσιν ἁλοῦσα, (Troy) *conquered under* (by) *our hands*.

B) with the *Genitive*:
  a) under, in space: ὑπὸ γῆς, *under the earth;* in the sense of dependency: ὑπ' αὐλητῶν χορεύειν, *to dance under* (the guidance of) *flute-players;* hence
  b) by, with Passives and verbs of Passive meaning: ἡ πόλις ἑάλω ὑπὸ τῶν Ἑλλήνων, *the city was taken by the Hellenes;* πολλοὶ ἀπέθανον ὑπὸ τῶν βαρβάρων, *many were killed by the barbarians.*
  c) from, because of : ὑπὸ γήρως ἀσθενὴς ἦν, *he was weak from old age.*

C) with the *Accusative:*
  a) under: Hom. ὣς εἰπὼν ὑπὸ πόντον ἐδύσετο κυμαίνοντα, *having thus spoken, he dived under the billowy sea;* ὑπὸ τὸ ὄρος ηὐλίζοντο, *they spent the night under* (at the foot of) *the mountain.*
  b) of time; toward (Lat. *sub*): ὑπὸ νύκτα, *toward night;* ὑπὸ τὴν νύκτα, *during the night.*

In compounds: *under, down under, gradually, secretly,* often untranslatable.

Chap. XVIII.—The Pronouns.

§ 469. 1. The Nominative of the *Personal Pronouns* is used, as in Latin, only when the person is to be mentioned with special emphasis: καὶ σὺ ὄψει αὐτόν, *tu quoque eum videbis, i. e.,* οὐ μόνον ἐγώ (*not merely I*).

§ 470. 2. The place of the *Possessive* Pronoun is frequently supplied by the article (§ 373). On the article with the Possessive Pronoun, § 388.

a) Instead of the Possessive Pronoun, the Greek likes to use the Genitive of the corresponding Personal Pronoun. Such a Genitive, when the substantive to which it belongs has the article, usually stands either *before* the article or *after* the substantive: σοῦ ὁ υἱός or ὁ υἱός σου, *thy son*, not ὁ σοῦ υἱός.

b) As the Possessive Pronoun approaches very near to a possessive Genitive (§ 408, 2), it may be qualified by a Genitive: τἀμὰ δυστήνου κακά, *my ills, the unfortunate one's* [*mea miseri mala*].

§ 471. 3. The *Reflexive Pronoun* refers either to the subject of the clause in which it occurs : ὦ ἀγαθέ, μὴ ἀγνόει σεαυτόν, *good friend, be not ignorant of thyself;* or, in dependent clauses, it refers back to the subject of the *leading* clause : εἱςιέναι ἐκέλευσεν, εἰ μέλλοις σὺν ἑαυτῷ ἐκπλεῖν, *he bade you enter, if you were going to sail away with him* (*secum*).

Obs. a)—Instead of the Reflexive Pronoun, the usual Personal Pronouns also *may* be employed : δοκῶ μοι οὐκ ἀπαράσκευος εἶναι, *I think myself not to be unprepared.*

Obs. b)—The simple Pronoun of the third person, οὖ, οἶ, ἔ, etc., is commonly used reflexively by the Attic writers, but in Hom. it is exactly like the English, of him, to him, him, etc. (like the Attic αὑτοῦ, αὑτῷ, αὑτόν, etc., according to § 474) : λέγεται Ἀπόλλων ἐκδεῖραι Μαρσύαν ἐρίζοντά οἱ περὶ σοφίας, *dicitur Apollo Marsyæ cutem detraxisse de arte secum certanti;* Hom. αὐτόματος δέ οἱ ἦλθε —Μενέλαος, *sponte sua ad eum venit Menelaus.*

Obs. c)—The Reflexive of the third person sometimes supplies the place of that of the first and second : δεῖ ἡμᾶς ἀνερέσθαι ἑαυτούς, *we must ask ourselves;* in like manner, the Possessive ὅς sometimes stands for the Possessive of the first two persons : Hom. οὐ γὰρ ἔγωγε ἧς γαίης δύναμαι γλυκερώτερον ἄλλο ἰδέσθαι, *for I can see nothing sweeter than my own country.*

§ 472. The following are used as *Possessives of the Reflexive Pronouns :*

a) the Genitives of the Reflexive Pronouns, especially in the Singular : ἐμαυτοῦ, σεαυτοῦ, ἑαυτοῦ. When the substantive to which they are joined has the article, the Genitives stand between the article and the substantive : Ζεὺς τὴν Ἀθηνᾶν ἔφυσεν ἐκ τῆς ἑαυτοῦ κεφαλῆς, *Zeus produced Athene out of his own head.*

b) the Possessives of the Personal Pronouns, especially

§ 475. DEMONSTRATIVE AND INTERROG. PRONOUNS. 269

in the plural: ἡμέτερος, ὑμέτερος : σφέτερος is exclusively Reflexive.

c) The Possessives in connection with the Genitives of αὐτός: ἡμέτερος αὐτῶν, etc.

§ 473. The *Reflexive Pronoun in the Plural* is also used instead of the *Reciprocal* Pronoun ἀλλήλων : διελεγόμεθα ἡμῖν αὐτοῖς, *we conversed with one another* (among ourselves).

§ 474. On αὐτός, *self*, and ὁ αὐτός, *the same*, see § 389.

αὐτός in the oblique cases, like the Lat. *is, ea, id*, is used as a Personal Pronoun referring to some person or thing mentioned before: ἐδέοντο αὐτοῦ παραμεῖναι, *they wanted him to remain*.

The Genitive αὐτοῦ, ἧς, ὧν, like the Lat. *ejus, eorum*, is the Engl. *his, her, their*, when it does not refer to the subject. Its position is that pointed out in § 470, *a*: ὁ υἱὸς αὐτοῦ or αὐτοῦ ὁ υἱός, *filius ejus*. Still the Genitive of αὐτός often supplies the place of the Reflexive of the third person.

§ 475. Of the *Demonstrative Pronouns*, οὗτος points more to what precedes and is already known; ὅδε to what follows and has not yet been named; so likewise are distinguished τοιοῦτος, *of such quality;* τοσοῦτος, *so great;* τηλικοῦτος, *so old*—from τοιόςδε, τοσόςδε, τηλικόςδε. On the article with these Pronouns, § 389.

On the demonstrative uses of ὅς, § 213, *Obs*.

§ 475*b*. The *Interrogative Pronouns* mentioned in § 216 : τίς, πότερος, ποῖος, etc., are used exclusively in direct questions. In indirect ones the compound Relatives ὅστις, ὁπότερος, ὁποῖος, etc., are employed. The former, however, are often used in indirect questions, though the latter never in a direct one: τίς εἶ; *who are you?* εἰπέ μοι, ὅστις εἶ, or τίς εἶ, *tell me who you are*.

On the *Attraction* with *Relative Pronouns*, §§ 597–603.

Chap. XIX.—The Voices of the Verb.

§ 476. 1. *The Active Voice.*

1. The Active voice not unfrequently has an intransitive as well as a transitive meaning. Thus ἐλαύνειν means *to drive* and *to ride;* ἔχειν, *to have, hold,* and *to be in a condition* (καλῶς ἔχει, *bene se habet*); πράττειν, *to do* and *to be* (εὖ πράττω, *I am doing well*); δηλοῦν, *to make* and *to become manifest.*

> In some verbs different tenses are assigned to the different meanings. See above, §§ 329, 330.

2. Simple verbs which are transitive often become intransitive when compounded: βάλλειν, *to throw*—μεταβάλλειν, *to change;* ἐςβάλλειν and ἐμβάλλειν, *to fall into, issue* (of rivers); διδόναι, *to give*—ἐνδιδόναι, *to give in;* ἐπιδιδόναι, *to grow;* κόπτειν, *to cut;* προκόπτειν, *proficere, make progress;* φέρειν, *to bear;* διαφέρειν, *differre, to differ* or *be distinguished.*

3. The Active often denotes an action which the subject accomplishes not *immediately,* but *mediately,* that is, *causes* or *allows* to be done by others: ὁ Κῦρος κατέκαυσε τὰ βασίλεια, *Cyrus had the royal castle burned down.* This is called the *Causative* use.

§ 477. 2. *The Middle Voice.*

Its primary meaning is *reflexive, i. e.,* the action of the verb in the Middle refers back to the subject from which it issues.

The Middle, in the first place, may be either *transitive* or *intransitive;* it is transitive when it can have an object in the Accusative: πράττομαι χρήματα, *I gain for myself money;* intransitive when it is incapable of having such an object: ἀπέχομαι, *I restrain myself.*

The Middle, farther, can vary much in its mode of referring back to the subject. We distinguish:

§ 478. 1. The *Direct* Middle, in which the subject is at the same time the *direct object* of the verb: λούομαι, *I wash myself;* τρέπομαι, *I turn myself;* ἐπιδείκνυμαι, *I show myself;* ἵσταμαι, *I place myself;* καλύπτομαι, *I hide myself.* This kind of Middle is the rarest. The Active with the reflexive pronoun in the Accusative is more generally used to express direct Reflexion.

Obs.—Through the direct Middle, several middle verbs have become intransitive or passive: παύω, *I cause to stop;* παύομαι, *I stop myself, cease;* φαίνω, *I show;* φαίνομαι, *I show myself, appear;* ἵημι, *I send;* ἵεμαι, *I send myself, hurry.*

§ 479. 2. The *Indirect*, or *Dative-like* Middle (§ 431), in which the subject is but indirectly affected by the action. Here the action takes place *for* or in the *interest* of the subject, so that in other languages the Dative may generally be used to denote the reflex influence: πορίζω, *I provide;* πορίζομαι, *I provide for myself*, e. g., χρήματα, *money;* ἄγομαι γυναῖκα, *I take a wife to myself;* μισθοῦμαι στρατιώτας, *I hire soldiers for myself* (but μισθοῦν, *hire out,* μισθοῦν ἑαυτόν, *to hire one's self out*); μεταπέμπομαί τινα, *I send for some one;* Hom. αὐτὸς ἐφέλκεται ἄνδρα σίδηρος, *the iron itself draws a man to it.* Hence the Athenian says: ὁ νομοθέτης τίθησι νόμους, *the lawgiver gives laws,* but ὁ δῆμος τίθεται νόμους, *the people gives laws to itself.*

Obs.—The interest of the subject sometimes consists in an object being removed *from* its reach: ἀμύνομαι κίνδυνον, *I ward off danger from me;* προίεμαί τινα, *I send some one away from me;* ἀποδόσθαι ναῦν (*to give away for one's interest*), *to sell a ship.* (Compare § 324, 7).

§ 480. 3. The *Subjective* or ethical Middle. This denotes that an action originates not only externally, but also internally from the subject, *i. e.*, from its means, power, or disposition: παρέχειν, *to furnish;* παρέχεσθαι, *to furnish from one's own means;* ποιεῖν εἰρήνην, *to make peace;* ποιεῖσθαι εἰρήνην, *to strive to make peace;* λαμβάνειν τι, *to take something;* λαμβάνεσθαί τινος, *to lay hold of something;* σκοπεῖν, *to look at;* σκοπεῖσθαι, *to reflect.*

Obs.—The subjective Middle is formed also from intransitive verbs; it then expresses a state more intensively than the active: πολιτεύειν, *to be a citizen;* πολιτεύεσθαι, *to act as a citizen;* βουλεύειν, *to give advice;* βουλεύεσθαι, *to deliberate with one's self.*

§ 481. 4. The *Causative* Middle.

As the Causative Active (§ 476, 3) expresses an action only *occasioned* by the subject, so the Middle is often used to denote that the subject *has* an action *done for* or *on* itself: ὁ πατὴρ διδάσκεται τὸν υἱόν, *the father has his son instructed;* παρατίθεμαι δεῖπνον, *I have a meal placed before me;* δικάζομαι, *I have judgment pronounced for me;* ἀποτέμνομαι τὰς χεῖρας, *I have my hands cut off.*

§ 481b. As examples, the following more important verbs may be adduced, whose meaning in the Middle essentially differs in various ways from that of the Active: ἄρχω, *I am first,* ἄρχομαι, *I begin;* ὁ ῥήτωρ γράφει νόμον, *the orator proposes* (writes down) *a law;* ὁ κατήγορος γράφεται τὸν ἀδικήσαντα, *the accuser prosecutes* (has the name written down) *the wrong doer;* τιμωρῶ τινι, *I help one;* τιμωροῦμαί τινα, *I avenge myself on one;* αἱρῶ, *I take,* αἱροῦμαι, *I choose;* δανείζω, *I put out to interest;* δανείζομαι, *I borrow at interest;* πείθω, *I persuade,* πείθομαι, *I allow myself to be persuaded, I obey.*

One and the same Middle may occur in different senses: διδάσκομαι (4), *I cause to teach,* or (1) *I teach myself, learn;* τρέπομαι (1), *I turn myself,* or (2) *I turn to myself;* τρέπονται τὰς γνώμας, *they change their opinion;* τρέπονται τοὺς πολεμίους, *they turn away* (put to flight) *the enemy* (§ 479, *Obs.*).

§ 482. *Obs.*—The *deponents* are distributed among the different kinds of Middle verbs, and differ from the verbs mentioned only by having no active form. Thus ὑπισχνοῦμαι, *I pledge myself,* is a direct Middle; but δέχομαι, *I receive;* κτάομαι, *I acquire,* are indirect; ἀγωνίζομαι, *I contend ;* οἴμαι, *I think*, are subjective : ἀναβιώσασθαι, *to revive*, is causative. On the Passive Deponents, § 328.

§ 483. 3. *The Passive Voice*

has a freer use in Greek than in Latin, viz. :

1. even such verbs as in the Active take a different case from the Accusative, form a Passive : καταφρονῶ τινος (§ 424), *I despise one ;* καταφρονεῖταί τις ὑπ' ἐμοῦ ; πιστεύουσι τῷ βασιλεῖ, *they trust the king ;* ὁ βασιλεὺς πιστεύεται ὑπ' αὐτῶν ; ἐπιβουλεύει τῷ πολεμίῳ, *he plots against the enemy ;* ὁ πολέμιος ἐπιβουλεύεται ὑπ' αὐτοῦ, *a plot is made against the enemy by him.*

2. Neuters of Passive participles may be formed even from intransitive verbs : τὰ στρατευόμενα, *the warlike measures ;* τὰ σοὶ πεπολιτευμένα, *your political course, your policy.*

3. The exclusively Passive forms even of Deponents are sometimes used in a Passive sense ; βιάζομαι, *I force,* ἐβιάσθην, *I was forced ;* in like manner a Passive may be formed from a Middle : αἱρέω, *I take*, αἱρέομαι, Pass., *I am chosen ;* μετεπέμφθη, *he was sent for*, μεταπέμπομαι, *I send for* (§ 479).

Chap. XX.—Use of the Tenses.

§ 484. In marking the time, the Greeks distinguished :

1. The ORDER of time. The three Orders of time being the *Present*, the *Past*, and the *Future*.

2. The KIND of time. In regard to the Kind of time, an action is either

a) *going on*, e. g., γιγνώσκειν (gradually), *to learn to know ;* or,

b) *momentary*, e. g., γνῶναι, *to perceive, know ;* or,

c) *completed*, e. g., ἐγνωκέναι, *to have learned*, to know (Lat. *nosse*).

Obs.—The momentary action may be compared to a *point*, the action going on to a *line*, and the completed action to a *surface*.

An action *going on* is indicated by the forms of the *Present-Stem*.

A *momentary* action is indicated by the forms of the *Aorist-Stems*.

A *completed* action is indicated by the forms of the *Perfect-Stem*.

The *Future* denotes the future *Order* of time of an action going on, as well as of a momentary action: γνώσομαι, *I shall* (gradually) *get to know*, and *I shall perceive;* the Third Future (*futurum exactum*) that of a completed action: ἐγνωκὼς ἔσομαι, *I shall have learned* (Latin *novero*).

In the Present, Aorist, and Perfect, *only the Indicative* indicates a definite *Order* of time; the other Moods, the Infinitive and the Participle, resemble the corresponding Indicative only in regard to the Kind, not in regard to the *Order* of time.

The following table presents a general view of these relations:

	Present.	Past.	Future.
Going on.	Ind. Pres.	Imperf.	
	Subj., Opt., Imperat., Inf., Part., *of the Present.*		*Future.*
Momentary.		Aor. Ind.	
	Subj., Opt., Imperat., Inf., of the *Aorist.*		
Completed.	Perf. Ind.	Pluperf.	Futurum exact.
	Subj., Opt., Imperat., Inf., Part., of the *Perfect.*		

§ 485. *Obs.*—As the English as well as the Latin language generally neglects the distinction between an action *going on* and a *Momentary* action, it is difficult to comprehend it. A similar distinc-

§ 488. THE PRESENT INDICATIVE. 275

tion, however, may be perceived in some English verbs, as *flee* (φεύγειν) and *escape* (φυγεῖν); *flicker* and *flash*; *fear* (φοβεῖσθαι) and *be frightened* (φοβηθῆναι, δεῖσαι); *wonder* (θαυμάζειν) and *to be surprised* (θαυμάσαι); *to be busy about* (πράσσειν) and *to accomplish* (πρᾶξαι); γελᾶν, *to be laughing*, and γελάσαι, *to burst out laughing*.

1. FORMS OF AN ACTION IN PROGRESS.

a) *The Present Indicative.*

§ 486. The Present Indicative denotes, as in English and Latin, an action going on or in progress *at the present time:* ἱκετεύομέν σε πάντες, *we all implore thee.* Hence by the Present are expressed general assertions, valid for all times, and therefore also for the Present: ἔστι Θεός, *there is a God.*

Obs.—Actions whose commencement indeed belongs to the Past, but whose effects extend to the Present, are sometimes expressed by this tense: ἀκούω, *I hear*, also in the sense, *I have heard* and still bear in mind; νικάω, *I conquer, i. e.*, I am *victorious*; φεύγω, *I am banished*; ἀδικέω, *I am wrong* (have done wrong); θνήσκει, *he is dead.* In this sense alone are used ἥκω, *I am come*; οἴχομαι, *I am gone.*

§ 487. By a lively apprehension a past action may be represented as present, hence the use, very frequent in Greek, of the *Historical* Present, which frequently alternates with past tenses: poet. καὶ πῶς ὁρᾶται καὶ ᾑρέθη; *and how is she seen, and was she captured?* ἐπεὶ ἡγεῖτο Ἀρχίδαμος καὶ ἐπορεύετο ἐπὶ τοὺς ἀντιπάλους, ἐνταῦθα οὗτοι οὐκ ἐδέξαντο τοὺς περὶ τὸν Ἀρχίδαμον, ἀλλ᾽ ἐγκλίνουσιν, *as Archidamus took the lead and marched against the enemy, the latter did not wait for the troops of Archidamus, but retreat.*

§ 488. *b) The Imperfect*

is the Preterite of an action in progress, like the Latin Imperfect.

The Greek therefore uses the Imperfect where he wishes to *describe* past states or past actions in their progress, in their continuance along with others, or in their frequent, continued repetition: Hom. οἱ μὲν ἄρ' οἶνον ἔμισγον ἐνὶ κρητῆρσι καὶ ὕδωρ, οἱ δ' αὖτε σπόγγοισι πολυτρήτοισι τραπέζας νίζον καὶ προτίθεν, τοὶ δὲ κρέα πολλὰ δατεῦντο, *some were mingling wine and water in mixing-bowls, others cleaning tables with porous sponges, and placing them, the rest were carving much meat;* τοὺς μὲν οὖν πελταστὰς ἐδέξαντο οἱ βάρβαροι καὶ ἐμάχοντο, *the barbarians met the peltasts, and then were fighting,*—Hom. ὄφρα μὲν ἠὼς ἦν καὶ ἀέξετο ἱερὸν ἦμαρ, τόφρα μάλ' ἀμφοτέρων βέλε' ἥπτετο, πῖπτέ τε λαός, *as long as it was morning, and holy day increasing, so long the darts of both were striking and people falling.* —οὔποτε μεῖον ἀπεστρατοπεδεύοντο οἱ βάρβαροι τῶν Ἑλλήνων ἑξήκοντα σταδίων, *the barbarians* (did not encamp) *used never to encamp less than sixty stadia from the Hellenes.*

§ 489. *Obs.* 1.—The Imperfect frequently expresses a merely attempted but not accomplished action: πρῶτος Κλέαρχος τοὺς αὑτοῦ στρατιώτας ἐβιάζετο ἰέναι, οἱ δὲ αὐτὸν ἔβαλλον, ὕστερον δὲ ἐπεὶ ἔγνω ὅτι οὐ δυνήσεται βιάσασθαι, συνήγαγεν ἐκκλησίαν, *first Clearchus tried to force his soldiers to go, but they shot at him; afterward, however, as he perceived he would not be able to force them, he summoned a meeting.* So ἐδίδου sometimes means *he offered to give,* to distinguish it from ἔδωκεν, *he gave.*

§ 490. *Obs.* 2.—The Imperfects of the verbs which denote *should* and *must* are used, just as in Latin, to denote what *should* be done in opposition to what was done: ἔδει τοὺς λέγοντας μήτε πρὸς ἔχθραν ποιεῖσθαι τὸν λόγον μήτε πρὸς χάριν, *the speakers ought to have made their speeches neither from fear nor from favor* (Lat. *oportebat*); so χρῆν, *it ought;* εἰκὸς ἦν, *it would be fair.*

On the Imperf. with ἄν, § 494, *Obs.* 1, and § 537, etc.

§ 491. *c) The Subjunctive, Optative, Imperative, Infinitive, and Participle Present*

simply express an action in progress, whether it lie in the present, past, or future: μαινόμεθα πάντες, ὁπόταν ὀργιζώμεθα, *we are all mad when we are angry;* ἔλεγον τῷ Εὐθυδήμῳ, ὅτι πάντες ἕτοιμοι εἶεν μανθάνειν, *they told Euthydemus that they were all ready to learn;* οὕτω ποιήσω,

§ 492. THE AORIST INDICATIVE. 277

ὅπως ἂν σὺ κελεύῃς, *I will do as you may bid me* (*sic agam, ut tu me agere jubebis*); ταῦτα λέγων θορύβου ἤκουσε, διὰ τῶν τάξεων ἰόντος καὶ ἤρετο, τίς ὁ θόρυβος εἴη, *saying this, he heard a noise pass through the ranks, and asked what the noise was.*

Obs.—These Present forms sometimes, like the Imperfect (§ 489), express a mere attempt: τὸ ἀποδιδράσκοντα μὴ δύνασθαι ἀποδρᾶναι πολλὴ μωρία, *for a man not to be able to run away when he tries to run away is great stupidity.*

§ 492. 2. FORMS OF A MOMENTARY ACTION.

a) The Aorist Indicative

is the Preterite of a Momentary action, and therefore denotes the actual beginning of an action in the past, similar to the Historical Perfect of the Latins.

The Greeks employ the Aorist Indicative when they wish to *narrate* past facts, to state past actions simply as having happened, or to represent them as individual facts without reference to other actions: μετὰ τὴν ἐν Κορωνείᾳ μάχην οἱ Ἀθηναῖοι ἐξέλιπον τὴν Βοιωτίαν πᾶσαν, *after the battle at Coronea the Athenians left all Bœotia;*—Παυσανίας ἐκ Λακεδαίμονος στρατηγὸς ὑπὸ Ἑλλήνων ἐξεπέμφθη μετὰ εἴκοσι νεῶν ἀπὸ Πελοποννήσου, ξυνέπλεον δὲ καὶ Ἀθηναῖοι τριάκοντα ναυσὶ καὶ ἐστράτευσαν ἐς Κύπρον καὶ αὐτῆς τὰ πολλὰ κατεστρέψαντο, *Pausanias was sent out from Lacedæmon as general by the Hellenes, with twenty ships from the Peloponnese, but Athenians also accompanied him* (accompanying circumstance) *with thirty ships, and they proceeded to Cyprus and subdued the greater part of it;* τοξικὴν καὶ ἰατρικὴν καὶ μαντικὴν Ἀπόλλων ἀνεῦρεν, *Apollo invented the arts of archery, medicine, and prophecy;*—

Hom. τὴν δὲ πολὺ πρῶτος ἴδε Τηλέμαχος θεοειδής, βῆ δ' ἰθὺς προθύροιο, νεμεσσήθη δ' ἐνὶ θυμῷ ξεῖνον δηθὰ θύρῃσιν ἐφεστάμεν, ἐγγύθι δὲ στὰς χεῖρ' ἕλε δεξιτερὴν καὶ ἐδέξατο χάλκεον ἔγχος, *but her first Telemachus of form divine beheld, and he went straight to the porch, and was grieved at heart that a stranger stood a long time at the door, and going near he took him by the right hand and eased him of his brazen spear.*

§ 493. As the Aorist Indicative simply expresses an action as having taken place in the past, it answers to all the different Preterites in other languages, especially often in subordinate sentences to the Latin and English *pluperfect:* Δαρεῖος Κῦρον μεταπέμπεται (§ 487) ἀπὸ τῆς ἀρχῆς ἧς αὐτὸν σατράπην ἐποίησεν, *Darius has Cyrus sent for from the province, over which he had made him satrap (fecerat).* Thus the Aorist is used with the Conjunctions of time, ἐπεί, ὡς, ὅτε, *as, when,* like the Latin Perfect with *postquam, ubi, ut:* ὡς ὁ Κῦρος ᾔσθετο κραυγῆς, ἀνεπήδησεν ἐπὶ τὸν ἵππον ὥσπερ ἐνθουσιῶν, *when Cyrus perceived (ut audivit) a cry, he sprang upon his horse like one inspired.*

§ 494. The Aorist Indicative is used in *statements of experience* implying that a thing once *happened,* but admitting an application to all times: poet. τῷ χρόνῳ ἡ δίκη πάντως ἦλθ' ἀποτισαμένη, *with time avenging justice always came* (and hence always comes); καὶ βραδὺς εὔβουλος εἷλεν ταχὺν ἄνδρα διώκων, *even a slow man, when well advised, overtook* (overtakes) *by pursuit a quick man.* In English we employ the Present in such general assertions, and often add such adverbs as *usually, commonly, always,* etc.: τὰς τῶν φαύλων συνουσίας ὀλίγος χρόνος διέλυσεν, *a short time usually dissolves the associations of the bad.* This Aorist is called the *gnomic* Aorist, because it is often used in gnomes, proverbs, or maxims. In Hom. it is often also used in comparisons.

Obs. 1.—In expressing what *usually* happens, the Aorist sometimes has ἄν in order to express the case as one *that may have occurred,* and therefore *may occur oftener:* ἔλεξεν ἄν, *he may have said.* In the same way the Imperfect is used, but referring to an action in progress: ἀναλαμβάνων αὐτῶν τὰ ποιήματα διηρώτων ἄν, τί λέγοιεν, *taking up their poems I would ask what they meant.*

Obs. 2.—The Aorist Indicative, especially in the 1 Pers. Sing., is frequently used to express actions and states beginning only at the moment of speaking: ἐγέλασα, *I burst out laughing;* poet. ἐπῄνεσ' ἔργον καὶ πρόνοιαν ἣν ἔθου, *I praise the deed and the prudence which you have exercised.*

On the Hypothetical Aorist, § 537, etc.

§ 496. THE AOR. SUBJ., OPT., IMPERAT., AND INFIN. 279

§ 495. *b) The Aorist Subjunctive, Optative, Imperative, and Infinitive*
denote a Momentary action *simply*, whether of the present, past, or future : οἱ τριάκοντα προςέταξαν ἀπαγαγεῖν Λέοντα, ἵν' ἀποθάνοι, *the Thirty commanded to take Leon away to die;* ἀπορῶ, τί πρῶτον μνησθῶ, *I am in doubt what first to mention;* μὴ θαυμάσητε, ἐὰν παράδοξον εἴπω τι, *be not surprised if I say something strange;* σύ μοι ἀπόκριναι, ὦ παῖ, *give me an answer, boy;* μέγα οἶμαι ἔργον τὸ ἀρχὴν καταπρᾶξαι, πολὺ δ' ἔτι μεῖζον τὸ λαβόντα διασώσασθαι, *I deem it a great thing to found a government, but a still greater to maintain it after acquiring it.*

Obs.—The Subjunctive, Optative, Imperative, and Infinitive Aorist, therefore, differ from the corresponding forms of the Present, just as the Aorist Indicative differs from the Imperfect ; the Aorist forms express a single fact, conceived as a point, the Present, as a *state* or condition, sometimes of long duration : χαλεπὸν τὸ ποιεῖν, τὸ δὲ κελεῦσαι ῥᾴδιον, *it is difficult to do; easy to command;* εἴ πῃ ἔχεις ἀντιλέγειν, ἀντίλεγε · εἰ δὲ μή, παῦσαι πολλάκις λέγων τὸν αὐτὸν λόγον, *if you have any thing to say in reply, reply* (even in a long speech), *if not, cease* (at once) *frequently repeating the same statement.*

§ 496. The *Aorist Participle* regularly expresses something which *took place earlier* or *before* the act of the principal verb : Κροῖσος Ἅλυν διαβὰς μεγάλην ἀρχὴν καταλύσει, *Crœsus, after crossing the Halys, will overthrow a great empire;* παθὼν δέ τε νήπιος ἔγνω (§ 494), *after suffering* (by suffering) *even a fool becomes knowing.*

Obs.—As the Aorist generally indicates the moment at which an action actually *begins* (§ 485), so the Aorist Participle also only expresses that the *beginning* of an action took place before another action, while its progress may continue simultaneously with that other : γελάσας εἶπε, *he began to laugh and said* (laughing) [*risu oborto dixit*]. Hom. ὧδε δέ τις εἴπεσκεν ἰδὼν ἐς πλησίον ἄλλον, *thus would say many a one while looking at his neighbor;* χάρισαί μοι ἀποκρινάμενος, *answer and oblige me*, inasmuch as the χαρίσασθαι follows immediately after the beginning of the answer.

§ 497. As the Aorist Indicative may frequently be translated by the Pluperfect (§ 493), so also the Aorist *Optative* and *Infinitive* in assertions generally denotes something which *took place before*: οἱ 'Ινδοὶ ἔλεξαν ὅτι πέμψειε σφᾶς ὁ 'Ινδῶν βασιλεύς (Ind. ὅτι ἔπεμψε), *the Indians said that the king of the Indians had sent them;* Κύκλωπες λέγονται ἐν Σικελίᾳ οἰκῆσαι, *the Cyclops are said to have dwelt in Sicily.*

§ 498. Many verbs whose Present-Stem expresses a *state*, denote in all the Aorist forms the *entrance into this state*: ἄρχειν, *to rule,* ἄρξαι, *to obtain dominion;* βασιλεύειν, *to be king,* βασιλεῦσαι, *to become king;* ἰσχύειν, *to be strong,* ἰσχῦσαι, *to become strong;* σιγᾶν, *to be silent,* σιγῆσαι, *to become silent;* ἔχειν, *to have,* σχεῖν, *to obtain;* φαίνεσθαι, *to appear,* φανῆναι, *to become apparent;* νοσεῖν, *to be ill,* νοσῆσαι, *to become ill;* πολεμεῖν, *to be at war (bellum gerere),* πολεμῆσαι, *to begin war (bellum inferre).* (Compare § 485.)

Obs.—This meaning, however, is not always attached to these forms; and ἐπολέμησαν may also signify simply *bellum gesserunt* (§ 492).

§ 499. 3. THE FUTURE expresses the futurity both of an action in progress and of a Momentary action: ἄρξω, *I shall become ruler, and I shall rule.*

Obs. 2.—The 2 Person Future with οὐ nearly resembles the negative Imperative: οὐκ ἐπιορκήσεις, *thou wilt (shalt) not swear falsely.*

§ 500. The Future Indicative in relative clauses, and in clauses with ὅπως, *that,* is worthy of notice, for there the Future denotes what *may* or *should* happen: οὐκ ἔχομεν ὅτου σῖτον ὠνησόμεθα, *we have nothing with which we can buy food (non habemus, quo cibum emamus)*; δεῖ ἅπαντα ἄνδρα τοῦτο παρασκευάζεσθαι, ὅπως ὡς σοφώτατος ἔσται, *every man should take care to be (that he shall be) as wise as possible* (compare § 553). The Participle is similarly used: ἡ χώρα πολλὴ καὶ ἀγαθὴ ἦν καὶ ἐνῆσαν οἱ ἐργασόμενοι, *the land was large and good, and there were people to (who could) cultivate it;* τίς ἔσται ὁ ἡγησόμενος; *who will be there to (who can) guide us?* (compare §§ 380, 578).

Obs.—ἄν (Hom. κέ) is sometimes added to the Future Indicative to denote that a case may possibly occur: εὖ οἶδ' ὅτι ἄσμενος ἄν

§ 503. THE PERFECT INDICATIVE. 281

πρὸς ἄνδρα οἷος σὺ εἶ ἀπαλλαγήσεται, *I well know that he will be glad to be reconciled to a man such as you are;* Hom. ὁ δέ κεν κεχολώσεται ὅν κεν ἴκωμαι, *and he will doubtless be in wrath whom I come upon.*

§ 501. The verb μέλλω is used with the Present, Future, or, though more rarely, the Aorist Infinitive, to express an *immediately approaching*, or, at least, intended action: μέλλω ὑμᾶς ἄγειν εἰς Ἀσίαν, *I am going to lead you to Asia* (*in Asiam vos ducturus sum*). This is called the *periphrastic Future*.

Obs. 1.—μέλλω may also be used in other tenses than the Present with an Infinitive, like *esse* in Latin, with the Part. Fut. : πλησίον ἤδη ἦν ὁ σταθμὸς ἔνθα ἔμελλον καταλύσειν, *jam prope aderat statio ubi deversuri erant, where they wished to rest.*

Obs. 2.—πῶς or τί οὐ μέλλω, is elliptical in the sense of *Why should I not?*

4. FORMS OF A COMPLETED ACTION.

§ 502. *a) The Perfect Indicative* is the *Present* of a completed action, *i. e.*, by the Perfect the Greeks denote an action completed *for* and *with reference to the Present:* poet. λόγος λέλεκται πᾶς, *the whole speech has been spoken* [*dixi*]; εὕρηκα, *I have found, I have it;* Hom. ἤδη γὰρ τετέλεσται ἅ μοι φίλος ἤθελε θυμός, *for now has been finished what my dear soul desired;* ἡ πόλις ἔκτισται παρὰ τῶν Κορινθίων, *the city has been founded by the Corinthians* (of a still existing city); τὰ χρήματα τοῖς πλουσίοις ἡ τύχη οὐ δεδώρηται ἀλλὰ δεδάνεικεν, *Fortune has not given, but lent* (at interest) *their money to the rich.*

§ 503. *Obs.*—Several Perfects have an entirely Present meaning, inasmuch as they present in a completed state the action of which the gradual accomplishment is expressed by the present: μιμνήσκομαι, *I remind myself;* μέμνημαι, *I bear in mind, remember* (*memini*) ; καλέομαι, *I am named;* κέκλημαι, *my name is;* πείθομαι, *I follow;* πέποιθα, *I confide in;* ὄλλυμι, *I am perishing;* ὄλωλα, *I am lost;* κτάομαι, *I acquire;* κέκτημαι, *I possess;* ἵσταμαι, *I place myself;* ἕστηκα, *I stand;* βαίνω, *I go;* βέβηκα, *I am gone.*

§ 504. *b) The Pluperfect*
is the *Preterite* of a completed action, *i. e.*, by the Pluperfect the Greeks express an action completed for and with reference to *a past time :* Hom. δὴ τότε γ' ἀτρέμας εὗδε λελασμένος ὅσσ' ἐπεπόνθει, *then truly he slept quietly, forgetting what he had suffered ;* ἐν τοῖς Δράκοντος νόμοις μία ἅπασιν ὥριστο τοῖς ἁμαρτάνουσι ζημία θάνατος, *in Draco's laws death had been appointed for all criminals as the only punishment —* says an Athenian after the laws were abolished. (As long as they were in force : ὥρισται.)

*Obs.—*The Pluperfects of the Perfects enumerated in § 503 are to be translated by Imperfects.
On the Aorist in the sense of the Latin Pluperfect, § 493.

§ 505. *c)* THE FUTURE PERFECT (FUTURUM EXACTUM) is the *Future* of a completed action, *i. e.*, it denotes an action which will be completed in the future. It is only in the Middle that the Greeks have a special form for this Third Future, which has generally a Passive meaning. In the Active, the circumlocution by means of the Perfect Participle and the Future of εἶναι must be used (§ 291): ἂν ταῦτ' εἰδῶμεν, τὰ δέοντα ἐσόμεθα ἐγνωκότες, *when we know this, we shall* (thence) *have got to know our duty ;* Hom. ἐμοὶ δὲ λελείψεται ἄλγεα λυγρά, *but I shall have gloomy woes left me.*

*Obs.—*The *Future Perfect* of the Perfects mentioned in § 503 serves as a common Future : μεμνήσομαι, *meminero,* etc.

§ 506. *d) The Perfect of all the Moods, of the Infinitive, and of the Participle,*
expresses a completed action generally, and may refer to any of the three Orders of time : οὐ βουλεύεσθαι ὥρα ἀλλὰ βεβουλεῦσθαι, *now is not the time to consult, but to have consulted* (to be resolved); Ξέρξης ὡς ἐπύθετο τὸν Ἑλλήσποντον ἐζεῦχθαι, προῆγεν ἐκ τῶν Σάρδεων, *when Xerxes*

§ 511. USE OF THE MOODS. 283

learned that the Hellespont had been bridged over (and was still provided with a bridge, ὅτι ἔζευκτο), *he marched forward from Sardis;* ταῦτα μὲν οὖν προειρήσθω, *thus much be said beforehand* (now to something else); Hom. ἔσσεται ἦμαρ ὅτ᾽ ἄν ποτ᾽ ὀλώλῃ Ἴλιος ἱρή,᾽ *a day will come when holy Ilios will be lost* (has been lost); χρήσιμόν τι ἐσκεμμένος ἥκω, *I am come after having devised something useful.*

Chap. XXI.—Use of the Moods.
A) The Moods in Simple Sentences.
§ 507. 1. *The Indicative.*

The Indicative, in accordance with the usage of other languages, is employed simply to state something positively or negatively, or simply and directly to ask a question: poet. τῆς ἀρετῆς ἱδρῶτα θεοὶ προπάροιθεν ἔθηκαν, *the gods placed sweat before virtue;* Hom. πόθεν εἰς ἀνδρῶν; *from what class of men are you?*

Obs.—On the Indicative in hypothetical sentences with or without ἄν, § 536, etc.; in sentences expressing a wish, § 515. On the Aorist Ind. with ἄν, to express what usually happens, see § 494.

2. *The Subjunctive.*

§ 508. The Subjunctive expresses what *ought to* take place; it always refers to the present, to reality. Hence it is used in the following cases:

§ 509. 1. as *a challenge* in the first person: ἴωμεν, *let us go* [*eamus*]; φέρε δή, τὰς μαρτυρίας ὑμῖν ἀναγνῶ, *well, come! let me read you the testimonies* [*recitem*].

§ 510. 2. with the negative μή in *prohibitions* and in negative admonitions (compare § 518): μὴ τοῦτο ποιήσῃς, *ne hoc feceris, you ought not to do this.*

§ 511. 3. In *hesitating questions,* where it is asked what

should be done: τί φῶ; *what am I to say?* Hom. πῶς τίς τοι πρόφρων ἔπεσιν πείθηται Ἀχαιῶν; *how shall any of the Achæans willingly trust thy words?* δέξεσθε ἡμᾶς ἤ ἀπίωμεν; *will you receive us, or are we to depart?*

§ 512. 4. with μή in sentences expressing *fear* or *anxiety:* μὴ ἀγροικότερον ᾖ τὸ ἀληθὲς εἰπεῖν, *if it be not rather rude to say the truth.* If the anxiety is to be negatively expressed, μὴ οὐ is used: Hom. μή νύ τοι οὐ χραίσμῃ σκῆπτρον καὶ στέμμα θεοῖο, *lest the staff and wreath of the god should not help thee, i. e.*, it will certainly be of little help to thee [Lat. *vereor ne non* or *ut te juvet*]. Compare §§ 533, 616, *Obs.* 3, § 621, *a.*

§ 513. *Obs.*—The Homeric language employs the Subjunctive of future events, quite like the Fut. Ind., to express a thing that is to be expected (§ 545): οὐ γάρ πω τοίους ἴδον ἀνέρας οὐδὲ ἴδωμαι, *for never yet did I see such men nor may* (shall) *I see them.* ἄν is sometimes added in Hom. to this Subjunctive: οὐκ ἄν τοι χραίσμῃ κίθαρις τά τε δῶρ' Ἀφροδίτης, *the lyre and Aphrodite's gifts would not help thee.* Compare § 500, *Obs.*

3. *The Optative.*

§ 514. 1. The Optative alone (without the particle ἄν) is used to express a *wish* that something *may* take place: poet. ὦ παῖ, γένοιο πατρὸς εὐτυχέστερος, *O boy! may you be happier than your father* [Lat. Pres. or Perf. Subj.].

The particles used (like Latin *utinam*) to introduce a wish are: εἰ (Hom. αἰ), εἴθε (Hom. αἴθε), εἰ γάρ, ὡς.

§ 515. *Obs.*—If it is to be intimated that a wish is *not to be realized*, it is referred to the past, and expressed by the *Imperfect* or *Aorist Indicative:* εἴθ' ἦσθα δυνατὸς δρᾶν ὅσον πρόθυμος εἶ, *would that you were able to do what you wish;* εἴθε σοι τότε συνεγενόμην, *would that I then had met you.* The same kind of wish is expressed by the Aorist ὤφελον (properly "I owed") and the Infinitive: ὀλέσθαι ὤφελον τῇδ' ἡμέρᾳ, *would that I had perished on that day* [Lat. Imperf. and Plup. Subj.]. Compare § 587.

§ 516. 2. The Optative with the particle ἄν (Hom. κέ or

§ 519. THE IMPERATIVE MOOD. 285

κέν) expresses *possibility*: τοῦτο γένοιτ' ἄν, *that* (could) *might be;* τί γὰρ γένοιτ' ἂν ἕλκος μεῖζον ἢ φίλος κακός; *what greater evil could there be than a bad friend;* ποῦ δῆτ' ἂν εἶεν οἱ ξένοι; *why! where can the strangers be?* [Latin Pres. and Perf. Subj.]. The Optative with ἄν is therefore called the *potential Optative*.

§ 517. *Obs*. 1.—Hence the Optative with ἄν is used in modestly expressed assertions: οὐκ ἂν λέγοιμι, *I would not say* [*non dixerim*]; ὥρα ἂν συσκευάζεσθαι εἴη, *it is perhaps time to break up;* οὐκ ἂν δύναιο μὴ καμὼν εὐδαιμονεῖν, *you could not, without taking trouble, be happy.*

Obs. 2.—In the poets the Optative in a potential sense is also used without ἄν: Hom. ῥεῖα θεός γ' ἐθέλων καὶ τηλόθεν ἄνδρα σαώσαι, *a god who is willing can easily save a man even afar off*. But this use of the Optative to denote a possible and merely imaginary case is originally peculiar to this mood, and hence is preserved in dependent clauses, §§ 528, 529, 532, *Obs.*, 546, 552, *Obs.*

§ 518. 4. *The Imperative.*

The Imperative is the mood of command, and, with negatives, of prohibition.

A prohibition in the second person can be expressed *only* in two ways, viz., *either* with μή and the *Present Imperative:* μὴ πρᾶττε, of a *continued* action, *or* with μή and the *Aorist Subjunctive:* μὴ πράξῃς, of a *Momentary* action, *do not do:* ταῦτά μοι πρᾶξον, τέκνον, καὶ μὴ βράδυνε μηδ' ἐπιμνησθῇς ἔτι Τροίας, *do me this, child, and delay not nor think farther of Troy.*

In the third person also μή with the *Aorist Imperative* is admissible: μηδεὶς ὑμῶν προςδοκησάτω ἄλλως, *let none of you expect otherwise.*

On the Infinitive instead of the Imperative, see § 577. On the Imperative as a substitute for a hypothetical clause, § 545, *Obs*. 3.

B) THE MOODS IN COMPOUND SENTENCES.

§ 519. Preliminary remarks on the connection of sentences with one another.

1. Two simple sentences (§ 361, 2) may be combined in two ways, viz., either

a) so that the one may be quite independent of the other —this combination is called *Co-ordination,* or Parataxis (παράταξις).

b) so that they mutually are referred to each other, and express a complete thought only in their combination— this combination is called *Subordination,* or Hypotaxis (ὑπόταξις).

2. Of two *Co-ordinate* sentences each is a principal sentence, and in every respect independent of the other: κοινὴ ἡ τύχη καὶ τὸ μέλλον ἀόρατον, *fortune is common, and the future invisible;* τοῦτο ἐγὼ οὔτ' εἴρηκα, οὔτε λέγοιμι ἄν, *I have neither said that, nor could I say it.*

On the manner in which co-ordinate sentences may be combined, § 624, *a.*

3. By *Subordination* two sentences are combined in such a way that one expresses the principal idea, the other a secondary one. The former is called the *leading* sentence, the latter the secondary, dependent or *Subordinate.* One leading sentence often has several subordinate ones dependent on it. The moods of subordinate sentences are in many ways determined by the leading sentence: Τισσαφέρνης διαβάλλει τὸν Κῦρον πρὸς τὸν ἀδελφόν, ὡς ἐπιβουλεύοι αὐτῷ, *Tissaphernes brings a calumny against Cyrus before his brother,* (saying) *that he was plotting against him;* Hom. σοὶ ἅμ' ἑσπόμεθ', ὄφρα σὺ χαίρῃς, *we have followed thee that thou mayst rejoice.*

4. The *Correlative* connection of sentences is a special kind of subordination. Of two correlative sentences, one always refers to the other. The one is called the *Protasis,* and the other the *Apodosis.* The Protasis, which requires to be completed by another sentence, is subordinate (3). The Apodosis is a leading sentence, which furnishes the necessary completion: Hom. ὡς ἴδεν, ὥς μιν ἔδυ χόλος,

§ 520. THE MOODS IN COMPOUND SENTENCES. 287

as he saw it wrath seized him ;. Hom. ὁπποῖόν κ' εἴπησθα ἔπος τοῖόν κ' ἐπακούσαις, *the kind of word you speak, such you will hear.*

Obs. 1.—This correlation is frequently expressed by two Pronouns or Particles referring to each other (§§ 216, 217), as in the examples just quoted, but not always: εἴ πῃ ἔχεις ἀντιλέγειν, ἀντίλεγε, *if you can in any way reply, reply.*

Obs. 2.—The Apodosis often precedes the Protasis: οὗτος βέλτιστος ἂν εἴη ὅστις κοσμιώτατα τὰς συμφορὰς φέρειν δύναται, *he would be the best who can bear calamities with most dignity.*

5. From the subordination of one clause to another there arises a *compound* sentence.

Obs. 1.—The same thought may often be as well expressed in two Co-ordinate sentences as in one Compound sentence: μηδενὶ συμφορὰν ὀνειδίσῃς, κοινὴ γὰρ ἡ τύχη, *reproach no one with a calamity, for fortune is common ;* or ἐπεὶ ἡ τύχη κοινή ἐστι, μηδενὶ συμφορὰν ὀνειδίσῃς, *since fortune is common, reproach no one with a calamity.* The Homeric language abounds in series of Co-ordinate sentences (the paratactic arrangement).

Obs. 2.—Frequently a word belonging to the Dependent sentence is drawn into the Principal sentence, where it may appear in different cases. If the Principal sentence stands first, the arrangement is called *prolepsis* (πρόληψις, *taking beforehand*) : καί μοι τὸν υἱὸν εἰπέ, εἰ μεμάθηκε τὴν τέχνην = καί μοι εἰπέ, εἰ ὁ υἱὸς μεμάθηκε τὴν τέχνην (§ 397). Hom. Τυδείδην δ' οὐκ ἂν γνοίης, ποτέροισι μετείη, *you could scarce perceive on which side Tydides stood;* καὶ τῶν βαρβάρων ἐπεμελεῖτο, ὡς πολεμεῖν ἱκανοὶ εἴησαν, *he also took care that the barbarians should be capable of carrying on war.* On the other hand, a substantive may pass from the Principal to the Subordinate sentence : Hom. μετὰ δ' ἔσσεται ἣν τότ' ἀπηύρων κούρην Βρισῆος, *among them also will be the daughter of Brises, whom I then took away* (compare § 602).

6. On the different kinds of sentences according to their *substance*, § 624, etc. Only those kinds will here be noticed which are most important in regard to the use of the Moods.

§ 520. The use of the Moods in Dependent sentences is subject to the following *general* rules:

1. The *Indicative* in Greek is very extensively used

even in Dependent sentences, the Greeks merely annexing or inserting many sentences without any mark of dependence where the Latin language marks the dependence by the Subjunctive or Infinitive: μή μ' ἀνέρῃ, τίς εἰμι, *ask me not who I am* [*ne me interroges, quis sim*].

§ 521. 2. The *Subjunctive* in Dependent sentences also denotes always that which *ought* to take place, and can generally be employed only when the leading sentence contains a principal tense.

Every verbal form is regarded as a Principal tense which connects the action with the *present;* hence the *Present* (except the Historical Present, § 487), the *Perfect*, and the *Future* Indicative, and all tenses of the *Subjunctive* and *Imperative*.

§ 522. 3. The *Optative* (without ἄν) denotes something merely conceived or supposed (§ 517, *Obs.* 2), and generally can be employed only when the Principal sentence contains an *Historical tense*.

Every verbal form, however, is regarded as an Historical tense which connects the action with the past, hence the *Historical Present* (§ 487), the *Indicative* of the *Aorist*, the *Imperfect* and *Pluperfect*.

A Dependent clause, moreover, frequently has the Optative when this mood occurs in the Principal sentence.

§ 523. 4. In *indirect speech* (*oratio obliqua*) the *Optative* (without ἄν), but only after an *Historical tense*, is used to denote something which is to be stated, not as the opinion of the speaker, but of another person: οἱ Ἀθηναῖοι Περικλέα ἐκάκιζον, ὅτι στρατηγὸς ὢν οὐκ ἐπεξάγοι ἐπὶ τοὺς πολεμίους, *the Athenians reproached Pericles because, being a general, he did not lead them out against the enemy* [*quod non duceret*]; εὔξαντο σωτήρια θύσειν ἔνθα πρῶτον εἰς φιλίαν γῆν ἀφίκοιντο, *they vowed to offer thank-offerings whenever they should first come to a friendly land;* εἴ τις πόλις ἐπὶ πόλιν στρατεύσοι, ἐπὶ ταύτην ἔφη ἰέναι, *si qua civ-*

§ 526. MOODS IN DEPENDENT ASSERTIONS, ETC. 289

itas contra [*aliam*] *civitatem pugnatura esset, contra hanc se dixit ituram*.

In this case, however, the Indicative also is admissible according to § 520, but *never* the Subjunctive, even after a Principal tense, its employment being limited to the case mentioned in § 527.

§ 524. 5. The *Potential Optative* (with ἄν) may occur in Dependent, in the same sense as in Independent, sentences (§ 516), to denote something as merely possible: λέγω, ὅτι τοῦτο οὐκ ἂν γένοιτο, *I say that this probably could not happen*.

The farther use of the Moods in Dependent sentences is treated of specially in what follows, according to the different kinds of Dependent sentences.

I. MOODS IN DEPENDENT ASSERTIONS AND IN DEPENDENT INTERROGATIVE SENTENCES.

§ 525. Sentences containing Dependent assertions are those which annex the substance of a speech or opinion to a Principal sentence by means of the conjunctions, ὅτι, ὡς, *that;* Dependent or indirect Interrogative sentences are connected with the Principal sentence by means of εἰ, *if;* πότερον... ἤ [*utrum... an*], *whether... or* (in double questions), or Interrogative Pronouns (§ 214) or Adverbs.

§ 526. 1. The *Indicative*
is used in those sentences which, when conceived independently, would have the Indicative, and thus,

a) when the leading sentence has a *Principal tense*, the Indicative *must* be used (§ 521): εἰπέ μοι, τίνα γνώμην ἔχεις, *tell me, what opinion you have* (direct: τίνα γνώμην ἔχεις) [Lat. *dic mihi, quam sententiam habeas*] ;

b) when the leading sentence has an *Historical tense* the Indicative *may* be used (§ 522): εἶπον, ἥντινα γνώμην εἶχον, *dixi quam sententiam haberem ;* ἧκεν ἀγγέλλων τις, ὡς Ἐλάτεια κατείληπται, *some one came bringing the news that Elatea was taken* (direct: Ἐλάτεια κατείληπται). Besides the Indicative, the Optative also is in this case admissible, § 528, *a*.

§ 527. 2. The *Subjunctive* can not occur at all in Dependent assertions, and in Dependent Interrogative sentences *only* if, when conceived as independent, they would necessarily have the Subjunctive, and thus

a) when the leading sentence has a *Principal tense* the Subjunctive *must* remain: βουλεύομαι, πῶς σε ἀποδρῶ, *I am planning how to escape from you* (direct according to § 511: πῶς σε ἀποδρῶ [*delibero, quo modo te effugiam*];

b) when the leading sentence has an *Historical tense* the Subjunctive *may* sometimes occur: ἐβουλευόμην, πῶς σε ἀποδρῶ; but the Optative is more frequent in this case than the Subjunctive (§ 528, *b*). The Subjunctive in Dependent Interrogative sentences accordingly is to be translated by *may* or *shall*.

§ 528. 3. The *Optative* (without ἄν) may occur in such sentences:

a) as a substitute for the *Indicative* (§ 526, *b*), i. e., when there is an Historical tense in the leading sentence, in case the Dependent sentence, if conceived independently, ought to have the Indicative: εἶπον, ἥντινα γνώμην ἔχοιμι (direct: εἶχον) [Lat. *dixi, quam sententiam haberem*]; ἔγνωσαν ὅτι κενὸς ὁ φόβος εἴη, *they knew that the fear was groundless* (direct: ὁ φόβος κενὸς ἦν), compare § 523.

b) as a substitute for the *Subjunctive* (§ 527, *b*), i. e., when an Historical tense occurs in the leading sentence, in case the Dependent sentence, if conceived independently, ought to have the Subjunctive: ἐβουλευόμην, πῶς σε ἀποδραίην (direct: πῶς σε ἀποδρῶ) [Lat. *deliberabam, quo*

§ 530. MOODS IN SENTENCES OF PURPOSE. 291

modo te effugerem], *I was reflecting how I should escape you.*

In the second case the Optative is to be translated by *should*.

Obs.—Which of the two meanings belongs to the Optative is generally perceived from the connection quite as easily as in the Latin *nesciebat quid faceret, he knew not what he did or what he should do.*

§ 529. The Optative as a substitute for the Indicative is found also without a Conjunction in the continuation of a direct speech: ἔλεγον πολλοί, ὅτι παντὸς ἄξια λέγει (§ 526, b), χειμὼν γὰρ εἴη καὶ οἴκαδε ἀποπλεῖν οὐ δυνατὸν εἴη, *many said that he says what is worthy of the utmost regard, for that it was winter, and that it was impossible to sail home.*

On the Infinitive in assertions, § 560. On the Participle in assertions, § 593.

Mixed examples:

Πυθαγόρας ὁ Σάμιος πρῶτος ἐν τοῖς ῞Ελλησιν ἐτόλμησεν εἰπεῖν, ὅτι τὸ μὲν σῶμα τεθνήξεται (§ 291), ἡ δὲ ψυχὴ ἀναπτᾶσα (§ 316, 5) οἰχήσεται ἀθάνατος καὶ ἀγήρως, *Pythagoras the Samian was the first among the Greeks who ventured to maintain that the body will be dead, but the soul, flying upward, will depart immortal and ever young;* Θεμιστοκλῆς νέος ἔτι ὢν ἔλεγεν, ὡς καθεύδειν αὐτὸν οὐκ ἐῴη τὸ τοῦ Μιλτιάδου τρόπαιον, *Themistocles, when still young, used to say that the trophy of Miltiades would not let him sleep ;* Ἀπορῶ, τοῦ (§ 214, *Obs.* 1) πρῶτον μνησθῶ, *I am at a loss what to mention first;* οἱ Ἐπιδάμνιοι τὸν θεὸν ἐπήροντο, εἰ παραδοῖεν Κορινθίοις τὴν πόλιν, *the Epidamnians asked the god whether they should give up their city to the Corinthians.*

II. MOODS IN SENTENCES OF PURPOSE, OR FINAL SENTENCES.

§ 530. Sentences which express an object or a purpose are introduced by the Conjunction ἵνα (Hom. ὄφρα), ὡς, ὅπως, *in order that, that, in order to,* μή, or ὅπως μή, ἵνα μή, *in order that not.*

As such sentences express something which *is expected* to happen, they take:

§ 531. 1. The *Subjunctive*

a) *necessarily* when the leading sentence has a Principal tense: εἰς καιρὸν ἥκεις, ὅπως τῆς δίκης ἀκούσῃς, *you have come at the right time to hear the trial* [*in tempore ades, ut causam audias*].

b) *more rarely* when the leading sentence has an Historical tense: εἰς καιρὸν ἧκες, ὅπως τῆς δίκης ἀκούσῃς [*aderas ut audires*]; ἐπίτηδές σε οὐκ ἤγειρον, ἵνα ὡς ἥδιστα διάγῃς, *I purposely did not wake you, that you might pass your time as pleasantly as possible.*

> *Obs.*—The Conjunctions ὡς, ὅπως, sometimes have ἄν (Hom. κέ, κέν) added to them in this sense: τοῦτ' αὐτὸ νῦν δίδασχ', ὅπως ἂν ἐκμάθω, *explain that very thing now that I may learn it*. The purpose is thereby represented as one whose attainment depends on conditions (as here, if you explain it). Compare § 554.

§ 532. 2. The *Optative*
as a regular substitute for the Subjunctive (§ 531, b), when the leading sentence has an Historical tense: ἐπίτηδές σε οὐκ ἤγειρον, ἵνα ὡς ἥδιστα διάγοις; Hom. Τυδείδῃ Διομήδεϊ Παλλὰς Ἀθήνη δῶκε μένος καὶ θάρσος ἵν' ἔκδηλος μετὰ πᾶσιν Ἀργείοισι γένοιτο, *to Tydides Diomedes Pallas Athene gave strength and courage that he might be distinguished among all the Argives* [*Diomedi Minerva animos dedit, ut insignis fieret inter cunctos Argivos*].

> *Obs.*—The distinction between the Subjunctive and Optative in sentences of purpose after an Historical tense consists in the rarer Subjunctive expressing the sentence more as an object or demand that may be attained, the Optative more as the thought or conception of the acting person (compare §§ 521, 522).
> On the Future Indicative with ὅπως, §§ 500, 553. On the hypothetical Indicative in Sentences of Purpose, § 500. On the non-intended consequence (ὥστε), § 565.

§ 533. Sentences expressive of *fear*, introduced by μή (Lat. *ne*) or μὴ οὐ (Lat. *ut*), follow the construction of sentences of purpose (compare § 512). They have the *Subjunctive* necessarily when dependent

§ 536. MOODS IN CONDITIONAL SENTENCES. 293

on a *Principal tense*: οὐ φοβεῖ, μὴ ἤδη πρεσβύτερος ᾖς ; *do you not fear to be already too old* [*nonne times, ne ætate provectior sis*] ? The *Optative* is commonly used after an Historical tense: ἐφοβοῦντο, μή τι πάθοι, *they feared he might suffer somewhat* [*verebantur ne quid illi accideret*] ; but not unfrequently also the Subjunctive : οἱ Ἀθηναῖοι τοὺς ξυμμάχους ἐδεδίεσαν, μὴ ἀποστῶσιν, *the Athenians were alarmed lest the allies should revolt* (compare § 519, 5, *Obs.* 2).

Obs.—μή and ὅπως μή after verbs of fearing seldom have the Future *Indicative*, oftener the Perfect Indicative when the fear refers to a completed action : φοβούμεθα, μὴ ἀμφοτέρων ἡμαρτήκαμεν, *we fear we have failed in both*.

Mixed examples:

τοῦτο οὐ προῄρημαί λέγειν, ἵνα τισὶν ὑμῶν ἀπεχθάνωμαι, *I have not chosen to say this in order to be hateful to some of you ;* Κῦρος φίλων ᾤετο δεῖσθαι, ὡς συνεργοὺς ἔχοι, *Cyrus thought friends necessary that he might have helpers ;* Δέδοικα, μὴ ἐπιλαθώμεθα τῆς οἴκαδε ὁδοῦ, *I am afraid lest we should forget the way home ;* Φίλιππος ἐν φόβῳ ἦν, μὴ ἐκφύγοι τὰ πράγματα αὐτόν, *Philip was in fear lest the affairs might escape him.*

III. The Moods in Conditional Sentences.

§ 534. Conditional or hypothetical sentences belong to the *Correlative* sentences (§ 519, 4). The *Protasis* states a condition under which something is to occur ; the *Apodosis* states that something happens under a certain condition. Both sentences together form a *Hypothetical Period*.

§ 535. In the *Protasis*, εἰ (Hom. αἰ), ἐάν (*i. e.*, εἰ-ἄν), contracted to ἤν or ἄν (Hom. εἴ κε-ν), *if*, are employed ; in the Apodosis the particle ἄν is sometimes used to show that it is true only under certain conditions.

In Greek there are *four* principal forms of the Hypothetical Period :

§ 536. 1. in the Protasis εἰ with the *Indicative*, in the Apodosis the *Indicative without ἄν*, or the Imperative.

This form of the Hypothetical Period is employed when the relation between the Protasis and Apodosis is to be represented as one *absolutely necessary, actual,* without any opinion being expressed by the speaker as to the probability or improbability of the case: εἰ θεοί εἰσίν, ἔστι καὶ ἔργα θεῶν, *if there are gods, there are also works of gods;* σοὶ εἴ πῃ ἄλλῃ δέδοκται, λέγε καὶ δίδασκε, *if you have any different opinion, speak and explain.*

> *Obs.*—All tenses may be used in this form, consequently also Historical tenses. If these latter occur, care must be taken not to confound this first principal form with the second: ἐξῆν σοι ἀπιέναι ἐκ τῆς πόλεως, εἰ μὴ ἤρεσκόν σοι οἱ νόμοι, *you were free to leave the city if its laws did not please you* (in the present: ἔξεστι —εἰ μὴ ἀρέσκουσι); εἴ τι τῶν δεόντων ἐπράχθη, τὸν καιρόν, οὐκ ἐμέ φησιν αἴτιον γεγενῆσθαι, *if any thing right was done, he says that the occasion, not I, was the cause.* A sure sign of the second principal form is the particle ἄν in the apodosis.

§ 537. 2. in the Protasis, εἰ with the Indicative of an *Historical* tense; in the Apodosis, ἄν with the Indicative of an *Historical* tense.

This form of the Hypothetical Period is applied when the relation between the Protasis and Apodosis is to be represented indeed as one *quite necessary,* but at the same time *neither of them as real.* The Indicative in such conditional sentences is called *the Hypothetical Indicative,* which, therefore, always denotes the *opposite to reality* (compare § 515).

In such Conditional Sentences, a sentence contradictory of the Protasis may always be supplied in thought.

Hence the *Protasis* may have the following forms:

§ 538. *a)* The *Imperfect* is used when a condition is stated as *not* existing *at present:* εἰ τὸν Φίλιππον τὰ δίκαια πράττοντα ἑώρων, σφόδρα ἂν θαυμαστὸν ἡγούμην αὐτόν, *if I saw* (were to see) *Philip acting justly, I should deem him very admirable.* Here we may oppose to the Protasis the thought νῦν δὲ οὐχ ὁρῶ τὰ δίκαια πράττοντα, *but now*

§ 541. MOODS IN CONDITIONAL SENTENCES. 295.

I see him not act justly. The verb of this contradiction to be supplied is in the *Present*. To this form corresponds in Latin the Imperfect Subjunctive: *si viderem, putarem*.

§ 539. *b*) The *Aorist* Indicative is used when a condition is stated which did *not* take place in the *past*: ἀπέθανον ἄν, εἰ μὴ ἡ τῶν τριάκοντα ἀρχὴ κατελύθη, *I should have died if the government of the thirty had not been overthrown*. Here we may oppose to the Protasis the thought κατελύθη δέ, *but it was overthrown*. The verb of this contradiction to be supplied is in the *Aorist*. To this form corresponds in Latin the Pluperfect Subjunctive: *periissem, nisi dominatio eversa esset*.

§ 540. *c*) The *Pluperfect* is used when a *non-completed* condition is stated: εἰ τοῦτο ὡμολόγητο ἡμῖν, ῥᾳδίως ἂν διεμαχόμεθα, *if in this we had been agreed, we should easily carry the contest through*. Here we may oppose to the Protasis the thought ἀλλ' οὐχ ὡμολόγηται, *but we have not been agreed*. The verb of this contradiction to be supplied is in the *Perfect*. To this form corresponds in Latin the Pluperfect Subjunctive: *si inter nos convenisset*.

§ 541. The *Apodosis* to a Hypothetical Protasis of this kind may have either the *Imperfect* or the *Aorist Indicative*, or the *Pluperfect* with ἄν [Hom. κέ-ν], and that quite independently as to which of the three tenses occurs in the Protasis. In this case, also, the Imperfect corresponds to the Latin Imperfect Subjunctive; the Aorist and Pluperfect, to the Latin Pluperfect Subjunctive: εἰ τότε ἐβοηθήσαμεν, οὐκ ἂν ἠνώχλει νῦν ὁ Φίλιππος, *if we then had rendered help, Philip would not now be troublesome;* εἰ αὐτάρκη τὰ ψηφίσματα ἦν, Φίλιππος πάλαι ἂν ἐδεδώκει δίκην, *si plebiscita per se sufficerent, Philippus dudum poenam dedisset*.

§ 542. *Obs.* 1.—The particle ἄν is sometimes omitted in the apodosis : ᾐσχυνόμην, εἰ ὑπὸ πολεμίου γε ὄντος ἐξηπατήθην, *I should be ashamed if I had been deceived by an enemy.*

§ 543. *Obs.* 2.—The Imperfect sometimes refers to a past time when the continuance of an action is to be made particularly emphatic : εἰ τοῦτ' ἐποίει (not ἐποίησεν) ἕκαστος, ἑνίκων ἄν, *if each had been acting so, they would be victorious.* On the other hand, the *Aorist* is sometimes used referring to present time, when the rapid commencement of an action is to be indicated : εἴ τίς σε ἤρετο, τί ἂν ἀπεκρίνω (not ἀπεκρίνου) ; *if any one asked you, what answer would you give?*

§ 544. *Obs.* 3.—A Hypothetical Apodosis may stand alone, the Protasis being supplied in thought or deduced from the context : ἐβουλόμην ἄν, *I should like* (εἰ ἐδυνάμην, *if I could, dared*); δι' ὑμᾶς αὐτοὺς πάλαι ἂν ἀπολώλειτε, *you would long since have perished through yourselves* (*i. e.*, if left to yourselves).

§ 545. 3. in the *Protasis*, ἐάν (ἤν, ἄν, Hom. εἴ κε-ν) with the *Subjunctive ;* in the *Apodosis*, the *Indicative* of a *Principal tense* or the Imperative.

This form of the Hypothetical Period is used to express or prescribe something in regard to a case that is *to be taken for granted* and *expected.* It is admissible only in connection with *present and future time* (§ 521), and is met with chiefly in maxims or proverbs : δεῖ τὰ βέλτιστα ἀντὶ τῶν ἡδέων, ἂν μὴ συναμφότερα ἐξῇ, λαμβάνειν, *you must choose what is best rather than what is agreeable, when both together are not allowed ;* ἂν τὰ παρεληλυθότα μνημονεύῃς, ἄμεινον περὶ τῶν μελλόντων βουλεύσει, *if you remember the past, you will judge better about the future.*

Obs. 1.—The Aorist Subjunctive in such conditional sentences often comes very near to the Latin *Future Perfect :* νέος ἂν πονήσῃς, γῆρας ἕξεις εὐθαλές, *si juvenis laboraveris, senectutem habebis jucundam.*

Obs. 2.—We find εἰ with the Subjunctive in Homer, and occasionally also in Attic writers, in the same sense as ἐάν, εἰ ἄν, and εἴ κε-ν : Soph. ἄνδρα, κεἴ τις ᾖ σοφός, τὸ μανθάνειν πόλλ', αἰσχρὸν οὐδέν, *for a man, even if he is wise, to learn much, is no disgrace.*

Obs. 3.—The Subjunctive in Conditional sentences is akin to the

§ 548. MOODS IN CONDITIONAL SENTENCES. 297

Subjunctive of Challenging (§ 509). The speaker thereby puts or demands an assertion, to which, for the present, he requires the hearer's assent: τοῦτο ἐὰν σκοπῆτε, εὑρήσετε, ὅτι πάντων ἄριστα ἔχει, *if you consider this you will find that it is the best of all;* which is almost identical with the challenge: consider this, etc. [compare Lat. *Naturam expellas furca, tamen usque recurret*]. In a similar way the *Imperative* sometimes takes the place of a Hypothetical Protasis: Poet. πλούτει τε γὰρ κατ' οἶκον, εἰ βούλει, μέγα καὶ ζῆ τύραννον σχῆμ' ἔχων, ἐὰν δ' ἀπῇ τούτων τὸ χαίρειν, τἆλλ' ἐγὼ καπνοῦ σκιᾶς οὐκ ἂν πριαίμην, *for be rich, if you will, at home, and live in the splendor of a great ruler; but if joy be wanting to it, I would not give the shadow of smoke for the rest.* (Compare § 549.)

§ 546. 4. in the Protasis, εἰ with the *Optative;* in the Apodosis, ἄν (κέ-ν) with the *Optative.*

This form of the Hypothetical Period is employed intentionally to represent what is said as quite uncertain, as *merely possible*, as a merely conceived case: εἴ τις κεκτημένος εἴη πλοῦτον, χρῷτο δὲ αὐτῷ μή, ἆρ' ἂν εὐδαιμονοῖ; *should any one possess wealth and not make use of it* (suppose any one possessed), *would he be happy?* Compare §§ 516, 517, *Obs.* 2. The *Present* or *Perfect* Subjunctive in Latin corresponds to this form: *si possideat* (or *possederit*), *num beatus sit?*

Obs.—In Homer the Protasis of such a period also sometimes has κέ-ν or ἄν: εἰ τούτω κε λάβοιμεν, ἀροίμεθά κεν κλέος ἐσθλόν, *if we should get these two, we should get glorious fame.* The Attic writers very rarely use ἄν in the Protasis.

§ 547. Since εἰ with the Optative intimates that a thing is merely possible, it expresses in reference to the past what possibly might have been, *i. e.*, a *repeated* case (compare § 494, *Obs.* 1); the Apodosis then usually has the Indicative: εἴ που ἐξελαύνοι Ἀστυάγης, ἐφ' ἵππου χρυσοχαλίνου περιῆγε τὸν Κῦρον, *if ever Astyages rode out* (might ride out), *he took Cyrus with him on a horse with a golden bridle.*

§ 548. εἰ with the Optative in the *oratio obliqua* takes the place, according to § 523, of εἰ with the Ind. (1), or

298   MOODS IN CONDITIONAL SENTENCES.   § 549.

ἐάν with the Subjunctive (3), when a Hypothetical sentence depends on a *Historical tense*: ᾔδει Κῦρος, ὅτι εἴ τι μάχης ποτὲ δεήσοι, ἐκ τῶν φίλων αὐτῷ παραστάτας ληπτέον εἴη, *Cyrus knew that, if ever any battle should be necessary, he would have to take his supporters from his own friends.* In direct language, Cyrus would say, ἤν ποτε δεήσῃ or εἴ ποτε δεήσει—ληπτέον ἐστί. If, in its relation to the time of the governing verb, the condition lies in the Future, the Future Optative is used. We seldom, in this case, find ἐάν with the Subjunctive.

The following general remarks also are to be observed in regard to Conditional sentences. °

§ 549. 1. The two members of a Hypothetical Period are not so dependent on each other as that the one necessarily requires a special form in the other. A Protasis of one form may, on the contrary, be joined with the Apodosis of another form. It occurs very frequently that a Protasis is in the first or third form, and the Apodosis in the fourth, in order to represent the Assertion which it contains as *merely possible:* εἰ τοῦτο λέγεις, ἁμαρτάνοις ἄν, *if you mean this, you would be in error;* ἐὰν ἐθελήσητε πράττειν ἀξίως ὑμῶν αὐτῶν, ἴσως ἂν μέγα τι κτήσαισθε ἀγαθόν, *if you should be disposed to act in a manner worthy of yourselves, you would perhaps gain great good.* The connection of a Protasis of the second form with an Apodosis of the fourth is rare: Hom. καί νύ κεν ἔνθ᾽ ἀπόλοιτο ἄναξ ἀνδρῶν Αἰνείας, εἰ μὴ ἄρ᾽ ὀξὺ νόησε Διὸς θυγάτηρ Ἀφροδίτη, *and now assuredly Æneas, ruler of men, would there have perished, if Zeus's daughter Aphrodite had not kept a sharp lookout.*

§ 550. 2. A Hypothetical Period may partly or entirely be inserted in another sentence. The most peculiar in this respect are sentences expressing a purpose, when connected with Conditional sentences: εἰ γὰρ ὤφελον οἷοίτε εἶναι οἱ πολλοὶ τὰ μέγιστα κακὰ ἐξεργάζεσθαι, ἵνα οἷοίτε ἦσαν αὖ καὶ ἀγαθὰ τὰ μέγιστα, *I would that the many were capable of doing* (to a man) *the greatest evil,* in order that they *might also, on the*

§ 552. MOODS IN RELATIVE SENTENCES. 299

other hand, be capable of (effecting) *the greatest good* (instead of: for if they were capable, they would also be capable). The Hypothetical Indicative here denotes the impracticable purpose (§§ 515, 537). On the Hypothetical Participle, §§ 583, 595. On the Hypothetical Infinitive, § 575, etc.

Mixed examples:

Εἰ ὑπὸ φίλων ἐθέλεις ἀγαπᾶσθαι, τοὺς φίλους εὐεργετητέον, *if you wish to be loved by your friends, you must benefit your friends;* Εἰ τὸ ἔχειν οὕτως ὥσπερ τὸ λαμβάνειν ἡδὺ ἦν, πολὺ ἂν διέφερον εὐδαιμονίᾳ οἱ πλούσιοι τῶν πενήτων, *if having were as sweet as getting, the rich would be greatly distinguished above the poor in blessedness;* Poet. Εἰ πᾶσι ταὐτὸ καλὸν ἔφυ σοφόν θ' ἅμα, οὐκ ἦν ἂν ἀμφίλεκτος ἀνθρώποις ἔρις, *if the same things were to all beautiful and wise, people would have no bitter disputes;* Πλάτων πρός τινα τῶν παίδων, μεμαστίγωσο ἄν, ἔφη, εἰ μὴ ὠργιζόμην, *Plato said to one of his servants, you would have been flogged if I were not angry;* Ἐὰν μέν τι ὑμῖν δοκῶ ἀληθὲς λέγειν, ξυνομολογήσατε, *if you think I utter any truth, agree with me;* Εἰ πόλις ἀνδρῶν ἀγαθῶν γένοιτο, περιμάχητον ἂν εἴη τὸ μὴ ἄρχειν, ὥςπερ νυνὶ τὸ ἄρχειν, *if there were a state* (consisting) *of good men, it would be an object of contention to avoid ruling* (how one might not rule), *as now to rule;* Ἦν τῶν στρατιωτῶν δόγμα, εἴ τις, ὁπότε ἡ στρατιὰ ἐξίοι, ἰδίᾳ ληίζοιτο, δημόσια εἶναι τὰ ληφθέντα, *it was a decision of the soldiers, if, when the army went out, any one took booty by himself, what he took was common property* (direct ἐὰν ληίζηται—δημόσια ἔστω).

IV. THE MOODS IN RELATIVE SENTENCES.

§ 551. *Relative sentences* are those which are connected with others by means of Relative pronouns (§§ 213, 214, 216) or Relative adverbs (§ 217).

§ 552. In Relative sentences *all* moods are possible in the same meanings as in independent or hypothetical sentences: οὐκ ἔχω ὅ τι πρῶτον λάβω, *I have* (know) *not what I shall take first* (§ 511, compare § 527); ὁρῶ σε διώκοντα ὧν μὴ τύχοις, *I see you pursuing what, I pray, you may not attain* (§ 514); ὑμεῖς ἐστε παρ' ὧν ἂν κάλλιστά τις τοῦτο μάθοι, *you are they from whom any one might best learn this* (§ 516); οὐκ ἤθελον λέγειν πρὸς ὑμᾶς τοιαῦτα οἷ' ἂν ὑμῖν ἥδιστ' ἦν ἀκούειν, *I did not wish to say to you such things as might be pleasantest to you to hear.* Compare § 544.

Obs.—Sometimes, especially in the Poets, Relative sentences have the Optative without ἄν in an indefinite assertion, very much like the potential Optative with ἄν: ὃν πόλις στήσειε, τοῦδε χρὴ κλύειν, *whom the state may appoint, him we must listen to* (compare § 517, *Obs.* 2).

§ 553. On the *Future Indicative* in Relative sentences expressive of purpose, see § 500. ὅπως, *how, that, in order that,* very frequently has the Future Indicative (yet, according to § 531, also the Subjunctive of other tenses) after verbs which denote *looking after, caring for, striving, avoiding:* σκόπει, ὅπως τὰ πράγματα σωθήσεται, *see that the affairs* (the state) *shall be safe;* δεῖ ἐκ παντὸς τρόπου ἅπαντα ἄνδρα τοῦτο παρασκευάζεσθαι, ὅπως ὡς σοφώτατος ἔσται, *every one ought to take care in every way to* (that he shall) *become as wise as possible.*

Obs.—ὅπως is often used in challenges and warnings in such a manner that the governing sentence has to be supplied: ὅπως παρέσει εἰς τὴν ἑσπέραν, *that you shall be here for the evening* (more completely somewhat like: σκόπει ὅπως, *see that you,* etc.); ὅπως περὶ τοῦ πολέμου μηδὲν ἐρεῖς, *that you shall say nothing about the war* (supply something like: φυλάττου, *take care*).

§ 554. The particle ἄν (Hom. κέ-ν) is added to the Relative when the Relative sentence expresses something *merely conceived,* so that the assertion contained in the leading sentence is true only when what is asserted in the Relative sentence really occurs. Such a Relative is called a *Hypothetical Relative.* The Hypothetical Relative with ἄν in

§ 555. MOODS IN RELATIVE SENTENCES. 301

general is used only where the verb in the leading sentence is in a *principal tense*, and is then accompanied by the *Subjunctive*. Such a Relative sentence may easily be changed to a Hypothetical sentence of the third form (§ 545); πᾶν ὅ τι ἂν μέλλῃς ἐρεῖν πρότερον ἐπισκόπει τῇ γνώμῃ, *whatever you may be about to say* (= ἐάν τι ἐρεῖν μέλλῃς), *examine it first in your mind;* in which it is left quite undecided whether one wishes to say any thing; ἕπεσθε ὅπῃ ἄν τις ἡγῆται, *follow wherever any one may lead you* (= ἐάν τίς πῃ ἡγῆται), where you must first wait to know whether any one leads.

Obs. 1.—As the Relative is generalized by the addition of ἄν, it may often in English be translated by *ever* (Lat. *cunque*) : ὅς ἂν τούτων τι δρᾷ τεθνάτω, *quicunque horum aliquid fecerit, perito ;* λέγε ὅσ' ἂν θέλῃς, *say whatever you wish* (compare ἐάν . τι θέλῃς λέγε).

Obs. 2.—In the same sense the Poets use the Subjunctive with a Relative without ἄν (or κέ-ν) : τῶν δὲ πημονῶν μάλιστα λυποῦσ' αἱ φανῶσ' αὐθαίρετοι, *the sufferings afflict most which appear self-caused* (compare εἰ with the Subj., § 545, *Obs.* 2). Homer has also the Fut. Ind. with κέ and the Relative (§ 500, *Obs.*).

§ 555. If the verb in the leading sentence is an *Historical tense* or an *Optative*, the Relative *without* ἄν with the *Optative* is used, quite in the same sense, as a substitute for the Subjunctive (§§ 522, 523). These Relative sentences take the place of those mentioned in § 554, in the same way as the *fourth* kind of Conditional sentences takes the place of the third (§ 548): ἐκέλευσεν αὐτοῖς ἕπεσθαι, ὅποι τις ἡγοῖτο, *he bade them follow wherever any one might lead.* Thus we read in Homer: ὅν δέ κ' ἐγὼν ἀπάνευθε μάχης ἐθέλοντα νοήσω μιμνάζειν, οὔ οἱ ἔπειτα ἄρκιον ἐσσεῖται φυγέειν κύνας ἠδ' οἰωνούς, *but whomsoever I may see inclined to remain away from the battle, to him there shall be no security of escaping dogs and birds* (*i. e.*, death), but: ὅντινα μὲν βασιλῆα καὶ ἔξοχον ἄνδρα κιχείη, τὸν δ' ἀγανοῖς ἐπέεσσιν ἐρητύσασκε, *but whatever* (where a) *king or prominent man he might meet with, him he* soothed with gentle words. Hom. ὡς ἀπόλοιτο καὶ ἄλλος ὅ τις τοιαῦτά γε ῥέζοι, so may any other perish who shall do such things (but ὃς ἂν ῥέζῃ—ἀπολέσθω).

Obs. 1.—This Optative often implies repetition: ὅντινα κιχείη, as often as he might find one (§ 547).

Obs. 2.—The Subjunctive and the Relative with ἄν occur only exceptionally after an Historical tense, and the Optative with the Relative and ἄν, in the same case (compare § 546, *Obs.*).

V. THE MOODS IN TEMPORAL SENTENCES.

§ 556. Temporal Sentences, *i. e.*, those which indicate time, are properly only a particular kind of Relative sentences, and follow them almost entirely in the use of the Moods. The particles of time employed in such sentences are: ἐπεί, ἐπειδή, ὡς (*when, after, as*); ὅτε, ὁπότε, ἡνίκα, *when, as;* ἕως, ἔςτε, μέχρι-ς, *till;* πρίν, *before;* in Hom. ὄφρα, *as long as, till;* ἦμος, *when;* and besides the Relative expressions: ἀφ' οὗ, ἐξ οὗ, *since;* ἐν ᾧ, *whilst;* ἄχρι οὗ, εἰς ὅ, *until.*

In these sentences the *Indicative* is used when any thing *actual* is stated; the *Optative* may supply the place of the Indicative in indirect speech after an Historical tense (§ 522).

§ 557. When a Temporal sentence states something merely *conceived*, occurring only conditionally, the particle of time, like the Relative, has ἄν (κέ-ν) joined to it (§ 554). This occurs usually only when the leading sentence has a *principal tense*, and the *Subjunctive* must then follow. By combination with ἄν are formed the Hypothetical particles of time: ὅταν, ὁπόταν, ἐπεάν or ἐπήν, ἐπειδάν: ἐπειδὰν πάντα ἀκούσητε, κρίνατε, *when ye have heard all, judge;* ἕως ἂν σώζηται τὸ σκάφος, τότε χρὴ καὶ ναύτην καὶ κυβερνήτην καὶ πάντ' ἄνδρα προθύμους εἶναι, *as long as the vessel is safe, the sailor, the pilot, and every one ought to be zealous.*

Obs.—Here also ἄν is sometimes wanting (§ 554, *Obs.* 2).

§ 558. MOODS IN TEMPORAL SENTENCES. 303

§ 558. If the leading verb is in an *Historical tense*, the particle of time with the Optative without ἄν occurs in the same sense: ἔλεγεν ὅτι, ἐπειδὴ πάντα ἀκούσειαν, κρίνειαν.

Obs. 1.—Here, too, the Optative often implies repetition (compare § 554, *Obs.*, and § 547), so that ὅτε, ὁπότε, ἐπεί, with the Optative, may be translated by "as often as," "whenever:" ὁπότε οἱ Ἕλληνες τοῖς πολεμίοις ἐπίοιεν, ῥᾳδίως ἀπέφευγον, *as often as the Hellenes went up to the enemy, the latter readily fled.*

Obs. 2.—Here, too, exceptionally, ἄν and the Subjunctive sometimes occur after an Historical tense (§ 555, *Obs.* 2).
On πρίν with the Infinitive, § 565.

Mixed Examples of Relative and Temporal Sentences.

Ἡμεῖς πάντα λογισάμενοι ταῦτα χειροτονεῖθ', ὅ τι ἂν ὑμῖν δοκῇ μάλιστα συμφέρειν τῇ πόλει, *after having weighed all this, vote for what you think will most benefit the state;* Οἱ τῶν βαρβάρων ἱππεῖς, ᾧτινι ἐντυγχάνοιεν Ἕλληνι, πάντας ἔκτεινον, *the cavalry of the barbarians, whatever Greek they met, killed them all;* Μέχρις ἂν ἐγὼ ἥκω, αἱ σπονδαὶ μενόντων, *till I come, let the treaty remain;* Poet. Μήποτ' ἐπαινήσῃς, πρὶν ἂν εἰδῇς ἄνδρα σαφηνῶς, ὀργὴν καὶ ῥυθμὸν καὶ τρόπον ὅστις ἂν ᾖ, *never praise a man before you clearly know his temper, and bearing, and character;* Ἐπειδή τι ἐμφάγοιεν, ἀνίσταντο καὶ ἐπορεύοντο, *after having eaten something, they rose and proceeded;* Ὁ Σωκράτης τοὺς συνόντας ἐποίει, οὐ μόνον ὁπότε ὑπὸ τῶν ἀνθρώπων ὁρῷντο, ἀπέχεσθαι τῶν ἀδίκων καὶ αἰσχρῶν, ἀλλὰ καὶ ὁπότε ἐν ἐρημίᾳ εἶεν, *Socrates caused his disciples to abstain from what was unjust and shameful, not only when they were seen by men, but also when they were in solitude.*

Chap. XXII.—The Infinitive.

A) *The use of the Infinitive generally.*

§ 559. 1. The Infinitive is a *verbal noun* (§ 225, 5) which, as such, has certain properties in common with a verb, others with a noun.

With a *noun* the Infinitive agrees

a) in expressing the action of a verb in general, like the *nomina actionis* (§ 342): ποιεῖν, πράττειν, *doing;* compare ποίησις, πρᾶξις.

b) in the fact that it may have the article like nouns: τὸ ποιεῖν, τὸ πράττειν, *the doing;* compare ἡ ποίησις, ἡ πρᾶξις.

With the verb, on the other hand, the Infinitive agrees

a) in its power of denoting different *times:* ποιεῖν, ποιῆσαι, πεποιηκέναι, and of being formed from the Active, the Middle, and the Passive: ποιῆσαι, ποιήσασθαι, ποιηθῆναι.

b) in being occasionally joined with ἄν, and thereby sharing the functions of mood (§ 575, etc.).

c) in governing the same case as the verb to which it belongs: ποιεῖν τὰ δέοντα, *doing your duty;* χρῆσθαι τοῖς ὅπλοις, *making use of arms.*

d) in being qualified, like the finite verb, by *adverbs*, never by adjectives: καλῶς πράττειν, *doing nobly;* but καλὴ πρᾶξις, *a noble action.*

2. The Infinitive is used very extensively in Greek. Very often, besides the more definite mode of expression, by means of a Conjunction with a *finite verb*, the less definite, by means of the Infinitive, is admissible.

§ 560. The Infinitive serves to complete and qualify different sorts of verbs, viz.:

1. those which express the occasion, capability, modality of an action: δύνανται ἀπελθεῖν, *they can go away;* μεῖζόν

τι ἔχει εἰπεῖν, *he has something greater to say* (can say);
Poet. οὗτοι συνέχθειν ἀλλὰ συμφιλεῖν ἔφυν, *I am born not
to join in hating but in loving;* ἄρχομαι λέγειν, *I begin
to speak;* ἐπιτρέπω σοι ποιεῖν ὅ τι ἂν βούλῃ, *I leave you to
do whatever you wish;*

2. such verbs as denote appearance, perception, opinion:
δοκεῖς ἁμαρτεῖν, *you seem to have erred;*

3. such verbs as denote striving after something, impelling toward, or frightening, deterring, preventing something: μὴ σπεῦδε πλουτεῖν, *do not hasten to be rich;* Hom.
κέλεαί με μυθήσασθαι, *you bid me to speak;* πάντες αἰτοῦνται τοὺς θεοὺς τὰ φαῦλα ἀποτρέπειν, *omnes homines
precantur deos, ut mala avertant;* φοβοῦμαι διελέγχειν σε,
I am afraid of refuting you; ἔλεγόν σοι μὴ γαμεῖν, *dixi
tibi, ne uxorem duceres;* τίς αὐτὸν κωλύσει δεῦρο βαδίζειν;
quis eum impediet, quominus huc veniat? ἀνεβάλλετό μοι
διαλεχθῆναι, *he put off conversing with me.*

§ 561. Even the *purpose* of an action may be expressed
by the mere Infinitive, as in English by the Infinitive with
to or *in order to:* Ξενοφῶν τὸ ἥμισυ τοῦ στρατεύματος
κατέλιπε φυλάττειν τὸ στρατόπεδον, *Xenophon left half the
army behind to guard the camp;* παρέχω ἐμαυτὸν τῷ ἰατρῷ
τέμνειν καὶ καίειν, *I give myself up to the physician to cut
and burn* (me); πιεῖν διδόναι τινί, *to give any one* (something) *to drink.*

Obs.—Not only with verbs of this kind, but also with those mentioned in § 560, this Infinitive has a much wider application in
Homer: ἀριστεύεσκε μάχεσθαι, *he used to be the first in fighting;* εἰσὶ
καὶ οἵδε τάδ' εἰπέμεν, *these too, then, are* (able) *to say this;* βῆ ἰέναι,
he started to go; ξυνέηκε μάχεσθαι, *he urged* (them) *to fight.*

§ 562. The Infinitive serves to complete or qualify *adjectives* of different kinds, partly in the sense of the English Infinitive with *to,* partly corresponding to the Latin
supine in *u:* χαλεπὸν εὑρεῖν, *difficult to find* [*difficile inventu*]; οἰκία ἡδίστη ἐνδιαιτᾶσθαι, *a house very pleasant to*

live in; ἄξιός ἐστι πληγὰς λαβεῖν, *he deserves to get blows;* ὀξύτατοί ἐστε γνῶναι τὰ ῥηθέντα, *you are very keen in perceiving what is said;* δεινὸς λέγειν, *powerful in speaking;* ὁ χρόνος βραχὺς ἀξίως διηγήσασθαι τὰ πραχθέντα, *the time is short for worthily narrating what has happened.*

Obs.—In Homer such Infinitives are particularly frequent: μέγα καὶ ἐσσομένοισι πυθέσθαι, *great also for posterity to learn;* θείειν ἀνέμοισιν ὅμοιοι, *like the winds in running;* so with some substantives: θαῦμα ἰδέσθαι, *a wonder to see.*
On οἷος, οἷόςτε, and ὅσος, with the Inf., § 601.

§ 563. The Infinitive, as in English and Latin, is used as the *Subject* of a sentence to which the predicate is a neuter adjective, a substantive, or an intransitive verb: πᾶσιν ἀδεῖν χαλεπόν, *to please all is difficult;* κίνδυνός ἐστιν ἡττᾶσθαι, *there is danger of being worsted;* σὸν ἔργον λέγειν, *speaking is your business.*

§ 564. The Infinitive is used in a freer way, without depending on a particular word, with and without the particle ὡς, in several phrases almost like a free Accusative (§ 404): ὡς εἰπεῖν, *so to speak;* ἐμοὶ δοκεῖν, *as seems to me;* ὀλίγου δεῖν, *almost;* τὸ νῦν εἶναι, *for the present;* κατὰ τοῦτο εἶναι, *in this respect.*
On ἑκὼν εἶναι, § 570, *Obs.*

§ 565. The *Conjunctions* ὥστε, *so that;* πρίν, *before,* and its Homeric synonym πάρος, are joined with the Infinitive: Φιλομαθέστατος ἦν ὁ Κῦρος, ὥστε πάντα πόνον ἀνατλῆναι τοῦ ἐπαινεῖσθαι ἕνεκα, *Cyrus was very fond of learning, so as to endure any trouble for the sake of being praised;* πρὶν τὴν ἀρχὴν ὀρθῶς ὑποθέσθαι, μάταιον ἡγοῦμαι περὶ τῆς τελευτῆς ὁντινοῦν ποιεῖσθαι λόγον, *before properly establishing the foundation, I deem it useless to make any words whatever about the end.*

Obs. 1.—These conjunctions may also be joined with the finite verb (compare § 556); ὥστε with the indicative represents a sentence as an actual consequence more independent and by itself, and may accordingly be often translated by *therefore, hence :* εἰς τὴν ὑστεραίαν οὐχ ἧκεν, ὥςθ' οἱ Ἕλληνες ἐφρόντιζον, *he came not on the following day, therefore the Hellenes became anxious.*

§ 567. THE INFINITIVE. 307

Obs. 2.—For πρίν we also find πρὶν ἤ, *prius-quam;* properly πρίν, when it means *sooner than*, is always to be regarded as an abbreviation for πρὶν ἤ, πρίν originally answering entirely to the Latin *prius*. On the Infinitive after ἤ, *than*, see the following §.

On ἐφ' ᾧτε, *on condition that*, with the Infin., § 601.

§ 566. After a comparative, the Infinitive is preceded by ἤ ὥστε or ἤ alone in the sense of *than that:* φοβοῦμαι μή τι μεῖζον ἤ ὥςτε φέρειν δύνασθαι κακὸν τῇ πόλει συμβῇ, *I fear lest too great an evil should befall the state for it to be able to bear* (greater than that it should be able).

On the Genitive of the Infinitive with the Article, which also is possible here, § 574, 3, *Obs.*

B) *The case of the Subject and Predicate with the Infinitive.*

§ 567. The *Subject* of the Infinitive is that word from which the action of the verb in the Infinitive proceeds. When the Subject is to be expressed with the Infinitive, it appears:

1. *most generally,* as in Latin, in the *Accusative,* which gives rise to the construction of the *Accusative* with the *Infinitive:* ἤγγειλαν τὸν Κῦρον νικῆσαι, *nuntiabant Cyrum vicisse.* The use of the Accusative with the Infinitive, like that of the Infinitive alone (§ 559, etc.), is more common in Greek than in Latin. Not only can the substance of a statement or perception—which, however, may be also expressed in one of the forms discussed, § 525, etc.—be given in this construction, but also the effect and consequence of an action. Hence the Accusative with the Infinitive also occurs after verbs of happening, and is admissible after verbs of commanding, demanding, forbidding: πάντες ὁμολογοῦσι τὴν ὁμόνοιαν μέγιστον ἀγαθὸν εἶναι, *all agree that concord is a very great good;* συνέβη μηδένα τῶν στρατηγῶν παρεῖναι, *it happened that none of the generals was present;* ἔγραψα ἀποπλεῖν τὴν ταχίστην τοὺς πρέσβεις, *proposui ut quam celerrime legati proficiscerentur.*

The Accusative with the Infinitive is properly dependent on the verb of the leading sentence (compare the English: I hear you sing, I bid you go), and is explained by the *prolepsis* mentioned in § 519, 5, *Obs.* 2. Instead of ἤγγειλαν ὅτι ὁ Κῦρος ἐνίκησεν, we might have : ἤγγειλαν τὸν Κῦρον ὅτι ἐνίκησεν ; and for ὅτι ἐνίκησεν, νικῆσαι, according to § 560, 2 ; thus we obtain ἤγγειλαν τὸν Κῦρον νικῆσαι. If the governing verb is intransitive or passive, the Accusative is of a freer kind (§ 404) : ἐλπίς ἐστι πάντα καλῶς ἔχειν, *there is hope that all is well.*

Obs. 1.—The impersonal verbs δεῖ and χρή, *it is necessary*, are joined with the Accusative and Infinitive like the Latin *oportet:* χρὴ τολμᾶν χαλεποῖσιν ἐν ἄλγεσι κείμενον ἄνδρα, *the man that lies in painful sufferings ought to be courageous.*

Obs. 2.—As a continuation of an Accusative with the Infinitive, the same construction may be employed in indirect speech in Relative sentences and after Conjunctions, denoting time and circumstances : τοιαῦτ' ἄττα σφᾶς ἔφη διαλεχθέντας ἰέναι · ἐπεὶ δὲ γενέσθαι ἐπὶ τῇ οἰκίᾳ τῇ Ἀγάθωνος, ἀνεῳγμένην καταλαμβάνειν τὴν θύραν, *he said that after such conversation they went ; but that, when they reached Agathon's house, they found the door open.*

§ 568. 2. A Predicate referring to such a Subject must necessarily be in the Accusative : τὸν ἄδικον καὶ πονηρὸν ἄνδρα φημὶ ἄθλιον εἶναι, *I maintain that the unjust and bad man is miserable.*

Not unfrequently a Predicative expression requires an indefinite Subject (τινά) to be supplied : τὰ τοιαῦτα ἔξεστι (τινα) μετρήσαντα καὶ ἀριθμήσαντα εἰδέναι, *one may know such things by measuring and counting.*

§ 569. 3. When the Subject of an Infinitive is *the same* as that *of the leading sentence*, it is usually *not* expressed *at all :* νομίζω νενικηκέναι, *puto me vicisse, I think I have conquered ;* ἐλπίζεις τεύξεσθαι ὧν ἂν δέῃ, *you hope to obtain what you need ;* ὑπέσχετο παρέσεσθαι εἰς τὴν ἑσπέραν, *promisit se affuturum ad vesperam.*

Obs.—For greater emphasis, especially when opposition to something else is to be expressed, the subject may be added, and that either in the Accusative or Nominative : Herod. οἱ Αἰγύπτιοι ἐνόμιζον ἑωυτοὺς πρώτους γενέσθαι ἀνθρώπων, *the Egyptians thought that they first of all men came into existence ;* εἰ οἴεσθε Χαλκιδέας ἢ Μεγαρέας τὴν Ἑλλάδα σώσειν, ὑμεῖς δὲ ἀποδράσεσθαι τὰ πράγματα,

§ 571. THE INFINITIVE. 309

οὐκ ὀρθῶς οἴεσθε, *if you think the Chalcidians and Megarians will save Greece, but you escape from trouble, you are mistaken.*

§ 570. 4. *Predicative* qualifications referring to the *Principal Subject* are in the *Nominative :* ὁ 'Αλέξανδρος ἔφασκεν εἶναι Διὸς υἱός, *Alexander dicebat se esse Jovis filium ;* ἐγὼ οὐκ ὁμολογήσω ἄκλητος ἥκειν, ἀλλ' ὑπὸ σοῦ κεκλημένος, *I will not acknowledge that I am come uninvited, but invited by you ;* οἱ δοκοῦντες σοφοὶ εἶναι, *they who seem to be wise.*

Obs.—From the Predicate, ἑκών, joining the freer Infinitive, εἶναι (§ 564), arises the combination ἑκὼν εἶναι : τοῦτο ἑκὼν εἶναι οὐ ποιήσω, *this* (if I am) *to be of free will I will not do.*

§ 571. 5. In many cases a *personal* instead of an *impersonal* form of expression is used in Greek, the Subject of the Infinitive being made the Subject of the leading sentence ; so, instead of the English "it was announced that Cyrus had conquered" (ἠγγέλθη τὸν Κῦρον νικῆσαι), we have, ὁ Κῦρος ἠγγέλθη νικῆσαι, *Cyrus was announced to have conquered.* This form of expression occurs not only—as in Latin with *dicitur, videtur*—with δοκεῖ, ἔοικε, *it seems ;* λέγεται [*dicitur, traditur*] ; ἀγγέλλεται, *it is announced ;* ὁμολογεῖται, *it is agreed,* but also with συμβαίνει, *it happens,* and with several adjectives with εἰμί, as : δίκαιος, *just ;* ἐπιτήδειος, ἐπικαίριος, *fitting ;* ἐπίδοξος, *probable ;* ἀναγκαῖος, *necessary ;* αὐτός μοι δοκῶ ἐνθάδε καταμενεῖν, *it appears to me that I myself shall remain here ;* δίκαιος εἶ ἄγειν ἀνθρώπους, *it is just that you should lead men* (you are justified in leading men); ἐπίδοξοί εἰσι τὸ αὐτὸ πείσεσθαι, *it is to be expected that they will suffer the same ;* Poet. πρέπων ἔφυς πρὸ τῶνδε φωνεῖν, *it becomes you to speak in their presence.*

The personal construction is explained, like that of the Accusative with the Infinitive (§ 567), by prolepsis (§ 519, 5, *Obs.* 2). For ἠγγέλθη ὅτι ὁ Κῦρος ἐνίκησε there might be ἠγγέλθη ὁ Κῦρος ὅτι ἐνίκησε, and for this again ἠγγέλθη ὁ Κῦρος νικῆσαι; for ἐπίδοξόν ἐστιν ὅτι τὸ αὐτὸ πείσονται—ἐπίδοξοί εἰσι ὅτι τὸ αὐτὸ πείσονται, and hence ἐπίδοξοί εἰσι τὸ αὐτὸ πείσεσθαι.

Obs.—The Accusative construction, however, is almost every where applicable: λέγεται τὸν Κῦρον νικῆσαι, *dicunt Cyrum vicisse.*

§ 572. 6. Predicative qualifications referring to a *Genitive* or *Dative* may be in these cases: ἦλθον ἐπί τινα τῶν δοκούντων σοφῶν εἶναι, *I came to one of those who seem to be wise;* ἔλεγον τοῖς δοκοῦσι σοφοῖς εἶναι, *I said to those,* etc.; Κύρου ἐδέοντο ὡς προθυμοτάτου γενέσθαι, *they begged Cyrus to be as ready as possible;* παντὶ ἄρχοντι προςήκει φρονίμῳ εἶναι, *it becomes every ruler to be judicious.*

Still the Predicate is often in the Accusative: συμφέρει αὐτοῖς φίλους εἶναι μᾶλλον ἢ πολεμίους, *it is to their advantage rather to be friends than enemies.*

C) *The Infinitive with the Article.*

§ 573. The Substantive nature of the Infinitive is made more manifest by prefixing the *Article.* Yet the Infinitive with the Article must nevertheless have a noun in the case required by the verb to which the Infinitive belongs: τὸ τὰς ἡδονὰς φεύγειν, *the shunning of pleasures;* the Infinitive in this case also is qualified by adverbs: τὸ καλῶς ζῆν, *living rightly.*

The rules given §§ 567–572 for the case of the Subject and Predicate are applicable also to the Infinitive with the Article. Thus the Accusative with the Infinitive is often preceded by the Article: τὸ προειδέναι τὸν θεὸν τὸ μέλλον καὶ τὸ προσημαίνειν ᾧ βούλεται, καὶ τοῦτο πάντες καὶ λέγουσι καὶ νομίζουσι, *God's foreknowing the future and pointing it out beforehand to whom he will, all assert and believe.*

§ 574. By having the Article prefixed the Infinitive becomes *declinable,* and thus answers to the Latin Gerund.

§ 574. THE INFINITIVE. 311

1. *Nominative :*

Poet. τὸ φρονεῖν εὐδαιμονίας πρῶτον ὑπάρχει, *to be thoughtful is the first step to happiness;* τὸ ἁμαρτάνειν ἀνθρώπους ὄντας οὐδὲν θαυμαστόν, *that those should commit errors who are human is nothing surprising.*

2. *Accusative :*

αὐτὸ τὸ ἀποθνήσκειν οὐδεὶς φοβεῖται, *dying itself no one dreads.* Especially to be noticed is the Accusative with the Prepositions εἰς, κατά, *in reference to;* διά, *on account of, because;* πρός, ἐπί, *besides :* Κῦρος διὰ τὸ φιλομαθὴς (Nominative according to § 570) εἶναι πολλὰ τοὺς παρόντας ἀνηρώτα, *Cyrus, through being eager for knowledge, asked those present about many things;* πρὸς τὸ μετρίων δεῖσθαι καλῶς πεπαίδευμαι, *I have been well trained to require what is moderate.*

Obs.—This Accusative of the Infinitive with the Article has sometimes a freer connection with a verb or adjective after the manner of the freer Accusative (§ 404) : οἱ Πελοποννήσιοι ἀνέλπιστοί εἰσι τὸ ἐς τὴν γῆν ἡμῶν ἐςβάλλειν, *the Peloponnesians have no hope in regard to invading our country.*

3. *Genitive :*

ἐπιθυμία τοῦ πιεῖν, *desiderium bibendi;* τὸ εὖ πράττειν παρὰ τὴν ἀξίαν ἀφορμὴ τοῦ κακῶς φρονεῖν τοῖς ἀνοήτοις γίγνεται, *prosperity without merit is an occasion to fools of base sentiments;* ἐμοὶ οὐδὲν πρεσβύτερον τοῦ ὅτι βέλτιστον ἐμὲ γενέσθαι (§ 416), *nothing is more important to me than my becoming as good as possible.* Especially to be noticed is the Genitive with the prepositions ἐκ, *from;* πρό, *before;* ἕνεκα, *because, on account of;* ὑπέρ, *for, for the sake of, in order to;* διά, *by, through;* ἄνευ, *without;* οἱ ἄνθρωποι πάντα ποιοῦσιν ὑπὲρ τοῦ μὴ δοῦναι δίκην, *people do every thing in order not to suffer punishment.*

Obs.—Purpose is often expressed by the Genitive of the Infinitive even without a preposition : τοῦ μὴ διαφεύγειν τὸν λαγὼν ἐκ τῶν δικτύων σκοποὺς καθίσταμεν, *we place scouts that the hare may not escape from the nets.* (Compare the rare use of the Lat. Genitive of the Gerundive : *arma cepit opprimundæ libertatis.*)

4. Dative.

The Dative is especially frequent to express *instrumentality* (§ 438); it is then, like the Latin Ablative of the Gerund, to be translated, *by:* Φίλιππος κεκράτηκε τῷ πρότερος (§ 570) πρὸς τοὺς πολεμίους ἰέναι, *Philip has gained the victory by going first against the enemy* [compare the Latin *docendo discimus*]; also with the prepositions ἐν, *in;* ἐπί, *on, on condition that;* πρός, *besides,* and others: πρὸς τῷ μηδὲν ἐκ τῆς πρεσβείας λαβεῖν τοὺς αἰχμαλώτους ἐκ τῶν ἰδίων ἐλυσάμην, *besides gaining nothing from the embassy, I set free the captives at my own expense.*

D) *The Infinitive with* ἄν.

§ 575. By the addition of ἄν the Infinitive acquires a potential or hypothetical meaning, and denotes therefore either that something only *might happen,* or that under certain circumstances something *would happen* or *would have happened.* Here two cases are possible:

1. the Infinitive with ἄν can be replaced by the *Optative with* ἄν: μάλιστα οἶμαι ἂν σοῦ πυθέσθαι (πυθοίμην ἄν), *I think I could learn it best from you;* δοκεῖτέ μοι πολὺ βέλτιον ἂν περὶ τοῦ πολέμου βουλεύσασθαι (βέλτιον ἂν βουλεύσαισθε), εἰ τὸν τόπον τῆς χώρας πρὸς ἣν πολεμεῖτε ἐνθυμηθείητε, *it seems to me you would much better settle about the war, if you took into account the localities of the country against which you are making war.*

This Infinitive with ἄν therefore answers either to the Potential Optative (§ 516), or to the apodosis of a Hypothetical Period of the fourth form (§ 546).

§ 576. 2: The place of an Infinitive with ἄν can be supplied by the *Hypothetical Indicative with* ἄν: Κῦρος εἰ ἐβίωσεν, ἄριστος ἂν δοκεῖ ἄρχων γενέσθαι (ἄριστος ἂν ἐγένετο), *if Cyrus had lived, it seems he would have become one of the best of rulers;* τοὺς ταῦτα ἀγνοοῦντας Σωκράτης ἀνδραποδώδεις ἂν κεκλῆσθαι ἡγεῖτο (εἴ τινες ταῦτα ἡγνόουν,

§ 578. THE PARTICIPLES. 313

ἐκέκληντο ἂν ἀνδραποδώδεις), *Socrates thought that, if any did not know this, they would be called slavish.*

This Infinitive with ἄν thus answers to the apodosis of a Hypothetical Period of the second form (§ 537, etc.).

Obs.—The context must show into which of the two forms the Infinitive with ἄν is to be resolved.

E) *The Infinitive instead of the Imperative,*

§ 577, belongs almost entirely to poetry; it is used for the second, and rarely for the third person. The Subject and Predicate are in the *Nominative*: Hom. θαρσῶν νῦν, Διόμηδες, ἐπὶ Τρώεσσι μάχεσθαι, *courageously now, Diomede, fight against the Trojans;* παῖδα δ' ἐμοὶ λῦσαί τε φίλην τά τ' ἄποινα δέχεσθαι, *deliver up to me my dear child and accept the ransom.*

Chap. XXIII.—The Participles.

Preliminary Remark.

A Participle, like the Infinitive (§ 559, 1), is a *verbal-noun* (§ 225, 5). It has the same things in common with the verb as the Infinitive, the same points also in common with the noun; but it is distinguished from the Infinitive inasmuch as the latter resembles a *nomen actionis*, whereas the Participle has the nature of an adjective.

A) *Their Attributive Use.*

§ 578. A Participle, corresponding to an adjective or to a relative sentence, is joined to a substantive, to ascribe to it a permanent quality: πόλις εὐρείας ἀγυιὰς ἔχουσα, *i. e.*, Hom. εὐρυάγυια or ἣ εὐρείας ἀγυιὰς ἔχει, *a city having broad streets;* αἱ καλούμεναι Αἰόλου νῆσοι, *the so-called islands of Æolus;* ὁ παρὼν καιρός, *the present opportunity* (compare § 361, 11).

O

314 THE PARTICIPLES. § 579.

Obs.—Like an adjective, the Participle also becomes a substantive by having the article prefixed: οἱ παρόντες, *those present* (compare § 379): ὁ τυχών, *the first comer*. Such participles may often be translated by substantives: ὁ δράσας, *the doer;* οἱ λέγοντες, *the speakers;* τὸ συμφέρον, *the advantage;* τὰ δέοντα, *the duty;* πρὸς τὸ τελευταῖον (§ 361, 8) ἐκβὰν ἕκαστον τῶν πρὶν ὑπαρξάντων κρίνεται, *every thing that happened before is judged of in accordance with its final result.*

On the peculiar use of the Fut. Part. with the Article, § 500.

B) *Their Appositive Use.*

§ 579. The Participle serves to ascribe to a substantive a merely transient quality or activity. In this case the Participle is a shorter and less definite mode of expression for what is otherwise expressed by subordinate clauses with conjunctions of the most different kinds (compare § 583, *Obs.*).

A Participle used in this way is:

§ 580. 1. Temporal, with the distinctions of time mentioned in Chap. XX. (esp. § 496): προςέχετε τούτοις ἀναγιγνωσκομένοις τὸν νοῦν, *give attention to this while being read;* Hom. ὣς ἄρα φωνήσας ἀπεβήσετο = ἐπεὶ ὣς ἐφώνησε, *after having thus spoken he went away.* Observe especially ἔχων and φέρων in descriptions, which may frequently be translated by the English *with :* τὰς ναῦς ἀπέστειλαν ἔχοντα Ἀλκίδαν, *they sent away Alcidas with* (having) *the ships;* χρώμενος, in a similar sense: πολλῇ τέχνῃ χρώμενος, *with* (using) *much skill.* So, also, ἀρχόμενος, *at first;* τελευτῶν, *at last;* διαλιπὼν χρόνον, *after a time;* εὖ ποιῶν, *fortunately;* καλῶς ποιῶν, *justly.* The Participle ὤν can not be omitted when *being* is to be ascribed to a substantive: Ἀλκιβιάδης ἔτι παῖς ὢν ἐθαυμάζετο, *while yet a boy* (Lat., merely *puer*) *Alcibiades was admired* (§ 428, *Obs.*).

§ 581. 2. Causal and final, where the Participle is to be resolved by *since, by* or *by*

§ 583. THE PARTICIPLES. 315

the fact that, when referring to the present or past, and by *that*, *in order that*, when referring to the future : οὐκ ἔστιν ἀδικοῦντα δύναμιν βεβαίαν κτήσασθαι, *firm power is not to be gained by acting unjustly;* τὸν ἀδικοῦντα παρὰ τοὺς δικαστὰς ἄγειν δεῖ δίκην δώσοντα, *he who acts unjustly ought to be brought before the judges in order that he may suffer punishment.*

§ 582. 3. Concessive,

a somewhat rarer use : τὸ ὕδωρ εὐωνότατον ἄριστον ὄν, *water is the cheapest though it is the best;* ὑμεῖς ὑφορώμενοι τὰ πεπραγμένα καὶ δυςχεραίνοντες ἤγετε τὴν εἰρήνην ὅμως, *though suspicious of what had been done, and indignant, you still maintained the peace.*

§ 583. 4. Hypothetical,

a very frequent use, where the Participle is to be resolved by *if*, and corresponds to one of the forms of the Hypothetical *Protaseis* mentioned in § 534, etc. : τοὺς φίλους εὐεργετοῦντες καὶ τοὺς ἐχθροὺς δυνήσεσθε κολάζειν, *if you benefit your friends you will be able also to punish your enemies* (ἐάν); also with the article : ὁ μὴ δαρεὶς ἄνθρωπος οὐ παιδεύεται, *a person is not educated if he has not been beaten.* Such a Participle with μή may often be translated by *without :* οὐκ ἔστιν ἄρχειν μὴ διδόντα μισθόν, *a man can not rule without giving pay.*

Obs.—With the varied use of the Appositive Participles, it must not be overlooked that such a Participle of itself does not clearly express any of the meanings developed in §§ 580-583, but that we make use of the one or the other turn in translating only in order to express in a more precise way what is simply suggested by the Participle. Hence there are many transitions between these meanings, especially between the Temporal and Causal, but also between the Temporal and Hypothetical meanings, just as in Latin sentences introduced by *quum :* πάντα ταῦτα συνιδόντας ἅπαντας (ὑμᾶς) δεῖ βοηθεῖν, *it becomes every one of you, when you have considered all these things, to render help;* νομίζω ἄμεινον ἂν ὑμᾶς περὶ ὧν νῦν ἐρῶ κρῖναι, μικρὰ τῶν πρότερόν ποτε ῥηθέντων μνημονεύσαντας, *I think you would better judge about what I am now going to say, when you remember a little what was said before.*

C) *The Participle with an Absolute Case.*

§ 584. The Participle with a noun or pronoun in the Absolute Genitive (§ 428) or Accusative serves to point out the circumstances mentioned in §§ 579-583. The noun or pronoun to which the Participle refers may be regarded as its *subject*, since from it proceeds the action expressed by the Participle. This construction, therefore, may be resolved by a separate clause, beginning with a conjunction, in which the word in the Genitive or Accusative must appear in the Nominative: τούτων ἀναγιγνωσκομένων τὸν νοῦν προςέχετε, *attend while this is being read* (compare § 580).

1. *The Absolute Genitive* (compare § 428), for which may be substituted clauses with temporal, causal, concessive, or hypothetical conjunctions: Περικλέους ἡγουμένου πολλὰ καὶ καλὰ ἔργα ἀπεδείξαντο οἱ 'Αθηναῖοι, *as long as Pericles led them (Pericle duce), the Athenians produced many and splendid works;* ναυμαχίας γενομένης τέτταρας τριήρεις λαμβάνει Γοργώπας, *navali pugna facta Gorgopas quattuor triremes capit;* ὅλης τῆς πόλεως ἐν τοῖς πολεμικοῖς κινδύνοις ἐπιτρεπομένης τῷ στρατηγῷ, μεγάλα τά τ' ἀγαθὰ κατορθοῦντος αὐτοῦ, καὶ τὰ κακὰ διαμαρτάνοντος εἰκὸς γενέσθαι, *as the whole state in the dangers of war is committed to the care of the general, it is natural both that great good should happen when he is successful, and great evil when he fails.* Poet. γένοιτ' ἂν πᾶν θεοῦ τεχνωμένου, *all may be done if a God contrives it* (εἰ τεχνῷτο).

§ 585. The Absolute Genitive differs from the corresponding Latin construction of the *Ablative Absolute* in the following points:

a) The subject of the Participle is more frequently omitted in Greek when it is either easily understood from what precedes, or from the meaning of the verb, or when it remains indefinite (compare § 361, 3, *Obs.* 2): προϊόντων, *as (they) went forward;* ὕοντος, *when he* (Zeus) *rains;* ἐξαγγελθέντων, *when it had been announced.*

b) On the necessity of the Participle of εἶναι—σοῦ παιδὸς ὄντος [Lat. *te puero*], see §§ 580, 482, *Obs.* An exception occurs in the case of the adjectives ἑκών and ἄκων, which very much resemble Participles: ἐμοῦ ἑκόντος, *with my will;* ἐμοῦ ἄκοντος, *me invito.* The Poets take other licenses.

c) As the Greeks have two active Participles to express a past action, they use the Absolute Genitive of a Passive Participle less fre-

§ 587. THE PARTICIPLES. 317

quently than the Romans do their Absolute Ablative : ὁ Κῦρος, τὸν Κροῖσον νικήσας, κατεστρέψατο τοὺς Λυδούς, *Cyrus, Crœso victo, Lydos sibi subjecit.*

d) The Absolute Genitive is employed even where the subject of the Participle is mentioned also in the leading sentence : ταῦτ' εἰπόντος αὐτοῦ ἔδοξέ τι λέγειν τῷ Ἀστυάγει, *after thus speaking he seemed to Astyages to say something* (of importance). [Lat. *ita locutus—visus est.*]

§ 586. 2. *The Absolute Accusative* is usual in the case of some impersonal verbs, especially δέον, *it being a duty ;* ἐξόν, παρόν, *it being allowed, feasible ;* προςῆκον, *it being befitting ;* δόξαν, *it having been decided ;* οὐδεὶς ἐξὸν εἰρήνην ἄγειν πόλεμον αἱρήσεται, *no one, being allowed to be at peace, will choose war ;* πολλάκις ὑμῖν ἐξὸν πλεονεκτῆσαι οὐκ ἠθελήσατε, *though it was often easy for you to gain more, you were unwilling ;* οἱ Συρακούσιοι κραυγῇ οὐκ ὀλίγῃ ἐχρῶντο, ἀδύνατον ὂν ἐν νυκτὶ ἄλλῳ τῳ σημῆναι, *the Syracusans raised no small shout, it being impossible to make a signal during the night by any thing else.*

D) *Supplements to Participles.*

§ 587. For the sake of greater clearness, certain particles are added to Appositive Participles, as well as to Participles joined with an absolute case ; they give more distinct prominence to the idea expressed by the Participle. Such *Supplements* to *Participles* are :

1. ἅμα, *at the same time*, denoting contemporaneousness : οἱ Ἕλληνες ἐμάχοντο ἅμα πορευόμενοι, *the Hellenes fought while marching.*

2. μεταξύ, *between, amidst*, with pretty nearly the same meaning : ἐπέσχε με λέγοντα μεταξύ, *he checked me in the midst of my speech.*

3. αὐτίκα and εὐθύς, to express immediate succession : τῷ δεξιῷ κέρᾳ εὐθὺς ἀποβεβηκότι ἐπέκειντο, *they pressed upon the right wing immediately after its landing.*

4. τότε, εἶτα (κᾆτα), ἔπειτα, οὕτως, are added to the principal verb to indicate that the action of the Participle was past before, and take up the substance of it with various accessory ideas : καταλιπὼν φρουρὰν οὕτως ἐπ' οἴκου ἀνεχώρησεν, *after having left a garrison, he thus went*

away home; Poet. μὴ νῦν φυγόντες εἶθ' ἁλῶμεν ὕστερον, lest though now escaping we should afterward be caught.

5. καίπερ (more rarely καί alone), with a Participle, to be translated though, renders prominent the concessive meaning: καίπερ οὕτω σοφὸς ὢν βελτίων ἂν γένοιο, though so wise, you might perhaps become better; Homer often separates καί from περ: οἱ δὲ καὶ ἀχνύμενοί περ ἐπ' αὐτῷ ἡδὺ γέλασσαν, and though vexed they heartily laughed at him; ὅμως, in the same sense though or yet, is used with the principal verb: Herod. ὕστερον ἀπικόμενοι τῆς συμβολῆς ἱμείροντο ὅμως θεήσασθαι τοὺς Μήδους, though they did not come till after the engagement, yet they desired to see the Medes.

6. ἅτε, with a Participle (like οἷον, οἷα δή), answers to the English in as far as, since, and brings into prominence its causal meaning: κατέδαρθε πάνυ πολὺ ἅτε μακρῶν τῶν νυκτῶν οὐσῶν, he slept a great while since the nights were long. [Compare Lat. quippe quum, quippe qui.]

§ 588. 7. ὡς and ὥςπερ added to a Participle suggest that what is expressed in the participle is subjective, i. e., is the opinion, the conception, the view of the principal subject. Both particles are joined to the Appositive Participle as well as to a Participle connected with an absolute case, either the absolute Genitive or the absolute Accusative. The latter case in this connection is far more extensively used than without those particles (§ 586). If the opinion expressed in the Participial construction is to be characterized at once as false, ὡς and ὥςπερ may be translated by as if: δεδίασι τὸν θάνατον ὡς εὖ εἰδότες ὅτι μέγιστον τῶν κακῶν ἐστιν, they fear death as if they well knew that it was the greatest of evils; but by in the belief that, since, in the feeling that, etc., if the correctness of the opinion is to be left undecided: ἡμεῖς πάντες ἐβλέπομεν πρὸς αὐτὸν ὡς αὐτίκα μάλα ἀκουσόμενοι θαυμασίους τινὰς λόγους, we all looked at him, expecting immediately to hear some wonderful statements; Poet. ἔξεστι φωνεῖν ὡς ἐμοῦ μόνης πέλας, you may speak out since (in the conviction that) I alone am near; λέγει ὡς διδακτοῦ οὔσης τῆς ἀρετῆς, he speaks thinking that virtue is capable of being taught; ἀπεβλέψατε πρὸς ἀλλήλους ὡς αὐτὸς μὲν ἕκαστος οὐ ποιήσων τὸ δόξαν, τὸν δὲ πλησίον πράξοντα (absolute

§ 590. THE PARTICIPLES. 319

Accusative), *you looked at one another thinking that each one of you would not do what was decided upon, but that his neighbor would.*

E) *The Predicative Participle.*

§ 589. The Participle, like the Infinitive (§ 560), serves to complete a verb, by attributing to a word contained in the sentence something which is not a mere addition, but an essential part of the statement. The Supplementary or Predicative Participle may refer either

1. to the *subject* of the sentence (§ 361, 5, 7, 8): παύεσθε ἀεὶ περὶ τῶν αὐτῶν βουλευόμενοι, *cease always consulting about the same things;* ἴσθι λυπηρὸς ὤν, *know that you are troublesome,* or

2. to a *dependent word* in the sentence (compare § 361, 10, and § 403): ὁ πόλεμος ἔπαυσε τοὺς Ἀθηναίους ἀεὶ περὶ τῶν αὐτῶν βουλευομένους, *the war caused the Athenians to cease from always consulting about the same things;* οἶδα αὐτὸν λυπηρὸν ὄντα, *I know him to be troublesome.*

In English such Predicative Participles are mostly expressed by the Infinitive with *to*, or by sentences with *that*, sometimes also in other ways. In some cases, however, the English language also makes use of a Participle in a similar way: *I feel myself affected by it, he found him armed* (compare § 361, 10, *Obs.*).

The verbs which admit of a Supplementary Participle may be classified as follows:

§ 590. 1. Verbs which express *a condition*, as: ἔχω, *I am in a condition;* τυγχάνω, *I chance to be* (Poet. κυρέω); λανθάνω, *I escape notice;* φαίνομαι, δηλόω, φανερός, δῆλός εἰμι, *I am manifest;* ἔοικα, *I seem;* διατελέω, διάγω, *I continue;* ἀνέχομαι, καρτερέω, *I hold out, endure;* κάμνω, *I grow weary;* ἀπαγορεύω, *I despair;* as well as the verbs which denote the *beginning, interrupting,* or *ending* of a condition; ἄρχομαι, *I begin;* φθάνω,

320   THE PARTICIPLES.   § 591.

I am beforehand; οἴχομαι, *I depart, I am off;* ἐπι-, δια-λείπω, *I break off, I suspend;* παύω, *I make to cease* (παύομαι, *I cease*). In translating we frequently change the Participle into the principal verb, and render the principal Greek verb by an adverb. Examples: κηρύξας ἔχω (more emphatic than ἐκήρυξα, compare Latin *nuntiatum habeo*), *I have announced;* τίς ἔτυχε παραγενόμενος; *who happened to be present?* διατελῶ εὔνοιαν ἔχων πᾶσιν ὑμῖν, *I continue cherishing a kindly feeling for you all;* μὴ καμῇς φίλον ἄνδρα εὐεργετῶν, *don't grow weary of benefiting a friend;* ἄλλα μυρία ἐπιλείπω λέγων, *I refrain from saying innumerable other things;* Hom. ᾤχετ' ἀποπτάμενος, *he was gone flying away.*

Obs.—Even the verb εἰμί may be joined with a Participle: ἢ τοῦτο οὐκ ἔστι γιγνόμενον παρ' ἡμῖν; *is this not happening* (usual) *among us?* A Participle is necessarily so used with εἰμί to complete certain verbal forms (compare §§ 287, 291), especially the Participle of the Perfect or Aorist with εἰμί instead of the *Future Perfect:* δεδωκὼς or δοὺς ἔσει = *dederis.*

§ 591. 2. Verbs of *perceiving,*
as: ὁράω, *I see* (περιοράω, *I overlook, endure*); ἀκούω, *I hear;* οἶδα, *I know;* μανθάνω, *I learn;* γιγνώσκω, *I get to know;* αἰσθάνομαι, *I perceive;* εὑρίσκω, *I find;* μέμνημαι, *I remember.* In several of these the object is in the Genitive, according to § 420. Examples: ὡς εἶδον αὐτοὺς πελάζοντας, οἱ λεηλατοῦντες εὐθὺς ἀφέντες τὰ χρήματα ἔφευγον, *cum eos appropinquantes vidissent, praedantes praeda statim relicta fugam capessiverunt;* ἤκουσά ποτε Σωκράτους περὶ φίλων διαλεγομένου, *I once heard Socrates discoursing about friends* [*audivi Socratem disputantem*]; Χερρόνησον κατέμαθε πόλεις ἔνδεκα ἢ δώδεκα ἔχουσαν, *he learned that the Chersonese had eleven or twelve cities;* ἄνθρωποι καλοὶ κἀγαθοὶ ἐπειδὰν γνῶσιν ἀπιστούμενοι (compare § 483, 1), οὐ φιλοῦσι τοὺς ἀπιστοῦντας, *when good men perceive that they are distrusted, they do not like those who distrust them.*

§ 595.   THE PARTICIPLES.   321

Obs.—With σύνοιδά μοι, *I am conscious*, the Participle may be connected with the Nominative of the Subject or the Dative (μοί): ἐμαυτῷ συνῄδειν οὐδὲν ἐπιστάμενος or ἐπισταμένῳ, *I was conscious of knowing nothing*. In the sense of "to be aware" it may also have the Accusative with the Participle.

§ 592. 3. Verbs of *emotion*,
as : χαίρω, ἥδομαι, τέρπομαι, *I rejoice ;* ἀγαπάω, *I am satisfied ;* χαλεπῶς φέρω, *ægre fero ;* ἄχθομαι, *I am dissatisfied ;* ἀγανακτέω, *I am vexed ;* αἰσχύνομαι, *I am ashamed ;* μεταμέλομαι or μεταμέλει μοι, *I repent*. Examples: Hom. ὁ δὲ φρεσὶ τέρπετ᾽ ἀκούων, *but he rejoiced in heart at hearing* (it); μεταμέλει αὐτῷ ψευσαμένῳ, *he repents having told a lie*.

§ 593. 4. Verbs of *pointing out* and *asserting*,
as : δείκνυμι, ἀποφαίνω, *I show ;* ἐξελέγχω, *I prove, convict ;* ἀγγέλλω, *I announce ;* ὁμολογέω, *I assent*. Examples: Φίλιππος πάντα ἕνεκα ἑαυτοῦ ποιῶν ἐξελήλεγκται, *it has been proved that Philip does every thing for his own sake ;* ἀποφαίνουσι τοὺς φεύγοντας πάλαι πονηροὺς ὄντας, *they make manifest that the banished had long been base*.

§ 594. *Obs.*—The Infinitive, according to § 560, may be used as well as the Participle with many of the verbs enumerated in §§ 590–593, but in a somewhat different sense : ἄρχομαι διδάσκων, *I begin to be a teacher ;* ἄρχομαι διδάσκειν, *I begin to teach* (my teaching) ; αἰσχύνομαι λέγων, *I am ashamed though I say it ;* αἰσχύνομαι λέγειν, *shame prevents me from saying*.

F) *The Participle with* ἄν.

§ 595. By the addition of the Particle ἄν the Participle, in every case like the Infinitive (§§ 575 and 576), acquires the meaning of *possibility* or that of an *Apodosis* in a *Hypothetical Sentence*, and may therefore be resolved in two ways:

1. by the *Optative* with ἄν (§§ 516 and 546):
ἐγώ εἰμι τῶν ἡδέως μὲν ἂν ἐλεγχθέντων, ἡδέως δ᾽ ἂν ἐλεγξάντων, *I am one of those who would gladly be refuted* (οἳ ἂν ἐλεγχθεῖεν), *and would gladly refute* (οἳ ἂν ἐλέγ-

O 2

ξειαν); εὑρίσκω ταύτην ἂν μόνην γενομένην τῶν μελλόντων κινδύνων ἀποτροπήν, *I find this would be the only prevention of the coming dangers* (ὅτι ἂν γένοιτο); ἴσμεν καὶ ὑμᾶς ἂν καὶ ἄλλους, ἐν τῇ αὐτῇ δυνάμει ἡμῖν γενομένους, δρῶντας ἂν αὐτό, *we know that you as well as others in the same position would do the same thing*, i. e., ὅτι εἰ γένοισθε δρῷτε ἄν.

2. By the *hypothetical Indicative* with ἄν (§ 536, etc.): Φίλιππος Ποτίδαιαν ἑλὼν καὶ δυνηθεὶς ἂν αὐτὸς ἔχειν, εἰ ἐβουλήθη, Ὀλυνθίοις ἀπέδωκεν, *when Philip had taken Potidæa, and might have* (ὅτε ἐδυνήθη ἄν) *kept it himself, if he had wished, he gave it back to the Olynthians*.

G) *The Verbal Adjectives.*

§ 596. Verbal Adjectives are, like Participles, verbal nouns of an adjective kind, but differ from participles by a usage much more restricted, and referring to no special time, which has been treated of generally in § 300.

The Verbal Adjectives in -τέος, implying *necessity*, are worthy of notice. A double construction is here possible:

1. The *object* of a necessary action becomes the *subject*, and the Verbal Adjective agrees with it: ὁ πατήρ σοι τιμητέος ἐστίν, *pater tibi venerandus est;* ἡ πόλις τοῖς πολίταις ὠφελητέα, *the state must be assisted by its citizens.* In this construction the subject is emphatic.

2. The Neutral or impersonal construction, where the necessity of the *action* is made specially prominent; the object of the action is in each instance in the case required by the verb: διωκτέον τὴν ἀρετήν, *we must pursue virtue;* εἰρήνην ἀκτέον ἐστίν, *pax agenda est;* ἁπτέον τοῦ πολέμου, *you must try war;* βοηθητέον ἡμῖν ἐστι τοῖς πράγμασιν, *we must help the state*.

The person who is to, or must do something, is in both cases in the Dative: in the second, according to the analogy of δεῖ (§ 567, *Obs.* 1), sometimes in the Accusative:

§ 597. PECULIARITIES OF RELATIVE SENTENCES. 323

οὐδενὶ τρόπῳ ἑκόντας ἀδικητέον, *in no way must you willingly do injustice.*

Obs. 1.—The Verbal Adjective sometimes has the meaning of a Middle : πειστέον ἐστίν, *we must obey* (πείθομαι, not πείθω).

Obs. 2.—In the Neuter construction we often find the Plural : *πολεμητέα ἐστίν, *we must fight* (compare § 364).

CHAP. XXIV.—SOME PECULIARITIES OF RELATIVE CLAUSES.

A) *Attraction.* —

§ 597. 1. The Relative Pronoun in general follows the rule that it agrees in Gender and Number with its antecedent, that is, with the word to which it refers, but in Case with what *follows;* that is, it accommodates itself to the sentence in which it stands : μέμνησθε τοῦ ὅρκου ὃν ὀμωμόκατε, *be mindful of the oath which you have sworn.*

2. An exception from this rule is the *Attraction,* or the process by which the Relative is *attracted* in Case also by the word to which it refers, so as to take its case : μέμνησθε τοῦ ὅρκου οὗ ὀμωμόκατε.

3. With Attraction another process is frequently combined, viz., *shortening*. This consists in the Article or the Demonstrative Pronoun being left out, and the Relative, with the word to which it refers, being drawn together into a single clause : μέμνησθε οὗ ὀμωμόκατε ὅρκου.

4. If the word referred to by the Relative is a mere pronoun, the Relative remains quite alone, but stands in the case which the Demonstrative would have had : μέμνησθε οὗ ὀμωμόκατε = μέμνησθε τούτου ὃ ὀμωμόκατε; *remember that which you have sworn;* ἀμελῶ ὧν με δεῖ πράττειν = ἀμελῶ τούτων ἃ με δεῖ πράττειν, *I neglect what I should do.*

§ 598. Attraction, however, can occur only under the following conditions:

1. The *Relative clause* must be closely connected with the word to which it refers, must be an *essential* part of it. Attraction is inadmissible in a Relative clause, which only loosely adds a remark to a substantive, which might quite as well be wanting, or be annexed by means of καί and a demonstrative pronoun.

2. The sentence must be such as would have the Relative pronoun in the *Accusative*, but its antecedent in the *Genitive* or *Dative*: τίς ἡ ὠφέλεια τοῖς θεοῖς τυγχάνει οὖσα ἀπὸ τῶν δώρων ὧν παρ' ὑμῶν λαμβάνουσιν, *what advantage have the gods from the presents which they receive from you?* εἰςφέρετε ἀφ' ὅσων ἕκαστος ἔχει, *contribute from what each has* (ἀπὸ τοσούτων ὅσα); λέγεις οὐ σύμφωνα οἷς τὸ πρῶτον ἔλεγες, *you do not say what harmonizes with what you first said* (τούτοις ἅ); τῷ ἡγεμόνι πιστεύσομεν ᾧ ἂν Κῦρος δῷ, *we shall trust the commander whom Cyrus gives* (us) (τούτῳ ὅν).

Obs.—Attraction very seldom takes place with other cases: ὧν ἐντυγχάνω μάλιστα ἄγαμαι σέ, *i. e.*, τούτων οἷς, *I admire you most of all I meet.*

§ 599. All clauses subordinate to a Relative Sentence, so far as they consist of words referring to the Relative, and are capable of inflexion, must likewise be modified in the Attraction: οἷς οὖσιν ὑμετέροις ἔχει, τούτοις πάντα τἆλλα ἀσφαλῶς κέκτηται, *i. e.*, ἃ ὄντα ὑμέτερα ἔχει, τούτοις, *he keeps all the rest in safety by means of what he has of yours.*

§ 600. οἷος, and sometimes ὅσος and ἡλίκος, have quite a peculiar attraction; viz., εἶναι is often omitted when it would stand with οἷος in the nominative, and the latter is put in the same case as its antecedent: οἴῳ γε ἐμοὶ παντάπασιν ἄπορον τοῦτο, *i. e.*, τοσούτῳ οἷος ἐγώ εἰμι, *that is quite impossible to such a man as I am.* Sometimes the article is prefixed at the same time: τοῖς οἴοις ἡμῖν, *to such as we.* By the same ellipsis ὁςτιςοῦν acquires the fixed meaning, *whoever, i. e., any whatever:* οὐκ ἔστι δικαίου ἀνδρὸς βλάπτειν ὁντινοῦν ἀνθρώπων, *it is not a just man's nature to injure any person whatever* (*i. e.*, any one, whoever he may be). [Compare Lat. *cuicunque homini nocere.*] So ὅςτις βούλει means the same as οὗτος ὃν βούλει, like *quivis.*

§ 601. Other Relative expressions, all involving either Shortening or Attraction, are: ἀνθ' ὧν, *because*, i. e., ἀντὶ τούτων ἅ, or ἀντὶ τούτων ὅτι: σὺ εὖ ἐποίησας ἀνθ' ὧν ἔπαθες, *you did good because you received good* (for that which you received).

ἐφ' ᾧ, ἐφ' ᾧτε (Herod. ἐπὶ τούτῳ, ἐπ' ᾧτε), *for the purpose of, on condition that,* i. e., ἐπὶ τούτῳ ὥςτε, often with the Infinitive: οἱ τριάκοντα ᾑρέθησαν ἐφ' ᾧτε συγγράψαι νόμους, *the thirty were chosen for the purpose of drawing up laws.*

ἐξ οὗ, ἀφ' οὗ, *ex quo, since,* i. e., since the time that. On ἐν ᾧ, εἰς ὅ, ἄχρι οὗ, § 556.

οἷος, more complete τοιοῦτος οἷος, with the Infinitive, *of the kind that, of the kind to,* and οἷόςτε, with the Infinitive, *able, possible:* οὐκ ἦν ὥρα οἵα ἄρδειν τὸ πεδίον, *it was not the season to water the field;* οὐχ οἷοίτε ἦσαν βοηθῆσαι, *they were not able to render help* (compare § 562). ὅσον, for τοσοῦτο ὅσον, *enough to,* with the Infinitive: ἔχομεν ὅσον ἀποζῆν, *we have enough to live on.*

§ 602. An *inverted* Attraction takes place when a noun or pronoun is put in the same case as the Relative which refers to it: τὴν οὐσίαν ἣν κατέλιπε τῷ υἱεῖ οὐ πλείονος ἀξία ἐστίν, *the property which he left his son is not worth more,* instead of ἡ οὐσία ἥν; Poet. τάςδε δ' ἅςπερ εἰςορᾷς ἥκουσι πρὸς σέ, *those whom you see* (the girls) *have come to you* (αἵδε ἅς). So οὐδείς, μηδείς, become one word, as it were, with ὅςτις οὐ: οὐδενὶ ὅτῳ οὐκ ἀποκρίνεται, properly οὐδείς ἐστιν ὅτῳ οὐκ, *nobody whom he does not answer.* Observe also such expressions as: θαυμαστὸς ὅσος, i. e., θαυμαστόν ἐστιν ὅσος, *wonderfully great;* θαυμαστῶς ὡς, i. e., θαυμαστόν ἐστιν ὡς, *it is wonderful how.* Compare § 519, 5, *Obs.* 2.

§ 603. A singular anomaly is presented by Relative sentences after ἔστι, in the sense of "there is." ἔστι is in the Singular even when the relative is in the Plural: ἔστιν οἵ, there are those who, i. e.; some; ἔστιν οἷς οὐχ οὕτως ἔδοξεν, there are some to whom it did not appear so. So ἔστιν ὅτε (=ἐνίοτε), sometimes; ἔστιν οὗ, in some places; ἔστιν ᾗ, in some ways.

B) *Complication.*

§ 604. In translating Greek Relative clauses into English, difficulties sometimes arise through the particular relations of the sentences:

1. When the Relative as an *Accusative of the Subject* belongs to an Infinitive: οἱ πολέμιοι, οὓς ᾤοντο ἀποφυγεῖν, ἐξαίφνης παρῆσαν, *hostes, quos aufugisse putabant, subito aderant, the enemy, whom they thought to have fled, were suddenly there.*

2. When the Relative depends on a *participle:* καταλαμβάνουσι τεῖχος ὃ τειχισάμενοί ποτε Ἀκαρνᾶνες κοινῷ δικαστηρίῳ ἐχρῶντο (=ᾧ ἐχρῶντο τειχισάμενοι αὐτό), *they take possession of the fort which the Acarnanians, after building it, used as a common judgment hall.*

3. When the Relative is in the *Genitive* dependent on a *comparative:* ἀρετή, ἧς οὐδὲν κτῆμα σεμνότερον, *virtue, than which no possession is more venerable* (§ 416).

4. When the Relative depends on the verb of an inserted clause: αἱρούμεθα αὐτομόλους, οἷς ὁπόταν τις πλείονα μισθὸν διδῷ, μετ' ἐκείνων ἀκολουθήσουσιν (duces) *eligimus transfugas, quibus si quis plus stipendii præbuerit illos sequentur* (i. e., οἵ, ὁπόταν τις — διδῷ, ἀκολουθήσουσιν, *qui, si iis—præbuerit, sequentur), we choose deserters, who, if any one gives them more pay, will follow him.*

Obs.—In the cases enumerated under 2 and 4, as well as those discussed in § 605, and others besides, the Greek language satisfies itself with putting *only once* a word which has to be supplied in different cases for several clauses belonging to one another.

§ 605. C) *Combination of several Relative Clauses.*

When several Relative clauses follow one another, the Relative pronoun need be expressed only once, even when, the second time, it would require to be in a different case: Hom. ἄνωχθι δέ μιν γαμέεσθαι

§ 606. INTERROGATIVE SENTENCES. 321

τῷ ὅτεῳ τε πατὴρ κέλεται καὶ ἀνδάνει αὐτῇ, *bid her marry whomsoever her father urges and* (who) *pleases herself;* 'Αριαῖος, ὃν ἡμεῖς ἠθέλομεν βασιλέα καθιστάναι καὶ [ᾧ] ἐδώκαμεν καὶ [ἀφ' οὗ] ἐλάβομεν πίστα, οὗτος ἡμᾶς κακῶς ποιεῖν πειρᾶται, *Ariæus, whom we wished to make king, and* (to whom we) *gave and* (from whom we) *received pledges of fidelity, attempts to ill use us.*

Obs.—Sometimes, instead of the repeated Relative, αὐτός is substituted in the case required by the construction of the sentence. So likewise μίν in Homer : οἱ πρόγονοι, οἷς οὐκ ἐχαρίζονθ' οἱ λέγοντες οὐδ' ἐφίλουν αὐτούς, ὥςπερ ὑμᾶς οὗτοι νῦν, πέντε καὶ τετταράκοντα ἔτη τῶν Ἑλλήνων ἦρξαν ἑκόντων; *your ancestors, whom the speakers did not gratify, nor did they flatter them, as these now do you, ruled forty-five years over the readily submitting Hellenes.* Hom. : ἀντίθεον Πολύφημον, ὅου κράτος ἐστὶ μέγιστον πᾶσιν Κυκλώπεσσι, Θόωσα δέ μιν τέκε νύμφη, *godlike Polyphemus, whose power is the greatest among all the Cyclops, and him* (whom) *the nymph Thoösa bore.*

CHAP. XXV.—INTERROGATIVE SENTENCES.

§ 606. 1. The simple direct question may be introduced by the Interrogative pronouns or adverbs mentioned § 214, etc. In Greek several different questions may be included in one interrogative sentence : Hom. τίς πόθεν εἶς ἀνδρῶν ; *what man, whence are you?* ἀπὸ τούτων φανερὸν γενήσεται, τίς τίνος αἴτιός ἐστιν, *from this it will be clear who is chargeable with what* (who is chargeable and with what).

Obs. 1.—An Interrogative pronoun may be joined with a demonstrative : ἀγγελίαν φέρω βαρεῖαν · τίνα ταύτην ; *I bring heavy tidings; what* (is) *that?* (τίς αὕτη ἐστίν ;)

Obs. 2.—A question may also be expressed in a subordinate clause and by a participle : πότε ἃ χρὴ πράξετε ; ἐπειδὰν τί γένηται ; *when will you do your duty? when what shall happen?* τί ἰδὼν τὸν Κριτόβουλον ποιοῦντα ταῦτα κατέγνωκας αὐτοῦ ; *what have you seen Critobulus doing that you have charged him with this?* οἱ πάλαι Ἀθηναῖοι οὐ διελογίσαντο, ὑπὲρ οἷα πεποιηκότων ἀνθρώπων κινδυνεύσουσιν, *the old Athenians did not calculate how much people have* done for whom they were going to incur risk. Of this kind also are the phrases: τί παθών; what have you passed through, that? τί μαθών; what have you got to know, that? τί παθὼν ἀδικεῖς τὴν πατρίδα; what have you passed through to make you act unjustly toward your country?

§ 607. 2. When the question refers not to a single word, but to a whole sentence, it may be indicated

a) merely by the *tone* of voice: οὐ φοβεῖ μὴ ἤδη πρεσβύτερος ᾖς; *do you not fear that you are already too old?*

b) by *Interrogative particles*, which, in translating into English, can not always be expressed by separate words, but often may be rendered by the position of the words and the tone of pronunciation. The most important Interrogative particles are ἆρα and ἦ, both comparable to the Latin affix -ne. Which answer is expected is indicated by neither of these particles: ἆρ᾽ εἰμὶ μάντις; *am I a prophet?* ἦ οὗτοι πολέμιοί εἰσιν, *are those enemies?*

Obs.—If an *affirmative* answer is to be specially indicated οὐ is added; if a *negative*, μή is added to ἆρα. Hence ἆρα οὐ corresponds to the Latin *nonne*. ἆρα μή to the English *surely not*.

§ 608. Of other Interrogative expressions the following may be noticed: ἦ γάρ; *isn't it?* ἦ που; *surely?* ἄλλο τι ἤ, properly ἄλλο τι ἔστιν ἤ; *does any thing else happen than?* hence, also with ἤ omitted (compare § 626, *Obs.*), like the Lat. *nonne*, where an affirmative answer is expected: ἄλλο τι ἢ ἀδικοῦμεν; *are we not doing wrong?* ἄλλο τι οὖν πάντα ταῦτα ἂν εἴη μία ἐπιστήμη; *would not this, then, be all one science?* οὐ put in a question also anticipates an *affirmative* answer, and may be compared with *nonne* and the English *not*. The opposite to it is μή, which may often be translated by *surely*, as μῶν, formed from μὴ οὖν, *surely not*, always points to a negative answer. μὴ ᾽Αχιλλέα οἴει φροντίσαι θανάτου καὶ κινδύνου; *surely you do not think Achilles cared about death and danger?*

§ 609. 3. The indirect question in Greek, according to § 520, is by no means clearly distinguished in regard to Mood from the direct. So likewise the direct Interrogatives, pronouns and adverbs, are often used instead of the indirect ones: αἱ γυναῖκες ἠρώτων αὐτούς, τίνες εἶεν, *the women asked them who they were* (§ 475, *b*).

§ 610. 4. The English indirect Interrogative *if* or *whether* is represented by εἰ (§ 525, etc.), more rarely by ἐάν (with the Subj.), sometimes by ἆρα, and in Homer by ἦ (ἠέ). *Whether or not* or *whether perhaps* may be rendered by μή : σκοπεῖτε, εἰ δικαίως χρήσομαι τῷ λόγῳ, *see whether I speak justly;* ὅρα, μὴ παίζων ἔλεγεν, *see whether or not he spoke in jest.*

On the subject of the Interrogative Sentence being drawn proleptically into the principal sentence, see §§ 397, 519, 5, *Obs.* 2.

§ 611. The direct *double question* (disjunctive question) is most generally introduced by πότερον (πότερα)—ἤ, Lat. *utrum—an :* πότερον δέδρακεν ἢ οὐ ; πότερον ἄκων ἢ ἑκών ; *has he done it or not ? willingly or unwillingly ?* In an indirect double question the same Interrogatives may be used, but also εἰ—ἤ, *whether—or,* and εἴτε—εἴτε : ἀποροῦμεν, εἴτε ἄκων εἴτε ἑκὼν δέδρακεν, *we are in doubt whether he did it willingly or unwillingly.*

Obs.—The Homeric language has for the direct, but more frequently for the indirect double question, the conjunctions ἤ (ἠέ), ἤ (ἠέ) : ἢ ὕμμ' ἐν νήεσσι Ποσειδάων ἐδάμασσεν, ἢ που ἀνάρσιοι ἄνδρες ἐδηλήσαντ' ἐπὶ χέρσου ; *did Poseidon overpower you in your ships, or have hostile men injured you on land ?* εἰπὲ δέ μοι μνηστῆς ἀλόχου βουλήν τε νόον τε, ἠέ μένει παρὰ παιδὶ καί ἔμπεδα πάντα φυλάσσει, ἢ ἤδη μιν ἔγημεν Ἀχαιῶν ὅςτις ἄριστος, *tell me the purpose and inclination of the wooed wife, whether she remains with the son and guards all carefully, or whether he who is the best of the Achæans has already married her.* ἤ (ἠέ) is also used for ἤ (ἠέ) in the second member.

CHAP. XXVI.—THE NEGATIVES.

A) *Simple Negative*.

§ 612. The Greeks have two different negatives, οὐ and μή. Numerous compounds and derivatives are formed.

from each, as: οὔτε, μήτε, οὐδείς, μηδείς, οὐδαμῶς, μηδαμῶς. The principal distinction between οὐ and μή is that οὐ *denies*, but μή *declines*. Hence arise the following special rules:

§ 613. 1. οὐ is used in all direct statements, whether the reality of something is denied by the *Indicative*, or the possibility or probability of something by the *Optative with ἄν*: Φίλιππος οὐκ ἄγει εἰρήνην, *Philip does not maintain peace;* οὐκ ἂν ἄγοι εἰρήνην, *he would not (will hardly) maintain peace;* οὐκ ἂν δύναιο μὴ καμὼν εὐδαιμονεῖν, *you could not be happy without laboring* (§ 516).

Obs.—οὐ is also used in the peculiar Subjunctive of the Homeric language mentioned § 513.

2. οὐ is used in direct questions to which an affirmative answer is expected (§ 608), but μή when a negative answer is expected (§ 608).

§ 614. 3. In independent sentences μή is used with the *Subjunctive* (§§ 510, 512), with the *Optative of wishing* (§ 514), with the *Indicative of wishing* (§ 515), and with the *Imperative*: μὴ θορυβήσητε, *do not make a disturbance;* μὴ γένοιτο, *may it not happen;* Hom. ὡς μὴ ὤφελλε γενέσθαι, *would it never happened!* μήποτ' ἐπ' ἀπρήκτοισι νόον ἔχε, *never devote your thoughts to what is impracticable.*

Obs.—In these cases μή generally corresponds to the Latin *ne*. It is often used in negative oaths with the Indicative, in so far as the swearer declines something (§ 612): Hom. ἴστω νῦν τόδε Γαῖα . . . . μὴ δι' ἐμὴν ἰότητα Ποσειδάων . . . . πημαίνει Τρῶας, *let Gœa now know this . . . . not with my consent does Poseidon afflict the Trojans.*

§ 615. 4. οὐ in general is used in all those dependent sentences which do *not* express a negative *purpose* or a *condition:* ᾔδειν, ὅτι οὐ ῥᾴδιον εἴη, *I knew it was not easy;* ἃ οὐκ ἐᾶτε τοὺς παῖδας ποιεῖν, ταῦτα αὐτοὶ ποιεῖτε, *what you do not allow your children to do you do yourselves.*

§ 616. THE NEGATIVES. 331

Obs. 1.—In indirect questions οὐ as well as μή may be used with εἰ in the sense of *whether*: σκοπῶμεν, εἰ πρέπει ἢ οὐ, *let us consider whether it is becoming or not;* πειράσομαι μαθεῖν, εἰ ἀληθές ἢ μή, *I will try to learn whether it is true or not.*

Obs. 2.—In such Relative Sentences as contain quite a general idea, μή may be used: ἃ μὴ οἶδα, οὐδὲ οἴομαι εἰδέναι, *what I do not know, I do not think I know.*

§ 616. 5. μή in general is used in all those dependent sentences in which a *negative purpose* or a *condition* is expressed; hence μή is the negative in *sentences denoting intention or purpose* (§ 530), in those indirect Interrogative and Relative sentences where a purpose of *hindering* is implied, in all the *Protaseis of Hypothetical Periods* (§ 534, etc.), and lastly in *Hypothetical Relative* (§ 554) clauses, as well as in Hypothetical Temporal clauses (§§ 556, 557): ἐάν τις κάμῃ, παρακαλεῖς ἰατρόν, ὅπως μὴ ἀποθάνῃ, *when any one is ill, you send for a physician, that he may not die;* ψηφίσασθε τοιαῦτα ἐξ ὧν μηδέποτε ὑμῖν μεταμελήσει, *vote for such things as will never cause you to repent* [*ea quorum numquam vos pœniteat*]; ὅρα, ὅπως μή σοι ἀποστήσονται, *see that they do not abandon you;* ἐξῆν σοι ἀπιέναι ἐκ τῆς πόλεως, εἰ μὴ ἤρεσκόν σοι οἱ νόμοι, *it was at your choice to leave the state, if its laws did not please you;* θεάσασθε, ὡς σαθρόν ἐστι πᾶν, ὅ τι ἂν μὴ δικαίως ᾖ πεπραγμένον, *see, how rotten every thing is, which is not justly done;* μεγίστη γίγνεται σωτηρία, ὅταν γυνὴ πρὸς ἄνδρα μὴ διχοστατῇ, *it is the greatest safety when a wife is not at variance with her husband.*

Obs. 1.—In sentences of this kind, sometimes οὐ is used to negative a *single word*: πάντως οὕτως ἔχει, ἐάν τε οὐ φῆτε ἐάν τε φῆτε, *it is entirely so whether you deny or assert it.*

Obs. 2.—The Optative expressing repetition likewise has μή (§ 547).

Obs. 3.—With verbs of fearing, μή, like the Latin *ne*, signifies *lest* or *that*: δέδοικα, μὴ ἐπιλαθώμεθα τῆς οἴκαδε ὁδοῦ, *I fear lest we forget the way home* (compare § 533). Even without a governing verb the fear that something may happen is introduced by μή, which in this case is to be translated *if only not,* or *if but not:* μὴ ἐπιλαθώμεθα τῆς οἴκαδε ὁδοῦ, *if only we do not forget the way home* (compare §§ 620, 621, and 512).

§ 617. ϐ. The *Infinitive* generally has μή, particularly when the Infinitive has the article: τὰς ὁμοίας χάριτας μὴ ἀντιδιδόναι αἰσχρόν, *not to return equal thanks is base;* σοὶ τὸ μὴ σιγῆσαι λοιπὸν ἦν, *it remained for you not to be silent.*

Obs. 1.—οὐ may be put with the Infinitive after verbs of declaring and conceiving: ὁμολογῶ οὐ κατὰ τούτους εἶναι ῥήτωρ, *I acknowledge I am not an orator in their sense.*

Obs. 2.—ὥςτε, *so that*, when joined with the Infinitive generally has μή, more rarely οὐ.

Obs. 3.—After verbs of hindering, forbidding, refusing, denying, and others which contain the idea of declining (§ 612), μή is usually added to the Infinitive, and is rendered in English by *from*, or not expressed at all: κωλυόμεθα μὴ μαθεῖν, *we are hindered from learning;* ἠρνοῦντο μὴ πεπτωκέναι, *they denied having fallen.*

§ 618. 7. With *Participles* μή is used when they are to be understood hypothetically, *i. e.*, in the sense of a *Hypothetical Protasis* (§ 583): οὐκ ἂν δύναιο μὴ καμὼν εὐδαιμονεῖν, *i. e.*, εἰ μὴ κάμοις (§ 613); so, likewise, when the Participle has the article, if it can be resolved into a hypothetical or a hypothetical relative clause: ὁ μὴ δαρεὶς ἄνθρωπος οὐ παιδεύεται, *i. e.*, ἐάν τις μὴ δαρῇ, or ὃς ἂν μὴ δαρῇ (§ 583).

Obs. 1.—When μή is added as a Negative to single words, they are likewise to be taken hypothetically: τὸ μὴ ἀγαθόν, *the not good*, *i. e.*, ὃ ἂν μὴ ἀγαθὸν ᾖ.

Obs. 2.—With Participles as well as with other words μή often occurs as a Negative on account of the prohibitive, declining, or hypothetical nature of the whole sentence: ψηφίσασθε τὸν πόλεμον μὴ φοβηθέντες τὸ αὐτίκα δεινόν, *determine upon the war without fearing the immediate danger.*

B) *Several Negatives combined.*

§ 619. 1. A Negative is not neutralized by a subsequent *compound* Negative of the same kind, but only continued. In translating, the Negative is employed *only once* in En-

§ 621. THE NEGATIVES. 333

glish, and the place of the other Negative is supplied by an indefinite: Poet. οὐκ ἔστιν οὐδὲν κρεῖσσον ἢ νόμοι πόλει, *there is not any thing better for a state than laws;* οὐδεὶς πώποτε Σωκράτους οὐδὲν ἀσεβὲς οὐδὲ ἀνόσιον οὔτε πράττοντος εἶδεν, οὔτε λέγοντος ἤκουσεν, *no one ever either saw Socrates doing or heard him saying any thing impious or unholy.*

Obs.—A Negative is neutralized by a subsequent *simple* Negative of the same kind: οὐδεὶς ἀνθρώπων ἀδικῶν τίσιν οὐκ ἀποδώσει, *no one who does wrong will not* (i. e., every one will) *pay the penalty.*

§ 620. 2. οὐ followed by μή with the Subjunctive or Future Indicative is an *emphatic* negative. This mode of speaking is to be explained by the idea of fear being supplied after οὐ (compare § 616, *Obs.* 3): οὐ μὴ ποιήσω, about the same as οὐ φοβητέον μὴ ποιήσω, *there is no fear that I shall do it,* i. e., I shall *certainly not* do it: οὐδεὶς μήποτε εὑρήσει τὸ κατ᾽ ἐμὲ οὐδὲν ἐλλειφθέν, *no one will ever find that any thing, as far as depends on me, is neglected;* οὐ μήποτε ἔξαρνος γένωμαι, *I shall certainly never deny.*

§ 621. 3. μή followed by οὐ is used in very different ways:

a) After verbs of *fearing*, μὴ οὐ corresponds to the Lat. *ne non* or *ut*, and is to be translated by *that not :* δέδοικα, μὴ οὐ θεμιτὸν ᾖ, *vereor, ne non justum sit, I fear that it is not just* (compare § 616, *Obs.* 3); also without a governing verb, μὴ οὐ θεμιτὸν ᾖ, if it be but not *not right,* i. e., if it be only not *wrong* (compare § 512, and § 616, *Obs.* 3); Hom. μή νύ τοι οὐ χραίσμῃ σκῆπτρον καὶ στέμμα θεοῖο, *the god's staff and garland will surely not help you.*

b) In indirect questions where μή would mean *if perhaps* (§ 610), μὴ οὐ means *if* or *whether perhaps not :* ἄθρει μὴ οὐ τοῦτο ᾖ τὸ ἀγαθόν, *look whether perhaps this is not the good.*

Obs.—In the cases adduced under *a* and *b*, μή is a Negative Conjunction, and οὐ the Negative to a special word.

c) μὴ οὐ is used with the Infinitive after *Negative* expressions, in the sense of *so as not*, or *not to :* οὐδεὶς οἷόςτε ἄλλως λέγων μὴ οὐ καταγέλαστος εἶναι, *no one speaking otherwise is able not to be ridiculous.*

d) μὴ οὐ is farther used with the Infinitive after *negative* verbs, or questions containing verbs of hindering, forbidding, denying, refusing (§ 617, *Obs.* 3). The Infinitive in this case is often preceded by the Article. In English the negative is not expressed: οὐ κωλυόμεθα μὴ οὐ μαθεῖν, *we are not hindered from learning;* μὴ παρῇς τὸ μὴ οὐ φράσαι, *do not omit saying it;* τίνα οἴει ἀπαρνήσεσθαι μὴ οὐχὶ ἐπίστασθαι τὰ δίκαια ; *who do you think will deny at all understanding what is just?*

Obs.—οὐ is here only a repetition of the Negative contained in the principal sentence.

C) Some Negative Phrases.

§ 622. 1. οὐδέν, μηδέν, and οὔτι, μήτι, *nothing*, are often used as free Accusatives, like the Latin *nihil*, meaning *not, not at all;* compare § 404, *Obs.*

2. οὔπω, μήπω, *not yet*, are to be carefully distinguished from οὐκέτι, μηκέτι, *no longer :* οὔπω πεποίηκα, *nondum feci;* οὐκέτι ποιήσω, *non amplius faciam.*

3. οὐχ ὅτι stands for οὐ λέγω ὅτι, *I do not say that, not to mention;* καὶ οὐχ ὅτι ὁ Κρίτων ἐν ἡσυχίᾳ ἦν, ἀλλὰ καὶ οἱ φίλοι αὐτοῦ, *and not to mention* (*i. e., not only*) *Crito was quiet, but his friends also were.*

4. μὴ ὅτι for μὴ εἴπω ὅτι (μὴ ὅπως) means *don't suppose, nedum*, by which the mention of something is declined as unnecessary, and hence may sometimes be translated in Negative sentences by *not only not :* μὴ ὅτι θεός, ἀλλὰ καὶ ἄνθρωποι οὐ φιλοῦσι τοὺς ἀπιστοῦντας, *don't suppose that only God, but men also do not love the faithless* [*non homines infidos amant; nedum deus*]. In like manner οὐχ ὅπως, properly *not that, don't suppose*, may frequent-

ly be rendered in connection with Negatives by *not only not.*

5. μόνον οὐ, μόνον οὐχί, *only not,* is equivalent to *almost, nearly;* ὅσον οὐ, temporal [*tantum non*], *nearly, almost :* καταγελᾷ ὑπ' ἀνδρῶν οὓς σὺ μόνον οὐ προςκυνεῖς, *you are ridiculed by men whom you almost worship.*

6. οὐ μήν or οὐ μέντοι ἀλλά, *however, notwithstanding,* is to be explained by an ellipsis : ὁ ἵππος μικροῦ ἐκεῖνον ἐξετραχήλισεν · οὐ μὴν (viz., ἐξετραχήλισεν) ἀλλὰ ἐπέμεινεν ὁ Κῦρος, *the horse nearly threw him off, (did) not, however, but Cyrus kept his seat.*

On οὔτε, μήτε, οὐδέ, μηδέ, § 625.

Chap. XXVII.—The Particles.

§ 623. Particles are also indeclinable words which serve partly to connect sentences, partly to give emphasis to particular parts of a sentence, and to enliven language. The Particles which serve to connect sentences are called *Conjunctions;* those which give prominence to particular parts of a sentence, or impart animation by making entire sentences prominent, are called *emphatic particles.*

In regard to position, they are either *prepositive, i. e.,* take the first place in a sentence, or *postpositive, i. e.,* always stand after at least one other word in a sentence.

Obs.—The Conjunctions are divided into various classes according to their meaning. Several Conjunctions, however, belong equally to different classes. They will be arranged according to their original or primitive signification.

A) *Conjunctions.*

Preliminary Remark.

§ 624. *a.* The Conjunctions are here enumerated without regard to the formal relation of sentences to one another (§ 519). But

1. *Co-ordination* is implied in all Copulative and Disjunctive Conjunctions, the Adversative Conjunctions with the exception of ὅμως, which is used principally in the Apodosis, among the Causal Conjunctions γάρ, and all Illative Conjunctions except ὥςτε;

2. *Subordination* is implied in all the rest.

Obs.—Much more rarely than in modern languages, more rarely also than in Latin, is one word or one sentence added to another in Greek without some Conjunction. The *Asyndeton* (ἀσύνδετον, *want of connection*) takes place more frequently only in an *Epexegesis* (ἐπεξήγησις), *i. e.*, a subsequent explanatory addition to something already alluded to in the previous sentence: εἰμί τις γελοῖος ἰατρός· ἰώμενος μεῖζον τὸ νόσημα ποιῶ, *I am an odd physician; by curing the disease I make it worse.* Wherever the Asyndeton occurs in other cases, the speaker generally intends to produce a special effect by it.

I. *Copulative Conjunctions.*

§ 624. *b.* 1. The two Copulative Conjunctions are καί, which in general corresponds to the Latin *et*, and the postpositive enclitic τέ, which in general corresponds to the Latin *que*. The language of poetry has besides ἠδέ and 'ἰδέ, with the meaning *and* [compare *atque*].

2. The Greeks, like the Romans, are fond of expressing the idea of addition in two connected parts of a sentence, either by καί—καί or τέ—καί, or τέ—τέ: καὶ κατὰ γῆν καὶ κατὰ θάλασσαν, *both by land and by water;* Hom. Ἀτρεῖδαί τε καὶ ἄλλοι ἐϋκνήμιδες Ἀχαιοί, *ye Atridæ as well as ye other well-greaved Achæans;* Hom. αἰεὶ γάρ τοι ἔρις τε φίλη πόλεμοί τε μάχαι τε, *for strife is always pleasant to you, and wars and battles.* We may farther add the Epic ἠμέν—ἠδέ, *as well—as also.*

Obs.—In single instances we also find τέ—δέ, where the second member is made more prominent by contrast.

3. καί has, moreover, the meaning *also:* Hom. παρ' ἔμοιγε καὶ ἄλλοι, οἵ κέ με τιμήσουσι, *with me are also others, who will honor me.*

§ 625. THE PARTICLES. 337

In this sense, also, καί is frequently used in both the connected parts of a sentence: καὶ ἡμῖν ταὐτὰ δοκεῖ ἅπερ καὶ βασιλεῖ, *we also approve the same thing as the king* (*does also*). The meaning *also* by intensification becomes *even :* καὶ λίαν, *even very much ;* and in the opposite case *even but :* καὶ βραχὺν χρόνον, *even but a short time.* καὶ δέ answers to the English *and also :* δίκαιον καὶ πρέπον δὲ ἅμα, *just and at the same time also becoming.* After words of resemblance or likeness καί means *as :* ὁμοίως καί, *æque ac.*

4. ἄλλως τε καί properly means "both in other respects, and also;" it serves to give prominence to the subsequent word or words, and may be translated by *especially :* χαλεπόν ἐστι διαβαίνειν τὸν ποταμὸν ἄλλως τε καὶ πολεμίων πολλῶν ἐγγὺς ὄντων, *it is difficult to cross the river, especially as many of the enemy are near.* καὶ δὴ καί is used to make the last part of a series emphatic : Herod. Κροίσου βασιλεύοντος ἀπικνέονται ἐς Σάρδις ἄλλοι τε οἱ πάντες ἐκ τῆς Ἑλλάδος σοφισταί, καὶ δὴ καὶ Σόλων, *during the reign of Crœsus there came from Hellas both all the other wise men and especially Solon* [Lat. *cum—tum*].

5. In the Epic Dialect τέ is frequently employed to indicate the agreement not only of separate parts of a sentence, but of whole sentences, often, too, in connection with other Particles, such as καί, μέν, δέ, ἀλλά, and with relatives (ὅςτε, ὅςοςτε). In these cases τέ must generally be left untranslated or rendered with an unaccented *also :* Hom. ὅς κε θεοῖς ἐπιπείθηται μάλα τ' ἔκλυον αὐτοῦ, *whoever obeys the gods they greatly listen to him also.*

Obs.—The τε in ὥςτε, οἷόςτε, which occurs also in prose, is of the same origin.

6. The rising climax is also expressed by οὐ μόνον—ἀλλὰ καί, *not only—but also.* On οὐχ ὅτι, μὴ ὅτι, οὐχ ὅπως, see § 622.

§ 625. 1. The Particles οὐδέ, μηδέ and οὔτε, μήτε, serve to form a negative series. Two different meanings belong to οὐδέ and μηδέ, viz. :

a) *nor either, and not ;* in this sense they are used to connect a single member of a sentence with a preceding one negatively : Hom. βρώμης οὐχ ἅπτεαι οὐδὲ ποτῆτος, *you touch not meat nor drink either ;* πρὸς σοῦ οὐδ' ἐμοῦ φράσω, *to your advantage and not to mine I will speak.*

P

b) also not, not even : ἐλπίζω οὐδὲ τοὺς πολεμίους μενεῖν ἔτι, *I hope that the enemy also will not longer stay ;* οὐδὲ τοῦτο ἐξῆν, *not even this was allowed* [*ne hoc quidem licebat*].

2. οὔτε—οὔτε, μήτε—μήτε, are used with mutual reference to each other, and may be translated *neither—nor :* Hom. οὔτε ποτ᾽ ἐς πόλεμον πωλέσκετο, οὔτε ποτ᾽ εἰς ἀγορήν, *he neither went to war nor to the assembly.* Sometimes a negative member of a sentence is brought into relation with a positive one by means of οὔτε or μήτε—τέ [Latin *neque — et*] : ὤμοσαν μήτε προδώσειν ἀλλήλους σύμμαχοί τε ἔσεσθαι, *they swore not to betray one another and to be allies.*

Obs.—If something else be added to two members connected by οὔτε—οὔτε, or μήτε—μήτε, it may be done by οὐδέ, μηδέ. When, on the contrary, οὐδέ or μηδέ corresponds to a preceding οὔτε or μήτε, it must be called an irregularity (compare τέ—δέ, § 624, 2, *Obs.*), and the member thus added is emphatic : ἀλλὰ γὰρ οὔτε τούτων οὐδέν ἐστιν ἀληθές, οὐδὲ γ᾽ εἴ τινος ἀκηκόατε, ὡς ἐγὼ παιδεύειν ἐπιχειρῶ ἀνθρώπους, *but neither is any of these things true, nor even if you have heard from any one that I undertake to train men.*

II. *Disjunctive Conjunctions.*

§ 626. 1. ἤ, carefully to be distinguished from ᾖ (§§ 643, 607), means

a) or, and in this sense is often doubled : ἤ—ἤ, *either—or,* for which ἤτοι—ἤ is used when greater emphasis is to be given to the first member of a sentence : ἢ ἀστός τις ἢ ξένος, *either some citizen or a stranger.*

b) than, after comparatives and comparative adjectives like ἄλλος, *alius ;* ἕτερος, *alter ;* διάφορος, *different ;* ἐναντίος, *opposed to,* etc. : τίνι ἂν μᾶλλον πιστεύσαιμι ἢ σοί ; *whom should I trust more than you ?* οὐδὲν ἄλλο ἐπιτηδεύουσιν ἢ ἀποθνήσκειν, *they think upon nothing else than dying.*

Obs.—After πλέον (πλεῖον, contracted πλεῖν), *more,* and ἔλαττον, μεῖον, *less,* ἤ is sometimes omitted with numerals, just as *quam* is after

§ 629. THE PARTICLES. 339

plus: ἔτη γεγονὼς πλεῖον ἑβδομήκοντα, *more than seventy years old* [*plus septuaginta annos natus*]. The same is the case also after ἄλλο τι in questions (§ 608).

§ 627. 2. εἴτε—εἴτε, ἐάντε—ἐάντε, are used like the Latin *sive—sive*, when it is to be left undecided which of two sides is to be chosen: εἴτε ἀληθὲς εἴτε ψεῦδος, οὐ καλόν μοι δοκεῖ τοῦτο τοὔνομα ἔχειν, *whether true or false, it seems to me not fair to have this name.*

III. *Adversative Conjunctions.*

§ 628. 1. δέ expresses so slight a contrast or opposition that, though it is generally rendered by *but*, it may also, and especially in Hom., be translated by *and*. The Greeks, however, also like to indicate the first of two sentences which are contrasted to one another, and this they do by μέν, *in truth, truly, indeed;* but it may often be left untranslated: Hom. ἄλλοι μέν ῥα θεοί τε καὶ ἀνέρες ἱπποκορυσταὶ εὗδον παννύχιοι, Δία δ' οὐκ ἔχε νήδυμος ὕπνος, *the other gods, indeed, and the horse-hair crested men slept through the night, but sweet sleep did not hold Zeus.* As here, μέν—δέ express a contrast, so elsewhere they indicate only a difference: Δαρείου καὶ Παρυσάτιδος γίγνονται παῖδες δύο, πρεσβύτερος μὲν Ἀρταξέρξης, νεώτερος δὲ Κῦρος, *Darius and Parysatis had two children, the elder Artaxerxes, the younger Cyrus;* Hom. περὶ μὲν βουλῇ Δαναῶν περὶ δ' ἔστε μάχεσθαι, *in council on the one hand, and in battle on the other, you are distinguished among the Danai.*

Obs.—In Homer an Apodosis also may be opposed to its Protasis by means of δέ, especially when the Protasis is introduced by a temporal conjunction : ἕως ὁ ταῦθ' ὥρμαινε κατὰ φρένα καὶ κατὰ θυμόν, ἦλθε δ' Ἀθήνη, *while he pored on this in his mind and spirit Athene came.* This is founded on a combination of co-ordination and subordination. Compare § 519, 1 and 5, *Obs.*

§ 629. 2. ἀλλά, *yet, but* (originally Acc. Plur. Neut. of ἄλλος), denotes a stronger contrast than δέ : Hom. ἔνθ' ἄλλοι μὲν πάντες ἐπευφήμησαν Ἀχαιοί—ἀλλ' οὐκ Ἀτρείδῃ Ἀγαμέμνονι ἥνδανε θυμῷ, ἀλλὰ κακῶς ἀφίει, *then all the* other Achæans assented, yet it did not meet the feelings of Atrides Agamemnon, but he harshly dismissed him.

Obs. 1.—After a hypothetical sentence either expressed or understood, ἀλλά, sometimes with a strengthening γέ added to it, may frequently be rendered by *but* or *yet at least:* εἰ μὴ πάντα, ἀλλὰ πολλά γ' ἴστε, *if not all, yet you know at least much;* Poet. ὦ θεοὶ πατρῷοι συγγένεσθέ γ' ἀλλὰ νῦν, *oh gods of my fathers, be with me at least now* [if not before].

Obs. 2.—ἀλλά frequently serves to break off a long discussion and emphatically to introduce a request: Hom. ἀλλὰ πίθεσθε καὶ ὕμμες, *but do you also follow me.*

Obs. 3.—After negatives ἀλλ' ἤ or ἀλλά alone means *except:* ἀργύριον μὲν οὐκ ἔχω ἀλλ' ἢ μικρόν τι, *I have no money except a little.* On οὐ μὴν ἀλλά, § 622, 6.

§ 630. Other Conjunctions which point out a contrast or a transition to something different are:

3. αὖ, αὖτε, properly *again*, then *on the other hand, yet.*
4. Hom. αὐτάρ, and ἀτάρ, *but, on the contrary, yet.*
5. μέντοι, *certainly, however,* see § 643, 13.
6. καίτοι, *and yet, still.*
7. ὅμως, *nevertheless, yet,* denotes a strong contrast [Lat. *tamen, nihilominus*]. On ὅμως as a supplement to a participle, § 587, 5.

IV. *Conjunctions of Comparison.*

§ 631. 1. ὡς, *as* (Lat. *ut*), is properly the adverb of ὅς, ἥ, ὅ. It differs in accent from ὥς, *so* or *thus* (§ 99), except when in poets and the Homeric Dialect it is placed after the word compared (§ 98, *a*), in which case it is oxytone: πατὴρ ὡς ἤπιος ἦεν, *he was gentle as a father.* Like the Lat. *ut,* it is employed in very different ways:

a) In its original *comparative* sense ὡς means *as* or *how,* and is used in *comparisons:* ὡς βούλει, *as you wish;* μακρὸν ὡς γέροντι, *far for me an old man* (Lat. *tanquam*); Hom. ὥς μοι δέχεται κακὸν ἐκ κακοῦ αἰεί (*how with me one evil always follows another,* Lat. *quam*); with superlatives

§ 632. THE PARTICLES. 341

like the Lat. *quam :* ὡς τάχιστα, *quam celerrime, as quickly as possible* (compare ὅτι). In statements of number and measure it means *about, nearly :* ὡς δέκα, *about ten ;* ὡς ἐπὶ τὸ πολύ, *for the most part ;* with verbs of motion or action it indicates what is merely intended, apparent : ἀπῄει ὡς εἰς τοὺς πολεμίους, *he went away in the direction of the enemy* (as if he went against the enemy); hence it occurs with *participles* in the manner described § 588. On its use with the Infinitive, § 564, and on ὡς as a preposition, § 450.

b) In a *temporal* sense ὡς means *when, as soon as* (compare Lat. *ut*): Hom. ὡς εἶδ', ὥς μιν μᾶλλον ἔδυ χόλος, *when he saw him, anger pierced him the more ;* ὡς τάχιστα ἕως ὑπέφαινεν, ἐθύοντο, *as soon as dawn appeared, they sacrificed* [Lat. *ut primum*].

c) In a *causal* sense ὡς means *as* (Latin *quum*), *since,* and with subsequent statement of the reason, *for :* δέομαι σοῦ παραμεῖναι, ὡς ἐγὼ ἥδιστα ἀκούσαιμι σοῦ, *I beg you to stay here, as I should hear you with the greatest pleasure.*

d) After verbs of saying and declaring ὡς means *that :* ἧκεν ἀγγέλλων τις, ὡς 'Ελάτεια κατείληπται, *some one came announcing that Elatœa has been taken.* § 526, *b*.

e) ὡς is rarely used in a *consecutive* sense, *so that* (ὥςτε).

f) In a *final* sense ὡς means *in order that :* ὡς μὴ πάντες ὄλωνται, *in order that all may not perish.* Compare § 530, etc.

g) On ὡς expressing a wish (Lat. *utinam*), see § 514.

§ 632. **2.** ὥςπερ, *as,*
is only a strengthened ὡς (compare § 641, **3**), and is used only in a comparative sense.

3. ὅπως, *how, that, in order that,*
is principally used as a *final* Conjunction, and may then

be translated by *that*, or *in order that*, compare § 530, etc. On οὐχ ὅπως, § 622, 4.

4. ὥστε, *as, so that*, has rarely the comparative meaning *as*, generally the consecutive *so that*, when it is followed either by an Infinitive or a finite verb. Compare § 565.

5. Hom. ἠύτε, *as, just as, like*, only in comparisons.

§ 633. V. *Declarative Conjunctions.*

1. ὅτι, *that, because* [Lat. *quod*], is originally nothing but the Neuter of the pronoun ὅςτις, ὅ τι, on the distinction of which from ὅτι, compare § 214, *Obs.* 2. Like the Latin *quod*, ὅτι has two principal meanings, the *declarative that* and the *causal because*.

a) ὅτι means *that* after verbs of saying and declaring (compare § 525): Ἡράκλειτος λέγει, ὅτι πάντα χωρεῖ καὶ οὐδὲν μένει, *Heraclitus says that every thing moves, and nothing is stationary.* Hence the phrase δῆλον ὅτι (also written δηλονότι), *it is clear that, manifestly.*

Obs.—Sometimes, also, a direct speech is introduced by ὅτι, so that the Conjunction is, as it were, a mere sign of quotation: ἐδήλου ἡ γραφή, ὅτι Θεμιστοκλῆς ἥκω παρὰ σέ, *the letter stated (that) I Themistocles am come to you.*

b) *because, that* [Lat. *quod*] : Hom. χωόμενος, ὅτ᾽ ἄριστον Ἀχαιῶν οὐδὲν ἔτισας, *angry that you have not honored the best of the Achæans.* The use of ὅτι (or ὅ τι) with a superlative deserves attention : ὅτι τάχιστα like ὡς τάχιστα, *as quickly as possible;* and ὅτι μή, *except, besides:* οὐκ ἦν κρήνη ὅτι μὴ μία, *there was no fountain except one.*

2. ὡς, *that*, § 631, *d.*

3. διότι, *that*, § 636, 2.

4. οὕνεκα, *that*, § 636, 3.

VI. Temporal Conjunctions.

§ 634. (Respecting the Moods, see § 556, etc.)

1. ὅτε, ὁπότε, *when, as* [*quando, cum*]: ὅταν, ὁπόταν, *when, if:* ἦν ποτε χρόνος, ὅτε θεοὶ μὲν ἦσαν, θνητὰ δὲ γένη οὐκ ἦν, *there once was a time when gods existed, but mortal races did not exist;* Hom. οἱ δ' ὅτε δὴ λιμένος πολυβενθέος ἐντὸς ἵκοντο, ἱστία μὲν στείλαντο, *but when they got within the deep harbor they furled the sails.* ὅτε and ὁπότε with the Optative, according to § 558, *Obs.* 1, mean *whenever, as often as:* Hom. ἔνθα πάρος κοιμᾶθ' ὅτε μιν γλυκὺς ὕπνος ἱκάνοι, *where formerly he used to lie down whenever sweet sleep came upon him.* Sometimes ὅτε has the causal meaning *since.*

2. Hom. εὖτε = ὅτε.

3. ἡνίκα, ὁπηνίκα, *when, at the time when* (§ 217), denotes rather a point of time : ἡνίκα ἦν δείλη, ἐξαπίνης ἐπιφαίνονται οἱ πολέμιοι, *when it was evening the enemy suddenly appeared.*

4. ἦμος, poet. *when :*

Hom. ἦμος δ' ἠέλιος μέσον οὐρανὸν ἀμφιβεβήκει, καὶ τότε δὴ χρύσεια πατὴρ ἐτίταινε τάλαντα, *when* (at the moment) *the sun had entered mid heaven, just then the father raised the golden scales.*

§ 635. 5. ἐπεί, *after, when, as :* ἐπεάν, ἐπήν, ἐπάν, *when ;* Hom. αὐτὰρ ἐπεὶ πόσιος καὶ ἐδητύος ἐξ ἔρον ἕντο, *but when they had quenched the desire for food and drink;* Κῦρος ὑπέσχετο ἀνδρὶ ἑκάστῳ δώσειν πέντε ἀργυρίου μνᾶς, ἐπὰν εἰς Βαβυλῶνα ἥκωσιν, *Cyrus promised to give each man five silver minæ when they should come to Babylon.* ἐπεί frequently introduces a *reason*, and then is to be translated by *because* or *for :* Hom. ἀλλὰ πίθεσθε καὶ ὕμμες, ἐπεὶ πείθεσθαι ἄμεινον, *but do you also obey me, for it is better to obey..*

6. ἐπειδή, *now since, since:* ἐπειδάν, *when,* is ἐπεί strengthened by δή (§ 642), and points more strongly to the reason

assigned than ἐπεί: ἐπειδὴ ἀνεῴχθη τὸ δεσμωτήριον, εἰσ-ήλθομεν, *now since the prison was opened we entered.*

7. ἕως, *as long as, till* [*quamdiu, dum, donec*]: ἕως ἔτι ἐλπίς, *as long as there is still hope;* περιεμένομεν ἕως ἀνοιχθείη τὸ δεσμωτήριον, *we waited till the prison should be opened.*

8. ἔστε
9. μέχρι, ἄχρι (compare § 455) } = ἕως.

10. poet. ὄφρα, *as long as, till :*

Hom. ὄφρα μὲν ἠὼς ἦν, *as long as it was morning;* Hom. ἔχει κότον, ὄφρα τελέσσῃ, *he nurses wrath till he fulfills it.* ὄφρα is very often a Particle of purpose or intention, and then to be translated by *that, in order that :* Hom. ὄφρα μὴ οἶος ἀγέραστος ἔω, *in order that I may not be alone unhonored.*

11. πρίν, *before, sooner* [*priusquam*] (compare § 565), is joined sometimes with the Infinitive, sometimes with a finite verb. Its original adverbial meaning, *previously, earlier,* has been preserved, especially in τὸ πρίν, *formerly.* In Hom. the Conjunction πρίν may refer back to the adverb πρίν: οὐδ' ὅγε πρὶν Δαναοῖσιν ἀεικέα λοιγὸν ἀπώσει, πρίν γ' ἀπὸ πατρὶ φίλῳ δόμεναι ἑλικώπιδα κούρην, *and he will not avert the dreadful suffering from the Danai before they have given back the quick-eyed maiden to her father.*

12. πάρος, Hom. = πρίν.

VII. *Causal Conjunctions.*

§ 636. 1. ὅτι, § 633, *b.*

2. διότι, *because,* properly διὰ τοῦτο ὅτι, *for this reason that,* or *that.*

3. οὕνεκα, *because,* poet., from οὗ ἕνεκα, for τούτου ἕνεκα ὅτι, *for this reason that;* *because,* also declarative *that.* So likewise ὁθούνεκα from ὅτου (οὗτινος) ἕνεκα.

4. ἐπεί, § 635, 5.

5. ὅτε, § 634, 1.

6. γάρ (always postpositive), *for, namely, to wit.* Special peculiarities in the use of γάρ are:

§ 637. THE PARTICLES. 345

a) In animated discourse the sentence containing a reason is often put before the one for which the reason is given, especially after a Vocative : Hom. Ἀτρείδη, πολλοὶ γὰρ τεθνᾶσι καρηκομόωντες Ἀχαιοί—τῷ σε χρὴ πόλεμον παῦσαι, *Atrides, for many rich-haired Achæans have died, therefore you ought to put an end to the war.*

b) By *namely*, γάρ may be translated when it introduces the substance of a speech or opinion before announced, so especially after τεκμήριον δέ, μαρτύριον δέ (supply ἔστι), *for that there is a proof, a testimony.*

c) In answers γάρ may often be rendered by *yes, certainly*, but must in reality be explained by an ellipsis: ἀγωνιστέον μὲν ἄρα ἡμῖν πρὸς τοὺς ἄνδρας; ἀνάγκη γάρ, ἔφη, *must we then contend with the men? yes, it is necessary, said he*—the complete answer would be, *we must contend, for it is necessary.*

d) In animated questions γάρ serves to give emphasis like the Lat. *nam :* τί γάρ; *quidnam? how so?* ἦ γάρ; οὐ γάρ; *is it not so?* πῶς γὰρ οὔ; *how could it be otherwise?* εἰ γάρ is the Lat. *utinam.* ἀλλὰ γάρ [*at enim*] corresponds to the English *but surely;* οὐ γὰρ ἀλλά properly : *for it is not so, but,* hence *however.*

VIII. *Inferential Conjunctions.*

§ 637. 1. ἄρα (Ep. ἄρ and enclitic ῥά, poet. also ἆρα, postpositive), *then, therefore, accordingly,* always refers to something known or resulting from what has gone before. It is most frequently used in Homer to connect sentences slightly : ὣς ἄρ' ἔφη, *thus then he spoke;* Ἀτρείδης δ' ἄρα νῆα θοὴν ἅλαδε προέρυσσεν, *and Atrides accordingly drew the fleet ship to the sea* (as was to be expected). οὐκ ἄρα often means *not forsooth,* εἰ ἄρα *if then* or *if perhaps,* and in indirect questions *whether perhaps.*
On the Interrogative ἆρα, § 607, *b.*

2. οὖν (New Ion. ὦν, postpositive), *then, consequently,* is

P 2

more emphatic than ἄρα: Hom. ἤτοι νόστος ἀπώλετο πατρὸς ἐμοῖο· οὔτ' οὖν ἀγγελίῃ ἔτι πείθομαι, εἴ ποθεν ἔλθοι, οὔτε θεοπροπίης ἐμπάζομαι, surely my father's return is lost, therefore I no longer believe a message, if one comes from any where, nor concern myself about prophecy. μὲν οὖν (compare § 643, 12), no doubt, certainly, well then; δ' οὖν, certainly; ἀλλ' οὖν, but certainly; γὰρ οὖν, yet surely. When joined to relatives, οὖν has the generalizing meaning of the Lat. cunque: ὅςτιςοῦν, whoever, quicunque (§§ 218, 600).

By combination with οὖν we obtain the *Negative* οὔκουν, *not then*, to be carefully distinguished from οὐκοῦν, which is properly an Interrogative, *not then?* but as an *affirmative* answer is expected after an interrogative with οὐ (§ 608), it has acquired the *positive* meaning, *therefore, accordingly, now*: οὔκουν ἔμοιγε δοκεῖ, *hence I do not think so*; Poet. οὐκοῦν ὅταν δὴ μὴ σθένω, πεπαύσομαι, *well, then, I will cease when I really have no strength*.

3. νύν (enclitic, postpositive), a weakened νῦν, corresponds to the unaccented English *now*.

4. τοίνυν, *hence, therefore, surely*, is a νύν strengthened by the assuring τοί (§ 643, 10).

5. τοίγαρ, *so then, therefore, yet;* more emphatic τοιγάρτοι, τοιγαροῦν.

6. ὥςτε, *so that*, § 632, 4.

IX. *Final Conjunctions.*

(Respecting the Moods, § 530, etc.)

§ 638. 1. ἵνα, *that, in order that, in order to* [Lat. *ut*], as an adverb also signifies *where* in a relative sense and in indirect questions: οὐχ ὁρᾷς ἵν' εἶ κακοῦ; *do you not see in what* (position of) *evil you are?* ἵνα as a Particle of *purpose* is elliptical in ἵνα τί; where γένηται must be supplied, *i. e., that what* may happen? *why?*

§ 639. THE PARTICLES. 347

On 2. ὡς and
3. ὅπως, see §§ 631, 632, 3.
4. ὄφρα, § 635, 10.
5. μή = Lat. *ne, that not, in order that not*, §§ 530, etc., 614; after verbs of fearing, § 616, *Obs.* 3.

X. Hypothetical Conjunctions.

(Respecting the Moods, § 535, etc.)

§ 639. 1. εἰ, *if*,
in indirect questions *whether*, § 610; in wishes (where εἴθε, εἰ γάρ are also used), *if only, if but*, § 514. Observe also εἰ μή in the sense of *except*, like the Lat. *nisi:* ἡμῖν οὐδέν ἐστιν ἀγαθὸν ἄλλο εἰ μὴ ὅπλα καὶ ἀρετή, *we have no other good except weapons and valor;* εἰ μὴ εἰ, *nisi si, unless;* εἴπερ, *siquidem, if indeed, certainly if*, contains an emphatic assurance: Poet. ἦ καὶ γεγηθὼς ταῦτ᾽ ἀεὶ λέξειν δοκεῖς; εἴπερ τί γ᾽ ἔστι τῆς ἀληθείας σθένος, *do you really think you will always speak thus joyously?* (answer) *if indeed* (certainly if) *there is any force in truth.*

2. ἐάν, *i. e.*, εἰ ἄν (ἄν, ἤν), *if;*
in indirect questions, *whether*, § 610.

3. ἄν, *I suppose, perhaps* (postpositive), always denotes that something may happen only under certain conditions, and hence is often untranslatable.

On ἄν with the (potential) Optative, § 516.
" " (hypothetical) Indicative, § 537.
" " Indicative, denoting repetition, § 494.
" " Future Indicative, § 500, *Obs.*
" " Subjunctive with relatives, § 554.
" " " with particles of time, § 557.
" " Infinitive, §§ 575, 576.
" " Participles, § 595.

Obs.—ἄν is often used twice in the same clause: οὐκ ἂν ὀρθῶς οὐδ᾽ ὑγιῶς ὁ τοῦτο ποιήσας περὶ οὐδενὸς ἂν λογίσαιτο, *he who did this would not, I suppose, judge correctly or soundly about any thing.*

4. Hom. κέ, κέν (enclitic and postpositive) is used almost entirely like ἄν.

XI. *Concessive Conjunctions.*

§ 640. 1. εἰ καί (ἐὰν καί), *if even, although,* denotes a simple concession: poet. πόλιν, εἰ καὶ μὴ βλέπεις, φρονεῖς δ᾽ ὅμως, οἵᾳ νόσῳ ξύνεστιν, *though you have not sight, yet you are aware in what misery the city is involved.*

2. καὶ εἰ (καὶ ἐάν, κἄν), *even if, even though,* denotes an emphatic concession, like *etiamsi :* ἡγεῖτο ἀνδρὸς εἶναι ἀγαθοῦ ὠφελεῖν τοὺς φίλους, καὶ εἰ μηδεὶς μέλλοι εἴσεσθαι, *he deemed it to belong to a good man to benefit his friends, even if no one should know it.*

Obs.—The distinction between εἰ καί and καὶ εἰ consists mainly in the former giving the emphasis of the καί to the Protasis, the latter to the Apodosis. Hence the meaning is in many cases almost the same.

3. καίπερ with the participle, § 587, 5.

In the Apodosis, the Concessive Conjunctions are often followed by ὅμως, *notwithstanding,* § 630, 7.

B) *Particles of Emphasis.*

§ 641. 1. γέ (enclitic and postpositive), *at least* [Latin *quidem*], gives the word before it greater weight, and is often represented in other languages merely by a more emphatic accent on the word to which γε is attached: Hom. εἴπερ γὰρ Ἕκτωρ γε κακὸν καὶ ἀνάλκιδα φήσει, ἀλλ᾽ οὐ πείσονται Τρῶες, *for if Hector shall call (you) base and effeminate, yet the Trojans will not believe* (it); Hom. ἀλλὰ σύ, εἰ δύνασαί γε, περίσχεο παιδός, *but do you, if you can, protect your son;* τοῦτό γε οἶμαι ὑμᾶς ἅπαντας ᾐσθῆσθαι, *this at least I think you all have perceived;* Hom. ὅτις τοιαῦτά γε ῥέζοι, *whoever should do such things.* γε is very frequently affixed to pronouns: ἔγωγε, *ego qui-*

§ 642. THE PARTICLES. 349

dem, ὅγε (Hom. *he, he specially*); ὅςγε strengthened ὅς, *qui quidem.*

2. γοῦν (postpositive), *at least* [Lat. *certe*], is compounded of γέ and οὖν, and hence more emphatic than γε alone.

3. πέρ (enclitic and postpositive), *just, exactly, very,* shortened from the adverb περί, *very* (§ 466), serves to give precision to the relative : ὅςπερ (§ 218), *the very one who ;* ὡςπερ, *just as.* In Homer it is added to participles in a sense similar to that of καίπερ (§ 587, 5): μηδ' οὕτως ἀγαθός περ ἐὼν θεοείκελ' Ἀχιλλεῦ κλέπτε νόῳ, *be not so stealthy in purpose, divine Achilles, though you are so very noble* (*ironical*).

§ 642. 4. δή (*certainly, to be sure, well then, therefore*), points to what is *obvious* in a single idea or in a whole sentence. δή is used principally in three ways :

a) to emphasize single words : ποῖά ἐστιν ἃ ἡμᾶς ὠφελεῖ ; ὑγίεια καὶ ἰσχὺς καὶ κάλλος καὶ πλοῦτος δή, *what kind of things are those which benefit us ? health, and strength, and beauty, and, certainly, wealth ;* δῆλα δή, *to be sure it is clear ;* νῦν ὁρᾶτε δή, *now you surely see ;* ἄγε δή, *well !* *come ;* τί δή ; *what then ?* μάλιστα δή, *very much so,* at the beginning of an apodosis ; καὶ τότε δή, *now, just then.* On καὶ δὴ καί, § 624, 4.

b) to confirm a sentence by referring to what precedes : τὸν μὲν δὴ πέμπει, *him, then, he sends ;* Poet. οἱ τηλικοίδε καὶ διδαξόμεσθα δὴ φρονεῖν πρὸς ἀνδρὸς τηλικοῦδε ;· *we even at such an age are, then* (according to the preceding speeches), *to be taught wisdom by a man of such an age ?* ὡς ἔν τινι φρουρᾷ ἐσμεν οἱ ἄνθρωποι, καὶ οὐ δεῖ δὴ ἑαυτὸν ἐκ ταύτης λύειν, *we men are, as it were, placed at some post, and it is therefore not proper to abandon it.*

c) referring to time, very much like the particle of time, ἤδη, Lat. *jam :* καὶ πολλὰ δὴ ἄλλα λέξας εἶπεν, *and after having already stated many other things, he said ;* νῦν δή, *just now.* Hom. τὰ δὴ νῦν πάντα τελεῖται, *all that is just now being done.*

5. δήπου, *surely, I suppose,* also δήπουθεν,
is often used ironically in assertions which admit of no reply: τρέφεται δὲ ψυχὴ τίνι; μαθήμασι δήπου, *the soul is nourished by what?* (answer) *surely by learning.* τί δήπου, *well, then, what do you suppose?*

6. δῆτα, *certainly,*
negative οὐ δῆτα, *certainly not;* τί δῆτα, *well! what then?*

7. δῆθεν, *clearly, evidently.*

8. δαί,
another form of δή, but only used in questions: τί δαί; *well! what? how so?*

§ 643. 9. ἦ, *verily, truly*
(to be distinguished from ἤ, *or, than,* § 626), strengthens an assurance. ἦ μήν (Hom. ἦ μέν) is the common form of an oath: ὤμοσαν ὅρκους ἦ μὴν μὴ μνησικακήσειν, *they swore that they would truly not cherish revenge.* On the Interrogative ἦ, §§ 607, 608.

In Homer ἦ is appended to ἐπεί and τί, to add strength to them: ἐπεὶ ἦ, τί ἦ, for which also ἐπειή, τιή is written.

10. τοί (enclitic and postpositive), *I assure you, let me tell you.* οὔτοι, *truly not;* strengthened forms: τοίγαρ, τοιγαροῦν, τοιγάρτο (§ 637, 5).

11. ἤτοι, *verily, faith* (ἤ and τοί),
serves as a naïve assurance in Epic poetry: ἤτοι ὅγ' ὡς εἰπὼν κατ' ἄρ' ἕζετο, *now when he had so spoken he sat down.*
On the disjunctive ἤτοι—ἤ, *either, or,* see § 626, *a.*

12. μήν (Hom. μάν, μέν), *verily, truly* [Latin *verum, vero*],
Hom. ὧδε γὰρ ἐξερέω, καὶ μὴν τετελεσμένον ἔσται, *for so will I speak out, and truly it will be fulfilled;* τί μήν; *why! what? why not?* (compare § 404, *Obs.*).

13. μέντοι, *yet, however, certainly,* Lat. *vero,*
from μέν, the weaker form of μήν: ἐς Οἰνιάδας ἐστράτευσαν καὶ ἐπολιόρκουν, οὐ μέντοι εἷλόν γε, ἀλλ' ἀνεχώρησαν ἐπ' οἴκου, *they made an expedition against Œniadæ, and be-*

§ 643. THE PARTICLES. 351

sieged it; yet they did not conquer it, but returned home.

14. ναί, *yea, in fact.*

15. νή, *truly,*
followed by the names of gods in the Accusative, who are invoked as witnesses in an oath: νὴ Δία, *by Zeus.*

16. μά, *truly,*
in negative oaths: οὐ μὰ Δία, *no, by Zeus;* also in positive ones, when ναί precedes: ναὶ μὰ Δία, *truly by Zeus* (§ 399, *Obs.*).

17. Hom. θήν (enclitic), *truly, surely,*
similar to the Attic δήπου (§ 642, 5), often with an ironical meaning: οὔ θήν μιν πάλιν αὖτις ἀνήσει θυμὸς ἀγήνωρ νεικείειν βασιλῆας, *his courageous heart will surely not again incite him to taunt kings.*

APPENDIX.

VERSIFICATION.

§ 644. In poetry, regard is had in the selection and arrangement of words to the quantity of syllables. The regular recurrence of long and short syllables creates *rhythm*, or measure, by which each verse has a regular movement and flow of its own.

1. VERSE.—Each single line is a *verse*.
2. FEET.—A verse is composed of arrangements of syllables by twos, threes, etc., called *feet*.
3. METRE.—The arrangement of feet by which a verse is constituted is called *metre*, and the kind of metre is named from the prevailing foot. Thus iambic metre signifies a metre of which the iambus is the fundamental foot.

Obs.—In the terms *monometer, dimeter*, etc., "meter" signifies the number of times a foot or a group of feet is used in the verse; *e. g.*, in dactylic, Ionic, and bacchic metres one foot forms a "meter;" and a dactylic, Ionic, or bacchic dimeter, trimeter, tetrameter, hexameter, is a metre of two, three, four, and six feet respectively. In all other verse two feet form a "meter;" and an iambic dimeter, for example, or trimeter, tetrameter, or hexameter, is a metre of four, six, eight, and twelve feet respectively. For rules of quantity, compare §§ 74-78.

§ 645. KINDS OF FEET.
1. Four Dissyllabic:
 ‾ ‾ Spondee (two long syllables).
 ‾ ˘ Trochee (one long and one short syllable).
 ˘ ‾ Iambus.
 ˘ ˘ Pyrrhic.

2. Eight Trisyllabic:
 – – – Molossus.
 ᴗ – – Bacchius.
 – – ᴗ Antibacchius.
 – ᴗ ᴗ Dactyl.
 ᴗ ᴗ – Anapæst.
 – ᴗ – Creticus.
 ᴗ – ᴗ Amphibrach.
 ᴗ ᴗ ᴗ Tribrach.

3. Sixteen Tetrasyllabic:
 ᴗ ᴗ ᴗ ᴗ Proceleusmatic.
 – ᴗ ᴗ ᴗ First Pæon.
 ᴗ – ᴗ ᴗ Second Pæon.
 ᴗ ᴗ – ᴗ Third Pæon.
 ᴗ ᴗ ᴗ – Fourth Pæon.
 – – ᴗ ᴗ Ionicus a Majore.
 ᴗ ᴗ – – Ionicus a Minore.
 – ᴗ ᴗ – Choriambus.
 ᴗ – – ᴗ Antispast.
 ᴗ – ᴗ – Diiambus.
 – ᴗ – ᴗ Ditrochee.
 ᴗ – – – First Epitritus.
 – ᴗ – – Second Epitritus.
 – – ᴗ – Third Epitritus.
 – – – ᴗ Fourth Epitritus.
 – – – – Dispondee.

§ 646. RESOLUTION AND CONTRACTION.—A long syllable is considered equal in time to two short ones. Hence a long quantity may be resolved into two short ones, or two short ones may be contracted into a long one. Thus a dactyl by contraction may be replaced by a spondee, or a spondee by resolution by a dactyl; and a dactyl, first by contraction, then by resolution, may pass over into an anapæst.

§ 647. 1. ARSIS AND THESIS.—One syllable of every

§ 647. APPENDIX. 355

foot receives a stronger emphasis—ictus—than the others. This emphasis is called the *arsis* (ἄρσις, raising). The *thesis* (θέσις, laying down) is the lowering of the voice which occurs in the pronunciation of the other syllables.

 a. The syllable upon which the arsis occurs is said to stand in arsis, and those upon which the thesis, in thesis. Less properly the syllables themselves are called arsis and thesis.
 b. Each foot properly has its own arsis, but when a foot stands for another (§ 646) it takes the arsis of that foot. Thus, in anapæstic metre, a dactyl taking the place of an anapæst will receive the arsis upon the second syllable instead of the first.

2. CÆSURA.—The regular arrangement of syllables in feet has the effect, in most kinds of verse, of dividing each verse into two rhythmical parts. The pause between the two is called a *cæsura*, a cutting (cædo, to cut). It, of course, always occurs at the end of a word, never in a word; while it may occur either in a foot, separating one part from another, or at the end of a foot.

 a. The ending of a word at any time before the ending of a foot is a cæsura of the foot. When the cæsura falls between the arsis and thesis of a foot, it is a cæsura also of the rhythm. The principal cæsura, which divides a verse into two equal or nearly equal parts, is called the cæsura of the verse. There are, therefore, three cæsuræ:
  1. Cæsura of the foot.
  2. Cæsura of the rhythm.
  3. Cæsura of the verse.

3. CATALECTIC, ACATALECTIC, AND HYPERCATALECTIC.—If the last foot of a verse is not complete, the verse is called *catalectic* (καταληκτικός, leaving off, stopping). A complete verse is *acatalectic*, and one more than complete is *hypercatalectic*.

4. SYNCOPE.—Sometimes one or more theses will be omitted, and thus a modification of rhythm occurs; this is called *syncope*.

5. ANACRUSIS.—An unaccented syllable prefixed to a

verse beginning with an accented syllable is called an *anacrusis*. It sometimes consists of two short syllables.

6. BASIS AND ECBASIS.—A trochee, iambus, tribrach, or spondee may be used to introduce a verse in the same way as the anacrusis, and is then called a *basis* (step). The same placed at the end of a verse is called *ecbasis*.

Note.—*Anacrusis*, *basis*, and *ecbasis* are extra rhythmic, i. e., count as no part of the metre.

§ 648. ARRANGEMENT OF VERSES.—Verses may be arranged—

1. *by the line*, i. e., by the continued repetition of one kind of verse, as in dactylic hexameter or iambic trimeter;

2. *by distichs* (δίστιχος, double row), i. e., by couplets of verses, the one differing from the other in length or in kind, or both, as in elegiac verse (difference in length), and in lyric verse when an iambic verse will alternate with a trochaic;

3. *by systems*, i. e., a number of verses in connected series, concluding with a verse either catalectic or of particular rhythm, and thus forming a whole; for example, an anapæstic system is a succession of anapæstic dimeters acatalectic, with sometimes a monometer, and always ending with the dimeter catalectic (parœmiac);

4. *by strophe and antistrophe.* A strophe (στροφή, a turning) is a combination of several verses, either like or different, into a rhythmical whole. It may be repeated. When repeated once only, the second is called an *antistrophe*.

The strophe was sung by the chorus in tragedy or comedy when making an evolution from right to left of the orchestra, and the antistrophe in making the return movement.

a. To a strophe and antistrophe a third strophe differing in form may be added as a conclusion, and is called an *epode;* or it may precede, and is then called a *proöde;* or it may come between, and is then called a *mesode.*

DIFFERENT KINDS OF VERSE.

§ 649. DACTYLIC VERSE.—The fundamental foot is the dactyl. By contraction of the last two quantities into one, a long syllable may take the place of the two short ones, and so a spondee replace a dactyl. The long quantity, however, as a rule, can not be resolved into two short ones, so that only in rare cases does a proceleusmatic ($\smile\smile\smile\smile$) replace a dactyl. The *arsis* falls upon the first syllable. The rhythms commonly used are the following:

1. Dimeter (compare § 644, 3, *Obs.*):

ἐξανύσεις χρέος, $-\smile\smile-\smile\smile$, Soph. Œd. Tyr., 157.

ὦ μεγάλα φάτις, ὦ, $-\smile\smile-\smile\smile-$ (hypercatalectic or penthemimeris), Soph. Ajax, 173.

ὧδε πρόκειμαι, $-\smile\smile-\smile$ (catalectic), Soph. Ajax, 427.

2. Trimeter:

μᾷ κράτος ἀντίπαλον Ζεὺς, $-\smile\smile-\smile\smile-\smile\smile$, Æsch. Pr. Vinct., 537.

εἴτ' ἐπὶ τὰς ἀνύδρους, $-\smile\smile-\smile\smile-$ (catalectic or penthemimeris; same as dimeter hypercatalectic), Eur. Alc., 115.

3. Tetrameter:

ἤ ῥά σε Ταυροπόλα Διὸς Ἄρτεμις, $-\smile\smile-\smile\smile-\smile\smile-\smile\smile$, Soph. Ajax, 172.

καρποφόρου Λιβύας, ἱερὰν, $-\smile\smile-\smile\smile-\smile\smile-$ (catalectic), Pind. Pyth. IV., 6.

τῶν μεγάλων Δαναῶν ὕπο κληζομέναν, $-\smile\smile-\smile\smile-\smile\smile-\smile\smile-$ (hypercatalectic), Soph. Ajax, 225.

4. Pentameter (the pentameter *acatalectic* does not occur):

Αἴλινον, Αἴλινον εἰπὲ, τὸ δ' εὖ νικάτω, $-\smile\smile-\smile\smile-\smile\smile-\smile\smile-\smile$
(catalectic in dissyllabam), Æsch. Agam., 121.
(The catalectic in syllabam = tetrameter hypercatalectic.)

5. Hexameter:

τῷ ἴκελος πολέεσσιν ὀχήσατο κύμασιν Ἑρμῆς,
$-\smile\smile-\smile\smile-\smile\smile-\smile\smile-\smile\smile-$, Odyss., 5:54.

6. Elegiac distich consists of a dactylic hexameter and a dactylic pentameter (so called, really two catalectic trimeters):

ᾤχετο μὲν Πίστις, μεγάλη θεός, ᾤχετο δ' ἀνδρῶν
Σωφροσύνη, Χάριτές τ', ὦ φίλε, γῆν ἔλιπον.

– ‿ ‿ – – – ‿ ‿ – ‿ ‿ – ‿ ‿ – –
– ‿ ‿ – ‿ ‿ – | – ‿ ‿ – ‿ ‿ –

§ 650. HEXAMETER.—This is the metre of Epic poetry, *e. g.*, of the Iliad and Odyssey of Homer. It is therefore called Epic or Heroic hexameter. A spondee may stand in any place, or in all the places at once. It always stands in the last place. A dactyl regularly occupies the fifth place, but sometimes a spondee, and then the verse is called spondaic. The cæsura regularly occurs after the arsis of the third foot, but sometimes in the thesis of the third foot or after the arsis of the fourth. A cæsura after the fourth foot is called the bucolic, from its frequent use in pastoral poetry.

§ 651. TROCHAIC VERSE.—The fundamental foot is the trochee. By protraction of the short quantity, a spondee may replace the trochee, or, by resolution of the long, a tribrach may replace the trochee. The arsis falls on the first syllable. The rhythms used are the following:

1. Monometer, not used alone, but always with other rhythms. Compare Logaœdic Verse.

2. Tripody (ithyphallicus):

ἦν ὁ ταῦτα πράσσων, – ‿ – ‿ – ⏒, Soph. El., 200.

3. Dimeter:

παῖδες ἐν τιμαῖς ἐμίχθεν, – ‿ – ⏒ – ‿ – ‿, Pind. Isth., 2, 29.
κλίνατ', οὐ σθένω ποσίν, – ‿ – ‿ – ‿ – (catalectic), Eur. Alc., 266.

4. Trimeter:

θεύμοροι νίσσοντ' ἐπ' ἀνθρώπους ἀοιδαί, – ‿ – ⏒ – ‿ – ⏒ – ‿ – ⏒,
Pind. Ol., 3, 10.
ζῶν κακῶς, εὔκλειαν αἰσχῦναι θέλει, – ‿ – ⏒ – ‿ – ⏒ – ‿ – (catalectic), Soph. El., 1082.

§ 652. APPENDIX. 359

5. Tetrameter:

τίς νιν ἀνθρώπων τέκεν; ποίας δ' ἀποσπασθεῖσα φύτλας,
$-\smile-\bar{\smile}-\smile-\bar{\smile}-\smile-\bar{\smile}-\smile-\smile$, Pind. Pythag., 9, 33.

κλεινὸς Αἰακοῦ λόγος, κλεινὰ δὲ καὶ ναυσικλυτὸς,
$-\smile-\smile-\smile-\bar{\smile}-\smile-\bar{\smile}-\smile\overset{\smile}{-}$, Pind. Frag. Isth., 4, 1.

§ 652. LOGAŒDIC VERSE.—Dactyls and trochees together formed a simple rhythm, which, from its similarity to the rhythm of common speech, was called logaœdic (λογαοιδικός). The same was true of anapæsts and iambi. Hence there are two kinds of logaœdic verse,

a. the dactylic logaœdic;
b. the anapæstic logaœdic.

1. Dactylic Logaœdic Verse.

This may consist of only two feet, but never more than six. In case of more than one dactyl, the dactyls are never separated. The trochees may be arranged together before or after the dactyls, or separated, and stand part before and part after, but never between them.

1. One dactyl and one trochee—ADONIC VERSE:

πλησίον "Αιδας, $-\smile\smile-\smile$, Eur. Alc., 268.
τοῦτον, στόμα, ῥῖψον ·, $-\ |\ -\smile\smile-\smile$ (same with anacrusis), Pind. Ol., 9, 36.

2. One dactyl and two trochees—PHERECRATEAN:

εὐπατριδᾶν τ' ἀρωγαί, $-\smile\smile-\smile-\smile$ (1st form), Soph. El., 859.
δαρὸν οὐκ ἀπόνητοι, $-\smile-\smile\smile-\smile$ (2d form), Soph. El., 1065.
ἢ πόλις ἢ φίλων, $-\smile\smile-\smile-$ (1st form catalectic), Eur. Med., 847.
ἐντὶ τραυματίαι, $-\smile-\smile\smile-$ (2d form catalectic), Pind. Frag., 141 (208).
κακά νιν ἕλοιτο μοῖρα, $\smile\ |\ -\smile\smile-\smile-\smile$ (1st form with anacrusis, parœmiac), Soph. Œd. Tyr., 887.
καὶ τὸ πρὶν ἐπαρκέσει, $-\ |\ -\smile\smile-\smile-$ (1st form catalectic with anacrusis), Soph. Antig., 612.

3. One dactyl and trochaic penthemim—GLYCONIC:

ἥμενος ὃν φρόνημά πως, $-\smile\smile-\smile-\smile-$ (1st form), Æsch. Sup., 94.
δώσουσ' ἀντιφόνους δόκας, $-\bar{\smile}-\smile\smile-\smile-$ (2d form), Soph. El., 248.

φῶτα βάντα πανσαγίᾳ, $-\smile--\smile-\smile-$ (3d form), Soph. Antig., 107.

ξυμμάρτυρας ὕμμ' ἐπικτῶμαι, $-|-\smile\smile-\smile-\overset{\smile}{-}.-$ (1st form with anacrusis), Soph. Antig., 846.

4. One dactyl and three trochees:

καὶ παραμειβόμεσθ' ἀδέρκτως, $-\smile\smile-\smile\smile-\overset{\smile}{-}$, Soph. Œd. Col., 130.

στέγειν; ἢ τί λέγειν πρὸς ἀνδρ' ὑπόπταν; $\smile-|-\smile\smile-\smile-\smile-\smile$ (same with basis), PHALACEAN, Soph. Phil., 136.

5. One dactyl and four trochees—SAPPHIC (*hendecasyllable*):

παῖ Δίος, δολόπλοκε, λίσσομαί σε, $-\smile--\smile\smile-\smile--$, Sappho, 1, 2.

τὸ δηὖτε κῦμα τῶν προτέρων ὄνω, $\smile|-\smile-\smile-\smile--$ (same catalectic with anacrusis), ALCAIC (*hendecasyllable*), Alc., 19.

6. Two dactyls and one trochee=dactylic trimeter catalectic.

7. Two dactyls and two trochees—ALCAIC (*decasyllable*):

ναΐ φορήμεθα σὺν μελαίνᾳ, $-\smile\smile-\smile\smile-\smile-\overset{\smile}{-}$, Alc., 18.

8. Two dactyls and three trochees:

ὦ πόλις, ὦ γενεὰ τάλαινα, νῦν σε, $-\smile\smile-\smile\smile--\smile-\smile$, Soph. El., 1413.

9. Three dactyls and two trochees—PRAXILLEAN:

ἀντιτύπᾳ δ' ἐπὶ γᾷ πέσε τανταλωθείς, $-\smile\smile-\smile\smile-\smile\smile-\smile-\overset{\smile}{-}$, Soph. Antig., 134.

SYNCOPATED FORMS.

10. PHERECRATEAN CATALECTIC is sometimes repeated, the two making one verse.

11. PHERECRATEAN CATALECTIC, second form followed by first form, constitutes the ASCLEPIADEAN VERSE.

12. The GREATER ASCLEPIADEAN is the same two pherecratean verses with a choriambus between.

13. The PRIAPEAN is the glyconic and pherecratean joined.

§ 652. APPENDIX. 361

14. The EUPOLIDEAN is a glyconic and a trochaic dimeter catalectic.

2. *Anapæstic Logaœdic Verse.*

Like the dactylic logaœdic, it can never have more than six feet. The arsis of both anapæst and iambus is on the long syllable.

1. One anapæst and one iambus:
   βοτάνα τέ νιν, ⌣ ⌣ – ⌣ –, Pind. Nem., VI., 43.

2. One anapæst and two iambi:
   πόλιν ἀλλ' ἀνάσχου, ⌣ ⌣ – ⌣ – ⌣ (catalectic), Eur. Heracl., 380.

3. One anapæst and three iambi:
   τό τ' ἔπειτα καὶ τὸ μέλλον, ⌣ ⌣ – ⌣ – ⌣ – ⌣ (catalectic), Soph. Antig., 611.

4. One anapæst and four iambi:
   διάπειρά τοι βροτῶν ἔλεγχος, ⌣ ⌣ – ⌣ – ⌣ – ⌣ – ⌣ (catalectic), Pind. Ol., IV., 18.

5. Two anapæsts and one iambus:
   πρὶν 'Ολύμπιος ἀγεμών, ⌣ ⌣ – – ⌣ ⌣ – –, Pind. Ol., IX., 57.

6. Two anapæsts and two iambi:
   φόνιόν τ' ἀπόπαυσον "Αιδαν, ⌣ ⌣ – ⌣ ⌣ – ⌣ – – (catalectic), Eur. Alc., 225.

7. Two anapæsts and three iambi:
   τὸν ἀνάλιον οἶκον οἰκετεύοις, ⌣ ⌣ – ⌣ ⌣ – ⌣ – – (catalectic), Eur. Alc., 437.

8. Two anapæsts and four iambi:
   τίς ἐφαμερίων ἄρηξις; οὐδ' ἰδέρχθης, ⌣ ⌣ – ⌣ ⌣ – ⌣ – ⌣ – ⌣ – –
   (catalectic), Æsch. Prom. Vinc., 556.

9. Three anapæsts and one iambus:
   ἀσεβοῦσ', ἀδικοῦσί τε τὴν πόλιν, ⌣ ⌣ – ⌣ ⌣ – ⌣ ⌣ – ⌣ –, Arist. Thesm., 367.

10. Three anapæsts and two iambi:
    ποτὲ μὲν κακὸν, ἄλλοτ' ἐπ' ἐσθλὸν ἕρπει, ⌣ ⌣ – ⌣ ⌣ – ⌣ ⌣ – ⌣ – –
    (catalectic), Soph. Antig., 367.

Q

11. Four anapæsts and one iambus:
μεγάλων προσορῶσα δόμοισι βλάβαν νέων,
⏑⏑−⏑⏑−⏑⏑−⏑⏑−⏑−, Soph. Trach., 842.

12. Four anapæsts and two iambi:
ἀτελέστατα γὰρ καὶ ἀμάχανα τοὺς θανόντας,
⏑⏑−⏑⏑−⏑⏑−⏑⏑−⏑−⏓ (catalectic), Stesich., 51.

§ 653. Iambic Verse.—The fundamental foot is the iambus. The arsis falls upon the long syllable. By protraction the short may become long, and accordingly a spondee often replaces an iambus, but only in the odd places (first, third, etc.). By resolution (§ 646) the tribrach may appear, and by both protraction and resolution the dactyl, and by protraction and then resolution the anapæst. When these feet replace iambi, the anapæst has its usual arsis; the others receive it upon the second syllable, as follows: the tribrach ⏑ ⏑́ ⏑,
spondee − ⏑́,
dactyl − ⏑́ ⏑,
anapæst ⏑ ⏑ ⏑́.
The "meter" is two feet. A dimeter therefore is a verse of four feet, and a trimeter of six feet, and so on. This measure is very common, and easily recognized.

1. Monometer, ⏑ − ⏑ −, occurs mostly in connection with systems or other rhythms.

2. Dimeter, ⏑ − ⏑ − ⏑ − ⏑ −, occurs frequently as a single verse, and also in systems.

ὅμοιον ὥστε ποντίαις, ⏑ − ⏑ − ⏑ − ⏑ −, Soph. Antig., 586.

3. Trimeter, known also by the Latin name *senarius*, ⏑ − ⏑ − ⏑ − ⏑ − ⏑ − ⏑ −, is most common, being the metre of the dialogue in tragedy and comedy; *e. g.:*

φέρ' εἰπὲ δὴ τὸ δεινόν. εἰ γὰρ τῶνδέ μοι
μεῖζόν τι λέξεις, οὐκ ἂν ἀντείποιμ' ἔτι.—Soph. El., 376, 377.

καλῶς δὲ σῶσαι παῖδα κεὐκλεῶς θανεῖν.
μόνος γὰρ αὐτοῖς ἦσθα, κοὔτις ἐλπὶς ἦν
σοῦ κατθανόντος ἄλλα φιτύσειν τέκνα.—Eur. Alc., 292, 293, 294.

§ 657. APPENDIX. 363

ὁρῶ, Προμηθεῦ, καὶ παραινέσαι γέ σοι
θέλω τὰ λῷστα, καίπερ ὄντι ποικίλῳ.—Æsch. Prom. Vinc., 315, 316.

The cæsura is commonly in the third foot, sometimes in the fourth, rarely at the end of the third, and sometimes is wanting.

§ 654. *Scazon.*—The satirists often substituted a spondee for the last iambus of the trimeter. The rhythmical break had a humorous effect. The verse was then called *claudus*, lame, or *scazon*, hobbling.

§ 655. *Ischiorrhogic* (limping) verse was iambic tripody in which spondees occurred irregularly in the second or third place.

§ 656. Syncopated forms in each kind of iambic verse also occur.

§ 657. ANAPÆSTIC VERSE.—The fundamental foot is the anapæst, which is the reverse of the dactyl, as the iambus is of the trochee. The arsis falls on the long syllable. By contraction of the two shorts into one long, a spondee may replace an anapæst, and by contraction of the two shorts and resolution of the long a dactyl often occurs. Sometimes, also, by the resolution of the long, a proceleusmatic may be used. The arsis in such case falls
on the last syllable of the spondee, $- \acute{-}$,
on the second syllable of the dactyl, $- \acute{\smile} \smile$, and
on the third of the proceleusmatic, $\smile \smile \acute{\smile} \smile$.
The " meter" consists of two feet. Monometers and tripodies are used, also the tetrameter (catalectic in Aristophanes), but the most common are the following.

1. Dimeter, the principal element in anapæstic systems:

τί σὺ πρὸς μελάθροις; τί σὺ τῇδε πολεῖς, $\acute{\smile} \smile - \smile \smile \acute{-} \smile \smile - \smile \smile -$,
Φοῖβ'; ἀδικεῖς αὖ τιμὰς ἐνέρων, $- \smile \smile - - - - \smile \smile -$, Eur. Alc., 29, 30.

2. Dimeter catalectic, PARŒMIAC, which always forms the close of an anapæstic system:

αὐτὴ προθανεῖν Πελίου παῖς, $- - \smile \smile - \smile \smile - \overset{\smile}{-}$, Eur. Alc., 37.

§ 658. Anapæstic systems are classed as *strict* and *free*.

a. The *strict* system consists of dimeters, sometimes interrupted by monometers, with a parœmiac (which is often preceded immediately by a monometer) for a close. The verse itself also is so far restricted as never to allow a proceleusmatic, or even a dactyl followed by an anapæst.

b. The *free* system consists of dimeters concluded not only by a parœmiac, but having a parœmiac at the beginning and middle, and sometimes repeated. The verse also will often consist of spondees only, or of dactyls only.

§ 659. CHORIAMBIC VERSE.—The choriambus occurs only by syncope (§ 647, 4) in dactylic, logaœdic, and anapæstic verses. There are thus formed, however, a choriambic dimeter, trimeter, and tetrameter.

1. Dimeter :

οὔτε βαθειᾶν κυλίκων, $-\smile\smile--\smile\smile-$, Soph. Ajax, 1200.

νεῖμεν ἐμοὶ τέρψιν ὁμιλεῖν, $-\smile\smile--\smile\smile.--$ (hypercatalectic), Soph. Ajax, 1201.

2. Trimeter :

εἰ δὲ κυρεῖ τις πέλας οἰωνοπόλων, $-\smile\smile--\smile\smile--\smile\smile-$, Æsch. Sup., 56.

3. Tetrameter :

δεινὰ μὲν οὖν, δεινὰ ταράσσει σοφὸς οἰωνοθέτας,
$-\smile\smile--\smile\smile--\smile\smile--\smile\smile-$, Soph. Œd. Tyr., 483.

ἄλλα δ' ἐπ' ἄλλοις ἐπενώμα στυφελίζων μέγας Ἄρης,
$-\smile\smile--\smile\smile-\cdot-\smile\smile--\smile\smile--$ (hypercatalectic), Soph. Antig., 139.

§ 660. CRETIC VERSE.—Syncopation (§ 647, 4) in trochaic, iambic, and logaœdic rhythms gives rise to cretic rhythms. There are cretic rhythms proper, in which the creticus is the fundamental foot. By resolution a first or fourth pæon ($-\smile\smile\smile, \smile\smile\smile-$) may replace a creticus. The arsis occurs upon the first syllable, with a slighter ictus on the third. The following are the common forms :

§ 661. APPENDIX. 365

1. Dimeter (occurs singly and in connection with other rhythms):

ὣ κτανόντας τε καὶ, $- \smile - - \smile -$, Soph. Antig., 1263.
τί δῆτ' ἐμοῦ βλεπτὸν, ἢ, $\smile \mid - \smile - - \smile -$ (with anacrusis), Soph. Œd. Tyr., 1337.

2. Trimeter:

φράζε τᾷ δυσπλάνῳ παρθένῳ, $- \smile - - \smile - - \smile -$, Æsch. Prom. Vinc., 626.

3. Tetrameter (often used by comic poets):

αὐτόματα πάντ' ἀγαθὰ τῷδέ γε πορίζεται,
$- \smile \frown - \smile \frown - \smile \frown - \smile -$, Arist. Ach., 978.

4. Pentameter:

οἵ ἔχει σπεισάμενος ἐμπορικὰ χρήματα διεμπολᾶν,
$- \smile - - \smile \frown - \smile - - \smile \frown - \smile -$, Arist. Ach., 972.

§ 661. IONIC VERSE.—The fundamental foot is the Ionic a minore ($\smile \smile - -$), with the arsis on the first long. It gives the verse a "character of discord and wild enthusiasm" (Munk), and is used in erotic poetry, and Dionysiac hymns, and songs to Cybele; also in the choruses of dramatists.

1. Dimeter:

μέτα μὲν πλείονα τίκτει, $\smile - - \smile \smile - -$,
σφετέρᾳ δ' εἰκότα γέννᾳ, $\smile \smile - - \smile \smile - -$ (1st form, pure), Æsch. Agam., 734, 735.
τί με φεύγεις τὸν γέροντα; $\smile \smile - - - \smile - \smile$ (2d form, *polyschematist*), Anacr., 64.
δότε μοι λύρην Ὁμήρου, $\smile \smile - \smile - \smile - \simeq$ (3d form, with anaclasis), ANACREONTIC, Anacr., 48.

a. In the *polyschematist* (many-formed) the quantities are preserved, but assume the trochaic form in the second foot.

b. Anaclasis (ἀνάκλασις, a breaking) occurs by an interchange of the last long of the first foot with the first short of the second foot. The form thus produced is the most common of the three. It is chiefly the form of the Anacreontic verse.

2. Trimeter:

ἀπό μοι θανεῖν γένοιτ'. οὐ γὰρ ἂν ἄλλη,
⏑ ⏑ – ⏑ – ⏑ – – ⏑ – – (anaclasis), Anacr., 48.

3. Tetrameter:

παρακλίνασ' ἐπέκρανεν δὲ γάμου πικρὰς τελευτὰς,
⏑ ⏑ – – ⏑ ⏑ – – ⏑ ⏑ – – ⏑ ⏑ – –, Æsch. Agam., 721.

a. The tetrameter catalectic is the *Galliambic* verse, the verse of the songs of the priests of Cybele.

§ 662. DOCHMIAC RHYTHMS.—A dochmius consists of a bacchius and an iambus, ⏑ – – ⏑ –. The arsis falls upon the first long, with a secondary ictus upon the last long. By production of the shorts and resolution of the longs, a great variety of forms was produced, which were freely used.

1. Monometer:

ἄφυκτοι κύνες, ⏑ – – ⏑ –, Soph. El., 1388.
ἰὼ δυσπότμων, ⏑ – – ⏑ –, Soph. Antig., 869.
στερεὰ θανατόεντ', ⏑ ⏑ ⏑ ⏑ ⏑ ⏑ –, Soph. Antig., 1262.
Ἑλλάνων ἄναξ, – – – ⏑ –, Soph. El., 483.
εἴδομεν ἃ θρηνεῖς, – ⏑ ⏑ – – –, Soph. El., 853.
τοὺς ἐμὸς ἴδε πατὴρ, – ⏑ ⏑ ⏑ ⏑ ⏑ –, Soph. El., 205.

2. Dimeter:

τὸ δυσέριστον αἷμα φυσῶν Ἄρης, ⏑ ⏑ ⏑ – ⏑ – ⏑ – – ⏑ –, Soph. El., 1385.

3. Trimeter:

ὤμοι ἐμᾶς ἄτας, οἷος ἄρ' αἱμάχθης, ἄφαρκτος φίλων,
– ⏑ ⏑ – – – | – ⏑ ⏑ – – – | ⏑ – – ⏑ –, Soph. Ajax, 910.

§ 663. BACCHIC RHYTHMS.—The bacchius, as the fundamental foot of a verse, was not freely used. The following are examples:

1. Monometer:

ζύναινεῖς, ⏑ – –,
τί μὴν οὔ; ⏑ – –, Soph. El., 1279, 1280.

§ 663. APPENDIX. 367

2. Dimeter:
πεπρᾶσθαι πεπρᾶσθαι, ˘ - - ˘ - -, Aristoph. Ach., 735.

3. Tetrameter:
τίς ἀχὼ, τίς ὀδμὰ προσέπτα μ' ἀφεγγὴς,
˘ - - ˘ - - ˘ - - ˘ - -, Æsch. Prom. Vinc., 115.

ALPHABETICAL LIST OF VERBS.

ἀάω, Aor. Pass. (Hom.) ἀάσθην, § 298.
ἄγαμαι, § 312, 8; § 328, 2.
ἀγγέλλω, § 252; pp. 122, 123.
ἀγείρω, § 253; § 257, D.
ἀγήοχα, § 279.
ἀγινέω, § 323, D. 39.
ἄγνυμι, § 319, 13; § 275, 2; § 330, 1.
ἄγω, 2d Aor., § 257 — 1st Aor., § 268, D.—Perf., § 279.
ἀδήσω, § 322, D. 23.
ᾄδω, § 266.
ἀέξω, § 322, D. 13.
ἄεσα, § 327, D. 17.
ἄημι, § 313, D. 3.
αἰδέομαι, § 301, 1; § 326, 10, and D. —Fut. Hom., § 261, D.
αἰνέω, § 301, 3.
αἴνυμαι, § 319, D. 27.
αἱρέω, § 327, 1; § 275, D. 1.
αἴρω, § 262; § 270, Obs.
αἰσθάνομαι, § 322, 11.
αἴσθομαι, § 322, 11.
αἰσχύνω, § 286, D.
ἀκάχημαι, § 319, D. 30.
ἀκαχίζω, § 319, D. 30.
ἀκαχμένος, § 47, D.
ἀκέομαι, § 301, 1.
ἀκήκοα, § 275, 1; § 280, Obs.
ἀκηχέδατο, § 287, D.
ἀκούω, Perf. Act., § 275, 1; § 280, Obs.—Perf. Mid., § 288.
ἀκροάομαι, Fut., § 261.
ἀλάλημαι, § 275, D. 1.
ἄλαλκον, § 326, D. 11.
ἀλάομαι, § 328, 2; § 275, D. 1.

ἀλαπάζω, § 251, D.—Fut., § 261, D.
ἀλδαίνω, ἀλδήσκω, § 324, D. 30.
ἀλέασθαι, ἀλεύασθαι, § 269, D.
ἀλείφω, § 275, 1, p. 120.
ἄλεν, ἀλήμεναι, § 325, D. d.
ἀλέξω, § 326, 11.
ἀλέω, § 301, 1.
ἄλθομαι, § 326, D. 39.
ἀλίσκομαι, § 324, 17—Perf., § 275, 2 —2d Aor., § 316, 12.
ἀλιταίνω, § 323, D. 37.
ἀλλάσσω, Perf., § 279, Obs. 2—2d Aor., § 294, Obs.
ἄλλομαι, § 252—1st Aor., § 270, Obs. —2d Aor., § 316, D. 32.
ἄλμενος, § 316, D. 32.
ἀλύσκω, § 324, 27.
ἀλφάνω, § 323, D. 38.
ἀλῶναι, § 324, 17; § 316, 12.
ἁμαρτάνω, § 322, 12, and D.
ἀμβλίσκω, § 324, 18.
ἄμεναι, § 312, D. 13.
ἀμιλλάομαι, § 328, 2.
ἀμπέχομαι, ἀμπισχνοῦμαι, § 323, 36.
ἀμπλακίσκω, § 324, 23.
ἀμπνύνθη, § 298, D.
ἄμπνυτο, § 316, D. 29.
ἀμφιέννυμι, § 319, 5, and D.—Augm., § 240.
ἀμφιῶ, § 319, 5.
ἀναβιώσκομαι, § 324, 11.
ἀναγιγνώσκω, § 329, D.
ἀναλίσκω, ἀναλώσω, § 324, 19.
ἀνδάνω, § 322, 23, and D.—Imp., § 237, D.
ἀνέχομαι, Augm., § 240.

ἀνέψγα, § 279, Obs. 1.
ἀνέψχα, § 275, 2 ;. § 279, Obs. 1.
ἀνήνοθεν, § 275, D. 2.
ἀνοίγνυμι, Perf., § 275, 2 ; § 275, Obs. 1.
ἀνοίγω, Augm., § 237.
ἀνορθόω, Augm., § 240.
ἀντιβολέω, Augm., § 239.
ἄνυμι, § 319, D. 28.
ἄνωγα, § 317, D. 11—Perf., § 283, D.
ἀπαντάω, Fut., § 266.
ἀπαυράω, § 316, D. 18.
ἀπαφίσκω, § 324, D. 33.
ἀπεῖπον, § 327, 13, Obs.
ἀπεχθάνομαι, § 322, 16.
ἀπόερσα, § 270, D. 1.
ἀπολαύω, Fut. Mid., § 266.
ἀπούρας, § 316, D. 18.
ἀραίρηκα, § 275, D. 1 ; § 327, D. 1.
ἀραρίσκω, § 324, D. 34—Perf., § 275, D. 1.
ἀραρυῖα, § 324, D. 34 ; § 280, D.
ἀρέσκω, § 324, 10.
ἄρηρα, § 275, D. 1 ; § 324, D. 34.
ἀρήροται, § 275, D. 1.
ἀρηρώς, § 280, D.
ἀρκέω, § 301, and D.
ἄρμενος, § 324, D. 34.
ἁρμόττω, § 250, Obs.—Fut., § 260, 3.
ἀρνέομαι, § 328, 2.
ἄρνυμαι, § 319, D. 29.
ἀρόω, § 301, 1—Perf. Pass., § 275, D. 1.
ἀρύω, § 301, 1.
ἄρχω, p. 116.
ἄσμενος, § 316, D. at end.
αὐξάνω, αὔξω, § 322, 13, and D.
ἀφάσσω, § 250, D.
ἀφίημι, § 313, 1.
ἀφύσσω, Fut. and 1st Aor., § 269, D.
ἄχθομαι, § 326, 12 ; § 328, 2.
ἄχνυμαι, § 319, D. 30 ; § 287, D.

βαδίζω, Fut. Mid., § 266.
βαίνω, § 321, 1, and D.—2d Aor., § 316, 1, and D.—Perf., § 317, 1, and D.—1st Aor. Mid., § 268, D. —Signif., § 329, 2.
βάλλω, § 254 ; § 255, 2, and D. ;

§ 316, D. 19 — Perfect, § 282 ; § 287, D.
βάπτω, § 249.
βέβληκα, § 282 ; § 285.
βέβουλα, § 326, D. 14.
βεβρώθω, § 324, D. 13.
βεβρώς, § 317, D. 16.
βείομαι, βέομαι, § 265, D.
βείω, § 316, D. 1.
βῇ, § 316, D. 1.
βιβάς, § 312, D. 14.
βιβρώσκω, § 324, 13, and D.—Aor., § 316, D. 23—Perf. Part., § 317, D. 16.
βιόω, § 316, 13.
βιώσκομαι, § 324, 11.
βλάβεται, § 249, D.
βλάπτω, § 249—Perf., § 279, 1— Aor. Pass., § 299.
βλαστάνω, § 322, 14.
βλεῖο, § 316, D. 19.
βλῆσθαι, § 316, D. 19.
βλίττω, § 250, Obs.
βλώσκω, § 324 ; § 51, D.
βοάω, Fut. Mid., § 266.
βόλεται, § 326, D. 14.
βόσκω, § 326, 13.
βούλομαι, § 326, 14—Augm., § 234, Obs. ; § 233, D. 5, 6 ; § 328, 2.
βράσσω, § 250, Obs.
βυνῶ, § 323, 32, and D.
βώσας, § 35, D. 1.

γαμέω, § 325, 1, and D.
γάνυμαι, § 319, D. 31.
γέγαμεν, § 317, 2, and D.
γέγονα, § 327, 14.
γεγωνέω, § 325, D. a.
γεγώς, § 317, 2, and D. ; § 327, D. 14.
γείνομαι, § 329, 8.
γελάω, § 301, 1—Aor. Pass., § 298— Fut. Mid., § 266.
γενέσθαι, § 327, 14.
γενήσομαι, § 327, 14.
γέντο, § 316, D. 33.
γηθέω, § 325, 2.
γηράσκω, § 324, 1—Inf. Aor., § 316, 2, and D.

APPENDIX. 369

γίγνομαι (γίνομαι), § 327, 14—Perf., § 317, 2, and D.
γιγνώσκω, § 324,14—Aor., § 316, 14.
γνῶναι, § 316, 14.
γνώω, § 316, 14, D.
γοάω, § 325, D. n.
γράφω, Perf., § 278.
δαήσομαι, § 326, D. 40.
δαΐζω, § 251, D.
δαίνυμι, § 319, D. 32.
δαινῦτο, § 318, D.; § 319, D. 32.
δαίω, § 253, D.—Perf., § 330, D. 9.
δάκνω, § 321, 8.
δαμείω, § 293, D.
δάμνημι, § 312, D. a — Subj. Aor. Pass., § 293, D.
δαρθάνω, § 322, 15, and D.
δατέομαι, § 325, D. b—1st Aor. Inf., § 269, D.
δέατο, § 312, 14 b.
δέγμαι, § 273, D.
δέδαον, § 324, D. 28; § 326, D. 40.
δεδάηκα, § 326, D. 40.
δέδεγμαι, § 318, D.
δέδηχα, § 321, 8.
δέδια, § 317, 5, and D.
δέδμημαι, § 312, D. a.
δέδοικα, § 317, 5, and D.
δέδρομα, § 327, D. 11.
δειδέχαται, § 318, D.
δείκνυμι, § 318, 2 and 4, and D.
δεῖσαι, § 317, 5—Augm., § 234, D.; § 77, D.
δέξω, § 318, D.
δέρκομαι, § 257, D.; § 59, D.; § 328, 2.
δεύομαι (δέομαι), § 326, D.15; § 328, 2.
δέχθαι, § 316, D. 34.
δέχομαι, Perfect, § 273, D.—Aorist, § 316, D. 34; § 328, 4.
δέω, § 301, 2; § 244, Obs. 1.
δέω, δέομαι, § 326, 15.
δήξομαι, § 321, 8.
διαιτάω, Augm., § 240.
διαλέγομαι, Perfect, § 274, Exc.; § 328, 2.
διδάσκω, § 324, 28, and D.—Aor., § 326, D. 40.
δίδημι, § 313, 2.

δίδωμι, § 305, and D.; § 307; § 308.—Aor., § 310—Fut., § 310, D.
διδράσκω, § 324, 2—Aor., § 316, 3, and D.
δίεσαν, § 313, D. 4.
δίζημαι, δίζω, § 313, D. 5.
διψάω, § 244, 2.
διώκω, § 338, D.
δοάσσατο, § 312, D. 14 b.
δοκέω, § 325, 3.
δουπέω, § 325, D. c.
δραμοῦμαι, § 327, 11.
δρατός, § 300, D.
δράω, Aor. Pass., § 298.
δύναμαι, § 312, 9—Augm., § 234, Obs.—Accent of Subj. and Opt., § 309; § 328, 2.
δύω, δυνω, § 321, 7, and D.; § 301, 4—1st Aor. Mid., § 268, D.—2d Aor,, § 316, 16, and D.—Signif., § 329, 4.

ἔαγα, § 275, 2; § 319, 13.
ἔαδα, § 322, D. 23.
ἑάλων, § 316, 12; § 324, 17.
ἑάνδανον, § 237, D.
ἔαξα, § 319, 13.
ἔαται, εἵαται, § 315, D. 2.
ἐάω, Augm., § 236.
ἔβρων, § 324, D. 13.
ἐγδούπησα, § 325, D. c.
ἐγείρω, 2d Aor., § 257, D.—Perfect, § 275, 1; § 317, D. 12; § 330, 2.
ἔγοον, § 325, D. n.
ἔγρετο, § 257, D.
ἐγρήγορα, § 275, 1; § 317, D. 12.
ἐγρηγόρθασι, § 317, D. 12.
ἔδδεισα, § 234, D.
ἔδηδα, ἐδήδοται, § 327, D. 4.
ἔδμεναι, § 315, D. 3; § 327, D. 4.
ἔδομαι, § 265; § 327, 4.
ἔδραθον, § 322, D. 15.
ἔδρακον, § 257, D.
ἔδραμον, § 327, 11.
ἐείσατο, § 314, D. 1; § 327, D. 8.
ἱέρχατο, § 287, D.
ἑέσσατο, § 269, D.; § 319, D. 5.
ἕζομαι, § 251 b; § 326, 21.
ἐήνδανον, § 237, D.

Q 2

370   APPENDIX.

ἐθέλω. See θέλω.
ἐθίζω, Augm., § 236—Perf., § 278.
ἔθρεξα, § 327, D. 11.
εἶδον, § 327, 8, and D.
εἰκάθω, § 338, D.
εἶκε, εἴκτον, § 317, D. 7.
εἰλέω, § 325, D. d.
εἰλήλουθα, § 40, D.; § 317, D. 13; § 327, D. 2.
εἴληφα, § 274, Exc.; § 322, 25.
εἴληχα, § 274, Exc.; § 322, 27.
εἴλοχα, § 274, Exc.; § 279.
εἶλον, § 327, 1.
εἴλω, § 253, D.—1st Aor., § 270, D. 1.
εἶμαι, § 319, D. 5.
εἵμαρται, § 274, Exc.
εἰμί, § 315, 1, and D.
εἶμι, § 314, 1, and D.; § 327, 2.
εἶνυον, § 319, D. 5.
εἴξασι, § 317, 7.
εἶπον, § 327, 13; Imper. Accent, § 333, 12.
εἴργνυμι, εἴργω, § 319, 15, and D.
εἴργω, Perf. and Pluperf., § 287, D.; § 338, D.
εἴρηκα, § 274, Exc.; § 327, 13.
εἴρομαι, § 326, D. 16.
εἰρύαται, § 314, D. 2.
εἴρω, 1st Aor., § 270, D. 3—Perf. and Pluperf. Mid., § 275, D. 2; § 327, D. 13.
εἶσα, § 269, D.
εἰσάμην, § 314, D. 1.
ἐΐσκω, § 324, D. 35.
εἴσομαι, § 314, D. 1.
εἴωθα, § 275, 2; § 278.
ἐκέκλετο, § 61, D.; § 257, D.
ἔκιον, § 319, D. 34.
ἐκκλησιάζω, Augm., § 239, Exc.
ἐκληθάνω, § 322, D. 26.
ἔκρησα, § 319, D. 1.
ἔκταν, § 316, D. 4.
ἐλάμφθην, § 322, D. 25.
ἐλαυνω, § 321, 2, and D.—Perfect, § 275, 1—Pluperf., § 287, D.—Fut., § 263.
ἐλέγχω, Perf. Mid., § 275, 1; §.286, Obs.

ἐλεῖν, § 327, 1.
ἐλεύσομαι, § 327, 2.
ἔλησα, § 322, D. 26.
ἐληλάδατο, § 287, D.; § 321, D. 2.
ἐλήλυθα, § 327, 2.
ἐλθεῖν, § 327, 2; § 333, 12.
ἐλίσσω, Augm., § 236; § 250 a.
ἑλκύω, ἕλκω, Augm., § 236; § 301, 1.
ἕλπω, Perf., § 275, D. 2.
ἔλσα, § 270, D. 1; § 325, D. d.
ἐμέμηκον, § 283, D.
ἐμέω, § 301, 1.
ἔμμεναι, § 315, D. 1.
ἔμμορα, § 274, D.
ἐμνήμυκα, § 275, D. 1.
ἔμολον, § 324, 12.
ἐναίρω, Augm., § 239, Exc.
ἐναντιοῦμαι, Augm., § 239, Exc.; § 328, 2.
ἔνασσα, § 329, D.
ἐνδυνέω, § 321, D. 7.
ἐνείκαι (ἐνείκοι), § 327, D. 12.
ἐνένιπον, § 257, D.
ἐνέπω, § 327, D. 13.
ἐνήνοθεν, § 275, D. 2.
ἐνήνοχα, § 327, 12.
ἐνήνεγμαι, § 327, 12.
ἐνίπτω, § 250, D.; § 257, D.
ἐνίσπω, § 327, D. 13.
ἐνίσσω, § 250, D.
ἔννεπε, § 327, D. 13.
ἔννυμι, § 319, 5, and D.
ἐνοχλέω, Augm., § 240.
ἔοικα, § 317, 7, and D.
ἔολπα, § 275, D. 2.
ἔοργα, § 275, D. 2; § 327, D. 3.
ἑορτάζω, Augm., § 237.
ἐπαυρίσκομαι, § 324, 24, and D.
ἐπηῦρον, § 324, D. 24.
ἐπιέσασθαι, § 319, 5.
ἐπίσταμαι, § 312, 10 — Accent of Subj. and Opt., § 309; § 328, 2.
ἔπλητο, § 312, D. f.
ἕπομαι, § 327, 5, and D.—Augm., § 236.
ἔπορον, § 285, D.
ἔπραθον, § 257, D.
ἔπτην, § 316, 5.
ἐπώχατο, § 327, D. 6.

APPENDIX. 371

ἔραμαι, § 312, 11.
ἐράω, Aor. Mid., § 301, D.
ἐργάζομαι, Augm., § 236,
ἔργαθον, § 319, D. 15.
ἔρδω, § 327, 3, and D.
ἐρείπω, § 329, D.
ἐρέσσω, § 250, Obs.—Fut., § 260, 3.
ἐρεύγομαι, § 323, D. 40.
ἐρηρέδαται, § 287, D.
ἑρπύζω, ἕρπω, Augm., § 236.
ἐρράδαται, § 287, D.
ἔρρω, § 326, 17.
ἔρρωγα, § 278; § 319, 24.
ἐρυγγάνω, § 323, D. 40.
ἐρύκω, 2d Aor., § 257, D.
ἔρυσθαι, § 314, D. 2.
ἐρύω, Aor., § 301, D.
ἔρχαται, § 319, D. 15.
ἔρχομαι, § 327, 2.
ἐρῶ, § 327, 13.
ἐσθίω, ἔσθω, § 327, 4, and D.; § 315, D. 3.
ἔσκλην, § 316, 10.
ἔσκον, § 337, D.
ἔσπεισμαι, § 286, 1, Obs.
ἑσπόμην, § 327, 5.
ἕσπον, § 327, D. 13.
ἔσπωμαι, § 327, D. 5.
ἔσσαι, ἔσσας, § 269, D.
ἔσσυμαι, § 274, D.
ἔσταμεν, § 317, 4.
ἑστεώς, § 317, D. 4.
ἑστήξω, § 291; § 311.
ἑστιάω, Augm., § 236.
ἐτάθην, § 298.
ἐτάφην. See θάπτω.
ἔτορον, § 326, D. 44.
εὔαδον, § 322, D. 23.
εὔδω, § 326, 18.
ἐϋκτίμενος, § 316, D. 25.
εὑρίσκω, § 324, 25; § 333, 12.
ἔχεα, § 269.
ἔχευα, § 269, D.
ἔχω, § 327, 6, and D.—Augm., § 236
—Aor. Imper., § 316, 11.
ἕψω, § 326, 19, and D.
ἔωθα, § 275, D. 2.
ἔωμεν, § 312, D. 13.
ἐῳνοχόει, § 237, D.

ἔψξα, § 319, 19.
ἑώρων, § 237.
ζάω, § 244, 2.
ζεύγνυμι, § 319, 16.
ζέω, § 301, 1.
ζώννυμι, § 319, 9.
ἥ, § 312, 1.
ἡβάσκω, § 324, 3.
ἤγαγον, § 257.
ἠγερέθοντο, § 338, D.
ᾖα, ᾖειν, § 314.
ἠείδης, § 317, D. 6.
ἤειρα, § 270, D. 3.
ἠερέθονται, § 338, D.
ᾔικτο, § 317, D. 7.
ἦκα, § 313, 1.
ἤκαχον, § 319, D. 30.
ἤλιτον, § 323, D. 37.
ἠλλάγην, § 294, Obs.
ἤλυθον, § 327, D. 2.
ἤλων, § 316, 12; § 324, 17.
ἦμαι, § 315, 2, and D.
ἤμβλωσα, ἤμβλωκα, § 324, 18.
ἤμβροτον, § 322, D. 12.
ἡμί, § 312, 1.
ἤμπισχον, § 323, 36.
ἤμπλακον, § 324, 23.
ἡμύναθον, § 338, D.
ἡμύω, Perf., § 275, D. 1.
ἠμφίεσα, § 319, 5.
ἤν. See εἰμί and ἠμί.
ἤναρον, § 239, Exc.
ἤνεγκ-ον,-α, § 327, 12.
ἤνεικα, § 327, 12, D.
ἠνειχόμην, § 240.
ἠνίπαπον, § 257, D.
ἤνυτο, § 319, D. 28.
ἤνωγον, § 283, D.
ἠνώρθουν, § 240.
ἠνώχλουν, § 240.
ἦξα, § 319, D. 13.
ἤπαφον, § 324, D. 33.
ἤρατο, § 319, D. 29.
ἤραρον, § 324, D. 34.
ἤριπον, § 329, D.
ἠρόμην, § 326, 16.
ἤρρηκα, § 326, 17.

ἡρύκακον, § 257, D.
ἠφίει, § 313, 1.
ἦχα, § 279, 1.

θάλλω, Perf., § 277, D.
θανεῖν, § 324, 4.
θάπτω, § 54 c; § 249; § 298.
θέλω (ἐθέλω), § 326, 20.
θέρομαι, Fut., § 262, D.
θέω, § 248—Fut., § 260, 2.
θιγγάνω, § 322, 24.
θλάω, § 301, 1.
θνήσκω, § 324, 4—Perf., § 317, 3—Perf. Part., § 276, D.—Fut. Perf., § 291.
θόρνυμαι, § 324, D. 15.
θρεκτέον, § 327, 11.
θρύπτω, § 54 c.
θρώσκω, § 324, 15, and D.; § 59, 1.
θύω, § 301, 2; Aor. Pass., § 53 b.

ἰάομαι, § 328, 4.
ἰαύω, § 327, D. 17.
ἰδέ, § 327, 8; § 333, 12.
ἴδμεν, § 317, D. 6.
ἱδρύω, Aor. Pass., § 298, D.
ἰδυῖα, § 317, D. 6.
ἱζάνω, ἵζω, § 322, 17.
ἵζομαι, § 326, 21.
ἵημι, § 313, 1, and D.—Perf., § 311.
ἱκάνω, § 323, 33.
ἵκμενος, § 323, D. 33.
ἱκνέομαι, § 323, 33, and D.—Aor., § 268, D.
ἱλάσκομαι, § 324, 5—Imperat., § 312, D. 15.
ἱμάσσω, § 250, D.
ἶξον, § 268, D.; § 323, D. 33.
ἴσκε, § 324, D. 36.
ἵστημι, § 305, and D.—Perf., § 317, 4.

καθεδοῦμαι, § 326, 21.
καθεύδω, § 326, 18—Augm., § 240.
κάθημαι, § 315, 2—Augm., § 240.
καθίζω, § 326, 21—Augm., § 240.
καθίστημι, § 329, 1, Obs.
καίνυμαι, § 319, D. 33.
καίω, § 35, Obs.; § 253, Obs.—Fut., § 260, 2—1st Aor., § 269, D.

καλέω, § 301, 3.
καλύπτω, § 249; p. 120.
κάμνω, § 321, 9, and D.—Perfect, § 282.
κάμπτω, Perf. Mid., § 286, 1, Obs.
κατηγορέω, Augm., § 239.
καύσω, § 260, 2.
κάω. See καίω.
κεῖαι, § 269, D.
κεῖμαι, § 314, 2, and D., Obs.
κείρω, Fut., § 262, D.
κεκαδήσω, κέκαδον, § 326, D. 41.
κέκασμαι, § 319, D. 33.
κέκμηκα, § 282.
κεκορηώς, § 319, D. 6.
κεκοτηώς, § 277, D.
κέκτημαι, § 274, Exc.; § 289.
κελαδέω, § 325, D. e.
κελεύω, Perf. Mid., § 288 — Aorist Pass., § 298.
κέλλω, Fut., § 262, Exc.
κέλομαι, Aor., § 257, D.
κεντέω, § 325, D. f.
κεράννυμι, § 319, 1, and D.—Subj. Mid., § 312, D. 16.
κερδαίνω, Perf., § 322, Obs. 1—Aor., § 270, Obs.
κέσκετο, § 337, D.
κέχανδα, § 323, D. 41.
κεχαρήσω, § 326, D. 38.
κεχάροντο, § 326, D. 38.
κέχυκα, § 281.
κῆαι, § 269, D.
κήδω, § 326, D. 41.
κηρύσσω, § 250—Perf., § 279.
κικλήσκω, § 324, D. 31.
κίννυμαι (κινέω), § 319, D. 34.
κίρνημι, § 312, D. 16 b.
κιχάνω, § 322, 18.
κίχημι, § 313, D. 6.
κιών, § 319, D. 34.
κλάζω, § 251, Obs.—Perf., § 276, D.
κλαίω, § 326, 22; § 253, Obs.—Fut., § 260, 2.
κλάω, § 301, 1.
κλείω, κλήω, Perf. Mid., § 288.
κλέπτω, Perfect, § 279—Aor. Pass., § 295.
κλίνω, Perf., § 282.

APPENDIX. 373

κλύω, Aor., § 316, D. 27.
κνάω, § 244, 2.
κομίζω, Fut., § 263; p. 118.
κόπτω, § 249—Perf., § 279; § 277, D.
κορέννυμι, § 319, 6, and D.
κορέω, Aor., § 301, D.
κορύσσω, § 250, D.—Perfect Pass. Part., § 286, D.
κοτέω, § 301, D. — Perfect Part., § 277, D.
κράζω, § 251—Perf., § 278; § 317, 8.
κρέμαμαι, § 319, 2; § 312, 12—Accent of Subj. and Opt., § 309.
κρεμάννυμι, § 319, 2.
κρεμόω, § 319, D. 2.
κρήμναμαι, § 312, D. 16 c.
κρίνω, § 253, Obs.—Perf., § 282; § 286, Obs.
κρούω, Perf. Mid., § 288.
κρύπτω, § 249.
κτάομαι, Perf., § 274, Exc. ; § 289.
κτείνω, Aor., § 316, 4, and D.
κτέωμεν, § 316, D. 4.
κτίζω, § 316, D. 25.
κτίννυμι, § 319, 17.
κτυπέω, § 325, D. 8 g.
κυίσκω, § 324, 21.
κυνέω, § 323, 34, and D.
κυρέω, κύρω, § 325, 4—Fut., § 262, Exc.
κύσσα, § 323, D. 34.

λαγχάνω, § 322, 27, and D.—Perf., § 274, Exc.
λαμβάνω, § 322, 25, and D.—Perf., § 274, Exc.
λάμψομαι, § 322, D. 25.
λανθάνω, § 322, 26, and D.
λάξομαι, § 322, D. 27.
λάσκω, § 324, 29, and D.
λέγω, Perf., § 274, Exc. ; § 279—2d Aor. Mid., § 316, D. 35.
λείπω, § 248; § 254—Perf., § 278; p. 120.
λέκτο, § 316, D. 35.
λέκτο, λέγμενος, § 316, D. 36.
λελαβέσθαι, § 322, D. 25.
λελακυῖα, § 324, D. 29.
λέλασμαι, § 322, D. 26.

λέλαχον, § 322, D. 27.
λέληκα, § 324, 29.
λέλογχα, § 322, D. 27.
λελῦτο, § 289, D.
λέξεο, § 268, D. 3.
λεύω, § 288.
λήθω, § 322, 26.
ληκέω, § 324, D. 29.
λήξομαι, § 322, 27.
λήψομαι, § 322, 25.
λίσσομαι, § 250, D. — Augm., § 234, D.
λόε, § 244, D. 4.
λόεσσα, § 269, D.
λούω, § 244, 4—1st Aor., § 269, D.
λύω, pp. 103-109 ; § 231 ; § 301, 2 —Opt. Perf. Mid., § 289, D.— Aor. Mid., § 316, D. 28.

μαθεῖν. See μανθάνω.
μαίομαι, § 253, D.
μανθάνω, § 322, 28.
μάρναμαι, § 312, D. 16 d.
μαρτυρέω, § 325, 5.
μαστίζω, § 251, Obs.—Fut. according to § 260, 3.
μάχομαι, § 326, 23, and D.
μέδω, § 326, D. 42.
μεθύσκω, § 324, 22.
μείρομαι, Perf., § 274, D.
μέλει, § 326, 24, and D.—Augm., § 234, Obs.
μέλλω, § 326, 25—Augm., § 234, Obs.
μέλομαι, § 326, 24.
μέματον, μέμαμεν, § 317, D. 9 ; § 326, D. 26.
μέμβλεται, § 326, D. 24.
μέμβλωκα, § 51, D.; § 282, D.; § 324, D. 12.
μεμετιμένος, § 313, D. 2.
μέμνημαι, § 274, Exc. ; § 284, D.— Subj. and Opt., § 289, D.
μένω, § 326, 26, and D.
μερμηρίζω, § 251, D.
μηκάομαι, § 325, D. o.
μίγνυμι, § 319, 18, and D.; § 327, 7.
μιαίνω, pp. 122, 123.
μῖκτο, § 316, D. 37.

μιμέομαι, Aor. Pass., § 328, 4.
μιμνήσκω, § 324, 6 ; § 274, Exc.; § 289, D.
μίσγω, § 327, 7—Aor. Mid., § 316, D. 37.
μνάομαι, § 243, D. 3 b.
μολεῖν, μολοῦμαι, § 324, 12.
μύζω, § 326, 27.
μυκάομαι, § 325, D. p.

ναιετάω, Contract., § 243, D. 1.
ναίω, § 253, D. ; § 329, D.
νέμω, § 326, 28.
νέω, § 248.
νίζω, § 251, Obs.

ξέω, § 301, 1.
ξυρέω, ξύρομαι, § 325, 6.
ξύω, Perf. Mid., § 288.

ὄδωδα, § 275, D. 1; § 326, 29.
ὄζω, § 251; § 326, 29—Perf., § 275, D. 1.
οἴγνυμι, οἴγω, § 319, 19, and D.
οἶδα, § 317, 6, and D.
οἰδάνω, οἰδέω, § 322, 19.
οἴμαι, § 244, 4.
οἰμώζω, § 251, Obs.—Future Mid., § 266.
οἰνοχοέω, Augm., § 237, D.
οἴομαι, § 326, 30, and D.—2d Sing. Pres., § 233, 3.
οἶσε, § 268, D.
οἴσω, § 327, 12.
οἰχνέω, § 326, D. 31.
οἴχομαι, § 326, 31, and D.
ὀλέκω, § 319, D. 20.
ὀλέσκετο, § 337, D.
ὀλισθάνω, ὀλισθαίνω, § 322, 20.
ὄλλυμι, § 319, 20, and D.—Iterat., § 337, D.
ὄμνυμι, § 319, 21, and D.
ὀμόργνυμι, § 319, 22.
ὀνίνημι, § 312, 2—Accent of Subj. and Opt. Aor. Mid., § 309—Redupl., § 308.
ὄνομαι, § 314, D. 2.
ὀξύνω, Perf. Mid., § 286, Obs.
ὀπτός, § 327, 8.

ὄπωπα, § 275, D. 1.
ὁράω, § 327, 8, and D. — Augm., § 237—Perf., § 275, D. 1.
ὀργαίνω, 1st Aor., § 270, Obs.
ὀρέγνυμι, ὀρέγω, § 319, D. 36.
ὀρέοντο, § 319, D. 37.
ὄρμενος, § 316, D. 38.
ὄρνυμι, § 319, D. 37—2d Aor. Mid., § 316, D. 38—Imperat., § 268, D.
ὄροντο, § 327, D. 8.
ὀρόω, etc., § 243, D. A 3 a.
ὄρσο, ὄρσεο, § 268, D. ; § 316, D. 38.
ὀρύσσω, § 250—Perf., § 275, 1; § 278.
ὄρωρα, § 319, D. 37.
ὀρωρέχαται, § 319, D. 36.
ὀρώρυχα, § 275, 1 ; § 278.
ὀσφραίνομαι, § 322, 21, and D.
οὐλόμενος, § 319, D. 20.
οὐρέω, Augm., § 237.
οὐτάω, § 316, D. 20.
ὀφείλω, § 326, 32 ; § 253, Obs.
ὀφέλλω, 1st Aor., § 270, D. 2 ; § 253, Obs. and D.
ὀφλισκάνω, § 322, 22.
ὄχωκα, § 327, D. 6.
ὄψομαι, § 327, 8.

παθεῖν. See πάσχω.
πάλλω, Aor., § 257, D.—Aor. Mid., § 316, D. 40.
παράκειμαι, § 314, 2.
παρανομέω, Augm., § 239.
παροινέω, Augm., § 240.
παρρησιάζομαι, Augm., § 239.
πάσσω, § 250, Obs.—Fut. according to § 260, 3.
πάσχω, § 327, 9, and D.—Perfect, § 317, D. 14.
πατέομαι, § 325, 7.
παύω, Aor. Pass., § 298.
πείθω, Aor., § 257, D.—Perf., § 317, D. 15 ; § 330—Fut. and Aor. Part., § 326, D. 43 ; p. 118.
πεινάω, § 244, 2.
πείσομαι, § 327, 9.
πελάζω, § 316, D. 22—Imperat. of 1st Aor., § 268, D.
πέμπω, Perf., § 279 ; p. 120.
πεπαλών, § 257, D.

πέπιθον, § 257, D.
πέποιθα, § 317, D. 15.
πέπομαι, § 327, 10.
πέπονθα, § 317, D. 14.
πέποσθε, § 327, D. 9 ; § 317, D. 14.
πέπρωται, § 285, D.
πέπταμαι, § 274, Exc.; § 319, 3.
πεπτεώς, § 317, D. 17.
πεπτηώς, § 316, D. 21.
πέπτωκα, § 274, Exc.; § 317, D. 17;
§ 327, 15.
πέπωκα, § 327, 10.
πέρδομαι, § 326, 33.
πέρθω, 2d Aor., § 257, D.; § 59, D.
—Inf. Aor. Mid., § 316, D. 41.
πέρνημι, § 312, D. e.
πεσεῖν, § 327, 15.
πεσοῦμαι, § 327, 15.
πέσσω, § 250, Obs.
πετάννυμι, § 319, 3.
πέτομαι, § 326, 34—2d Aor., § 61 c;
§ 257, D.; § 316, 5, and D.
πετῶ, § 319, 3.
πεύθομαι, § 322, 29.
πεφήσομαι, § 321, D. 10.
πεφιδέσθαι, § 257. D.
πεφιδήσομαι, § 257, D.
πέφνον, § 257, D.
πέφραδον, § 257, D.
πεφύασι, § 277, D.
πεφυζότες, § 277, D.
πήγνυμι, § 319, 23—Aor. Mid., § 316,
D. 39; § 330, 4.
πιέζω, πιεζέω, § 325, D. h.
πῖθι, § 316, 15.
πίλναμαι, § 312, D. 16 f.
πίμπλημι, § 308 ; § 312, 3.
πίμπρημι, § 308 ; § 312, 4.
πίνω, § 321, 4 ; § 327, 10—2d Aor.,
§ 316, 15, and D.
πίομαι, § 265; § 327, 10.
πιπίσκω, § 324, 20; § 329, 7.
πιπράσκω, § 324, 7.
πίπτω, § 327, 15—Perf., § 317, D. 17.
πίσω, § 324, 20.
πιτνέω, πίτνω, § 323, 35.
πίτνημι, § 312, D. g.
πιφαύσκω, § 324, D. 32.
πλάζω, § 251, Obs.

πλάσσω, § 250, Obs.—Fut., § 260, 3.
πλέκω, p. 116—Aor. Pass., § 295.
πλέω, § 248—Fut., § 260, 2 ; § 264
Perf. Mid., § 288.
πλήθω, § 312, 3.
πλήσσω, 2d Aor. and Fut. Pass.,
§ 295—Perf., § 278.
πλῆτο (πελάζω), § 316, D. 22.
πλῆτο (πίμπλημι), § 312, D. 3.
πλώω, § 316, D. 24.
πνέω, § 248—Fut., § 260, 2 ; § 264
— Perf. Mid., § 285, D.—Aor.,
§ 316, D. 29.
ποθέω, § 301, 4.
πολεμίζω, § 251, D.—Fut., § 261, D.
πονέω, § 301, 4.
πορεῖν, § 285, D.
ποτάομαι, Plup. Mid., § 287, D.
πράττω, § 250—Perf., § 279, Obs. 1.
πρήθω, § 312, 4.
πρίασθαι, § 316, 8—Accent of Subj.
and Opt., § 309.
πρίω, Perf., § 288.
προθέουσιν, § 305, D.
πτάς, § 316, 5.
πτέσθαι, § 257, D.
πτήσσω, § 316, D. 21.
πτίσσω, § 250, Obs.—Fut., § 260, 3.
πτύω, § 301, 1.
πυθέσθαι, § 322, 29.
πυνθάνομαι, § 322, 29, and D.

ῥαίνω, Perf. Mid., § 287, D.
ῥέζω, § 327, 3, and D.
ῥερυπωμένος, § 274, D.
ῥέω, § 248 ; § 326, 35.
ῥήγνυμι, § 319, 24 ; § 330, 5.
ῥηθήσομαι, § 327, 13.
ῥιγέω, § 325, D. i.
ῥιγόω, ῥιγῶν, § 244, 3.
ῥιπτέω, ῥίπτω, § 325, 8, and D.
ῥυήσομαι, § 326, 35.
ῥῦσθαι, etc., § 314, D. 2.
ῥώννυμι, § 319, 10.

σαλπίζω, § 251, Obs.
σβέννυμι, § 319, 7—2d Aor., § 316,
9; § 318, 5.
σέβομαι, Aor. Pass., § 328, 2.

σείω, Perf. Mid., § 288.
σεύω, § 248, D.—1st Aor., § 269, D.
—Perf. Mid., § 274, D.; § 285, D.
—2d Aor. Mid., § 316, D. 30.
σημαίνω, Aor., § 270, Obs.
σήπω, § 330, 6—Aor. Pass., § 295.
σιγάω, Fut. Mid., § 266.
σιωπάω, Fut. Mid., § 266.
σκεδάννυμι, § 319, 4.
σκεδῶ, § 319, 4.
σκέλλω, Aor., § 316, 10; § 329, 6.
σκίδνημι, § 312, D. 16 h; § 319, 4.
σκλῆναι, § 316, 10.
σμάω, § 244, 2.
σπάω, § 301, 1—Perf. Mid., § 288.
σπείρω, § 253; p. 122.
σπείσω, § 260, 1.
σπένδω, Fut., § 260, 1—Perf. Mid., § 286, 1, Obs.
σπέσθαι, § 327, 5.
σπουδάζω, Fut. Mid., § 266.
σπών, § 327, 5.
στάζω, § 251, Obs.—Fut. according to § 260, 3.
στείβω, § 326, 36.
στέλλω, Perfect, § 282—Aor. Pass., § 295.
στενάζω, § 251, Obs.—Fut., § 260, 3.
στερίσκω, στερῶ, § 324, 26, and D.
στέρομαι, § 324, 26.
στίζω, § 251, Obs.—Fut., § 260, 3.
στορέννυμι, § 319, 8.
στόρνυμι, § 319, 25.
στρέφω, Perf. Mid., § 285 — Perf., § 278—Aor. Pass., § 328, 3.
στρώννυμι, § 319, 11.
στυγέω, § 325, D. 8 k.
στυφελίζω, § 251, D.—Fut., § 261, D.
σύτο, § 316, D. 30.
σφάλλω, § 252.
σφάττω, § 250.
σχεθέειν, § 338, D.
σχεῖν, etc., § 327, 6.
σχές, § 316, 11; § 327, 6.
σχίζω, § 251.
σώζω, 1st Aor. Pass., § 298.

τάνυμαι, τανύω, § 319, D. 38.
ταράσσω, § 250—Perf., § 277, D.

τάσσω, § 250—Perf., § 287; p. 116.
τεθηλώς, § 277, D.
τέθναμεν, § 317, 3.
τιθνεῶτος, § 317, D. 3.
τεθνήξω, § 291; § 324, 4.
τείνω, Perf., § 282—1st Aor. Pass., § 298.
τελέω, § 301, 1—Perf. Mid., § 288—1st Aor. Pass., § 298.
τέμει (τέμνω), § 321, D. 10.
τέμνω, § 321, 10, and D.
τέξομαι. See τίκτω.
τέρπω, Aor. Pass., § 59, D.; § 295, D.—Aor. Mid., § 257, D.
τεταγών, § 257, D.
τέτακα, § 282.
τετάρπετο, § 257, D.
τετεύχαται, § 322, D. 30.
τέτλαμεν, § 317, D. 10.
τέτληκα, § 317, D. 10.
τέτμηκα, § 321, 10.
τέτμον, § 257, D. 2.
τετορήσω, § 326, D. 44.
τετραίνω, Aor., § 270, Obs.
τέτρηχα, § 277, D.
τετυκεῖν, § 322, D. 30.
τεύχω, § 322, 30—Perf. Mid., § 285, D.; § 322, D. 30.
τήκω, § 330, 7—Aor. Pass., § 295.
τίθημι, p. 124; § 305, and D.; § 307—Aor. Pass., § 53 b—Aor., § 310—Perf., § 311.
τίκτω, § 249.
τίνυμι, § 319, D. 35.
τίνω, § 321, 5, and D.
τιτράω, § 327, 16.
τιτρώσκω, § 324, 16, and D.
τιτύσκομαι, § 322, D. 30; § 324, D. 37.
τλῆναι, § 316, 6, and D.
τμήγω, § 321, D. 10.
τραπέω, τραπείομεν, § 295, D.
τρέπω, Aor., § 257; § 294—Perf., § 279—Perf. Mid., § 285.
τρέφω, § 54 c—Perf., § 285—2d Aor. Pass., § 295—Aor., § 329, D.
τρέχω, § 54 c; § 327, 11, and D.
τρήσω, § 327, 16.
τρίβω, p. 120.
τρώγω, 2d Aor., § 257.

APPENDIX. 377

τρώω, § 324, D. 16.
τυγχάνω, § 322, 30, and D.
τύπτω, § 326, 37, and D.; § 249.
τύφω, § 54 c.
τυχεῖν, § 322, 30.
ὑπισχνοῦμαι, § 323, 36.
ὑποπτεύω, Augm., § 239, Exc.
φαάνθην, § 321, D. 10.
φαγεῖν, § 327, 4.
φάε(ν), § 321, D. 10.
φαείνω, § 321, D. 10.
φαίνω, § 253; § 321, D. 10; § 258; § 267; § 273; § 292 — Perf., § 282; § 278—Aor. Pass., § 298, D.; § 328, 3.
φάσκω, § 324, 8.
φείδομαι, Aor., § 257, D.; § 326, D. 45.
φέρτε, § 315, D. 4; § 327, D. 12.
φέρω, § 327, 12, and D.—Imperat. 1st Aor., § 268, D.
φεύγω, § 322, 31—Fut. Mid., § 264 —Perf. Act., § 278—Perf. Mid., § 285, D.
φημί, § 312, 5; § 92, 3.
φθάνω, § 321, 3, and D.—2d Aor., § 316, 7, and D.
φθείρω, Perf., § 282; § 330, D. 11.
φθίνω, § 321, 6, and D.—Aor. Mid., § 316, D. 26.
φιλέω, § 325, D. l.
φιλοτιμέομαι, Aor. Pass., § 328, 2.
φράγνυμι, φάργνυμι, § 319, 26.
φράζω, 2d Aor., § 257, D.
φράσσω, § 319, 26.

φυγγάνω, § 322, 31.
φυλάσσω, § 250.
φύρω, Fut., § 262, D.
φύω, Aor., § 316, 17, and D.; § 329, 3.
χαίρω, § 326, 38, and D.
χαλάω, § 301, 1.
χανδάνω, § 323, D. 41.
χανοῦμαι, § 324, 9.
χάσκω, § 324, 9.
χείσομαι, § 323, D. 41.
χέω, § 248 — Fut., § 265 — Perf., § 281—1st Aor., § 269—Aor. Mid., § 316, D. 31.
χραισμέω, § 325, D. 8. m.
χράω, χράομαι, § 244, 2—Fut., § 261.
χρεών, § 312, 6.
χρή, § 312, 6.
χρίω, Perf. Mid., § 288.
χρώννυμι, § 319, 12.
ψάω, § 244, 2.
ψεύδω, Mid. and Pass., p. 118.
ὤγμαι, § 327, D. 6.
ὠθέω, § 325, 9—Augm., § 237.
ὤμμαι, § 327, 8.
ὠνάμην, etc., § 314, 2, D.
ὠνέομαι, Augm., § 237 — Perfect, § 275, 2.
ὤξυμμαι, § 286, 1, Obs.
ὤρορον, ὤρσα, § 319, D. 37.
ὠσφρόμην, § 322, 21.
ὠφείλω, § 326, 32.
ὤφελλα, § 270, D. 2.
ὤφθην, § 327, 8.
ὤφλον, § 322, 22.

ENGLISH INDEX.

(The numbers indicate the §, not the pages.)

ABODE.
"*Abode*," to be supplied, 411.
Absolute Genit., 428; 584—Acc., 586.
Abstracts in the Plur., 362, Obs.—mostly Fem., 103.
Accent, 17, etc.— General rules, 79, etc.— of Nouns, 107, etc.; 118; 123; 148—of Comparatives, 171—of Pron., 207—Irregularities in the declensions, 121; 123; 131; 133; 142; 163; 166; 181; 183—in Adverbs, 201; 165—in Verbs, 229; 331, etc.—in the Strong Aor., 255—in the Perf., 276; 284—in the Strong Pass. Stem, 293—irreg., 332, etc.— in derivation, 340, Obs. 4, etc.
Accusative, orig. ending, 173, Obs.— meaning, 395—of the outer obj., 396, etc.—of the inner obj., 400, etc.—of double obj., 402, etc.—of the predicate, 403—free Acc., 404, etc.—Adverbial, 201; 203; with Prep., 447, 1—with the Inf., 567, etc.
"*Accustomed to*," expressed by Aor. and Imperf. Ind., with ἄν, 494, Obs. 1.
"*Acquainted with*," or "*ignorant of*," with Genit., 414, 3.
Action, Suffixes for, 342.
Active, 476—Act., Mid., Pass. meaning, 328.
Acute Accent, 17; 80, etc.—87, 2.
"*Adapted for*" Suffix, 351.
Adjectives, declens., 114; 126; 154; 164, etc.— Compar., 197—Genders, 180, etc.—of 3 Endings, 185, etc.— of 2 Endings, 182; 189—of 1 Ending, 190—Derived, 350—Contr., 183—Subs. fem., 127, 4—with Art., 379—follow the Genit., 412, Obs.
Adverbs, 201, etc.— Correlative, 217, etc.—Num. Adv.,

ATTRIBUTE.
223—with the Art., 379—as Adject., 382.
"*Aim*," expressed by Acc., 406.
Alphabet, 3.
Anastrophe, 90.
Aorist, weak, with transitive meaning, 329—with κ, 310—strong with intransitive meaning, 329—of proverbs and gnomes, 494—Ind., 492, etc.—in Condit. sentences, 543—in Condit. sentences, 539; 541—Moods, 495, etc.—Subj. in cond. sent., 545, Obs. 1—Opt. and Inf. 497—Part., 496.
Apocope, 64, D.
Apostrophe, 15; 64; 65, D.
Apposition, 361, 12; 385—Appositive Partic., 579; 583.
Article, 106—Crasis, 65—without Accent, 97, 1—as Demonstr. Pron., 212, D.—for the Relative, 213, D.—Origin in Homer, 368; 370, Obs.—omitted, 376, etc.—Meaning, 369, etc.—Neut., with Genit., 381; 410—Position, 383-390.
Aspirates, 32; 52, etc.—at the begin. of two successive syll., 53; 274, 1—Reduplicated by Tenues, 62.
Aspiration dropped or removed, 52, D.—thrown back, 54—omitted, 52, D.—in the strong Perf., 279.
Assimilation, 45; 47, etc.; 50 b; 51; 56.
Asyndeton, 624 a, Obs.
Atona, 97—before Enclit., 93 e; 98.
"*Attempting* an action," expressed by the Imperf., 489.
Attic Decl., 132—Ending, 157—Future, 263—Reduplic., 275, 1; 278.
Attraction, 597, etc.—inverted, 604.
Attribute, 361, 11—Attributive Adjective Art., 384—

COMPLETED.
Attrib. compounds. 359, 2, and Obs. (Comp. 360)—Attributive additions, 383—386—Attrib. Partic., 578.
Augment, 234, etc.—Omitted, 234, D.; 235—Double, 237; 240—in Compounds, 238, etc.—irreg., 270, D.
Barytones, 19.
"*Be*," "become," "make," etc., 417; 361, 7.
"*Begin*," "interrupt," "end," verbs with Part., 590—with Genit., 419 b.
"*Benefiting*," Verbs of, 396.
"*Buy*," Verbs with Genit., 421.
"*Capability*," etc., Verbs with Inf., 560, 1.
Cardinal Num., 220.
Case, 100—Use of, 392, etc.—Endings, 100—Acc., 142; 153—in Comps., 354, Obs.
"*Cause*," in the Genit., 408; 7—422; 426—Dat., 439—Part., 581.
Challenge or Command—in the Subjunc., 509—by ὅπως, 553, Obs.
Characteristic, 249.
Circumflex, 21; 80; 83, etc.; 87 a.
Classes of Verbs in ω, 247-250; 320-327; of Verbs in μι, 305-319.
Collective Sing., 362.
Common Gend., 127, 5; 140.
"*Community*," expressed by Dat. 436.
Comparative, 192, etc.— declens., 170, etc.—irreg., 199—Adv., 203—with Genit., 416, Obs. 3; 423.
Compensation by lengthening, 42—for ν, 49, Obs. 3; 147, 1; 233, 2—for ντ, νθ, νδ, 50; 147, 1; 187—for σ, 270.
Completed Action in Verbs, 484; 435; 502-506.

ENGLISH INDEX.

COMPOUNDS.

Compounds, Divis. of Syll., 78 — Accent, 85; 131; 165; 183; 332 — Adj., 182, etc.; 189, 3 — Augm. in Comp. Verbs, 238, etc. — treated as simple Verbs, 402 — with Genitive, 424 — with Dat., 437.
Concessive Participle, 582.
Conditional Sentences, 534, 549 — negat., 616.
Conjunctions, 623, etc.
Connecting Vowels, 233, 1, 2, 5; 262, etc.; 275.
Consonants, Divis. of, 30, etc., 44 — in dividing Syll., 71, etc.
Contraction, 36, etc. — in Declens., 118; 122; 128; 130, etc.; 163, D.; 166; 168 — Double, 167 — Omitted, 35, D. 1; 165; 160, D.; 233, D. 4; 243, D.; 263, D. — of the Pres. Stem, 243, etc. — of Adv., 201 — Contr. Syll. ₒ long, 75, Obs. — Accent, 87; 163; 331 — Contr. Fut., 259; 262, etc.
Co-ordination, 519, 1 *a,* 2.
Coronis, 16; 65.
Correlation, 519, 4 — Correl. Pron. 216; 218 — Adv., 217, etc.
Crasis, 16; 65 — Accent in, 89.

Dative, Perispome, 109 — Oxytone, 133, 2 — in Monosyll., 142 — in σι(ν), 68; 165, D. — represented by φιν, 178, D. — Meaning, 429, etc. — with Prepos.,447,3 — of advant. and disadv., 431 — of interest, 431, etc. — ethical, 433 — of community, 436, etc. — of instrument, 438, etc. — of measure, 440 — free, 441-443.
"Declaration," Verbs of — with Acc. and Inf., 567 — with Inf., 560, 2 — with Part., 593 — with οὐ, 617, Obs. 1 — Sentences of, 525.
Decomposites, Augment in, 239.
Defectives in Compar., 200.
Defining Object, 400 *c* — Inf., 562.
Demonstrative Article, 369 — Pron., 212; 216; 475 — follows the predicate, 367 — Art. with, 389.
Denominatives, 339.
Dental Cons., 30 — dissim. 46 — become σ, 47; 67 — mutes dropped before σ, 49; 147, 1; 149; 260 — in Perf., 281 — Charact. in Verbs, 250, Obs. — Fut., 260, 3.

GENDER.

*Deponents,*482 — Pass., 328, 2 — Pass. Mean., 328, 4; 483, 3.
Derivative Ending in Comparatives, 357.
Description expressed by the Imperf., 488.
Desideratives, 353, Obs. 2.
Determinative Comps., 359, 1, and Obs. (Comp. 360).
Diæresis, 9; 22, Obs.
Digamma, 3, D.; 34, D.; 35, D. 2; 63, D.; 75, D.; 160; 237; 233, Obs.; 360, Obs.
Diminutives, 347; 104.
Diphthongs, Pronunciation, 8 — Origin, 26; 35, 2 — before Vowels, 35, Obs.; 160; 248, Obs. — without Augm., 235 — spurious, 27.
Disjunctive questions. (See Double question.)
Dissimilation, 46.
Distributives, 223.
Doric Fut., 264.
Doubling of Conson., 62; 34.
Double questions, 611 — οὐ and μή, 615, Obs. 1.
Dual represented by Pl., 365.

Effect and Consequence expressed by Acc. and Inf., 567.
Elision, 64 — Accents, 88 — before Enclit., 96, 3.
Enclitics, 92, etc. — retaining the Accent, 96.
Ending, 100 — changed in Comps. 355 — of the 1st Declens., 134 — of 2d, 172.
Enjoying, verbs of, with Genitive, 419 *d.*
Epexegesis, 624 *a,* Obs.
Ethical Dative, 433.
Exclamations, 393 — in Acc., 399, Obs. — in Genit., 427.
Extent, exp. by Acc., 405.

Fear and Anxiety, 533; 512; 616, Obs. 3.
Feeling, verbs of, with Acc., 399 — with Dat., 439, Obs. — with Genitive, 422, Obs. — with Part., 592.
Feminines, 103; 127; 138; 163.
Final letters, 67, etc. — Syll. long — bef. vowels short, 75, D. 2 — Contr. Accent, 87; 183.
Future, 499, etc., 484 — Act. with trans. Meaning, 329 — periphrastic, 501 — Fut. Perf., 505 — Ind. with κέ, 554, Obs. 2 — Particip. with Art., 500.

Gender, known by general rules, 101, etc.; 127 — by ending of Stem, 125; 137,

INTERROGATIVE.

etc. — by Declens., 105; 122 — in A Declens., 122 — in O Declens., 127 — in Conson. Declens., 137, etc.
Generic Article, 375.
Genitive Perispome, 100; 118 — Oxytone, 133, 2 — Paroxytone, 181 — in Monosyll., 142 — represented by θεν and φιν, 178, D.; 118 — Meaning, 407 — with Prepos., 447, 2 — with Subst., 408, etc. — with Adj. and Adv., 414, etc. — with Verbs, 417, etc. — free Genit., 425, etc.
Gentile Names, 349; 350.
Grave accent, 19, etc.; 86.
Gutturals, 30 — with σ form ξ, 48; 260 — before μ, become γ, 47 — with ι, become σσ, 57 — Charact. of Pres., 250; 251, D.

Heteroclites, 174.
Hiatus, 63 — apparent, 63, D. 4.
Hypothetical Sent. (See Conditional Sent.).

Imperative, 228 — 1 Aor., 53 — 268, D.; 518 — in Cond. Sent., 545, Obs. 3 — exp. by 2 Pers. Fut. with οὐ, 499, Obs. — supplied by Inf., 577.
Imperfect, 488, etc. — in Cond. Sent., 543 — in Prot. and Apod., 538; 541.
Inclination, 91, etc.
Incomplete Action, 484, etc.
Indefinite Subject, 361, 3, Obs. 2 — in Neut., 364.
Indefinite Pronouns, 214, etc.; 216 — Adv., 92, 4.
Indicative, 467 — in Depend. Sent., 520; 523 — in depend., declar., and interrog. Sent., 526 — in Condit. Sent., 536, etc., 545 — in temp. Sent., 556 — hypoth. Ind. in Cond. Sent., 537 — in Sent. of purpose, 550.
Indirect Object, 430 *a.*
Individualizing Article, 371, etc.
Infinitive Act., in μεναι, μεν, 233, D. 3; 255, D. — in ναι Aor. and Perf. Accent, 333, 1-5; 268, Obs. 1 — Use, 559 — with Art., 379 — as Subject, 563; 574, 1 — Acc., 2 — Gen., 3 — Dat., 4 — with μή, and οὐ, 617 — with μὴ οὐ, 621 *c, d* — for Imper., 577.
"Injure," Verbs — with Acc., 396.
Instrument, suffix, 344 — Dative of, 438; 574, 4.
Interest or Advantage, Dat. of, 431, etc. — Middle of, 479.
Interrogative Pron., 214 ;- 216

ENGLISH INDEX. 381

IRREGULAR.
—direct and indirect, 475 b;
609—in depend. Sent., 525
—joined with Demonstr., 606, Obs. 1.
Irregular Nouns, 177—Verbs, 320, Obs.
Iterative form, 334, D., etc.—
in Imperf. and Aor., 335, D.

Judicial Proceedings, Verbs of—with Genit., 422.

Kinds of Verbs, 225, 2.-

Labials, 30—before μ, 47—before σ, 48; 260—verbal stem. 249.
Lengthening, 40, etc. ; 147 ; 155; 165; 173, Obs. — in Pres., 248—in the Fut., 260, 2; 261 — in Redupl., 275 (Comp., 273, D. ; 278)—of Vowels, 243, D. 3 ; 263, D.
Liquids, 33—in divis. of Syll., 72, 1.
Locative, 179.
Long by Nature, 75.

Manner, exp. by Dat., 441.
Masculines, 102; 137—disting. from Fem., 113 ; 122 ; 134 ●—for Fem. , 362, Obs. 2.
Material, suffix, 352, 3, 4 — Genit., 408, 3 ; 414, 2 ; 418.
Measure, in Dat., 440.
Mediæ, 32.
Metaplasm, 175.
Metathesis, 59 ; with strong Aor. Act. and Mid., 257 ; D., 282, 285 ; with strong Aor. Pass., 295, D.
Middle, 477, etc.—direct, 478 — indirect, 479 — Subjective, 480—Causative, 481—Aor. with Mid. meaning, 255, 2 ; 271—Fut. with Act. meaning, 264 ; 266 ; 328, 1 —with Pass. meaning, 266.
Modesty of Assertion, exp. in Opt., with ἄν, 517, Obs. 1.
Momentary Action, 484 ; 492- 498.
Monosyllabic Stems, lengthened, 142 b—in λ, ν, ρ, Perf., 282—Accent of Mon. words, 142—with Enclit., 94.
Moods, 225, 4.
Multiplicatives, 223.
"*Must*" and "*Should*," Verbs of, in Imperf., 490.
Mutes, 31, etc.—Assimilation, 49, D. ; 52—before Liquids and Nasals, 78—Stems of Verbs, 248.

Name in Genit., 408, 9 — of Animals, Gender, 140.
"*Name*," "Select," etc., Verbs of, 361, 7, 10 ; 392; 403.

PASSIVE.
Narrative in Aor. Ind., 492.
Nasals, 33—in divis. of Syll., 72, 1.
Necessity, expressed by Verbal Adj., 300.
Negatives, 619, and Obs.
Negative Pron. and Adv., 219.
Neuters, 104 ; 139 — Dental Stems, 147 b ; — Liquid Stems, 151—Sigma Stems, 165—Marks of, 105, 3 ; 125 ; 136—Accent, 340, Obs. 4 — as Adv., 201 ; 203 ; 401 — Plu. with Sing. Verbs, 363 —Adj. as Predic., 366.
Nominal Predicate, 361, 4, etc.
Nominative Dual oxytone, 131, 1—for Voc., 129 ; 393— meaning, 392.
Nouns from Verbal Stems, 245.
Numbers, 100, 1 ; 225, 1 — "two" in the Pl., 365.
Numerals, 220, Obs. — with Art., 374.

Objective Inf., 561 — Genit., 574, 3, Obs.—Part., 581 ; 361, 9 ; 395.
Objective Comp̃s., 359, 3, and Obs.—Genit., 408, 5 b ; 413.
"*Opinion* to be of," Verb, with Inf., 560, 2 ; 567.
Optative, 228 — Pres., 2 Pers. Sing. in οῑο, 233, D. 1 — Perf. Mid., 289-514 — potential with ἄν, 517, Obs. 2 ; 552, Obs.—in dep. sent., 524 —Opt. in dep. Sent., 522, etc. —in indir. Speech, 523—in depend., declar., and inter. Sent., 525—in Sent. of purpose, 532—in Sent. of fear, 533—in Condit. Sent., 546, etc.—in Relat. Sent., 555— in tempor. Sent., 556 ; 558 —exp. interest, 430.
Ordinal Numbers, 220 — in Acc., 405, Obs. 1.
Oxytones, 17—before Enclit., 93 a.
Paroxytones, 17— in Crasis, 89—before Enclit., 93 c.
Participles, Declens., 187 — Voc. Sing., 148—Perf. Act., 276, D. — Fem., 188 ; 277, D.—Pres., Aor., and Perf. Mid., 333, 6-10—with Art., 379, etc. ; 578, Obs. — in Dat., 435, Obs. — hypoth. with μή, 583, 618.
Particles, 92, 5 ; 623, etc.
Partitive Genitive, 408, 4 ; 412 ; 419.
Passive, 483 — with Dative, 434—Aor. in Active verbs with Mid. meaning, 328, 3.

PRESENT.
Patronymics, 348.
Peculiar Charact. Suffix, 351 —Genit., 408, 8.
"*Perceive*," Verbs of, with Genit., 420 ; 417, Obs. — with Infin., 560, 2 — with Part., 591.
Perfect, weak, 277, D. ; 280, etc.—strong, 277, etc.—intrans. meaning, 330—trans. and intrans. meaning, 329 —use of the Ind., 502 — Moods, Inf., Part., 506 — Perfects with Pres. meaning, 503.
Period, hypoth., 534 — interposed, 550—Negative, 616.
Perispomes, 21 — before Enclit., 93 b.
Personal Endings, 226—Pronoun, 250, etc. ; 92, 2 — Meaning, 469—Genit., 470 a —for reflec. pron., 471, Obs. a, b—Personal Constr., 571.
Place, Suffix of, 345—Genit. of, 412 ; 415 ; 425—Dative, 442—Adv. with Genit., 415 —Desig. of, 82, 2 ; 179 ; 412.
Plenty and Want, Adject. of, 414, 2—Wishes, 418.
Plural, 3 Pers. Pl. Mid. in -αται, -ατο, 226, D. ; 283, D. 6—1 Mid. in μεσθα, 233, D. 5 ; 362, etc.
Position, 71, etc. ; 193.
Possessive Article, 373 — Pron., 208—with Art., 388 ; 470 — of the reflective, 472 b, c—Poss. exp. by Genit., 408, 2 ; 414, 1—by Dat., 422.
Possibility, exp. by Verb Adj., 300—by Opt. with ἄν, 516, etc. ; 546 — by Part. with ἄν, 595.
Predicate, 361, 3, etc. — dependent, 361, 10 ; 589, 2 — without Art., 378, 387.
Predicative Acc., 403—Genit., 417— Acc. with Inf., 570— Gen. or Acc., 572 — Part., 589.
Prepositions, lose their Accent, 88—Elision in dissyl., 64 ; 90 ; 238—Anastrophe, 90—Augm. aft. Prep., 238, etc.—Use, 444—Adverbial, 446 — with Acc., 449 f— Genit., 451, etc.—Dat., 456, etc.—Genit. and Acc., 458— with three cases, 462, etc.— spurious, 445.
Present Ind., 486, etc. — Moods, Inf. Part., 491 — hist., 487 — exp. by Ind. Aor., 494, Obs. 2—enlargement of, 246—Stem, 231— like the Verb Stem, 247— with lengthened Stem Vowel, 248 — from Verb

382 ENGLISH INDEX.

PRIMITIVE.
Stem with τ, 249 — with ι, 250, etc.
Primitive words, 339.
Principal Conjugations, 230 —first, 231, etc.; 320, etc. — second, 302–319 — Declensions, 111—first, 112–134—second, 135.
Proclitics (see Atona).
"Prohibition," 518; 510; 499 — Prohibit, Hinder, Deny, etc.—have the Infin. with μή, 617, Obs. 3—with μὴ οὐ, 621 d.
Prolepsis, 519, 5, Observ. 2 (Comp., 567; 571).
Pronunciation, 4, etc.
Proparoxytones, 17 — before Encl., 93 d.
Properispomes, 21 — before Encl., 93 d.
Proper Names in -α, 115, D. 2 —ης, 174 — κλῆς, 167 — with Art., 371, Obs.; 375, Obs.; 387, Obs.
"Property," Suffix of, 346; 343, Obs.

Quantity, in Crasis, 65—in Monosyll., 142 — doubtful, 75, D., 1—reversing quant., 37, D., 2; 161, Obs.
Quantitative Adj. and Adv., 224—with Art., 374.
Questions, dubious in the Subj., 511.

Reciprocal Pron., 211.
Reduplication, 53, 10 a — in the Perf., 273, etc.—in the 2 Aor., 257 d—in Verbs in μι, 308.
Reflective Pron., 210—Meaning, 471—3d for 1st and 2d Pers., Obs. c — to denote possession, 472 — for Reciprocal, 473.
Relative Adj., 414.
Relative Pron., 213; 216 — Crasis, 65—Compound, 214, Obs. 2—Hypoth., 554—follows the Predic. Subst., 367 —used once only, 605.
Relative Sentences, 551—with Future Ind., 500—with μή, 615, Obs. 2—complication, 604—Connection, 605.
"Reference to," exp. by the Acc., 404.
Rejection of letters, 61—of a Vowel at begin., see Syncope—of a vowel at end, see Elision.
Repetition, exp. by the Opt., 547 (Negative, 616, Obs. 2) 555, Obs. 1; 558. Obs. 1.

SUBJUNCTIVE.
Result of an Act, 343—in the Acc., 400 d.
Root, 245.
"Scare," "Obstruct," a d other Verbs, with the Inf., 560, 3.
Semivowels, 31.
Sentences, Compound, 519, 3, 5—Principal, Subordinate, 519, 4—Moods of, 525, etc. —Condit., 534; 549, etc.— Negat., 616—of Experience in Aor. Ind., 494—Interr., 525—of Purpose, 530–533— Negat., 616.
Shortening, at the beginn., 74, D. — of the final syll., 75, D. 2—in the Perf., 285, D.—in the Subj., 228, D.; 233, D. 2 — in Rel. Sent., 597, 3.
"Should," exp. in depend. Sent. by the Subj., 527 b, Opt., 528 b.
"Show," Verbs of with Part., 593; 580.
Sigma, future, 259; 260, etc. —Aor., 260.
Singular, 3 Pers. in ε (ν), 68, 4—Accent on Imp. Mid., 268, 2—Accent on 2 Aor. Imper. Act. and Mid., 333, 11, 12, 362.
"Space," exp. by the Accus., 399 b.
Spiritus, position, 12; 22 — with ρ and ρρ, 13 — Spir. Asper, 60 b—in Augment, 235, Obs.—Spir. Lenis, 11.
Stem, 100—St. Vowel lengthened, 147, 2; 248; 253, Obs.; 261, 270, changed to ε, 157.
"Strive," "Aim at," Verbs with Genitive, 419 c—with Inf., 560, 3.
Subject, 361, 3—Omitted, Obs. 2—with Genit. Abs., 585 a —of a Subordinate Sent. as Object of the Principal Sent., 397; 519, 5—Obs. 2— Subj. of Prin. Sent. in the Subord. Sent., 602; 519, 5, Obs. 2.
Subjective Genit., 408, 5 a.
Subjunctive, 228—Shortened, 233, D. 2; 255, D. 1; 302, D. —of the Perf. Mid., 289 — of verbs in μι, accent, 309—Meaning, 508, etc.—similar to Fut., 513—in dep. sent., 521—in depend. assert. and interrog., 527—in sent. of purpose, 531, 532, Obs.— exp. fear, 533 — in condit. sent., 545, 554, 555, Obs. 2

WORTH.
—in tempor. sent., 557, 558, Obs. 2.
Subordination, 519, 3.
Substantive, degrees of, 199, D.—joined to the Dat., 430, Obs., 432, Obs.
Suffixes, 340; 178.
Superlatives, Adv., 203—with Genit., 416, Obs. 2—with ὡς, 635 a—with ὅτι, 633, 1 b.
Supplements to the Part., 361, 8.
Supplementary Aorist, 270, etc.
Syllabic Augm., 234 — with initial vowel, 237 — omitted, 283.
Syllables of both quantities, 75, D., 1; 77.
Synizesis, 39; 66; 243, D., 3.
Syncope, 61 c; 257, D.

"Taking part in," with Genitive, 414, 5; 419 a.
Temporal Adj., 352, 4, Obs.— Augm., 234 b; 235.
Tenses, 225; 3 Prin. Tenses, 521—Subord., 522—Tense Stems, 227.
Tenues, 32—for Aspirates, 32, D.
Time, in Acc., 399 b; 405 ♣ in Genit., 426—in Dat., 443 Adv. of with Genit., 415— kinds, degrees of, 484, 1, 2.
Transitive and Intransitive Meaning, 329, etc.; 476 — Mid., 477.
"Touch," and other Verbs with Genitive, 419 b.

Uncontracted Syll., 35, D., 1.

Verba Contracta among Iteratives, 336 d—V. pura, impura, 247.
Verbal Pred., 361, 4—Nouns, 225, 5 — Stem, 245, etc. — Pres. Stem, 246; 260, 3.
Vocal Stems, 1 Perf. 280.
Vowels, 24, etc.—in divis. of Syll., 470 — before others, 74—long without Augm., 235—Changes, 40, etc.—in 2 Perf., 278—in derivation, 340, Obs. 3.

Weakening of Conson., 60.
"When," expressed by Dat., 443.
"Whither," expressed by Accusative, 406.
"Wish," expressed in the Opt., 514, etc.
Worth and Price, in the Genitive, 408, 6; 421.

GREEK INDEX.

ἀ.
ἀ for η, 24, D. 2; 41, D.; 115, D. 1; 121, D. 2; 235 D.; 270, Obs.
ἀ for η, 277, D.
a bec. ω, 268; 278—bec. o, 268.
a bec. η. 40; 115, 1, c; 116, d; 235; 270; 268; 278; 303.
a bec. ε, 37, D. 2; 169 D.; 243, D. 3.
a bec. αι, 24, D. 3.
ἀ from αο, αω, see αο.
ἀ after ε, ι, ρ, 41; 115, 1, α; 116, c; 121; 180; 261; 270; 278.
a before vowels, 235.
α, connecting vowel, 276; 336, D.; 338, D.—in the 3 Plur., 302, 3.
α, characteristic of the First or Weak Aorist, 268.
α, privative, 360—in Adj. with the Genit. 414; Obs. 5.
-α, ending of the Accus., 141; 156; 173, Obs.; 181; 276.
-α, quantity of, 117; 121; 161; 169; 181, 1.
-α, Plur. ending of Neuters, 125, 2; 136; 141; 173.
-α, Adverbs in, 202.
-α, Nom. of Substant. in, 172.
-α, from αο in the Genit., 122, Obs.
ἀγαθός, Comparison, 199, 1.
ἄγαμαι (ἀγάομαι), 312, 8—Pass. Depon., 328, 2.
ἀγανακτέω, with the Particip., 592.
ἀγαπῶ, with the Dative, 439, Obs.—with the Partic., 592.
ἀγγέλλομαι, construed personally, 571—ἀγγέλλω, with a Partic., 593.
ἄγε δή, 642, 4 α.
ἀγείρω, 2 Aor., 257, D.—Perf., 275, 1.
ἀγήοχα, 279.
ἀγινέω, 323, D. 39.
ἄγνυμι, 319, 13—Perf., 275, 2—Signif. 330, 1.
ἄγχι, Comparison of, 203, D. —with the Genit., 415.
ἄγω, 2 Aor., 257—Imper. of 1 Aor., 268, D.
ἀδελφός, Voc. Sing., 129.

ἀκούω.
ἀδικέω, with the Accus., 396 —Signif., 486, Obs.
αε (αη) into ᾱ, 38; into η, 243, D. 2—into αα, 336, D.
αει into ᾳ, 38—into α, 243, Obs.—into αι, 38, Obs.
αέξω, 322, D. 13.
ἄεσα, 327, D. 17.
-αζω, Verbs in, 353, 6—Fut. 263.
ἀηδών, Gen. Sing., 163.
ἄημι, 313, D. 3.
ἀήρ, Masc., 140.
αι, in the Compar. for o or ω, 195—into η, 235.
-αι, Elided, 64, D.—Short in regard to the Accent, 83, Obs. 2; 108; 229; 268, Obs. 1.
αἰ, αἴθε, see εἰ, εἴθε.
αἰδέομαι, αἴδομαι, 301, 1; 326, 10—Pass. Depon., 328, 2—with the Accus., 399.
Ἀΐδης, 177, D. 19—ἐν, εἰς, Ἅιδου, 411.
αἰδώς, 163.
-αιν, in the Dual, 173, 4.
-αινα, Fem. ending, 115, 1 b.
αἰνέω, 301, 3.
αἴνυμαι, 319, D. 27.
-αινω, Verbs in, 353, 7.
αἴξ, of both genders, 140.
αἱρέω, 327, 1—Perf., 275, D. 1 —Distinct between Act. and Mid., 481 b—Passive meaning, 483, 3.
αἴρω, Aor., 270, Obs.
-αις, Subst. in, 172.
-αις, in the Dat. Pl., 119.
αἰσθάνομαι, 322, 11—with the Gen., 420—with the Partic., 591.
αἰσχρός, Comparison of, 198.
αἰσχύνομαι, with Acc., 399— with Dat., 439, Obs.—with Partic., 592—with the Inf., 594—αἰσχύνω, Perf., 286, D.
αἰτέω, with double Acc., 402.
αἰτιάζω, 319, D. 30.
ἀκέομαι, 301, 1.
ἀκήκοα, 275, 1; 280, Ob
ἀκηχέδατο, 287, D.
ἀκούω, Perf. Act., 275, 1— Perf. Mid., 288—with the Nom., 392, Obs.—with

ἄμεναι.
Gen., 420, and Obs.—with Partic., 591.
ἄκρατος, Comparison of, 196 b.
ἀκρόαομαι. Fut., 261 — with Gen., 420.
ἄκων, Gen. Abs., 585 b.
ἄλαλκον, 326, D. 11.
ἀλάλημαι, 275, D.
ἀλάομαι, Pass. Depon., 328, 2 —Perf., 275, D. 1.
ἀλγεινός, Comparative of, 199, 8.
ἀλδήσκω, 324, D. 30.
ἀλέασθαι, 269, D.
ἄλειφαρ, 176.
ἀλείφω, Perf., 275, 1.
ἀλεκτρυών, of both genders, 140.
ἄλεν, ἀλήμεναι, 325, D. d.
ἀλέξω, 326, 11.
ἀλέω, 301, 1.
ἄληθες, 165.
ἀλθομαι, 326, D. 39.
ἆλις, with Gen., 414, 2.
ἀλίσκομαι, 327, 17—Perf., 275, 2—Aor., 316, 12—with the Genit., 422.
ἀλιταίνω, 323, D. 37.
ἀλκή, Dat. Sing., 175, D.
ἀλλά, 629—ἀλλὰ γάρ, 636, 6, d; ἀλλ' ἤ, 629, Obs. 3—ἀλλ' οὖν, 637, 2.
ἀλλάσσω, 1 Aor. Pass., 294, Obs.
ἀλλήλων, etc., 211.
ἄλλομαι, 1 Aor., 270, Obs.— 2 Aor., 316, D. 32.
ἄλλος, 211—ἄλλο τι ἤ; ἄλλο τι; 608.
ἄλλως τε καί, 624, 4.
ἅλς, 150.
ἀλύσκω, 324, 27, Obs.
ἀλφάνω, 323, D. 38.
ἁλῶναι, 324, 17.
ἀλώπηξ, irr'g. Nom. Sing., 145.
ἅμα, with Dat., 436 c—with Part., 587. 1.
ἁμαρτάνω, 322, 12—with Gen., 419 e.
ἀμβλίσκω, 324, 18.
ἀμείβομαι, with Acc., 398.
ἀμείνων, Signif., 109, 1, Obs.
ἀμελέω, with Genit., 420.
ἄμεναι, 312, D. 13.

334 GREEK INDEX.

ἀμιλλάομαι.
ἀμιλλάομαι, Depon. Pass., 328, 2.
ἀμνήμων, with Genit., 414, 3.
ἄμοιρος, with Genit., 414, 5.
ἀμός, ἀμός, 208, D.
ἀμπέχω, 53, d.
ἀμπισχνοῦμαι, 323, 36.
ἀμπλακίσκω, 324, 23.
ἀμπνύνθη, 298, D.—ἄμπνυτο, 316, D. 29.
ἀμφί, 462 — without Anastrophe, 90.
ἀμφιέννυμι, 319, 5 — Augm., 240—with double Acc.,402.
ἄμφω, ἀμφότεροι, ἀμφότερον, 221 — ἀμφοτέρωθεν, with Genit., 415.
-αν-, affixed to form the Present Stem, 322.
ἀν-, privative, 360.
'ἀν, see ἐάν.
'ἀν, 639, 3—with particles of time, 557—in the Apodosis of Conditional Sentences, 535; 537; 541; Comp. 542; 546—with Aor., 494, Obs. 1 — with Subj., 513 — with Fut. Ind., 500, Obs.—with Imperf., 494, Obs. 1—with Ind., 536, etc.—with Inf., 575, etc.—with Opt., 516; 546—with Part., 595—with Relatives, 554; 555, Obs. 2.
-αν, Nom. Masc. and Neut., 172.
-αν for άων, Gen. Plur. of α-Decl., 118, D.
ἄνα, see ἄναξ.
ἀνά, 461—Apocope, 64, D.— without Anastrophe, 90.
ἀναβάλλομαι, with Inf.,560, 3.
ἀναβιώσκομαι, 324, 11.
ἀναγκαίης εἰμί, construed personally, 571.
ἀναλίσκω, ἀναλώσω, 324, 19.
ἀναμιμνήσκω, with double Acc., 402.
ἄναξ, Voc. Sing., 148, D.
ἀνάξιος, with Genit., 414, 4.
ἀνδάνω, 322, 23—Augm., 237.
ἀνδράποδον, Dat. Pl., 175, D.
ἀνέγνων, ἀνέγνωσα, Diff. of Signif., 329. D.
ἄνευ, 445; 455, 5.
ἀνέχομαι, double Augm., 240 —with Part., 590.
ἀνέωγα, ἀνέῳχα, 319, 19—Distinction, 279.
ἀνήνοθεν, 275, D.
ἀνήρ, 153; 177, 1—Genit., 51, Obs. 2.
ἀνήρ, 65, Obs. 1.
ἀνθ' ὧν, 601.
ἀνοίγω, Augm., 237 — Perf., 275, 2; 279.
ἀνορθόω, double Augm., 240.
ἄντα, ἄντην, ἀντικρύ, see ἀντί.
ἀντέχομαι, with Genit., 419 b.

ἀρχήν.
ἀντί, 451 — without Anastrophe, 90.
ἄνω, Compar., 204 — with Genit., 415.
ἄνωγα, 517, D. 11—Pluperf., 283, D.
ἄξιος, with Genit., 414, 4— with Inf., 562.
ἀξιόχρεως, 184.
ἀο into ᾱ, 37, D. 3; 122, D. 2 —into ω, 37; 122, D. 3 c— into εω, 37, D. 2; 122, D. 3 b; 132; 243, D. 3.
-αο, Genit. Sing., 122, Obs., etc., D. 3 b.
ἀοι, into ῳ, 37.
ἀου, into εω, 243, D. 3 b.
ἀπαγορεύω, with Part., 590.
ἀπαντάω, Fut. Mid. with Act. meaning, 266.
ἀπαφίσκω, 324, D. 33.
ἀπεῖπων, 327, 12.
ἄπειρος, with Genit., 419 e.
ἀπεχθάνομαι, 322, 16.
ἀπέχομαι, with Genit., 414, 3.
ἀπό, 452—Apocope, 64, D.; Compar., 204.
ἀποδίδομαι, with Genit., 421.
ἀποδιδράσκω, with Acc., 398.
ἀποέρσα, 270, D.
ἀπολαύω, Fut. Mid. with Act. meaning, 266—with Genit., 419 d.
'Απόλλων, Acc., 171; Voc. 148, Obs.
ἀποστερέω, with Doub. Acc., 402.
ἀποτυγχάνω, with Genitive, 419 e.
ἀπούρας, 316, D. 18.
ἀποφαίνω, with Part., 593.
ἀπόχρη, 312, 6.
ἄπτομαι, with Genit., 419 b.
-αρ, Subst. in, 172.
ἄρα and ἄρα, Distinction, 99.
ἄρα (ἄρ'), Apocope, 64, D.; 637, 1.
ἄρα, in questions, 607 b—indirect, 610; ἆρ' οὐ, ἆρα μή, 607, Obs.
ἀραρίσκω, 324, D. 34—Perf., 275, D. 1.
ἀρείων, ἄριστος, 199, 1, and Obs.
ἀρέσκω, 324, 10.
ἀρηρώς, 280, D.
"Αρης, 177, 2.
-αριον, Neuters in, 347, Obs.1.
ἀρκέω, Aor., 301, 1.
ἁρμόττω, 260, Obs. — Fut., 260, 3.
ἀρνέομαι, Depon. Pass., 328,2.
ἀρνός, etc., 177, 3.
ἄρνυμαι, Aor., 319, D. 29.
ἄρρωμι, 301, 1—Perf. Pass., 275, D. 1.
ἀρόω, 301, 1.
ἀρχήν, 405, Obs. 2.

βασιλεύς.
ἄρχομαι and ἄρχω, Distinction, 481 b.
ἄρχομαι, with Genit., 419 b —with Inf., 560, 1—with Part., 590—with Inf. and Part., 594.
ἄρχω, with Genit., 423—Diff. of Pres. and Aor., 498.
-ας, Ending of the Acc. Pl., 141.
-άς, Fem. in, 138.
-ας, Neut. in, 139.
-ας, Subst. in, 172.
ἄσμενος, 319, D. — Compar., 196 b.
ἆσσον, ἀσσοτέρω, 203, D.
ἀστήρ, Dat. Pl., 153.
ἄστυ, 158—Gend., 139.
-αται, -ατο, 3 Pl. Mid., 226, D.; 233, D. 6; 287, and D.
ἀτάρ, αὐτάρ, 630, 4.
ἅτε, with Part., 587, 6.
ἄτερ, 455, 5.
ἄττα, ἅττα, 214.
αὖ, αὖτε, 630, 3.
αὐξάνω, αὔξω, 322, 13.
-αυς, Fem. in, 172.
αὐτίκα, with Part., 587, 3.
αὐτός, 200—position with the Art., 389—with Dat., 441, Obs.—in the Genit. with Possess., 474—for the Rel., 605, Obs. — ὁ αὐτός, with Dat., 436 b.
ἀφαιρέομαι, with doub. Acc., 402.
ἀφάσσω, 250, D.
ἀφίημι, 313, 1—Augm. 240.
ἀφ' οὗ, 556; 601.
ἀφύσσω, 1 Aor., 269, D.
ἄχαρις, compar. 193, D.
ἄχθομαι, 326, 2 — Depon. Pass., 328, 2—with Part., 592.
ἄχνυμαι, 319, D. 30 — Plup. 287, D.
ἄχρι(ς), 69, Obs. 3; 445; 455 b; without Elision, 64, Obs. 1—ἄχρι οὗ, 556.
-αω, Verbs in, 353, 2, and Obs. 2—lengthening, 243, D. 3.
-αω, Fut. in, 263, D.

β, inserted between μ and ρ, 51, Obs. 2, and D.; β for μ, sec μ.
βαδίζω, Fut. Mid. with Act. meaning, 266.
βαίνω, 321, 1, and D—Perf., 317, 1—2 Aor., 316, 1—i Aor. Mid., 268, D.—meaning, 329, 2—of the Perf., 503.
βάλλω, Aor., 316, D. 19— Perf., 282—Signif., 476, 2.
βάρδιστος, 198, D.
βασίλεια and βασιλεία, 117.
βασιλεύς, 161, D.

GREEK INDEX.

βασιλεύω, with Genit., 423—Diff. of Pres. and Aor., 498.
βεβρώθω, 324, D. 13.
βείομαι, βέομαι, 265, D.
βείω, βίῃ, etc., 316, D. 1.
βελτίων, βέλτιστος, 199, 1.
βιάζομαι, Pass. meaning, 483, 3.
βιβάς, 312, D. 14.
βίβλος, Fem., 127, 5.
βιβρώσκω, 324, 13—Aor., 316, D. 23—Perf. Part., 317, D. 16.
βιόω, Aor., 316, 13.
βλ, Redup., 274, Ex.
βλάβεται. Hom. Pres., 249, D.
βλάπτω, Aor. Pass., 299—with Acc., 396.
βλαστάνω, 322, 14.
βλῆσθαι, etc., 316, 19.
βλίττω, 250, Obs.
βλώσκω, 324, 12; 51, D.
βοάω, Fut. Mid. with Act. meaning, 236.
βόλεται, 366, D. 14.
βορρᾶς, Genit. Sing., 122, Obs.
βόσκω, 326, 13.
βότρυς, Masc., 140.
βούλομαι, 326, 14—Augm., 234, Obs.—2 Sing. Pres. Mid., 233, 3—Depon. Pass., 328, 2.
βοῦς, 159; 160; 35, Obs.—of two Genders, 140.
βράσσω, 250, Obs.
βράσσων, 198, D.
βραχύς, with Inf., 562.
βροτός, 51, D.
βυνώ, 323, 32.
βώσας, 35, D. 1.

γ, Pronunt., 4—Character of Verbs, 251, Obs. — their Fut., 260, 3—Perf., 279.
γαμέω, 325, 1.
γάνυμαι, 319, D. 31.
γάρ, 636, 6—γὰρ οὖν, 637, 2.
γαστήρ, 153—Fem., 140.
γγ, Char. of Verbal Stems, 251, Obs.
γέ, 641, 1—Affix, *ibid.*
γέγονα, 327, 14.
γεγωνέω, 325, D. *a.*
γείνομαι, Signif., 329, 8.
γελάω, 301, 1—Aor. Pass., 298 — Fut. Mid. with Act. meaning, 266.
γέλως, 169, D.
γέμω, with Genit., 418.
γενέσθαι, γενήσομαι, etc., 327, 14.
γέντο, 316, D. 33.
γεραιός, Compar., 194.
γεύω, with Genit., 419, D.
γηθέω, 325, 2.
γηράσκω, 324, 1—Aor., 316, 2.
γι into ζ, 58; 251.
γίγνομαι, 327, 14—Perf., 317,

δεύτερος.
2—with Genit., 417—with Dat., 432.
γιγνώσκω, 324, 14—Aor., 316, 14—with Part., 591.
γλ, γν, Redupl. with, Ex.
γοάω, 325, D. *n.*
γόνυ, 177, 4.
γοῦν, 641, 2.
γραῦς, 159.
γράφομαι, with Genit., 422.
γράφομαι and γράφω, Diff., 481 *b.*
γυνή, 177, 5.

δ inserted betw. ν and ρ, 51, Obs. 2; 287, D.; 612—Character, 251. See Dentals.
δαί, 642, 8.
δαίμων, of two Genders, 140.
δαίνυμι, 319, D. 32 — Opt., 318, D.
δαίω, meaning, 330, D. 9.
δάκνω, 321, 8.
δάκρυον, 175.
δάμαρ, 147, 1, Ex.
δάμνημι, 312, D. *a*—Aor. Subj. Pass., 293, D.
δανείζω, Diff. of Act. and Mid., 481 *b.*
δαρθάνω, 322, 15.
δᾷς, Accent. of Genit. Pl. and Dual, 142, 3.
δατέομαι, 325, D. *b*—1 Aor. Inf., 269, D.
-δε, affixed, 94; 212; 216—Enclitic, 92, 5—Local Suffix, 178.
δέ, 628—δ᾽ οὖν, 637, 2.
δ᾽ ατο, 269, D.
δέγμαι, 312, D. 14, *b.*
δέδαον, 324, D. 28; 326, D. 40.
δέδεγμαι, δέξω, etc., 318, D.
δέδια, δέδοικα, 317, 5, and D.
δεῖ (see δέω), with Acc. and Inf., 567, Obs. 1—ἔδει, 490.
δείδω, forms Position, 17, D.—doubling of the δ, 234, D.
δείκνυμι, 318—with Partic., 593.
δεῖνα, Indef. Pronoun, 215.
δεινός, with Inf., 562.
δείρη, 115.
δένδρον, 175.
δέομαι, Depon. Pass., 328, 2. See δέω.
δέον, 586.
δέπας, Dat. Pl., 169, D.
δέρκομαι, Depon. Pass., 328, 2—2 Aor., 257, D.; 59, D.—with Acc., 400 *c.*
δεσμός, Nom. and Acc. Pl., 175, D.
δεσπότης, Voc. Sing. 121—Acc. Sing. 174, D.
δεύομαι, Depon. Pass., 328, 2.
δεύτατος, 199, D. (Defectives).
δεύτερος, with Genitive, 416, Obs. 3.

ὁρατός.
δέχομαι, Perf., 273, D—2 Aor., 316, D. 34—Aor. Pass. Signif., 328, 4.
δέω (I bind), 301, 2—Contraction, 244, 1.
δέω, δέομαι (I am in want of), 326, 15—with Genit., 418.
δή, 642, 4—Affix, 218.
δ᾽, θεν, 642, 7.
δῆλον ὅτι, 633, 1 *a.*
δηλόω, Meaning, 476, 1—δηλόω and δῆλός ε·μι, with Part., 590.
Δημήτηρ, 153.
δήν, makes position, 77, D.
δήποτε, Affix, 218.
δήπου, δήποθεν, 642, 5.
-δης, Masc. in, 348.
δῆσα, 326, D. 15.
δῆτα, 642, 6.
δι into ζ, 58; 251.
διά, 448; 485—without Anastrophe, 90—with Inf. and Article, 574, 2, 3.
δία, 181, D.
διάγω, διαλείπω, διατελέω, with Part., 590.
δίαιτα, 115.
διαιτάω, with double Augm., 240.
διακονέω, with doub. Augm., 240.
διαλέγομαι, Depon. Pass., 328, 2—Redupl., 274, Ex.—with Dat., 436 *a.*
διάλεκτος, Fem., 127, 5.
διαφέρομαι, 436 *a.*
διαφέρω, 423; 440.
διάφορος, 436 *b.*
διδάσκω, 324, 28, Obs.—Aor., 326, D. 40 — with double Acc., 402—διδάσκομαι, 481.
δίδημι, 313, 2.
δίδωμι, Compounds — Meaning, 476, 2—with Inf., 561.
διδράσκω, 324, 2—Aor., 316, 3.
δίεσαν, etc., 313, D. 4.
δίζημαι, δίζω, 313, D. 5.
δικάζομαι, Meaning, 481.
δίκαιος εἰμί, construed personally, 571.
δίκην, free Acc., 404, Obs.
δ ὅτι, 636, 2.
διπλάσιος, δισσός, etc., 223—with Genit., 416, Obs. 3.
δίχα, 445.
διώκω, with Genit., 422.
δμώς, Gen. Pl. and Dual, 142, 3.
δοίω, etc., 313, D. 2.
δοκέω, 325, 3—with Inf., 560, 2—constr. personally, 571.
δοκός, Fem., 127, 5.
δόξαν, with Acc. Abs., 586.
δόρυ, 177, 6.
δόσαν, 313, D. *c.*
δραμεῖν, δραμοῦμαι, etc., 327, 11.
ὁρατός, 300, D.

R.

386 GREEK INDEX.

δράω, Aor. Pass., 298.
δρόσος, Fem., 127, 5.
δύναμαι, 312, 9—Augm., 234,
 Obs.—Subj., Opt., Accent,
309—Depon. Pass., 328, 2—
 with Inf., 560, 1.
δύς, Compounds with, 360,
 Obs.—Augm., 241.
δύω, δύνω, 321,7; 301, 4—1 Aor.
 Mid., 268, D.—2 Aor., 316,
 15—Meaning, 329, 4.

ε for α, 263, D.—bec. α, 257;
 282; 285; 295; 298.
ε bec. η, 40; 147, 2; 151; 161,
 D.; 233, 4; 235; 293.
ε bec. ει, 24, D. 3; 42; 147, 1;
 236; 243, D. B.; 270; 293, D.
ε bec. o, 165; 278; 340, Obs. 3
 —bec. ω, 278.
ε for digamma, 34, D. 4;
 237, D.
ε inserted, 264; 269, D.
ε rejected, 153; 243, D. B.;
 257, D.—in Synizesis, 59, D.
ε contr. with preceding vowel, 166, D.
ε affixed to the Stem, 322,
 Obs.; 324, Obs.; 325, etc.—
 considered as Stem-vowel,
 43.
ε in the Augm., 236; 275.
 See Syllabic Augm.
ε in Redupl.,275—as Redupl.,
 274, 3, 4.
ε connecting vowel, 233, 1,
 and D. 3, 6; 262; 336, D.;
 338, D.
-ε in Nom. Acc. and Vocative
 Dual, 141.
εα bec. ᾶ, 130—bec. η, 38.
-εα for εια, 185, D.—for νν in
 Acc. Sing., 185—in ι and
 υ Stems, 157—in Diphth.
 Stems, 161—bec. η and α,
 ibid.—bec. η in the Acc.
 Pl., ibid.—bec. ᾶ or η in
 Fem. of Adj., 183—Ending
 of the Plup., 283, D.
ἔᾳ᾽α, 275, 2; 319, 13.
εαι bec. η, 38—bec. ει, ibid.,
 Obs.
ἐάν, 639, 2—in Condit. Sent.,
 535; 545; 548—"whether,"
 610—Comp. εἰ.
ἐάντε-ἐάντε, 627.
ἔαξα, 319, 13.
-εας bec. -εις in Acc. Pl., 157
 —from ηας, 161, Obs.
ἔαται, etc., 315, D. 2.
ἑαυτοῦ, 210—used as a possessive, 472 α.
ἐάω, Augm., 236.
ἐγγύς, Compar., 204 — with
 Genit., 415.
ἐγδούπησα, 325, D. c.
ἐγείρω, 2 Aor., 275, D.—Perf.,
 275, 1; 317, D. 12—Meaning, 330, 2.

εἶπον.
ἐγρήγορα, 275.
ἔγχελυς, 158.
ἐγώ, Synizesis, 66 — ἐγώγε,
 641, 1.
ἔδμεναι, 315, D. 3; 327, D. 4.
ἔδομαι, Fut., 265. See ἐσθίω.
εε bec. ει, 36—bec. ει and η,
 243, D. B. — bec. η in the
 Dual. See -η.
ἐέρχατο, 287, D.
-εες bec. εις in Nom. Pl., 157
 —bec. εις and ης, 161 d.
-εη for -εια, 185, D.
ἔης, 213, D.
ἐθίζω, Augm., 236.
ει for ε, 24, D. 3—for αι, 267,
 etc.—from ε, ι, see ε, ι.
ει, Redupl., 274, etc.—in the
 Plup., 283.
-ει in the Dat. Sing., 157;
 161 b—connecting vowel,
 233, 1—3 Sing. Ind. Act.,
 233, 2—2 Sing. Ind. Mid.,
 233, 3.
εἰ, 639, 1—Atonon, 97, 3—in
 Cond. Sent., 535 — with
 Ind., 536—with Opt., 546,
 etc.—for ἐάν, 545, Obs. 2.
εἰ, εἴθε, εἰ γάρ, in a wish, 514
 —"whether" in Depend.
 Interr. Sent., 525; 610.
εἰ-ή, 611—εἴ κεν, see ἐάν—
 εἰ ἄρα, 637, 1—εἰ γάρ, 637,
 6 d—εἰ καί, 640, 1—εἰ μή,
 639, 1.
-εια, Fem. in, 185—Quantity,
 117; 341, Obs.; 342, Obs.
εἴατο, 315, D. 2.
εἴδον, 327, 8.
-ειη, Fem. in, 115, D. 2.
εἴκε, εἴκτον, 317, D. 7.
εἰκοσί(ν), 68, 3; 220.
εἴκω, with Genit., 419 c.
εἰκών, Genit., 163.
εἰλέω, 625, D. d.
εἰλήλουθα, 40, D.; 317, D. 13.
εἴληφα, εἴληχα, 274, Ex.
εἴλοχα, 274, Ex.; 279.
εἶλον, etc., 327, 1.
εἴλω, 253, D.—1 Aor., 270, D.
εἷμαι, 319, D.—5.
εἵμαρται, 274, Ex.
εἰμί, 315, 1—Enclit., 92, 3;
 315, Obs. 2—with Partic.,
 287; 289; 291; 505; 590,
 Obs. — with Genit., 417 —
 with Dat., 432—Accent of
 compounds of εἰμί, 315, Obs.
 Obs. 3—ὧν, 428, Obs.; 580;
 585 b—τῷ ὄντι, 441.
εἶμι, 314, 1 — Meaning, 314,
 Obs.
εἵνεκα, see ἕνεκα.
εἴνυον, 319, D. 5.
εἴξασι, 317, 7.
-ειον, Neuters in, 345, 2.
εἴπερ, 639, 1.
εἰπόν, 327, 13—Aor. Imper.
 Accent, 333, 12.

ἔμπειρος.
-ειρ, Subs. in, 172.
εἴργνυμι, 319, 15.
εἴργω, Perf. and Plup., 287, D.
 —with Genit., 419 c.
εἴρηκα, 274, Ex.; 327, 13.
εἴρομαι, 326, D. 16.
εἴρω, 1 Aor., 270, D.—Perf.
 and Plup., 275, D. 2.
εἰς, 2 Sing. of εἰμί, 92, D.
εἰς, ἐς, 448; 449—Atonon, 97,
 2—with Inf. and Art., 574,
 2—εἰς ὅ, 556.
-εις, Nom. Pl., 157; 161 d.
-εις, Masc. and Fem. in, 172.
-εις, 2 Sing. Ind. Act., 233, 2.
-εις-εσσα-εν, Adj. in, 352, 5:
 187—Dat. Plur., 50, Obs. 1;
 149.
εἶσα, def. Aor., 269, D.
εἴσκω, 324, D. 35.
εἴσομαι, etc., 314, D. 1.
εἴσω, with Genit., 415.
εἶτα, with Part., 587, 4.
εἴτε, 94—εἴτε-εἴτε, 611; 627.
εἴωθα, 275, 2; 278.
ἐκ, ἐξ, 69, Obs. 2; 448; 453—
 with Augm., 238—Atonon,
 97, 2—with Inf. and Art.,
 574, 3—unaltered, 45, Obs.;
 47, Ex.—ἐξ οὗ, 556; 601.
ἐκάς, Compar., 203, D.
ἐκεῖνος, 212.
ἐκέκλετο, 257, D.; 61, D.
ἐκεχειρία, 53, 10 d.
ἐκκλησιάζω, Augm., 239.
ἐκλείπω, with Acc., 398.
ἐκληθάνω, 322, D. 26.
ἐκπλήττομαι, with Acc., 399.
ἐκτός, 327, 6.
ἱκών, Genit. Abs., 585 b —
 ἑκών ἑκών, 70, Obs.
ἐλάσσων, ἐλάχιστος, 199, 4
 —ἔλαττον, without ἤ, 626,
 Obs.
ἐλαύνω, 321, 2—Fut., 263—
 Perf., 275, 1—Plup., 287, D.
 —Meaning, 476, 1.
ἐλέγχω, Perf. Mid., 275, 1;
 286, Obs.
ἐλεῖν, 327, 1.
ἐλευθερόω, with Genit., 419 c.
ἐλθεῖν, ἐλεύσομαι, 327, 1.
ἐλλάδατο, 287, D.
ἐλίσσω, 236.
ἑλκύω, ἕλκω, 301, 1—Augm.,
 236.
ἔλμινς, 50, Obs. 2.
ἐλπίζω, with Inf., 569.
ἕλπω, Perf., 275, D. 2—Meaning, 330, D. 10.
ἕλσα, 270, D.; 325, D. d.
ἐμαυτοῦ, 210—Poss., 472 α.
ὑμέμηκον, 283, D.
ἔμμεναι, 301, 1.
ἔμμεναι, 315, D. 1.
ἔμμορα, 274, D.
ἐμνήμυκα, 275, D. 1.
ἔμπειρος, with Genit., 414, 3.

GREEK INDEX. 387

ἔμπλεως.
ἔμπλεως, with Genit., 414, 2.
ἔμπροσθεν, with Genit., 415.
ἐν (ἐνί), 448; 456—unaltered in compounds, 49, Obs. 1—bef. ρ, 51, Obs. 2—Atonon, 97, 2—with Inf. and Art., 574, 4—ἐν ᾧ, 556.
-ε(ν), 3 Sing., 68, 4.
-εν, Nom. of Neuters, 272.
-εν, 3 Pl. Aor. Pass., 293, D.
-έναι, Inf., 276.
ἐναίρω, Augm., 239.
ἐναντιόομαι, Depon. Pass., 328, 2—Augm., 239.
ἐναντίος, with Dat., 436 b.
ἔναυσα, Meaning, 329, D.
ἐνδεής, with Genit., 414, 2.
ἐνδύω, with double Acc., 402 —Meaning, 329, 4.
ἐνείκαι (ἐνεῖκοι), 327, D. 12.
ἕνεκα, 445; 448; 445, 8—with Inf. and Art., 574, 3.
ἐνέπω, ἔνεπε, ἔνισπω, etc., 327, D. 13.
ἐνέρτεροι, 199, D. (Defect.).
ἐνήνοθεν, 275, D. 2.
ἐνήνοχα, 327, 12.
ἔνι, 90.
ἐνίπτω, 2 Aor., 257, D.
ἐνίσσω, 250, D.
ἔννυμι, 319, 5.
ἐνοχλέω, double Augm., 240.
ἐντός, with Genit., 415.
ἐντρέπομαι, with Genit., 420.
ἐξελέγχω, with Part., 593.
ἐξικνοῦμαι, with Genit., 419 c.
ἐξόν, 586.
ἔξω, Comparative, 204—with Genit., 415.
εο bec. ου, 37—bec. ευ, 37, D. 1; 165, D.; 233, D. 4; 243, D. B., C.
ἔο, εὖ, εἶο, etc., 205, D.
ἐοι bec. οι, 37.
ἔοικα, 317, 7; 275, 2—construed personally, 571—with Part., 590.
ἔολπα, 275, D. 2.
ἔοργα, 327, D. 3.
ἑορτάζω, Augm., 237.
ἑοῦς, 208, D.
-εος, Genit. in, 161, D.
-εος, Adj. in, 352, 4; 183—for -εως, 184, D.
εου bec. ου, 37—bec. ευ, 37, D. 1; 243, D. B.
ἐπαυρίσκομαι, 324, 24.
ἐπεί, 556—ἐπείν, ἐπήν, ἐπάν, 557; 635, 5—in Synizesis, 66—with Aor. Ind., 493—"whenever,",558, Obs. 1.
ἐπειδή, 556 ; 635, 6.
ἔπειτα, with Part., 587, 4.
ἐπί, 448; 463—with Inf. and Art., 574, 2, 4.
ἐπίδοξος, ἐπικαίριός εἰμι, construed personally, 571.
ἐπιέσασθαι, 319, 5.
ἐπιθυμέω, with Genit., 420.

ἐτάθην.
ἐπιλαμβάνομαι, ἐπιλανθάνομαι, with Genit., 419 b; 420.
ἐπιλείπω, with Part., 590.
ἐπιμέλομαι, Depon.Pass.,328, 2—with Genit., 420.
ἐπίσταμαι, 312, 10—Accent. of Subj. and Opt.,309—Depon. Pass., 328, 2.
ἐπιστήμων, with Genit.,414, 3.
ἐπιτήδειός εἰμι, construed personally, 571.
ἐπιτρέπω, with Inf., 560, 1.
ἔπλητο, 312, D. ƒ.
ἕπομαι, 327, 5—Augm., 236.
ἔραζε, 178, D.
ἔραμαι, 312, 11.
ἐράω, Aor. Mid.,301, D.—with Genit., 420.
ἐργάζομαι, Augm., 236.
ἐργαθον, 319, D. 15.
ἔρδω, 327, 3.
ἐρέσσω, 250, Obs.—Fut., 260, 3.
ἐρεύγομαι, 322, D. 40.
ἐρηρέδαται, 287, D.
ἐρίζω, with Dat., 436 a.
ἔριφος, Nom. Pl., 175, D.
ἕρπω, ἑρπύζω, Augm., 236.
ἐρράδαται, 287, D.
ἔρρω, 326, 17.
ἔρρωγα, 278 ; 319, 24.
ἐρρωμένος, Compar., 196 b.
ἔρση, 115.
ἔρσην, 189, D.
ἐρυγγάνω, 323, D. 40.
ἐρύκω, 2 Aor., 257, D.
ἔρυσθαι, etc., 314, D.
ἐρύω, Aor., 301, D.
ἔρχαται, etc., 319, D. 15.
ἔρχομαι, etc., 326, 1.
ἐρῶ, 327, 13, and Obs.
ἔρως, 177, D. 20.
ἐρωτάω, with doub. Acc., 402.
-ες, Nom. of Neuters, 172.
-ες, Ending of Nom. Pl., 141; 173, 8, 2.
ἐσθίω, 315, D. 3 (ἔσθω) ; 327, 4 —with Genit., 419 d.
ἔσκον, 387, D.
ἔσπειμαι, 286, 1, Obs.
ἑσπόμην, etc., 327, 5.
ἔσπον, 327, D. 13.
-εσσα, Fem. of Adj., 187.
ἔσσαι, etc., 269, D.
-εσσι(ν), Dat. Pl., 141, D. ; 153, D. ; 158, D. ; 165, D.
ἔσσυμαι, 274, D.
ἔσσων, 199, D. 2.
ἔστε, "until," 556.
-ἔστερος, -ἔστατος, Compar. Ending, 196.
ἐστί, Accented, 96 ; 315, Obs. 2—ἔστιν οἵ, οὗ, etc., 603.
ἑστιάω, Augm., 236 — with Acc., 402 d. c—with Genit., 419 d.
ἔσχατος, 200; 391.
ἔσω, Compar., 204. See εἴσω.
ἐτάθην, 298.

ζώννυμι.
ἐτάφην, see θάπτω.
ἕτερος,with Genit.,416,Obs.3.
ἐτήσιαι, Genit. Pl., 123.
ἔτορον, 326, D. 44.
εὖ bec. εϝ; 35, D. 2: 248, Obs. —from εο, εου, see εο, εου.
εὖ, 202 — Augm. in Compounds, 241—εὖ ποιέω,with Acc., 396.
εὔαδον, 322, D. 23.
εὔδιος, Compar., 195.
εὐεργετέω, with Acc., 396.
εὐθύ, with Genit., 415—εὐθύς, with Part., 587, 3.
εὐκτίμενος, 316, D. 25.
εὐλαβέομαι, Depon.Pass.,328, 2—with Acc., 399.
εὔνους, Accent, 183—Compar., 196 c.
εὑρίσκω, 324, 25—with Part., 591.
εὐρύς, Acc. Sing., 157, D.
-ευς, Genit. in, 161, D.; 165, D.
-εύς, Nom. Sing., 341, 1; 349, 1; 137 ; 172.
εὖτε, see ὅτε.
εὐφαίνω, Meaning of the Aor. Pass., 328, 3.
-ευω, Verbs in, 353, 4.
ἔφαγον, 327, 4.
ᾧ ᾧ, ἐφ' ᾧτε, 601.
ἔχεα, 269.
ἐχθρός, Compar., 198.
ἔχω, 327, 6 — Augm., 236 — Meaning, 476, 1 — Diff. of Pres. and Aor., 498—with Inf., 560,1—with Part., 590 — ἔχων, 580 — ἔχομαι, with Genit., 419 b.
ἕψω, 326, 19.
εω for αο, see αο—in the Attic Declens., 132, etc.—in Contracted Verbs, 243, D., Herod.—as one Syll., 121, D. 3 b; 133, 1 ; 157.
ἕω, Genit. Sing., 121, D. 3 b; 177, 11 — Verbs in, 248 ; 253, 3 — Fut., 260, 2 ; 264 ; 263.
ἕωθα, 275, D. 2.
ἕωμεν, etc., 312, D. 13.
-εων, Genit. of a - Declens., 118, D.
ἕως ("till"), 556 ; 635, 7.
ἕως, Decl., 163.
-εως, Genit., 161, Obs.

ζ, Pronunt., 5—Pres. Stems in, 251, Obs.
ζάω, Contract., 244, 2.
-ζε, Local Suffix, 178.
ζεύγνυμι, 319, 16.
Ζεύς, 177, 7.
ζέω, 301, 1.
ζηλόω, with Acc., 398.
-ζω, Char. of Verbs, 251, Obs. and D.—Fut.,260,3. Comp. 263.
ζώννυμι, 319, 9.

GREEK INDEX.

η.

η for ᾱ, 24, D. 1; 115, D. 2; 180, D.; 244, 2; 161, D.; 270, Obs. See ε.
η after ο, 180, Ex.—bec. ω, 43.
η, Syll. Augm., 234, Obs.
-η, Voc. Sing., 121—in Acc. Pl., 157—in the Dual, 158; 166—in the Acc. Sing., 161, D.: 166—Conn. Vowel, 233, 1—Ending of 1 and 3 Plur. Plup., 283.
-η, 2 Sing. Ind. and Subj. Mid., 233, 3, 4.
ἤ and ἥ, Synizesis, 66—Diff., 99; 643, 9.
ἤ (ἠέ)-ἤ (ἠέ), 611, Obs.
ἤ, in indir. questions, 610— ἤ and ἤ-ἤ, 626 a, and Obs. —ἤ and ἤ ὥστε, with Inf., 506.
ἤ, Interr., 607 b—"really?" 643, 9—ἤ γάρ, ἤ που, 608; 636, 6 d—ἤ μήν, 643, 9.
ἤ, "he spoke," 312, 1.
ἤα, ἤειν, 314.
ἠβάσκω, 324, 3.
ἠγαγον, 257.
ἠδέ, 624 b, 1.
ἤδομαι, Depon. Pass., 328, 2—with Dat., 439, Obs.—with Part., 592.
ἠδύς, Fem., 185, D.
ἤειρα, 270, D.
ἤκα, 313.
ἤκιστα, 199, 2.
ἤκω, Meaning, 486, Obs.
ἡλίκος, Attr. in, 600.
ἤλιτον, 323, D. 37.
ἤλυθον, 327, 2.
ἤμαι, 315, 2.
ἠμβροτον, 322, D. 12.
ἠμέν-ἠδέ, 624 b, 2.
ἠμί, ἤν, ἤ, 312, 1.
ἦμος, 556; 634, 4.
ἤμπισχον, 323, 36.
ἠμφίεσα, 319, 5.
-ην, Nom., 172.
ἤν, see ἐάν.
ἤνεγκον, ἤνεικα, 327, 12.
ἐνίκα, 556; 634, 3.
ἐνίπαπον, 257, D.
ἤνυτο, 319, D. 28.
ηο bec. ω, 37 —ηος, ηα, ηας, 161, Obs.—ηου bec. ω, 37.
ἤπαρ, 176.
ἤπαφον, 324, D. 33.
-ηρ, Nom. 172.
ἤρ, 142, 4.
Ἡρακλῆς, 167, D.
ἤραρον, 324, D. 34.
ἤριπον, Meaning, 329, D.
ἠρόμην, 326, 16.
-ης, Nom. Pl., 161 d.
-ης, Nom. Sing., 172; 174, D.
-ης, Prop. Names in, 174.
-ης, Adj. in, 355—Comp., 197.
-ησι(ν), Dat. Plur. of α-Decl., 119, D.

ι.

ἥσσων, 199, 2.
ἥσυχος, Compar., 195.
ἤτοι, 94; 643, 11—ἤτοι- ἤ, 626 a.
ἦτορ, Gender, 189.
ἡττάομαι, with Genit., 423.
ἤττων, 199, 2.
ἠύτε, 632, 5.
ἰφίει, 240; 313, 1.
ἤχα, 279.
ἤχι, 217, D.
ἰ, ὡς, 163, D.

θ, Pronunt., 7—in the Perf.; 286, 4—in the Weak Pass. Stem, 298—Nom. Sing. of Stems in, 147, Obs. 2—Affixed to Pres. and 2 Aor. Stems, 338, D.—bec. σ, 307. See also Dentals.
θανεῖν, 324, 4.
θάπτω, 54 c; 298.
θαρρέω, with Acc., 399.
θᾶσσον, see ταχύς.
θάτερον, 65, Obs. 1.
θαυμάζω, with Genit., 417, Obs.; 422, Obs.
θαυμαστός ὅσος, etc., 602.
θεά, 115, D. 2; 117.
θέλω, ἐθέλω, 326, 20.
θέμις, 177, D. 21.
-θε(ν), Suffix, 178, 2; 68, D.— for the Genitive, 205, D.; 178, D.
θεός, Voc. Sing., 129, D.
θέρειος, 350.
θέρομαι, Fut., 262, D.
θέω, 248—Fut., 260, 2.
θῆλυς, as Fem., 185, Obs.
θήν, Enclit., 92, 5; 643, 17.
θηράω, with Accus., 398.
θι bec. σσ, 57.
-θι, Loc. Suff., 178, 1—Ending of 2 P. Imper., 228; 302, 5; 307.
θιγγάνω, 322, 24.
θλάω, 301, 1.
θνῄσκω, 324, 4—Perf., 317, 3— Perf. Part., 276, D.—3 Fut., 291—Signif., 486, Obs.
θοἰμάτιον, 65, Obs. 1.
θόρνυμαι, 324, D. 15.
θρίξ, 54 a; 145.
θρύπτω, 54 c.
θρώσκω, 59; 324, 15.
θυγάτηρ, 153.
ἐν- προ- θυμέομαι, Depon. Pass., 328, 2.
θύρασι(ν), 179.
θύω, 301, 2—Aor. Pass., 53, 10 b.
θώς, Genit., Pl. and Du., 142, 3.

ι, Pronunt., 4—Long by Nat., 83, Obs. 1—Lengthened, 253, Obs.—ι bec. ῑ, ει, οι, 40; 278—ι of the Stem bec. ε, 157—Changes, 55; 168; 250, etc.

ἴσος.

-ι, Locative Ending, 179—Demonst., 212—Neut. in, 139; 172.
-ι, Nom. Ending in the Pl., 134, 9—Dat. Sing., 141; 173, 2.
ι, Sign of the Opt., 228—Redupl., 308; 327, D. 17—Connect. Vowel, 348; 351—Affixed to the Stem in the Dat. Pl., 119; 134, 8.
ι, Subscribed, 8: 12; 27; 65, Obs. 2—Dat. Sing., 134, 3; 169; 173, 2.
ι, Verbs in the Pres. with, 250, etc.; 322, Obs.—their Fut., 260, 3; 262.
ια for ιο, 348.
-ια, Fem. in, 346, 3; 185, etc.
ἴα, ἴης, ἰῇ, ἰῷ, 220, D. 1.
ἰάομαι, Meaning of the Aor. Pass., 328, 4.
ἰάω, 327, D. 17.
-ιαωι, Verbs in, 353, Obs. 2.
ἰδέ (Conj.), 624 b, 1—(Imper.), 327, 8; 333, 12.
-ίδιον, Neut. in, 347, 1, Obs.
ἴδιος, with Genit., 414, 1—with Dat., 436 b.
ἴδρις, 158; 189, 3.
ἱδρύω, Aor. Pass., 298, D.
ἱδρώς, 169, D.
ἱερός, with Genit., 414, 1.
ἰζάνω, 322, 17.
ἵζομαι, 326, 21.
-ίζω, Verbs in, 353, 5—Fut., 263.
ιη, Char. of the Opt. 293; 302, 4.
ἴθυς, Superl., 193, D.
ἱκμένος, 316, D.; 323, D. 33.
ἱκνέομαι, ἱκνοῦμαι, 323, 33— 1 Aor., 268, D.
-ικός, Adj. in, 351—with Genit., 414, 6.
ἱλάσκομαι, 324, 5—Imper., 312, D. 15.
ἱμάσσω, 320, D.
-ιν, Subs. in, 172—-ιν, Dual Ending in Genit. and Dat., 134, 6; 173, 4.
ἵνα, 638, 1—in Sentences of Purpose, 530.
-ινος, Adj. in, 352, 3, 4, Obs.
-ιο, Genit. Ending, 128, D.
-ιον, Neut. in, 347, 1.
-ιος, Adj. in, 350.
-ιον, 323, D. 33.
ἰπός, 35, D. 1.
-ις, Nom. of Fem. in, 138; 172—Barytones in Acc. Sing., 156.
ἴσκε, 324, D. 36.
-ισκος, -ισκη, Subs. in, 347, 2.
ἴσος, Compar., 195—with Dat., 436 b.

GREEK INDEX. 389

-ιστερος.
-ιστερος, -ιστατος, Compar., 197.
ἴστημι, Perf., 317, 4—Meaning, 329,1—of the Perf.,503.
ἰσχύω, Diff. of Pres. and Aor., 498.
ἰχθύς, Dat. Sing., 158, D.—Acc. Pl., 158—Masc., 140.
ἰχώρ, Acc. Sing., 175, D.
-ιων, Nom. of Masc. in, 348, Obs.
-ιων, -ιστος, Compar., 198.

κ, in οὐκ, 69, Obs. 1—New-Ion. for π, 216, D—Asp. in the Perfect, 279. See also Gutturals.
-κα, 1 Aor. in, 310.
καθεδοῦμαι, 326, 21.
καθεύδω, 326, 18—Augm., 240.
κάθημαι, 315, 2—Augm., 240.
καθίζω, Fut., etc., 326, 21—Augm., 240.
καί, 624 b—Crasis, 65—with Numbers, 222—with Part., 587, 5—καί ὅς, καί τόν, 369, 2—καί δέ, 624, 3—καί-καί, 624, 2, 3—καὶ δ᾽) καί, 624, 4 —καὶ εἰ, 640, 2—καὶ τότε δή, 642, 4 a.
καίνυμαι, 319, D. 33.
καίπερ, with Part., 587, 5.
καίτοι, 630, 6; 94.
καίω, 35, Obs.; 253, Obs.—Future, 260, 2—1 Aorist, 269, D.
κακὸν λέγω, κακῶς ποιέω, with Acc., 402; 396.
κακός, Compar., 199, 2.
καλέω, 301, 3.
καλός, Compar., 199, 6.
κάμνω, 321, 9—Perfect, 282—with Acc., 400 b — with Part., 590.
κάνεον, κανοῦν, 131, 3.
κάρα, 177, D. 22.
καρτερέω, with Part., 590.
κατά, 448; 459—Apocope, 64, D. — with Inf. and Art., 574, 2.
καταπλήττομαι, with Acc., 399.
κατηγορέω, Augm., 239.
κάτω, Compar., 204.
κεῖαι, etc., 269, D.
κεῖμαι, 314, 2.
κεῖνος, see ἐκεῖνος.
κείρω, Fut., 262, D.
κέκασμαι, 320, D. 33.
κέκλημαι, Meaning, 503.
κέκτημαι, 274, Ex. — Moods, 289—Meaning, 503.
κελαδέω. 325, D. c.
κελεύω, Perf., 288.
κέλλω, Fut., 266, Ex.
κέλομαι, Aor., 257, D.
κε(ν), 68, D.—Enclit., 92, 5. See ἄν.
κεντέω, 325, D. f.

κυνέω.
κεράννυμι, 319, 1—Sub. Mid., 312, D. 16.
κερδαίνω, Aor., 270, Obs.—Perf., 322, Obs.
κέσκετο, 337, D.
κῆαι, etc., 269, D.
κήδω, 326, D. 41.
κῆρυξ, 83, Obs. 1; 145.
κικλήσκω, 324, D. 31.
κίνυμαι, 319, D. 34.
κίρνημι, 312, D. b.
κιχάνω, 321, 18.
κιχημι, 313, D. 6; 322, 18.
κίχρημι, 312, 7.
κιών, etc., 319, D. 34.
κλάζω, 251, Obs.—Meaning of the Perf. Act., 276, D.
κλαίω, 253, Obs.; 326, 22—Fut., 260, 2.
κλάω, 301, 1.
κλείς, Acc., 156.
κλείω, κλήω, Perf. Mid., 288.
κλέπτης, Compar., 197.
κλέπτω, Perfect, 279—Aorist Pass., 295.
-κλ ̆ς, Proper Names in, 167; 174.
κλίνω, Perf., 282.
κλύω, Aor., 316, D. 27.
κνάω, Contr., 244, 2.
κνίσση, 115, D. 2.
κοινός, κοινωνέω, with Genit., 414, 1; 419 a—with Dat., 436 a, b.
κοῖος, κόσος, etc., 216, D.
κολακεύω, with Acc., 396.
κόπτω and compounds, Meaning, 476, 2.
κορέννυμι, 319, 6.
κορέω, Aor., 270, D.
κόρη, κόρρη, 115.
κορύσσω, 250, D. — Perfect, 236, D.
-κύς, Adj. in, 351.
κοτέω, Aor., 301, D. — Perf. Part., 277, D.
κράζω, 251—Perf., 317, 8.
κρατέω, with Geuit., 423.
κρᾶτός, etc., see κάρα.
κρατύς, Positive, 199, D. 1.
κρείσσων, κράτιστος, 199, 1, Obs.
κρεμάννυμι, κρέμαμαι, 319, 2: 312, 12—Acc. of Sub. and Opt., 309.
κρεμόω, 319, D. 2.
κρέσσων, 199, D. 1.
κρήμναμαι, 312, D. c.
κρίνω, 253, Obs.—Perf., 282; 286, Obs.
κρούω, Perf. Mid., 288.
κρύπτω, with double Acc.,402.
κτείνω, Aor., 316, 4.
κτίννυμι, 319, 17.
κτυπέω, 325, D. g.
κυίσκω, 324, 21.
κυκεών, Acc. Sing., 171, D.
κυλίω, Perf. Mid., 288.
κυνέω, 323, 34.

μακράν.
κύντερος, 199, D.
κυρέω, κύρω, 325, 4—Future, 262, Ex.—with Part., 590.
κύσαι, κύσσα, 323, D. 34.
κύων, 177, 8.
κωλύω, with Inf., 560, 3.

λ doubled after the Syll.
Augm., 234, D. — Character, 252.
λ, μ, ν, ρ, Metathesis, 59 — Position, 77, f. and D.—
Redupl., 274, 2 — Fut. of Stems in, 262—Aor., 270—
Perf., 280.
λ,ν,ρ,Monos. Stems in, Perf., 282—Aor. Pass., 298.
λαγχάνω, 322, 27—with Genit. and Acc., 419, Obs.
λαγώς, 174.
λήθρα, with Genit., 415.
λᾶλος, Compar.,197.
λαμβάνω, 322, 25—Perf., 274, Ex.—with Genit., 419 b—Meaning, 480.
λάμψομαι, 322, D. 25.
λανθάνω, 322, 26—with Acc., 398—with Part., 550.
λᾶς, 177, 9.
λάσκω, 324, 29, and Obs.
λέγομαι, construed personally, 571.
λέγω (collect), Perf., 279—2 Aor. M., 316, D. 35.
λείπομαι, with Genit., 423.
λέκτο, λέγμενος, etc., 316, D. 36; 268, D.
λέλημκα, 324, 29.
λέλογχα, 322, D. 27.
λεύω, Perf. Mid., 288.
λήθω, 322, 26.
λήκομαι, 322, D. 29.
λήξομαι, 322, 27.
λήψομαι, 322, 25.
λι bec. λλ, 56 ; 252.
λίσσομαι, 250, D.
λλ, Pres. Stems in, 252.
λέε, 244, D. 4.
λόεσσα, 269, D.
τὸ λοιπόν, 405, Obs. 2.
λοῖσθος, λοίσθιος, 199, D.
-λος, Adj. in, 352, Obs.
λούω, Constr., 244, 4—1 Aor.;
λυποῦμαι, with Dat., 439,Obs.
λύω, 301, 2—Perf. Opt. Mid., 289, D.—Aor., 316, D. 28—with Genit., 419 e.
λωΐων, λῷστος, 199, 1.

μ bef. ρ, 51, Obs. 2—bef. λ bec. β, 51, D.—Change of preceding Cons., 47; 286, 1—doubled after the Syll.
Augm.; 284, D.
μά, 648, 16.
-μα, Nom. of Neuters, 343, 1; 139.
μακράν, 405, Obs. 2.

GREEK INDEX.

μάλα, μᾶλλον, μάλιστα, 202—
μάλιστα δή, 642 a.
μάν, see μήν.
μανθάνω, 322, 28—with Part.,
 591.
μάντις, of both Genders, 140.
μάρναμαι, Imper., 312, D. d.
μαρτυρέω, 325, 5.
μάρτυς, 177, 10.
μάσσων, μήκιστος, 198, D.
μαστιζώ, 251, Obs.—Future,
 260, 3.
μάστιξ, 177, D. 23.
μάχομαι, μαχέομαι, 326, 23,
 aud D.—with Dat., 436 a.
μέγας, 191 — Compar., 198—
 μέγα, 401.
μέδομαι, 326, D. 42.
μεθύσκω, 324, 22.
μείρομαι, Perf., 274, D.
μεις, 177, D. 24.
μείων, see μικρός—μεῖον without ή, 626, Obs.
μέλας, 186.
μέλει, 326, 24—with Genit.,
 420.
μέλλω, 326, 25—Augm , 234,
 Obs.—as Fut.,501—πῶς, τι
 οὐ μέλλω, 501, Obs. 2.
μέματον, etc., 217, D. 9.
μέμβλεται, etc., 326, D. 24.
μέμβλωκα, 51, D.; 282, D.;
 324, D. 12.
μεμετιμένος, 313, D. 1.
μέμνημαι,274,Ex.—Sub.Opt.,
 289, D.—Meaning, 503—
 with Part., 591.
μέν, comp. μέν—μέν- δέ, 628—
 μέν οὖν, 637, 2.
-μεν, 1 Pers. Dual and Plural
 Act., 226.
-μεναι, -μεν, Inf. Act., 233,
 D. 3 ; 255, D.—Aor. Pass.,
 293, D.— in Verbs in μι,
 302, D.
μέντοι, 630, 5.
μένω, 326, 26.
μεσημβρία, 51, Obs. 2.
μέσος, Compar., 195—Meaning, 301.
μεστος, with Genit., 414, 2.
μετά, 448 ; 464—Adverb, 446.
μεταδίδωμι, μεταλαμβάνω,
 with Genit., 419 a.
μεταμέλομαι, Dep. Pass., 328,
 2—with Part., 592.
μεταξύ,445; 448; 455, 7—with
 Part., 587, 2.
μεταπέμπομαι, Pass. mean.,
 483, 3—Indir. Mid., 479.
μετέχω, μέτοχος, with Genit.,
 419 a, aud Obs. : 414, 5.
μέχρι(ς), 69, Observ. 3 : 445 ;
 448; 455, 6 ; 556—without
 Elision, 64, Obs. 1.
μή, Synizesis, 66—Neg., 612,
 etc.—in sentences of purpose, 530—with Verbs of
 prohibiting.518: 510—with

νέατος.
Verbs of fearing,512 ; 533 ;
 616, Obs. 3—with Future
 and Perf. Ind., 533, Obs.—
 with Hypoth. Part., 583—
 in questions,608—"whether perchance," 610—μὴ οὐ,
 621 ; 512 ; 533 — μὴ ὅτι,
 622, 4.
μηδείς, μήπω, etc., see οὐδείς,
 οὔπω, etc.
μηκάομαι, 325, D. o.
μήν, 643, 12.
μήτηρ, 150, 153.
-μι, 1 Pers. Sing. Act., 226 ;
 302, 1 — Subj., 233, D. 1 ;
 255, D.
μίγνυμι, 319, 18.
μικρός, Compar., 199, 3.
μιμέομαι, Meaning, 328, 4—
 with Acc., 398.
μιμνήσκω, 274, Ex.; 324, 6—
 μιμνήσκομαι, with Genit.,
 420.
μίν, 205. D.
Μίνως, Acc. Sing., 163, D.;
 174, D.
μίσγω,327, 7—Aor. Mid., 316,
 D. 37.
μν, in divis. of Syll., 72,1.
μνᾶ, Genit. Sing., 116 c.
μνημῶν, with Genit., 414, 3.
μολοῦμαι, 324, 12.
μόνον οὐ, οὐχί, 622, 5.
μονοφάγος, comp , 197.
-μος, Masc. in, 342, 2—Adj.
 in, 352, Obs.
μύζω, 326, 27.
μυκάομαι, 325, D. p.
μῦς, Masc., 140.

ν, before σ (and ζ) dropped,
 49 ; 147, 1 ; 149 ; 187—bef.
 other Conson., 51—bec. γ,
 51 ; 282—Present Stems in,
 253 — dropped in Perfect
 Stems. 282 ; 286, 1, Obs.—
 298, D.—affixed to Verb.-
 Stem, 321—doubled after
 the Syll. Augm., 234, D.—
 doubled in the Pres. Stem,
 318, 3—movable, 68. .
-ν, in the Acc. Sing.; 134, 4 ;
 141 ; 155, etc. ; 173, 3—in
 Neuters,125—1 Pers. Sing.
 in Hist. Tenses Act., 226—
 3 Pl. in Hist. Tenses, 226 ;
 302, D.
-να, affixed to Verb.-Stems,
 312, D.
-ναι, Inf., 302, 6 ; 333, 1.
ναί, 643, 14.
ναιετάω, Contr., 243, D. 1.
ναῦς, 177, 11.
νδ, νθ, ντ, dropped before σ,
 50—147, 1 ; 149.
-νε, affixed to Verb.-Stems,
 323.
νέατος. 200.

οἴκαδε.
νέμω, 326, 28.
νέω, 248—Fut., 260, 2.
νή, 643, 15.
νίζω, 251, Obs.
νικάω 'Ολύμπια, 400 c—Meaning, 486, Obs.
νίν, 205, D.
.πο-, δια-, ἐν-, προ- νοέομαι,
 Dep. Pass., 328, 2.
νομίζω, with Genitive, 417—
 with Inf., 569.
-νος, Adj. in, 352, Obs.
νοσέω,Diff. of Pres. and Aor.,
 498.
νόσος, Fem., 127, 5.
-ντι, 3 Plnr. of Princ. Tenses
 Act., 226.
-ντων, 3 Pl. Imper. Act., 228.
-νυ affixed to Verb.-Stems,
 304, 2 ; 318, 1.
νύμφα, Voc. Sing., 117, D. 3.
νύ(ν), 68, D.—Enclit., 92, 5—
 Diff. of νύν and νῦν, 99 ; 637,
 3—νῦν δή, 642, 4 c.
νωίτερος, 208; D.

ξ, 34 ; 48 ; 260.
-ξ, Masc. and Fem. in, 172.
ξέω, 301, 11.
ξυρέω, 325, 6.
ξύω, Perf. Mid., 288.

o, bec. ου, 24, D. 3 ; 42 ; 147, 1 ;
 bec. οι, 24, D. 3—bec. ω, 40 ;
 147, 2 ; 151 ; 193 ; 233, 4—
 bec. ε, 24, D. c—dropped
 after αι, 194—for α, 268, D. ;
 354—Conn.Vowel,178 ; 233,
 1 : 354.
-o, Genit. Ending, 122, Obs. ;
 128 ; 131, D.
ὅ, for ὅς, 213, D.—Neut. for
 ὅτι, 633, 1—Crasis, 65.
ὁ μέν—ὁ δέ,369,1—τὸν καὶ τόν,
 369, 2. See τό.
oa bec. ω, 37—bec. α, 183.
ὅδε, 212 ; 475. See also Demonst. Pron.
ὁδύρεσθαι, with Acc., 400 c.
ὅδωδα, 275, D. 1.
οε bec. ου, 37.
οει bec. οι or ου, 37 ; 243, Obs.
-οεις, Adj. in, 359, 2, Obs.
ὄζω, 326, 29—Perf. 275, D. 1.
ἔθι, πόθι, τόθι, 217, D.
οθούνεκα, 636, 3.
οι from ι, 40—bec. ω, 235.
-οι.dropped, 64, D.—Short in
 regard to Acc., 83, Obs. 2 ;
 108—Voc; ending, 163.
ὁ γνυμι, 319, 16.
οἶδα, 317, 6—with Part., 591.
-οιεν, Genit. and Dat. Dual,
 128, D. ; 141, D.
οἴκαδε. 94 ; 178.

GREEK INDEX. 301

οἰκεῖος.
οἰκεῖος, with Genit., 414, 1—
 with Dat., 436 b.
οἴκοι, 179.
ὀ κτρός, Compar., 198.
οἴμαι, 244.
οἰμωϊζω, 251, Obs.—Fut., 260, 3
 —Mean. of Fut. Mid., 266.
-οιν, ending of Genitive and
 Dative Dual, 141; 173, 4.
ο.νοχοέω, Augm., 237, D.
-οιο, in the Genit., 128, D.—
 2 Pers. Sing. Opt. Mid.,
 233, 5.
οἶο, 213, D.
οἴομαι,οἴομαι,326,30—2Pers.
 Sing. Pres., 233, 3—Dep.
 Pass., 328, 2.
οἷος, Attr. and Article, 600—
 with Inf., 601—ο᾽όστε, 94
 —οἷον, οἷα δή, with Part.,
 587, 6.
οἷς, 160.
οἶσε, 268, D.—οἴσει, 327, 12.
-οισι(ν), Dat. Pl., 128, D.
ο σω, etc., 327, 12.
οἴχομαι, οἰχνέω, 326, 31, and
 D.—Meaning, 486, Obs.—
 with Part., 590.
ὀλέκω, 319, D. 20.
ὀλίγος, Compar., 199, 4.
ὀλιγωρέω, with Genit., 420.
ὀλισθάνω, 322, 20.
ὄλλυμι, 319, 20—Meaning of
 Perf., 329, 9; 503 — Iterative, 337, D.
ἷλος, Position, 390.
'Ολύμπια, 400 c.
ὁμιλέω, with Dat., 436 a.
ὄμνυμι, 319, 21 — with the
 Acc., 399.
ὅμοιος, ὁμοιόομαι, ὁμολογέω,
 ὁμοῦ, etc., with Dat., 436 a,
 b, c.
ὁμολογέομαι, constr. personally, 571.
ὑμόργνυμι, 319, 22.
ὀμώνυμος, with Dat., 436 b.
ὅμως,630,7—after Participle,
 587, 5.
-ον, Num. of Neuters, 172.
ὄνειρος, 175.
ὀνίνημι, 312, 2—Acc. of Aor.
 Sub. and Opt. Mid., 309—
 with Accus., 396.
ὄνομαι, 314, D.
ὀξύνω, Perf. Mid., 286, Obs.
οο bec. ου, 36; 130.
-οος, Adj. in, 183.
ὅου, 213, D.
ὁπηνίκα, 634, 3.
ὄπισθεν, with Genit., 415.
ὁπότε, ὁπόταν, 556 ; 634, 1—
 "as often as," 558, Obs. 1.
ὅπωπα, 275, D. 1.
ὅπως, 632, 3—in sentences of
 purpose, 530—with ἄν, 531
 b, Obs.—with Future Ind.,
 500; 553 — in Challenges
 and Warnings, 553, Obs.—

οὐξ.
ὅπως μή, with Verbs of
 Fearing, 533, Obs.
ὁράω,327, 8—Double Augm.,
 237—Perf., 327, 8; 275, D. 1
 —with Part., 591.
ὀργαίνω, Aor., 270, Obs.
ὀρέγνυμι, 319, D. 36.
ὀρέγομαι, with Genit., 419 c.
ὀρέοντο, 320, D. 37.
ὄρνις,177, 12—Acc. Sing.,156.
ὄρνυμι, 319, D. 37—2 Aorist
 Mid., 316, D. 38.
ὄρονται, 327, D. 8.
ὀρόω, 243, D. 3 a.
ὄρσεο, 268, D.
ὀρύσσω, Perf., 275, 1.
ὤρωρα, 320, D. 37.
-ος, Neuters in, 243, 2, and
 Obs. ; 139 ; 172—Ending of
 Genit., 141 ; 157, D. ; 173,
 8, 1.
ὅς, Relative, 213—Demonst.,
 212, D. ; 213, Obs., and D.—
 for the Possess. of 1 and 2
 Pers., 471, Obs. c.; 208, D.
ὅσος, Attr., 600—ὅσον, 601—
 ὅσον οὐ, 622, 5.
ὁσσάτιος, 216, D.
ὅσσε, 177, D. 25.
ἔστις, 94—214, Obs. 2—ἧστις
 and ὁστισοῦν, Mean., 600.
ὀσφραίνομαι, 322, 21, and Obs.
ὅτε, ὅταν, 556; 634, 1—with
 Aor. Ind., 493—"as often
 as," 558, Obs. 1.
ὅτι and ὅ τι, 214, Obs. 2.
ὅτι, 633, 1—without Elision,
 64, Obs. 1—in Dependent
 Declarative Sentences, 525
 —ὅτι μή, 633, 1 b.
ὅτιη, 218.
ὅτις, 214, D.
ου from ο. See ο.
-ου, Genitive ending, 122, 2 ;
 128 ; 134, 2—Conn. Vowel,
 233, 1—2 Pers. Sing. Imper.
 and Perf. Mid., 233, 5.
οὐ, οὐκ, οὐχ, 69, Obs. 1; 52, D.
 —Atonous, 97, 4; 612, etc.
 —with Prohibitives, 499,
 Obs.—in questions,608—οὐ
 γάρ, οὐ γὰρ ἀλλά, 596, 6 d.
 —οὐ δῆτα, 642, 6—οὐκ ἄρα,
 637, 1—οὐ μή, 620—οὐ μήν
 (μέντοι) ἀλλά, 622, 6 — οὐ
 μόνον-ἀλλὰ καί, 624, 6.
οὔ, οἵ, ἕ, etc., Meaning, 471,
 Obs. 5.
οὐδέ, 625, 1.
οὐδείς, 221—Attr., 602—οὐδέν,
 622, 1.
οὐκέτι, 622, 2.
οὐκοῦν and οὔκουν, Diff. 99 ;
 637, 2.
οὐλόμενος, 319, D. 20.
οὖν, 637, 2—Affixed, 218.
-οῦν, Acc. Sing., 163, D.
οὕνεκα, 636, 3.
οὐξ, 65, D.

πάσχω.
οὔπω, 622, 2.
οὐρέω, Augment, 237.
-ους, Adj. in, 183 ; 352, 4—
 Nom. of Subs., 172.
οὖς, 177, 13 ; 142, 3—Neut.,
 140.
οὐτάω,Aor., 316, 20, D.
οὔτε,94—οὔτε-οὔτε,οὔτε-οὐδέ,
 625, 2, and Obs.
οὔτι, 622, 1.
οὔτοι, 648, 10.
οὗτος,212 ; 475 ;—in addressing, 393—οἱτοσί, 212.
οὕτω(ς),69,Obs.3—withPart.,
 587, 4.
οὐχί, 97, Obs.
οὐχ ὅτι, οὐχ ὅπως, 622, 3, 4.
ὀφείλω and ὀφέλλω,D.ff.,253,
 Obs.
ὀφείλω, 326, 32.
ὀφέλλω, 1 Aor., 270, D.
ὀφλισκάνω, 322, 22.
ὄφρα, 556 ; 635, 10. —See ἵνα.
ὀφρύς, Acc. Pl., 158.
ὄχος, Pl., 174, D.
ὄχωκα, 327, D. 6.
ὄψιος, Comp., 195.
ὄψομαι, 327, S.
ὀψοφάγος, Compar., 197.
-οω, Length. in Contr. Verb,
 243, D. A. 3—Attic Fut.,
 263, D.—Verbs in, 353, 1,
 and Obs. 1.

π, doubled, 217, D. (62, D.)—
 Aspir. in Perf., 279.
πα ς, Genit., Plur. and Dual,
 142, 3—Voc. Sing., 148—of
 two Genders, 140.
παίω, Perf. Mid., 288.
παλαιός, Compar., 194.
πάλιν, in Compos. before σ,
 49, Obs. 1.
πάλλω, Aor. 257, D.—2 Aor.
 Mid., 316, D. 40.
πᾶν, 142, b—in Compos. before σ, 49, Obs. 1.
παντάπασι(ν); 68, 3.
παρά, παραί; πάρ, 448, III. ;
 465—Apoc., 64, D.
πάρα, 90.
παρανομέω,irreg. Augm.,239.
παραπλήσιος, with Dat., 436
 b—Compar., 195.
παρατίθεμαι, 481.
παρέχω,with Genit.,419 e.
παρέχω and παρέχομαι, 480.
παρέχω, with Inf., 561.
παροινέω, double Aug., 240.
παρόν, 586.
πάρος, 625 ; 635, 12.
παρρησιάζομαι, Augm., 239.
πᾶς, Genit. and Dat. Accent.,
 142, 2—meaning with and
 without Art., 390, and Obs.
πάσκω, 250, Obs.—Fut. 260, 3.
πάσσων, 198, D.
πάσχω, 327, 9—Perf., 317, D.
 14.

GREEK INDEX.

πατέομαι.	πράττω.	σ.
πατέομαι, 325, 7.	πιπράσκω, 324, 7.	πράττομαι, with double
πατήρ, 153.	πίπτω, 327, 15 — Perf. Part.,	Acc., 402.
παύομαι, Aorist, 298 — with	317, D. 17.	πρέσβυς, 177, 15.
Genit., 419 e — with Part.	πίσυρες, 220, D. 4.	πρήθω, 312, 4.
mean., 590.	πιτνέω, 323, 35.	πρίαμαι, 2 Aorist, 316, 8 —
πείθω, Aorist, 257, D.—Perf.,	πίτνημι, 312, D. g.	Accent. of Aor. Sub. Opt.,
317, D. 15—Fut. and Aor.	πιφαύσκω, 324, D. 32.	309.
Part., 326, D. 43 — Mean-	πίων, Compar., 196 a.	πρίν, 556 ; 635, 11—with Inf.,
ing, 330, 3 ; 503.	πλάζω, 251, Obs.	565, and Obs. 1, 2.
πεινάω, Contr., 244, 2.	πλάσσω, 250, Obs.—Future,	πρίω, Perf. Mid., 288.
πείσομαι, 327, 9.	260, 3.	πρό, 448, B ; 454 — Crasis, 65
πελάζω, 1 Aor. Imper., 268, D.	πλείων, πλεῖστος, 199, 5 —	—with Augm., in Compos.,
πέλεκυς, Masc., 140 ; 157.	πλέον, without ἤ, 626, Obs.	238 — with Inf. and Art.,
πέμπω, Perf., 279.	—πλεῦν, 199, D. 5.	574, 3—πρὸ τοῦ, 369, 3.
πένης, Compar., 192 — with	πλέκω, Aor. Pass., 295.	πρός (ποτί, προτί), 448, III ;
Genit., 414, 2.	πλέω, 248—Fut., 260, 2 ; 264	467—Adv., 446—with Inf.
πέποιθα, 317, D. 15.	—Perf. Mid., 288.	and Art., 574, 2, 4.
πέπονθα, 317, D. 14.	πλέως, 184 — with Genitive,	πρόσθεν, πρόσω, with Genit.,
πέπραγα and πέπραχα, Diff.,	414, 2.	415.
330.	πλίθω, 312, 3 — with Genit.,	προσ.κον, 586.
πέπρωται, 285, D.	418.	πρόσωπον, Nom. Acc. Plur.,
πέπταμαι, 274, Ex.	πλήν, 445 ; 455, 9.	175, D.
πέπτωκα, 274, Ex. ; 327, 15.	πλήρης, πληρόω, with Genit.,	πρότερος, πρῶτος, 200.
πέπωκα, 327, 10.	414, 2 ; 418.	προῦργου, Compar., 195.
πέπων, Compar., 196 a.	πλησίον, Compar., 195—with	πρώϊος, Compar., 195.
πέρ, 641, 3 —Enclit., 92, 5 —	Genit., 415.	πτήσσω, 316, D. 21.
Affix, 218.	πλήσσω, 2 Aorist and Future	πτίσσω, 250, Obs. — Future,
πέρα, with Genit., 415—Com-	Pass., 205.	260, 3.
par., 200.	πλῆτο, 316, D. 22.	πτύω, 301, 1. .
πέρδω, 326, 33.	-πλοῦς, in Multiplicat., 223.	πτωχός, Compar., 197.
πέρθω, 2 Aor., 257, D. ; 59, D.	πλούσιος, with Genit., 414, 2.	πυθέσθαι, 322, 20.
—Aor. Inf. Mid., 316, D. 41.	πλύνω, Perf., 282.	Πυκνός, 177, 14.
περί, 448, III. ; 466—without	πλώω, Aor., 316, D. 24.	πύματος, 190, D. (Defect.).
Elision, 64, Obs. 1—Anastr.,	πνέω, 248 — Fut., 260, 2 ; 264	πυνθάνομαι, 322, 29 — with
446 — Adverb, ibid. — with	—Perf., 285, D. — with Acc.,	Genit., 420.
Augm., 238.	400 c.	πῦρ, 142 b ; 151 ; 175 ; Neut.,
περιβάλλομαι, with double	Πνύξ, 177, 14.	140.
Acc., 402.	ποδός, see πούς.	πώ, πώ(ς), Encl., 92, 4.
περιγίγνομαι, περίειμι, with	πόθεν, Eucl., 92, 4.	πῶς, with Genit., 415 — πῶς
Genit., 423.	ποθέω, 301, 4.	γὰρ οὔ, 636, 6 d.
πέρνημι, Part., 312, D. e.	ποθί, see πού.	
πέρυσι(ν), 68, 3.	ποί, Encl., 92, 4.	ρ, doubled, 62 — after the
πεσεῖν, 327, 15.	ποιέω and ποιέομαι, 480 —	Augm., 234—after Redupl.,
πέσσω, 250, Obs.	with Genit., 417.	274, 4—Metathesis, 59—in
πετάννυμι, 319, 3. .	πόλις, 157, D.—Gender, 138 b	2 Aor., 257, D.—ῥ, ρρ, 13.
Πετεώς, Genit. Sing., 131, D.	—Compos., 189, 3.	ῥά, Eucl., 92, 5.—See ἄρα.
πέτομαι, 326, 34—2 Aor., 61 c;	πολιτεύω and πολιτεύομαι,	ῥάβδος, Fem., 127, 5.
257, D. ; 316, 5.	480, Obs.	ῥᾴδιος, Compar., 199, 7.
πείθομαι, 322, 29.	πολλάκι(ς), 69, Obs. 3 ; 224.	ῥαίνω, Plup., 287, D.
πέφνον, 257, D.	πολύς, 191 — Compar., 199, 5	ῥέζω, 327, 3.
πεφυζότες, 277, D.	—πολύ, 404, Obs.—πολλῷ,	ῥερυπωμένος, 274, D.
πῆ, Enclit., 92, 4.	with Compos., 440.	ῥέω, 248 ; 326; 35—Fut., 260, 2.
πήγνυμι, 319, 23 — 2 Aorist	πονέω, 301, 4.	ῥήγνυμι, 319, 24 ; 278—Mean-
Mid., 316, D. 39—Meaning,	πόρρω, with Genit., 415.	ing, 330, 5.
330, 4.	Ποσειδῶν, Acc. Sing., 171 —	ῥηθήσομαι, etc., 327, 14.
πηνίκα, with Genit., 415.	Voc., 148, Obs.	ῥιγέω, 325, D. ἴ.
πῖ, χυς, Masc., 140 ; 154.	ποτέ, Encl., 92, 4.	ῥίγιον, 199, D.
πιεζέω, πιέζω, 325, D. h.	πότερον ἤ, 611 — in Depend.	ῥιγόω, Contr., 244, 3.
πίθι, 316, 15.	Interr. Sentences, 625.	ῥίπτω, ῥίπτω, 325, 8.
πιλναμαι, Aor., 312, D. f.	ποτί, see πρός.	ῥύσθαι, etc., 314, D.
πίμπληβι, 312, 3—with Gen-	ποῦ, with Genitive, 415.	ῥώννυμι, 319, 10.
itive, 418.	πού (ποθί), Encl., 92, 4.	
πίμπρημι, 312, 4. .	πουλύς, Fem., 185, D.	σ, 2 ; 33 c—effect on preced-
πίνω, 321, 4 ; 327, 10—Future,	πούς, 147, 1 ; Ex. —	ing Vowel and Cons., 46,
265—Aor., 321, 4 ; 316, 15—	Dat. Plur., 49, D. ; 141, D. ;	etc. ; 260, etc. ; 286—Com-
Meaning, 329, 7—with Gen-	149, D.—in Compos., 160—	bin., 48—Assim. to ρ, 50 b
itive, 419 d, and Obs.	Masc., 140.	—to λ, μ, ν, ρ, 270, D.—bec.
πίομαι, 265 ; 327, 10.	πρᾶος, 191.	Spir. Asp., 60 b ; 308 ; 327,
πίπισκω, 324, 20.	πράττω, Meaning, 476, 1 —	5. Obs.—from τ, see τ.

GREEK INDEX. 3J3

σ, dropped, 61 a, b—in Sigma Stems,166—in Pres.Stems, 233, 3, 4, 5—in the Future, 262, Obs., etc. — in the 1 Aor., 268 ; 269, D. ; 270 — in the 2 Aor. Mid., 307—in the Perf. and Plup. Mid., 284, D.
σ, inserted in the Perf., 288 —in the Weak Pass. Stem, 298—in the Verb. Adj., 300 —in Deriv., 340, Obs. 2—in Compos., 358, 2.
σ, doubled in the Dat. Plur., 158, D.—in the Fut., 261, D.—in the 1 Aor., 269, D.— after Syl. Augm., 234, D.
ς, dropped, 69, Observ. 3—in Compar., 204.
ς, ending of Nom. Sing., 173, 1 ; 113 ; 122, 1 ; 134, 1 ; 141 ; 145 ; 147, 1 ; 155 ; 160 — wanting, 122, D. 1 ; 147, 2 ; 151 ; 163.
ς, ending of Dat. Plur., 119 ; 134, 8—of Acc. Pl., 134, 10 ; 173, 7—of 2 Person Sing. in Hist. Tenses Act., 226 —Nom. of Fem., 348 ; 349, Obs.
-σα, Fem. ending, 187.
σαλπίζω, 251, Obs.
-σαν, 3 Pl. in Preter., 302, 7.
Σαρπηδών, 174, D.
σβέννυμι, 319, 7—2 Aor., 316, 9 ; 318, 5—Meaning, 329, 5.
-σε, Local Suffix, 178.
σεαυτοῦ, 210—Poss., 472 a.
σέβομαι, Dep. Pass., 328, 2.
-σείω, Verbs in, 353, Obs. 2.
σείω, Perf. Mid., 288.
σεύω, 248, D.—1 Aor., 269, D. —Perf. Mid., 274, D., 285, D.—2 Aor., 316, D. 30.
σήπω, Mean. of Perf., 330, 6.
σῆς, Gen., Pl. and Du., 142, 3.
σθ, after Cons., 61 a ; 286, 4.
-σθαι, in the 2 Pers. Sing. Sub. and Opt., 233, D. 1 ; 255, D. 1—Ind., 302, D.—in the 1 Person Plur. Pres. Mid., 233, D. 5.
-σθε, 2 Pers. Plural, Imper. Mid., 228.
-σθον, 1 Pers. Du. Pres. Mid., 233, D. 5 — 3 Person Dual Imperf., 233, D. 7—2 Pers. Du. Imper. Mid., 228.
-σθω, -σθων, -σθωσαν, 3 Pers. Sing. Du. Pl. Imper. Mid., 228.
-σι, 2 Pers. Sing. of Princ. Tenses Act., 226 ; 302, 2.
-σι(ν), Dat. Plur., 68, 1 ; 119 ; 134, 8 ; 141 ; 160 ; 173, 6 — 3 Pers. Sing. Pres. Subj., 233, D. 1 ; 255, D. 1—Local ending, 179 ; 68, 2—3 Pers. Plur. and Sing., 68, 5.

σφέ.

-σια, -σις, Fem. in, 342, 1.
σιγάω, Diff. of Pres. and Aor., 498 — Mean. of Fut. Mid., 266.
-σιμος, Adj. in, 352, Obs.
σιωπάω, Meaning of Fut. Mid., 266.
σκ, in forming Inchoatives, 324—Iteratives, 334, D., etc.
σκεδάννυμι, 319, 4.
σκέλλω, Aor., 316, 10—Meaning, 329, 6.
σκίδνημι, 312, D. h; 319, 4.
σκοπέω and ἐομαι, 480.
σκότος, 174.
Σκύλλη, 115, D. 2.
σκώρ, 176.
σμάω, Contr., 244, 2.
-σο, 2 Person Sing. Imper. Mid., 228.
σπάω, 301, 1—Perf. Mid., 288.
σπένδω, Fut., 260, 1 — Perf. Mid., 286, Obs.
σπέος, 166, D.
σπέσθαι, etc., 327, 5.
σπεύδω, with Inf., 560, 3.
σπουδάζω, Meaning of Fut. Mid., 266.
σσ, 57 ; 250.
-σσω, Verbs in, 250—Future, 260, 3.
-στα, 307.
στάζω, 251, Obs.—Fut., 260, 3.
στάχυς, Masc., 140.
στείβω, 326, 36.
στέλλω, Perf., 282 — Aorist Pass., 295.
στενάζω, 251, Obs.—Future, 260, 3.
στενωπός, Masc., 127, 2.
στέργω, with Dat., 439, Obs.
στερίσκω. 324, 26—with Genitive, 419 c.
στίζω, 251, Obs.—Fut., 260, 3.
στοά, 115 (Ex.).
στορέννυμι, 319, 8.
στόρνυμι, 319, 25.
στοχάζομαι, with Genitive, 419 c.
στρέφω, Perf., 285—Meaning of Aor. Pass., 328, 3.
στρώννυμι, 319, 11.
στυγέω, 325, D. k.
συμβαίνω, Constr.· personally, 571.
συμφωνέω, συνᾴδω, with Dat., 436 a.
σύν, ξύν, in Compos. bef. σ and ζ, 49, Obs. 1—in Distributives, 223.
-συνη, Fem., 346, 2.
σύνοιδά μοι, with Part., 591, Obs.
συνώνυμος, with Dat., 436 b.
σῦς, 142 b—of two Genders, 140.
σφάλλομαι, with Gen., 419, e.
σφέ, 205, D.—σφέτερος, 472 b —σφός, 208, D.

σφήξ, Masc., 140.
σχεθέειν, 338, D.
σχές, etc., 316, 11 ; 327, 6.
σχολαῖος, Compar., 194.
σώζω, 1 Aor. Pass., 298.
Σωκράτης, 174.
σῶς, 184.
σωτήρ, Voc. Sing., 152.

τ, Pronunt., 4 — bec. θ, 54 — becomes σ, 60 a ; 67 ; 187— dropped, 147, 2 ; 169 — in the Perfect, 281—changes before, 286, 3 — affixed to Verb. Stem, 249—movable, 169, D.
τάν, Defect., 177, 16.
τάννυμαι, 319, D. 38.
τάχα, 212—τήν ταχίστην, 405, Obs. 2.
ταχύς, Compar. θάσσων, 54 b; 198.
-τε, 2 Pers. Plur. Act., 226— 2 Plur. Imper. Act., 228.
-τέ, 624 b — Enclit., 92, 5 — Affix, 94 ; 624, 5 — τέ-καί, τέ-δέ, 624, 2, and Obs.
τεθνήξω, 291.
τείν, 205, D.,
τείνω, Perfect, 282—1 Aorist Pass., 298.
-τειρα, Fem., 341, 2.
τεκμήριον δέ, 636, 6 b.
τελέω, 301, 1—Perf. Mid., 288.
τέμει, 321, D. 10.
τέμνω, 321, 10.
τέο, τεῦ, τέω, etc., 214, D.
τέος, 208, D.
-τεος, Verb. Adj., 300 ; 596— with Dat., 434.
-τερος, Compar., 192 ; 208, Obs. ; 216.
τέρπομαι, Aorist, 59, D. ; 257, D. ; 295, D.—with Partic., 592.
τεταγών, 257, D.
τέτακα, 282.
τέτληκα, 317, D. 10.
τέτμον, 257, D.
τετραίνω, Aor., 270, Obs.
τέτρηχα, 277, D.
τετύκειν, 322, D. 30.
τεύχω, 322, 30 — Perf. Mid., 285, D.
τή, κω, Meaning, 330, 7.
τηλίκοτος, τηλικόσδε, 212 ; 475.
-την, Ending of the 3 Person Dual of the Hist. Tenses, Act., 226—of the 2 Person Dual, 233, D. 7.
-τηριον, Neut. in, 345, 1.
-τηρ, Nom. of Masc. in, 341, 2 ; 349, 2—Voc. Sing., 121 —Nom. of Fem. in, 346, 1 ; 138.
τι bec. σα, 57 — inserted in Derivation, 351.

394 GREEK INDEX.

-τι, 3 Pers. Sing. Act. in the Princip. Tenses, 226.
τί; why? 404, Obs.—τί γάρ; 636, 6 d — τί δή; 642, 4 a — τί, δήπου; 642, 5 — τί δῆτα; 642, 6—τί μαθών; τί παθών; 606, Obs. 2—τί μήν; 643, 12.
τίη, 218.
τίθημι, Aor. Pass., 53 b.
τίκτω, 249.
τιμάω, with Genit., 421.
τιμωρέομαι and -έω, 481 b— -έομαι, with Acc., 396.
τίνυμι, 319, D. 35.
τίνω, 321, 5.
τίπτε, 61, D.
Τίρυνς, 50 b, Obs. 2.
-τις, Nom. Fem., 341, 2; 342, 1.
τίς, τί, 214—for ὅστις, 609.
τίς, τί, 214—Encl., 92, 1—τινά, to be supplied, 568.
τιτράω, 327, 16.
τιτρώσκω, 324, 16.
τιτύσκομαι, 322, D. 30; 324, D. 37.
τλῆναι, etc., 316, 6.
τμῆγω, 321, D. 10.
τό, 379, Obs ; 104; 559 b—τὸ μέν, τὸ δέ, 369, Obs. — τὸ πρίν, 635, 11.
τόθι, τόθεν, τώς, 217, D.
τοί, 643, 10—Encl., 92, 5.
τοίγαρ, τοιγαροῦν, τοιγάρτοι, 643, 10; 637, 5 — τοίνυν, 637, 4.
τοῖο, etc., 212, D.
τοιοῦτος, τοιόσδε, 212; 475.
τοίσδεσι, 212, D.
τόλμα, 115 (Ex.).
-τον, 2 and 3 Pers. Du. Act., 226—3 Pers. Dual Imperf., 233, D. 7—2 Pers. Du. Imperf., 228.
-τός, Verbal Adj. in, 300.
τοσοῦτος, τοσόσδε, 212; 475.
τότε, with Part., 587, 4.
τοῦ, τῳ, 214, Obs. 1.
-τρα for -τερ in the Dat. Plur., 153.
-τρα, Fem. in, 344, Obs.
τρέπω, 2 Aorist Act., 257— 2 Aorist Pass., 294—Perf., 279 ; 285.
τρέφω, 254 c—Perf., 279 ; 285— Aor. Pass., 295—Aor. Act. Meaning, 329, D.
τρέχω, 54 c; 327, 11.
τρῆσα, Fem. in, 341, 2—Quantity, 117.
τριήρης, Genit. Pl., 166.
-τρις, Fem. in, 341, 2.
τριχός, see θρίξ.
-τρον, Neut. in, 344.
τρώγω, 2 Aor. Act., 257.
Τρώς, Gen. Pl. and Du., 142, 3.
τρώω, 324, D. 16.
ττ, -ττω, see σσ, -σσω.

φείδομαι.
τυγχάνω, 322, 30, etc. — with the Genitive, 419 c — with Part., 590.
τύνη, 205, D.
τύπτω, 326, 37.
τύφω, 54 c.
τυχεῖν, 322, 30.
-τω, -των, 3 Pers. Sing. and Du. Imper. Act., 228.
-τωρ, Nom. Masc. in, 341, 2; 137.
-τωσαν, 3 Pers. Plur. Imper. Act., 228.

ὑ bec. ῒ, 35, D. 2 ; 160; 248, Obs.—bec. ὔ, 40 — bec. εν, 40 ; 278 — bec. ου, 40, D.— of the Stem bec. ε, 157— Long by nature, 83, Obs. 1 —lengthened, 253, Obs.— dropped, 253 — not dropped, 64.
-υ, Neut. in, 139 ; 172.
ὑβρίζω, with Acc., 396.
ὑβριστής, Compar., 197.
-υδριον, Neut. in, 347, Obs. 1.
ὕδωρ, 176—Neut., 140.
ὑε bec. ὔ, 158.
υἱ, Diphth., 28.
-υια, Fem. of Perf. Partic., 188.
υἱός, 177, 17.
ὕμιν, ὕμιν, etc., 207 — ὑμός, 208, D.
-υν, Nom. of Masc. and Neut. in, 172.
-υνω, Verbs in, 353, 8.
ὑπαί, see ὑπό.
ὕπατος, 200.
ὑπέρ (ὕπειρ), 448, II., A. ; 460 —with Inf. and Art., 574, 3.
ὑπισχνοῦμαι, 323, 36 — with Inf., 569.
ὑπό, 448, III.; 468 —Apoc., 64, D.
ὑποπτεύω, Augm., 239.
-υς, Nom. Masc. and Fem., 172 — Barytones in Acc. Sing., 156.
ὑσμίνη, Dat. Sing., 175, D.
ὕστερος, ὕστατος, ὑστάτιος, 200; 199, D.
ὕστερος, ὑστερέω, with Gen., 416, Obs. 3 ; 423,

φ, Pronunt., 6.
φαάνθην, 321, D.
φαεινός, Superl., 193, D.
φαίνω, φαείνω, 321, D.—Perf., 282—Meaning, 330, 8—Aor. Pass., 298, D. — Meaning, 328, 3 — Diff. of Pres. and Aor., 498.
φαίνομαι, φανερός ε.μι, with Part., 590.
φάσκω, 324, 8.
φείδομαι, 326, D. 45—Aor. and Fut., 257, D.—with Genit., 419 e.

χρίω.
φέρτε, 315, D. 4.
φέρτερος, φέρτατος, φέριστος, 199, D. 1.
φέρω, 327, 12—Imperat. of 1 Aor. Act., 268, D.—Meaning, 476, 2—φίρων, 580.
φεύγω, 322, 31—Fut. Mid., 264 —Perf. Mid., 285, D.—with Acc., 398—with Genit., 422 —Meaning, 486, Obs.
φημί, 312, 5—Pres. Ind. Encl., 92, 3.
φθάνω, 321, 3—2 Aor., 316, 7 — with Acc., 398 — with Part., 590.
φθείρω, Perf., 282—Meaning, 330, D. 11.
φθίω, 321, 6—Aor. Mid., 216, D. 26.
φιλέω, 325, D. 1.
φίλος, Compar., 195.
φιλοτιμέομαι, Dep. Pass., 328, 2.
-φι(ν), 178, D.
φοβοῦμαι, Meaning of Aor., 328, 3—with Inf., 560, 3.
φοῖνιξ, 83, Obs. 1 ; 145.
φορῆναι, see φέρω.
φράγνυμι, φάργνυμι, 319, 26,
φράζω, Aor., 257, D.
φρέαρ, 176.
φρήν, Fem., 140.
φύγαδε, 178, D.
φυγγάνω, 322, 31, and Obs.
-φυής, Adj. in, Acc. Sing., 166.
φυλάττομαι, with Acc., 399.
φύω, Fut., 262, D.
φίω, Aor., 316, 17—Meaning, 329, 3.
φώς, φῶς, Genit. Plur. and Dual, 142, 3.

χαίρω, 326, 38—with Dat, 439, Obs.—with Part., 592.
χαλάω, 301, 1.
χαλεπαίνω, with Dat., 439, Obs.
χαλεπός, with Inf., 562.
χαλεπῶς φέρω. with Part., 592.
χανδάνω, 323, D. 41.
χανοῦμαι, 324, 9.
χάριν, 404, Obs.
χάρις, Compar. of compounds with, 197.
χάσκω, 324, 9.
χείρ, 177, 18—Fem., 140.
χείρων, χείριστος, 199, 2.
χέρης, etc., 199, D. 2.
χέω, 248 — Fut., 265 — Perf., 281 — 1 Aor., 269 — 2 Aor., 316, D. 31.
χράομαι, χράω, Contr., 244, 2 —Future, 261—with Dat., 438, Obs.
χρή, 312, 6—χρῄν, 490—with Acc. and Inf., 567, Obs. 1.
χρήστης, Genit. Pl., 123.
χρίω, Perf. Mid., 288,

GREEK INDEX. 395

χρόα, 115 (Ex.).
χρώννυμι, 319, 12.
χρώς, 169, D.
χωρίζω, with Genit., 419 e.
χωρίς, 455, 5.

ψ, 34 ; 48 ; 260.
-ψ, Subs. in, 172.
ψαύω, Perf. Mid., 288—with Genit., 419 b.
ψάω, Contr., 244, 2.
ψεύδομαι, with Genit., 419 e.

ω, for o, 276, D.—See Att. Declens.—from o, see o— from η, see η.
-ω, Fem. in, 138—Nom., 172
— Adv. in, 204 — Proper Names in Acc. Sing.,163,D.
—in the Genit., 122, D. 3 c
—Conn. Vowel, 233, 1 — 1
Pers. Sing. Ind. Act., 233,2.
ὤγμαι, 327, D. 6.
-ωδης, Adj. in, 359, 2 Obs.

ως.
ἰθέω, 325, 9 — Syll. Augm., 237.
ὦλλοι, 65, D.
ὤμμαι, 327, 8.
-ων, Nom. of Masc. and Fem., 172 ; 345, 3—Genit., 118 ;
134, 7 ; 141 ; 173, 5.
ὠνάμην, etc., 3 4, D.
ὦναξ, 65, D.
ὠνέομαι, Syll. Augm., 237—
Perf., 275, 2—with Genit., 421.
ὤξυμμαι, 286, 1, Obs.
-ωρ, Subs. in, 172.
ὠρασι(ν), 179.
-ως, Nom. 172 — Adj., 184 —
Perf.Part.,276; 188—Fem., 138—Adv., 201 ; 203—Ending of Genit. Sing. in, 161
—with ι- and υ- Stems,157
—in -ευ Stems, 161 a.
ὡς and ὥς, 217.
ὡς and ὥς, Diff., 99 ; 217, D. ;
631.

ὤφελον.
ὡς, Atonon, 97, 3 ; 98—with Compar., 631 a—with Inf.,
etc.,564—"as though,"etc.,
with Part., 588—"when,"
"as," 556—with Aor. Ind.,
493—"that,"in Dependent Declarative Sentences, 525
—"in order that," in Sentences of Purpose, 530 —
with ἄν, 631 b, Obs. — in expressing a wish, 514.
ὡς, Preposit., 445 ; 448, A. ; 450.
ὥσπερ, 632—with Part., 588.
ὥστε, 94 ; 566 ; 632, 4—with Inf., 566—joined with μή, 617, Obs. 2.
ὡτός, see οὖς.
ὠυ, Diphth., 26, D.
ὡυτός, etc., 209, D.
ὠφελέω, with Acc., 396.
ὤφελον, 326, 32— in expressing a wish, 515.

THE END.

www.ingramcontent.com/pod-product-compliance
Lightning Source LLC
Chambersburg PA
CBHW071437300426
44114CB00013B/1467